Where in the World?

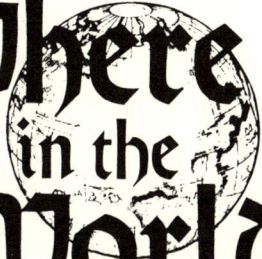

About the author

A fascination for the remote and little-known areas of the world is a motivating force often strong in stamp collectors, and Ken Wood is no exception. Stamps from such areas are what first attracted him to the hobby 50 years ago.

Born at Hastings, England, a few years after the famous battle, Wood served in the British Army during World War II, spending several years in Egypt, Cyrenaica, and the Mediterranean area.

After the war he traveled widely, living in what was then British Guiana, Trinidad, and Canada, before settling, with his wife Hilda, in the United States.

Editor of *Stamp Collector,* formerly *Western Stamp Collector,* from 1968 to 1980 and currently its editor emeritus, he is also author of *Basic Philately* and the philatelic encyclopedia *This is Philately.*

A Fellow of the Royal Philatelic Society, London, Wood is an American Philatelic Society-accredited judge and holder of the Phoenix Award, given by the Arizona State Philatelic Hall of Fame to out-of-state residents for service to philately.

In 1974 he was named Distinguished Philatelist of the Year by the Northwest Federation of Stamp Clubs, and in 1979 the American Topical Association elected him to its Roll of Distinguished Topical Philatelists.

This atlas reflects a marriage of Wood's love for stamps and his curiosity about the world's geography and history.

Where in the World?

AN ATLAS FOR STAMP COLLECTORS

by Kenneth A. Wood

Published by
Van Dahl Publications
Box 10,
Albany, OR 97321

iv

For Hilda

Who sympathized when it went slowly, cheered when it went well, and never complained. Without her support and help it would not have been possible.

First Printing 1983
Second Printing 1985

ISBN: 0-934466-06-8

Library of Congress Catalog Card Number: 83-90234
Printed in the United States of America.

Foreword
Why an atlas for stamp collectors?

This work has been created for two reasons: Partly because, to my knowledge, there has been no comprehensive atlas that looks at the world from the perspective of philately, but mostly because, like so many collectors, I have a curiosity about the places represented by those tiny paper fragments that we cherish.

Where are those little-known specks of land? Where were those long-gone kingdoms and colonies? What gave them such status as to send their names abroad by postal messenger, and what quirk of political, economic, or military fate caused them to recede into anonymity?

One would be sadly lacking in romantic sensibility not to be entranced at the thought of unknown lands looming on the horizon after weeks aboard some 17th-century galleon. And how could we not share the wonder experienced by men such as Marco Polo or Charles Darwin as they sought distant places to probe their mysteries?

Since few of us can realize such dreams, we must visit foreign parts via the stamps we collect and the friends we make while so engaged. But without a map, how can we know the way?

This book will, I hope, help you to steer a true philatelic course and take you in imagination to those lands of mystery and enchantment.

And that must be my answer to the question, "Why an atlas for stamp collectors?"

So come, stand watch with me on the bridge, albums and charts at hand, as we range the globe from Abu Dhabi to Zululand and all points in between.

Kenneth A. Wood, FRPSL

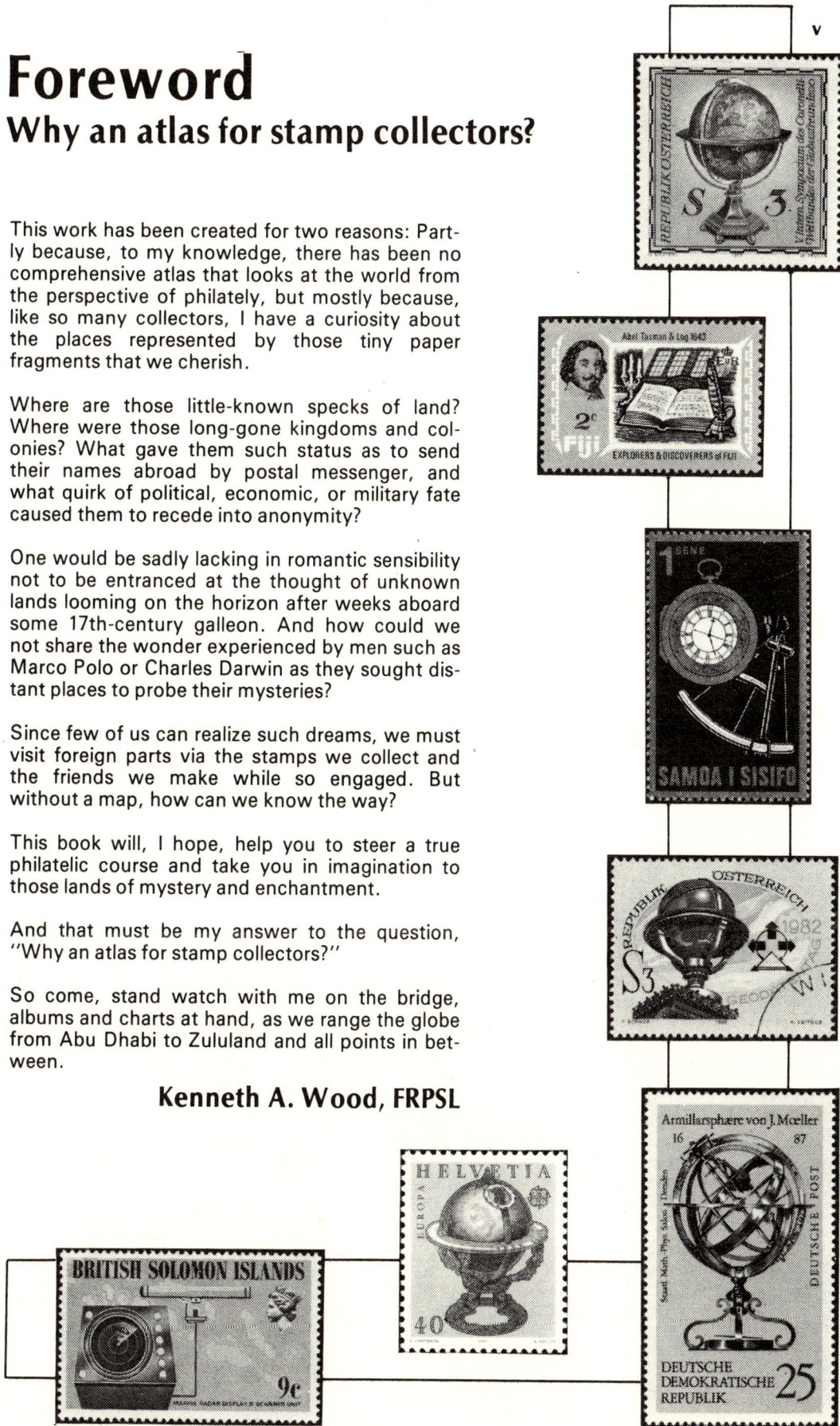

Appreciation

No work of this nature is a one-man show, and without the cartographers of the past, it would have been impossible to reconstruct yesterday's political entities.

I am grateful to those who helped locate sources and assisted in unraveling the often conflicting information they contained.

The responsibility for interpreting the information is entirely mine, and I would welcome comments and information, including sources. A list of references will be found at the end of the book.

Those who offered special help are:

Henry W. Beecher, Oregon.
Lorne W. Bentham, Ottawa, Canada.
Peter Collins, Bournemouth, England.
Don Clark, California.
Herman L. Halle, Maryland.
Philip Halward, Rickmansworth, England.
Harold D. Peterson, Oregon.
Maurice S. Stuckey, Defense Mapping Agency, Washington, D.C.
John Tucker, Pretoria, RSA.
Gordon D. Vaughn, Nova Scotia, Canada.
Joseph Zollman, New York, N.Y.

My thanks also go to William Bennett of CDE Stamps, Santa Fe, N.M., and to the United States Stamp Co. of San Francisco, Calif. for supplying some of the stamps illustrated.

At Van Dahl Publications, I am grateful to Michael Green for his editorial assistance, to Sue Storm, and to Production Manager Mary Meacham, Assistant Production Manager Mona Conley, and printing technicians Esther Miller and Kate Waters.

Chief Photographer Warren Burgess and Robert Bloodgood of the *Albany Democrat-Herald* newspaper applied their talents to producing the excellent photographic reproductions, and their efforts and patience are appreciated.

The final thanks must go to Arlene Van Dahl, to whom we all owe so much.

Contents

Section One

Gazetteer
A philatelic dictionary of the world since 1840.

This alphabetical listing of stamp-issuing areas past and present includes the many little-known and often long-gone political entities that have issued stamps since 1840. It also indicates the form in which they exist today and is designed to help you untangle their often complex histories.

Many areas have used stamps at various times. Some have changed through conquest or liberation; others began as colonies, to be traded back and forth among the colonial powers. Most have since become independent and constitute many of today's stamp-issuing areas.

The gazetteer is also an index to the pages featuring maps and an aid in identifying stamps by means of the many illustrations. The stamps pictured show the inscription used and will often include some national symbol that will help to identify other stamps of the same area.

Page numbers indicating the location of maps are placed ahead of the area names and for added convenience are also included in the cross references. This makes it possible to go directly to a map without having to follow a reference. Additionally, to make the search for an area easier, all letters begin on a righthand page.

Because they are referred to so frequently, World Wars I and II are indicated as WWI and WWII.

Considerable use has been made of the *quod vide* (q.v.) reference. When this appears, it means that additional or related information may be found listed under the name that precedes it.

The arrangement of the listing is alphabetical, and all multiword names are alphabetized as though they were one word.

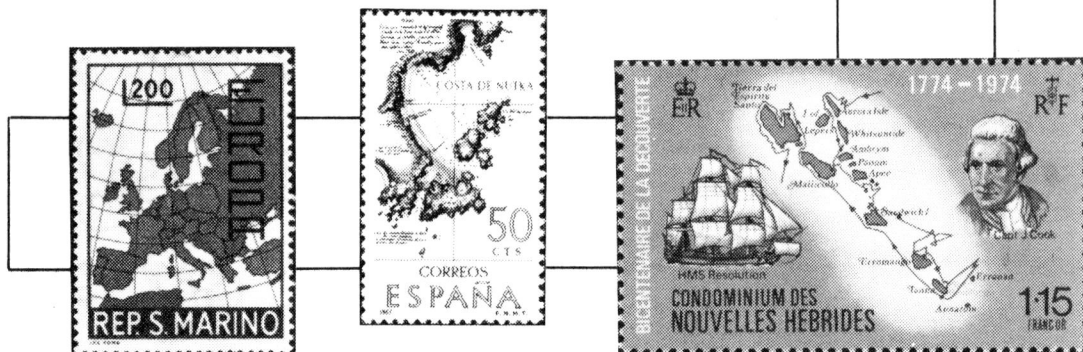

Ajman

Abu Dhabi

Aden

Afars and Issas

Aitutaki

Afghanistan

Alaouites

Albania

A

Alderney

157 ABIDJAN — See Dakar and Abidjan.

331 ABU DHABI
A sheikdom on the southern shore of the Persian Gulf. Once a trucial state, it is now one of the United Arab Emirates. For map see Trucial States.

90 ABYSSINIA
Former name of Ethiopia (q.v.).

92 ACAMBARO
A town in Mexico. For map see Aguascalientes.

90 ACAPONETA
A town in Mexico.

91 ADEN
A former coaling station and British naval base on the southern shore of Arabia. Once administered from British India, it became a crown colony in 1937. In 1962 it was included in the South Arabian Federation. Independence came in 1967 and it is now the capital city of the People's Democratic Republic of Yemen.

190 ADEN PROTECTORATE STATES — See Hadhramaut.

162 AEGEAN ISLANDS — See Dodecanese Islands.

91 AFARS AND ISSAS
The French Territory of Afars and Issas was located in East Africa facing on the Gulf of Aden at the mouth of the Red Sea. Formerly the French Somali Coast, since 1977 it has been independent as the Republic of Djibouti.

365 AFGHANISTAN
The Republic of Afghanistan is in central Asia and was once known as the Kingdom of Kabul. From 1891 to 1973 it was the Kingdom of Afghanistan. It is currently a republic in the process of being occupied by the Soviet Union.

92 AGUASCALIENTES
A state and city in Mexico.

222 AGUERA, LA — See La Aguera.

368 AITUTAKI
Located in the South Pacific, Aitutaki is one of the Cook Islands.

331 AJMAN
A sheikdom on the southern shore of the Persian Gulf. Once a trucial state, it is now one of the United Arab Emirates. For map see Trucial States.

383 ALAND ISLANDS
A group of islands at the mouth of the Gulf of Bothnia. Part of Finland, it was scheduled to have its own postage stamps beginning in 1984.

92 ALAOUITES
Located on the coast of Syria, this was a territory mandated to France following WWI. It became the Republic of Latakia in 1930 and part of Syria in 1937.

382 ALBANIA
The People's Socialist Republic of Albania is a Balkan state located on the Adriatic Sea.

385 ALDERNEY
One of the English Channel Islands, Alderney is a dependency of Guernsey.

2

Alexandretta

Alexandria

Algeria

Angra

Fr. Andorra

Allenstein

Angola

Anjouan

Alwar

Sp. Andorra

Alsace Lorraine

192 ALEXANDRETTA
An area of the former Turkish Empire under French control following WWI, it was located between Syria and Turkey. A portion was known as Hatay (q.v.). It was restored to Turkey in 1939. For map see Hatay.

93 ALEXANDRIA
A city in Egypt located on the Mediterranean coast.

160 ALEXANDROUPOLIS
Now a Greek city, it was named Dedeagh (Dedeagatz or Dedeagatch) while part of Turkey prior to WWI. For map see Dedeagh.

353 ALGERIA
The Democratic and Popular Republic of Algeria is a former French colony in North Africa. It became independent in 1962.

93 ALLENDE
A town in Mexico.

94 ALLENSTEIN
Formerly part of German East Prussia, it is now within Poland. It was a district centered on the town of Allenstein, now called Olsztyn.

94 ALSACE AND LORRAINE
Now located in France, these twin provinces were under German control from 1870 to the end of WWI and again during the WWII German occupation of France.

202 ALWAR
A feudatory state of India, located to the southwest of Delhi. Now part of the Republic of India. See Indian Feudatory States.

95 AMUR
A province in Siberia. The capital city is Blagoveshchensk.

ANATOLIA
Anatolia is that part of Turkey located in Asia.

95 ANCACHS (ANCASH)
A department of Peru.

96 ANDALUSIA
Andalusia is an area comprising the eight southernmost provinces of Spain.

96 ANDAMAN & NICOBAR IS.
Twin island groups in the Indian Ocean, they are now part of the Republic of India.

383 ANDORRA
A French-Spanish co-principality in the Pyrenees Mountains on the Franco-Spanish border.

353 ANGOLA
The People's Republic of Angola is a former Portuguese colony on the west coast of southern Africa. It became independent in 1975.

97 ANGORA
A town in Turkey under nationalist government during 1921. Now Ankara, the capital city of Turkey.

97 ANGRA
A district in the Azores, which is a Portuguese island group in the Atlantic, Angra comprised the islands of Graciosa, Sao Jorge, and Terceira.

371 ANGUILLA
A British dependent territory in the Leeward Islands of the Lesser Antilles. The island was one of the states constituting St. Kitts, Nevis, and Anguilla until declaring its separation in 1967.

98 ANHWEI
A province in the People's Republic of China.

98 ANJOUAN
An island in the Comoro group. Now part of the Republic of Comoros.

99 ANNAM AND TONKIN
Twin districts of French Indo-China. Now part of the Socialist Republic of Vietnam, with a portion in Laos.

99 ANNOBON
A former Spanish island off the west coast of Africa. Now part of the Republic of Equatorial Guinea. See also Corisco and Elobey.

372 ANTIGUA
A former British colony and associated state, Antigua is an island group in the Leeward Islands of the Lesser Antilles. It achieved independence in 1981 and includes the islands of Antigua, Barbuda, and Redonda.

100 ANTIOQUIA
One of the states of the former Granadine Confederation, now a department of Colombia.

100 APURIMAC
A department of Peru.

101 ARAD
A town and district in western Romania. Prior to WWI it was in the Austro-Hungarian Empire.

101 ARBE
An island off the coast of Yugoslavia. Now called Rab.

102 AREQUIPA
A department of Peru.

397 ARGENTINA
The Argentine Republic is located in the southern part of South America.

166 ARGYROKASTRON
A town in southern Albania. Now called Gjirokaster. For map see Epirus.

102 ARICA
A city in Chile, on the border with Peru.

103 ARMENIA
Formerly part of Russia and located between the Black and Caspian Seas, it achieved temporary independence after the 1917 Russian Revolution. It federated briefly in 1922-23 with Azerbaijan and Georgia as the Transcaucasian Federation. Now part of the Soviet Union.

103 ARWAD
An island off the coast of Syria, now part of that country. Also known as Rouad.

354 ASCENSION
A British island in the South Atlantic and a dependency of St. Helena.

314 ASCH
A town in Czechoslovakia. For map see Sudetenland.

162 ASTIPALAIA
A Greek island in the Aegean Sea. Also known as Stampalia. Occupied by Italy in 1912 and officially ceded to Italy by Turkey in 1920, it became Greek in 1947. See Dodecanese Islands.

Annam & Tonkin

Arwad

Annam

Annobon

Armenia

Antioquia

Astipalaia

Ascension

Antigua

Argentina

4

104 ASTURIAS
A region of Spain comprising the northern part of the province of Oviedo.

213 AUNUS
Finnish name for the Soviet town of Olonets. See Karelia.

368 AUSTRALIA
An island continent, the Commonwealth of Australia comprises the former British colonies of New South Wales, Queensland, South Australia, Tasmania, Victoria, and Western Australia, plus the Northern Territory and some island dependencies.

359 AUSTRALIAN ANTARCTIC TERRITORY
An area of Antarctica under Australian administration.

382 AUSTRIA
Once part of the Austro-Hungarian Empire, Austria became a republic after WWI. Occupied by Germany from 1938 to 1945, it was re-established as a republic by the Allies after WWII.

228 AUSTRIAN ITALY — See Lombardy and Venetia.

AUSTRIAN LEVANT
Collective name given to Austrian post offices that operated in the Turkish Empire until 1914.

105 AUSTRO-HUNGARIAN EMPIRE
An empire in central and eastern Europe until WWI.

104 AVILA
A town and province in Spain.

106 AYACUCHO
A department of Peru.

106 AZERBAIJAN
Formerly part of the Russian Empire, it achieved a temporary independence following the 1917 Russian Revolution. The area federated briefly with Armenia and Georgia as the Transcaucasian Federation. Now part of the Soviet Union. It is located between the Black Sea and the Caspian Sea.

107 AZERBAIJAN
A province of northern Iran. Not to be confused with the Soviet province of the same name.

97 AZORES
Part of Portugal, the Azores is an island group in the Atlantic Ocean. For map see Angra.

Australian Antarctic Territory

Australia

Azores

Austrian Levant

Azerbaijan

Austria

Austro-Hungarian Empire

Baden

Baghdad

Bahamas

Bahawalpur

Bahrain

Bamra

Bangladesh

Barbados

B

Barbuda

107 BADEN
A former grand duchy, now part of the Federal Republic of Germany.

108 BAENA
A town in the Spanish province of Cordoba.

108 BAGHDAD
The capital city of Iraq, Baghdad was occupied in WWI by British forces during the campaign against the Turkish Empire. Now the capital of Iraq.

395 BAHAMAS
The Commonwealth of the Bahamas is an island group in the Atlantic Ocean off the coast of Florida. A former British colony, it became independent in 1973.

109 BAHAWALPUR
A former Indian state in British India, it is now part of Pakistan.

366 BAHRAIN
Located in the Persian Gulf, Bahrain was a British protected territory until becoming independent in 1971.

109 BAJA CALIFORNIA
A long peninsula on Mexico's west coast.

106 BAKU
A city and province of Azerbaijan, in the USSR. For map see Azerbaijan.

202 BAMRA
A former feudatory state in India. Now part of the Republic of India. For map see Indian Feudatory States.

110 BANAT
Once a district in Hungary, following WWI Banat was divided between Yugoslavia and Romania.

110 BANGKOK
Capital city of Siam (Thailand).

361 BANGLADESH
The People's Republic of Bangladesh was formerly part of India until it became the eastern enclave of Pakistan. It broke from Pakistan and became independent in 1971.

111 BARANYA
A district of Hungary, it was occupied by Serbia after WWI and later returned to Hungarian control.

372 BARBADOS
A former British colony in the West Indies. It became independent in 1966.

371 BARBUDA
An island dependency of Antigua (q.v.).

134 BARCELONA
A city in Spain. For map see Cataluna.

Bergedorf

Barwani

Bavaria

Basutoland

Belgium

Belgian Congo

Benadir

Bechuanaland

Batum

Benin

Belize

Basel

401 BARDSEY

An island off the coast of Wales. See British Offshore Islands.

117 BARRANQUILLA

A city on the Caribbean coast of Colombia. For map see Bogota.

202 BARWANI

A former feudatory state in India, it is now part of the Republic of India. For map see Indian Feudatory States.

111 BASEL

A city and canton in Switzerland.

202 BASHAHR — See Bussahir.

112 BASUTOLAND

A territory in Africa formerly under British protection, later a crown colony. It became independent in 1966 as the Kingdom of Lesotho.

112 BATUM

A city in the Soviet Socialist Republic of Georgia. Occupied for a period by British forces following WWI.

T13 BAVARIA

A former kingdom in southern Germany. Now part of the Federal Republic of Germany.

113 BECHUANALAND

A British protectorate in central southern Africa. It gained independence in 1966 as the Republic of Botswana. Not to be confused with British Bechuanaland (q.v.).

271 BEIJING — See Peking.

116 BEIRUT

The capital city of the Republic of Lebanon.

Located on the Mediterranean coast. For map see Beyrouth.

114 BELGIAN CONGO

Established in 1885 as a kingdom under King Leopold II of Belgium, it was annexed as a colony of Belgium in 1908. It became independent in 1960 as Congo (Kinshasa). The name was changed to the Republic of Zaire in 1971. Located in central Africa.

382 BELGIUM

The Kingdom of Belgium is located in northwest Europe.

378 BELIZE

Formerly titled the Crown Colony of British Honduras, its name was changed to Belize in 1973. Independence came in 1981.

114 BENADIR

A former Italian colony in East Africa. It was made part of Italian Somaliland and is now in the Somali Democratic Republic.

115 BENGASI

Bengasi (Benghazi) is the capital city of Cyrenaica in Libya. It is that country's second city.

353 BENIN

A former French colony in West Africa, Benin became the French colony of Dahomey in 1899. Dahomey was incorporated into French West Africa during WWII. It gained independence in 1958 as the Republic of Dahomey changing its name to the People's Republic of Benin in 1975.

115 BERGEDORF

A German city on the Elbe River near Hamburg. It was owned jointly by Hamburg and Lubeck until 1868, when it was purchased by Hamburg. Now part of the Federal Republic of Germany.

384 BERLIN

Berlin was the German capital until the end of WWI. It was occupied by the Allied powers and divided into zones. The area comprising the British, French, and US zones is now enclaved in the German Democratic Republic, of which the Soviet zone of Berlin is the capital.

183 BERLIN-BRANDENBURG

A portion of the Soviet occupation zone of Germany. For map see Germany, Soviet Zone.

395 BERMUDA

A British colony comprising a group of islands in the Atlantic Ocean east of the North Carolina coast.

401 BERNERA

An island in the Outer Hebrides off the west coast of Scotland. See British Offshore Islands.

116 BEYROUTH — French spelling of Beirut.

202 BHOPAL

Formerly an Indian feudatory state, it is now part of the Republic of India. For map see Indian Feudatory States.

202 BHOR

Formerly an Indian feudatory state, it is now part of the Republic of India. For map see Indian Feudatory States.

362 BHUTAN

The Kingdom of Bhutan is located in the Himalayas between Tibet and the Republic of India.

116 BIAFRA

Biafra formed the eastern portion of the Republic of Nigeria. It attempted to gain its independence during the 1967-70 civil war, but was unsuccessful.

202 BIJAWAR

Formerly an Indian feudatory state, it is now part of the Republic of India. For map see Indian Feudatory States.

127 BILBAO

A town in northern Spain. For location see Burgos.

168 BIOKO

The name of the island formerly known as Fernando Po (q.v.). With Rio Muni it forms the Republic of Equatorial Guinea.

95 BLAGOVESHCHENSK

A city in Siberia, capital of Amur Province. For map see Amur.

348 BLUEFIELDS — See Zelaya.

117 BOCAS DEL TORO

City on an island off the Caribbean coast of the Republic of Panama. Capital of province of the same name.

117 BOGOTA

The capital city of Colombia.

Bermuda

Bernera Is.

Berlin

Bhopal

Bhutan

Biafra

8

118 BOHEMIA AND MORAVIA

Provinces of Czechoslovakia prior to the 1939 German invasion. They were made a protectorate by the Germans. Restored to Czechoslovakia in 1945.

118 BOLIVAR

A state in the Granadine Confederation, Bolivar became a department of Colombia in 1886.

397 BOLIVIA

The Republic of Bolivia is located in central South America.

356 BOPHUTHATSWANA

Established in 1977 as one of the black "homelands" within the Republic of South Africa. Comprises several separate areas. For map see South Africa (Homelands).

BORNEO — See Brunei, Sabah, Sarawak, Indonesia, Malaysia, and South Borneo.

119 BOSNIA & HERZEGOVINA

A Turkish province until annexation by Austria-Hungary in 1908. Now part of Yugoslavia.

353 BOTSWANA

The Republic of Botswana was under British protection as the Bechuanaland Protectorate until it became independent in 1966. Not to be confused with British Bechuanaland (q.v.).

119 BOYACA

Boyaca was a state in the Granadine Confederation until 1886, when it became a department of Colombia.

397 BRAZIL

The Federative Republic of Brazil is the largest nation in South America. It was previously a colony of Portugal.

401 BRECQHOU (BRECHOU)

An island off the west coast of Sark in the Channel Islands. See British Offshore Islands.

120 BREMEN

Once a city-state and member of the Hanseatic League, Bremen is located on the Weser River and is now within the Federal Republic of Germany.

359 BRITISH ANTARCTIC TERRITORY

Formed in 1962 and comprises territory in the Antarctic region south of 60 degrees south latitude, including the South Shetlands, South Orkneys, and Graham Land.

120 BRITISH BECHUANALAND

A colony in central southern Africa, it was absorbed into the Cape of Good Hope colony in 1895 and became a part of the Union of South Africa. Not to be confused with Bechuanaland Protectorate (q.v.).

121 BRITISH CENTRAL AFRICA

A territory of central Africa that was chartered to the British South Africa Company, it became the Nyasaland Protectorate in 1907. Between 1953 and 1963, it was part of the Central African Federation and in 1964 became the independent Republic of Malawi.

Bophuthatswana

Bohemia & Moravia

British Bechuanaland

Bolivia

Brazil

Botswana

Bosnia & Herzegovina

Bremen

British Antarctic Territory

British Central Africa

British India

British Columbia

British Levant

British Honduras

British Solomon Is.

British Indian Ocean Terr.

British New Guinea

Brit. Somaliland

British Guiana

Brit. South Africa

121 BRITISH COLUMBIA
Formerly a British colony, it is now the western-most province of Canada and includes the former colony of Vancouver Island.

122 BRITISH EAST AFRICA
A territory administered by the British East Africa Company. It became East Africa and Uganda Protectorate and later was part of Kenya. It is now within the Republic of Kenya.

122 BRITISH GUIANA
A former British crown colony on the north coast of South America. It became independent in 1966 and is now the Cooperative Republic of Guyana.

123 BRITISH HONDURAS
A former British crown colony on the east coast of Central America. Its name was changed to Belize in 1973, and it became independent in 1981.

200 BRITISH INDIA
That area of India not within a convention or feudatory state prior to the 1947 partition. For map see India, British.

123 BRITISH INDIAN OCEAN TERRITORY
A British crown colony formed in 1965 and comprising the Indian Ocean island groups of the Chagos Archipelago, plus Aldabra, Farquhar, and Desroches. The latter three were transferred to the Republic of the Seychelles in 1976.

BRITISH LEVANT
Collective name for British post offices operating in the Turkish Empire prior to WWI.

124 BRITISH NEW GUINEA
A British protectorate from 1888, British New Guinea comprised the southernmost part of the eastern half of the island of New Guinea. It became the Territory of Papua under Australian administration in 1905 and is now part of Papua New Guinea.

401 BRITISH OFFSHORE ISLANDS
Islands off the British coast that have issued local carriage or souvenir labels.

369 BRITISH SOLOMON ISLANDS
A British protectorate comprising 10 large islands and a number of smaller groups located to the east of New Guinea in the western Pacific. The name was changed to Solomon Islands in 1975, and independence came in 1978.

124 BRITISH SOMALILAND
A former British protectorate in East Africa, on the Gulf of Aden. It was occupied briefly by the Italians during WWII and became part of the Somali Democratic Republic in 1960.

125 BRITISH SOUTH AFRICA
A territory administered by the British South Africa Company. In 1924 it was divided into Northern and Southern Rhodesia. There was a period of federation with Nyasaland from 1953 to 1963. Southern Rhodesia is now the nation of Zimbabwe and Northern Rhodesia is the Republic of Zambia.

Brunei

Brit. Virgin Is.

Brunswick

Bundi

Bulgaria

Bussahir

Burundi

Buenos Aires

Burma

372 BRITISH VIRGIN ISLANDS
A group of islands in the Leeward Islands of the Lesser Antilles. It is a British colony.

362 BRUNEI
The State of Brunei is a British protected state comprising two enclaves on the northwest coast of Borneo.

125 BRUNSWICK
The Duchy of Brunswick joined the North German Confederation in 1868. It is now located mainly in the Federal Republic of Germany, with a portion in the German Democratic Republic (East Germany).

246 BUCHANAN
A town in Liberia. For map see Monrovia.

126 BUENOS AIRES
A province of the Argentine Republic.

382 BULGARIA
The People's Republic of Bulgaria was once a Turkish province, then a principality under the Turks. It became a kingdom in 1908 and a "people's republic" in 1946.

400 BUMBUNGA
The "province" of Bumbunga is an area in South Australia.

202 BUNDI
Formerly a feudatory state in India, it is now part of the Republic of India. For map see Indian Feudatory States.

126 BURGENLAND
A province of the Republic of Austria.

127 BURGOS
A province and town in northern Spain.

361 BURMA
The Socialist Republic of the Union of Burma was formerly part of British India. It was separated in 1937. Occupied by Japan during WWII, it became independent in 1948.

353 BURUNDI
The Republic of Burundi was originally part of German East Africa. Mandated to Belgium at the end of WWI, it became independent in 1962 as a monarchy. Following a revolution in 1967, the country became a republic.

127 BUSHIRE
A port city on the Persian Gulf coast of Iran.

202 BUSSAHIR (BASHAHR)
Formerly a feudatory state of India, it is now part of the Republic of India. For map see Indian Feudatory States.

Cambodia

Cameroon

Calf of Man

Calimno

Campione D'Italia

Canada

Canal Zone

C

128 CABINDA
Previously known as Portuguese Congo, Cabinda is that portion of the People's Republic of Angola located north of the River Congo.

128 CABO GRACIAS A DIOS
A port city and district of northern Nicaragua.

129 CADIZ
A province and city in southwestern Spain.

162 CALCHI
One of the islands in the Aegean Sea occupied by Italy in 1912. It became Greek following WWII. Now called Khalki. See Dodecanese Islands.

401 CALDEY
An island off the south coast of Wales. See British Offshore Islands.

401 CALF OF MAN
An island off the southern tip of the Isle of Man. See British Offshore Islands.

162 CALIMNO
One of the islands in the Aegean Sea occupied by Italy in 1912. It became Greek following WWII. Now called Kalimnos. See Dodecanese Islands.

162 CALINO — See Calimno.

280 CAMAGUEY — See Puerto Principe.

361 CAMBODIA
Once part of French Indo-China, Cambodia became independent in 1954. In 1971 it became the Khmer Republic, but reverted to the name of Cambodia in 1975. It is currently the Cambodian People's Republic.

353 CAMEROON
The United Republic of Cameroon was formerly the German colony of Kamerun. At the end of WWI, it was divided and mandated to Great Britain and France. The British mandate was administered as part of Nigeria until 1960, when a plebiscite resulted in the northern portion becoming part of Nigeria and the southern part joining what had been the French mandate as the Federal Republic of Cameroon. It adopted its present name in 1972.

CAMEROUN — French spelling of Cameroon.

129 CAMPECHE
A state in southern Mexico.

404 CAMPIONE D'ITALIA
An area of Italy enclaved in Switzerland.

394 CANADA
Canada generally forms that part of North America located to the north of the United States, except for Alaska. An independent nation within the Commonwealth, Canada was formed from the Province of Canada and the colonies of British Columbia and Vancouver Island, New Brunswick, Nova Scotia, and Prince Edward Island. Newfoundland became the 10th province when it joined Confederation in 1949.

130 CANAL ZONE
The Canal Zone comprised a strip of territory on either side of the Panama Canal. It was established under US administration in 1904 and restored to Panama in 1979.

130 CANARY ISLANDS
A group of Spanish islands off the northwest coast of Africa.

131 CANDIA
A district of Crete under British administration during the period of joint administration of the island by France, Great Britain, Italy, and Russia from 1898 to 1908. Now part of Greece, it is called Iraklion, but was also known as Heraklion.

151 CANEA — See La Canea.

401 CANNA
An island off the west coast of Scotland. See British Offshore Islands.

Cape Juby

Carinthia

Cape Verde

Castellorize

Cavalle

Caso

Canton

Caroline Is.

Cape of Good Hope

Cayman Islands

328 CANTON
A port in China at which there was a French post office. See Treaty Ports.

312 CAPE JUBY
A Spanish possession on the northwest coast of Africa that became part of Spanish Sahara. For map see Spanish Sahara.

131 CAPE OF GOOD HOPE
A former British colony at the southernmost tip of Africa, it became a province of the Union of South Africa in 1910. Now a province of the Republic of South Africa.

354 CAPE VERDE
The Republic of Cape Verde is an island group in the Atlantic Ocean off the African coast. Once a Portuguese colony, it achieved independence in 1975.

132 CARINTHIA
An area between Austria and the then-newly formed country of Yugoslavia. A plebiscite was held in 1920 to decide if it should be Austrian or join Yugoslavia. The vote was for the northern portion to become part of the new Republic of Austria, while the south joined Yugoslavia.

132 CAROLINE ISLANDS
A group of some 500 atolls and islands in the western Pacific that formed a German protectorate until WWI. Mandated to Japan by the League of Nations, it was occupied by the United States during WWII and is now administered as a Trust Territory.

133 CARPATHO-UKRAINE
Once a province of Czechoslovakia under the name of Ruthenia. The 1938 Munich "Agreement" made it autonomous, but its freedom was brief. In 1939 it was absorbed by Hungary and is now part of the USSR.

117 CARTAGENA
A city on the Caribbean coast of Colombia. For map see Bogota.

133 CARUPANO
A city on the coast of Venezuela.

162 CASO
One of the Aegean islands taken by Italy from Turkey in 1912. It became Greek following WWII. Now called Kasos. See Dodecanese Islands.

162 CASTELLORIZE (CASTELROSSO)
An island in the Mediterranean Sea off the Turkish coast to the east of the island of Rhodes. It was taken by France from Turkey during WWI and later ceded to Italy. It joined the Italian Dodecanese Islands in 1921 and went to Greece after WWII. Now called Kastellorizon. See Dodecanese Islands.

134 CATALUNA
A region of northeast Spain.

134 CATTARO
A town in Southern Yugoslavia. Now called Kotor.

135 CAUCA
Once a state, now a department of the Republic of Colombia.

135 CAVALLE
Cavalle (or Cavalla) is a Greek town on the northern shore of the Aegean Sea. A French post office operated there prior to WWI, when it was part of the Turkish Empire. Now Kavalla.

379 CAYMAN ISLANDS
A British crown colony, the Cayman Islands are located in the Caribbean Sea to the south of Cuba. Until 1962 the colony was a dependency of Jamaica.

207 CEFALONIA — See Cephalonia.

136 CELEBES
An island group to the east of Borneo. Now part of the Republic of Indonesia.

353 CENTRAL AFRICAN EMPIRE
Name of the Central African Republic from 1977 to 1979.

136 CENTRAL AFRICAN FEDERATION
The name sometimes applied to the 1953-1963 federation of Northern and Southern Rhodesia and Nyasaland.

353 CENTRAL AFRICAN REPUBLIC
Originally part of French Equatorial Africa, the area was administered by France. Known as Ubangi-Shari, it became independent in 1958 as the Central African Republic. From 1977 to 1979 it was known as the Central African Empire.

166 CENTRAL ALBANIA — See Epirus.

CENTRAL CHINA
An area of China under Communist control prior to the formation of the People's Republic of China in 1949. It included the provinces of Honan, Hupeh, Hunan, and Kiangsi. For maps see under individual province names.

137 CENTRAL LITHUANIA
An area of the former Russian Empire that was in-

dependent for a short time following WWI. It was taken by Poland and is now within the USSR.

207 CEPHALONIA AND ITHACA
These are two of the Ionian Islands (q.v.) in the Adriatic Sea off the coast of Greece that were occupied by Italy during WWII.

207 CERIGO
One of the Ionian Islands (q.v.).

137 CEYLON
An island off the southern tip of India. Formerly under British administration, it became fully independent within the British Commonwealth in 1972 and changed its name to the Republic of Sri Lanka.

138 CHACHAOPOYAS
A town in north central Peru.

353 CHAD
Once a dependency of Ubangi-Shari in central Africa, Chad became part of French Equatorial Africa in 1937 and achieved independence within the French Community in 1958 as the Republic of Chad. For map also see French Equatorial Africa.

138 CHAHAR
A province in northern China. Now part of the People's Republic of China.

139 CHALA
A town on the southern coast of Peru.

Central African Republic

Central Lithuania

Cephalonia & Ithaca

Central African Empire

Ceylon

Chad

14

201 CHAMBA
Formerly a convention state in India, it is now part of the Republic of India. See Indian Convention States.

385 CHANNEL ISLANDS
A group of British islands in the English Channel, near the French coast. It includes Jersey, Guernsey, Alderney, Brechou, Great Sark, Little Sark, Herm, Jethou, and Lithou (Lihou). For map see English Channel Islands.

202 CHARKHARI
A former Indian feudatory state, now part of the Republic of India. See Indian Feudatory States.

139 CHEKIANG
A province in the People's Republic of China.

140 CHIAPAS
The southernmost state of Mexico. Borders on Guatemala.

140 CHICLAYO
A town on the northern coast of Peru.

141 CHIHUAHUA
A state in northern Mexico.

397 CHILE
The Republic of Chile is a long, narrow strip of a country on the western coast of South America.

166 CHIMARRA
Now known as Himare, Chimarra (Khimara or Chimara) is located in Albania. For map see Epirus.

361 CHINA, PEOPLE'S REPUBLIC OF
A Communist government that has ruled China since 1949.

142 CHINA, REPUBLIC OF
A large country located in the eastern part of Asia. It became a republic in 1912. Following WWII, Communists took over and it became the People's Republic of China.

361 CHINA (TAIWAN) REPUBLIC OF
When the Communists took over China in 1949, the defeated government of the Republic of China moved to the island of Taiwan (Formosa) and continued as the Republic of China (Taiwan).

141 CHIOS
An island in the Aegean Sea. Now part of Greece.

143 CHITA
A city in Siberia.

362 CHRISTMAS ISLAND
Christmas Island in the Indian Ocean is located to the south of Sumatra. It was one of the British Straits Settlements, then administered from Singapore. In 1958 it was placed under the administration of Australia. For map see Asia and Far East.

404 CHRISTMAS ISLAND
Christmas Island in the Pacific Ocean is in the Ellice group and is now part of Tuvalu.

143 CHUNGKING
Chungking (Tchongking) is a city in the People's Republic of China. It was the site of a French Indo-Chinese post office from 1902 to 1922, and was the WWII capital of China.

Chamba

Charkhari

People's Rep. of China

Chile

Republic of China

Christmas Island (Indian Ocean)

Republic of China (pre-1949)

Christmas Island (Pacific Ocean)

Cilcia

Clipperton Island

Cochin

Ciskei

Cocos (Keeling) Is.

Colombia

Comoros

144 CILCIA
An area of Turkey located in the southeastern part of the country. It was occupied by France for a period following WWI.

356 CISKEI
A South African "homeland" formed in 1981. For map see South Africa, Homelands.

141 CIUDAD JUAREZ
A town in Mexico. For map see Chihuahua.

405 CLIPPERTON ISLAND
An island in the Pacific Ocean, off the coast of Mexico.

144 CLUJ
A city in Transylvania, once part of Hungary. It was taken and retained by Romania during WWI. Formerly known as Klausenburg and Kolozsvar.

280 COAMO
A town in Puerto Rico. For map see Puerto Rico.

202 COCHIN
A former Indian feudatory state. Now part of the Republic of India. See Indian Feudatory States.

145 COCHIN CHINA
A former French colony located at the nouthern tip of Indo-China, of which it later became part.

362 COCOS (KEELING) ISLANDS
A group of islands in the Indian Ocean, once administered from Singapore, but transferred to Australian control in 1955.

90 COLIMA
A town in Mexico. For map see Acaponeta.

397 COLOMBIA
The Republic of Colombia in northern South America was once a Spanish colony, but became independent in 1819. Its various states became the Granadine Confederation in 1858 and the United States of New Grenada in 1861. Later in the same year it assumed its present name.

COLOMBIAN STATES
The stamp-issuing entities that united to form the Republic of Colombia included Antioquia, Bolivar, Boyaca, Cauca, Cundinamarca, Santander, and Tolima. For maps see under individual state names.

176 COLUMBUS ARCHIPELAGO — See Galapagos Islands.

145 COMAYAGUA
A town in the Central American country of Honduras.

353 COMOROS
Located between the northwestern tip of Madagascar and the African mainland, the Republic of Comoros comprises the islands of Anjouan, Great Comoro, and Moheli. They are former French colonies. Another island, Mayotte, chose to become a department of France.

French Congo

Confederate States of America

State of Congo

People's Republic of Congo

Portuguese Congo

Cos

Cordoba

Cook Islands

Corfu

Corisco

146 CONFEDERATE STATES OF AMERICA
The Confederate States of America was formed in 1861. It was dissolved at the end of the Civil War and the states re-admitted to the United States. For towns issuing Postmasters' Provisionals in the CSA, see maps of individual states following the CSA map.

114 CONGO, BELGIAN — See Belgian Congo.

353 CONGO (BRAZZAVILLE) — See Congo, People's Republic of the.

114 CONGO FREE STATE — See Belgian Congo.

149 CONGO, FRENCH
A former colonial possession located in Central Africa. In 1888, Gabon was added and in 1894, Ubangi-Shari. Chad joined in 1900. In 1906, it was divided again, and French Congo ceased to exist.

114 CONGO, INDEPENDENT STATE OF THE
Established in 1885, under King Leopold II of Belgium as an independent kingdom, it was annexed to Belgium as the Belgian Congo in 1908. It is now the Republic of Zaire.

353 CONGO (KINSHASA)
Formerly the Belgian Congo. Now Republic of Zaire.

353 CONGO, PEOPLE'S REPUBLIC OF THE
It began as the French colony of Middle Congo, which had been one of the three colonies formed in 1906 from French Congo. It became part of French Equatorial Africa in 1937, achieving independence in 1958 as Congo (Brazzaville). Now known as the People's Republic of the Congo.

128 CONGO, PORTUGUESE
Now called Cabinda (q.v.), it is an enclaved portion of the People's Republic of Angola and is located north of the River Congo.

149 CONSTANTINOPLE
The former name of Istanbul, largest city and chief seaport of Turkey.

201 CONVENTION STATES — See Indian Convention States.

162 COO (COS)
One of the Aegean Islands ceded to Italy by Turkey at the end of WWI. See Dodecanese Islands.

368 COOK ISLANDS
The Cook Islands comprise two groups in the South Pacific. They are administered by New Zealand, although internally independent.

150 CORDOBA
A province in the Argentine Republic.

150 CORFU
One of the Ionian Islands (q.v.) located off the coast of Greece in the Adriatic Sea. It was briefly occupied by Italy in 1923 and again during WWII.

99 CORISCO
Together with the islands of Elobey and Annobon, it was a Spanish colony off the west coast of Africa. It became part of Spanish Guinea until 1960, when it was joined with Fernando Po. Now in the Republic of Equatorial Guinea. For map see Annobon.

151 CORRIENTES
A province in the northern part of Argentina.

162 COS — See Coo.

128 COSTA ATLANTICA
An area of Nicaragua known as Cabo Gracias a Dios (q.v.).

379 COSTA RICA

A republic since 1821, Costa Rica is located in Central American with coastlines on both Caribbean Sea and Pacific Ocean.

220 COURLAND — See Kurland.

177 CRACOW

Now the Polish city of Krakow. For map see General Gouvernement.

151 CRETE

A large island in the eastern Mediterranean, Crete was once part of the Turkish Empire. From 1898 to 1908 it was administered jointly by Britain, France, Italy, and Russia. It became Greek in 1908 and was invaded and occupied for a time by the Germans during WWII.

152 CRIMEA

A peninsula extending into the Black Sea from the north. Part of the USSR.

152 CROATIA

Now a state within the Federal People's Republic of Yugoslavia, Croatia is in the northern part of the country, bordering on the Adriatic Sea. It has formerly been part of the Austro-Hungarian Empire. During WWII, it was occupied by Axis forces and given semi-autonomous status.

153 CUAUTLA

A town in the Mexican state of Morelos.

378 CUBA, REPUBLIC OF

Located in the Caribbean Sea south of Florida, Cuba was a Spanish colony until taken by the US during the Spanish-American War of 1898. It became fully independent in 1934.

153 CUCUTA

A city in the South American Republic of Colombia.

154 CUERNAVACA

The capital city of the Mexican state of Morelos.

154 CUNDINAMARCA

One of the states forming the Granadine Confederation. It is now a department of Colombia.

155 CURACAO

Previously a Dutch colony in the Caribbean off the coast of Venezuela. Now part of the Netherlands Antilles.

Crete

Costa   Rica

Curacao

Spanish Cuba

Croatia

Republic of Cuba

155 CUZCO

A town and department of Peru.

384 CYPRUS

An island in the eastern Mediterranean Sea, it came under British administration in 1878 at the request of Turkey. It remained a colony until becoming independent as a republic within the British Commonwealth in 1960. In 1974 Turkey invaded the island and continues to occupy the northern portion.

156 CYRENAICA

An area of northern Africa to the west of Egypt. It was part of the territory taken by Italy during its 1911-12 war with Turkey. With Tripolitania and Fezzan it became the Italian colony of Libya. After much fighting Cyrenaica was liberated by British forces during WWII and administered as a military area until it became independent as part of the Kingdom of Libya in 1951. It is now within the Socialist People's Libyan Arab Jamahiriya.

382 CZECHOSLOVAKIA

The Czechoslovak Socialist Republic was once part of the Austro-Hungarian Empire and achieved its independence following WWI. Occupied by Germany before and during WWII, it regained its freedom at the end of the war, only to fall under the close control of the USSR.

Turkish Cyprus

British Cyprus

Republic of Cyprus

Cyrenaica

Italian
Cyrenaica

Czechoslovakia

Danish West Indies

Dahomey

Danzig

Denmark

Davaar

Dedeagh

D

156 DAHOMEY
Formerly a native kingdom in West Africa, Dahomey was annexed by France in 1894 and made a colony. It was administered as a unit of French West Africa and included the colony of Benin from 1899. It became independent as the Republic of Dahomey in 1958 and changed its name to the People's Republic of Benin in 1975.

157 DAIREN AND PORT ARTHUR
Towns located in Liaoning Province of the People's Republic of China. Dairen is now named Talien, and Port Arthur is known as Lu-shun. They are located on a peninsula jutting into the Gulf of Chihli.

157 DAKAR-ABIDJAN
These were the capital cities of the French West African colonies of Senegal and Ivory Coast, respectively. A French West African stamp was issued inscribed with their names in 1959 during the period when the various colonies making up French West Africa were becoming independent.

158 DALMATIA
Once part of the Austro-Hungarian Empire, Dalmatia is an area on the Adriatic coast of the Balkan Peninsula and includes some offshore islands. It was occupied by Italy following WWI and again during WWII. It is now part of the Socialist Federal Republic of Yugoslavia.

276 DAMAN — See Damao.

276 DAMAO
Formerly part of Portuguese India (q.v.), Damao is a city on the west coast of India, north of Bombay. It is now called Daman.

158 DANISH WEST INDIES
The Danish West Indies was a colony comprising a group of islands in the Lesser Antilles of the West Indies. It was purchased from Denmark by the US in 1917 and is now the American Virgin Islands.

159 DANZIG
A port city on the Polish coast, Danzig was German until WWI, then a Free City from 1920 to 1939, when it was again occupied by Germany. After its liberation it became Polish and is now called Gdansk.

159 DARDANELLES
The Dardanelles is a strait separating the Gallipoli Peninsula from Asian Turkey. The chief town on the strait is Canakkale (Kale Sultanieh), located on the Asian side.

331 DAS ISLAND
An island in the Persian Gulf. Now part of the sheikdom of Abu Dhabi within the United Arab Emirates. For map see Trucial States.

202 DATIA — See Duttia.

401 DAVAAR
An island off the Scottish coast. See British Offshore Islands.

160 DEBRECEN
A town and area of Hungary occupied by Romania following WWI. Restored after a brief occupation and now part of Hungary.

DECCAN
An area of central India, in which was located the state of Hyderabad (q.v.).

160 DEDEAGH (DEDEAGATZ OR DEDEAGETCH)
A Greek city now called Alexandroupolis.

382 DENMARK
A kingdom in northern Europe, Denmark comprises the peninsula of Jutland and a number of adjacent islands in the Baltic Sea.

20

Diego Suarez

Djibouti

Dodecanese Is.

Dominica

Dominican Republic

Dubai

Durazzo

Duttia

202 DHAR
A feudatory state in India, it is now part of the Republic of India. See Indian Feudatory States.

161 DIEGO-SUAREZ
A seaport of the northern tip of Madagascar. Until 1896, it was a separate French colony. Now part of the Democratic Republic of Madagascar.

276 DIU
Formerly part of Portuguese India (q.v.), Diu is an island and town on the north shore of the Gulf of Khambhat on the west coast of India.

91 DJIBOUTI
A city on the south shore of the Gulf of Tadjoura at the southern end of the Red Sea. It is now the capital of the East African Republic of Djibouti. For map see Afars and Issas.

353 DJIBOUTI
The Republic of Djibouti is an area of East Africa around the Gulf of Tadjoura at the southern end of the Red Sea. It was originally the French Somali Coast. In 1967 it became the French Territory of Afars and Issas (q.v.). Independence as the Republic of Djibouti came in 1977.

161 DOBRUDJA
An area of Romania occupied by Bulgaria during WWI.

162 DODECANESE ISLANDS
A group of islands in the Aegean Sea off the coast of Asian Turkey. They were occupied by Italy in 1912 and became Greek following WWII.

163 DOHA
The capital city of the Persian Gulf country of Qatar.

372 DOMINICA
The Commonwealth of Dominica is a former British colony in the Leeward Islands of the Lesser Antilles. It was transferred to the Windward Group in 1940 and became independent in 1978.

373 DOMINICAN REPUBLIC
A republic occupying about the eastern two thirds of the Caribbean island of Hispaniola in the Greater Antilles.

163 DORPAT
A city in the former independent country of Estonia. It is now called Tartu and is part of the Soviet Union.

331 DUBAI
A former Trucial state on the south shore of the Persian Gulf, Dubai is now one of the United Arab Emirates. For map see Trucial States.

164 DURAZZO
A town on the Adriatic coast of Albania. Now called Durres.

164 DURRES — See Durazzo.

254 DUTCH EAST INDIES — See Netherlands Indies.

398 DUTCH GUIANA — See Suriname.

202 DUTTIA
A former feudatory state in India, it is now part of the Republic of India. See Indian Feudatory States.

Eastern
Rumelia

Ecuador

Egypt

Elobey

Equatorial Guinea

E

El Salvador

EAST AFRICA
See British East Africa, German East Africa, and
Italian East Africa.

EAST CHINA
An area of China under Communist control prior
to the formation of the People's Republic of
China. It included Shantung, Kiangsu, Chekiang,
Anhwei, and Fukien. For maps see under in-
dividual province names.

343 EASTERN GALICIA — See Western Ukraine.

213 EASTERN KARELIA
An area of the USSR to the west of Lake Onega,
occupied by Finland for a period during WWII.
See Karelia.

164 EASTERN RUMELIA
Formerly part of the Turkish Empire, Eastern
Rumelia revolted and became known as South
Bulgaria. Now part of that country.

165 EASTERN SILESIA
An area of eastern Europe between
Czechoslovakia and Poland in which a plebiscite
was to have been held following WWI. However,
it was never held and the area was divided between the two countries by the League of Nations.

165 EASTERN SZECHWAN
The eastern portion of the Chinese province of
the same name.

382 EAST GERMANY — See German Democratic
Republic.

183 EAST SAXONY — See Germany, Soviet Zone.

277 EAST TIMOR — See Portuguese Timor.

398 ECUADOR
The Republic of Ecuador is located on the upper
west coast of South America.

162 EGEO
An overprint applied to Italian stamps for use in
the Dodecanese Islands (q.v.).

353 EGYPT
The Arab Republic of Egypt was under nominal
Turkish control until WWI, when it became a
British protectorate. It was made a kingdom in
1922 and became a republic in 1953. From 1958 to
1961 it was a joint republic with Syria as the
United Arab Republic. It assumed its present
name in 1971.

382 EIRE — See Ireland.

219 EKATERINODAR
A town in the USSR located between the Black
Sea and the Caspian Sea. It is now called
Krasnodar. For map see Kuban Territory.

368 ELLICE ISLANDS — See Tuvalu.

99 ELOBEY
A former Spanish colony off the western coast of
Africa, it is now part of the Republic of Equatorial
Guinea. See Annobon and Corisco. For map see
Annobon.

380 EL SALVADOR
A republic on the west coast of Central America.

382 ENGLAND
Part of the United Kingdom of Great Britain and
Northern Ireland. See Great Britain.

385 ENGLISH CHANNEL ISLANDS — See Channel
Islands.

166 EPIRUS
An undefined area located between northern
Greece and Albania. Now divided between them.

353 EQUATORIAL GUINEA
The Republic of Equatorial Guinea was formed in
1968 from the Spanish colonies of Fernando Po
(including Elobey, Annobon, and Corisco) and
Rio Muni.

Estonia

Eritrea

Ethiopia

Eynhallow

Eupen
and
Malmedy

166 ERITREA
A former Italian colony on the African coast of the Red Sea, Eritrea was administered by Great Britain following its liberation in 1941 until it federated with Ethiopia in 1952.

167 ESTONIA
Once part of the Russian Empire, Estonia gained its independence following WWI, only to lose it in 1940 when the Soviet Union invaded and took over the country.

353 ETHIOPIA
Formerly known as Abyssinia, Ethiopia is located in East Africa. From 1935 to 1941 it was an Italian colony. In 1952 it federated with the ex-Italian colony of Eritrea. For map see Abyssinia.

167 EUPEN AND MALMEDY
A portion of Germany occupied by Belgium at the end of WWI.

401 EYNHALLOW
An island in the Orkney Islands off the northern tip of Scotland. See British Offshore Islands.

Falkland Islands

Far Eastern Republic

Faridkot

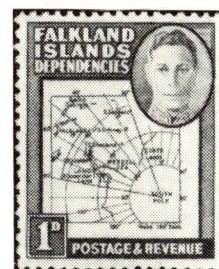
Falkland Is. Dependencies

Faroe Islands

Fernando Po

Federated Malay States

Fezzan

Fiji

F

398 FALKLAND ISLANDS
A British crown colony in the South Atlantic.

359 FALKLAND ISLANDS DEPENDENCIES
This administrative unit is currently made up of South Georgia (q.v.), and the South Sandwich Islands. Areas previously included are now part of the British Antarctic Territory. For map see Antarctica.

168 FAR EASTERN REPUBLIC
A short-lived, vaguely defined republic located in Siberia during the early 1920s. Now in the USSR.

202 FARIDKOT
Faridkot was an Indian convention state that later became a feudatory state. See Indian Convention States and Indian Feudatory States.

386 FAROE ISLANDS
A group of islands located in the North Atlantic. It is Danish but has a measure of self government. The islands were administered by Great Britain during WWII while Denmark was under German occupation.

169 FEDERATED MALAY STATES
A grouping of states on the Malay Peninsula from 1895 to the mid-1930s. Comprised the states of

Negri Sembilan, Pahang, Perek, Selangor, and Sungei Ujong. The latter previously had become part of Negri Sembilan.

237 FEDERATION OF MALAYA — See Malayan Federation.

168 FERNANDO PO
An island off the west coast of Africa, Fernando Po was part of Spanish Guinea until 1960. In 1968 it became part of the Republic of Equatorial Guinea. Its current name is Bioko, although for a short time it was called Macias Nguema Biyoga.

202 FEUDATORY STATES — See Indian Feudatory States.

170 FEZZAN
An undefined territory in the southern part of Libya. It was taken by Italy during its 1911-1912 war with Turkey. Free French forces liberated it from the Italians in 1942, and it was administered by France until it became part of Libya in 1951. See Ghadames.

368 FIJI
The Dominion of Fiji is a member of the British Commonwealth and is located in the South Pacific. It became a British crown colony in 1874 and gained independence in 1970.

Finland

Fiume

France

Fr. Equatorial
Guinea

French Guiana

French Guinea

Foochow

French India

382 FINLAND
The Republic of Finland is located on the eastern shore of the Baltic Sea and borders on the USSR. It was a Russian grand duchy until the 1917 Russian Revolution, when it gained its freedom.

170 FIUME
Fiume, a seaport on the Adriatic coast of Yugoslavia, is now called Rijeka. Previously in the Austro-Hungarian Empire, the city was occupied by the Allies in WWI. It was a Free State until 1924, when it was taken by Italy. It has been in Yugoslavia since WWII.

171 FOOCHOW
A town near the coast of the People's Republic of China, to the west of the northern tip of Taiwan. Now called Fu-chou.

361 FORMOSA — See China (Taiwan), Republic of.

382 FRANCE
A large country in Western Europe with coastlines on the English Channel, the Mediterranean Sea, and the Atlantic Ocean.

149 FRENCH CONGO — See Congo, French.

171 FRENCH EQUATORIAL AFRICA
Comprising the French colonies of Gabon, Middle Congo, Ubangi-Shari, and Chad, it was formed in 1936. In 1958 the four areas each became independent republics.

172 FRENCH GUIANA
Once a French colony, it is now a department of France located on the north coast of South America between Suriname and Brazil.

172 FRENCH GUINEA
Located on the west coast of Africa, French Guinea became part of French West Africa in 1944. It achieved independence as the Republic of Guinea in 1958.

173 FRENCH INDIA
French India comprised five widely scattered settlements around the coast of India. They were Chandernagor, Karikal, Mahe, Pondichery, and Yanaon. Between 1949 and 1954 they became part of the Republic of India.

205 FRENCH INDO-CHINA — See Indo-China.

FRENCH LEVANT

The collective name for French post offices in the Turkish Empire prior to WWI.

173 FRENCH MOROCCO

A French protectorate from 1912. In 1956 French Morocco, Spanish Morocco, and the International Zone of Tangier joined to form the Kingdom of Morocco.

174 FRENCH OCEANIC SETTLEMENTS

A French colony formed in 1903 from a number of French islands in the South Pacific. Became French Polynesia in 1956.

174 FRENCH POLYNESIA — See French Oceanic Settlements.

91 FRENCH SOMALI COAST

The French Somali Coast became the French Territory of Afars and Issas in 1967 and gained independence in 1977 as the Republic of Djibouti. For map see Afars and Issas.

359 FRENCH SOUTHERN AND ANTARCTIC TERR.

Formed in 1955, the French Southern and Antarctic Territories comprise Adelie Land in Antarctica, the Indian Ocean Kerguelen and Crozet archipelgos, and the islands of St. Paul and Amsterdam. Prior to 1955, the areas were dependencies of Madagascar.

174 FRENCH SUDAN

Formed from Upper Senegal and Niger, it was a French colony until 1899, when it was split among the neighboring French colonies of Dahomey, French Guinea, Ivory Coast, and Senegal and Niger. It was reconstituted in 1921, becoming part of French West Africa in 1944. In 1958 it became independent as the Sudanese Republic, and after a brief federation with the Republic of Senegal from 1959 to 1960 as the Federation of Mali, it became the independent Republic of Mali.

French
Levant

French Polynesia

French Morocco

French Sudan

French
Somali
Coast

French Southern
& Antarctic Terr.

91 FRENCH TERR. OF AFARS AND ISSAS — See Afars and Issas.

175 FRENCH WEST AFRICA
French West Africa was formed in 1944 from the French colonies of Dahomey, French Guinea, French Sudan, Ivory Coast, Mauritania, Niger, Senegal, and Upper Volta. These areas became individually independent in 1958.

171 FU-CHOU — See Foochow.

331 FUJIERA
One of the Trucial States, Fujeira is located on the Arabian coast of the Gulf of Oman. It is now one of the United Arab Emirates. For map see Trucial States.

171 FUKIEN
A province in the People's Republic of China. For map see Foochow.

175 FUNCHAL
A district of the Portuguese island of Madeira, located in the Atlantic Ocean off the northwest coast of Africa.

French West
Africa

Fujeira

Funchal

Fu-chou

Gabon

Georgia

The Gambia

General
Gouvernement

German
East
Africa

Geneva

German
New
Guinea

German
Democratic
Republic

G

353 GABON

Gabon was a French colony on the west coast of central Africa until 1937, when it became part of French Equatorial Africa. It gained independence in 1958 as the Gabonese Republic. For map see French Equatorial Africa.

353 GABONESE REPUBLIC — See Gabon.

401 GAIRSAY

An island in the Orkney Islands off the northern tip of Scotland. See British Offshore Islands.

176 GALAPAGOS ISLANDS

An island group in the Pacific Ocean off the west coast of South America. The islands have been a province of Ecuador since 1973.

354 GAMBIA, THE

The Gambia was a British colony on the coast of West Africa. It was made independent in 1965 and became a republic within the British Commonwealth in 1970. Early in 1982 it joined a form of limited federation with the Republic of Senegal under the name of Senegambia.

176 GAZA

A town and district facing on the southeast corner of the Mediterranean Sea. Currently occupied by Israel.

159 GDANSK — See Danzig.

177 GENERAL GOUVERNEMENT

An area of Poland under German occupation during WWII.

177 GENEVA

A city and canton in southwest Switzerland.

178 GEORGIA

Once part of the Russian Empire, Georgia enjoyed a period of freedom following the 1917 Russian Revolution. With Armenia and Azerbaijan it form-ed the Transcaucasian Federation during 1922. Now part of the USSR.

382 GERMAN DEMOCRATIC REPUBLIC

At the end of WWII, the Soviet Union occupied the eastern part of Germany. This area eventually became the German Democratic Republic (East Germany), with the Soviet Zone of Berlin as its capital.

178 GERMAN EAST AFRICA

A German colony until WWI, it was mandated to Great Britain as Tanganyika until 1961, when it became independent. In 1964 it united with the former British protectorate of Zanzibar to become the United Republic of Tanganyika and Zanzibar, later changing its name to the United Republic of Tanzania.

181 GERMAN EMPIRE — See Germany.

179 GERMAN KAMERUN

A German colony in Africa. Now the United Republic of Cameroon.

GERMAN LEVANT

The collective name for German post offices in the Turkish Empire.

238 GERMAN MARIANAS — See Mariana Islands.

239 GERMAN MARSHALL ISLANDS — See Marshall Islands.

179 GERMAN NEW GUINEA

German New Guinea comprised the northern portion of the eastern half of New Guinea. It was called Kaiser Wilhelm Land by the Germans and included the Bismarck Archipelago. Occupied by Australia during WWI, it was joined to Papua under Australian administration. Self government was achieved in 1973, and it is now part of Papua New Guinea.

German Samoa

German SW Africa

Germany

German
Togo

Federal
Republic of
Germany

Soviet Occupation
Zone of Germany

Ghana

180 GERMAN SAMOA

A German territory from 1899. Prior to that German Samoa had been administered jointly by the US, Germany, and Great Britain. Occupied by New Zealand in 1914, the islands were mandated to that country in 1920. Later known as Western Samoa, the South Pacific group became independent in 1962 and is now called Samoa.

180 GERMAN SOUTHWEST AFRICA

A former German colony in southern Africa, it was taken by South African forces in WWI and later mandated to South Africa. In recent years the Republic of South Africa has refused to give up its control of the territory, now called Namibia, despite United Nations demands.

GERMAN STATES

The old stamp-issuing states of Germany comprised Baden, Bavaria, Bergedorf, Bremen, Brunswick, Hamburg, Hanover, Lubeck, Mecklenburg Schwerin, Mecklenburg Strelitz, Oldenburg, Prussia, Saxony, Schleswig-Holstein, and Wurttemberg. See under individual names.

181 GERMAN TOGO

Until WWI, Togo was a German colony in West Africa. After the war it was divided and portions mandated to Great Britain and France by the League of Nations. The British mandate became part of the Gold Coast (now Ghana), and the French area achieved independence in 1958 as the Republic of Togo.

181 GERMANY

Formed from the North German Confederation (q.v.) in 1871, the German Empire lasted until it was defeated in WWI. It then became a republic until, under Hitler, it was again defeated. After WWII, the country emerged divided into the Soviet-controlled East Germany (German Democratic Republic) and the areas occupied by Britain, France, and the US, which became the Federal Republic of Germany (West Germany).

382 GERMANY, FEDERAL REPUBLIC OF

Country formed in 1949 from the British, French, and US zones of occupation in Germany.

183 GERMANY, SOVIET ZONE

Now the Communist German Democratic Republic, the post-WWII Soviet Occupation Zone included districts of Berlin-Brandenburg, Mecklenburg-West Pomerania, Saxony, West Saxony, East Saxony, and Thuringia.

183 GHADAMES

An area in the southern portion of the Italian colony of Tripolitania, Ghadames was occupied by Free French forces in 1943 and remained under French administration until 1951, when it was made part of what is now the Socialist People's Libyan Arab Jamahiriya. Now Ghudamis.

353 GHANA

The Republic of Ghana was once the British colony of the Gold Coast. It assumed its present identity in 1960.

386 GIBRALTAR

A British colony and naval base located near the southern tip of the Iberian Peninsula at the western entrance to the Mediterranean Sea.

184 GILBERT AND ELLICE ISLANDS

Comprising several island groups in the Pacific, the Gilberts included, among others, Makin, Tarawa, and Ocean, plus Phoenix Island and the Line Islands of Fanning, Washington, and Christmas. The Ellice Islands comprised a separate group. It was a British protectorate from 1892 until the colony was formed in 1915 at the request of the inhabitants. In 1976 the colony was divided, with the Gilbert Islands becoming one crown colony and the Ellice Islands, under the name of Tuvalu, becoming another. Both became independent in 1979, when the Gilbert Islands changed its name to Kiribati.

184 GILBERT ISLANDS — See Gilbert and Ellice Islands.

184 GIUMULZINA

A town in Thrace. Now the Greek town of Komotini.

276 GOA

Formerly part of Portuguese India (q.v.), Goa was an area on the west coast of the Indian peninsula, centered on what is now the town of Panaji in the Republic of India.

185 GOLD COAST

A former British colony in West Africa, the Gold Coast attained Dominion status in 1957, and in 1960 it became the independent nation of Ghana.

359 GRAHAM LAND

An area at the northern tip of the Antarctic Peninsula, which extends towards the southern tip of South America. It is included in the British Antarctic Territory (q.v.).

185 GRANADA

A town and province of southern Spain.

GRANADINE CONFEDERATION

The ex-Spanish colonial area in the northwest part of South America became independent in 1810 as the State of Greater Colombia. In 1832 Venezuela and Ecuador broke away, and the remaining portion became the Republic of New Granada. From 1858 to 1861 this was known as the Granadine Confederation. Following several subsequent name changes, the country adopted its present name, the Republic of Colombia. For maps of the constituent stamp-issuing states, see under their individual names.

186 GRAND COMORO

An island northwest of Madagascar, it was once a French colony and is now part of the Republic of the Comores.

Gibraltar

Gilbert and
Ellice Islands

Gilbert Islands

Gold Coast

Granadine
Confederation

Grand
Comoro

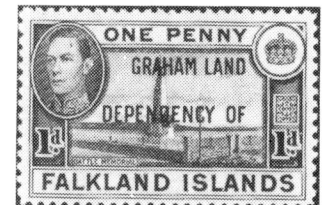

Graham Land

30

382 GREAT BRITAIN

Its full title is the United Kingdom of Great Britain and Northern Ireland, but it is commonly referred to as Great Britain, Britain, The United Kingdom, or simply the UK. It comprises a group of islands off the coast of northwest Europe between the Atlantic and the North Sea. The major island includes England, Scotland, and Wales; the second largest island contains the Republic of Ireland and the six counties that make up Northern Ireland. There are many lesser islands, the most important of which are the English Channel Islands off the French coast, the Isle of Man in the Irish Sea, the Isle of Wight, and the Orkney and Shetland islands and the Western Isles off the Scottish coast.

282 GREATER RAJASTHAN UNION

This union was formed in 1947-1949 by the merger of 14 states of India. Included were the stamp-issuing states of Bundi, Jaipur, and Kishangarh. It is now part of the Republic of India. For map see Rajasthan.

382 GREECE — See Hellenic Republic.

382 GREENLAND

The world's largest island, Greenland is located to the northeast of Canada. It is part of the Kingdom of Denmark, but enjoys a large degree of home rule.

373 GRENADA

A former British colony, Grenada became independent in 1974. It is located in the Lesser Antilles of the West Indies, to the north of Trinidad.

375 GRENADINES OF GRENADA

A chain of small islands running north from Grenada toward the island of St. Vincent. Administered from Grenada. The main islands are Petit Martinique and Carriacou.

375 GRENADINES OF ST. VINCENT

The northern portion of the Grenadine Islands between St. Vincent and Grenada. Administered from St. Vincent. The chief islands are Bequia, Mustique, Canouan, and Union.

246 GRENVILLE (GREENVILLE)

A town in Liberia. For map see Monrovia.

Great Britain

Greece

Grenadines of St. Vincent

Greenland

Grenada

Grenadines of Grenada

Guam

Guam Guard Mail

Guatemala

Guadeloupe

Guayana

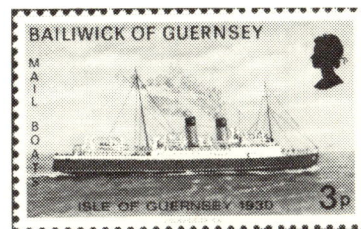

Guernsey

186 GRIQUALAND WEST

A British crown colony established in 1873, it was located in South Africa around the chief town of Kimberley. It was incorporated into Cape Colony in 1880 and is now part of the Republic of South Africa.

187 GRODNO

A district of South Lithuania. Now located within Belorussia, Soviet Union.

187 GUADALAJARA

A city in Mexico and the capital of the state of Jalisco.

188 GUADELOUPE

An island group in the Lesser Antilles of the West Indies, it comprises the two main islands of Basse Terre and Grande Terre, which are separated by the Salt River. Also included are islands of Marie-Galante, Les Saintes, Saint Barthelemy, Desirade, and the northern portion of the island of Saint Martin. It was a French colony until 1946, when it became a department of France.

188 GUAM

A US possession, Guam is an island in the Western Pacific. Until the Spanish-American War of 1898, it was a Spanish colony, and except for a period of Japanese occupation during WWII, it has remained under US control.

189 GUANACASTE

A province of the Central American country of Costa Rica.

378 GUATEMALA

The Republic of Guatemala is located in Central America bordering on Belize, El Salvador, Honduras, and Mexico. It became a republic in 1839 following a period as a state in the United States of Central America. Prior to that, it had been part of the Spanish Empire and then a state of Mexico.

189 GUAYANA

Located in the Republic of Venezuela, it was an administrative area in the province of Bolivar, based on the town of Ciudad Guayana.

385 GUERNSEY

The Bailiwick of Guernsey is an island with five lesser island dependencies located in the English Channel islands off the French coast. The dependencies are Alderney, Sark, Herm, Jethou, and Lithou (Lihou). For map see English Channel Islands.

32

Republic
of Guinea

Spanish Guinea

Guyana

401 GUGH
An island in the Scilly group off Land's End in the British Isles. See British Offshore Islands.

122 GUIANA, BRITISH — See British Guiana.

398 GUIANA, DUTCH — See Suriname.

172 GUIANA, FRENCH — See French Guiana.

353 GUINEA-BISSAU
The Republic of Guinea-Bissau is located on the coast of West Africa. It was Portuguese Guinea until achieving independence in 1974.

353 GUINEA, EQUATORIAL REPUBLIC OF — See Equatorial Guinea, Republic of.

172 GUINEA, FRENCH — See French Guinea.

276 GUINEA, PORTUGUESE — See Portuguese Guinea.

353 GUINEA, REPUBLIC OF
Formerly French Guinea, it became part of French West Africa in 1944 and achieved independence in 1958.

GUINEA, SPANISH — See Spanish Guinea.

190 GUIPUZCOA
A province in northern Spain.

397 GUYANA
The Cooperative Republic of Guyana was formerly the Crown Colony of British Guiana (q.v.), which became independent in 1966.

201 GWALIOR
Formerly a convention state in India, it is now part of the Republic of India. See Indian Convention States.

Hadhramaut

Haiti

Hamburg

Hatay

Hawaii

Harper

Hanover

Heligoland

Hellenic Republic

H

Hejaz

190 HADHRAMAUT
An area of Southern Arabia now within the People's Democratic Republic of Yemen. It included the Qu'aiti State in Hadhramaut, the Qu'aiti State of Shihr and Mukalla, and the Mahra Sultanate of Qishn and Socotra. Together with the Kathiri State of Seiyun, it was part of the Aden Protectorate until 1967.

191 HAINAN
An island off the coast of the People's Republic of China, Hainan was part of the Communist South China Liberation Area in 1949, prior to the formation of the People's Republic of China.

373 HAITI
The Republic of Haiti occupies the western third of the Greater Antilles island of Hispaniola, which it shares with the Dominican Republic.

191 HAMBURG
A seaport in the Federal Republic of Germany, Hamburg was once a Free City.

192 HANOVER
A kingdom in northeast Germany, Hanover joined Prussia in 1866. It is now in the Federal Republic of Germany.

246 HARPER
A town in Liberia. For map see Monrovia.

192 HATAY
A territory in the southeastern part of Turkey, Hatay came under French control at the end of WWI. It was returned to Turkey in 1939. The territory included the city of Alexandretta.

353 HAUTE VOLTA — See Upper Volta.

193 HAWAII
Located in the middle of the Pacific Ocean, the Hawaiian Islands were once called the Sandwich Islands. The group was an independent kingdom until 1893. It was annexed by the US in 1898 and became a US territory. It is now one of the United States.

193 HEILUNGKIANG-KIRIN
Provinces of Manchuria.

194 HEJAZ
Formerly part of the Turkish Empire, the area of Hejaz became an independent kingdom in 1916. It was taken by the Sultan of the Nejd and became part of the Kingdom of the Hejaz and Nejd, which was renamed the Kingdom of Saudi Arabia in 1932.

194 HELIGOLAND
An island in the North Sea off the coast of northern Germany. It was a British colony until 1890, when it was ceded to Germany, which made it part of the province of Schleswig-Holstein. It is now in the Federal Republic of Germany.

382 HELLENIC REPUBLIC
Commonly known as Greece, it is located in southeast Europe. It was part of the Turkish Empire until 1830, when it became an independent kingdom. It was a republic from 1924 to 1935, then became a kingdom again. Occupied by Germany during WWII, it was liberated by British forces and the monarchy re-established. Since 1973 it has been a republic.

195 HELSINKI
The capital city of Finland. Once known as Helsingfors.

Hoi-Hao

Horta

Honduras

Hong Kong

Hungary

Hutt River

Herm

Hyderabad

131 HERAKLION

A district of Crete under British administration during the period ending in 1908 when the population voted for union with Greece. See Candia.

401 HERM

A small island in the English Channel Islands. A dependency of Guernsey. For map see British Offshore Islands, and English Channel Islands.

109 HERMOSILLO

A town in Mexico. For map see Baja California.

119 HERZEGOVINA

A Turkish province until annexed by Austria-Hungary in 1908. It is now part of Yugoslavia. See Bosnia and Herzegovina.

401 HESTON (HESTEN)

An island off the Scottish coast near Dumfries. See British Offshore Islands.

401 HILBRE

A small island off the coast of Cheshire, near Liverpool, England. See British Offshore Islands.

191 HOI-HAO

A town on Hainan Island off the south coast of the People's Republic of China. An Indo-Chinese post office operated there until 1922. Now called Hai-k'ou. For map see Hainan Island.

191 HOIHOW

Spelling variation of Hoi-Hao (q.v.).

202 HOLKAR

Alternative name of Indore (q.v.).

HOLLAND, SOUTH AND NORTH

Provinces in the Kingdom of the Netherlands.

299 HOLSTEIN

Part of the territory known as Schleswig- Holstein at the base of the Jutland Peninsula. Danish from 1848, it was occupied by Prussia in 1864 and made a province of the country in 1866. For map see Schleswig-Holstein.

195 HONAN

A province in the People's Republic of China.

196 HONDA

A town in the central part of the Republic of Columbia.

378 HONDURAS

The Republic of Honduras is located in Central America bordering on Guatemala and Nicaragua.

362 HONG KONG

A British colony comprising a number of islands and a portion of the mainland on the coast of the People's Republic of China. Occupied by Japan during WWII.

196 HOPEH

A province in the People's Republic of China.

197 HORTA

The chief town on the island of Faial in the Azores.

197 HUACHO

A town in the South American country of Peru.

198 HUNAN

A province in the People's Republic of China.

382 HUNGARY

The Hungarian People's Republic is located in Eastern Europe and was once a partner in the Austro-Hungarian Empire. Following WWI, it was a short-lived republic before becoming a monarchy in 1920. After WWII, it came under Soviet control and continues as a satellite of the USSR.

198 HUPEH

A province in the People's Republic of China.

400 HUTT RIVER PROVINCE

A wheat farm in Western Australia, the owner of which "seceded" after a dispute with the Australian government over wheat quotas. The owner proclaimed himself "king" and issued local labels to frank mail to the nearest Australian post office.

202 HYDERABAD

A former feudatory state in India, it is now part of the Republic of India. Not to be confused with the city of the same name in Pakistan. For map see Indian Feudatory States.

Iceland

Idar

Ifni

India, British

Indo-China

India

Indonesia

Indore

199 ICARIA (NIKARIA or IKARIA)
A Greek island in the Aegean Sea, it is labeled Ikaria in current atlases. Formerly Turkish, it was occupied by Greece prior to WWI.

382 ICELAND
The Republic of Iceland is an island in the North Atlantic off the coast of Greenland. Previously a dual monarchy with Denmark, it became a republic in 1944.

202 IDAR
Formerly a feudatory state in India, it is now part of the Republic of India. For map see Indian Feudatory States.

199 IFNI
A former Spanish colony on the coast of Morocco. It became part of the Kingdom of Morocco in 1969.

199 IKARIA — See Icaria.

401 INCHOLM
An island in the Firth of Forth, Scotland. See British Offshore Islands.

361 INDIA
The Republic of India comprises what was formerly part of British India plus the many states. It was created from the Dominion of India in 1950. The dominion had been created in 1947 when India was divided into India and Pakistan. The areas of French and Portuguese India were later absorbed.

200 INDIA, BRITISH
The area of India under British control prior to the 1947 partition. It did not include feudatory or convention states.

201 INDIAN CONVENTION STATES
The stamp-issuing convention states of India were Chamba, Faridkot, Gwalior, Jind, Nabha, and Patiala.

202 INDIAN FEUDATORY STATES
The stamp-issuing feudatory states of India were Alwar, Bamra, Barwani, Bhopal, Bhor, Bijawar, Bundi, Bussahir (Bashahr), Charkhari, Cochin, Dhar, Duttia, Faridkot, Hyderabad, Idar, Indore (Holkar), Jaipur, Jammu and Kashmir, Jasdan, Jhalawar, Jind, Kishangarh, Las Bela, Morvi, Nandgaon (Rajnandgaon), Nowanuggur (Nawanagar), Orchha, Poonch, Rajasthan, Rajpipla, Sirmoor, Soruth, Travancore, Travancore-Cochin, and Wadhwan.

173 INDIAN SETTLEMENTS, FRENCH — See French India.

276 INDIA, PORTUGUESE — See Portuguese India.

205 INDO-CHINA
Formerly a French territory in Southeast Asia, Indo-China in 1949 was split into the independent states of Cambodia, Laos, and Vietnam. The area was under Japanese occupation during WWII.

361 INDONESIA
The Republic of Indonesia was previously known as the Dutch East Indies, Dutch Indies, or the Netherlands Indies. The United States of Indonesia was formed after WWII. It comprises the Netherlands Indies, Netherlands New Guinea, and Portuguese Timor, to form a nation made up of thousands of islands stretching from Sumatra in the west to the western half of New Guinea in the east. The present name was assumed in 1950.

202 INDORE
Formerly a feudatory state in India, it is now part of the Republic of India. See Indian Feudatory States.

Inhambane

Inini

Ionian Islands

Iraq

Iran

Ireland, Northern

Ireland

261 INGERMANLAND, NORTH — See North Ingermanland.

205 INHAMBANE
A town and district in the southern part of the People's Republic of Mozambique.

206 ININI
A territory that formed the greater part of the interior of French Guiana.

206 INNER MONGOLIA
An area of the People's Republic of China bordering on Mongolia. It was granted a degree of autonomy while under Japanese occupation prior to and during WWII.

210 IOANNINA — See Janina.

207 IONIAN ISLANDS
A chain of islands off the west coast of Greece, plus one — Cerigo, or Kithira — that lies to the south between the Greek mainland and the island of Crete. The other islands are Corfu (now Kerkira), Paxos, Levkas, Cephalonia (now Kefallinia), Ithaca (now Ithaki), and Zante (now Zakinthos). They were a British protectorate from 1814 to 1864, when they were presented to Greece. The islands were occupied at various times by Italy and Germany during WWII, and Italy had briefly occupied Corfu in 1923. All are now Greek.

131 IRAKLION — See Candia.

365 IRAN
The Islamic Republic of Iran is in western Asia bordering on the northern shore of the Persian Gulf and the Gulf of Oman, with frontiers on Afghanistan, Iraq, Pakistan, Turkey, and the USSR. It was once Persia.

365 IRAQ
The Republic of Iraq was a Turkish possession until WWI, when it was occupied by Britain. It is located to the north of the Persian Gulf and borders on Syria, Kuwait, Iran, Jordan, Saudi Arabia, and Turkey. Following WWI, it was mandated to Britain as Mesopotamia until 1932, when it became a kingdom. It has been a republic since 1958.

382 IRELAND
Once part of the United Kingdom of Great Britain, the Republic of Ireland, except for the six counties of Ulster, became a British Dominion as the Irish Free State in 1922. It declared its sovereignty in 1937 and withdrew from the Commonwealth in 1948.

389 IRELAND, NORTHERN
Northern Ireland, or Ulster, comprises the six northern counties of Ireland. The territory chose to remain part of Great Britain when the rest of Ireland separated as the Irish Free State in 1922.

253 IRIAN BARAT — See West Irian.

382 IRISH FREE STATE — See Ireland.

387 ISLE OF MAN
Located in the middle of the Irish Sea, the Isle of Man is part of the United Kingdom of Great Britain and Northern Ireland. It retains its ancient traditions of government and has a measure of autonomy.

365 ISRAEL
The State of Israel was formerly known as Palestine. It was part of the Turkish Empire until liberated by British forces during WWI. Following the war, it was mandated to Britain by the League of Nations until the formation of the State of Israel in 1948.

207 ISTRIA
A peninsula jutting into the Adriatic Sea at its northern end, just south of Trieste. Once part of Italy, it is now in Yugoslavia.

208 ITALIAN AUSTRIA
The name "Italian Austria" was applied to that part of Austria taken by Italy during WWI. It included Trentino, the city of Trieste, and Istria.

208 ITALIAN EAST AFRICA
An area of Italian colonies in East Africa including Eritrea, Ethiopia, and Italian Somaliland. It was combined into one administrative area in 1936, following Italy's invasion and conquest of Ethiopia. After the area was liberated by British forces during WWII, Ethiopian independence was restored and Eritrea and Italian Somaliland were placed under military administration. Eritrea is now part of Ethiopia, and Italian Somaliland is in the Somali Democratic Republic.

ITALIAN LEVANT
The collective name given to Italian post offices in the Turkish Empire prior to WWI.

ITALIAN SOCIALIST REPUBLIC
A puppet state set up in an undefined area of northern Italy by Germany in 1943, with the ousted Mussolini as its figurehead.

209 ITALIAN SOMALILAND
An Italian colony in East Africa. It included Benadir and Jubaland. Liberated by British forces in WWII, it was placed under United Nations supervision until, together with the British Protectorate of Somaliland, it became independent in 1960 as the Somali Democratic Republic.

ITALIAN STATES
Prior to the formation of the unified Kingdom of Italy in 1861, the area comprised a number of small states. The stamp-issuing states were Modena, Parma, Romagna, Roman States, Sardinia, Tuscany, and the Kingdom of the Two Sicilies. For maps see under individual state names.

Isle of Man

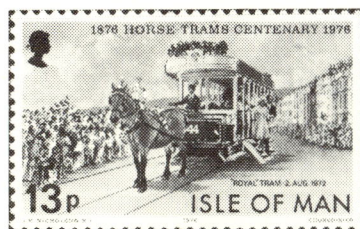

Israel

Italian
East
Africa

Italian
Socialist
Republic

Italian Somaliland

382 ITALY

Formally titled the Italian Republic, Italy was formed as a kingdom in 1861 from the Kingdom of Sardinia. It remained a kingdom until 1946.

207 ITHACA — See Ionian Islands.

207 ITHAKI — See Ionian Islands.

353 IVORY COAST

The Republic of the Ivory Coast was once a French colony in West Africa. It was made part of French West Africa in 1944 and became a republic within the French Community in 1958. In 1960 it achieved full independence.

Italy

Italy

Ivory Coast

Janina

Jaipur

Jamaica

Japan

Jethou

Jersey

J

209 JAFFA
A former city in Israel. Now part of the Tel Aviv-Yafo urban complex.

202 JAIPUR
A former feudatory state in India, Jaipur joined with Bundi and Kishangarh and several non-stamp-issuing states to form Rajasthan in 1949. It is now part of the Republic of India. See Indian Feudatory States.

380 JAMAICA
A onetime British colony in the Caribbean Sea, Jamaica became part of the short-lived British Caribbean Federation in 1958. In 1962 it was granted independence within the British Commonwealth.

202 JAMMU AND KASHMIR
A feudatory state in the north of India. It is now part of the Republic of India, although there is an unresolved border dispute with Pakistan. See Indian Feudatory States.

210 JANINA
A city in northern Greece. Now called Ioannina.

361 JAPAN
A country comprising a number of islands in the western Pacific off the coast of mainland Asia, east of China and the Korean Peninsula.

202 JASDAN
A feudatory state in India, Jasdan joined the Saurashtra Union in 1948. It is now part of the Republic of India. See Indian Feudatory States.

210 JAVA
One of the main islands of the Republic of Indonesia and site of the capital city of Jakarta (Batavia).

194 JEDDA (JIDDAH)
A city on the Red Sea coast of Saudi Arabia. For map see Hejaz.

385 JERSEY
One of the English Channel Islands. See Channel Islands.

211 JERUSALEM
Formerly a city in the Turkish Empire, Jerusalem was included in the area mandated to Great Britain following WWI. It is now the capital city of the State of Israel.

401 JETHOU
An island dependency of the Bailiwick of Guernsey. See British Offshore Islands, and English Channel Islands.

Johore

Jubaland

Jordan

Jind

Jugoslavia

202 JHALAWAR
A former feudatory state in India, it is now part of the Republic of India. See Indian Feudatory States.

202 JHIND — See Jind.

194 JIDDAH — See Jedda.

202 JIND
A former feudatory state in India, it later became a convention state and is now part of the Republic of India. See Indian Convention States and Indian Feudatory States.

237 JOHORE
A state on the Malay Peninsula, Johore is now part of Malaysia. See Malayan Federation.

365 JORDAN
The Hashemite Kingdom of Jordan is an area that was mandated to Britain following WWI, prior to which it had been a Turkish possession. It was known as Transjordan during the mandate period and became independent in 1946.

211 JUAN FERNANDEZ ISLANDS
A group of islands in the Pacific Ocean off the coast of Chile and belonging to that country.

212 JUBALAND
A district in East Africa ceded to Italy by Britain in 1925. It had been part of Kenya. It is now in the Somali Democratic Republic.

382 JUGOSLAVIA
Spelling variation of Yugoslavia (q.v.).

202 JUNAGARH — See Soruth.

Katana

Karelia

Kaulbach Is.

Kenya, Uganda, Tanganyika

Kelantan

K

Kenya

365 KABUL
The Kingdom of Kabul is the former name of the Republic of Afghanistan.

162 KALIMNOS — See Calimno.

179 KAMERUN — See German Kamerun.

361 KAMPUCHEA
A name used in reference to Cambodia.

212 KANSU
A province in the People's Republic of China.

213 KARELIA
An area in the northwestern part of the USSR. In 1921 the population made a try for freedom, and for a brief time Karelia was independent.

162 KARKI — See Calchi.

314 KARLSBAD
A town in Czechoslovakia. For map see Sudentenland.

162 KARPATHOS — See Scarpanto.

202 KASHMIR — See Jammu and Kashmir.

162 KASOS — See Caso.

162 KASTELLORIZON — See Castellorize.

213 KATANGA
A province in the Republic of Zaire in Central Africa. In 1960 it tried to break away, but after a period of civil war was reunited with Zaire.

190 KATHIRI STATE OF SEIYUN
A state in the Aden Protectorate States until 1967. Now part of the People's Democratic Republic of Yemen. See Hadhramaut.

405 KAULBACH ISLAND
An island off the Atlantic coast of Nova Scotia, Canada.

214 KAUNAS
A city in what was once the independent country of Lithuania. It was the capital city of Lithuania after Vilnius (q.v.) was occupied by Poland.

135 KAVALLA
Current Greek name for the city of Cavalla. See Cavelle.

237 KEDAH
A state on the Malay Peninsula and now part of Malaysia. See Malayan Federation.

362 KEELING ISLANDS — See Cocos (Keeling) Islands.

207 KEFALLINIA — See Ionian Islands.

237 KELANTAN
A state on the Malay Peninsula. Now part of Malaysia. See Malayan Federation.

353 KENYA
The Republic of Kenya is located in East Africa on the Indian Ocean. Until 1963 it was part of the British colony of Kenya, Uganda, and Tanganyika. It became independent in 1963.

214 KENYA, UGANDA, AND TANGANYIKA
From 1935 these three British areas in East Africa had a common postal system. Tanganyika became independent in 1961 and is now the United Republic of Tanzania. Uganda became the Republic of Uganda in 1962. Kenya gained its independence as the Republic of Kenya in 1963.

Kiribati

Kiautschou

Klaipeda

Kingdom of Two Sicilies

Kishangarh

215 KERASSUNDE
A town in the Turkish Empire, located on the Black Sea.

207 KERKIRA — See Ionian Islands.

162 KHALKI — See Dodecanese Islands.

151 KHANA — See La Canea.

361 KHMER REPUBLIC — See Cambodia.

331 KHOR FAKKAN
A dependency of Sharjah (q.v.). Sharjah was one of the Trucial States and is now a member of the United Arab Emirates. Khor Fakkan is located on the Gulf of Oman shore of Arabia. See Trucial States.

215 KIANGSI
A province of the People's Republic of China.

216 KIANGSU
An area of eastern China under Communist control prior to the takeover of the country in 1949.

216 KIAUCHAU — See Kiautschou.

216 KIAUTSCHOU (TSINGTAU)
An area on the south side of the Shantung Peninsula on the coast of the People's Republic of China. It was leased to Germany in 1898, following its seizure by that country a year earlier. It was taken by Japan in WWI and returned to China in 1922. It is now the Chinese city of Ch'ing-tao.

333 KIEV
Capital city of the Ukraine (q.v.).

217 KILIS
A town in Turkey, near the border with Syria.

304 KINGDOM OF TWO SICILIES — See Sicily.

217 KING EDWARD VII LAND
An area of the Antarctic continent.

218 KIONGA
A portion of German East Africa occupied by Portugal during WWI. It subsequently became part of the Portuguese colony of Mozambique and is now in the People's Republic of Mozambique.

368 KIRIBATI
Formerly the Gilbert Islands and previously part of the British colony of the Gilbert and Ellice Islands. The Pacific Ocean group became independent in 1979 and adopted its present name.

193 KIRIN
A province of Manchuria. For map see Heilungkiang.

202 KISHANGARH
A former feudatory state in India, it is now part of the Republic of India. See Indian Feudatory States.

207 KITHIRA (KITHYRA) — See Ionian Islands.

207 KITHYRA — See Ionian Islands.

243 KLAIPEDA — See Memel.

144 KLAUSENBURG — See Cluj.

343 KOLOMYYA
A town in western Ukraine (q.v.).

144 **KOLOZSVAR** — See Cluj.

314 **KONSTANTINSBAD**

A town in Czechoslovakia. For map see Sudentenland.

166 **KORCE**

A town in Albania. For map see Epirus.

KOREA

A peninsula on the coast of mainland Asia jutting south and located west of Japan. It was under Chinese control until 1910, when Japan took it. It did not gain its independence until the end of WWII. The Soviet Union prevented the establishment of a unified Korean state, and the peninsula became divided along the 38th parallel. The Korean War of the 1950s resulted from the invasion of the south by North Korea with Soviet and Chinese encouragement and assistance. The invasion failed, and South Korea remained free.

361 **KOREA, NORTH** — See North Korea.

361 **KOREA, SOUTH** — See South Korea.

166 **KORITSA (KORYTSA)**

A town in Albania, now called Korce. For map see Epirus.

166 **KORYTSA** — See Koritsa.

162 **KOS** — See Coo.

134 **KOTOR** — See Cattaro.

218 **KOUANG TCHEOU-WAN**

Also known as Kwangchow or Kwangchowan, Kouang Tcheou-wan is a port and district in southern China leased to France from 1898 to 1943. Now Chan-chiang.

177 **KRAKOW**

A city in Poland. For location see General Gouvernement.

219 **KRASNODAR**

Formerly Ekaterinodar (q.v.). For map see Kuban Territory.

338 **KRK**

An island off the Adriatic coast of Yugoslavia, once called Veglia (q.v.).

A stamp from South Korea (left) and one from North Korea.

Kotor (Cattaro): Stamps issued under Italian and German occupation in WWII

Kouang Tcheou-wan

44

169 KUALA LUMPUR
Capital city of Malaysia. For map see Federated Malay States.

219 KUBAN TERRITORY
An area of southern Russia controlled for a time by anti-Bolshevist forces during 1919-20.

219 KUNMING
A town in Yunnan province of China in which an Indo-Chinese post office operated from 1900 to 1922.

220 KUPA
An area comprising Fiume (Reijeka), Susak, and the Kupa river area that was under Italian occupation during WWII.

220 KURLAND (COURLAND)
An area of the once-independent country of Latvia.

366 KUWAIT
The State of Kuwait is an area at the head of the Persian Gulf. It was under British protection until 1961, when it became independent.

218 KWANGCHOWAN — See Kouang Tcheou-wan.

221 KWANGSI
A province in the People's Republic of China.

221 KWANGTUNG
A province in southern People's Republic of China.

222 KWEICHOW
A province in the People's Republic of China.

239 KWIDZYN
The current name of Marienwerder (q.v.), a former town and district of East Prussia. Now part of Poland.

Kurland

Kuwait

Laos

Latakia

Lebanon

Latvia

Labuan

Lagos

L

222 LA AGUERA

An undefined area of Spanish Sahara. Now part of the Kingdom of Morocco.

223 LABUAN

An island off the northwest coast of Borneo. It was acquired by Great Britain in 1846 and was a crown colony from 1848 to 1906, when it was incorporated into the Straits Settlements. It was part of North Borneo from 1946 and is now in Malaysia.

151 LA CANEA

A town on the island of Crete. Now called Khana (Canea). For location see Crete.

223 LAGOS

A British colony on the coast of Nigeria. Included in Southern Nigeria from 1906, it is now part of the Federal Republic of Nigeria.

230 LAIBACH

A province of Yugoslavia under the name of Lubiana (Ljubljana), it was under German and Italian occupation during WWII. See Lubiana.

361 LAOS

Once part of French Indo-China, Laos became independent in 1951 and is now the Lao People's Democratic Republic.

202 LAS BELA

A former feudatory state in India, it is now part of Pakistan. See Indian Feudatory States.

92 LATAKIA

Formerly known as Alaouites (q.v.), this state was independent from 1930 until being made part of Syria in 1937.

224 LATVIA

Once included in the Russian Empire, Latvia gained its independence following WWI, but lost it during WWII when the Soviet Union invaded and took the area.

366 LEBANON

The area of the Republic of Lebanon was part of the Turkish Empire until WWI. It was mandated to France and gained independence in 1941, but French troops remained in the country until the end of the war. In recent years it has been a battleground, and Syria has exercised much control over the tiny country.

Leeward Islands

Lemnos

Leros

Lesotho

Liechtenstein

Liberia

Libya

224 LEEWARD ISLANDS
A group of islands in the northern portion of the Lesser Antilles of the British West Indies. The group comprised Anguilla, Antigua, Dominica (until the end of 1939), Montserrat, Nevis, St. Kitts, and the British Virgin Islands.

207 LEFKAS (LEVKAS) — See Ionian Islands.

225 LEMNOS
An island in the Aegean Sea occupied by Greece prior to WWI, it is now known as Limnos.

92 LEON
A town in Mexico. For map see Aguascalientes.

162 LERO (LEROS) — See Dodecanese Islands.

162 LEROS — See Dodecanese Islands.

225 LESBOS
A Greek island in the Aegean Sea. Occupied by Greece prior to WWI, it is now known as Lesvos.

353 LESOTHO
The Kingdom of Lesotho was formerly the British Protectorate of Basutoland. It became an independent kingdom in 1966 and is enclaved within the Republic of South Africa.

226 LESSER SUNDAS
An island chain from Java to Timor in what was the Netherlands Indies. Now part of Indonesia.

225 LESVOS — See Lesbos.

224 LETTLAND — See Latvia.

207 LEVKAS — See Ionian Islands.

157 LIAONING
A postal administration area that included the cities of Dairen and Port Arthur (q.v.).

224 LIBAU (LIEPAJA)
The town of Liepaja (German Libau) is located on the coast of Latvia (now part of the USSR). Founded by Teutonic Knights about 1263, it has been under Lithuanian, Prussian, Swedish, and Russian control. Occupied by Germany April-June 1919, when German stamps were used overprinted "LIBAU."

353 LIBERIA
The Republic of Liberia is located on the west coast of Africa and was founded in 1822 as a homeland for freed slaves from the United States. It became a republic in 1847 with a constituton modeled on that of the US.

353 LIBYA
The Socialist People's Libyan Arab Jamahiriya was once part of the Turkish Empire. It became an Italian colony as a result of the 1911-12 war between Italy and Turkey. After the expulsion of Italian and German forces by the British in WWII, a monarchy was established in 1952. A military coup in 1969 placed the present regime in power.

387 LIECHTENSTEIN
The Principality of Liechtenstein is located between Austria and Switzerland.

401 LIHOU (LITHOU)
An "island" that is joined to Guernsey at low tide. See British Offshore Islands.

226 LIMA
The capital city of Peru.

225 LIMNOS — See Lemnos.

162 LIPSO — See Dodecanese Islands.

162 LIPSOI — See Dodecanese Islands.

162 LISSO — See Dodecanese Islands.

401 LITHOU — See Lihou.

227 LITHUANIA
Once part of the Russian Empire, Lithuania achieved its independence following WWI. It was located on the Baltic Sea between Latvia and East Prussia. Occupied by Germany in WWII, it came under Soviet domination and has since been taken by the USSR. This takeover has not been recognized by the United States.

137 LITHUANIA, CENTRAL — See Central Lithuania.

187 LITHUANIA, SOUTH — See Grodno.

227 LIVONIA
A district in what was once the independent country of Latvia. A portion was also absorbed into Estonia. The Latvian part was known as Vidzeme.

230 LJUBLJANA — See Lubiana.

228 LOGRONO
A town and province of Spain.

228 LOMBARDY AND VENETIA
An area formerly included in Austrian Italy. Lombardy was annexed to the Kingdom of Sardinia in 1859, and Venetia was taken by the Kingdom of Italy in 1866.

229 LONG ISLAND
An island off the coast of Asian Turkey. Occupied by British forces for a short time during WWI.

94 LORRAINE — See Alsace and Lorraine.

229 LOURENCO MARQUES
A district around the town of the same name (now Maputo) in the southern part of Mozambique.

334 LOWER AUSTRIA
A province of Austria. For map see Upper Austria.

230 LUBECK
Once a Free City in the Hanseatic League, Lubeck is located on the Baltic Sea. Now in the Federal Republic of Germany.

230 LUBIANA (LJUBLJANA)
The capital city of the province of Slovenia in Yugoslavia. It was occupied by Italy and Germany during WWII. Occupation stamps were inscribed either "LUBIANA" or "LJUBLJANA." It was known as Laibach by the Germans.

231 LUBLIN
A town in Poland.

A stamp of independent Lithuania (left) and one issued under German occupation.

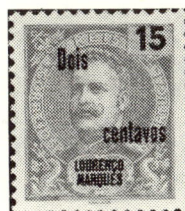

Lourenco Marques

Lombardy Venetia

Lubeck

48

406 LUNDY
An island off the coast of England in the Bristol Channel.

388 LUXEMBOURG
The Grand Duchy of Luxembourg is in Western

Europe between Belgium, the Federal Republic of Germany, and France. It was invaded and occupied by Germany during WWI and WWII.

231 LYDENBURG
A town in the Transvaal. Now in the Republic of South Africa.

Lundy

Luxembourg

Macao

Madagascar

Madeira

Mafeking

Malawi

Malaysia

M

Malacca

Malagasy

363 MACAO
A Portuguese colony located on the east coast of the People's Republic of China, near Hong Kong.

232 MACEDONIA
A loosely defined area in the central part of the Balkan peninsula. Portions are located in Greece, Bulgaria, and Yugoslavia. It is not a geographic entity.

168 MACIAS NGUEMA BIYOGA
For a short time, this was the name given to the island of Fernando Po, now Bioko.

353 MADAGASCAR
The Democratic Republic of Madagascar comprises a large island off the southeast part of Africa. A former French colony, it became the independent Malagasy Republic in 1958, incorporating the former French colonies of Diego Suarez, Nossi Be, and Ste. Marie de Madagascar. Its present name was adopted in 1975.

354 MADEIRA
A Portuguese island in the Atlantic Ocean off the Northwest coast of Africa. Administered as part of Portugal.

232 MADRID
District and capital city of Spain.

233 MADURA
An island off the north coast of Java. Now part of Indonesia.

233 MAFEKING
A town in the Republic of South Africa, west of Pretoria and near the border with Botswana.

234 MAFIA ISLAND
An island off the coast of East Africa, south of Dar es Salaam. Part of the United Republic of Tanzania.

234 MAGDALENA
A province in northern Colombia.

400 MAGNETIC ISLAND
An island off Townsville, Queensland, Australia.

190 MAHRA SULTANATE OF QISHN & SOCOTRA
— See Hadhramaut.

235 MAJORCA
An island in the Balearic group in the western Mediterranean. Part of Spain.

235 MAJUNGA
A town located on the northwest coast of Madagascar.

237 MALACCA
A former state on the west coast of the Malay Peninsula. Now part of Malaysia. For map see Malayan Federation.

236 MALAGA
A province and town on the south coast of Spain, to the east of Gibraltar.

353 MALAGASY REPUBLIC — See Madagascar.

353 MALAWI
The Republic of Malawi was originally known as British Central Africa. It was the Nyasaland Protectorate until 1954, when it joined the Central African Federation. In 1964 it became independent within the British Commonwealth as the Republic of Malawi.

237 MALAYAN FEDERATION
A federation of British states and settlements on the Malayan Peninsula, established in 1946 as the Union of Malaya. It included Johore, Pahang, Negri Sembilan, Selangor, Perak, Kedah, Perlis, Kelantan, Trengganu, Penang, and Malacca. In 1963 it was incorporated into Malaysia.

361 MALAYSIA
Formed in 1963, the independent state of Malaysia comprises the Malayan Federation, Sarawak, and Sabah (North Borneo). Singapore was also included until it became independent in 1965.

50

Maldive Is.

Malta

Mali

Manchuokuo

Manama

Marianwerder

Marshall Islands

Martinique

363 MALDIVES

The Republic of Maldives is a group of islands in the Indian Ocean off the southern tip of India. Initially a British protectorate administered from Ceylon (Sri Lanka), the group gained independence in 1965 and left the British Commonwealth.

353 MALI

The Republic of Mali was formed in 1960, when the Mali Federation broke up. It had previously been part of French West Africa as French Sudan.

236 MALI FEDERATION

A short-lived federation of the Republic of Senegal and the Sudanese Republic formed in 1959. In 1960 the federation broke up and the Sudanese Republic became independent as the Republic of Mali. Both had formerly been part of French West Africa.

167 MALMEDY — See Eupen and Malmedy.

388 MALTA

Located in the Mediterranean Sea to the south of Sicily, Malta comprises the main island of the same name plus Gozo and Comino. A former British colony, it became independent in 1974.

331 MANAMA

A dependency of Ajman, a state in the United Arab Emirates, Manama is located near the center of the peninsula jutting toward the Strait of Hormuz at the entrance to the Persian Gulf. Not to be confused with the city of the same name that is the capital of Bahrain. For map see Trucial States.

238 MANCHUKUO

In 1932 Japan set up a puppet government in Manchuria under the name of Manchukuo. Occupied by the Soviet Union at the end of WWII, it is now part of the People's Republic of China.

238 MANCHURIA — See Manchukuo.

387 MAN, ISLE OF — See Isle of Man.

406 MANIZALES

A town in Colombia.

229 MAPUTO — See Laurenco Marques.

238 MARIANA ISLANDS

Located north of Guam, the Mariana Islands were a German colony until WWI, when they were mandated to Japan. They were taken by the United States during WWII and now constitute a US Trust Territory.

239 MARIANWERDER

Formerly a town and district in East Prussia. Now the Polish town of Kwidzyn.

278 MARITIME PROVINCES, PRIAMUR AND

An area in eastern Siberia. See Priamur and Maritime Provinces.

239 MARSHALL ISLANDS

A former German colony comprising two groups of islands in the Pacific Ocean. The Marshall Islands are now a US Trust Territory.

240 MARTINIQUE

A former French colony in the Lesser Antilles of the West Indies. Now an overseas department of France.

92 MATEHUALA

A town in Mexico. For map see Aguascalientes.

240 MATURIN

A town in northeastern Venezuela.

353 MAURITANIA

The Islamic Republic of Mauritania was a French colony in West Africa. It became independent in 1960.

355 MAURITIUS

An island in the Indian Ocean, Mauritius was a British colony given self government in 1967 and independence in 1968.

241 MAYOTTE

An island in the Comoro group between Madagascar and the African coast. Mayotte chose to remain French when the rest of the group became the Republic of the Comoros. It is now an overseas department of France.

90 MAZATLAN

A town on the Pacific coast of Mexico. For map see Acaponeta.

241 MECKLENBURG-SCHWERIN

A former grand duchy in northern Germany. It is now part of the German Democratic Republic.

242 MECKLENBURG-STRELITZ

A former grand duchy in northern Germany. It is now part of the German Democratic Republic.

183 MECKLENBURG-WESTERN POMERANIA

An area of the Soviet Occupation Zone of Germany. See Germany, Soviet Zone.

242 MEDELLIN

A city in the South American country of Colombia.

194 MEDINA

A city in Saudi Arabia. For map see Hejaz.

237 MELAKA

Spelling variation of Malacca (q.v.).

312 MELILLA

A town in Morocco. For map see Spanish Morocco.

243 MEMEL (KLAIPEDA)

A port and district on the Baltic coast north of East Prussia. Memel was under Allied control after being taken from Germany during WWI. Lithuania occupied it in 1923. Hitler took it back, but lost it to the USSR, which kept it and it is now part of that country.

206 MENG CHIANG — See Mengkiang.

206 MENGKIANG (MENG CHIANG)

Also known as Inner Mongolia, it was an autonomous area in China established by Japan in 1937. It included Siuyuan, South Chahar, and North Shansi. Now part of the People's Republic of China. For map see Inner Mongolia.

246 MENGTSZ — See Mong-Tseu.

345 MERIDA

The capital city of Yucatan, Mexico. For map see Yucatan.

243 MESOPOTAMIA

A former Turkish province, Mesopotamia was taken by British forces during WWI. It was mandated to Great Britain following the war and became the major portion of the Kingdom of Iraq in 1932. It is now in the Republic of Iraq.

225 METELIN (MYTILENE)

A town on the Greek island of Lesbos (Lesvos). Now called Mitilini. For map see Lesbos.

Mauritania

Mecklenburg Strelitz

Memel (Klaipeda)

Mauritius

Mayotte

394 MEXICO
The United States of Mexico is a republic in the southern part of North America.

171 MIDDLE CONGO
In 1906 the French colony of Middle Congo was created from French Congo. In 1937 it was incorporated into French Equatorial Africa. It was included in Congo (Brazzaville) when that country was formed in 1958, and is now part of the People's Republic of the Congo. For map, see French Equatorial Africa and Congo, French.

235 MINORCA
One of the Balearic Islands. For map see Majorca.

292 MIQUELON, ST. PIERRE AND — See St. Pierre and Miquelon.

220 MITAU
A town in Kurland (q.v.).

225 MITILINI — See Metelin.

244 MODENA
A former duchy in northern Italy. Now part of the Italian Republic.

244 MOHELI
One of the islands in the Comoro group between Madagascar and the African coast. Now part of the Republic of the Comoros.

245 MOLDAVIA
The Principality of Moldavia was located in southeastern Europe. It joined with the Principality of Walachia in 1859 to form the country of Romania.

245 MOLUCCAS
An archipelago south of the Philippines. Part of the Republic of Indonesia.

389 MONACO, PRINCIPALITY OF
Monaco is an enclave on the Mediterranean coast of France. It includes the town of Monte Carlo.

232 MONASTIR
A town in southern Yugoslavia. Now called Bitola. For map see Macedonia.

361 MONGOLIA
The People's Republic of Mongolia is located in Central Asia between the USSR and the People's Republic of China. Formerly known as Outer Mongolia.

206 MONGOLIA, INNER — See Inner Mongolia.

361 MONGOLIA, OUTER — See Mongolia.

Mexico

Modena

Middle Congo

Moldavia

Moheli

Mongolia

Monaco

Mong-tseu

Montenegro

Morocco
Agencies

Morocco

Montserrat

Mozambique

Morvi

246 MONG-TSEU
A town in Yunnan Province, China, in which an Indo-Chinese post office operated from 1903 to 1922. Also spelled Mongtze and Mengtsz.

246 MONGTZE — See Mong-Tseu.

246 MONROVIA
The capital city of Liberia.

247 MONT ATHOS
A mountain and peninsula in what was the Turkish Empire. Now part of Greece.

247 MONTENEGRO
The Kingdom of Montenegro was located on the Adriatic coast of the Balkan Peninsula. Now part of Yugoslavia.

248 MONTERREY
A town in Mexico.

248 MONTEVIDEO
The capital city of the South American country of Uruguay.

373 MONTSERRAT
A British West Indian colony in the Leeward group of the Lesser Antilles.

249 MOQUEGUA
A district of the South American country of Peru.

118 MORAVIA, BOHEMIA AND — See Bohemia and Moravia.

249 MORELIA
A town in Mexico.

353 MOROCCO
The Kingdom of Morocco was formed in 1956 from French and Spanish Morocco and the International Zone of Tangier. The Spanish enclave of Ifni was added in 1969. Most of Spanish Sahara was annexed in 1976, with Mauritania taking the rest. Mauritania's part was later turned over to Morocco.

MOROCCO AGENCIES
British post offices operating in various towns in Morocco from the late 19th century to 1957.

173 MOROCCO, FRENCH — See French Morocco.

312 MOROCCO, SPANISH — See Spanish Morocco.

202 MORVI
A former feudatory state in India. Morvi is now part of the Republic of India. See Indian Feudatory States.

166 MOSCHOPOLIS
A town in Albania. For map see Epirus.

250 MOSUL
A town in northern Iraq.

353 MOZAMBIQUE
The People's Republic of Mozambique was created in 1975 from the former Portuguese colony in southern Africa.

250 MOZAMBIQUE COMPANY

Until 1942, the territories of Manica and Sofla in the Portuguese African colony of Mozambique were administered by the Mozambique Company.

251 MUSCAT

A sultanate in eastern Arabia. Now part of Oman.

365 MUSCAT AND OMAN

Now known as the Sultanate of Oman, it is located in eastern Arabia near the entrance to the Persian Gulf.

225 MYTILENE (METELIN)

The chief town on the Aegean island of Lesbos (Lesvos). It is now called Mitilini. For map see Lesbos.

Mozambique Company

Natal

Nauru

Negri
Sembilan

Naples

Netherlands

Nejd

Nepal

N

Netherlands Antilles

201 NABHA
A former Indian convention state. Now part of the Republic of India. See Indian Convention States.

407 NAGALAND
A province in northeastern India.

266 NAGYVARAD — See Oradea.

353 NAMIBIA
The area controlled by the Republic of South Africa, which calls it South-West Africa. The area had been mandated to South Africa following WWI, but that country has refused to give up control, despite United Nations demands.

251 NAN-CHING — See Nanking.

202 NANDGAON (RAJNANDGAON)
A former feudatory state in India. Now part of the Republic of India. See Indian Feudatory States.

251 NANKING
A town in the People's Republic of China on the Yangtze River. Now called Nan-ching.

252 NAPLES
A former kingdom, Naples was incorporated into the Kingdom of the Two Sicilies. Now part of Italy.

252 NATAL
Once a British colony on the coast of South Africa, Natal is in the Republic of South Africa.

369 NAURU
A former German colony, the western Pacific island of Nauru was under Australian administration until it became independent in 1968.

202 NAVANAGAR — See Nowanuggur.

202 NAWANAGAR — See Nowanuggur.

252 NEAPOLITAN PROVINCES
Group of provinces in southern Italy, which joined the new kingdom of Italy in 1861. See Naples.

169 NEGERI SEMBILAN — See Negri Sembilan.

169 NEGRI SEMBILAN
A state on the Malay Peninsula. Now part of Malaysia. Its name is also spelled "Negeri Sembilan." For map see Federated Malay States.

253 NEJD
A sultanate in Arabia that annexed Hejaz in 1926. In 1932 the combined area became the Kingdom of Saudi Arabia.

363 NEPAL
The Kingdom of Nepal is located in the mountains between the Republic of India and Tibet.

382 NETHERLANDS
Located in northwest Europe, the Kingdom of the Netherlands is bordered by the Federal Republic of Germany, Belgium, and the North Sea.

374 NETHERLANDS ANTILLES
Formerly called Curacao, the Netherlands Antilles is part of the Kingdom of the Netherlands. It comprises two widely separated groups of islands in the Caribbean Sea: the so-called "ABC group" consists of Aruba, Bonaire, and Curacao in the south, and the northern group includes St. Eustatius, Saba, and the southern portion of the island of St. Maarten (St. Martin).

Netherlands Indies

Netherlands
New Guinea

Nevis

New South Wales

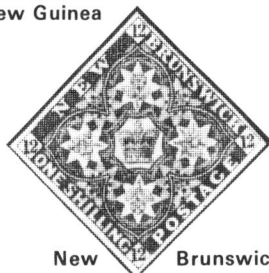
New Brunswick

Newfoundland

New Caledonia

New Zealand

New Hebrides

254 NETHERLANDS INDIES

The Netherlands Indies consisted of a large group of islands in the area north of Australia and south of the Philippines. It included Java, Sumatra, Lesser Sundas, Madura, much of Borneo, the Celebes Islands, and the Moluccas, plus many smaller islands. It became the Republic of Indonesia in 1950.

253 NETHERLANDS NEW GUINEA

This former Dutch colony occupied the western half of the island of New Guinea. It was administered by the United Nations from 1962 until, as West Irian, it became part of the Republic of Indonesia.

371 NEVIS

An island in the Lesser Antilles of the West Indies. It is a British colony in association with St. Kitts. See St. Kitts-Nevis.

255 NEW BRITAIN

An island off the north coast of New Guinea, it was formerly part of German New Guinea. Captured during WWI by Australian forces, it was joined to Papua and mandated to Australia. During WWII it was occupied by Japan. It is now part of the independent country of Papua New Guinea.

255 NEW BRUNSWICK

A former colony of Great Britain. It is now a province of Canada.

369 NEW CALEDONIA

A French overseas territory located in the South Pacific.

256 NEW CARLISLE

A town in the province of Quebec, Canada.

256 NEWFOUNDLAND

A former colony and dominion of the British Commonwealth. It is now a province of Canada.

397 NEW GRANADA — See Colombia, Republic of.

257 NEW GREECE

An area of Turkey occupied by Greece prior to WWI.

368 NEW GUINEA — See Papua New Guinea.

124 NEW GUINEA, BRITISH — See British New Guinea.

179 NEW GUINEA, GERMAN — See German New Guinea.

253 NEW GUINEA, NETHERLANDS — See Netherlands New Guinea.

257 NEW HEBRIDES

An island group in the South Pacific, it was under joint British-French administration as a condominium until 1980, when it became independent as the Republic of Vanuatu.

258 NEW REPUBLIC

A state set up by the Boers in South Africa in what had been Zulu territory. It became part of the Transvaal in 1888 and is now in the Republic of South Africa.

258 NEW SOUTH WALES

An ex-British colony in the southeast of Australia. Now a state in the Commonwealth of Australia.

368 NEW ZEALAND

An independent nation within the British Commonwealth. It is located on two large islands to the southeast of the Australian subcontinent.

378 NICARAGUA
The Republic of Nicaragua became independent in 1821. It is located in Central America between Honduras and Costa Rica.

199 NICARIA — See Icaria.

96 NICOBAR ISLANDS — See Andaman and Nicobar Islands.

353 NIGER
Located in West Africa to the north of Nigeria, the Republic of Niger was a French military territory that was incorporated into French West Africa in 1944. It became a republic in the French Community in 1959 and gained full independence in 1960.

265 NIGER COAST PROTECTORATE
A British African settlement, formerly the Oil Rivers Protectorate (q.v.), it combined with Southern Nigeria in 1894. It later joined the British colony of Nigeria. Now part of the Federal Republic of Nigeria. For map see Oil Rivers Protectorate.

353 NIGERIA
The Republic of Nigeria is a former British colony in West Africa.

174 NIGER, SENEGAMBIA AND — See Senegambia and Niger.

174 NIGER, UPPER SENEGAL AND — See Senegambia and Niger.

199 NIKARIA — See Icaria.

259 NIKOLAEVSK
A Siberian town about 22 miles from the mouth of the Amur River on its north bank.

259 NINGSIA
A former province of China.

162 NISIRO (NISIROS) — See Dodecanese Islands.

368 NIUAFO'OU
An island better known as "Tin Can Island," it is in the South Pacific and part of Tonga, although it is located far to the north, between Samoa and Fiji.

369 NIUE
Located in the Cook Islands, Niue was a dependency of New Zealand until it gained self-government in free association with New Zealand in 1974.

369 NORFOLK ISLAND
Located east of Australia, Norfolk Island is administered from that country. It was granted a measure of self-government in 1978.

260 NORTH BORNEO
The northern part of the island of Borneo was under the administration of the North Borneo Company from 1881 to 1946, when it became a British colony. It was joined by Labuan and the name was changed to Sabah shortly before it became part of Malaysia. The area was occupied by Japan during WWII.

NORTH CHINA
This area included the provinces of Honan, Hopeh, Shansi, Shantung, and Supeh (Northern Kiangsu). For maps see individual provinces.

NORTH CHINA LIBERATION AREA
An area of China under Communist control prior to the formation of the People's Republic of China. It included Hopeh, Chahar, Shansi, and Siuyuan. For maps see individual provinces.

Niger Coast Protectorate

Nicaragua

Niuafo'ou

Niue

Norfolk Island

Niger

Nigeria

North Borneo

NORTHEAST CHINA
An area of China under Communist control prior to the formation of the People's Republic of China. See Manchukuo.

NORTHEASTERN PROVINCES — See Northeast China.

166 **NORTHERN EPIRUS** — See Epirus.

389 **NORTHERN IRELAND** — See Ireland, Northern.

216 **NORTHERN KIANGSU (SUPEH)**
A province of northern China in the People's Republic. See Kiangsu.

260 **NORTHERN NIGERIA**
A British protectorate in West Africa, in 1914 it joined Southern Nigeria to form the British colony of Nigeria. Now part of the Federal Republic of Nigeria.

261 **NORTHERN RHODESIA**
A British colony, Northern Rhodesia was a member of the Central African Federation from 1953 to 1963. Independence came in 1964, and the country adopted the name Republic of Zambia.

181 **NORTH GERMAN CONFEDERATION**
Established in 1868, the North German Confederation preceded the formation in 1871 of the German Empire. For map see Germany.

261 **NORTH INGERMANLAND**
An area located between the old Russian Empire and Finland. It enjoyed a brief existence in 1920, when its population opted for freedom. The tiny area was quickly subdued by Soviet troops and has been within the USSR since then.

361 **NORTH KOREA**
The Democratic People's Republic of Korea (North Korea) is a puppet state established by the Soviet Union at the end of WWII in the northern part of the Korean peninsula. Its unsuccessful attempt to conquer South Korea has resulted in continued enmity between it and South Korea.

319 **NORTH MONGOLIA**
The area of North Mongolia (Tuva) was made part of the Soviet Union in 1944. For map see Tannu Tuva.

262 **NORTH VIETNAM**
A Communist government established in the north of what had been French Indo-China resulted in a long and bitter war with much US participation, climaxed by the withdrawal of US and Allied forces. The Communist regime then established itself throughout the area and calls itself The Socialist Republic of Vietnam.

NORTHWEST CHINA
An area of China under Communist control prior to the formation of the People's Republic of China. It included the provinces of Sinkiang, Tsinghai, Ningsia, and the western portion of Shensi. For maps see individual provinces.

262 **NORTH WEST PACIFIC ISLANDS**
A group of ex-German colonies captured by Australian forces during WWI. Areas included German New Guinea, islands in the Bismarck Archipelago, and Nauru. The territories were mandated to Australia by the League of Nations following the war and except for Nauru are now part of Papua New Guinea.

NORTHWEST RUSSIA
An area under the control of anti-Bolshevist forces during 1918-1920.

382 **NORWAY**
The Kingdom of Norway was a possession of Denmark until 1814. It was then ceded to Sweden and until 1905 the king of Sweden was also king of Norway. Since 1905 Norway has been an independent monarchy. It was occupied by Germany during WWII.

263 **NOSSI BE**
An island off the northwest coast of Madagascar, Nossi Be was a French Protectorate from 1840 to 1896, when it joined Madagascar.

263 **NOVA SCOTIA**
A former British colony, Nova Scotia is now a province of Canada.

202 **NOWANUGGUR**
Once a feudatory state in India, it is now part of the Republic of India. The name is also spelled Nawanagar or Navanagar. See Indian Feudatory States.

121 **NYASALAND PROTECTORATE**
Formerly British Central Africa, it was a member of the Central African Federation from 1953 to 1963. It became independent in 1964 as the Republic of Malawi. For map see British Central Africa.

264 **NYASSA COMPANY**
In 1894 the Nyassa Co. received a charter to administer an area in the northern part of the Portuguese colony of Mozambique. The area reverted to Portugal in 1929.

North Ingermanland

Nova Scotia

Nowanuggur

Nyassa Company

Grand Duchy
of Oldenburg

Sultanate of Oman

Obock

Orange
Free State

O

Orange
River Colony

264 OAXACA
A city and state in southern Mexico.

91 OBOCK
Obock was a port city and district on the north shore of the Gulf of Tadjoura in East Africa. It later became part of the French Somali Coast and subsequently of the French Territory of Afars and Issas. It is now located within the independent Republic of Djibouti. For map see Afars and Issas.

174 OCEANIC SETTLEMENTS — See French Oceanic Settlements.

265 ODESSA
A town in the USSR located on the northwest coast of the Black Sea.

265 OIL RIVERS PROTECTORATE
The Oil Rivers Protectorate was formed in June 1885. It became the Niger Coast Protectorate in 1893 and is now part of the Federal Republic of Nigeria in West Africa.

266 OLDENBURG
Once a grand duchy in the northern part of Germany with several enclaves. It became a member of the North German Confederation in 1868. Now part of the Federal Republic of Germany.

213 OLONETS
A town in the USSR. For map see Karelia.

94 OLSZTYN — See Allenstein.

212 OLTRE GIUBA
The Italian name for Jubaland (q.v.).

365 OMAN
The present Sultanate of Oman was previously called the Sultanate of Muscat and Oman. It is located in the eastern portion of Arabia facing on the Gulf of Oman.

266 ORADEA
A town in the Transylvanian area of Hungary prior to WWI. It was taken by Romania and remains in that country. It is also known as Nagyvarad.

267 ORANGE FREE STATE
An independent republic in South Africa from 1854, it became the British Orange River Colony in 1900. Now within the Republic of South Africa.

267 ORANGE RIVER COLONY — See Orange Free State.

202 ORCHHA
Once a feudatory state in India, it is now part of the Republic of India. See Indian Feudatory States.

267 ORENSE
A town and province located in the northwestern part of Spain.

171 OUBANGUI-CHARI — See Ubangi-Shari.

361 OUTER MONGOLIA
The area now known as the Mongolian People's Republic.

Through postage stamps one may view the geography, culture, and history of even the most remote and little-known area. This selection of stamps from the Sultanate of Oman, located on the southern shore of Arabia, provides us with such a glimpse.

Pahang

Pakhoi

Pakistan

Palau

Palestine

Panama

P

Papua

401 PABAY
An island off the coast of the island of Skye. See British Offshore Islands.

169 PAHANG
A former state on the Malay Peninsula, now part of Malaysia. For map see Federated Malay States.

268 PAITA
A town in the South American country of Peru.

268 PAKHOI
A city in the People's Republic of China. It is situated on the country's southern coast and is now known as Pei-hai.

365 PAKISTAN
Pakistan was created in 1947 when the Indian sub-continent was divided between Pakistan and India. Pakistan has been an Islamic republic since 1956. It withdrew from the Commonwealth in 1972. In 1971 its eastern enclave had declared its independence and is now the People's Republic of Bangladesh.

369 PALAU
The Republic of Palau is a group of small islands in the western Pacific. Until 1983 it was included in the US Trust Territory.

269 PALESTINE
Once part of the Turkish Empire, Palestine was liberated by Britain during WWI. The territory was mandated to Britain by the League of Nations until the creation of the State of Israel in 1948. It is located on the eastern Mediterranean Sea.

378 PANAMA
The Republic of Panama is in Central America astride the Panama Canal. The country came into being in 1903 when it broke away from Colombia with US support.

130 PANAMA CANAL ZONE — See Canal Zone.

269 PAPAL STATES
Comprising areas of what is now the Italian Republic, the Papal States were ruled from the Vatican until 1870, when they joined what was then the Kingdom of Italy.

124 PAPUA
The southern half of the eastern portion of the island of New Guinea, Papua was formerly British, but was handed to Australia and is now part of the independent country of Papua New Guinea. For map see British New Guinea.

Papua New Guinea

Paraguay

Parma

Patmos

Perak

Peking

Penang

Penrhyn

Perlis

Persia

368 PAPUA NEW GUINEA
Area comprising the eastern half of the island of New Guinea to the north of Australia, plus islands in the Bismarck group and the Solomons. These consist of the Admiralty Islands, New Ireland, New Britain, and Bougainville. The northern portion plus some of the islands constituted the former German colony of German New Guinea.

397 PARAGUAY
The Republic of Paraguay is located in the center of southern South America. It became independent from Spain in 1811.

270 PARMA
A former grand duchy in northern Italy, Parma united with the Kingdom of Sardinia prior to the formation of the Kingdom of Italy.

270 PASCO
Also known as Cerro de Pascoe, it is a town and province in Peru.

201 PATIALA
A former convention state in India, it is now part of the Republic of India. See Indian Convention States.

162 PATMO — See Patmos.

162 PATMOS
An island in the Italian Dodecanese group in the Aegean Sea, it became Greek following WWII. See Dodecanese Islands.

271 PATZCUARO
A town in central Mexico.

207 PAXOS — See Ionian Islands.

271 PECHINO — See Peking.

268 PEI-HAI — See Pakhoi.

271 PEKING
The capital city of the People's Republic of China. Also known as Beijing.

237 PENANG
A state on the Malay Peninsula. Once a member of the Malayan Federation, it is now part of Malaysia. For map see Malayan Federation.

368 PENRHYN ISLAND
An island in the northern group of the Cook Islands.

169 PERAK
A state on the Malay Peninsula. Once part of the Federation of Malaya, it is now in Malaysia. For map see Federated Malay States.

237 PERLIS
A state on the Malay Peninsula. Formerly a member of the Malayan Federation, it is now in Malaysia. For map see Malayan Federation.

272 PERSIA
Persia was the name of what is now the Islamic Republic of Iran.

397 PERU
The Republic of Peru is located on the west coast of South America.

361 PHILIPPINES
The Republic of the Philippines is a group of islands in the China Sea. It was a Spanish colony until the Spanish-American War of 1898, when the islands became a US possession. They were occupied by Japan during WWII. The country became independent in 1946.

272 PIETERSBURG
A town in the Transvaal. Now within the Republic of South Africa.

273 PISCO
A town in Peru.

162 PISCOPI — See Dodecanese Islands.

368 PITCAIRN ISLANDS
An isolated group of islands in the central south Pacific Ocean. Included is the island of Pitcairn and the uninhabited islets of Henderson, Ducie, and Oeno.

273 PIURA
A town and province in Peru.

207 POLA
A port town of Yugoslavia. Now called Pula. For map see Istria.

382 POLAND
The Polish People's Republic is located between the Soviet Union and the German Democratic Republic (East Germany) in northern Europe. An independent republic since 1918, it was brutally occupied by Germany in 1939 and made the location of Germany's "final solution" for what it termed the "Jewish problem." At the time of the German invasion, the Soviet Union also moved in and took large areas of Polish territory. The country is now firmly under Soviet control.

POLISH LEVANT
A Polish post office operated briefly in Constantinople (Istanbul) during 1919.

174 POLYNESIA, FRENCH — See French Oceanic Settlements.

280 PONCE
A US military postal station was opened at La Playa de Ponce in Puerto Rico in 1898, following the Spanish-American War, during which the island had been taken by the US. For map see Puerto Rico.

274 PONTA DELGADA
A district in the Azores, an Atlantic Ocean group that is part of Portugal.

274 PONTEVEDRA
A province in northwestern Spain.

202 POONCH
A former feudatory state in India. Now part of the Republic of India. See Indian Feudatory States.

157 PORT ARTHUR AND DAIREN — See Dairen and Port Arthur.

159 PORT GDANSK — See Danzig.

263 PORT HOOD
A town in Nova Scotia, Canada. For map see Nova Scotia.

275 PORT LAGOS
A town located on the coast of Greece on the north shore of the Aegean Sea. Formerly a Turkish city.

275 PORT SAID
An Egyptian port city at the northern end of the Suez Canal.

382 PORTUGAL — See Portuguese Republic.

PORTUGUESE AFRICA
General name given to Portuguese possessions in Africa.

Peru

Poonch

Pitcairn

Philippines

Poland

Ponta Delgada

Port Said

64

128 PORTUGUESE CONGO — See Cabinda.

276 PORTUGUESE GUINEA
Located on the bulge of West Africa between the former French colonies of Senegal and French Guinea, it is now the independent country of Guinea Bissau.

276 PORTUGUESE INDIA
Comprised settlements on the west coast of India. They were Goa, Damao, and Diu. The Republic of India took them in 1961.

382 PORTUGUESE REPUBLIC
A republic located on the west coast of the Iberian Peninsula, which it shares with Spain.

277 PORTUGUESE TIMOR
An area that comprised the eastern portion of the island of Timor plus an enclaved portion on the north coast of the western part, which was in the Dutch East Indies. The island is located to the north of Australia. It was administered from Macao until 1896 and was absorbed by Indonesia in 1976.

277 POSEN (POZNAN)
A town in the Polish People's Republic.

278 PRIAMUR AND MARITIME PROVINCES
An area of Siberia that had an anti-Bolshevist government during 1921-22.

278 PRINCE EDWARD ISLAND
A British colony, Prince Edward Island entered Canadian Confederation in 1873 as a province of the new country. It is an island in the Gulf of St. Lawrence off the coasts of New Brunswick and Nova Scotia.

279 PRISTINA
A town in southern Yugoslavia.

279 PRUSSIA
A former state in northern Germany, it became the dominant state in the North German Confederation and later, in the German Empire.

280 PUERTO PRINCIPE
A provincial capital city in Cuba. Now called Camaguey.

280 PUERTO RICO
The easternmost island in the Greater Antilles of the West Indies. It was a colony of Spain until 1898, when it was taken by the US, and is now a commonwealth associated with the US.

207 PULA — See Pola.

281 PUNO
A town in the South American country of Peru.

201 PUTTIALA
Spelling variation of Patiala (q.v.).

Portuguese Guinea

Portugal

Portuguese India

Prince Edward Island

Portuguese Timor

Prussia

Puerto Rico

Qu'aiti
State in
Hadhramaut

Qatar

Queensland

Quelimane

Q

365 **QATAR**
The State of Qatar is an independent sheikdom on the Persian Gulf. It comprises a peninsula on the south coast of the gulf, with the landward end bordering on Saudi Arabia and the United Arab Emirates.

190 **QISHN AND SOCOTRA** — See Hadhramaut.

190 **QU'AITI STATE IN HADHRAMAUT** — See Hadhramaut.

190 **QU'AITI STATE OF SHIR & MUKALLA** — See Hadhramaut.

281 **QUEENSLAND**
The northeastern state in the Commonwealth of Australia. It was formerly a British colony.

282 **QUELIMANE**
A district in the Portuguese colony of Mozambique. Previously part of Zambezia District, it is now included in the People's Republic of Mozambique.

92 **QUERETARO**
A town in Mexico. For map see Aquascalientes.

Once pearl fishing was the most important industry of tiny, arid Qatar, but as these stamps show, oil brought considerable wealth and the jet age soon came to the dusty peninsula in the Persian Gulf.

Ras al Khaima

Rajpipla

Reunion

Rhineland Palatinate

Rhodes

Rhodesia

67

R

101 RAB
An island off the coast of Yugoslavia in the Adriatic Sea. Formerly called Arbe (q.v.).

400 RAINBOW CREEK
Located in the Australian state of Victoria to the east of Melbourne. The owner of this self-proclaimed "state" issues local post labels.

282 RAJASTHAN
An area of India formed in 1948 from various Indian states including the stamp-issuing ones of Bundi, Jaipur, and Kishangarh. Now part of the Republic of India.

202 RAJNANDGAON — See Nandgaon.

202 RAJPEEPLA — See Rajpipla.

202 RAJPIPLA
A former feudatory state in India. Now part of the Republic of India. Also spelled Rajpeepla. See Indian Feudatory States.

283 RAROTONGA
An island in the Cook Islands, located in the central South Pacific.

331 RAS AL KHAIMA
A sheikdom on the Persian Gulf side of the Arabian Peninsula at the entrance to the gulf. Now one of the United Arab Emirates. See Trucial States.

407 RATTLESNAKE ISLAND
An island in Lake Erie off the Ohio shore that has issued local post labels.

371 REDONDA
A one-half square-mile islet in the Caribbean Sea. Part of Antigua, it is reported to be uninhabited.

314 REICHENBERG
A town in Czechoslovakia. For map see Sudetenland.

283 RETHYMNON
A district of the Mediterranean island of Crete.

284 REUNION
An island in the Indian Ocean east of Madagascar. Once a French colony, it is now an overseas department of France.

284 RHINELAND PALATINATE
An area of Germany located in the French Occupation Zone following WWII. Now part of the Federal Republic of Germany.

284 RHINELAND-PFALZ
German name for Rhineland Palatinate (q.v.).

162 RHODES — See Dodecanese Islands.

RHODESIA
A former British territory in Central Africa. In 1924 it was split into Northern and Southern Rhodesia. From 1953 to 1963 both were part of the Central African Federation together with Nyasaland Protectorate. In 1964 Northern Rhodesia became the Republic of Zambia; Southern Rhodesia became Rhodesia in 1965 and the Republic of Zimbabwe in 1980. For maps see Northern Rhodesia and Southern Rhodesia.

136 RHODESIA AND NYASALAND
Name sometimes used in reference to the Central African Federation.

285 RIAU-LINGGA ARCHIPELAGO
Twin groups of islands located to the south of Singapore and off the eastern coast of Sumatra. Now part of the Republic of Indonesia.

170 RIJEKA
The current name for the port city in Yugoslavia once known as Fiume (q.v.).

312 RIO DE ORO
Located on the northwest coast of Africa, Rio de Oro was the former name of Spanish Sahara. For map see Spanish Sahara.

Romania

Roman States

Romagna

Ruanda-Urundi

Russian
Empire

Rwanda

Ryukyu
Islands

234 RIO HACHA
A town on the coast of Colombia. For map see Magdalena.

285 RIO MUNI
Once a Spanish colony located on the west coast of Central Africa. Rio Muni was made part of Spanish Guinea together with Fernando Po and the islands of Annobon, Corisco, and Elobey. Now part of the Republic of Equatorial Guinea.

286 RIZE — See Rizeh.

286 RIZEH
A town on the Black Sea coast of Turkey. Now called Rize.

246 ROBERTSPORT
A town in Liberia. For map see Monrovia.

162 RODI (RHODOS)
Spelling variations of Rhodes. See Dodecanese Islands.

286 ROMAGNA
One of the Italian Papal States.

382 ROMANIA
The Socialist Republic of Romania became a nation with the merger of Moldavia and Walachia in 1859. It was a kingdom from 1881 and became a republic following WWII. It is located on the Black Sea in Eastern Europe.

ROMANIAN LEVANT
The collective name given to the Romanian post offices operating in the Turkish Empire prior to WWI.

269 ROMAN STATES
Name sometimes applied to the Papal States.

287 ROSS DEPENDENCY
A dependency of New Zealand, located in Antarctica.

103 ROUAD ISLAND — See Arwad.

382 ROUMANIA
Spelling variation of Romania.

287 RUANDA-URUNDI
Originally part of German East Africa, the area was occupied by Belgium during WWI. Mandated to Belgium after the war, in 1962 it became the independent countries of the Republic of Burundi and the Republic of Rwanda.

382 RUMANIA
Spelling variation of Romania.

314 RUMBERG
A town in Czechoslovakia. For map see Sudetenland.

288 RUSSIAN EMPIRE
An empire located in Central Europe and northern Asia until the Russian Revolution of 1917. It eventually became the Union of Soviet Socialist Republics, of which Russia is only a part. For maps see Russia in Europe and Russian Empire.

RUSSIAN LEVANT
The collective name given to Russian post offices operating in the Turkish Empire prior to WWI.

290 RUSTENBURG
A town in the Transvaal, Republic of South Africa.

133 RUTHENIA — See Carpatho-Ukraine.

353 RWANDA
The Republic of Rwanda in Central Africa was formed in 1962 from part of the Belgian-mandated area from German East Africa during WWI.

290 RYUKYU ISLANDS
A group of Japanese islands located in the Western Pacific Ocean between Japan and the island of Taiwan. Occupied by the US in 1945 and subsequently under US military administration. A semi-autonomous period followed until 1972, when the group reverted to Japan.

Saar

St. Christopher

Sabah

St. Christopher,
Nevis,
Anguilla

St. Helena

St. Kilda

Ste. Marie de
Madagascar

St. Lucia

St. Pierre & Miquelon

S

St. Thomas
and Prince

St. Vincent

291 SAAR
An area of the Federal Republic of Germany adjacent to where the borders of Luxembourg, Germany, and France meet. It was occupied by France following WWI until 1935, when a plebiscite favored return to Germany. It was occupied again by France at the end of WWII, and in 1956 it again voted to join Germany.

260 SABAH
Formerly known as North Borneo, the area comprises the northern portion of the island of Borneo and was administered by the British North Borneo Company until taken by Japan during WWII. It became a British crown colony in 1946. Its name was changed to Sabah shortly before it became part of Malaysia in 1963. See North Borneo.

298 SACHSEN — See Saxony.

375 ST. CHRISTOPHER
An island in the Lesser Antilles of the West Indies. Also known as St. Kitts. It is part of the Associated State of St. Kitts-Nevis.

375 ST. CHRISTOPHER, NEVIS, ANGUILLA
A British Associated State, from which the island of Anguilla seceded in 1967.

355 ST. HELENA
A British crown colony located in the South Atlantic Ocean.

401 ST. KILDA
An island in the North Atlantic about 50 miles west of the Outer Hebrides. See British Offshore Islands.

375 ST. KITTS-NEVIS — See St. Christopher, Nevis, Anguilla.

375 ST. LUCIA
An island in the Lesser Antilles of the West Indies. Formerly a British crown colony, it achieved Associated State status in 1967 and became independent in 1979.

291 STE. MARIE DE MADAGASCAR
An island off the east coast of Madagascar. Formerly a colony of France.

292 ST. PIERRE AND MIQUELON
A group of islands about 10 miles off the south coast of Newfoundland. It was a French colony until 1976, when it became an overseas department of France.

292 ST. THOMAS AND PRINCE ISLANDS
Islands off the west coast of Africa. Formerly a Portuguese colony, the pair is now the Democratic Republic of Sao Tome and Principe.

376 ST. VINCENT
An island in the Windward group of the Lesser Antilles in the West Indies. It was a British colony until 1969, when it gained Associated State status. Independence came in 1979.

70

Samoa

Sarawak

Santander

San Marino

Sardinia

375 ST. VINCENT GRENADINES — See Grenadines of St. Vincent.

293 SALAMANCA
A town and province of Spain.

92 SALAMANCA
A town in Mexico. For map see Aguascalientes.

293 SALONICA (SALONIKA)
A port city in northern Greece on the Aegean Sea. Now called Thessaloniki.

293 SALONIQUE — See Salonica.

380 SALVADOR — See El Salvador.

294 SALZBURG
A town and province of Austria.

368 SAMOA
An independent kingdom in the Pacific Ocean until 1889. After that year it was administered jointly by the US, Germany, and Great Britain. In 1899 the eastern group went to the US and the western group to Germany. In 1914 the German islands were taken by British forces and mandated to New Zealand by the League of Nations. They became the independent state of Western Samoa in 1962. In 1982 the country officially became Samoa. The US Samoan islands are still a possession of that country.

294 SAMOS
An island in the Aegean Sea off the Turkish coast. It belongs to Greece.

401 SANDA
An island off the west coast of Scotland. See British Offshore Islands.

295 SAN LUIS POTASI
A state and town in Mexico.

390 SAN MARINO
The Republic of San Marino is a tiny area enclaved in Italy, inland from the Italian town of Rimini on the Adriatic coast.

93 SAN PEDRO DE LAS COLONIAS
A town in Mexico. For map see Allende.

190 SAN SEBASTIAN
A town in northern Spain near the French border. For map see Guipuzcoa.

295 SANTA CRUZ DE TENERIFE
The chief town on Tenerife in the Canary Islands. It belongs to Spain.

207 SANTA MAURA
An island in the Ionian group, now called Levkas (Lefkas). See Ionian Islands.

296 SANTANDER
A state in the Granadine Confederation. Since 1886 it has been a department of the Republic of Colombia.

353 SAO TOME AND PRINCIPE
The Democratic Republic of Sao Tome and Principe (St. Thomas and Prince) comprises two islands off the west coast of Africa opposite Gabon. The pair was formerly a Portuguese colony and became independent in 1975.

296 SARAWAK
An independent state ruled by the Brooke family under British protection until the Japanese invasion and occupation of WWII. It became a British crown colony in 1946 and part of Malaysia in 1963.

297 SARDINIA, KINGDOM OF
The Kingdom of Sardinia included the Mediterranean island of the same name plus a large part of what is now northern Italy. Other states joined the kingdom, and it became the unified Kingdom of Italy in 1861. The counties of Nice and Savoy were ceded to France in 1860.

401 SARK
An island dependency of Guernsey in the English Channel Islands. For map see English Channel Islands and British Offshore Islands.

297 SASENO
An island in the Adriatic Sea off the coast of Albania. Occupied by Italy after WWI. Now called Sazan.

365 SAUDI ARABIA

The Kingdom of Saudi Arabia was under Turkish rule for many years. The area began to take its present form in 1926, when the Sultan of Nejd invaded and absorbed neighboring Hejaz to create the Kingdom of Hejaz and Nejd. The present name was adopted in 1932. The country occupies much of Arabia.

298 SAURASHTRA

The United States of Saurashtra was formed in 1948 by the merger of the stamp-issuing feudatory states of Jasdan, Morvi, Nowanuggur, and Wadhwan, together with 213 other Indian states. It is now part of the Republic of India.

298 SAXONY

A former kingdom in the southern part of Germany, Saxony joined the North German Confederation in 1868. It is now located within the German Democratic Republic (East Germany). For map of Soviet occupation of Saxony, see Germany, Soviet Zone.

297 SAZAN — See Saseno.

162 SCARPANTO — See Dodecanese Islands.

299 SCHLESWIG

The northern partner of the twin provinces of Schleswig-Holstein in north Germany. In 1920 a plebiscite was held; northern Schleswig went to Denmark, and the southern portion remained German. For map see Schleswig-Holstein.

299 SCHLESWIG-HOLSTEIN

This is now a part of the Federal Republic of Germany, except for the northern portion of Schleswig, which went to Denmark as a result of the 1920 plebiscite. The twin provinces had been Danish until occupied by Prussia in 1864.

299 SCHWEIZER-RENEKE

A town in Transvaal, Republic of South Africa.

300 SCINDE

A district of British India. Now in Pakistan.

390 SCOTLAND

A former kingdom, Scotland is united with England, Wales, and Northern Ireland to form the United Kingdom of Great Britain and Northern Ireland. Located north of England, it includes many islands especially off its west coast.

300 SCUTARI

A town in Albania, now called Shkoder.

301 SEGOVIA

A province of Spain.

190 SEIYUN — See Kathiri State of Seiyun.

169 SELANGOR

A state on the Malay Peninsula, Selangor is now part of Malaysia. For map see Federated Malay states.

353 SENEGAL

The Republic of Senegal is a former French colony that was made part of French West Africa in 1944. It became a state in the French Community in 1958 and joined with the ex-French Sudan in 1959 to form the short-lived Mali Federation. In 1960 it became independent under its present name.

SENEGAMBIA

The name of a form of limited federation formed in 1982 by the Republic of Senegal and The Gambia. It has not thus far had any philatelic effects.

174 SENEGAMBIA AND NIGER

A French colony in Africa that became Upper Senegal and Niger and subsequently French Sudan. For map see French Sudan.

Saudi Arabia

Saxony

Schleswig

Scotland

Scutari

Scarpanto

Selangor

Senegal

301 SERBIA

Located on the Balkan Peninsula, the Kingdom of Serbia joined then then-new Kingdom of Yugoslavia following WWI and is now part of the Socialist Federal Republic of Yugoslavia.

382 SERBS, CROATS, AND SLOVENES

The Kingdom of the Serbs, Croats, and Slovenes was established following WWI and included Serbia, Montenegro, Bosnia, Herzegovina, and part of Hungary. It became the Kingdom of Yugoslavia and since WWII has been known as the Socialist Federal Republic of Yugoslavia.

302 SEVILLE

A town and province in southwestern Spain.

355 SEYCHELLES

The Seychelles is a group of islands in the Indian Ocean off the coast of Africa. The group was attached to the colony of Mauritius until 1903, when it became the Crown Colony of the Seychelles. Internal independence came in 1975, and complete independence was achieved as the Republic of the Seychelles in 1976.

302 SHANGHAI

A Chinese city on the coast near the mouth of the Yangtze River.

303 SHANSI

A province in the People's Republic of China.

303 SHANTUNG

A province in the People's Republic of China.

331 SHARJAH

One of the Trucial States on the south coast of the Persian Gulf, it is now a member of the United Arab Emirates. It also includes the dependencies of Diba, Khor Fakkan, and Kalba. For map see Trucial States.

304 SHENSI

A province in the People's Republic of China.

SHENSI-KANSU-NINGSIA

An area of Communist administration in China prior to the formation of the People's Republic of China. For maps see individual provinces.

190 SHIR AND MUKALLA See Hadhramaut.

300 SHKODER — See Scutari.

401 SHUNA

An island off the west coast of Scotland. See British Offshore Islands.

361 SIAM — See Thailand.

288 SIBERIA

Siberia forms the bulk of the USSR in Asia. Following the 1917 revolution, there were several short-lived anti-Bolshevist governments scattered around the area. For map see Russian Empire.

304 SICILY

The island of Sicily, together with the mainland state of Naples, constituted the Kingdom of the Two Sicilies. It existed until 1860, when it was incorporated into the Kingdom of Sardinia and thence into Italy.

Serbia

Seychelles

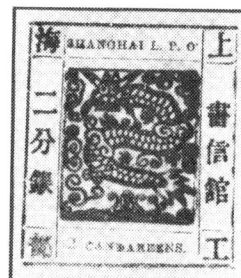

Shanghai

Sharjah

Siam

Siberia

Sicily

Sierra Leone

Simi

Singapore

Sirmoor

Somali Democratic
Republic

Slovakia

Smyrna

South
Africa

355 SIERRA LEONE
The Republic of Sierra Leone is a former British colony on the coast of West Africa. It became independent within the British Commonwealth in 1961.

305 SIKANG
A former Chinese province, now divided between Szechwan and Tibet.

SILESIA — See Silesia, Eastern, and Silesia, Upper.

162 SIMI — See Dodecanese Islands.

305 SINAI
An arid region between Egypt and Israel forming a peninsula jutting south to the Red Sea. Currently part of Egypt.

306 SINALOA
A state in northern Mexico.

363 SINGAPORE
The Republic of Singapore is an island at the southern tip of the Malay Peninsula. It was a member of the Straits Settlements until becoming a crown colony in 1946. In 1958 it became internally self-governing and from 1963 to 1965 was part of Malaysia.

306 SINKIANG
A province in the People's Republic of China, located between Tibet and Mongolia.

202 SIRMOOR
A former feudatory state in India, it is now part of the Republic of India. See Indian Feudatory States.

335 SKOPJE — See Uskub.

299 SLESVIG — See Schleswig.

307 SLOVAKIA
Located in Czechoslovakia, it was nominally independent under German "protection" from 1939 to 1945, when it was restored to Czechoslovakia.

307 SLOVENE COAST
An area of coast south of Trieste on the Adriatic Sea. Part of Yugoslavia. For map see Slovenia.

307 SLOVENIA
A province of Yugoslavia.

308 SMYRNA (SMYRNE)
A town on the Aegean coast of Asian Turkey. Now Izmir.

401 SOAY
An island off the Scottish coast. See British Offshore Islands.

369 SOLOMON ISLANDS
Formerly the British Solomon Islands.

91 SOMALI COAST — See French Somali Coast.

353 SOMALI DEMOCRATIC REPUBLIC
Formed in 1960 from what had been Italian Somaliland and the British Somaliland Protectorate. The present name was adopted in 1969.

124 SOMALILAND PROTECTORATE — See British Somaliland.

308 SONORA
A state in northern Mexico.

202 SORUTH
A feudatory state in India, in 1948 it joined with the stamp-issuing states of Jasdan, Morvi, Nowanuggar, Wadhwan, and 203 other states to form the Saurashtra Union. Now part of the Republic of India. See Indian Feudatory States.

356 SOUTH AFRICA AND HOMELANDS
Formed in 1910 from the British colonies of Cape of Good Hope, Natal, the Orange Free State, and the Transvaal, the Union of South Africa became a republic in 1961.

327 SOUTH AFRICAN REPUBLIC — See Transvaal.

190 SOUTH ARABIAN FEDERATION
Formed in 1963 around the former British colony of Aden and including territory of the Western Aden Protectorate and the Eastern Aden Protectorate, it became independent in 1967 as the People's Republic of Southern Yemen. It is now the People's Democratic Republic of Yemen. For map see Hadhramaut.

South
Australia

Southern Rhodesia

Southern
Nigeria

South Georgia

South Kasai

South Korea

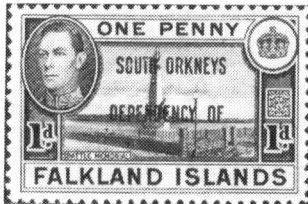
South Orkneys

South Shetlands

309 SOUTH AUSTRALIA
A former British colony in Australia, it is now a state in the Commonwealth of Australia.

254 SOUTH BORNEO
The Dutch area of Borneo controlled by Japan during WWII. For map see Netherlands Indies.

164 SOUTH BULGARIA — See Eastern Rumalia.

SOUTH CHINA
An area of China under Communist control prior to the formation of the People's Republic of China. It included Kwangtung, Kwangsi, and Hainan Island. For maps see individual provinces.

309 SOUTHERN CAMEROON
The United Kingdom Trust Territory of Southern Cameroon was the southern portion of the British-mandated area of the former German colony of Kamerun, which in 1960 had voted to become autonomous. A plebiscite in 1961 decided its future as part of the new United Republic of Cameroon.

310 SOUTHERN NIGERIA
An area of West Africa, it joined with Northern Nigeria in 1914 to form the British colony of Nigeria. Now in the Republic of Nigeria.

310 SOUTHERN RHODESIA
A former British colony in Africa. Now Zimbabwe.

365 SOUTHERN YEMEN
The People's Republic of Southern Yemen was formed in 1967 from the former British colony of Aden, the Aden States, and the South Arabian Federation. Now the People's Democratic Republic of Yemen.

359 SOUTH GEORGIA
A British island in the South Atlantic.

311 SOUTH KASAI
Part of the province of Kasai in the Republic of Zaire and centered on the town of Bakwanga (Mbuji-Mayi), it declared its independence in 1960, but returned to the control of the central government in 1962.

361 SOUTH KOREA
The area of the Korean Peninsula south of the 38th parallel. Now known as the Republic of Korea.

187 SOUTH LITHUANIA — See Grodno.

408 SOUTH MOLUCCAS
A short-lived republic in the Moluccas during 1951. Now part of Indonesia.

359 SOUTH ORKNEYS
A British island group in the South Atlantic.

359 SOUTH SANDWICH ISLANDS
A British island group southwest of South Georgia.

359 SOUTH SHETLANDS
A British island group in the South Atlantic.

311 SOUTH VIETNAM

The state of Vietnam was formed in 1945 from the French Indo-Chinese areas of Tonkin, Annam, and Cochin-China. In 1949 it became independent within the French Community. By 1954 it had been partitioned near the 17th parallel between the Communist north and the non-Communist Republic of South Vietnam. After the US pulled out following the abortive Vietnam War, North Vietnam took over the entire country, and it is now known as the Socialist Republic of Vietnam.

353 SOUTH-WEST AFRICA

Once German Southwest Africa, South-West Africa was mandated to South Africa following WWI. That country still administers the area now generally called Namibia.

SOUTHWEST CHINA

An area of China under Communist control prior to the formation of the People's Republic of China. Included the provinces of Kweichow, Szechwan, Yunnan, Sikang, and Tibet. For maps see individual provinces.

382 SPAIN

Spain is a kingdom comprising the greater part of the Iberian Peninsula, which it shares with Portugal. It was a republic during 1873-74 and again from 1931 to the end of the Spanish Civil War, when it became a fascist dictatorship under General Franco until his death in 1975. It then once more became a kingdom.

SPANISH GUINEA

A colony of Spain that comprised the islands of Fernando Po, Elobey, Annobon, and Corisco in the Atlantic, Spanish Guinea also included the African mainland area of Rio Muni. All are now combined in the Republic of Equatorial Guinea. For maps see individual areas.

238 SPANISH MARIANAS

A group of islands in the western Pacific Ocean that were Spanish until the Spanish-American War of 1898. Of the group, Guam was taken by the US and the rest were sold to Germany and became the German Mariana Islands. For map see Mariana Islands.

312 SPANISH MOROCCO

An area of North Africa across the Strait of Gibraltar from Spain, which became a Spanish Protectorate in 1912 under an arrangement with France and with British consent. It joined the Kingdom of Morocco in 1956.

361 SPANISH PHILIPPINES — See Philippines.

312 SPANISH SAHARA

A former Spanish territory on the northwest coast of Africa, of which the colonies of Rio de Oro and Cape Juby were a part. The area was divided between the Kingdom of Morocco and the Islamic Republic of Mauritania in 1976.

Mauritania later turned its portion over to Morocco, which is still fighting the nomadic tribes, and is believed to control only a small portion of ex-Spanish Sahara. The United Nations does not recognize Moroccan authority and refers to the area as Western Sahara.

SPANISH WEST AFRICA

This administrative area encompassed most of the Spanish area of northwest Africa, including Spanish Sahara (Rio de Oro, Seguiet el Hamra, and Cape Juby), Ifni, and La Aguera. For maps see under Ifni, La Aguera, and Spanish Sahara.

361 SRI LANKA

The Republic of Sri Lanka is the name of the former British colony of Ceylon.

401 STAFFA

An island off the Scottish coast. See British Offshore Islands.

Spain

South Vietnam

Spanish Morocco

Sri Lanka

South-West Africa

Staffa

162 STAMPALIA — See Dodecanese Islands.

343 STANISLAV — See Western Ukraine.

313 STELLALAND

A Boer republic set up in an attempt to gain territory from the Bechuana people. Established in 1884, it was eliminated in 1885 by the British and became part of British Bechuanaland.

401 STEEPHOLM

An island in the Bristol Channel off the English coast. See British Offshore Islands.

313 STRAITS SETTLEMENTS

A British crown colony created in 1867 comprising a portion of the Malay Peninsula and including offshore islands plus the island of Labuan off the coast of Borneo. The colony was disbanded in 1946. Areas constituting the colony were Labuan (from 1906), Malacca, Penang and Province Wellesley, Singapore, Christmas Island, and Cocos (Keeling) Islands.

401 STROMA

An island off the northern tip of Scotland. See British Offshore Islands.

314 STYRIA

A province of Austria.

353 SUDAN, DEMOCRATIC REPUBLIC OF

The Sudan is an area to the south of Egypt. It was an Anglo-Egyptian condominium until granted internal self-government in 1954. It became fully independent in 1956.

174 SUDAN, FRENCH — See French Sudan.

314 SUDETENLAND

An area of Czechoslovakia taken by Germany in 1938 and restored following WWII.

315 SUIYUAN

An area in Inner Mongolia under Communist control prior to the formation of the People's Republic of China.

315 SUMATRA

A large island that was formerly part of the Netherlands East Indies and is now in the Republic of Indonesia.

401 SUMMER ISLANDS

An island group off the west coast of Scotland. See British Offshore Islands.

226 SUNDAS ISLANDS — See Lesser Sundas.

169 SUNGEI UJONG

A state on the Malay Peninsula. In 1885 it became part of Negri Sembilan. For map see Federated Malay States.

216 SUPEH — See Northern Kiangsu.

398 SURINAME

The Republic of Suriname is a state on the north coast of South America between Guyana and French Guiana, with Brazil to the south. Previously known as Dutch Guiana, it became part of the Netherlands in 1954 and was granted independence in 1975.

170 SUSAK

Part of the Fiume and Kupa Zone of Axis occupation during WWII. Now part of Yugoslavia. For map see Fiume.

316 SUVALKI (SUWALKI)

A province in the Russian Empire bordering on German East Prussia. Later, it was mostly in the briefly independent country of Lithuania.

357 SWAZILAND

The Kingdom of Swaziland is located in southeastern Africa bordering on Mozambique and the Republic of South Africa. It was under British protection until achieving independence in 1968.

382 SWEDEN

The Kingdom of Sweden is located in Scandinavia on the Baltic Sea. It was united with Norway until 1905.

391 SWITZERLAND

A federal republic located in Europe, with borders on France, Germany, Italy, and Austria.

365 SYRIA

The Syrian Arab Republic is an area of the Middle East occupied by Turkey until WWI, when it was liberated by British forces. Mandated to France in 1920, it became a republic in 1934 and gained complete independence in 1942. From 1958 to 1961 it was united with Egypt as the United Arab Republic.

316 SZECHWAN

A province of the People's Republic of China.

317 SZEGED

A town in Hungary near the border with Yugoslavia and north of Belgrade.

Switzerland

Sudan

Sweden

Sungei Ujong

Straits Settlements

Tanganyika

Tangier

Tannu Tuva

Tanzania

Tchongking

Tasmania

T

Tete

Thailand

317 TACNA
A city and province in southern Peru.

174 TAHITI
An island in the Society Group, located in the South Pacific. See French Oceanic Settlements.

TAI HAN
Name once used for Korea.

361 TAIWAN (FORMOSA)
A large island off the coast of China. See China, Republic of.

318 TALCA
A town and province in central Chile.

214 TANGANYIKA
Formerly known as German East Africa, it was mandated to Great Britain following WWI. It became independent in 1961 and together with Zanzibar is now the United Republic of Tanzania. For map see Kenya, Tanganyika, and Uganda.

318 TANGIER
A town and province on the Atlantic coast of Morocco at the entrance to the Mediterranean Sea. From 1923 to 1956 it was an international zone, except for the period 1940-45, when it was under Spanish control. Now part of the Kingdom of Morocco.

319 TANNU TUVA
An area located between Mongolia and the USSR. Now the Tuva Autonomous Soviet Socialist Republic.

353 TANZANIA
The United Republic of Tanzania was formerly German East Africa. After WWI it became the British Mandated Territory of Tanganyika and achieved independence in 1961. Now united with Zanzibar.

163 TARTU
A town in what was the independent country of Estonia and is now in the USSR. Formerly named Dorpat. For map see Dorpat.

319 TASMANIA
An island to the south of Australia. Now an Australian state, it was the British colony of Van Diemen's Land until 1853, when it assumed its present name. It was one of the six British colonies that combined in 1901 to form the Commonwealth of Australia.

353 TCHAD — See Chad.

143 TCHONGKING
A town in China, known during WWII as Chungking, the capital city of the Nationalist regime. Also called Ch'un-ch'ing.

320 TEGUCIGALPA
The capital city of Honduras.

272 TEHRAN
Capital city of the Islamic Republic of Iran. For map see Persia.

320 TEMESVAR
A town in Romania, now called Timisoara. It was occupied by Serbia during WWI when it was part of the Austro-Hungarian Empire. Romanian forces later took over the occupation.

321 TERUEL
A city and province of Spain.

321 TETE
A town and district in the western part of the People's Republic of Mozambique.

322 TETUAN (TETOUAN)
A town in the Kingdom of Morocco. Now called Tetouan.

361 THAILAND
The Kingdom of Thailand is a country located in Southeast Asia. Formerly known as Siam.

293 THESSALONIKI
The current name of a seaport in northern Greece on the Aegean Sea. Formerly called Salonica. For map see Salonica.

Thessaly

Thurn & Taxis

Tobago

Thomond

Tibet

Tierra del Fuego

Timor

Togo

322 **THESSALY**

Now an area of Greece, Thessaly was ceded to that country by Turkey in 1881. In 1897 it was the main battlefield in a war between the two countries. It is located on the Aegean Sea, and the chief town is Larisa.

THOMOND

Although there are labels bearing the name "Principality of Thomond," they are bogus, and the country never existed.

184 **THRACE**

An area of the Balkan Peninsula, once part of the Turkish Empire. In 1878 the northern portion became autonomous under Turkey. It was known as Eastern Rumelia and later joined Bulgaria. The southern portion remained Turkish; today its eastern part is still Turkish, and the west is now in Greece. For map see Giumulzina.

183 **THURINGA** — See Germany, Soviet Zone.

323 **THURN AND TAXIS**

The House of Thurn and Taxis operated postal services in much of Europe until it declined following the Napoleonic Wars. During the years of stamp issuance from 1852 to 1867, it served a number of German states, principalities, and Free Cities.

324 **TIBET**

Formerly an independent state located to the north of the Republic of India and the Kingdom of Nepal. It was taken over by the People's Republic of China and is now part of that country.

324 **TIENTSIN**

A city in the People's Republic of China. Now called T'ien-ching, it is located on the Gulf of Chihli.

408 **TIERRA DEL FUEGO**

Located at the southern tip of South America, Tierra del Fuego is an island of which part belongs to Chile and part to Argentina.

178 **TIFLIS** — See Georgia.

162 **TILOS**

The present name of Piscopi. See Dodecanese Islands.

320 **TIMISOARA** — See Temesvar.

277 **TIMOR**

The eastern portion of Timor, plus a small enclave on the north coast of the western part of the island, constituted Portuguese Timor. The rest of the island was part of the Netherlands Indies until it became independent in the Republic of Indonesia. Indonesia annexed the Portuguese area in 1976. For map see Portuguese Timor.

325 **TLACOTALPAN**

A village in the Mexican state of Veracruz.

325 **TOBAGO**

An island in the West Indies to the northeast of Trinidad. Now part of the Republic of Trinidad and Tobago.

353 **TOGO**

Formerly a German colony in West Africa, the Republic of Togo was divided and mandated to Britain and France following WWI. The British-mandated area was merged into the colony of the Gold Coast (now Ghana); the French portion became a republic within the French Community in 1956 and became fully independent in 1958.

368 TOKELAU ISLANDS
The Tokelau Islands consist of three atolls some 300 miles north of Samoa. They were once known as the Union Islands and were part of the Gilbert and Ellice group. New Zealand took over their administration in 1949.

?26 TOLIMA
A state in the Granadine Confederation, Tolima became a department in the South American country of Colombia in 1886.

368 TONGA
Located in the South Pacific and sometimes known as the Friendly Islands, the Kingdom of Tonga is an independent country that was under British protection until 1970, when it became a member of the British Commonwealth.

368 TONGAREVA
The local name for Penrhyn Island (q.v.), one of the Northern Cook Islands.

99 TONKIN (TONKING)
Part of French Indo-China, located around the capital city of Hanoi. Now part of the Socialist Republic of Vietnam. For map see Annam and Tonkin.

319 TOUVA — See Tannu Tuva.

329 TRABZON — See Trebizonde.

168 TRANSBAIKAL PROVINCE — See Far East Republic, which superceded it.

TRANSCAUCASIAN REPUBLIC
A short-lived federation of Armenia, Azerbaijan, and Georgia. All are now located within the USSR between the Black Sea and the Caspian Sea. The federation existed for a brief period following the Russian Revolution. For maps see individual names.

326 TRANS-JORDAN
An area of the Middle East formerly under Turkish control, it was mandated to Great Britain along with neighboring Palestine following WWI. In 1946 it became the Hashemite Kingdom of Jordan.

356 TRANSKEI
One of the "homelands" established in South Africa. It was formed in 1976. For map see South Africa, Homelands.

327 TRANSVAAL
A republic established by the Boers in South Africa as the South African Republic. It was annexed by Great Britain in 1877, restored in 1881, only to be taken again in 1900. It is now part of the Republic of South Africa.

327 TRANSYLVANIA
Prior to WWI, Transylvania comprised the eastern portion of Hungary. It was incorporated into Romania following the war.

202 TRAVANCORE
A former feudatory state in India, Travancore joined with Cochin in 1949 to form the United States of Travancore and Cochin. It is now part of the Republic of India. See Indian Feudatory States.

202 TRAVANCORE AND COCHIN — See Travancore.

328 TREATY PORTS
Cities in the Orient (mostly in China) at which foreign post offices were operated under a treaty arrangement.

329 TREBIZONDE
A Turkish city on the Black Sea. Now called Trabzon.

237 TRENGGANU
Located on the Malay Peninsula, Trengganu was a state in the Federation of Malaya. It is now part of Malaysia. For map see Malayan Federation.

208 TRENTINO — See Italian Austria.

329 TRIESTE
A seaport located at the head of the Adriatic Sea near the Italian-Yugoslavian border. Formerly part of the Austro-Hungarian Empire, it became Italian after WWI. Trieste and surrounding territory was a Free City from 1947 to 1954, when it was divided between Italy and Yugoslavia, with the city going to Italy.

409 TRINIDAD
A small island in the South Atlantic about 700 miles from the coast of Brazil, to which it belongs.

Tonga

Transkei

Travancore

376 TRINIDAD

A large island off the coast of Venezuela near the mouth of the Orinoco River. Together with the island of Tobago it forms the Republic of Trinidad and Tobago. From 1958 to 1962 it was a member of the Caribbean Federation; before that it was a British crown colony.

376 TRINIDAD AND TOBAGO — See Trinidad.

330 TRIPOLI

Now the capital city of the Socialist People's Libyan Arab Jamahiriya, it had once been the capital of the Italian colony of Tripolitania. Italy had taken it from Turkey during its 1911-12 war with the Turkish Empire. For map see Tripolitania.

330 TRIPOLITANIA

Once part of the Turkish Empire and located on the north coast of Africa, it became an Italian colony as a result of the 1911-12 war between Italy and Turkey. It was occupied by British forces during WWII and remained under military administration until 1952, when it became part of the Kingdom of Libya, now the Socialist People's Libyan Arab Jamahiriya.

357 TRISTAN DA CUNHA

A group of islands located in the South Atlantic about midway between South America and Africa. The group is a dependency of the British island of St. Helena.

331 TRUCIAL STATES

A group of seven sheikdoms mostly on the Arabian shore of the Persian Gulf. The group broke up in 1963. The sheikdoms were Abu Dhabi, Ajman, Dubai, Fujeira, Ras al Khaima, Sharjah, and Umm al Qiwain, plus dependencies of Khor Fakkan (Sharjah) and Manama (Ajman). On Dec. 2, 1971, they joined to become the United Arab Emirates.

330 TSINGHAI

A province of the People's Republic of China.

216 TSINGTAU

A district of the People's Republic of China located on the southern side of the Shantung Peninsula. It was a German colony from 1897 to WWI. Now the Chinese city of Ch'ing-tao. See Kiautschou.

357 TUNISIA

The Republic of Tunisia was formerly a French Protectorate, becoming independent in 1956 and a republic a year later. It is located in North Africa between Algeria and Libya.

365 TURKEY

The Republic of Turkey was once the heart of an empire that covered most of the Middle East and much of southeastern Europe. The creaking empire finally collapsed during WWI, and the country is now confined to Asia Minor and a small area in Europe.

376 TURKS AND CAICOS ISLANDS

A pair of island groups located southeast of the Bahamas and north of the Greater Antilles island of Hispaniola. It was a dependency of Jamaica until 1962 and is now a British crown colony.

332 TURKS ISLANDS

A group of islands east of the Caicos group and with it forming the British Crown Colony of the Turks and Caicos Islands.

332 TUSCANY

Formerly an independent duchy located in central Italy. It became part of the Kingdom of Sardinia, then of the Kingdom of Italy.

319 TUVA ASSR

The Tuva Autonomous Soviet Socialist Republic was once known as North Mongolia, Tannu Tuva, or Tuva. It is lcoated between Mongolia and Siberia.

368 TUVALU

Previously known as the Ellice Islands and part of the Gilbert and Ellice Islands colony. The two groups split in 1976, with the Ellice Islands becoming Tuvalu.

304 TWO KINGDOMS OF SICILY — See Sicily, Two Kingdoms of.

294 TYROL

A province of Austria. For map see Salzburg.

Trinidad & Tobago

Tripolitania

Turkey

Turks Islands

Tuscany

Uganda

United
Arab
Emirates

Ukraine

Umm al Qiwain

United Arab
Republic

81

U

171 UBANGI-SHARI
Part of the Central African colony of French Congo from 1894 to 1910, Ubangi-Shari was absorbed into French Equatorial Africa. In 1958 it became independent as the Central African Republic. For map see French Equatorial Africa.

171 UBANGUI-CHARI — See Ubangi-Shari.

353 UGANDA
The Republic of Uganda was a former British protectorate in East Africa. It achieved independence within the British Commonwealth in 1962.

333 UKRAINE
Once part of the Russian Empire, it became the Ukrainian National Republic following the Russian Revolution of 1917. Its freedom was short-lived, however, and it was absorbed by the Soviet Union in 1923.

389 ULSTER — See Ireland, Northern.

331 UMM AL QIWAIN
A sheikdom on the southern shore of the Persian Gulf, it was one of the Trucial States and is now in the United Arab Emirates. For map see Trucial States.

333 UMM SAID
A town located on the east coast of Qatar.

368 UNION ISLANDS — See Tokelau Islands.

356 UNION OF SOUTH AFRICA — See South Africa.

331 UNITED ARAB EMIRATES
A federation of seven sheikdoms with their various dependencies located on the south shore of the Persian Gulf and the Oman Gulf coast of Arabia. The members are Abu Dhabi, Ajman, Dubai, Fujeira, Sharjah, Umm al Qiwain, and Ras al Khaima. For map see Trucial States.

334 UNITED ARAB REPUBLIC
A union between Egypt and Syria that existed from 1958 to 1961.

334 UNITED ARAB STATES
In 1959 the United Arab Republic admitted what is now the Yemen Arab Republic to its union. The merger lasted until 1961.

382 UNITED KINGDOM — See Great Britain.

394 UNITED STATES OF AMERICA
A union of 48 adjoining states plus the states of Alaska and Hawaii, the Commonwealth of Puerto Rico, Guam, the American Virgin Islands, American Samoa, the Trust Territory of the Pacific Islands, and a number of minor islands. For maps showing towns for which postmasters' provisional stamps were issued, see US Postmasters' Provisonals on page 336.

361 UNITED STATES OF INDONESIA
This was the name of the Republic of Indonesia for a few months after it became independent in 1949.

397 UNITED STATES OF NEW GRANADA — See Colombia.

298 UNITED STATES OF SAURASHTRA — See Saurashtra.

334 UPPER AUSTRIA
A province of Austria.

174 UPPER SENEGAL AND NIGER — See French Sudan.

Upper Silesia

Upper Volta

USSR

Uruguay

335 UPPER SILESIA

Prior to WWI, Silesia formed part of eastern Germany. A plebiscite held following the war was not decisive, and the League of Nations divided the area between Germany and Poland, with Upper Silesia going to Poland.

353 UPPER VOLTA

The Republic of Upper Volta is located in West Africa, north of Ghana. It was a French colony until 1933, when it was divided among the French colonies of Niger, French Sudan, and Ivory Coast. It was included in French West Africa from 1944, becoming self-governing in the French Community in 1958 and fully independent in 1960.

UPPER YAFA

A sultanate in Southern Arabia. Independent during 1967, it is now part of the People's Democratic Republic of Yemen.

398 URUGUAY

The Oriental Republic of Uruguay gained its independence from Spain in 1828. It is located in South America on the Atlantic Ocean, south of Brazil.

336 US POSTMASTER'S PROVISIONALS

335 USKUB

A town in southern Yugoslavia. It is now called Skopje.

382 USSR

The Union of Soviet Socialist Republics covers a huge area in eastern Europe and northern Asia, reaching to the Pacific Ocean. It was formed in 1923 out of the chaos of the Russian Revolution and currently comprises 15 so-called "republics," of which Russia is the largest.

Van Diemen's Land

Valona

Vancouver Is.

Vathy

Vanuatu

Vatican City

Venezuela

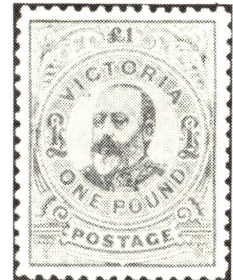
Victoria

Venda

V

235 VALENCIA
A city in Spain. For location see Majorca.

336 VALONA
A town in Albania. Now called Vlore.

337 VALLADOLID
A province in northern Spain.

319 VAN DIEMEN'S LAND — See Tasmania.

337 VANCOUVER ISLAND
A large island off the Pacific coast of Canada. Now part of the province of British Columbia, it was once a British crown colony.

368 VANUATU
Formerly known as New Hebrides, the South Pacific island group became independent in 1980 as the country of Vanuatu. It had been administered by Britain and France as a condominium since 1906. The islands are located about 500 miles slightly to the northwest of Fiji.

338 VASA (VAASA)
A city in Finland on the Gulf of Bothnia.

294 VATHY (VATHI)
A town on the Greek island of Samos in the Aegean Sea. Now called Vathi. For map see Samos.

392 VATICAN CITY
The State of the Vatican City is located in the Italian capital city of Rome. Formed in 1929, it has independence and sovereignty in foreign affairs.

338 VEGLIA
An island off the coast of Yugoslavia. Now called Krk.

356 VENDA
One of the so-called "homelands" located in the Republic of South Africa. For map see South Africa, Homelands.

228 VENETIA — See Lombardy and Venetia.

339 VENEZIA GIULIA
An area in northeast Italy, bordering on Yugoslavia.

397 VENEZUELA
The Republic of Venezuela is located on the north coast of South America. It became independent from Spain in 1811 and until 1830 was a unit in the State of Greater Colombia.

339 VICTORIA
Formerly a British colony in southeastern Australia, it is now a state in the Commonwealth of Australia.

340 VICTORIA LAND
An area in the Antarctic. Overprints on New Zealand stamps were made for the 1911 Scott expedition.

Vilnius

Virgin Islands, British

227 **VIDZEME** — See Livonia.

334 **VIENNA**

Capital city and district of Austria. For map see Upper Austria.

361 **VIETNAM**

The Socialist Republic of Vietnam was once part of French Indo-China. It became split between the Communists in the north and an anti-Communist regime in the south following WWII and the withdrawal of the French. Despite massive US intervention on the side of the south, in 1976 the entire area was united under a Communist government.

227 **VILNIUS**

Capital city of the former independent country of Lithuania when it was established following WWI. For map see Lithuania.

158 **VIRGIN ISLANDS, AMERICAN** — See Danish West Indies.

372 **VIRGIN ISLANDS, BRITISH** — See British Virgin Islands.

340 **VLADIVOSTOK**

A city on the Pacific coast of the USSR.

341 **VRYBURG**

A town in the Republic of South Africa, Vryburg is about 125 miles north of Kimberley.

Wenden

Wallis and Futuna

Wales

Western
Australia

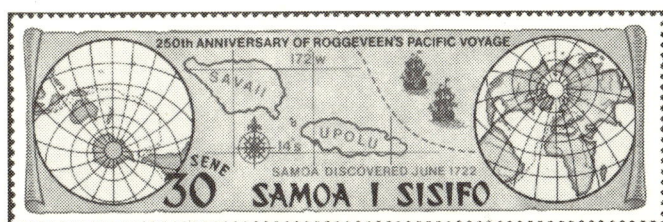
Western Samoa

Western
Ukraine

W

202 WADHWAN
A former feudatory state of India, it is now part of the Republic of India. For map see Indian Feudatory States.

341 WALACHIA
Together with Moldavia, it formed Romania in 1859.

392 WALES
The Principality of Wales is located in the western part of Great Britain. It is administered with England as one unit.

368 WALLIS AND FUTUNA ISLANDS
A group of French islands in the South Pacific, west of Samoa and northwest of Fiji. It is administered as a dependency of New Caledonia.

177 WARSAW
The capital city of Poland. For location see General Gouvernement.

342 WEI-HAI-WEI
A town and district on the north side of the Shantung Peninsula of China. It was leased by Great Britain from the Empire of China in 1898 and returned to China in 1930.

227 WENDEN
The town of Wenden was formerly part of the Russian Empire. After the 1917 Revolution it was included in the area of Livonia in Latvia. The town is now called Cesis and is located in the USSR as part of the Latvian SSR. For map see Livonia.

342 WESTERN AUSTRALIA
A former British colony comprising the western portion of Australia. Now a state in the Commonwealth of Australia.

312 WESTERN SAHARA — See Spanish Sahara.

368 WESTERN SAMOA — See Samoa.

316 WESTERN SZECHWAN
Comprises the western part of the Chinese province of the same name. For map see Szechwan.

343 WESTERN UKRAINE
Once part of the Austro-Hungarian Empire, it was briefly independent in 1918-19 before being absorbed by Poland. It is now part of the USSR.

Wurttemberg

382 WEST GERMANY — See Germany, Federal Republic of.

253 WEST IRIAN
The western portion of the island of New Guinea, formerly Netherlands New Guinea, now part of Indonesia. For map see Netherlands New Guinea.

253 WEST NEW GUINEA
When the Netherlands gave up Netherlands New Guinea, it was administered by the United Nations as West New Guinea during 1962-63, prior to becoming part of Indonesia as West Irian. For map see Netherlands New Guinea.

183 WEST SAXONY
For map see Germany, Soviet Zone.

343 WOLMARANSSTAD
A town in Transvaal. Now in the Republic of South Africa.

344 WURTTEMBERG
A former independent kingdom, it became part of the German Empire in 1870 and is now in the Federal Republic of Germany.

Yemen
People's
Democratic
Republic

Yugoslavia

Zaire

Zanzibar

Zambezia

Zambia

Zara

X Y Z

344 YCA

A town and district in Peru. Now called Ica.

366 YEMEN ARAB REPUBLIC

Located in the southwest part of the Arabian Peninsula on the Red Sea and bordering on Saudi Arabia to the north and east and the People's Democratic Republic of Yemen on the south. A kingdom until 1962. A civil war was fought between royalist and republican forces from 1962 to 1970. Both sides claimed sovereignty, but Saudi Arabia recognized the republicans, and the royalist faction collapsed.

365 YEMEN PDR

The People's Democratic Republic of Yemen was formed from South Arabia in 1967 as the People's Republic of Southern Yemen. The present name was adopted in 1970. See Aden, Hadhramaut.

345 YUCATAN

A state in southern Mexico.

382 YUGOSLAVIA

The Socialist Republic of Yugoslavia was established following WWI as the Kingdom of the Serbs, Croats, and Slovenes. It is located on the Balkan Peninsula with a coastline on the Adriatic Sea and was formed from Serbia, Montenegro, Bosnia, Herzegovina, and portions of Hungary.

345 YUNNAN

A town in the Chinese province of the same name, it is now called Kunming.

346 ZACATECAS

A town and state in Mexico.

347 ZADAR — See Zara.

353 ZAIRE

The Republic of Zaire was the Congo Republic (Kinshasa) until 1971. It had previously been the Belgian Congo.

ZAMBEZIA

A district in the then-Portuguese colony of Mozambique, Zambezia included Tete and Quelimane. For map see Tete and Quelimane.

353 ZAMBIA

The Republic of Zambia was formerly the British Central African colony of Northern Rhodesia. Part of the Central African Federation from 1953 to 1963, it became independent in 1964.

207 ZANTE (ZAKINTHOS) — See Ionian Islands.

346 ZANZIBAR

A former British protectorate comprising several islands off the East African coast, Zanzibar became independent in 1963. In 1964 it joined with the new Republic of Tanganyika as the United Republic of Tanganyika and Zanzibar. It is now the United Republic of Tanzania.

347 ZARA

A province on the north coast of Yugoslavia.

347 ZARAGOZA

A town and province in Spain.

Zil Elwagne Sesel

Zimbabwe

Zululand

Zurich

348 ZELAYA
A province of Nicaragua, located on the Caribbean coast.

357 ZIL ELOIGNE SESEL — See Zil Elwagne Sesel.

357 ZIL ELWAGNE SESEL
Comprises the outer islands of the Republic of Seychelles, located in the Indian Ocean to the north of Madagascar. Includes Aldabra, Coetivy, Farquhar, the Amirante Islands, Cosmoledo, Astove, Providence, and Cerf. Formerly spelled Zil Eloigne Sesel.

353 ZIMBABWE
The British colony of Rhodesia became independent in 1980 and assumed the name of Zimbabwe. It is located in southern Africa.

348 ZULULAND
Located in southeast Africa, Zululand was annexed by Great Britain in 1887 and incorporated into the colony of Natal. It is now part of the Republic of South Africa.

349 ZURICH
A town and canton of Switzerland.

Section Two
Dead Countries
Stamp-issuing areas of the past.

The philatelic term "dead country" is a rather in-elegant way of describing an area that once issued its own stamps, but which does so no longer.

This is usually because it has been absorbed into another political entity. Newfoundland, once a stamp-issuing colony and now a province of Canada, is an example.

However, for the purpose of arranging this atlas, I have considered as philatelically "dead" not only areas that have ceased issuing stamps, but also those that have changed their status and their name — the ex-colony of British Honduras, now independent as Belize, for example, or Palestine, now Israel.

Wherever possible, population figures have been given that are contemporaneous with the area's existence, as well as more recent figures for purposes of comparison.

Where there are various name spellings, those most familiar to collectors have been given prominence.

A fascination for the past exists in most of us, but more especially in those who collect and study the philately of yesterday's countries. Where was the Austro-Hungarian Empire, or the Ottoman Empire? What happened to Zanzibar and the island of Fernando Po? The appeal of such exotic places is obvious, and much is reflected in the stamps that they used.

So, let's away to Devil's Island, Kionga, or Kilis and browse among the world's forgotten "yesterdays."

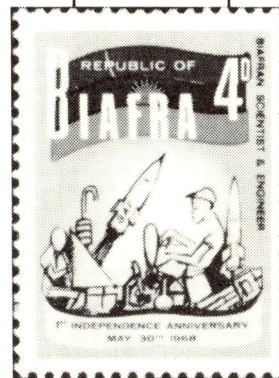

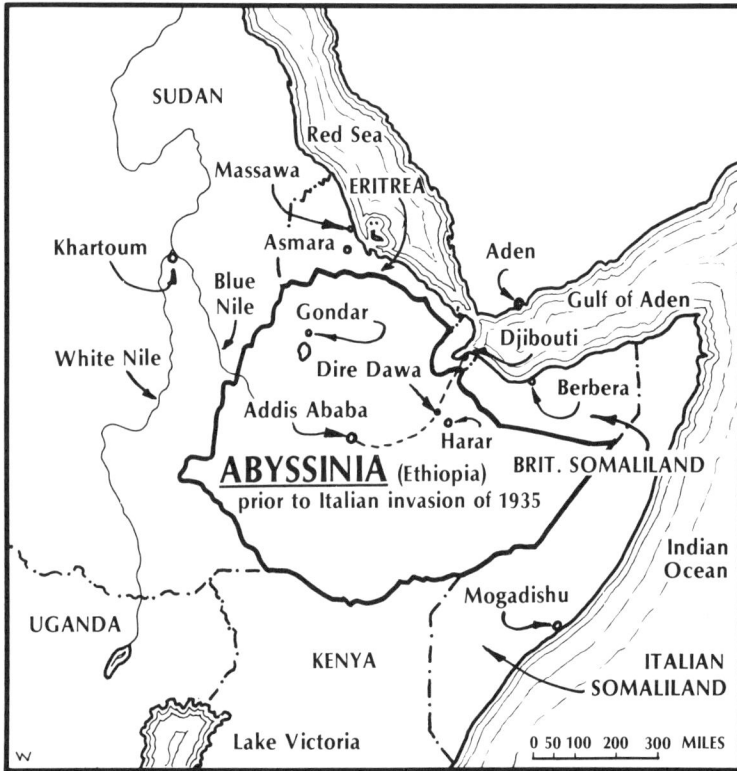

Area: 462,000 sq. miles
Pop: 5 million (1900)
33,300,000 (1981 est.)
Capital: Addis Ababa

An exception in what was once the colonial continent of Africa, Abyssinia has a long and proud history of independence. Now known as Socialist Ethiopia, the country had only one period in modern history when it was a colony, during the Italian occupation from 1935 to 1941.

———————————————— ACAPONETA, TOWN OF ————————————————

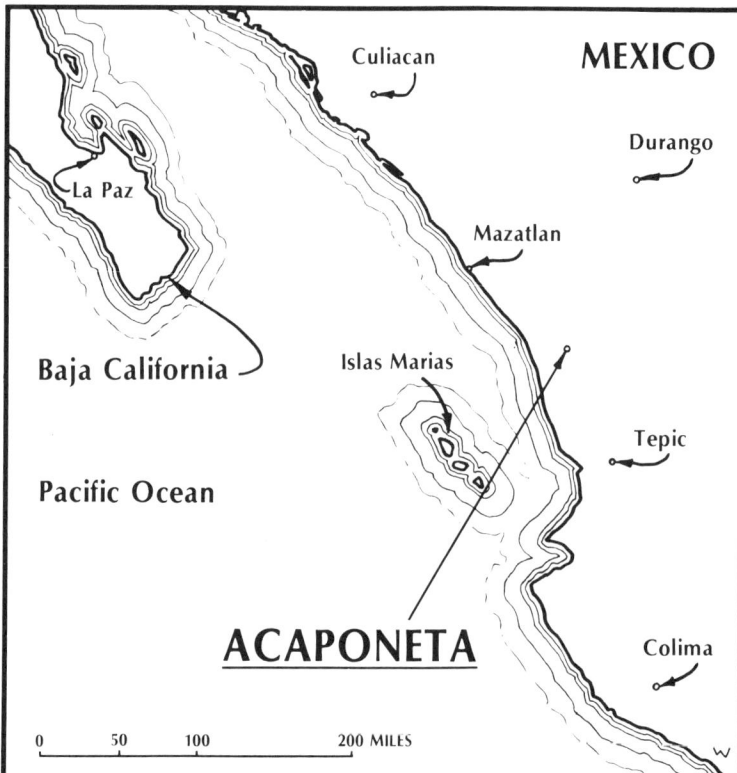

Pop: 18,994 (1894)
29,829 (1970)

Acaponeta is a town in the Mexican state of Nayarit, located on the Acaponeta River. In 1914, during the revolutionary period, a 5c orange stamp of the Mexican 1910 issue was overprinted with the town name as a revolutionary provisional.

Area: 80 sq. miles
Pop: 48,338 (1931 est.)
250,000 (town 1970 est.)

The coaling station and naval base of Aden had been administered from British India until it became a crown colony in 1937, when its first stamps appeared. Previously, Indian stamps had been used. The colony included five-square-mile Perim Island at the mouth of the Red Sea. On April 1, 1965, stamps of the Federation of South Arabia replaced those of Aden.

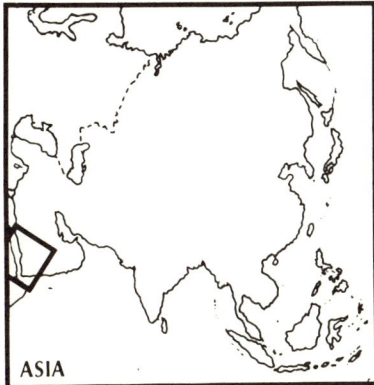

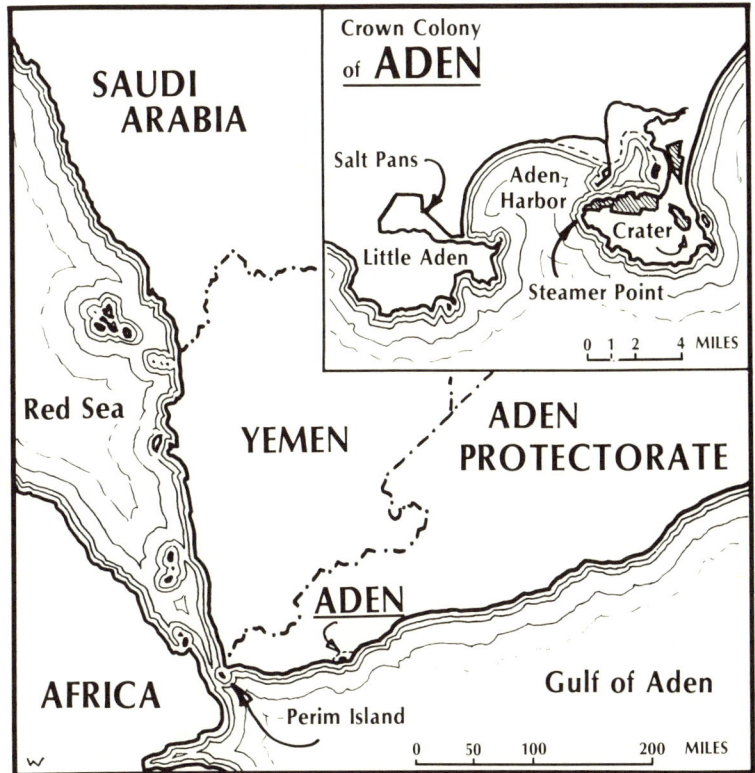

AFARS AND ISSAS, FRENCH TERRITORY OF

Area: 8,880 sq. miles
Pop: 95,000 (1970 est.)
460,000 (1981 est.)
Capital: Djibouti

For a 10-year period between 1967 and 1977, what had previously been the French Somali Coast was the French Territory of the Afars and Issas. It became the independent Republic of Djibouti in June 1977. The seaport of Djibouti is the terminus of a railway linking the Ethiopian capital of Addis Ababa with the sea.

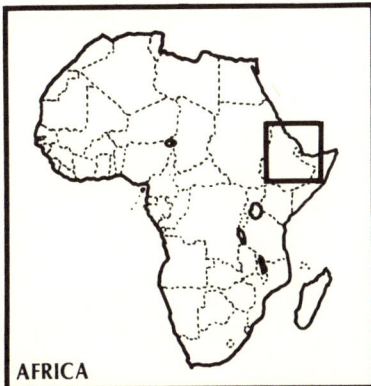

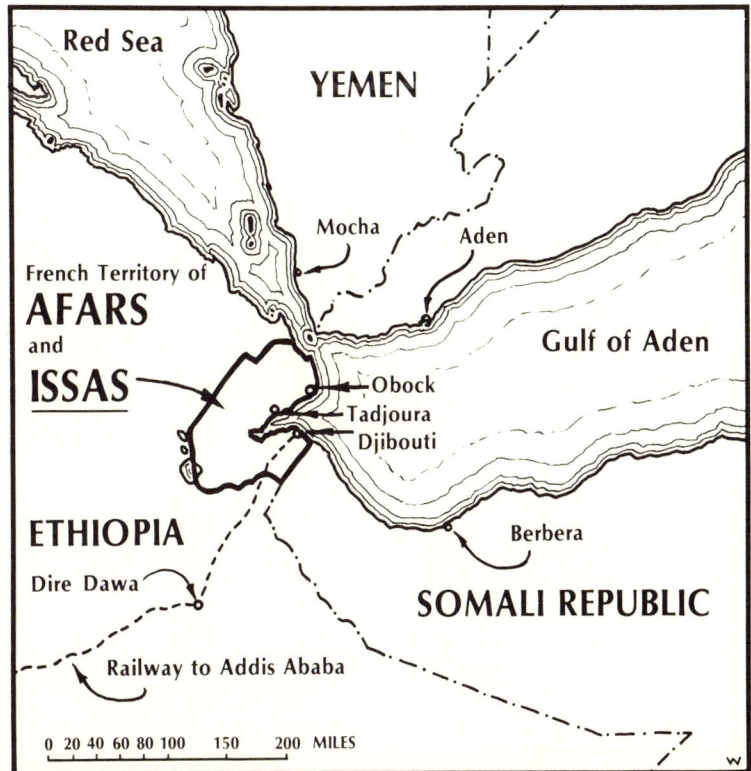

Area: 2,158 sq. miles
Pop: 334,936 (1970)

Aguascalientes is a state with a capital city of the same name in Mexico. Several revolutionary provisional stamps were created there during 1914. Gibbons notes a total of five postage stamps and one postage due label overprinted "GOBIERNO CONSTITU-CIONALISTA" and the name of the city. This was done by revolutionary forces as they captured towns.

———————— **ALAOUITES, STATE OF**————————

Area: 2,500 sq. miles
Pop: 278,000 (1930 est.)
Capital: Latakia

The State of Alaouites was part of the ex-Turkish territory mandated to France after WWI. French and Syrian stamps overprinted "ALAOUITES" were used from 1925 to 1930, when the area became the Republic of Latakia. It is now included within the Syrian Arab Republic.

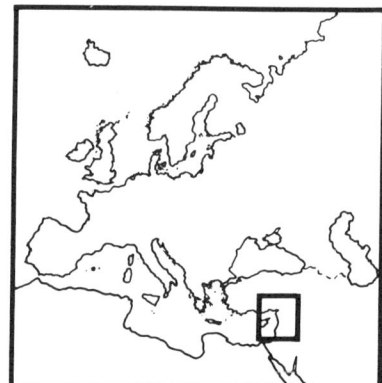

Pop: 319,700 (1897)
2,318,655 (1976)

A major city of Egypt, Alexandria is located west of the Nile delta. From 1899, a French post office in the city used French stamps overprinted "ALEXANDRIE." Later, specially inscribed stamps were used. The last such stamp was issued in 1928, although usage continued into the 1930s. Austria, Britain, Greece, Italy, and Russia also operated post offices there but did not use special stamps.

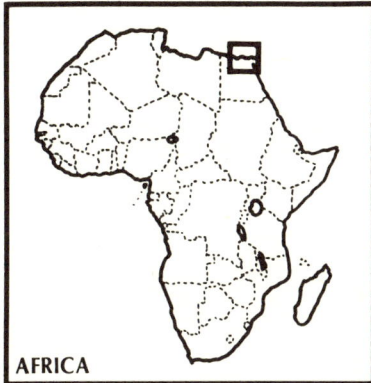

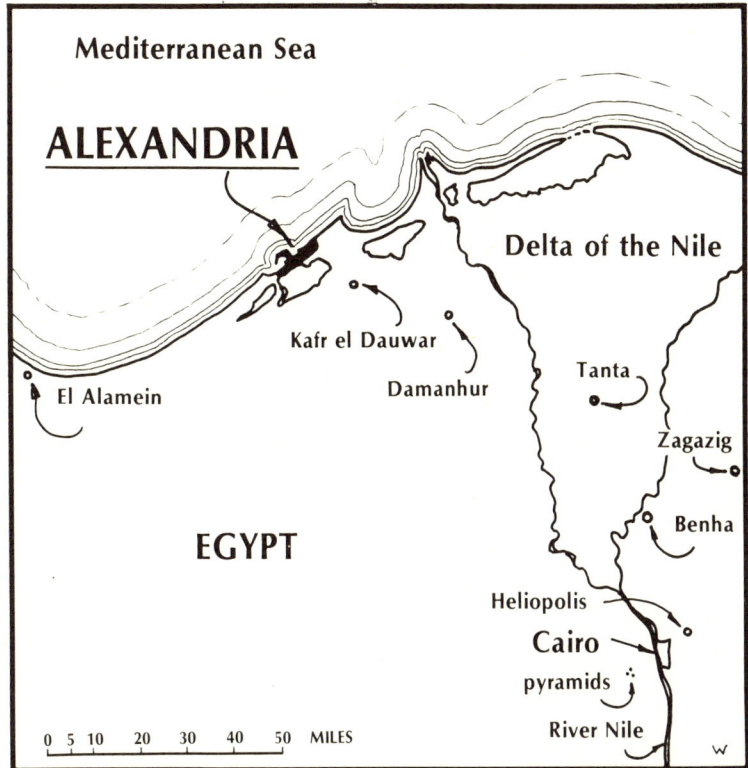

AFRICA

Mediterranean Sea

ALEXANDRIA

Delta of the Nile

Kafr el Dauwar

Damanhur

Tanta

Zagazig

El Alamein

Benha

EGYPT

Heliopolis

Cairo

pyramids

0 5 10 20 30 40 50 MILES

River Nile

ALLENDE, TOWN OF

Allende is a town in northern Mexico near the border with the United States. In 1914 a revolutionary provisional stamp was isued there. It was a 5-centavo stamp of the 1910 Mexican issue and was overprinted "ALLENDE."

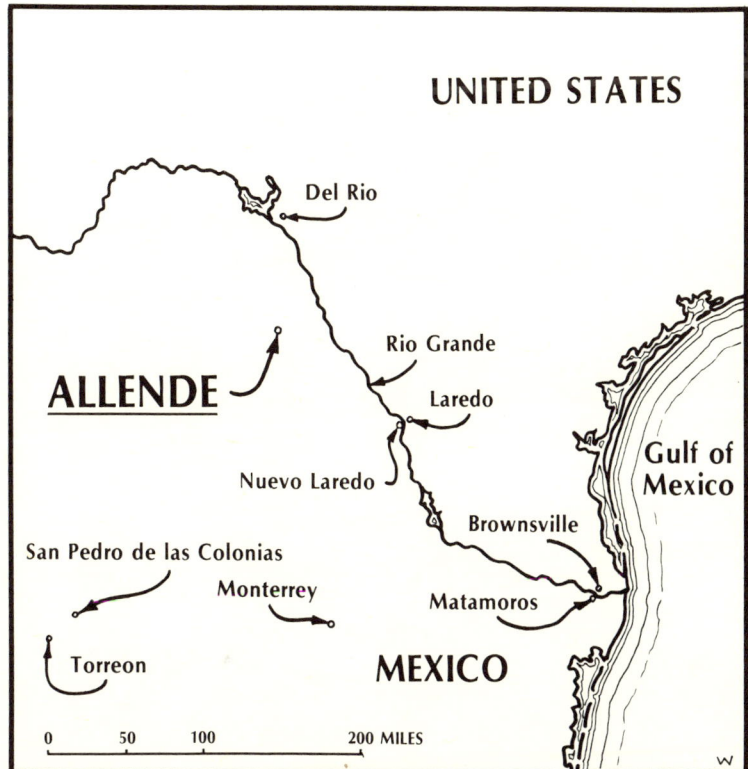

NORTH AMERICA

UNITED STATES

Del Rio

Rio Grande

ALLENDE

Laredo

Nuevo Laredo

Gulf of Mexico

Brownsville

San Pedro de las Colonias

Monterrey

Matamoros

Torreon

MEXICO

0 50 100 200 MILES

Baltic Sea

LITHUANIA

Memel (Klaipeda)

Konigsberg (Kaliningrad)
Danzig
(Gdansk)
EAST PRUSSIA

Polish Corridor

Allenstein
(Olsztyn)   Lyck

Tannenberg

ALLENSTEIN

Warsaw

GERMANY   **POLAND**

0 20 40 60 80 100 MILES

CZECHOSLOVAKIA

Area: 4,450 sq. miles
Pop: 550,000 (1920)
Capital: Allenstein

Allenstein was a district based on the former Prussian town of Allenstein (now Olsztyn). Following WWI, a plebiscite returned the area to Germany. Overprinted German stamps were issued during the plebiscite period. The area is now part of Poland.

EUROPE

———————— ALSACE AND LORRAINE ————————

BELGIUM

Luxembourg

LORRAINE
(LOTHRINGEN)

Mannheim

Metz   Saarbrucken

GERMANY

Nancy   Karlsruhe

ALSACE
(ELSAS)   Strasbourg

River Rhine

Colmar   Freiburg

FRANCE

Belfort   Mulhouse

Dijon   **SWITZERLAND**
Basel

0 10 20 30 40 50 MILES

The twin provinces of Alsace and Lorraine are a frontier region between France and Germany with Alsace bordering on the Rhine river. They were ceded to Germany by France in 1871, following French defeat in the Franco-Prussian War. They remained German until the end of WWI, when they returned to France under the Treaty of Versailles in 1919. During WWII, Germany again invaded and occupied them, along with much of France itself.

EUROPE

Area: 140,425 sq. miles
Pop: 793,000 (1970)
Capital: Blagoveshchensk

Amur is a province of the USSR in Siberia. Its capital city is located on the Amur River, which forms the border between the USSR and the People's Republic of China at this point. Stamps were issued in 1920 under a People's Revolutionary Committee, which was superseded by the formation of the Far Eastern Republic.

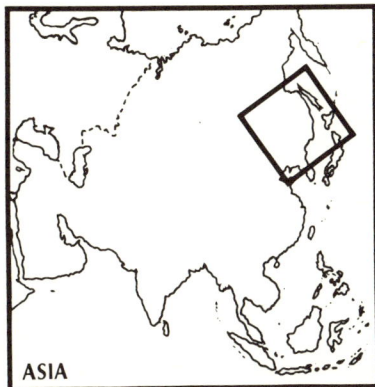

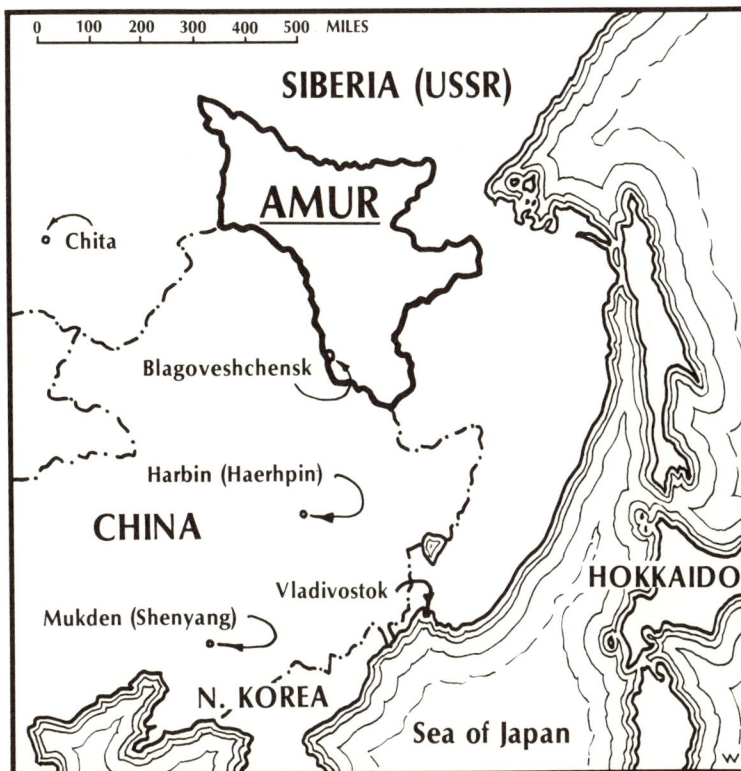

SIBERIA (USSR)

AMUR

Chita

Blagoveshchensk

Harbin (Haerhpin)

CHINA

Vladivostok

Mukden (Shenyang)

HOKKAIDO

N. KOREA

Sea of Japan

ASIA

— ANCACHS (ANCASH), DEPARTMENT OF —

Area: 14,019 sq. miles
Pop: 727,000 (1969 est.)
Capital: Huaraz

Ancachs (Ancash) is a department of Peru located on the coast of that country to the north of the capital city of Lima. A number of provisional stamps were issued there during a stamp shortage caused by the Chilean occupation of Lima and Callao, in the war between the two countries that was fought in the late 1870s and early 1880s.

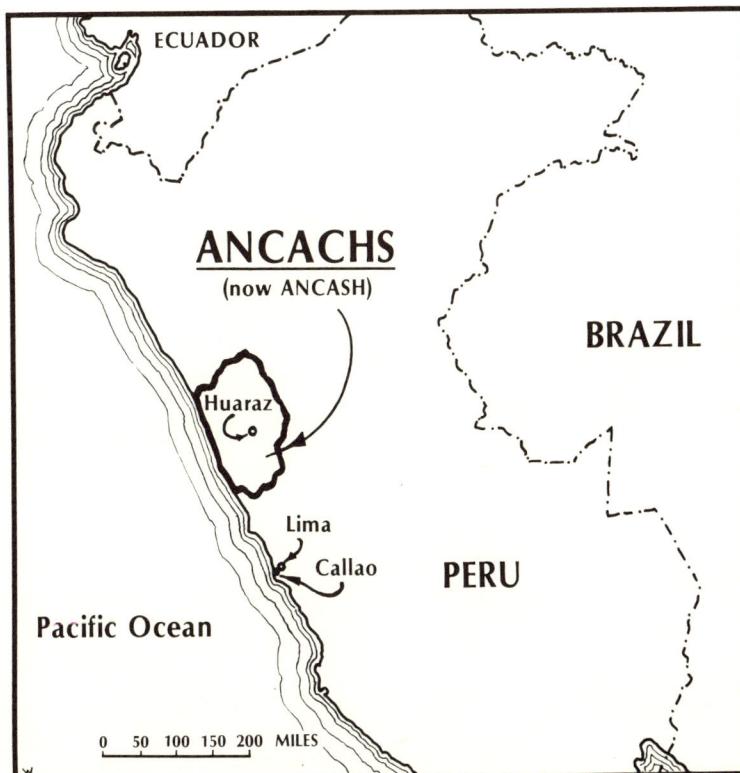

ECUADOR

ANCACHS
(now ANCASH)

BRAZIL

Huaraz

Lima

Callao

PERU

Pacific Ocean

SOUTH AMERICA

Area: 33,964 sq. miles
Pop: 5,894,000 (1960 est.)

Andalusia is a region comprising the eight southernmost provinces of Spain. It corresponds roughly to the old Roman province of Baetica and was divided into its present subdivisions in 1833. The climate ranges from subtropical to alpine and is similar to the corresponding area in Africa across the Strait of Gibraltar. A stamp issue was released there in 1868-69 by a provisional government.

EUROPE

ANDAMAN AND NICOBAR ISLANDS

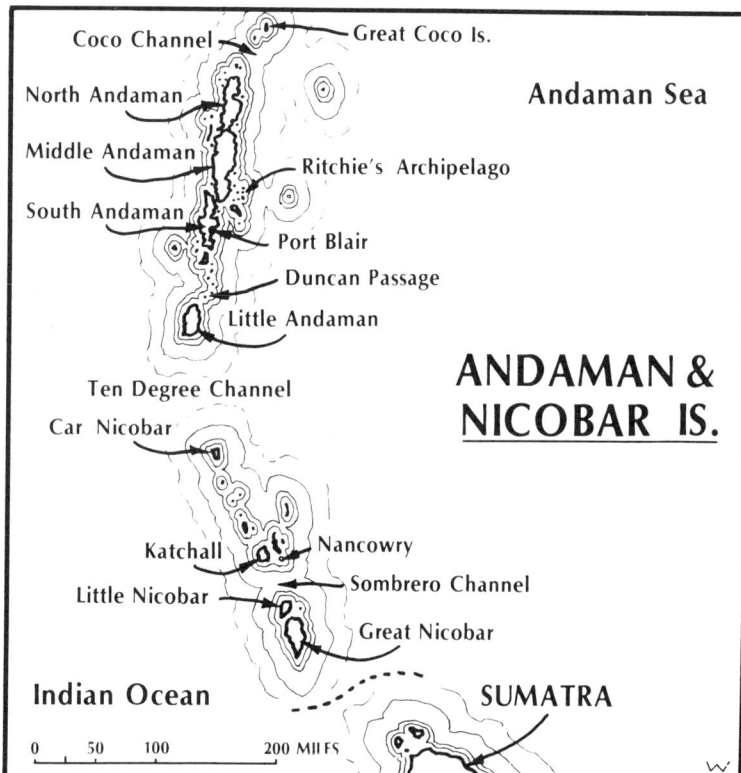

Area: Andaman 2,461 sq. miles
Nicobar 740 sq. miles
Pop: Andaman 48,985 (1961)
Nicobar 14,563 (1961)

The Andaman and Nicobar Islands are twin groups located in the Bay of Bengal. They are part of the Republic of India. During the WWII occupation of the islands by Japan, Indian stamps were overprinted by the occupying authorities.

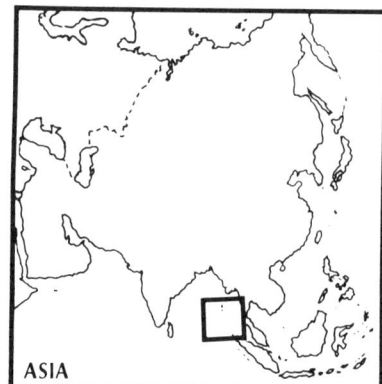

ASIA

Pop: 36,000 (1900 est.)
2.6 million (1979 est.)

Angora was the center of the Turkish Nationalist revolution following the WWI defeat by the Allies of the old Turkish Empire. It was made the capital city of the new republic of Turkey in 1923, and the name was officially changed to Ankara in 1930. Stamps were issued there by the Nationalists during the revolutionary period.

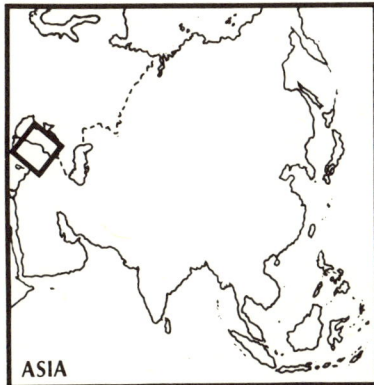

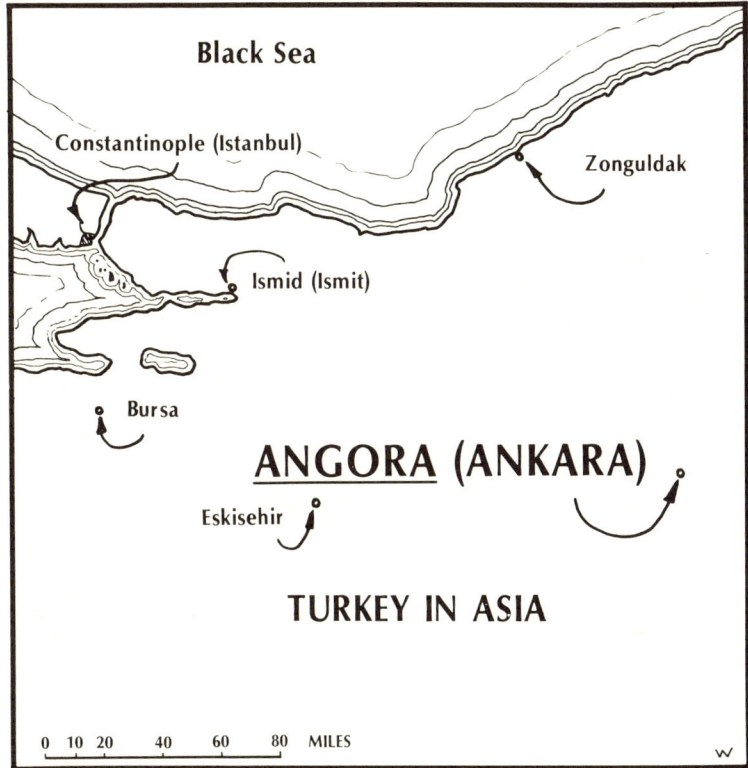

Black Sea

Constantinople (Istanbul)

Zonguldak

Ismid (Ismit)

Bursa

ANGORA (ANKARA)

Eskisehir

TURKEY IN ASIA

0 10 20 40 60 80 MILES

ASIA

ANGRA, DISTRICT OF

Area: 275 sq. miles
Pop: 11,067 (1890)
Capital: Angra do Heroismo

This administrative area of the Portuguese Azores comprised the islands of Graciosa, Sao Jorge, and Terceira. Stamps were issued from 1892 to 1906.

Santa Cruz da Graciosa

0 5 10 20 30 40 MILES

GRACIOSA

SAO JORGE

Praia da Vitoria

Rosais

Velas

Angra
do Heroismo

Calheta

Sao Sebastiao

St. Antao

TERCEIRA

Administrative District

of **ANGRA**

AZORES

Atlantic Ocean

CORVO

FLORES

GRACIOSA

TERCEIRA

SAO JORGE

SAO MIGUEL

FAIAL

PICO

SANTA MARIA

FORMIGAS

0 50 100 150 MILES

ATLANTIC

CHINA

Yellow Sea

Hsu-chou

Su-hsien

Peng-pu

Fu-yang

ANHWEI

Ho-fei

Nanking

Shanghai

An-ch'ing

Hangchow

Yangtze River

0 20 40 60 80 100   150   200 MILES

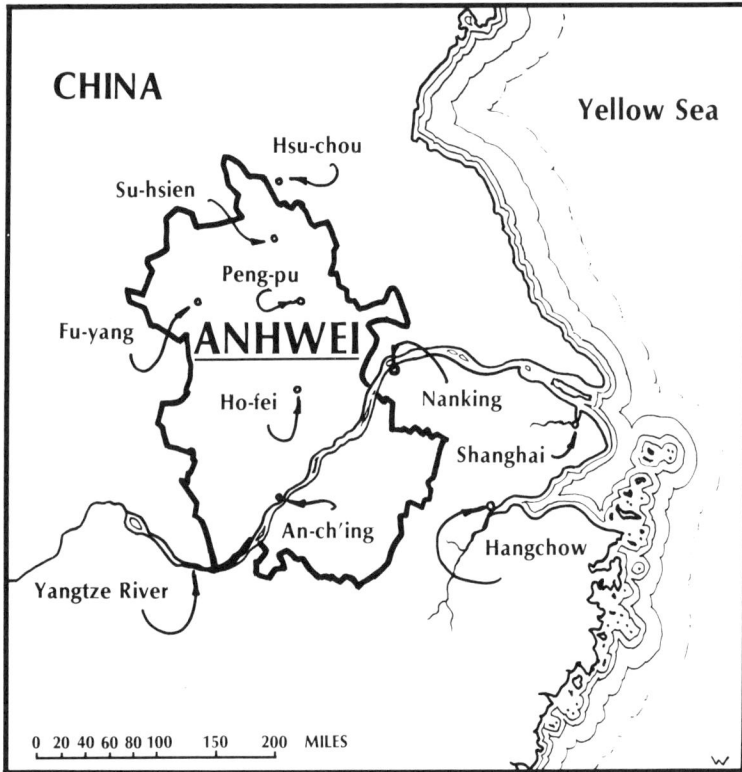

Area: 54,015 sq. miles
Pop: 35,810,000 (1896)
Capital: Ho-fei

Originally part of Kiang-nan and Kiangsu provinces, Anhwei became a separate province of China during the 17th century. Provisional stamps were issued for use in the province during the 1940s. In 1949, Anhwei became part of the Communist East China Liberation Area, and stamps for use in that area were issued. It is now part of the People's Republic of China.

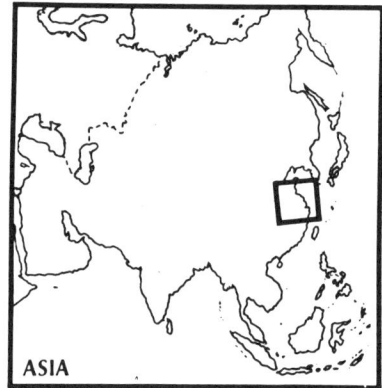

ASIA

———————— ANJOUAN, COLONY OF ————————

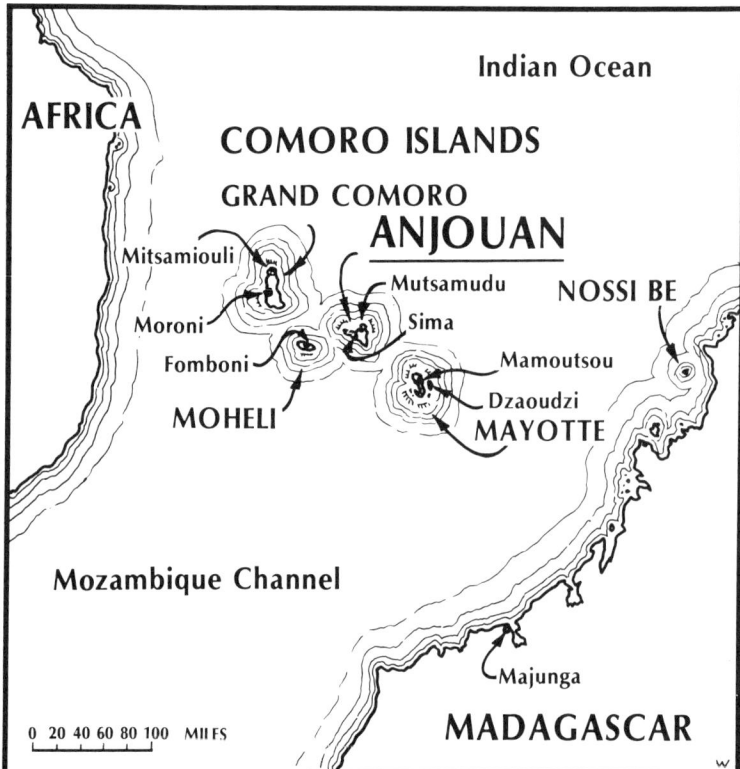

Indian Ocean

AFRICA

COMORO ISLANDS

GRAND COMORO

ANJOUAN

Mitsamiouli

Mutsamudu

NOSSI BE

Moroni

Sima

Fomboni

Mamoutsou

MOHELI

Dzaoudzi

MAYOTTE

Mozambique Channel

Majunga

MADAGASCAR

0 20 40 60 80 100 MILES

Area: 89 sq. miles
Pop: not recorded
Capital: Mutsamudu

This island in the Comoro group had its own stamps during the 1890s and early 1900s. It was later administered from Madagascar and is now part of the Republic of Comoros.

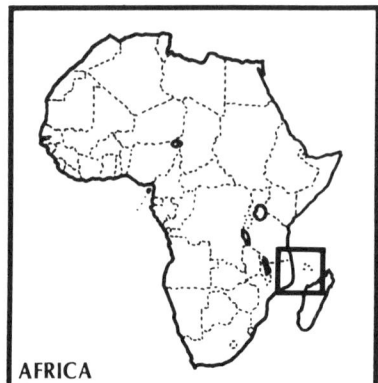

AFRICA

Area: 97,500 sq. miles
Pop: Annam, 5 million (1900 est.)
Tonkin, 9 million (1900 est.)
Capital: Hue (Annam)
Hanoi (Tonkin)

Twin provinces in what is now Vietnam, they were formerly part of French Indo-China. In 1888, stamps of the French Colonies were overprinted "A & T" and surcharged for use there.

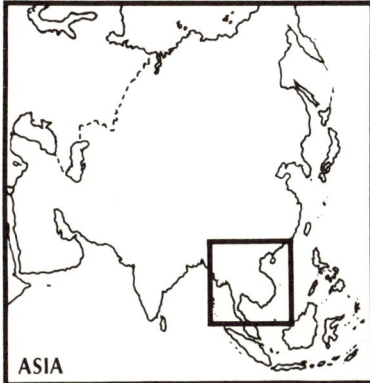

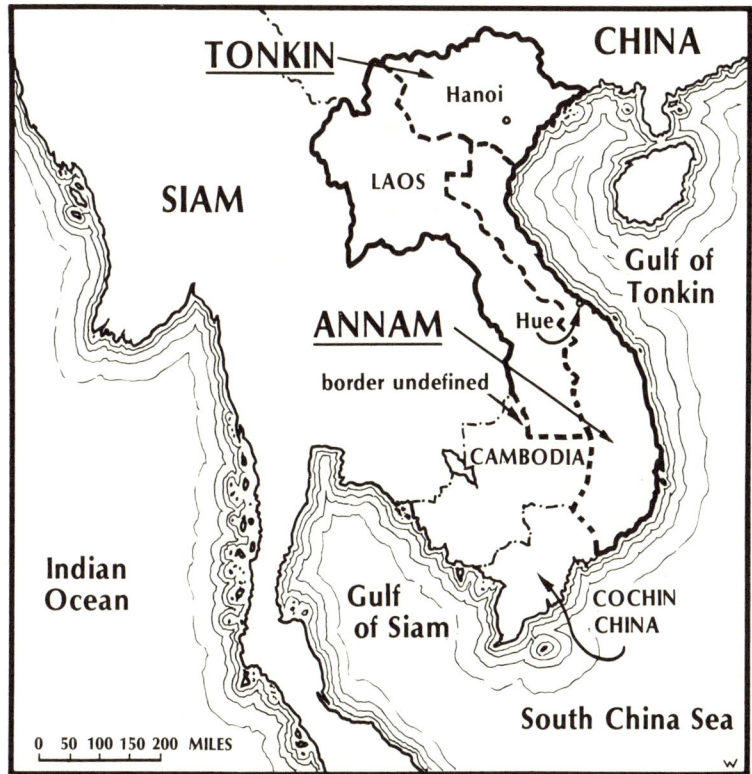

TONKIN

CHINA

Hanoi

SIAM

LAOS

Gulf of Tonkin

ANNAM

Hue

border undefined

CAMBODIA

Indian Ocean

Gulf of Siam

COCHIN CHINA

South China Sea

0 50 100 150 200 MILES

ASIA

ANNOBON, ISLAND OF

Area: 7 sq. miles
Pop: 1,436 (1965)

Annobon is one of the trio of former Spanish islands of Elobey, Annobon, and Corisco located off the African coast. A joint stamp issue was made in 1903 and continued until replaced by stamps of Spanish Guinea in 1909. Each island now uses stamps of Republic of Equatorial Guinea.

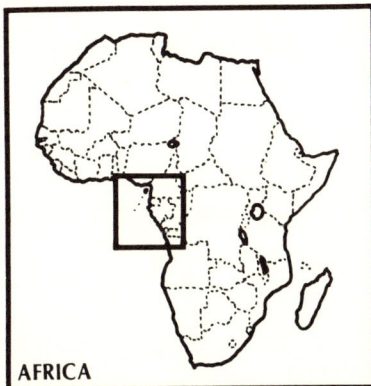

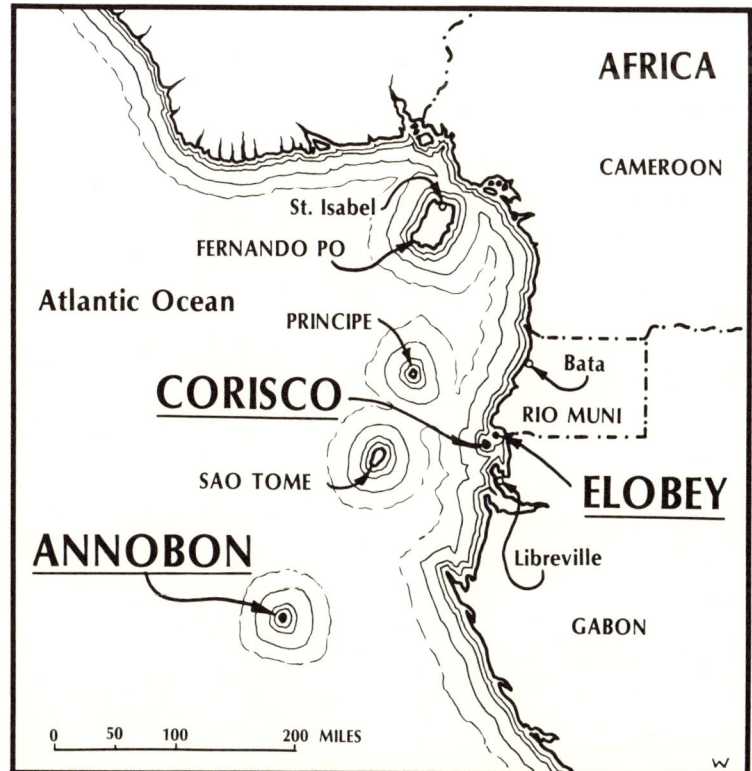

AFRICA

CAMEROON

St. Isabel

FERNANDO PO

Atlantic Ocean

PRINCIPE

Bata

CORISCO

RIO MUNI

SAO TOME

ELOBEY

ANNOBON

Libreville

GABON

0 50 100 200 MILES

AFRICA

Area: 24,274 sq. miles
Pop: 10,000 (1892)
Capital: Medellin

Antioquia was formerly a state in the Granadine Confederation and is now a department of the Republic of Colombia. Stamps were issued from 1868 to 1904, a right the ex-state retained although it became a department in 1886. A large variety exists, including registration, acknowledgement of receipt, and late fee stamps.

━━━━━━━━━ APURIMAC, DEPARTMENT OF ━━━━━━━━━

Area: 7,975 sq. miles
Pop: 119,246 (1876)
          327,000 (1979)
Capital: Abancay

A department of Peru, located to the southeast of Lima, Apurimac issued a single provisional stamp in 1885, to fill a need caused by the war between Chile and Peru in the late 1870s and 1880s. Chile had occupied Lima, thus cutting off stamp supplies to the rest of the country.

Area: 2,955 sq. miles
Pop: 42,052 (1890)
492,439 (1970 est.)
Capital: Arad

A county and city of Romania, Arad was formerly part of the Austro-Hungarian Empire. It was occupied by France in 1919, when Hungarian stamps were overprinted for use in the area. Soon thereafter it went to Romania. The city of Arad, located on the Muresul River, is an important transportation and commercial center.

CZECHOSLOVAKIA

USSR

Debrecen
(Debreezin or Debreczen)

Budapest

Szatmar-Nemeti (Satu Mare)

HUNGARY

Kolozsvar (Klausenburg, now Cluj)

Szeged

ARAD
PRIOR TO WORLD WAR I,
ARAD WAS PART OF
THE AUSTRO-HUNGARIAN EMPIRE.

Temesvar (Timisoara)

YUGOSLAVIA

ROMANIA

Belgrade

0 20 40 60 80 100 MILES

EUROPE

ARBE (RAB), ISLAND OF

Area: 36 sq. miles
Pop: 8,369 (1961 est.)

Located off the coast of Yugoslavia, the island of Arbe (Rab) has marble quarries and is a popular resort. In 1920, stamps of Fiume were issued overprinted "ARBE" during the period of D'Annunzio's occupation.

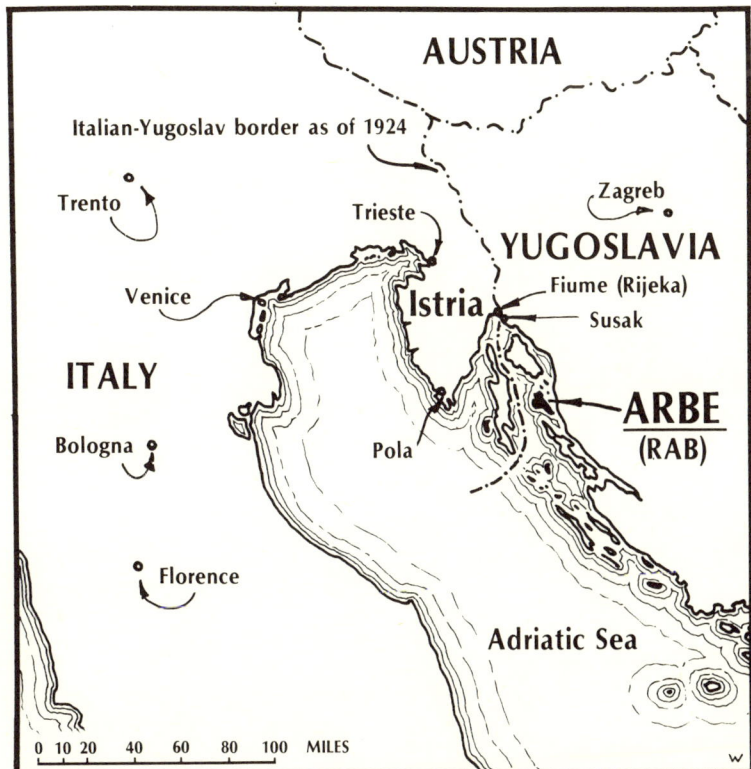

AUSTRIA

Italian-Yugoslav border as of 1924

Trento

Zagreb

Trieste

YUGOSLAVIA

Venice

Istria

Fiume (Rijeka)

Susak

ITALY

ARBE
(RAB)

Bologna

Pola

Florence

Adriatic Sea

0 10 20 40 60 80 100 MILES

EUROPE

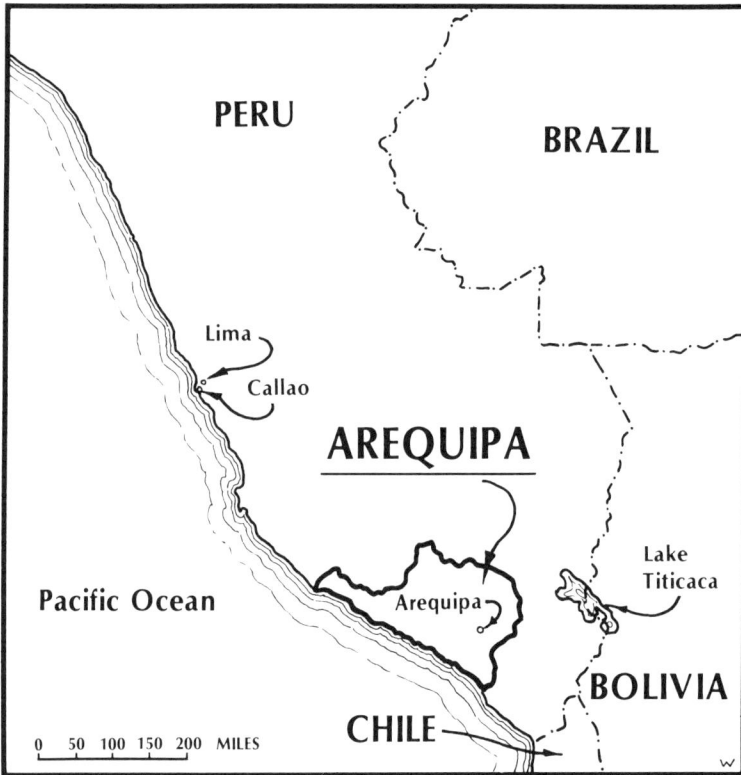

Area: 24,528 sq. miles
Pop: 160,000 (1876)
      504,200 (1969 est.)
Capital: Arequipa

A department of Peru, Arequipa is located in the southern part of the country. Provisional stamps were issued there in 1881-84, during a stamp shortage caused by the Chilean occupation of Lima in a war between the two countries in the late 1870s and 1880s.

——————— ARICA, SAN MARCOS DE ———————

Pop: 63,160 (1966 est.)

San Marcos de Arica is a seaport in the Chilean province of Tarapaca in the northern part of the country. Originally part of Peru, it was taken by Chile in the 19th century. For many years it was a source of dispute between the countries. A plebiscite was planned and in 1925, Peru released a plebiscite issue for use in the area. In 1927, Peru also issued postal tax stamps to raise funds to pay for the plebiscite.

Area: 11,506 sq. miles
Pop: 2,493,000 (1970)
Capital: Erivan

Armenia was part of the Russian Empire prior to the 1917 Revolution. It subsequently achieved a brief independence, then federated in 1922-23 with neighboring provinces of Georgia and Azerbaijan as the Transcaucasian Federation. Now it is a constituent republic of the USSR. Stamps were first issued in 1919 and continued until 1923.

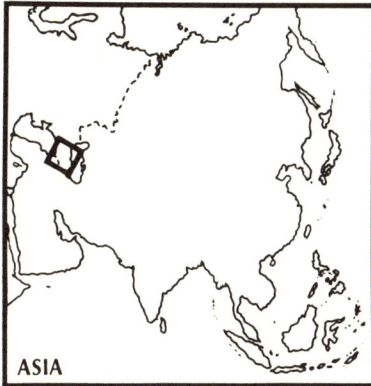

USSR
Caspian Sea
GEORGIA (GRUZIYA)
Tiflis (Tbilisi)
Leninakan
Gandzha (Kirovabad)
AZERBAIJAN (AZERBAYDZHAN)
ARMENIA (ARMENIYA)
Erivan (Yerevan)
Ararat
TURKEY
Nakhichevan
IRAN
Tabriz
0 10 20 40 60 80 MILES

ASIA

ARWAD (ROUAD), ISLAND OF

An island located about two miles off the coast of Syria. It was the site of a prosperous Phoenician seaport city. The island was occupied by French forces during WWI and a postal station was established there in 1916. Stamps were issued overprinted with the island's French name of "Ile Rouad." Following the war, Arwad became part of the French mandated area of Latakia.

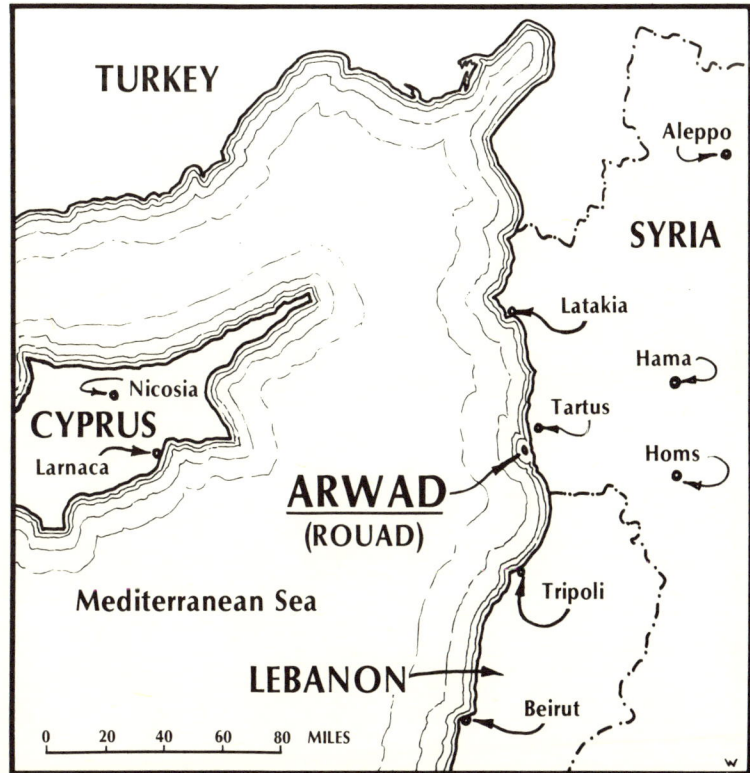

TURKEY
Aleppo
SYRIA
Latakia
Hama
Nicosia
CYPRUS
Tartus
Homs
Larnaca
ARWAD (ROUAD)
Tripoli
Mediterranean Sea
LEBANON
Beirut
0 20 40 60 80 MILES

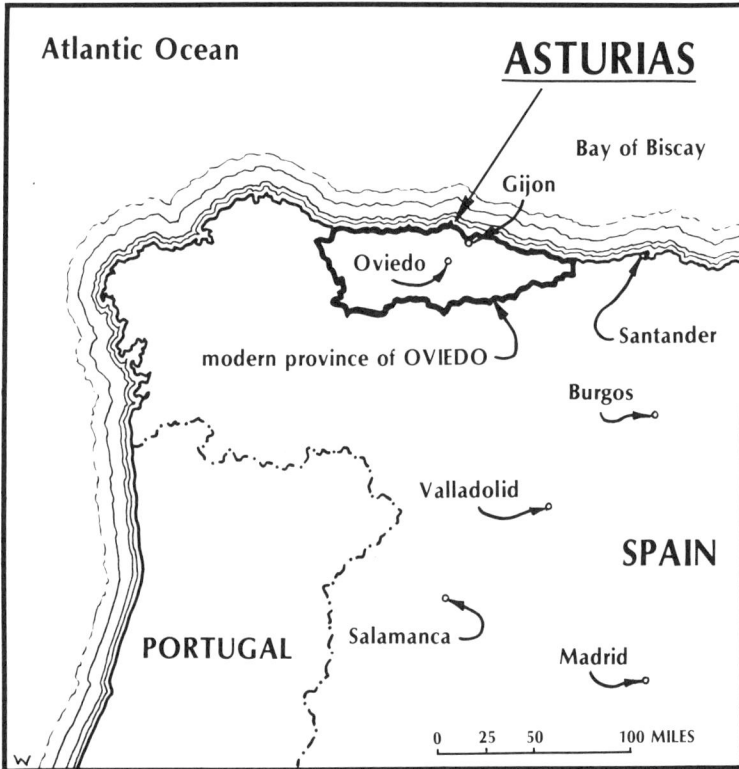

Area: 4,079 sq. miles

A region and ancient former Kingdom of Leon and Castile in northwestern Spain, Asturias now comprises the Spanish province of Oviedo. It was made a principality in 1388 and until 1931 belonged to the heir apparent to the throne of Spain. Its fertile valleys are used for cattle raising and horse breeding, and many crops are grown. Two provisional stamps were issued for the area in 1868-69.

━━━━━━━━━━━ AVILA, PROVINCE OF ━━━━━━━━━━━

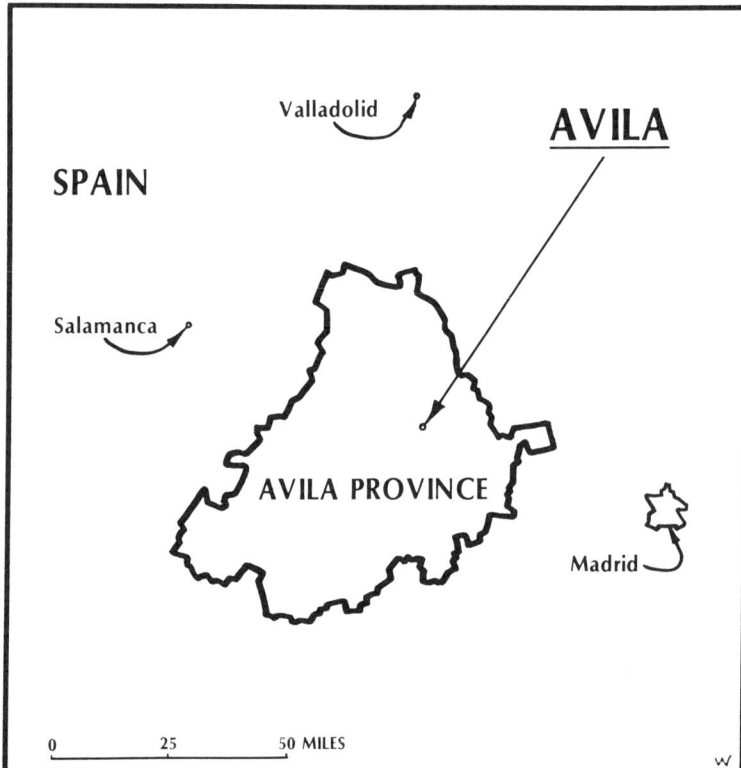

Area: 3,107 sq. miles
Pop: 203,798 (1970)
Capital: Avila

Avila is a province of Spain located in the central part of the country, to the west of Madrid. The capital city is the site of a university founded by Ferdinand and Isabella in 1455. The city itself dates from the late 11th century when a walled town was built there. Its 1970 population was 30,938.

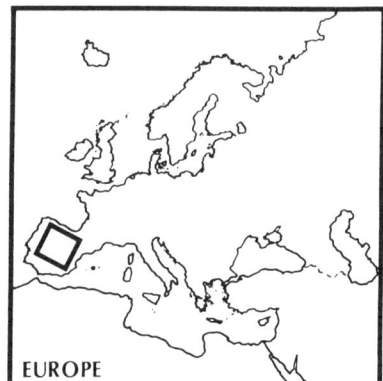

Area: 261,027 sq. miles
Pop: 45,242,889 (1900)
Capital: Vienna

The dual monarchy of the Austro-Hungarian Empire was formed in 1867 from the old Austrian Empire and the Kingdom of Hungary, following the Austrian defeat by Prussia in 1866. It included what is now Austria, Hungary, Czechoslovakia, Bukowina and Transylvania in Romania, the northwestern part of Yugoslavia, Polish Galicia, and the northeastern portion of Italy. The empire was a shaky combination of numerous unstable minorities barely held together by its aged Emperor Franz Josef, who reigned from 1848-1916. It was the Austro-Hungarian ultimatum to Serbia, following the assassination of Archduke Ferdinand at Sarajevo, that lit the fuse of WWI and resulted in the empire's complete destruction. From 1867 to 1871 both Austrian and Hungarian portions of the dual monarchy used the same stamps. Subsequently, Hungary had its own issues.

EUROPE

AUSTRIA-HUNGARY
PRIOR TO WORLD WAR ONE

RUSSIA

GERMANY

BOHEMIA

Prague (Praha)

SILESIA

GALICIA

Krakau (Krakow)   Lemberg (L'vov)

Brunn (Brno)

MORAVIA

UPPER AUSTRIA

LIECHTENSTEIN

Salzburg   Linz

LOWER
AUSTRIA

Vienna (Wien)

BUKOWINA

Debreczen
(Debracen)

SALZBURG

SWITZ.   Innsbruck
TYROL

STYRIA

Budapest   HUNGARY

Klausenburg (Cluj)

CARINTHIA

Trent
(Trento)

Laibach

Szegedin (Szeged)

Arad

TRANSYLVANIA

Trieste   CARNIOLA   Zagreb

Verona

Venice

CROATIA   SLAVONIA

Bucharest (Bucuresti)

ISTRIA   Pola (Pula)

BOSNIA
HERZEGOVINA

Belgrade

ROMANIA

DALMATIA

Sarajevo

SERBIA

ITALY

MONTENEGRO

BULGARIA

Adriatic Sea

TURKEY

0 20 40 60 80 100   150 MILES

W

Area: 17,658 sq. miles
Pop: 142,205 (1876)
       468,300 (1968 est.)
Capital: Ayacucho

Ayacucho is a department of Peru located to the southeast of the capital city of Lima. The city of Ayacucho produces textiles, wine, pottery, and is a mining center. It was founded in 1539 by Pizarro and had a 1969 estimated population of 27,900.

SOUTH AMERICA

━━━━━━━━━ AZERBAIJAN, PROVINCE OF ━━━━━━━━━

Area: 33,436 sq. miles
Pop: 5,111,000 (1970)
Capital: Baku

Part of the Russian Empire prior to the 1917 Revolution, Azerbaijan subsequently achieved a brief independence, then federated in 1922-23 with neighboring provinces of Armenia and Georgia as the Transcaucasian Federation. It is now a constituent republic of the USSR. Stamps were first issued in 1919 and continued until replaced by those of the Transcaucasian Federation.

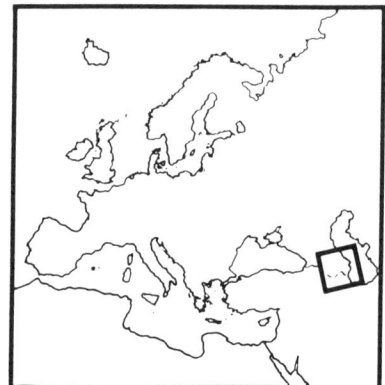

Area: 41,952 sq. miles
Pop: 3,683,620 (1966)
Capital: Tabriz

Formerly a province of Iran, it now is divided into East and West Azerbaijan. From May 1945 to March 1946, the USSR invaded and occupied it. Upon its withdrawal, an autonomous government existed, but the central government's authority was soon restored. During the brief independence, a set of 15 Iranian stamps was overprinted "NATIONAL GOVERNMENT OF AZERBAIJAN, 11TH MAY, 1945."

BADEN, GRAND DUCHY OF

Area: 5,817 sq. miles
Pop: 1,430,000 (1864)
Capital: Karlsruhe

A former grand duchy, Baden joined the North German Confederation in 1870 and became part of the German Empire in 1871. It issued its own stamps from 1851 until 1872. Stamps were also issued for a portion of Baden included in the French zone of occupation following WWII and are inscribed "Baden."

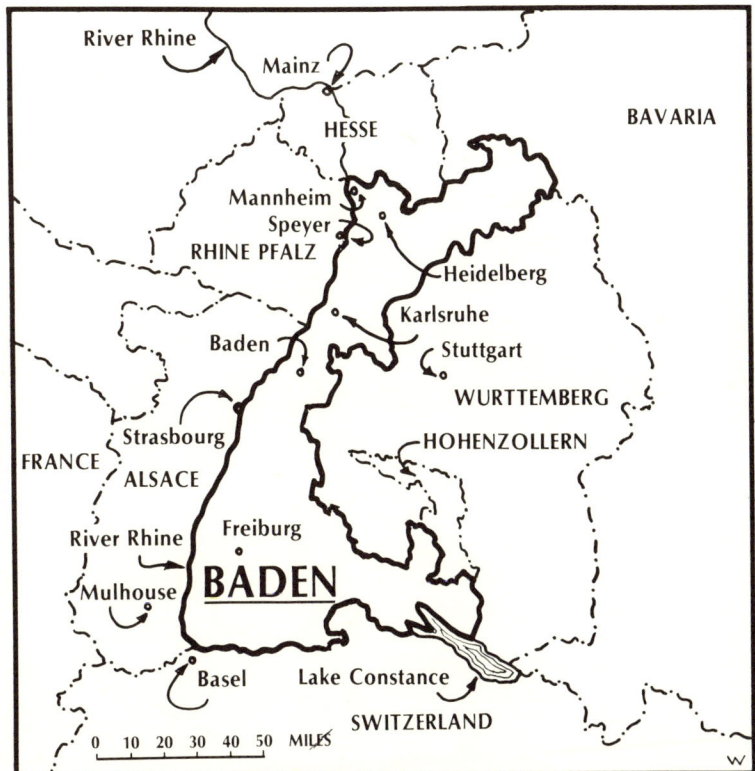

Cordoba Province

Cordoba

Seville

SPAIN

Malaga

| 0 | 25 | 50 MILES |

BAENA

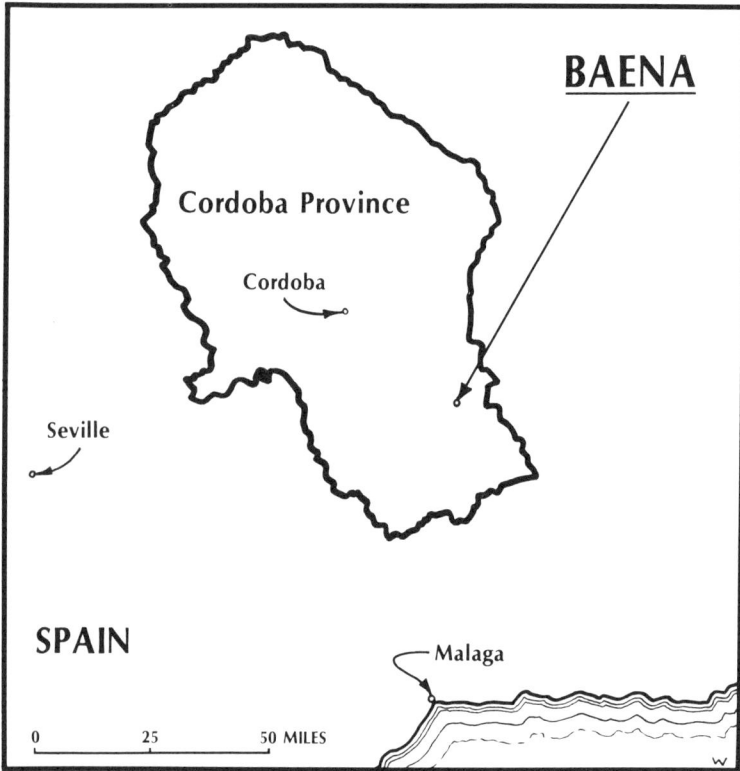

Pop: 10,781 (1970)

The city of Baena is located in the Spanish province of Cordoba about 30 miles southeast of the city of Cordoba and to the north of Malaga. The city is known for its Roman ruins. In 1937, during the Spanish Civil War, Spanish stamps were overprinted by the revolutionary forces to mark the anniversary of the landing at Cadiz and of the occupation of Baena.

EUROPE

━━━━━━━━ BAGHDAD, CITY OF ━━━━━━━━━━

TURKEY

Caspian Sea

SYRIA

Tigris River

Tehran

BAGHDAD

IRAN

Euphrates River

IRAQ

Abadan

Basra

KUWAIT

SAUDI ARABIA

Persian Gulf

| 0 | 50 | 100 | 150 | 200 | MILES |

Pop: 180,000 (1900 est.)
2,183,760 (1970 est.)

The capital city of Iraq, Baghdad is located on the Tigris River. A city rich in history and romance, it was the objective of British forces during the war against the Turkish Empire in 1915-17. It was taken from the Turks in 1917 and became the capital of a new country following a period of British mandate administration.

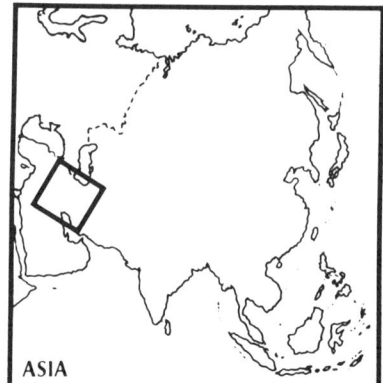

ASIA

Area: 17,494 sq. miles
Pop: 2,574,066 (1961)

Formerly an Indian state in the southwest Punjab, Bahawalpur is now part of Pakistan. It became an administrative division of that country in 1955. Its first stamps were issued in 1947. They were valid only within the state. Stamps of Pakistan have been used since 1949.

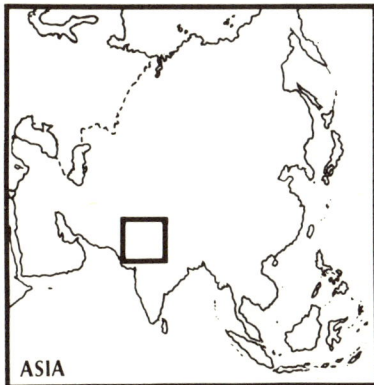

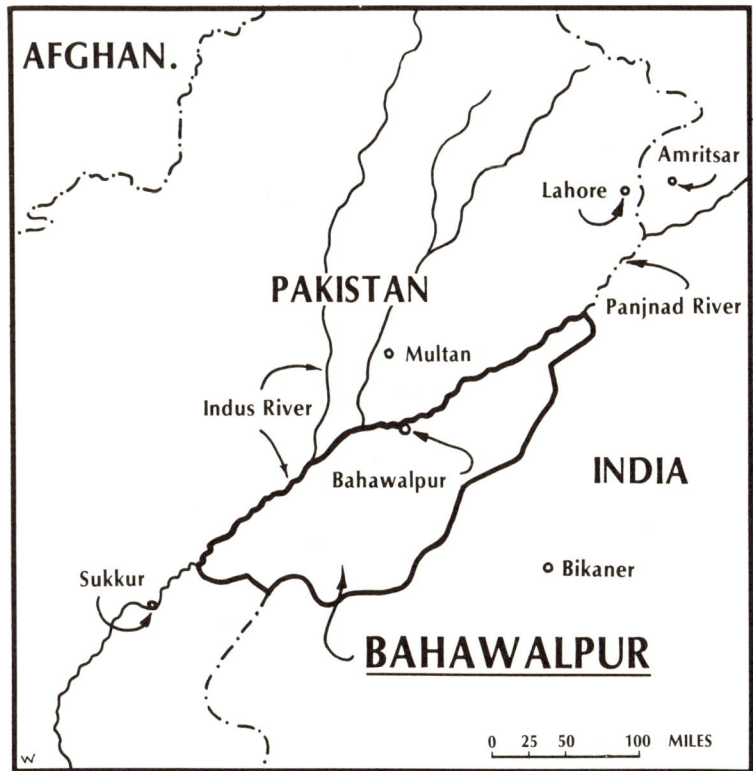

AFGHAN.

PAKISTAN

Amritsar

Lahore

Panjnad River

Multan

Indus River

INDIA

Bahawalpur

Sukkur

Bikaner

BAHAWALPUR

0 25 50 100 MILES

ASIA

BAJA CALIFORNIA, STATES OF

Area: 55,518 sq. miles (combined)
Pop: 980,559 (1970 combined)
Capital: Mexicali and La Paz

A long peninsula and state on the Pacific coast of northern Mexico, Baja California was divided into two states (Norte and Sur) in 1974. The name Baja California translates as Lower California. A single stamp was issued during the 1914 revolutionary period, and in 1915 a set of four imperf stamps was released inscribed "DISTRITO SUR DE LA BAJA CAL. MEXICO."

UNITED STATES

Tijuana Mexicali

Ensenada

MEXICO

Hermosillo

Guaymas

Ciudad Obregon

Navojoa

Sta. Rosalia

Rosarito

Los Mochis

Pacific Ocean

Gulf of California

BAJA CALIFORNIA

La Paz

0 50 100 200 MILES

NORTH AMERICA

Area: 7,224 sq. miles
(Romanian portion)

Formerly part of the Austro-Hungarian Empire, at the end of WWI the District of Banat was divided between the new Kingdom of Yugoslavia and Romania. Settled by Magyars and Serbs in the ninth-14th centuries, it came under Turkish rule from the mid-1500s to 1718, when it went to Austria. After several changes, it finally went to Hungary in 1860.

————————BANGKOK, CITY OF————————

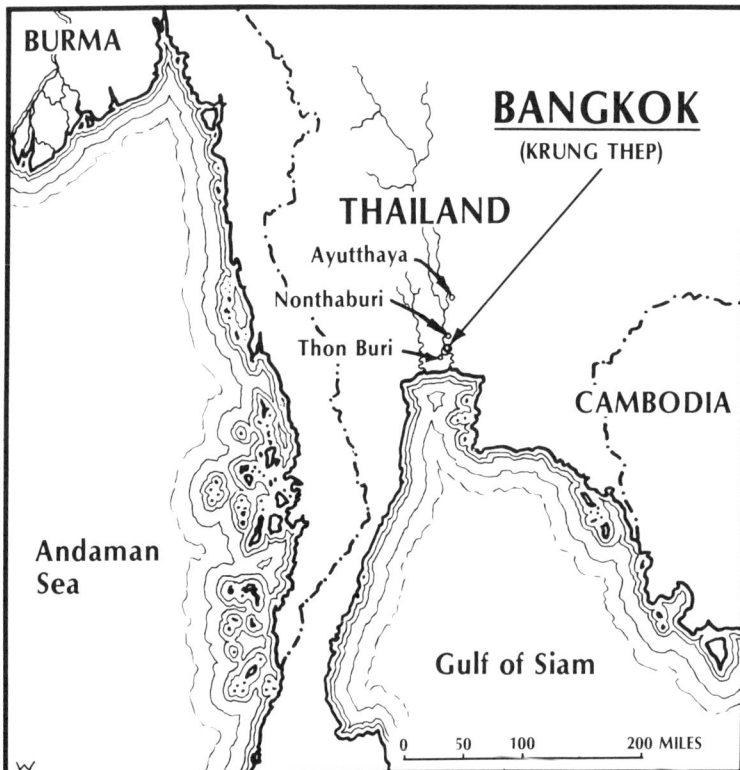

Pop: 700,000 (1900 est.)
2,132,000 (1970)

The capital city of Siam (now Thailand), Bangkok is located near the head of the Gulf of Siam. Stamps were issued beginning in 1882 for use at a British post office established in the city. They comprised stamps of the Straits Settlements overprinted with the letter "B" and were used until July 1, 1885, when stamps of Siam became the only stamps permitted within the country.

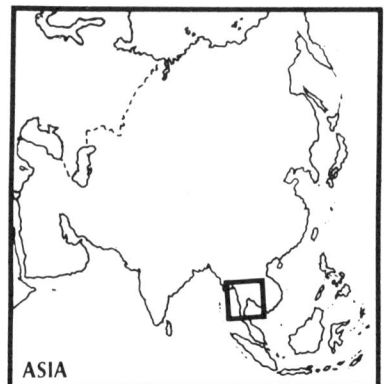

Area: 1,694 sq. miles
Pop: 279,715 (1970)

Baranya is an area of Hungary that was briefly occupied by Serbia at the end of WWI. Stamps were issued beginning in 1919 and comprised stamps of Hungary overprinted "1919 BARANYA." They were followed by stamps surcharged with new denominations. Semipostal stamps as well as special deliveries, a newspaper stamp, and postage due labels were also created.

BASEL, CANTON OF

Area: 179 sq. miles
Pop: 144,284 (1894 est.)
440,000 (1970 est.)
Capital: Basel

A canton of Switzerland, in 1833 Basel was divided into two demicantons named Basel-Stadt and Basel-Land. A stamp known as the "Basel Dove" was issued for use in the canton in 1845 and is one of the world's major philatelic rarities.

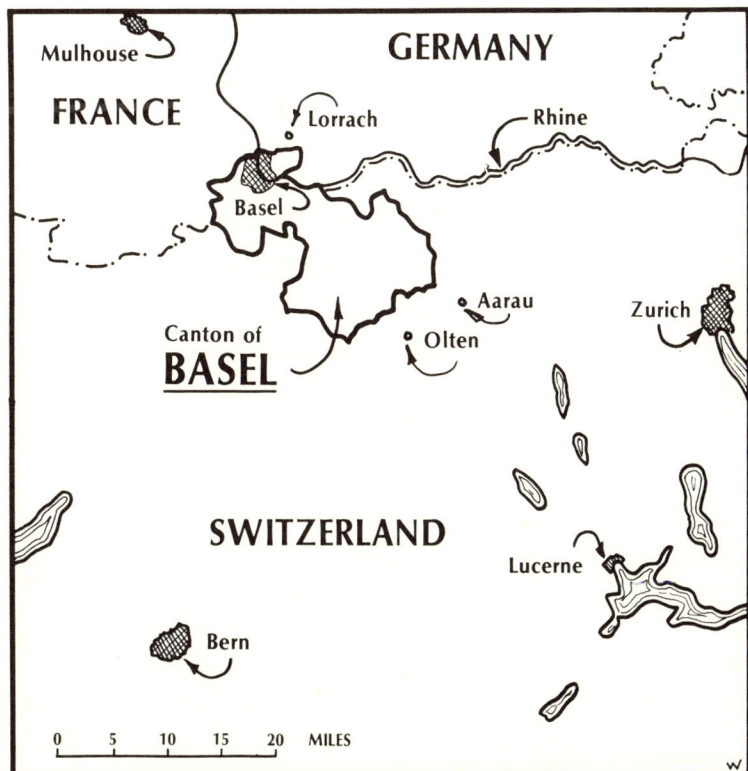

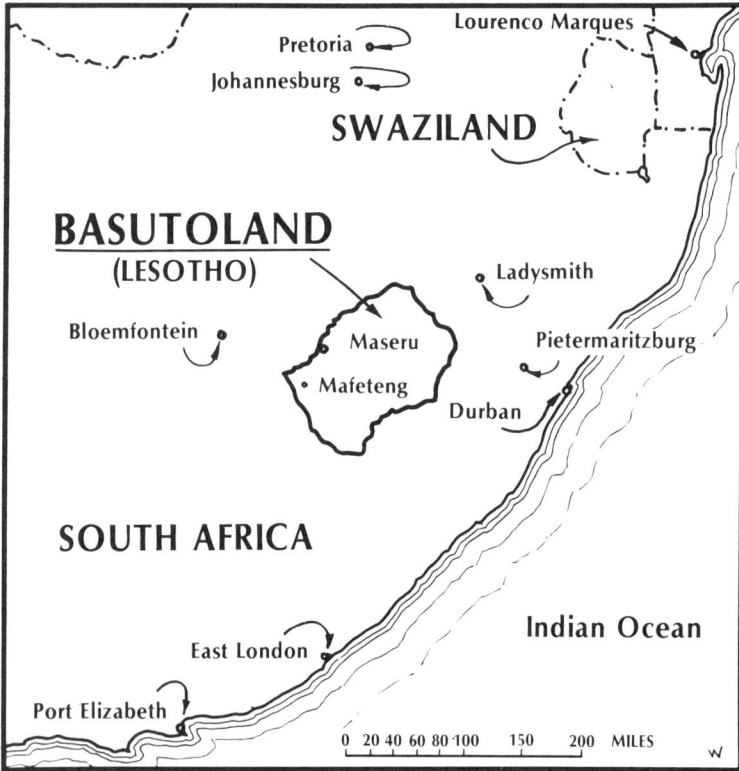

Area: 11,715 sq. miles
Pop: 218,902 (1891)
Capital: Maseru

Basutoland was a British crown colony enclaved in southern Africa from 1883. Stamps of the Cape of Good Hope were used in the colony from 1871 to 1910 and stamps of the Union of South Africa from 1910 to 1933, when stamps inscribed "Basutoland" went into use. It became independent as the Kingdom of Lesotho in 1966.

Pretoria

Johannesburg

Lourenco Marques

SWAZILAND

BASUTOLAND
(LESOTHO)

Ladysmith

Bloemfontein

Maseru

Pietermaritzburg

Mafeteng

Durban

SOUTH AFRICA

Indian Ocean

East London

Port Elizabeth

0 20 40 60 80 100   150   200 MILES

AFRICA

————— **BATUM, CITY OF** —————

Pop: 10,167 (1891)
        101,000 (1970)

A port city of the USSR and capital of the Adzhar ASSR, Batum is located at the eastern end of the Black Sea. It had long been a possession of Persia and Turkey, but was acquired by Russia in 1878. It was occupied by British forces from December 1918 to July 1920, and stamps were issued during the occupation. It is now a Soviet naval base and oil pipeline terminal.

GEORGIA

Black Sea

ADZHARSKAYA

BATUM

Tiflis (Tbilisi)

ARMENIA

TURKEY

Leninakan

Yerevan

0 10 20 40   60   80   100 MILES

EUROPE

Area: 30,500 sq. miles
Pop: 6,176,057 (1900)
Capital: Munich

A kingdom located in southern Germany, Bavaria joined the North German Confederation in 1870 and the German Empire a year later. Following German defeat in WWI, it became a republic within Germany. Stamps were first issued in 1849 and continued until its postal autonomy was lost March 31, 1920.

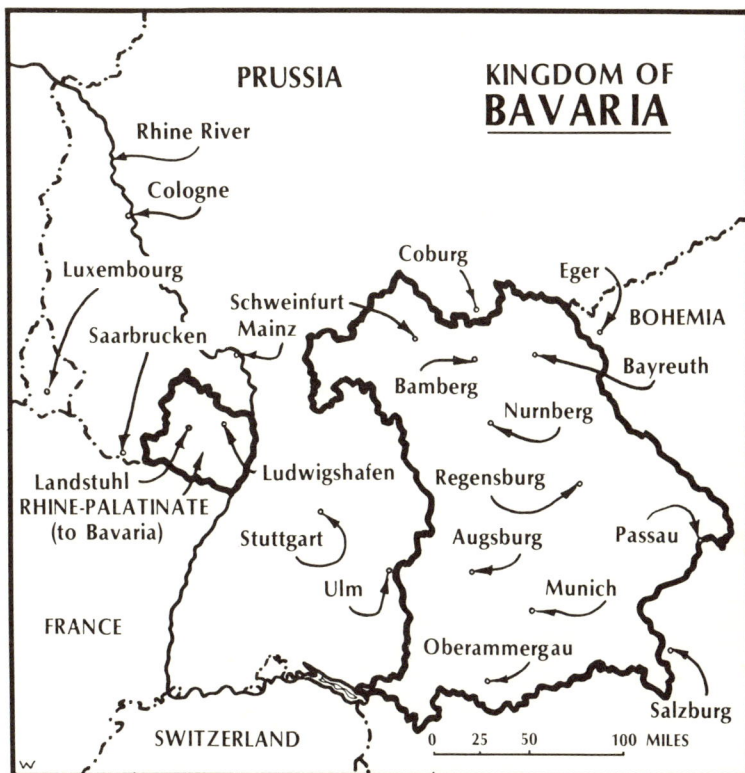

BECHUANALAND PROTECTORATE

Area: 219,916 sq. miles
Pop: 550,000 (1964 est.)

This area was that part of Bechuanaland to the north of the Molopo River that had been established in 1885. The part to the south of the river eventually became British Bechuanaland and was absorbed into the Union of South Africa. Bechuanaland Protectorate became independent as the Republic of Botswana on Sept. 30, 1966.

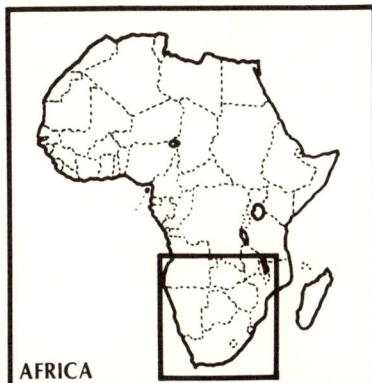

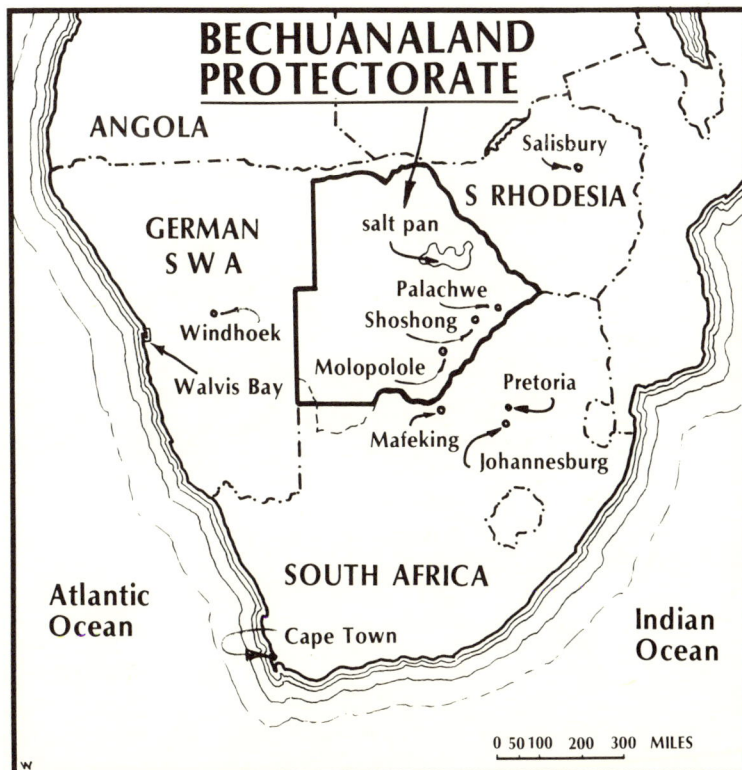

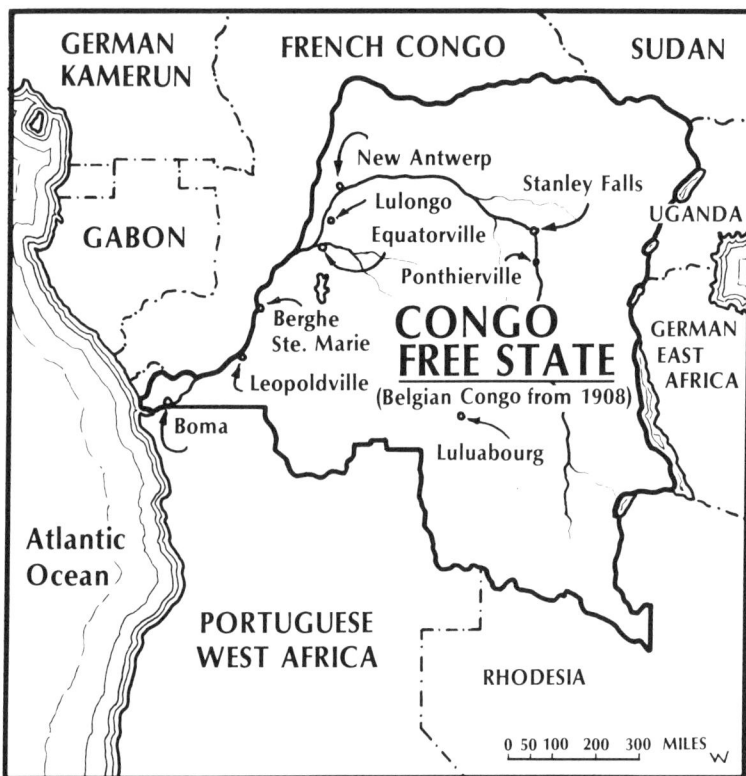

Area: 905,063 sq. miles
Pop: 12,660,000 (1956)
          16,585,944 (1969 est.)
Capital: Leopoldville

An independent kingdom founded in 1885 by King Leopold II of Belgium, it was annexed to Belgium in 1908 as the Belgian Congo. In 1960 it became independent as the Republic of the Congo and changed its name to the Republic of Zaire in 1971. The first stamps were issued in 1886.

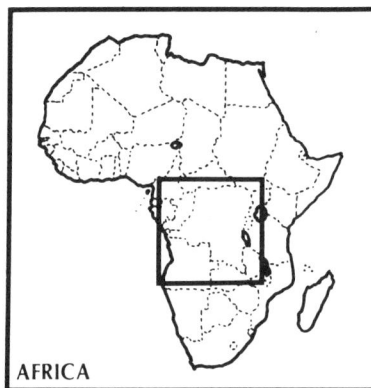

GERMAN KAMERUN
FRENCH CONGO
SUDAN
GABON
New Antwerp
Lulongo
Stanley Falls
Equatorville
UGANDA
Ponthierville
Berghe Ste. Marie
CONGO FREE STATE
(Belgian Congo from 1908)
GERMAN EAST AFRICA
Leopoldville
Boma
Luluabourg
Atlantic Ocean
PORTUGUESE WEST AFRICA
RHODESIA
0 50 100 200 300 MILES

AFRICA

━━━━━━━━━ **BENADIR, REGION OF** ━━━━━━━

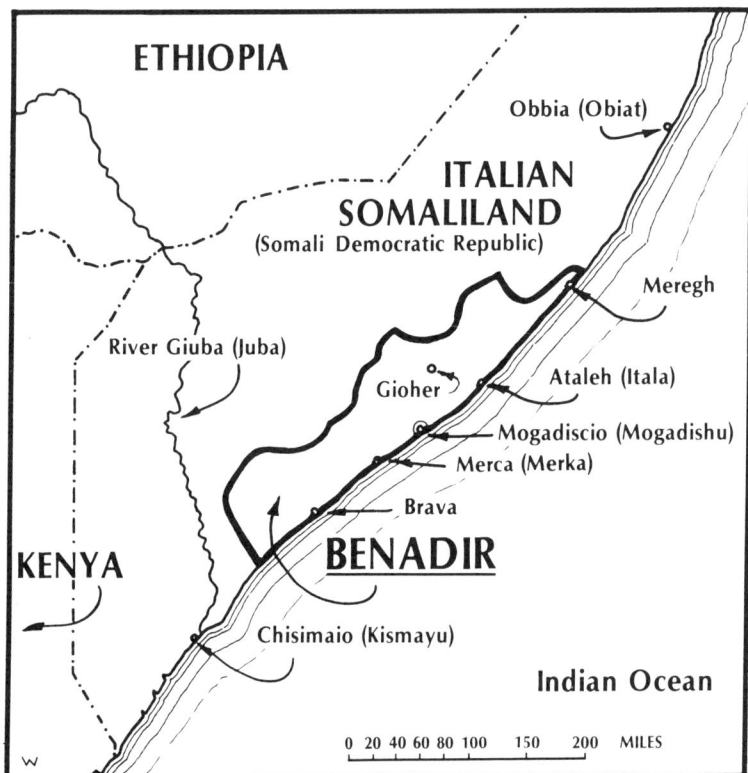

ETHIOPIA
Obbia (Obiat)
ITALIAN SOMALILAND
(Somali Democratic Republic)
Meregh
River Giuba (Juba)
Ataleh (Itala)
Gioher
Mogadiscio (Mogadishu)
Merca (Merka)
Brava
BENADIR
KENYA
Chisimaio (Kismayu)
Indian Ocean
0 20 40 60 80 100 150 200 MILES

Benadir comprised a coastal area of East Africa based on the town of Mogadishu. It became part of Italian Somaliland and was later absorbed into Italian East Africa. It was under British military administration from 1941-49, and after a period of UN supervised trusteeship under Italy it became the Somali Democratic Republic. It first issued stamps inscribed "BENADIR" in 1903.

AFRICA

Pop: 48,510 (1936)
170,000 (1970 est.)

A city on the coast of Libya, Bangasi was an administrative center for Cyrenaica when it was an Italian colony. A naval and air base, it changed hands a number of times during WWII. It later became a co-capital with Tripoli, of independent Libya. Prior to the Italian takeover in 1912, it had been part of the Turkish Empire. Italian stamps overprinted "BENGASI" were used at an Italian post office in the city from 1901.

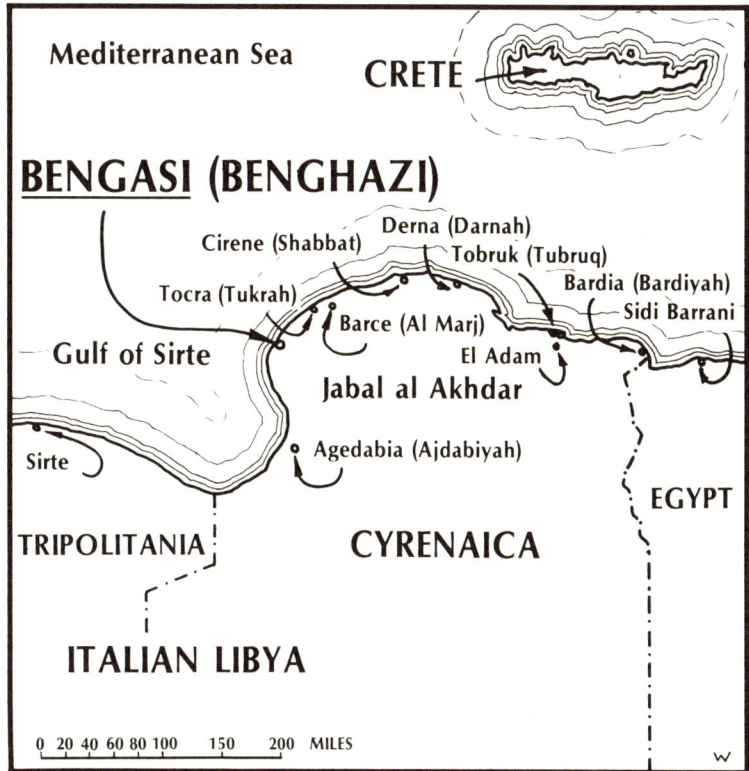

BERGEDORF, CITY OF

Pop: 3,000 (1860s)

A city in north Germany, Bergedorf was owned jointly by the Free Cities of Lubeck and Hamburg from 1420 to 1868, when it was bought by Hamburg. Stamps were issued from 1861 until superseded by those of the North German Confederation in 1868.

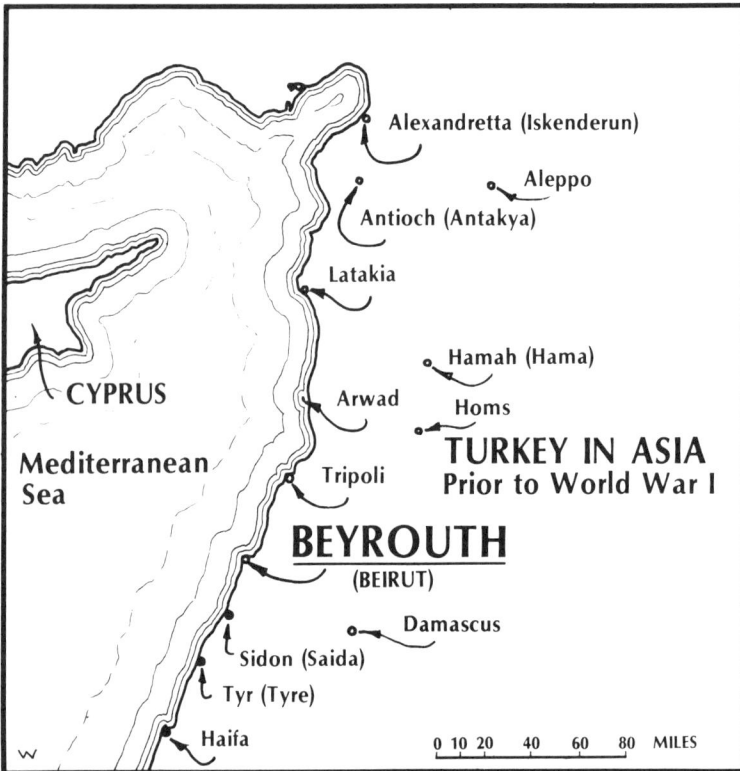

Pop: 105,400 (1889)

Now the capital city of Lebanon, Beirut (French — Beyrouth) was a city in the Turkish Empire up to WWI. During the pre-WWI period, a French post office operated in the city. In 1905 a stamp of French Levant was overprinted and surcharged for use there.

————————————————— BIAFRA —————————————————

The area of Nigeria known as Biafra comprised the former Eastern Region of the country. In 1967 it attempted to secede, and until 1970 the area fought a bloody civil war against Nigerian government forces. The attempt to gain independence failed, and Biafra was subsequently divided into the Nigerian states of East-Central, Rivers and South-Eastern. During its bid for freedom, Biafra issued a number of stamps. These are listed by Gibbons.

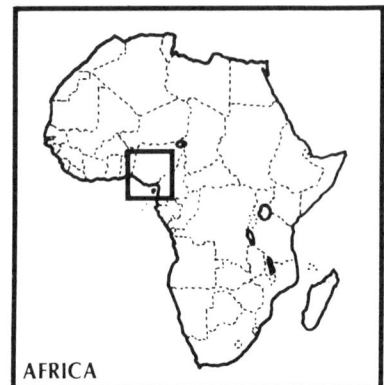

BOCAS DEL TORO, CITY OF

Pop: 9,636 (1970)

Bocas del Toro is a seaport and capital city of Bocas del Toro Province in the Republic of Panama. It is located on an island off the Caribbean coast of the country, near the border with Costa Rica. Exports include bananas, coffee, and cacao. In 1903-04 stamps were issued overprinted "R de Panama" for use there.

HONDURAS

Caribbean Sea

Tegucigalpa

NICARAGUA

Managua

BOCAS DEL TORO

COSTA RICA Limon

San Jose

Canal Colon

Panama

PANAMA

Pacific Ocean

0 20 40 60 80 100 150 200 MILES

CENTRAL AMERICA

BOGOTA, CITY OF

Area: 613 sq. miles (spec. dist.)
Pop: 100,000 (1891 est.)
966,341 (1968 est.)

The capital city of Colombia and of Cundinamarca Department, Bogota is located at an altitude of 8,500 feet. Local stamps were issued there during 1889-1896.

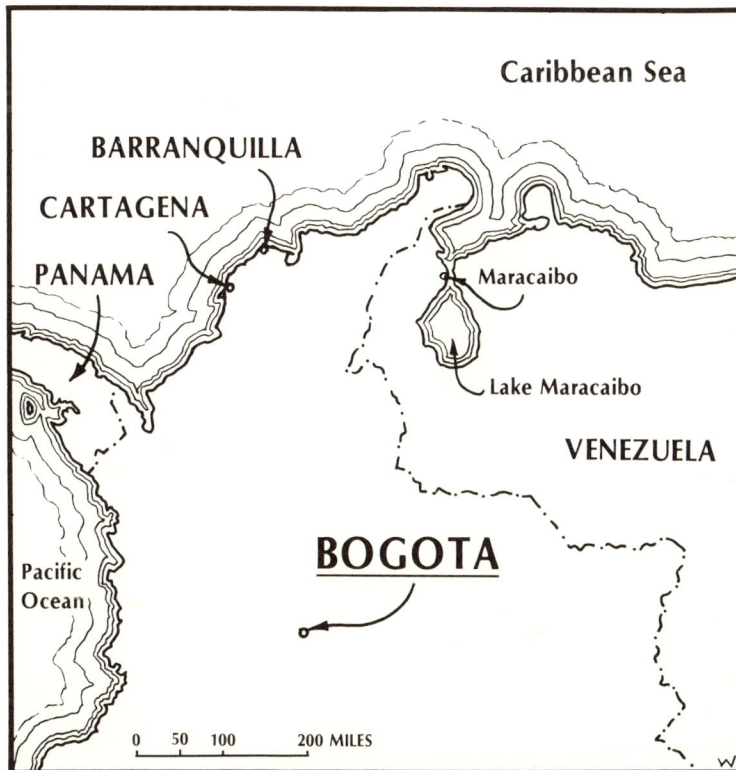

Caribbean Sea

BARRANQUILLA

CARTAGENA

PANAMA

Maracaibo

Lake Maracaibo

VENEZUELA

Pacific Ocean

BOGOTA

SOUTH AMERICA

0 50 100 200 MILES

Bohemia and Moravia was a German protectorate set up in March 1939 comprising the two western provinces in what was left of Czechoslovakia after the Sudentenland had been stripped away by Germany following the so-called Munich "Agreement." The area was restored to Czechoslovakia after WWII. Stamps were issued under the German occupation.

───── BOLIVAR, DEPARTMENT OF ─────

Area: 10,190 sq. miles
Pop: 350,000 (1885 est.)
   791,851 (1968 est.)
Capital: Cartagena

A department of Colombia, Bolivar was formerly a state in the Granadine Confederation. It issued its own stamps from 1863 to 1904. The first issue consisted of three extremely tiny stamps, one of which is noted as existing bisected!

Area: 23,000 sq. miles (approx.)
Pop: 1,568,092 (1895 est.)

A province of the Turkish Empire in the Balkans, Bosnia and Herzegovina was controlled by Austria-Hungary from 1879 until formally annexed in 1908. It is now part of Yugoslavia. Stamps were issued from 1879 to the end of WWI. They are noted for their fine engraving, especially the 1906 issue.

(Map of Bosnia and Herzegovina showing Croatia, Slavonia, Hungary, Zagreb, Banjaluka, Belgrade, Dalmatia, Spalato (Split), Sarajevo, Serbia, Mostar, Ragusa (Dubrovnik), Montenegro, Cetinje, Turkey, Adriatic Sea, Italy. Inset map of Europe. Scale 0-100 miles.)

BOYACA, DEPARTMENT OF

Area: 26,158 sq. miles.
Pop: 645,000 (1890 est.)
       1,144,415 (1968 est.)
Capital: Tunja

Boyaca was originally a state in the Granadine Confederation. It became a department of the Republic of Colombia in 1886. Stamps were issued for Boyaca from 1902 to 1904.

(Map of Colombia showing Caribbean Sea, Panama, Cartagena, Venezuela, Medellin, Tunja, Bogota, Boyaca, Colombia, Pacific Ocean, Ecuador, Brazil. Inset map of South America. Scale 0-150 miles.)

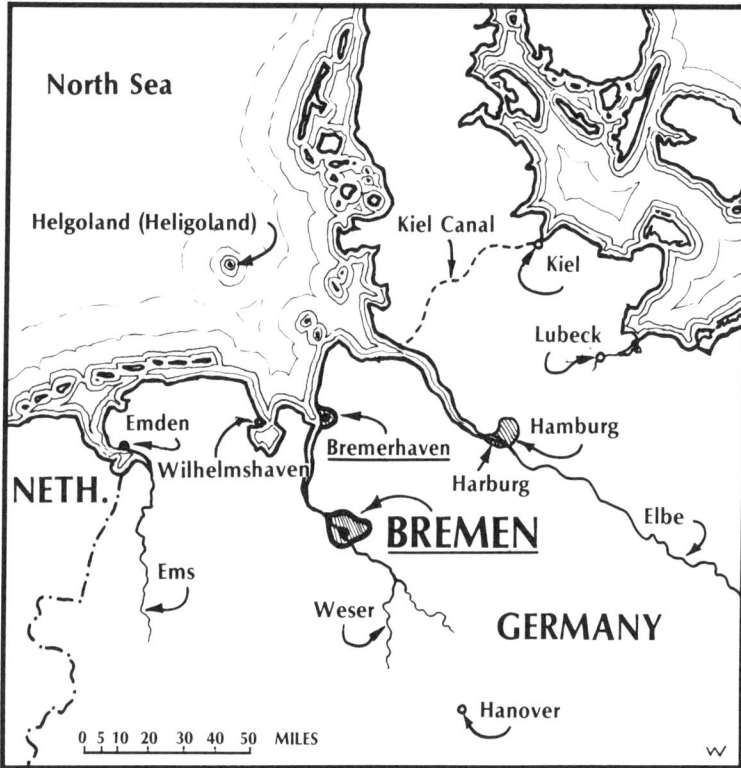

Area: 99 sq. miles
Pop: 224,882 (1900)

A former German state, Bremen included the port of Bremerhaven located some miles down the Weser River from Bremen. Both are important seaports. Bremen joined the North German Confederation in 1868 and became part of the German Empire in 1870. Stamps were issued from 1855 to 1868.

EUROPE

———BRITISH BECHUANALAND, CROWN COLONY OF———

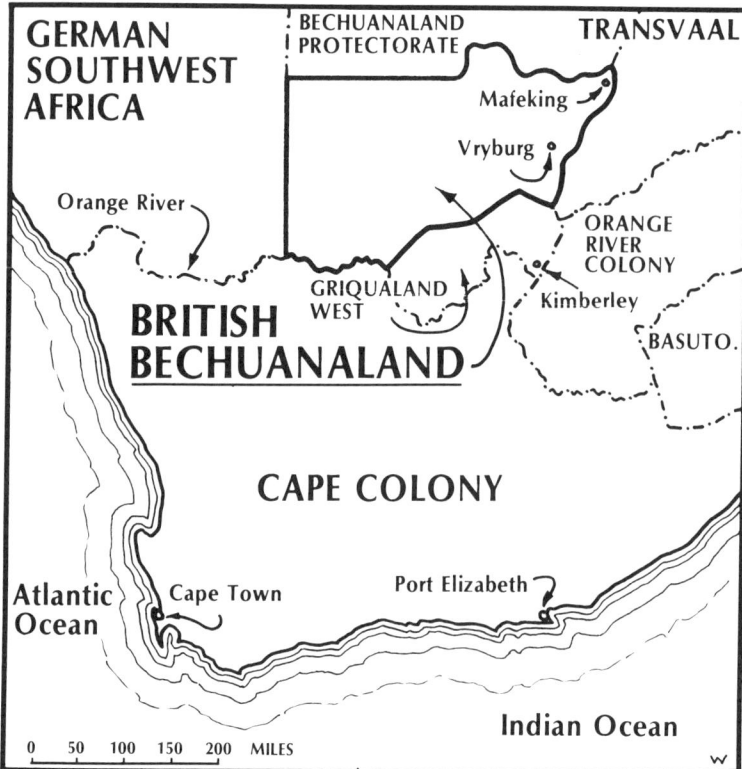

Area: 51,425 sq. miles
Pop: 84,200 (1904 est.)
Capital: Mafeking

A crown colony, British Bechuanaland was annexed to the Cape of Good Hope colony in 1895. It is now part of the Republic of South Africa. Stamps were issued from 1886 to 1897. Not to be confused with Bechuanaland Protectorate (q.v.).

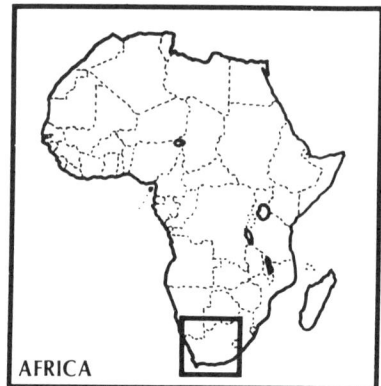

AFRICA

Area: 36,325 sq. miles
Pop: three million (1900 est.)
Capital: Zomba

Established in 1891, British Central Africa became the Nyasaland Protectorate in 1907. From 1953 to 1963 it was part of Central African Federation. It is now the independent country of Malawi. Stamps for British Central Africa were issued from 1891 to 1908.

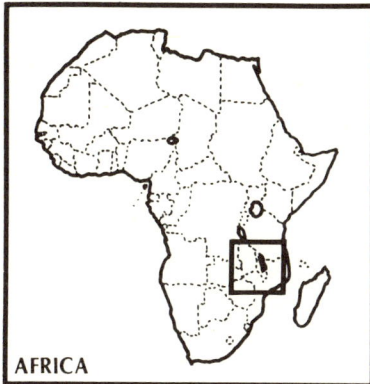

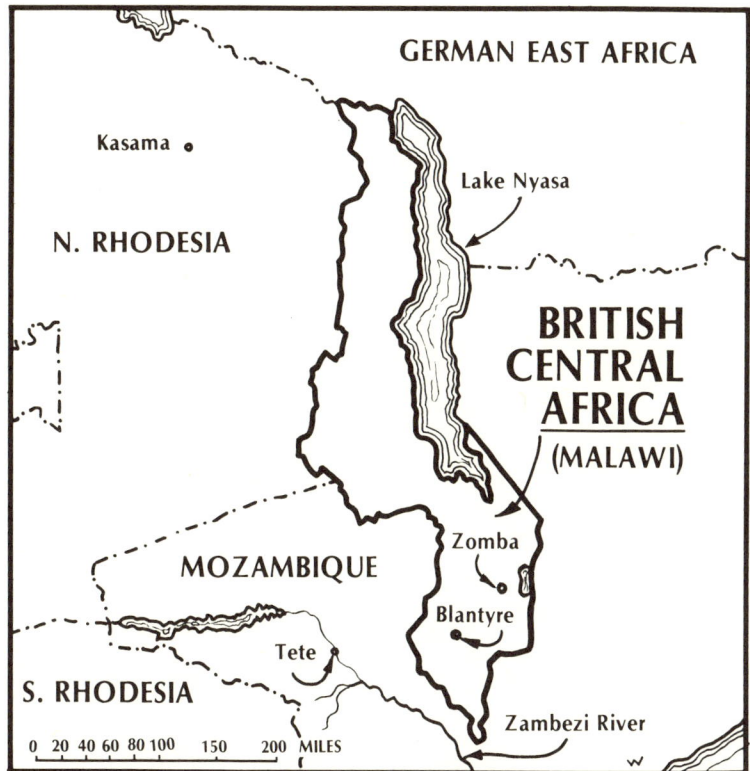

BRITISH COLUMBIA, COLONY OF

Area: 359,279 sq. miles
Pop: 178,657 (1901)
2,737,700 (1982)
Capital: New Westminster
(now Victoria)

A British crown colony from 1858, British Columbia was united with the colony of Vancouver Island in 1866. It is now a province of Canada. Stamps were issued from 1860 to 1871 when British Columbia joined the new country of Canada.

Pop: 6,620,000 (1901 est.)

British East Africa was administered by the British East Africa Company until 1904. Stamps were issued by the company up to that year, when the area became East Africa and Uganda Protectorate. The territory of Kenya was added later.

━━━━━━━BRITISH GUIANA, COLONY OF━━━━━━━

Area: 83,000 sq. miles
Pop: 310,933 (1931)
        850,000 (1981)
Capital: Georgetown

Ceded to Britain by the Dutch in 1814, the three areas of Essequibo, Berbice, and Demerara were united in 1831 as the Crown Colony of British Guiana. It became independent as Guyana 1966. The first stamps were issued in 1850. The colony, now nation, is famous for the "British Guiana 1c" of 1856 — the world's highest priced stamp.

Area: 8,866 sq. miles
Pop: 119,645 (1970)
Capital: New city of Belmopan, but formerly city of Belize.

British Honduras became a British colony administered from Jamaica in 1862, a full crown colony in 1884, achieved internal self-government in 1960, and became fully independent as Belize on Sept. 21, 1981. The first stamps were issued in 1886.

CENTRAL AMERICA

Caribbean Sea
Merida
Ticul
MEXICO
Belize
BRITISH HONDURAS (BELIZE)
GUATEMALA
Guatemala
HONDURAS
Tegucigalpa
EL SALVADOR
Pacific Ocean
NICARAGUA
0 20 40 60 80 100 150 200 MILES

BRITISH INDIAN OCEAN TERRITORY

Area: 22 sq. miles
Pop: 560 (1971)
Capital: Diego Garcia

The Crown Colony of British Indian Ocean Territory was formed on Nov. 8, 1965. It comprised the Chagos Archipelago, plus Aldabra, Farquhar, and Desroches Islands. The colony was disbanded in 1976 and all except the Chagos Archipelago was given to the Seychelles. The Chagos Archipelago is now administered from London.

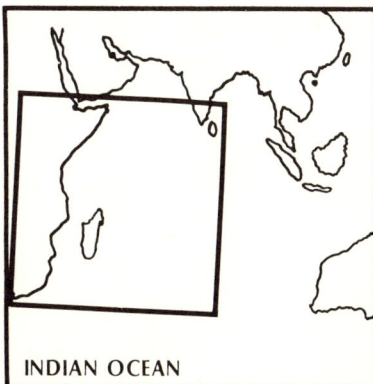

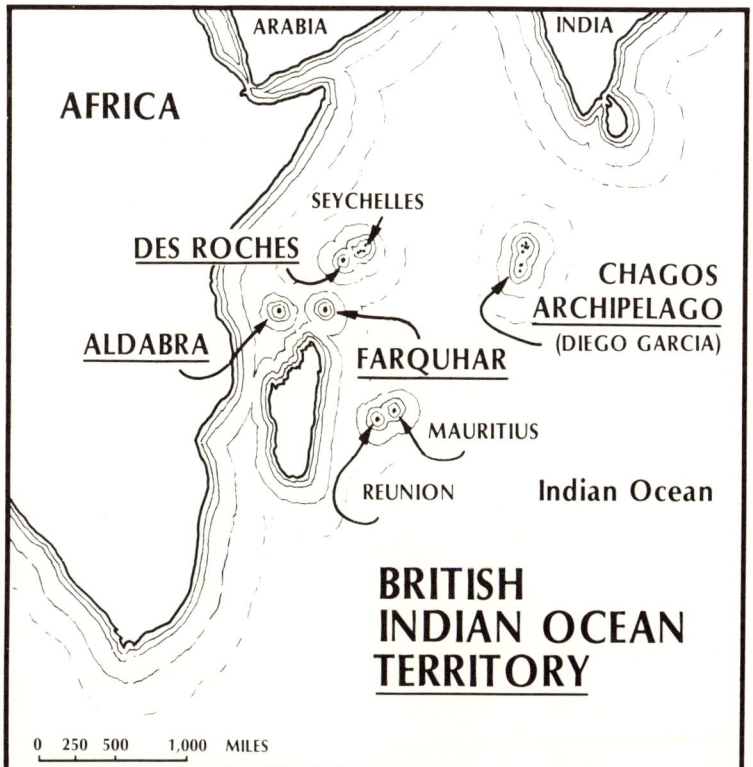

INDIAN OCEAN

ARABIA
INDIA
AFRICA
SEYCHELLES
DES ROCHES
CHAGOS ARCHIPELAGO (DIEGO GARCIA)
ALDABRA
FARQUHAR
MAURITIUS
REUNION
Indian Ocean
BRITISH INDIAN OCEAN TERRITORY
0 250 500 1,000 MILES

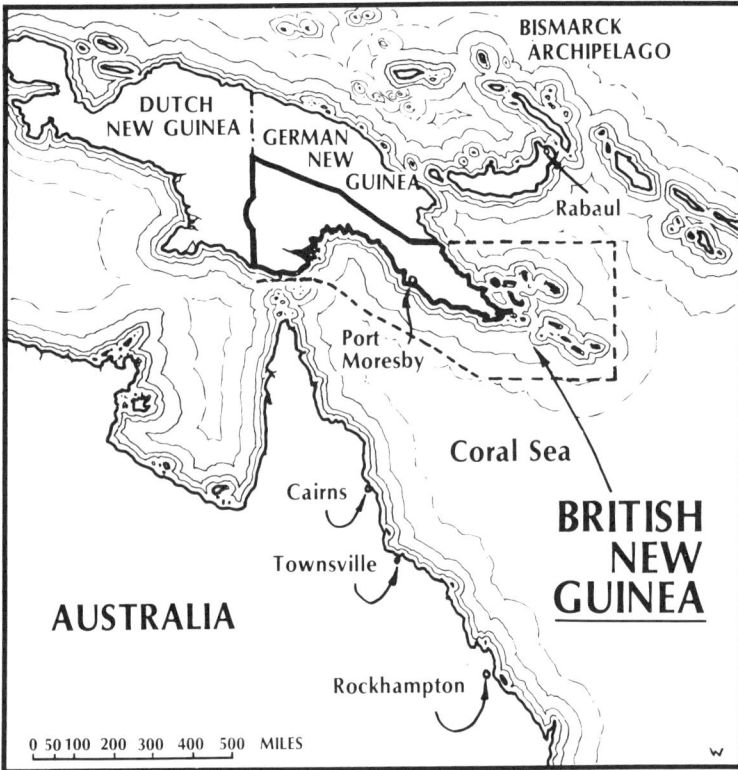

Area: 90,540 sq. miles
Pop: 598,825 (1968 est.)
Capital: Port Moresby

This area comprised the southern part of the eastern half of New Guinea. It was made a British protectorate in 1888. It transferred to Australian administration in 1905, and the name changed to Papua in 1906. Now part of Papua New Guinea.

───── BRITISH SOMALILAND, PROTECTORATE OF ─────

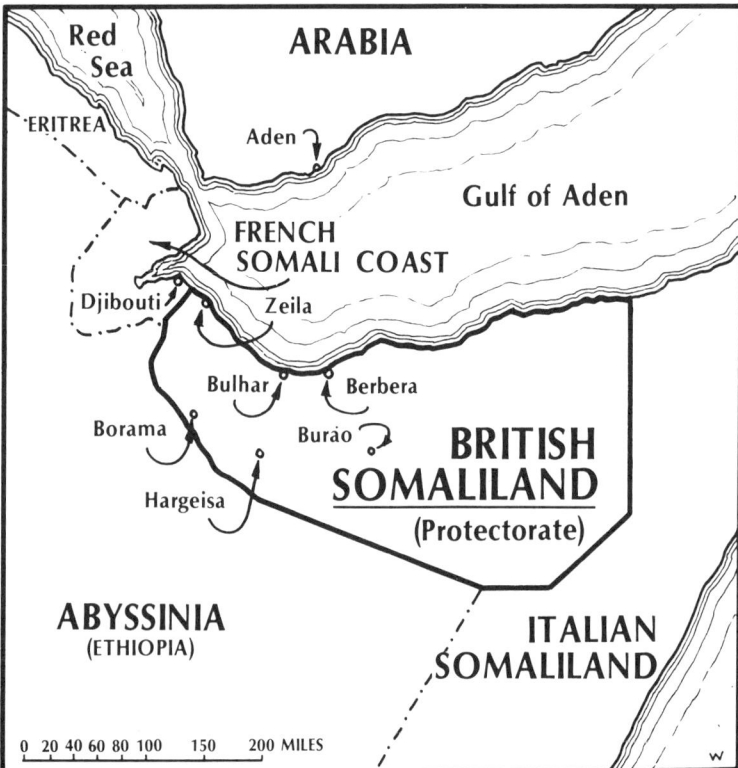

Area: 67,936 sq. miles
Pop: 350,000 (1938 est.)
Capital: Hargeisa

Administered from British India from 1894 to 1898, British Somaliland was under British Foreign Office until 1905. Subsequently a British protectorate. Merged with the former Italian Somaliland in 1960 as Somali Democratic Republic. Its first stamps were Indian stamps overprinted "BRITISH SOMALILAND" issued in 1903.

Area: 441,000 sq. miles
Pop: 1,738,000 (1921 est.)
Capital: Salisbury

The area of British South Africa was administered by the British South Africa Company from 1889 to 1923, when it was divided into Southern Rhodesia and Northern Rhodesia. In 1953, the two areas joined with the Nyasaland Protectorate to form the Federation of Rhodesia and Nyasaland, sometimes called the Central African Federation.

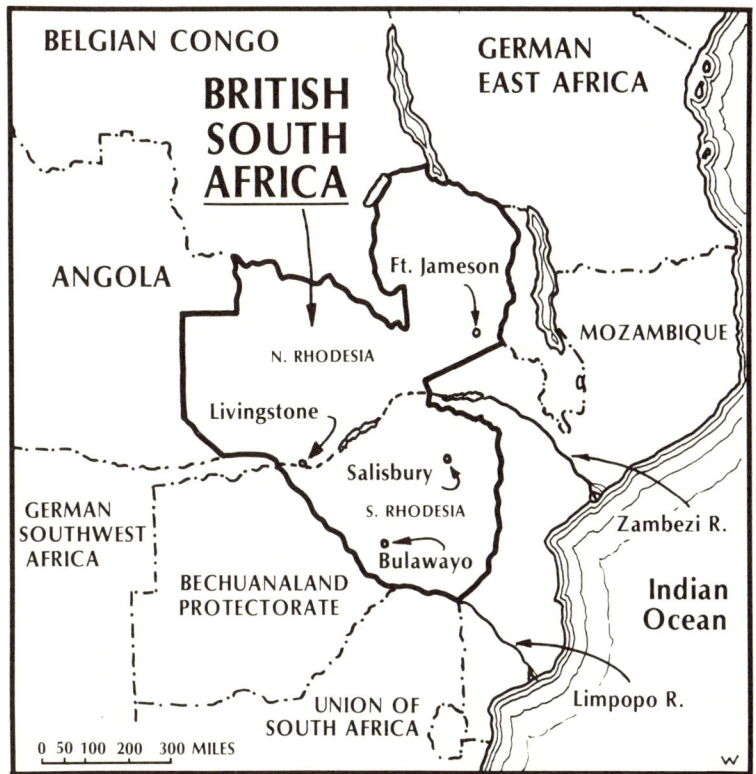

BRUNSWICK, DUCHY OF

Area: 1,417 sq. miles
Pop: 464,333 (1900)
Capital: Brunswick

A former German duchy, the Duchy of Brunswick joined the North German Confederation in 1868 and became part of the German Empire in 1870. It was declared a republic in 1918. Brunswick issued its own stamps from 1852 to 1868.

Rosario
URUGUAY
Pergamino
Montevideo
Chivilcoy
Buenos Aires
Pehuajo
BUENOS AIRES
ARGENTINA
Azul
Tandil
Tres Arroyos
Bahia Blanca
Mar del Plata

South Atlantic Ocean

0 20 40 60 80 100   150   200 MILES

SOUTH
AMERICA

Area: 118,843 sq. miles
Pop: 921,225 (1895)
8,774,529 (1970)
Capital: Buenos Aires

Buenos Aires is a province in Argentina. It was a stamp-issuing entity during 1858-62. A total of 13 stamps were issued, not counting varieties.

———————————BURGENLAND, PROVINCE OF———————————

POLAND
Prague
CZECHOSLOVAKIA
Danube
Vienna
Bratislava
AUSTRIA
Eisenstadt
Rechnitz
Andau
Sopron
Budapest
BURGENLAND
Oberwart
Gussing
ITALY
YUGOSLAVIA
HUNGARY

0 10 20   40   60   80   100 MILES

EUROPE

Area: 1,531 sq. miles
Pop: 272,000 (1971)
Capital: Eisenstadt

Burgenland is a province of Austria located in the eastern portion of the country. Prior to WWI it was part of Hungary. In 1945, a series of stamps was issued for use in Vienna, Lower Austria, and Burgenland.

Area: 5,509 sq. miles
Pop: 358,075 (1970)
Capital: Burgos

Burgos is a province of Spain, based on the city of the same name. The city, which had a 1970 population of 119,915, is noted for its cathedral, one of the finest examples of Gothic architecture in Europe. During the Spanish Civil War, Nationalist revolutionary forces issued stamps in the province.

BUSHIRE, CITY OF

Pop: 15,000 (1900 est.)

A port city of Persia (now Iran) on the country's Persian Gulf coast, Bushire was under British occupation for about two months in 1918. During that occupation, Persian stamps were overprinted for use from the city. The first issue was released on Aug. 15 and the second appeared in September. The overprint reads "BUSHIRE/ under British/ Occupation."

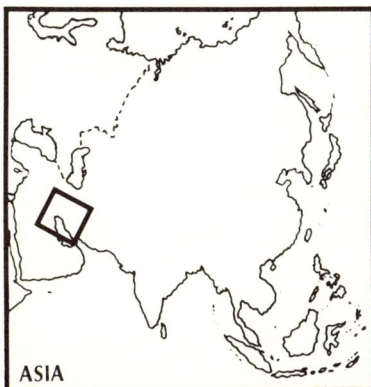

Area: 2,807 sq. miles
Pop: 10,000 (1900 est.)
Capital: Cabinda

Cabinda is an enclaved area of Angola to the north of the River Congo. Stamps were issued under the name of Portuguese Congo from 1894 until replaced by stamps of Angola in 1920. Cabinda now is part of the People's Republic of Angola.

CABO GRACIAS A DIOS, DISTRICT OF

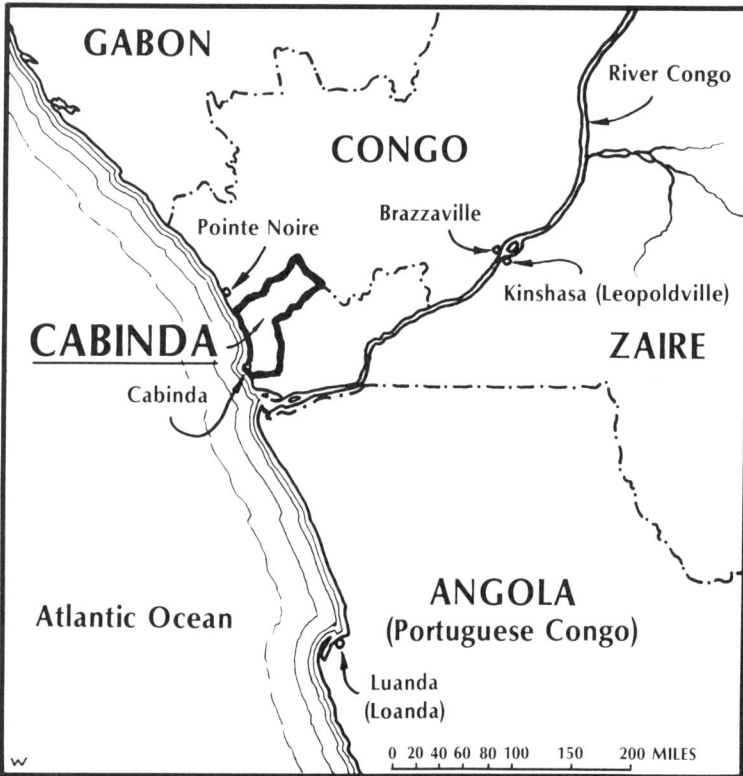

Pop: 6,166 (1970 est.)

Cabo Gracias a Dios is a district, with a port of the same name, in the northern part of Nicaragua. The name (Cape Thanks be to God) was applied by early Spanish explorers who had trouble finding landing places along the coast and who were relieved to come upon this haven. Separate stamps were issued during the early 1900s because the area used a currency that had a different value from that used in the rest of Nicaragua.

Area: 2,851 sq. miles
Pop: 885,433 (1970)
Capital: Cadiz

Cadiz is a province of Spain with a capital city of the same name. It was once a prosperous center for trade with the New World possessions. Stamps were issued there by Nationalist revolutionaries in 1936, during the Spanish Civil War.

EUROPE

SPAIN

Seville

Arcos de la Frontera

Malaga

San Fernando

Cadiz

CADIZ

Algeciras

Gibraltar

Atlantic Ocean

Strait of Gibraltar

Mediterranean Sea

Tangier

AFRICA

0 10 20 30 40 50 MILES

CAMPECHE, STATE OF

Area: 21,666 sq. miles
Pop: 90,458 (1895)
      250,391 (1970)
Capital: Campeche

Campeche is a state in southern Mexico. Provisional stamps were issued there in 1876, during the establishment of a Mexican government following the expulsion of the French from that country.

CENTRAL AMERICA

Gulf of Mexico

CAMPECHE

Merida

Ciudad del Carmen

Veracruz

Campeche

MEXICO

BELIZE

GUATEMALA

Pacific Ocean

EL SALVADOR

0 20 40 60 80 100 150 200 MILES

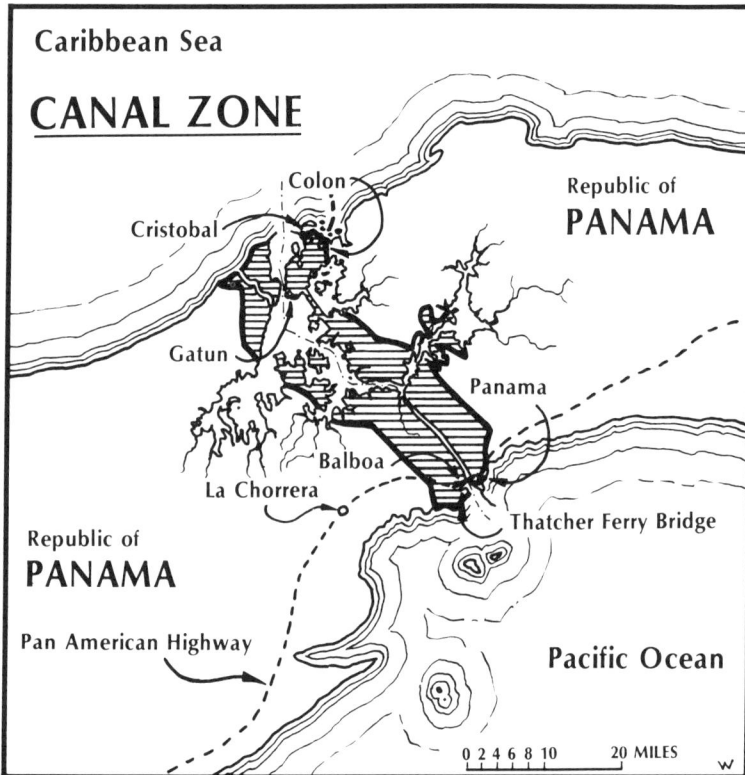

Area: 647 sq. miles
Pop: 44,650 (1970)
Capital: Balboa Heights

A strip of land across Panama on either side of the Panama Canal, the Canal Zone was granted to the US under a 1903 treaty with Panama. It was restored to Panama in October 1979. Stamps were issued by the Canal Zone Postal Service during the period of its operation.

─────── CANARY ISLANDS ───────

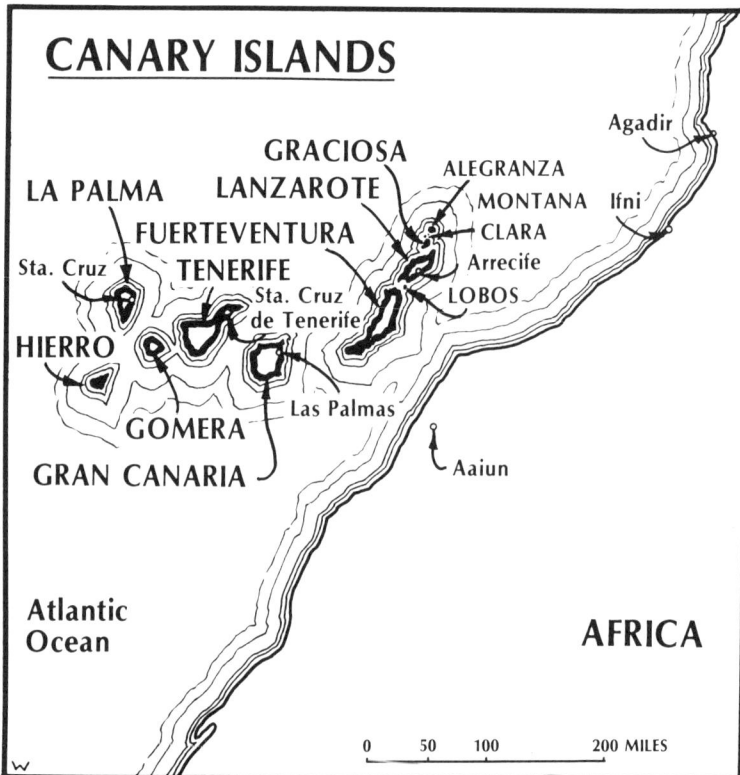

Area: 2,808 sq. miles
Pop: 1,170,224 (1970)

The Canary Islands is an island group belonging to Spain and located in the Atlantic Ocean off the northwest coast of Africa. It forms two Spanish provinces. Air mail stamps were issued there in 1936-38 for use on the German Lufthansa air service calling at the islands on its South American route. The stamps were overprints and surcharges on Spanish issues.

Area: 1,020 sq. miles
Pop: 209,652 (1971)
Capital: Candia (Iraklion)

Candia Province is located in the central part of the island of Crete. Its capital, Candia (now Iraklion), is on the north coast. Grapes and olives are the area's main products. The city was capital of Crete prior to 1841. Both city and province were devastated by the German invasion of May 1941.

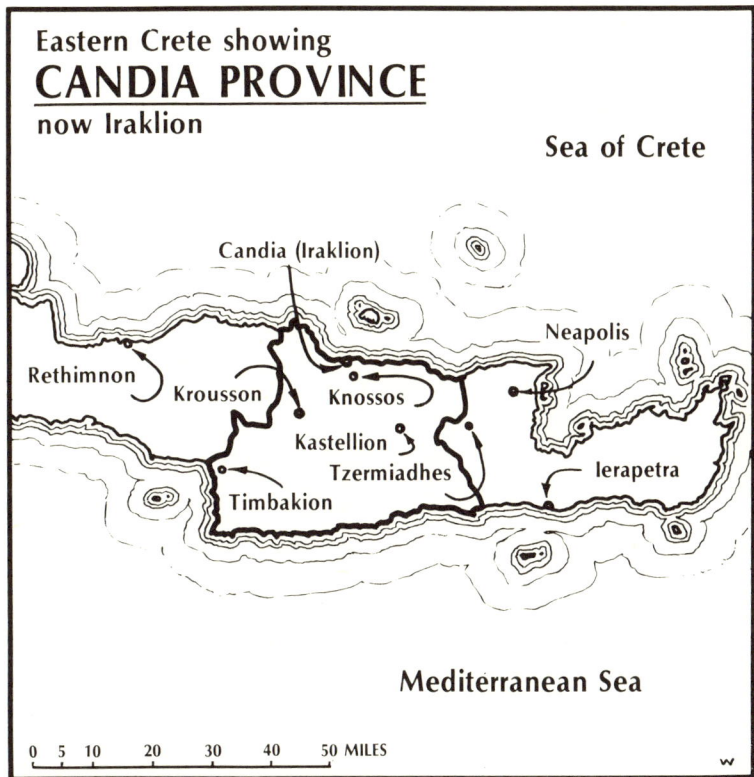

Eastern Crete showing
CANDIA PROVINCE
now Iraklion

Sea of Crete

Candia (Iraklion)

Neapolis

Rethimnon

Krousson

Knossos

Kastellion

Tzermiadhes

Timbakion

Ierapetra

Mediterranean Sea

0 5 10 20 30 40 50 MILES

EUROPE

CAPE OF GOOD HOPE, COLONY OF

Area: 276,993 sq. miles
Pop: 2,565,000 (1911 est.)
Capital: Cape Town

The Cape of Good Hope was a British colony at the southern tip of Africa. It existed as a colony from 1814 to the formation of the Union of South Africa on May 31, 1910. Stamps were first issued in 1853. These were the famous "Cape Triangulars." Stamps continued until replaced by those of South Africa.

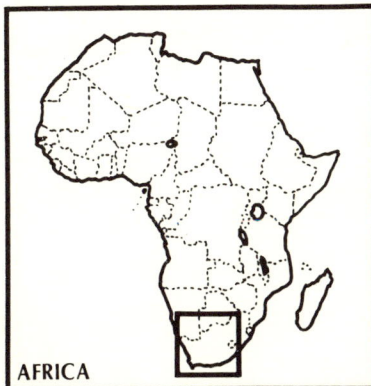

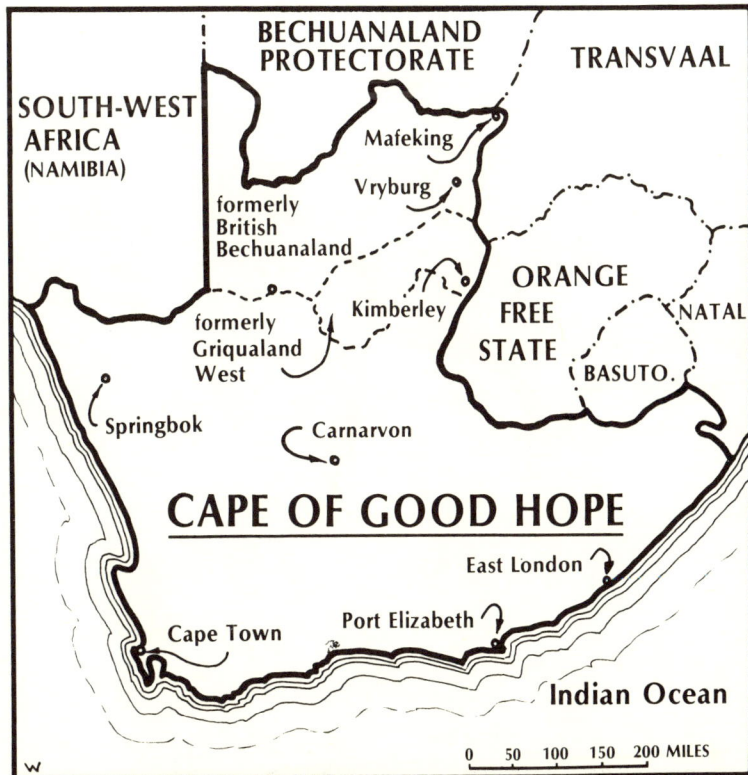

SOUTH-WEST
AFRICA
(NAMIBIA)

BECHUANALAND
PROTECTORATE

TRANSVAAL

Mafeking

Vryburg

formerly
British
Bechuanaland

Kimberley

ORANGE
FREE
STATE

NATAL

formerly
Griqualand
West

BASUTO.

Springbok

Carnarvon

CAPE OF GOOD HOPE

East London

Port Elizabeth

Cape Town

Indian Ocean

0 50 100 150 200 MILES

AFRICA

Carinthia is an area in southern Austria that was part of the Austro-Hungarian Empire until the end of WWI. The new country of Yugoslavia occupied the southern portion. This division was confirmed by a plebscite, and the northern part remained a province of Austria with the town of Klagenfurt as its capital. Stamps were issued during the plebscite.

CARINTHIA
showing present status as a province of Austria

EUROPE

————**CAROLINE ISLANDS, COLONY OF**————

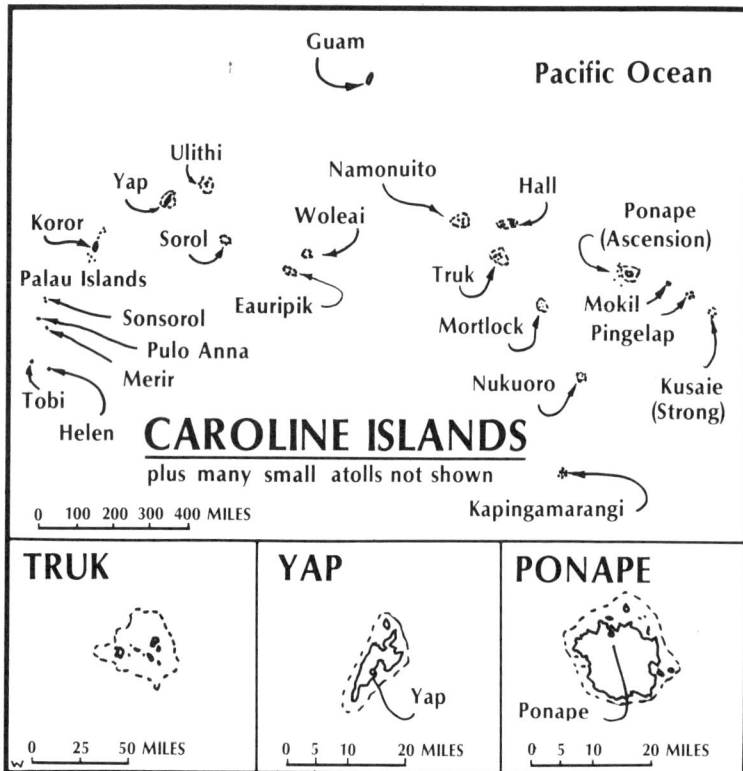

Area: 457 sq. miles
Pop: 40,000 (1915 est.)
   66,900 (1969 est.)

This is an extensive archipelago of some 500 atolls and islands in the southwestern Pacific. It was bought from Spain by Germany in 1899. Taken by Japan during WWI, it was mandated to that country. The US took the area during WWII, and it has remained a US Trust Territory. Stamps were issued during the German period.

CAROLINE ISLANDS
plus many small atolls not shown

TRUK

YAP

PONAPE

PACIFIC OCEAN

The province of Carpatho-Ukraine was in the easternmost part of Czechoslovakia. It was named Ruthenia up to WWII. The Germans granted it a form of autonomous status under the Munich "Agreement," which dismembered the country in a futile attempt to appease German expansionism. The province was quickly taken by Hungary, which later lost it to the USSR. It was never restored to Czechoslovakia. Its memorial is a single stamp issued March 15, 1939.

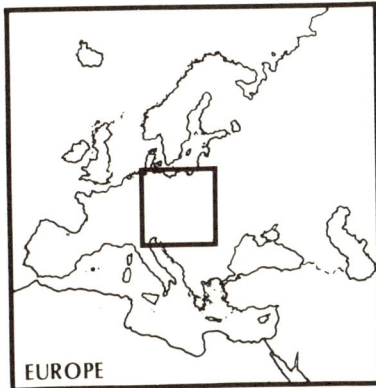

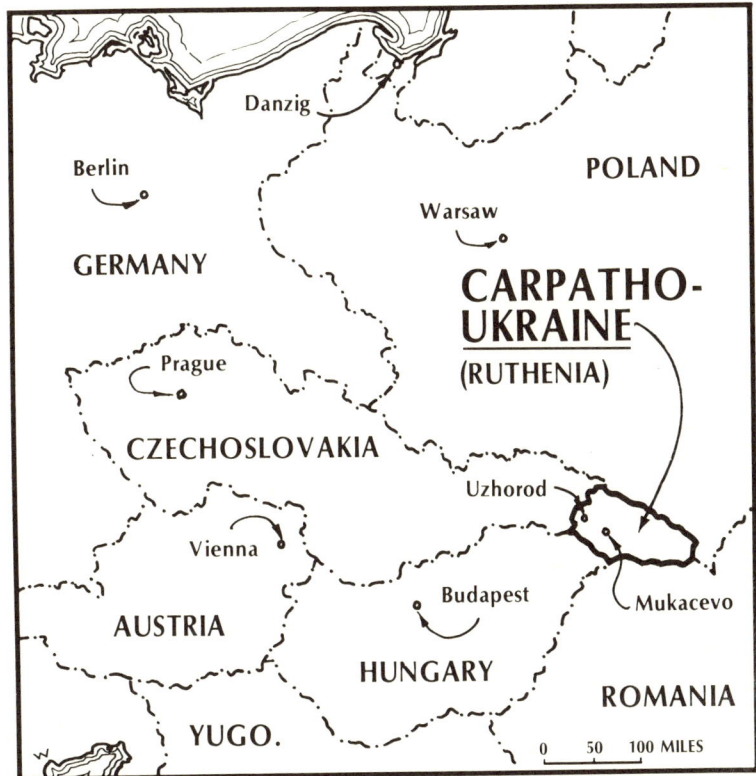

CARUPANO, CITY OF

Pop: 12,000 (1900 est.)
46,155 (1970 est.)

Carupano is a port city on the east coast of Venezuela, near Trinidad. During a stamp shortage there caused by a 1902 blockade of the port of La Guaira by British, German, and Italian naval forces, the city issued a number of local provisional stamps. The Scott catalog lists them, despite their local status.

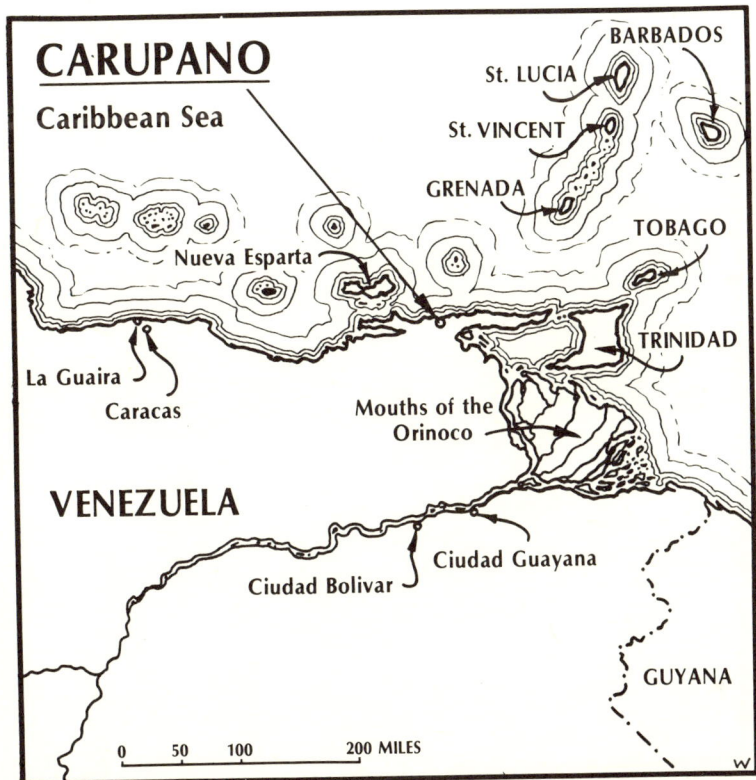

Area: 12,329 sq. miles
Pop: 5,122,567 (1970)

Cataluna is a region occupying the northeastern portion of Spain. During the 1870s, much of it was controlled by revolutionary Carlist forces, and civil war resulted. The Carlists issued stamps for use in the areas it controlled. These are listed by Scott under the heading of Carlist Issues. The stamps feature a portrait of Carlos VII, pretender to the Spanish throne.

———————— **CATTARO, PROVINCE OF**————————

Capital: Cattaro (Kotor)

Part of the Austro-Hungarian Empire prior to WWI, it became part of the new country of Yugoslavia following the war. The city of Kotor was an important naval base, and during WWII the area was occupied by Italian and German forces. The occupiers released stamps in the form of Italian and Yugoslav issues overprinted.

CAUCA, DEPARTMENT OF

Area: 11,774 sq. miles
Pop: 621,000 (1881 est.)
Capital: Popayan

Formerly a state of the Granadine Confederation, Cauca is now a department of the South American Republic of Colombia. It issued its own stamps from 1879. Although it joined Colombia in 1886, it retained the right to have its own stamps until 1904.

Caribbean Sea

VENEZUELA

COLOMBIA

Bogota

Popayan

CAUCA

0 25 50 75 100 MILES

BRAZIL

SOUTH AMERICA

CAVALLE (KAVALLA), CITY OF

Pop: 46,679 (1971)

A port city and capital of Kavalla Department, the city is now Greek. Previously it had been Turkish. During the period of Turkish rule, a French post office operated in the town. Stamps were issued for use from the post office from 1893 to 1903.

BULGARIA

Sofia

CAVALLE (Cavalla, now Kavalla)
Once Turkish, now in Greece.

YUGO.

GREECE

TURKEY

Salonica (Thessaloniki)

Thasos

Gallipoli

Aegean Sea

TURKEY

0 10 20 40 60 80 100 MILES

EUROPE

CELEBES ISLANDS

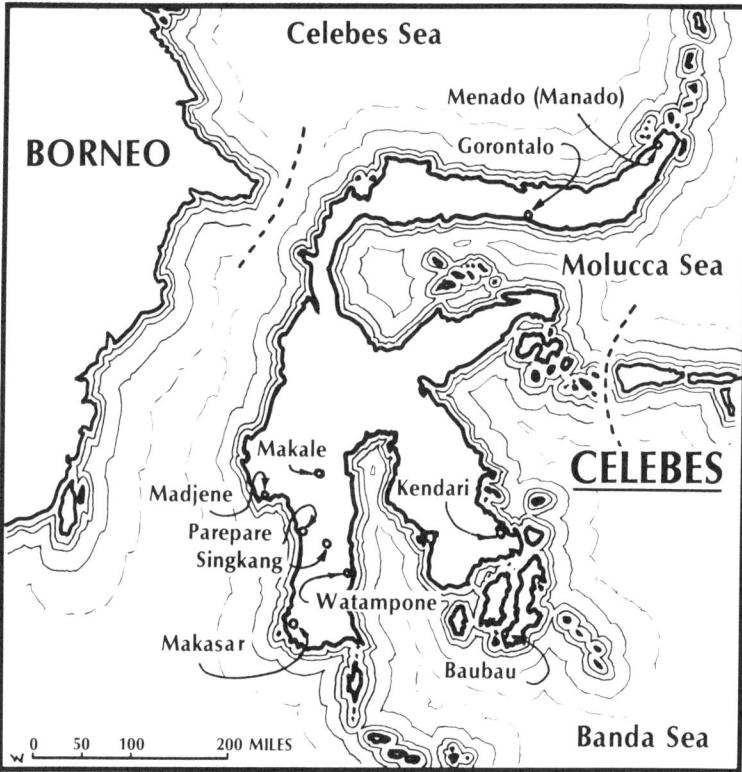

Area: 72,986 sq. miles
Pop: 8,925,000 (1970 est.)

The Celebes consists of a large single island and a number of smaller ones. Now part of Indonesia, they were once included in the Netherlands Indies. The area was overrun by the Japanese during WWII and occupied by them until liberated by Australian forces in September 1945.

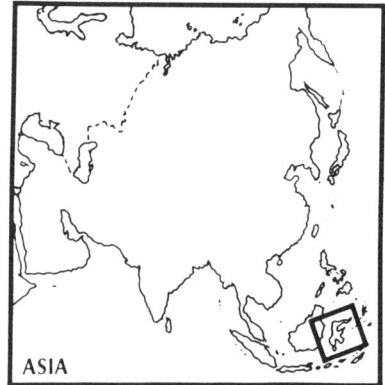

CENTRAL AFRICAN FEDERATION

Area: 486,975 sq. miles
Pop: 8,510,000 (1961 est.)
Capital: Salisbury

The Central African Federation was a grouping of Northern and Southern Rhodesia and the Nyasaland Protectorate that lasted from 1953 to 1963. It was known as Rhodesia and Nyasaland on the stamps issued for the federation. The three components are now independent as Zambia, Malawi, and Zimbabwe.

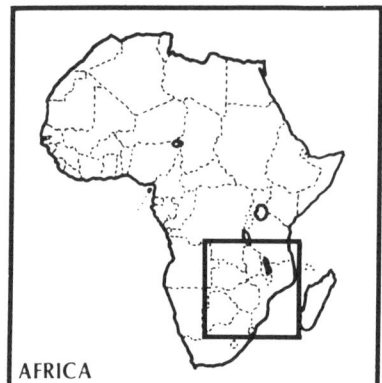

Capital: Vilnius

Following WWI, an area of the newly independent country of Lithuania, Central Lithuania was a former grand duchy. Soon after independence, Poland moved in and took it, forcing the Lithuanian capital to be moved from Vilnius to Kaunas. During a brief period of re-occupation by Lithuania, stamps were issued. But these ceased when Poland again took the area and kept it until WWII, when the USSR moved in and took it.

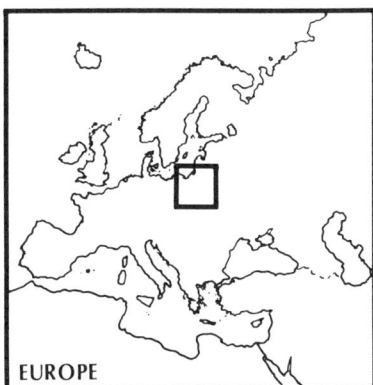

EUROPE

Baltic Sea • LATVIA • Danzig (Gdansk) • Klaipeda (Memel) • LITHUANIA • Kaunas • Vilnius (Wilno) • Konigsberg (Kaliningrad) • EAST PRUSSIA • Minsk

CENTRAL LITHUANIA
Polish from 1922 to 1939.

Warsaw • POLAND • USSR

0 20 40 60 80 100 MILES

CEYLON, COLONY OF

Area: 25,332 sq. miles
Pop: 12,514,000 (1970)
Capital: Colombo

An island off the southern tip of the Indian sub-continent, Ceylon became a British colony in 1833. The Portuguese had first claimed the island, and they were followed by the Dutch in 1658. The British arrived in 1796. Independence was granted in 1948, and the island joined the UN in 1955. It became the Republic of Sri Lanka on May 22, 1972.

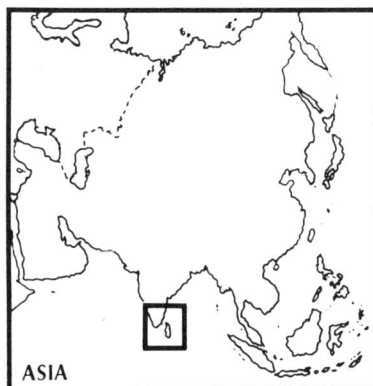

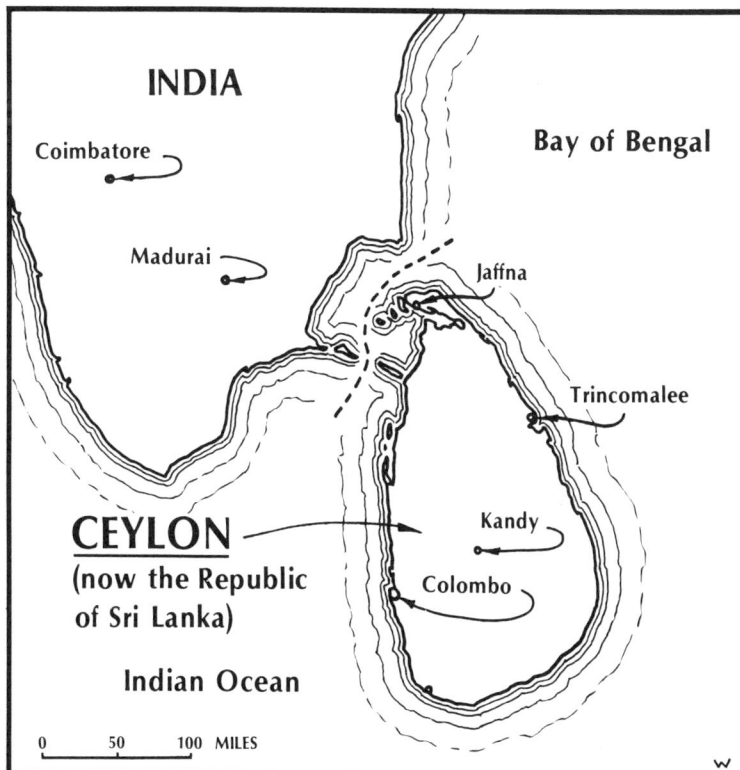

ASIA

INDIA • Coimbatore • Bay of Bengal • Madurai • Jaffna • Trincomalee • Kandy • Colombo

CEYLON
(now the Republic of Sri Lanka)

Indian Ocean

0 50 100 MILES

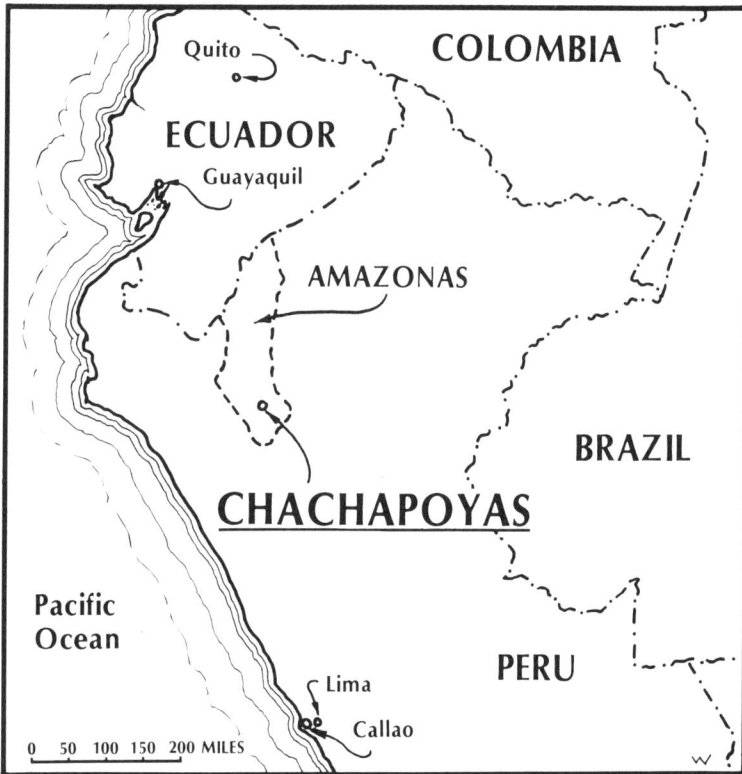

Pop: 5,000 (1900 est.)
6,860 (1961)

The city of Chachapoyas is the capital city of the Peruvian Department of Amazonas. The city is at an altitude of 7,600 feet and is described as an industrial center. A stamp was issued there in 1884, during a stamp shortage caused by the war with Chile, when that country occupied Lima and Callao.

CHAHAR, PROVINCE OF

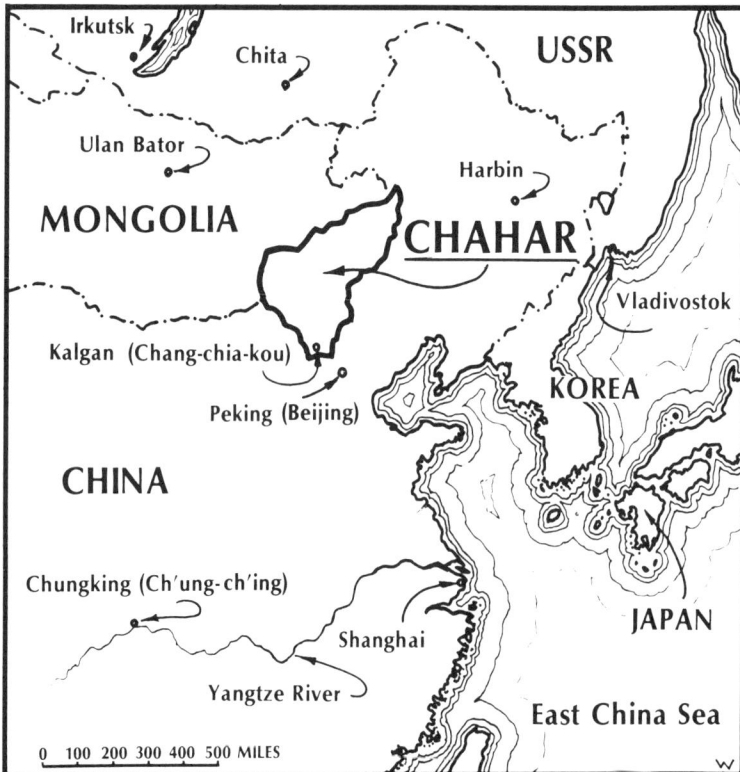

Capital: Kalgan

Chahar was a province of China that was included in the North China Liberation Area of the Communists, prior to the formation of the People's Republic of China in 1949. It had been taken by the Japanese in 1935. Stamps were issued for use in the area from 1946 to 1949. In 1952, the province was divided among neighboring provinces.

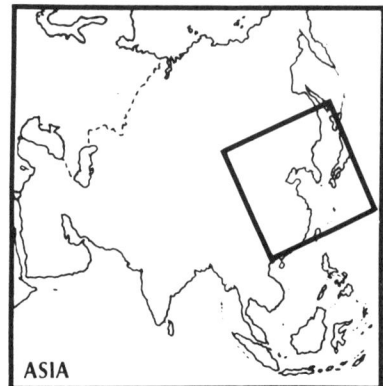

Chala is a city in the Arequipa department of Peru. Stamps were issued in the city during 1885, because of a shortage caused by the Chilean occupation of Lima and Callao in that country's war with Peru. Since the occupied cities were the source of stamps for the rest of the country, it was necessary for many centers to prepare provisional stamps as denominations of regular stamps ran out.

PERU

BRAZIL

Lima

Callao

CHALA

BOLIVIA

Lake Titicaca

Arequipa

Pacific Ocean

0 50 100 150 200 MILES

CHILE

SOUTH AMERICA

CHEKIANG, PROVINCE OF

Area: 39,305 sq. miles
Pop: 31 million (1968 est.)
Capital: Hang-chou

A province on the coast of China, Chekiang is one of the smallest of the Chinese provinces but among the most densely populated. It was included in the East China Liberation Area by the Communists, and stamps were issued for use there during 1948-49, prior to the establishment of the People's Republic of China.

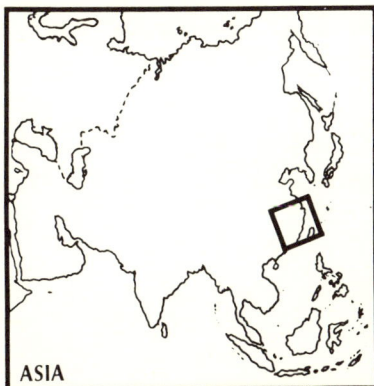

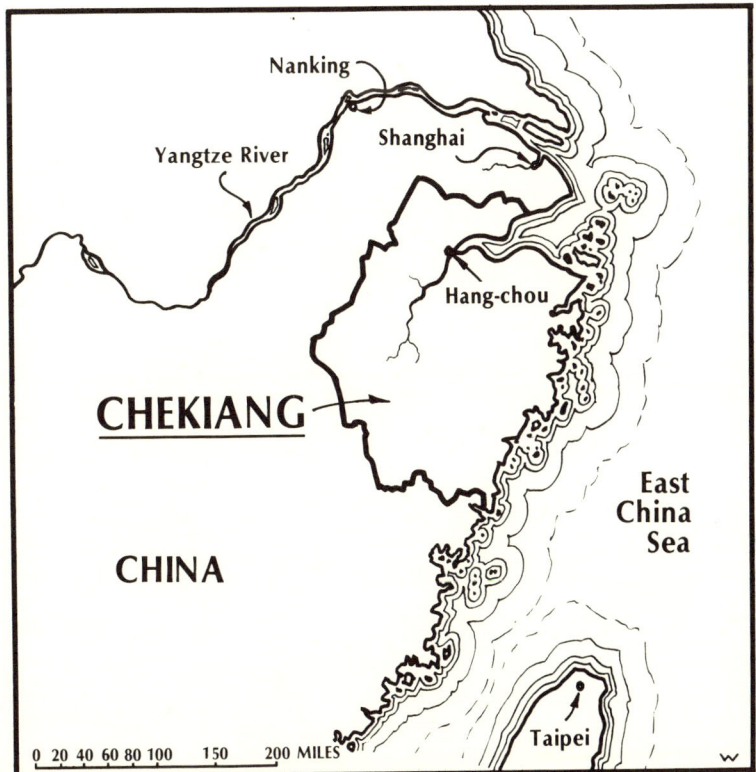

Nanking

Yangtze River

Shanghai

Hang-chou

CHEKIANG

East China Sea

CHINA

Taipei

0 20 40 60 80 100   150   200 MILES

ASIA

Gulf of Mexico

Merida

Campeche

Yucatan Peninsula

MEXICO

Villahermosa

Tuxtla Gutierrez

CHIAPAS

BELIZE

Tapachula

GUATEMALA

Pacific Ocean

Guatemala City

0   50   100   150   200 MILES

CENTRAL AMERICA

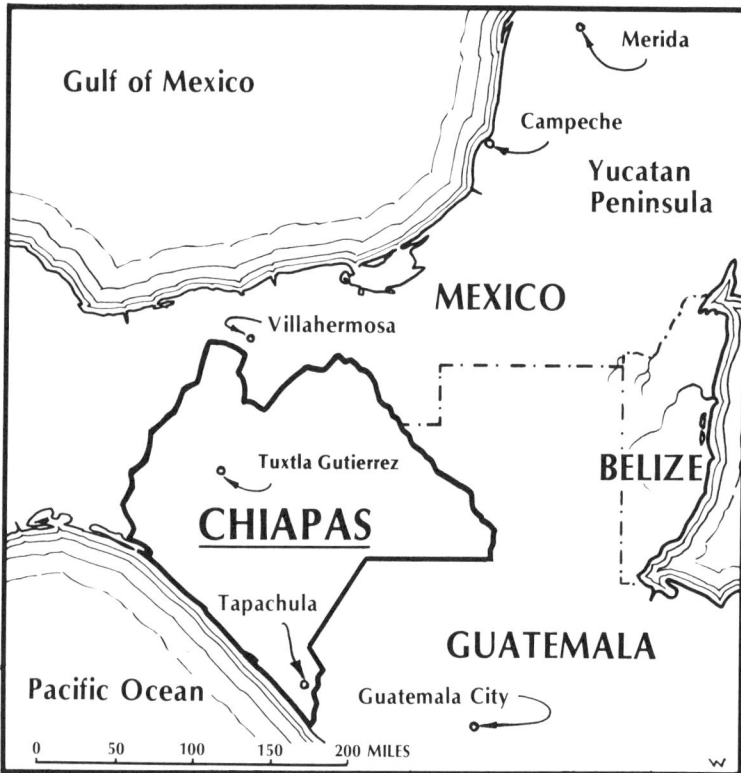

Area: 28,528 sq. miles
Pop: 313,678 (1895)
      1,578,180 (1970)
Capital: Tuxtla Gutierrez

Chiapas is a state in the south of the United States of Mexico, bordering on Guatemala. Stamps were issued there in 1886, during the unsettled period following the ousting of the French from Mexico. The issue takes the form of five denominations, which were typeset.

━━━━━━━━━━━ CHICLAYO, CITY OF ━━━━━━━━━━━

Quito

COLOMBIA

ECUADOR

Guayaquil

PERU

Lambayeque Province

CHICLAYO

BRAZIL

Pacific Ocean

Callao

Lima

0 50 100 150 200 MILES

SOUTH AMERICA

Pop: 14,000 (1900 est.)
      134,709 (1969 est.)

Chiclayo is a city in Peru and capital of Lambayeque Province. It is in the northwest part of the country in a rice and sugar-growing area. Provisional stamps were issued there in 1884, made necessary by the Chilean occupation of Lima and Callao, which were the normal sources of Peruvian stamps.

Pop: 363,850 (1970)

Located at an altitude of 4,600 feet, Chihuahua is a city in northern Mexico and capital of the state of the same name. It is the center of a rich silver-mining area. A university was founded there in 1954. In 1872 a primitive provisional stamp issue was released in the city. It consisted of an oval handstamp in denominations of 12c and 25c.

NORTH AMERICA

ARIZONA
NEW MEXICO
El Paso
Ciudad Juarez
TEXAS
MEXICO
CHIHUAHUA
Rio Grande
US-MEXICAN border
Ciudad Obregon
Chihuahua
Delicias
Hidalgo del Parral
Gulf of California
Los Mochis
0 25 50 100 MILES

CHIOS, ISLAND OF

Area: 325 sq. miles
Pop: 36,000 (1900 est.)
60,061 (1961)

Located in the Aegean Sea off the Turkish coast, Chios is the reputed birthplace of Homer. The island was Turkish up to 1912, when it was taken by Greece. With some adjacent islands, it is currently a department of Greece. It is a fruit-growing area, producing primarily figs. A stamp was issued there in 1913 by the Greek military authorities.

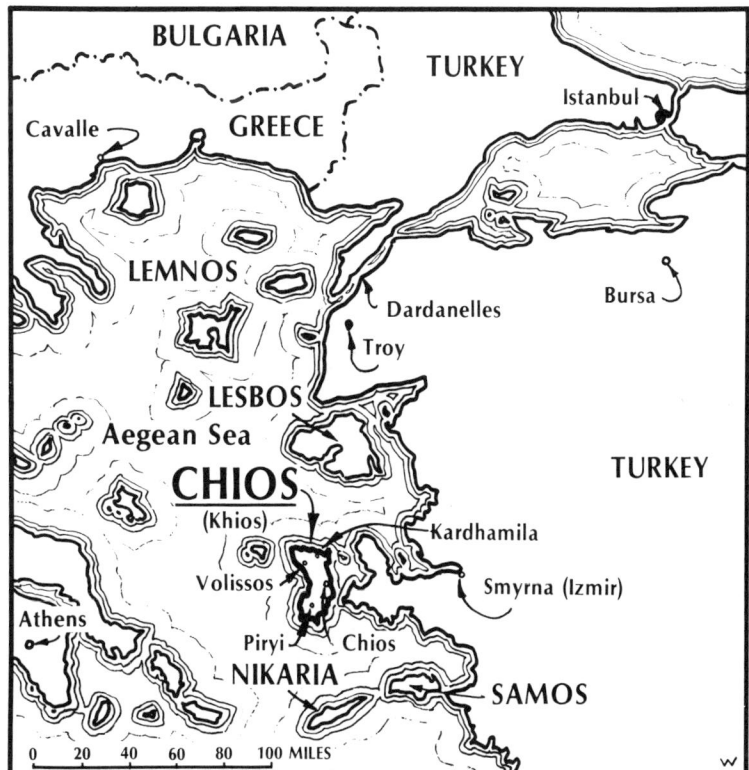

EUROPE

BULGARIA
TURKEY
Istanbul
Cavalle
GREECE
LEMNOS
Dardanelles
Bursa
Troy
LESBOS
Aegean Sea
CHIOS
(Khios)
TURKEY
Kardhamila
Volissos
Smyrna (Izmir)
Athens
Piryi
Chios
NIKARIA
SAMOS
0 20 40 60 80 100 MILES

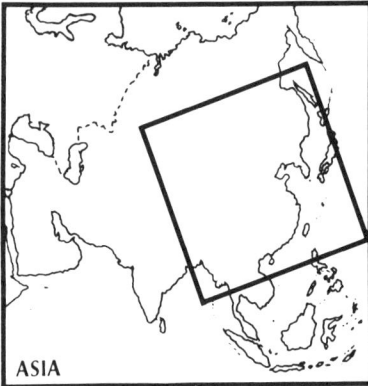

Area: 2,903,500 sq. miles
Pop: 402,680,000 (1897 est.)
1,004,000,000 (1981 est.)
Capital: Chungking (now Peking)

The Manchu dynasty was overthrown and the modern Chinese republic established in 1912. Following the civil war of 1920-26, a nationalist government was set up at Nanking in 1928 by Chiang Kai-shek. He was head of the government through WWII. While the 1937-45 war against the invading Japanese occupied the Chinese government, the Communists took the opportunity to gain power, until, by the end of WWII, they had virtual control of the country. In 1949, Chiang Kai-shek and the Nationalists were expelled to Taiwan. There they set up a second China, the present Republic of China (Taiwan). The first Chinese stamps appeared in 1878, and Chinese philately has been both complex and stimulating.

REPUBLIC OF CHINA
PRIOR TO WORLD WAR TWO

SIBERIA

USSR

USSR

Vladivostok

Ulan Bator

MANCHUKUO
Harbin

MONGOLIA

Hsinking

SINKIANG

Mukden

Sea
of Japan

INNER MONGOLIA

Tokyo

KOREA

Peking
(Beijing)

Great Wall

JAPAN

TIBET

Delhi

Nanking

Lhasa

Hankow

Chungking

Shanghai

NEPAL

Yangtze River

INDIA

BHUTAN

Yunnan (Kunming)

Calcutta

Canton

FORMOSA (TAIWAN)

BURMA

Hanoi

Pacific
Ocean

Hainan

Manila

Bay of
Bengal

THAILAND

South
China
Sea

PHILIPPINES

Bangkok

Rangoon

0   500   1,000 MILES

INDO-CHINA

Pop: 6,985 (1903 est.)
242,000 (1970)

Located on the Chita River near its junction with the Ingoda, Chita is one of Siberia's more important centers. It is on the Trans-Siberian Railway and has rolling stock works. It was founded in 1653 and is the capital city of Chita Oblast. Chita was the capital of the short-lived Far East Republic following the Russian Revolution of 1917.

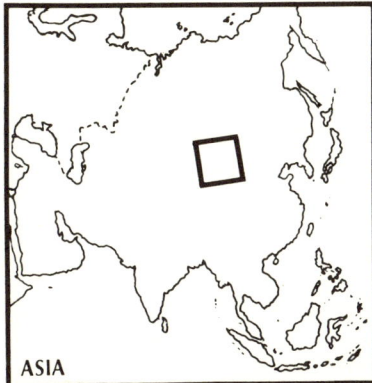

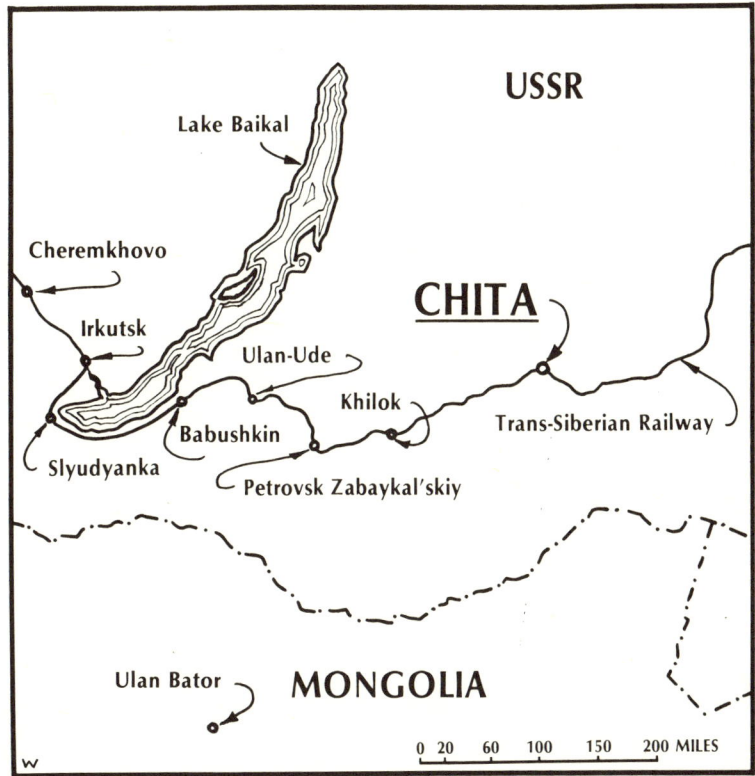

ASIA

USSR
Lake Baikal
Cheremkhovo
Irkutsk
Ulan-Ude
CHITA
Khilok
Slyudyanka
Babushkin
Trans-Siberian Railway
Petrovsk Zabaykal'skiy
Ulan Bator
MONGOLIA
0 20 60 100 150 200 MILES

CHUNGKING, CITY OF

Pop: 300,000 (1898)
3,500,000 (1970)

A city in China, Chungking was the national capital from 1937 to 45. It is located in Szechwan Province on the Yangtze River. During WWII it was the site of a US air base. Stamps were issued there in 1903-1919 for use at a French Indo-Chinese post office in the city.

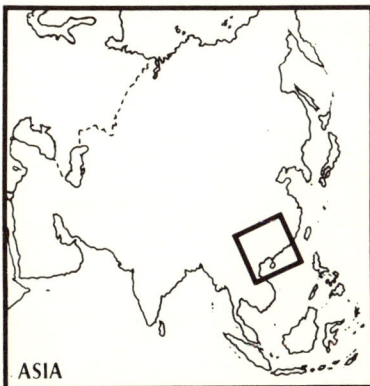

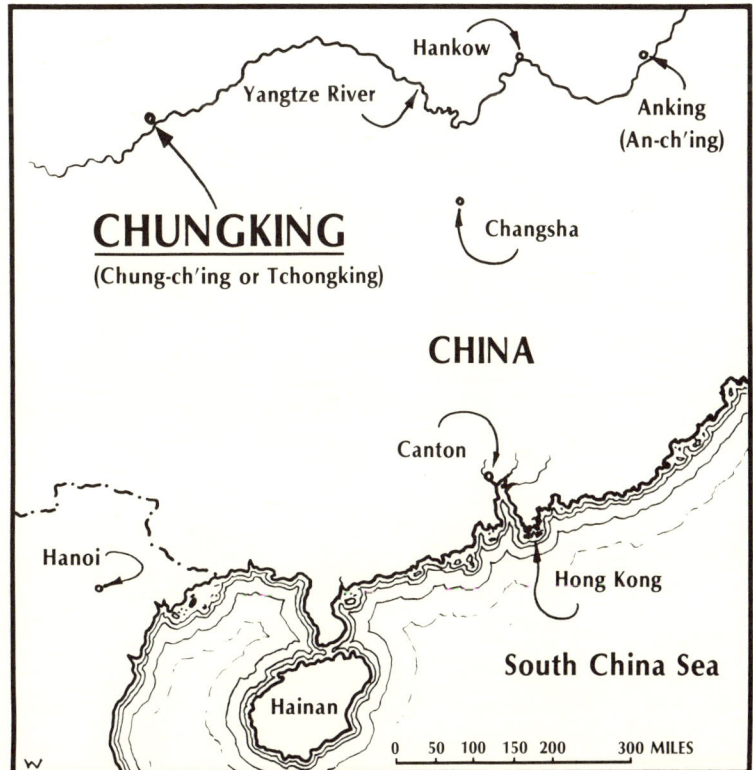

ASIA

Hankow
Yangtze River
Anking
(An-ch'ing)
CHUNGKING
(Chung-ch'ing or Tchongking)
Changsha
CHINA
Canton
Hanoi
Hong Kong
South China Sea
Hainan
0 50 100 150 200 300 MILES

Area: 6,300 sq. miles approx.
Pop: 384,000 est.

Cilicia is the ancient name for a region of southeast Turkey. The area was occupied by British and French forces for a brief period following WWI. It was mandated to France until 1923, when it was restored to Turkey. Stamps were issued during the occupation period.

———————————————CLUJ, CITY OF———————————————

Pop: 35,850 (1890)
   202,715 (1970)

Cluj, a city in Transylvania, was also known as Kolozsvar or Klausenburg. Once Hungarian, it is now in Romania. Stamps were issued there in 1919, during the Romanian occupation following the WWI defeat of the Austro-Hungarian Empire. The area was later made part of Romania.

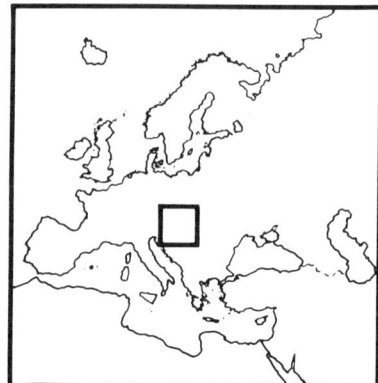

Area: 29,974 sq. miles
Pop: 2,034,000 (1891 est.)
Capital: Saigon

Comprising the area of the Mekong Delta, Cochin China was ceded to France by the Treaty of Saigon in 1862. The colony was united administratively with Annam, Tonkin, and Cambodia to form French Indo-China. It was incorporated into Vietnam in 1949. Stamps were issued from 1886 to 1892.

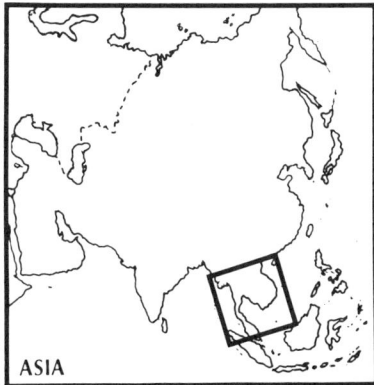

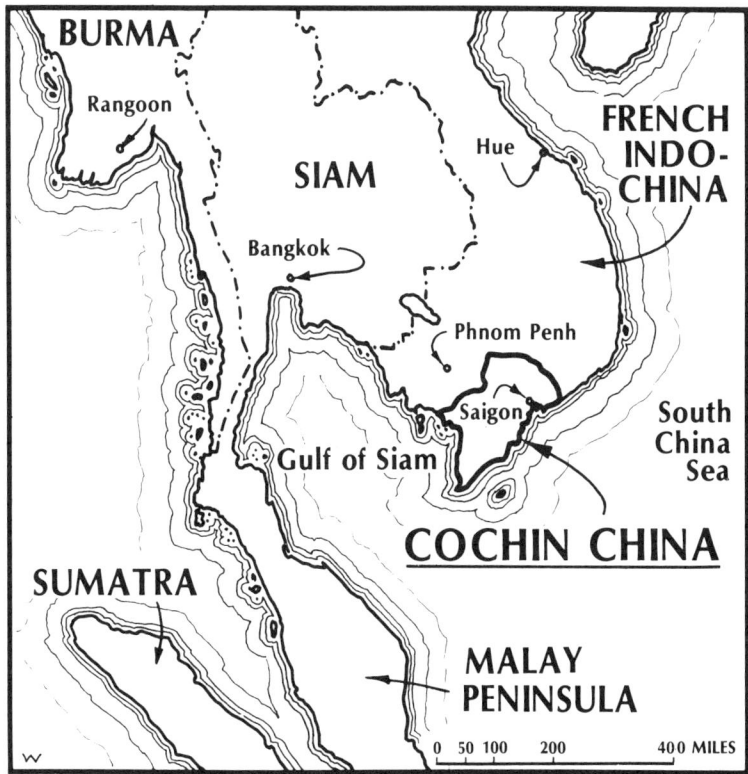

COMAYAGUA, CITY OF

Pop: 10,000 (1887)
        8,473 (1961)

Comayagua is a town in Honduras and was once its capital city. An 1877 stamp issue of Honduras is known as the Comayagua Issue. The city is about 35 miles northwest of Tegucigalpa, the present capital city.

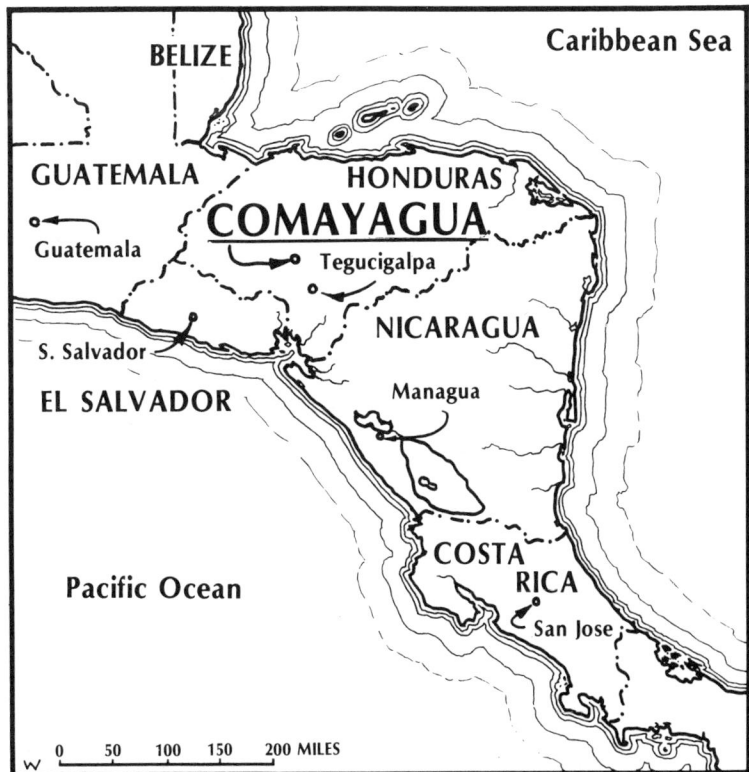

The Confederate States of America was formed beginning in 1861, when the states of South Carolina, Mississippi, Florida, Alabama, Georgia, and Louisiana seceded from the United States. The states of Texas, Arkansas, North Carolina, Virginia, and Tennessee were admitted later. West Virginia was created when that area of Virginia refused to approve the secession. It was admitted to the Union as a state in 1863. The Con-federacy was dissolved at the end of the Civil War and the states re-admitted to the United States. The individual state maps show towns at which postmasters' provisional stamps were generally issued prior to the introduction of general CSA stamp issues in October 1861. The use of United States stamps had ceased in June of the same year. Postmasters' provisional stamps were also used at times when CSA stamps were not available.

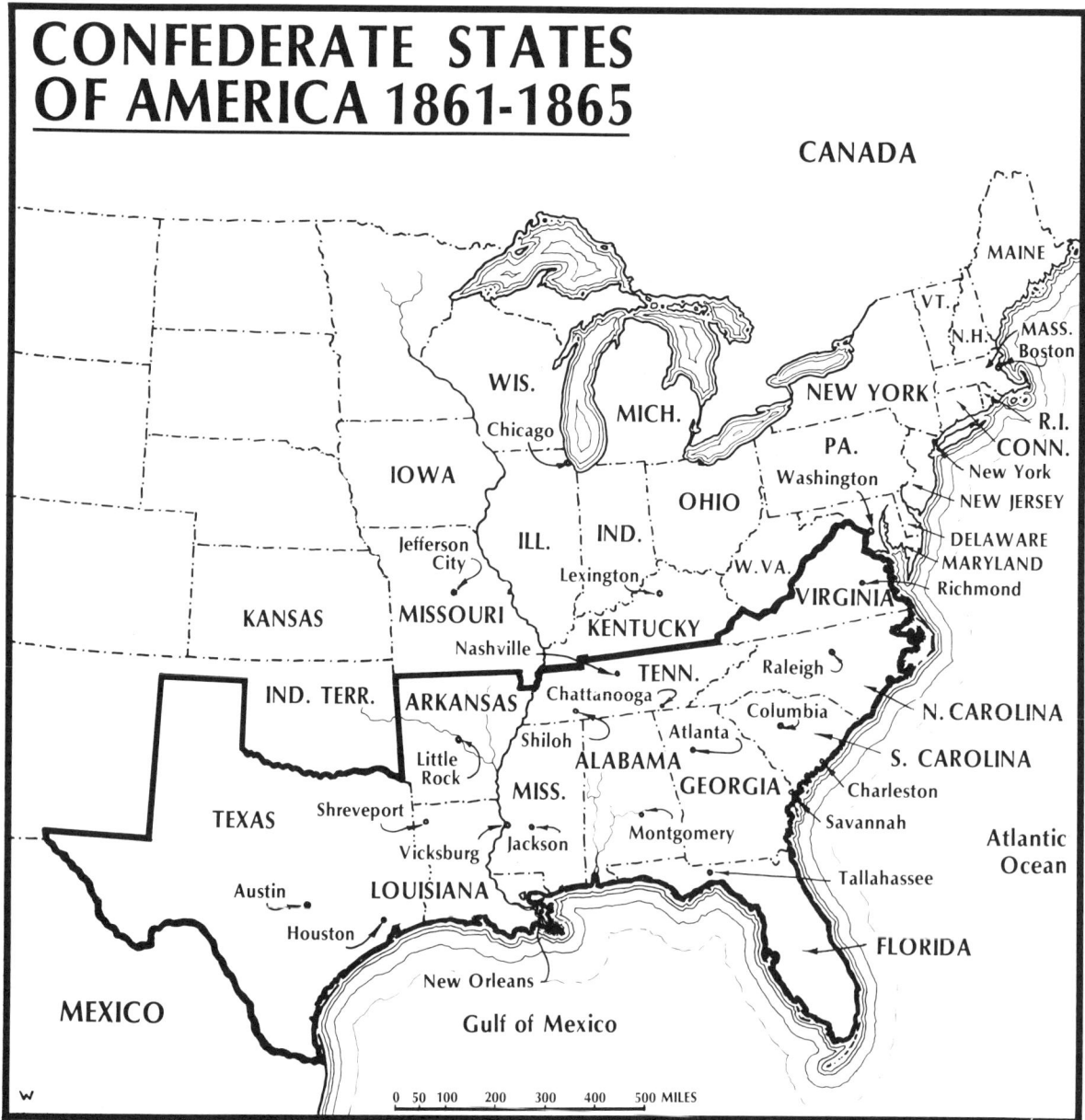

NORTH AMERICA

CONFEDERATE STATES OF AMERICA 1861-1865

CANADA

MAINE

VT.

N.H.

MASS. Boston

NEW YORK

R.I.

CONN.

New York

NEW JERSEY

DELAWARE

MARYLAND

Richmond

PA.

Washington

OHIO

W.VA.

VIRGINIA

WIS.

MICH.

Chicago

IOWA

ILL.

IND.

Jefferson City

Lexington

MISSOURI

KENTUCKY

Nashville

TENN.

Raleigh

N. CAROLINA

KANSAS

Columbia

S. CAROLINA

Chattanooga

Atlanta

Charleston

IND. TERR.

ARKANSAS

Shiloh

ALABAMA

GEORGIA

Savannah

Little Rock

MISS.

Montgomery

Atlantic Ocean

Shreveport

Vicksburg

Jackson

Tallahassee

TEXAS

Austin

LOUISIANA

Houston

New Orleans

FLORIDA

MEXICO

Gulf of Mexico

0 50 100 200 300 400 500 MILES

147

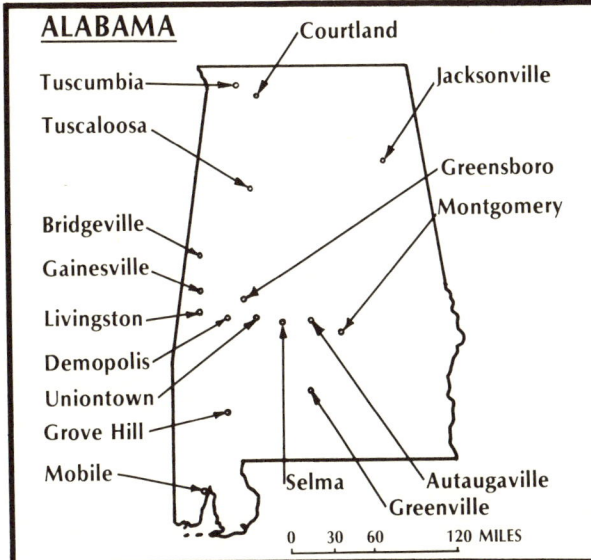

ALABAMA

Courtland
Tuscumbia
Jacksonville
Tuscaloosa
Greensboro
Montgomery
Bridgeville
Gainesville
Livingston
Demopolis
Uniontown
Grove Hill
Mobile
Selma
Autaugaville
Greenville

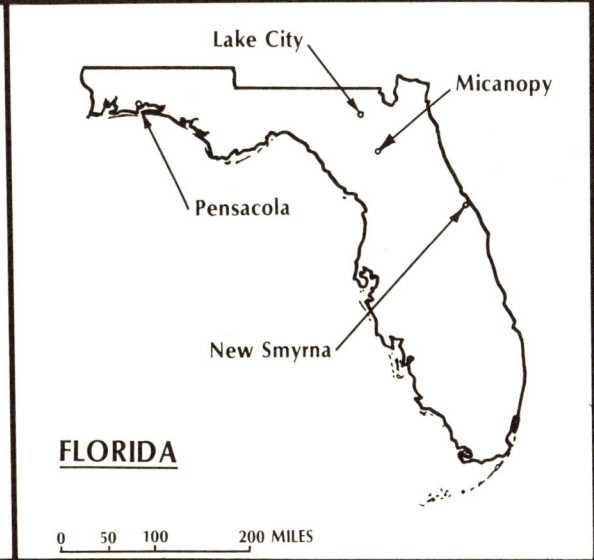

FLORIDA

Lake City
Micanopy
Pensacola
New Smyrna

0 50 100   200 MILES

0 30 60   120 MILES

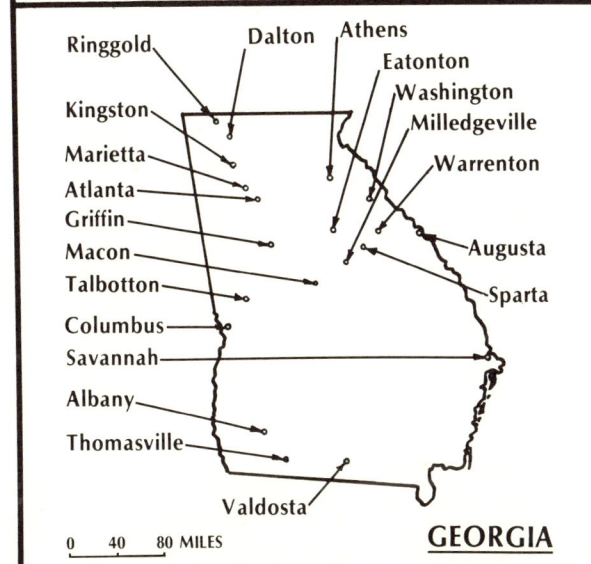

GEORGIA

Ringgold
Dalton
Athens
Eatonton
Washington
Kingston
Milledgeville
Marietta
Warrenton
Atlanta
Griffin
Macon
Augusta
Talbotton
Sparta
Columbus
Savannah
Albany
Thomasville
Valdosta

0 40 80 MILES

LOUISIANA

Mount Lebanon
Baton Rouge
New Orleans

0 40 80 MILES

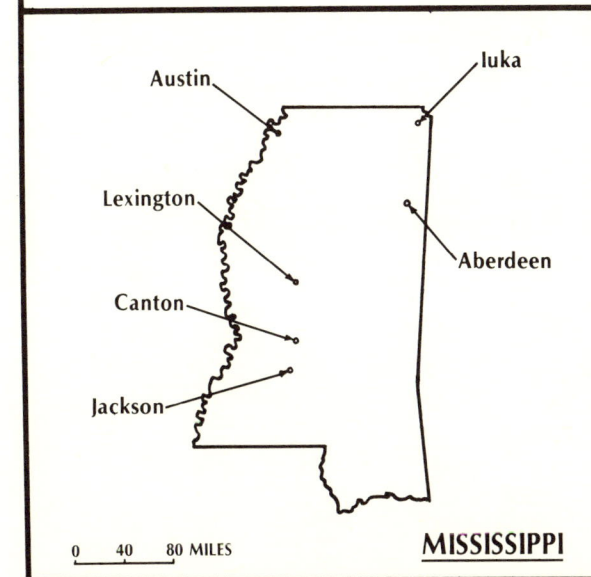

MISSISSIPPI

Austin
Iuka
Lexington
Aberdeen
Canton
Jackson

0 40 80 MILES

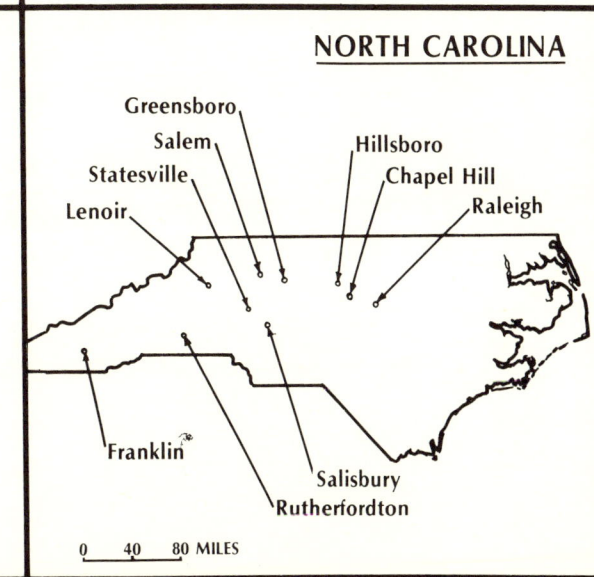

NORTH CAROLINA

Greensboro
Salem
Hillsboro
Statesville
Chapel Hill
Lenoir
Raleigh
Franklin
Salisbury
Rutherfordton

0 40 80 MILES

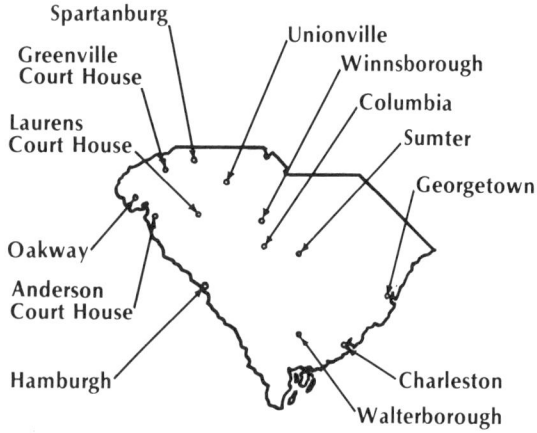

SOUTH CAROLINA

Spartanburg
Greenville
Court House
Unionville
Winnsborough
Laurens
Court House
Columbia
Sumter
Georgetown
Oakway
Anderson
Court House
Hamburgh
Charleston
Walterborough

0   40   80 MILES

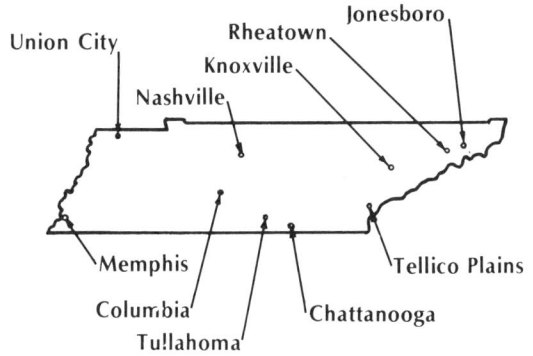

TENNESSEE

Union City
Rheatown
Jonesboro
Knoxville
Nashville
Memphis
Columbia
Tullahoma
Chattanooga
Tellico Plains

0   50   100 MILES

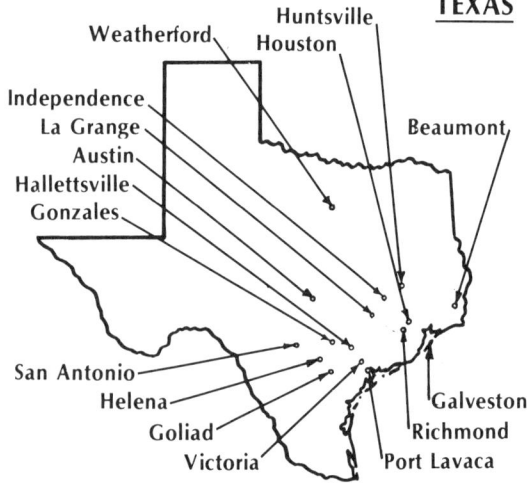

TEXAS

Weatherford
Huntsville
Houston
Independence
La Grange
Austin
Hallettsville
Gonzales
Beaumont
San Antonio
Helena
Goliad
Victoria
Galveston
Richmond
Port Lavaca

0   90   180 MILES

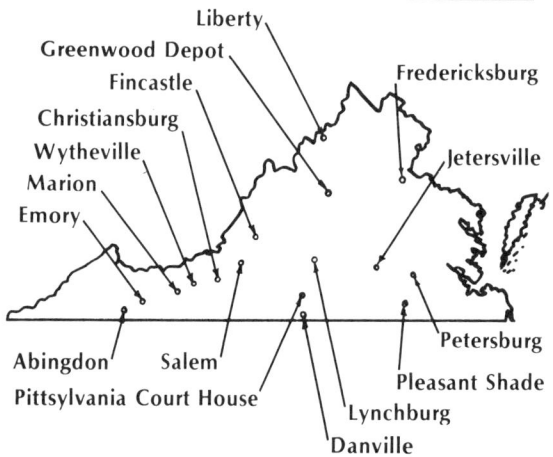

VIRGINIA

Liberty
Greenwood Depot
Fincastle
Christiansburg
Wytheville
Marion
Emory
Fredericksburg
Jetersville
Abingdon
Salem
Pittsylvania Court House
Petersburg
Pleasant Shade
Lynchburg
Danville

0   40   80 MILES

Pop: 12 million (1900 est.)
Capital: Brazzaville

French Congo was an area of Central Africa. A former French colony, it was divided among neighboring French territories in 1906. Stamps of the French Colonies general issue were overprinted "CONGO FRANCAIS" and surcharged in 1891. These were followed by several attractive pictorial designs until 1906.

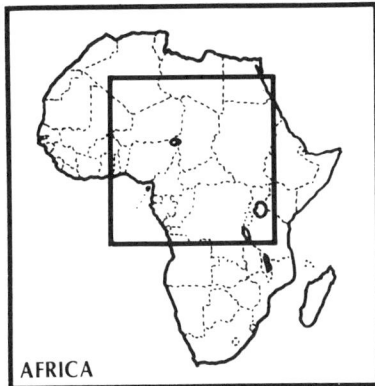

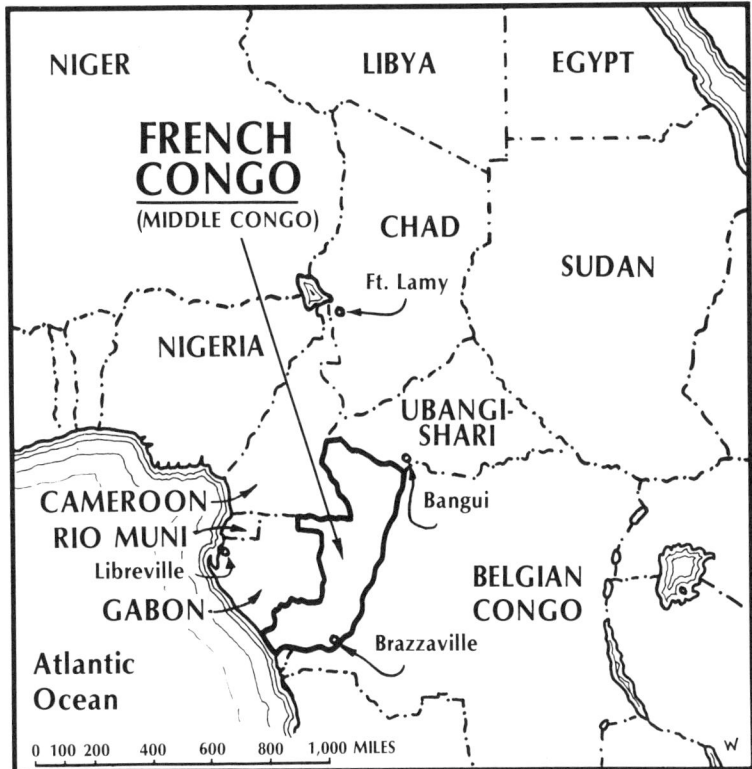

NIGER LIBYA EGYPT

FRENCH CONGO
(MIDDLE CONGO)

CHAD

SUDAN

Ft. Lamy

NIGERIA

UBANGI-SHARI

Bangui

CAMEROON
RIO MUNI

Libreville

BELGIAN CONGO

GABON

Brazzaville

Atlantic Ocean

0 100 200 400 600 800 1,000 MILES

AFRICA

CONSTANTINOPLE (ISTANBUL), CITY OF

Pop: 873,565 (1885)
2,312,751 (1970)
3,900,000 (1979 est.)

Located on the European side of the stretch of water between the Black Sea and the Mediterranean, Constantinople was a city of great importance as long ago as the days of the Byzantine Empire, of which it was the capital from AD 395 to 1453. Several foreign post offices operated there prior to WWI.

BULGARIA Black Sea

CONSTANTINOPLE
(Istanbul)

TURKEY

Beykoz
Uskudar

Sea of Marmara

Izmit

Gallipoli

Bursa

Canakkale

TURKEY

Lesbos

0 10 20 40 60 80 100 MILES

EUROPE

Area: 65,161 sq. miles
Pop: 351,745 (1895)
2,060,065 (1970)
Capital: Cordoba

Cordoba is a province located in the north-central part of the South American Argentine Republic. The capital city is a textile and transportation center and has an astronomical observatory founded in 1573. Two stamps were issued for the province in 1858 and feature the provincial coat of arms.

———————— CORFU, ISLAND OF ————————

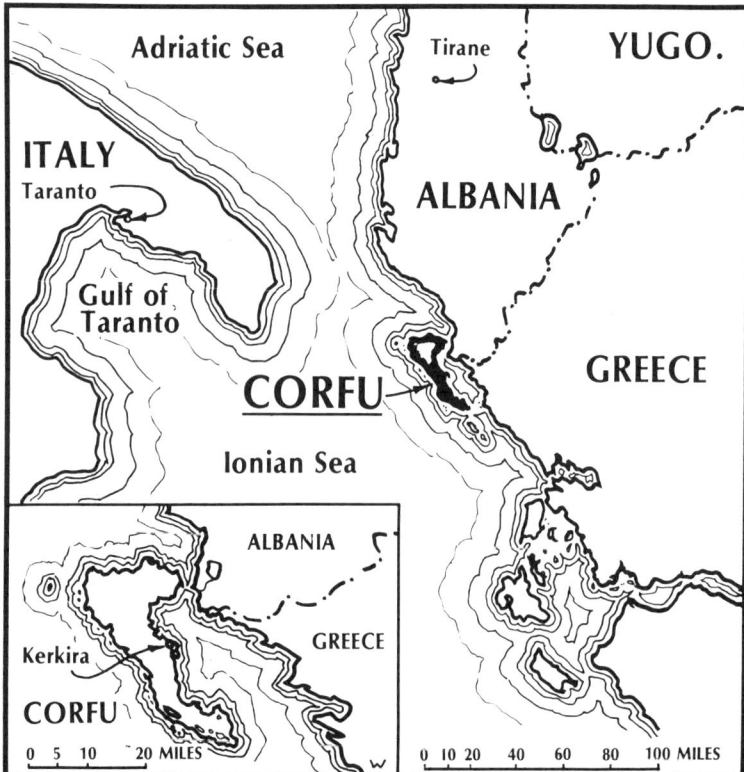

Area: 229 sq. miles
Pop: 94,686 (1895)
97,412 (1961)

An island in the Ionian group off the west coast of Greece, Corfu was under Italian occupation during 1923 and again in WWII. Italian stamps were overprinted during the first occupation, and Greek stamps were similarly treated during the WWII occupation.

Area: 34,054 sq. miles
Pop: 239,570 (1895)
564,147 (1970)
Capital: Corrientes

Corrientes is a province in north-eastern Argentina. Stamps were issued from 1856-78. The first issue is remarkable for its similarity to the first stamps of France, and it seems obvious that they are copies.

CRETE, ISLAND OF

Area: 3,189 sq. miles
Pop: 294,192 (1885)
483,075 (1961)

A Greek island in the Mediterranean Sea, Crete was once part of the Turkish Empire. During a period of instability from 1898 to 1908 it was under the joint administration of Britain, France, Italy, and Russia. In 1908 it became Greek. Stamps were issued by the various powers as well as the Cretan government.

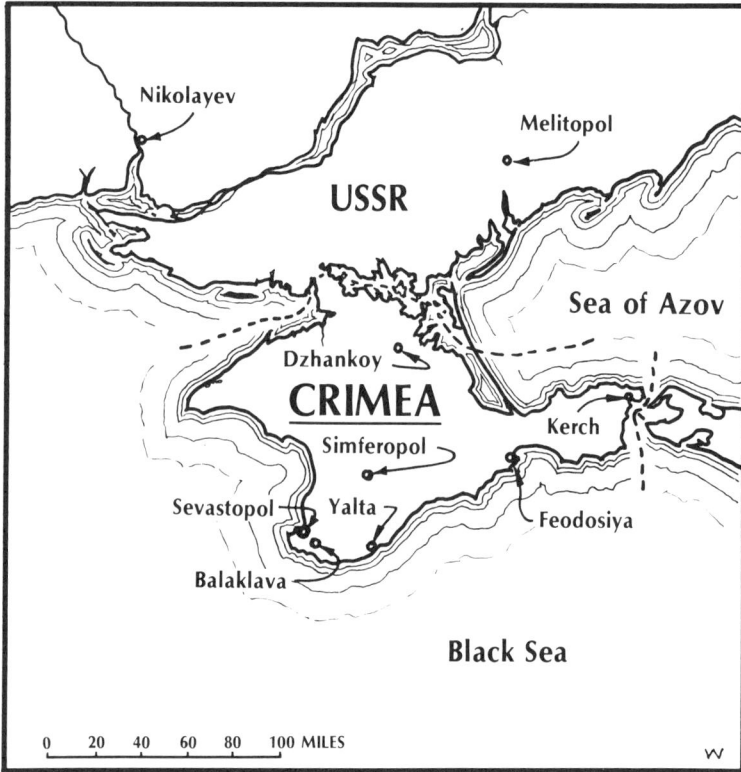

Area: 10,425 sq. miles
Pop: 1,814,000 (1970)
Capital: Simferopol

The Crimea is a peninsula extending into the Black Sea from its northern shore. Part of the USSR, it is joined to the mainland by the Isthmus of Perekop. The area was the scene of the Crimean War in 1854-56 fought by Britain, France, and Sardinia against the Russians. It also was the site of bitter fighting during WWII. Stamps were issued for use there during 1919-20.

─────── CROATIA, CONSTITUENT REPUBLIC OF ───────

Area: 21,829 sq. miles
Pop: 4,422,564 (1971)
Capital: Zagreb

Croatia was an area of the Austro-Hungarian Empire that became part of Yugoslavia following WWII. During WWII, it was made nominally independent by the German and Italian occupiers, and stamps were issued during that period. After the war it was reunited with Yugoslavia as a constituent republic.

Pop: 5,113 (1894)
67,869 (1970)

Cuautla is a resort town containing sulfur springs in the Mexican state of Morelos. It is about 18 miles south southeast of Cuernavaca at an altitude of about 4,350 feet. A provisional stamp was issued there in 1867, during the unsettled period following the ouster of the French from Mexico.

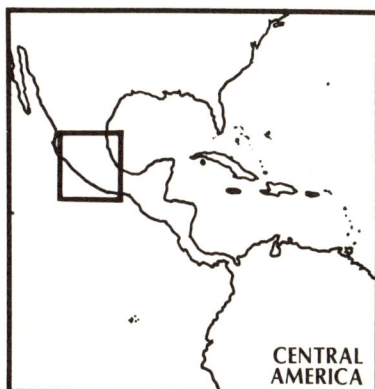

CENTRAL AMERICA

Tampico

Gulf of Mexico

Queretaro

Veracruz

Federal District
Mexico City
Cuernavaca
Puebla
Taxco
MORELOS
CUAUTLA

Acapulco

MEXICO

Pacific Ocean

0 25 50 100 MILES

CUCUTA, CITY OF ————————

Pop: 167,404 (1968)

Cucuta is the capital city of Norte de Santander Department in the Republic of Colombia. The city was rebuilt after being largely destroyed by an earthquake in 1875. Provisional government stamps were issued in the city during 1900. The first issue is inscribed "GOBIERNO PROVISORIO." The second issue bears the inscription "GOBIERNO PROVISIONAL."

SOUTH AMERICA

Caribbean Sea

Cartagena

PANAMA

Norte de Santander

VENEZUELA

CUCUTA

Medellin

Bogota

COLOMBIA

0 50 100 200 MILES

Pop: 8,554 (1895)
44,278 (1969)

Cuernavaca is a resort town in Morelos State, Mexico, located at an altitude of about 5,050 feet. The Cacahuamilpa Caverns, among the largest in North America, are nearby. A handstamped provisional stamp was issued in the town in 1867, during the unsettled period following the ouster of the French from Mexico.

——————CUNDINAMARCA, DEPARTMENT OF——————

Area: 8,638 sq. miles
Pop: 595,000 (1900 est.)
1,165,095 (1968)
Capital: Bogota

Formerly a state in the Granadine Confederation, Cundinamarca is now a department of Colombia. Stamps were issued from 1870 to 1904, under an arrangement whereby the department retained stamp-issuing rights.

Area: 182 sq. miles
Pop: 143,778 (1969 est.)
Capital: Willemstad

An island in the Caribbean Sea off the coast of Venezuela, Curacao is part of the Netherlands Antilles. Stamps for use in Curacao and other islands in the Netherlands Antilles were inscribed ''CURACAO'' from 1873 to 1949. It now uses stamps of the Netherlands Antilles.

──────CUZCO, DEPARTMENT OF──────

Area: 29,430 sq. miles
Pop: 238,445 (1876)
    742,100 (1969 est.)
Capital: Cuzco

Cuzco is a department in the southern part of Peru. The capital city of the same name is located at an altitude of 11,000 feet and was once the capital of the Inca Empire. Provisional stamps were issued there from 1881 to 1885, during the shortage caused by the Chilean occupation of Lima and Callao.

Mediterranean Sea

Derna (Darnah)
Apollonia
Barce (Al Marj)
Tocra
Cyrene
Bengasi (Benghazi)
Bomba
Marble Arch
Jabal al Akhdar
El Adem
Agedabia
El Agheila
Giarabub (al Jaghbub)
Tobruk (Tubruq)
Bardia
Sidi Barrani

LIBYA

EGYPT

CYRENAICA

Continues south to
border with Chad

0   50   100   150   200 MILES

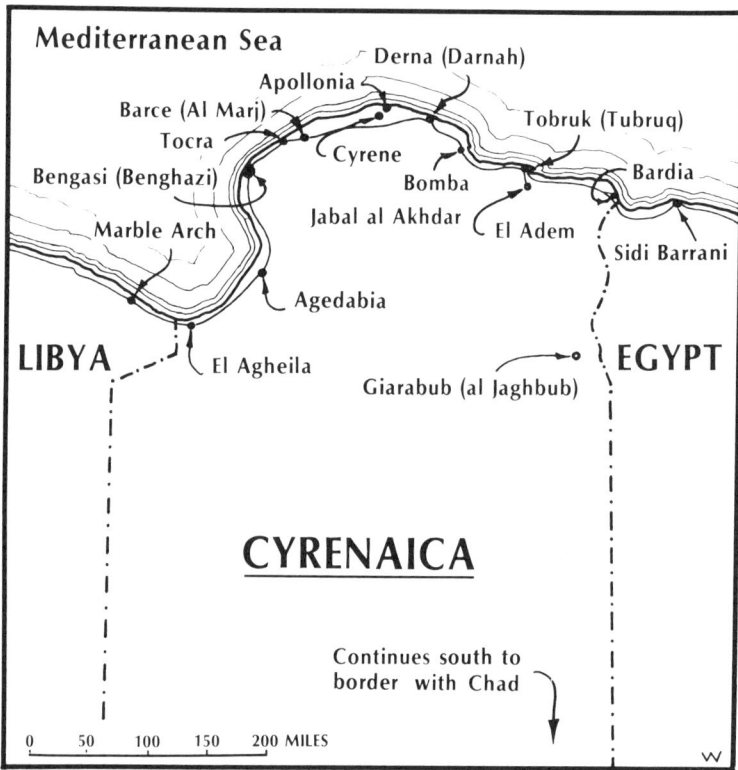

Area: 330,258 sq. miles
Pop: 350,024 (1963)
Capital: Bengasi

Formerly part of the Turkish Empire, Cyrenaica was taken by Italy during its 1911-12 war with Turkey and made an Italian colony. Along with Tripolitania, it later became part of Libya. It borders on Egypt on the east and much development took place along the coast during the Italian occupation.

AFRICA

━━━━━━━━ DAHOMEY, COLONY OF ━━━━━━━

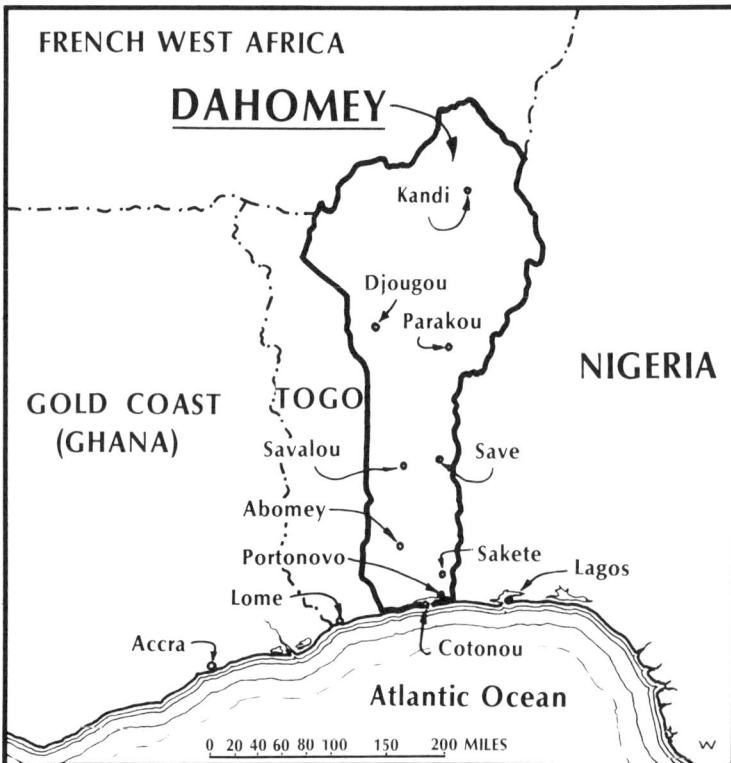

FRENCH WEST AFRICA

DAHOMEY

Kandi

Djougou
Parakou

NIGERIA

GOLD COAST
(GHANA)

TOGO

Savalou
Save

Abomey

Portonovo
Sakete
Lagos

Lome

Accra
Cotonou

Atlantic Ocean

0 20 40 60 80 100   150   200 MILES

Area: 43,483 sq. miles
Pop: 2,718,000 (1970)
Capital: Portonovo

Dahomey was a French colony in West Africa from 1894 to 1946, when it was made an Overseas Territory of France. It achieved independence in 1958 and in 1975 changed its name to the People's Republic of Benin. Stamps were issued from 1899 to 1945, when stamps of French West Africa went into use.

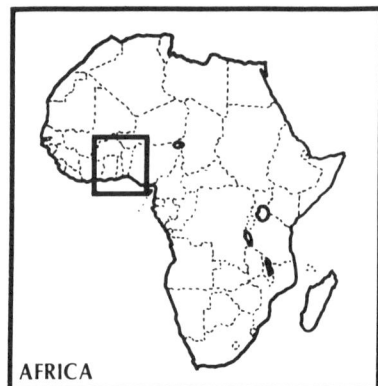

AFRICA

Pop: 4 million (1970 combined)

Twin cities on the Liao-tung Peninsula, Dairen and Port Arthur are now known as Ta-lien and Lu-shun, respectively. They were made a postal district of China in 1946. Formerly in the puppet state of Manchukuo, the area is now part of the People's Republic of China. Stamps were issued from 1946 and comprised overprints on issues of Manchukuo.

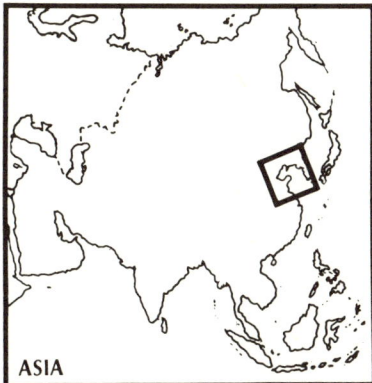

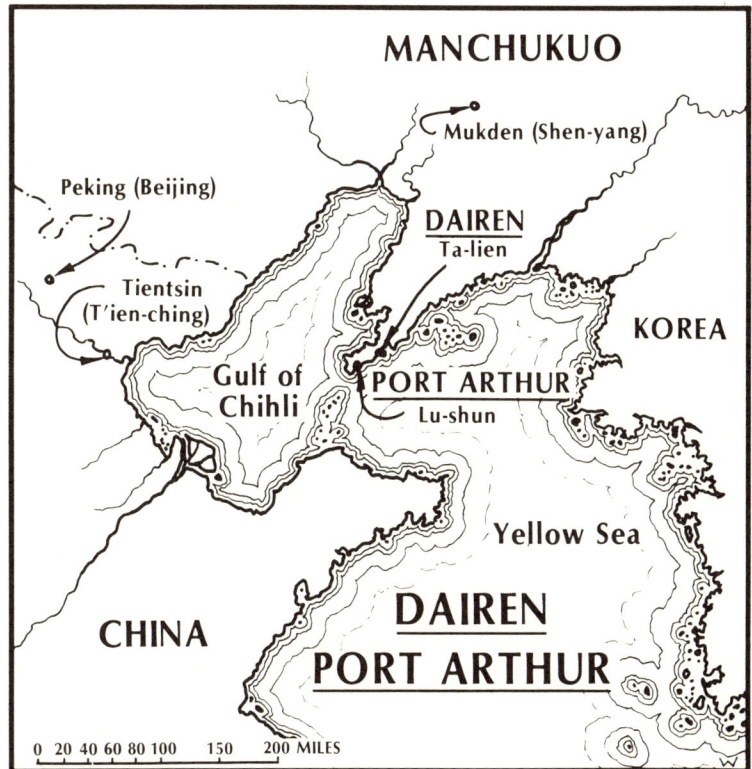

MANCHUKUO

Mukden (Shen-yang)

Peking (Beijing)

DAIREN
Ta-lien

Tientsin
(T'ien-ching)

KOREA

Gulf of
Chihli

PORT ARTHUR
Lu-shun

Yellow Sea

CHINA

DAIREN
PORT ARTHUR

0 20 40 60 80 100   150   200 MILES

ASIA

DAKAR-ABIDJAN, CITIES OF

Dakar and Abidjan were the capital cities of the French colonies of Senegal and Ivory Coast, respectively. Both were part of French West Africa. During the period when the various units were becoming independent, a French West African stamp was released on March 21, 1959, inscribed with the names of the two cities.

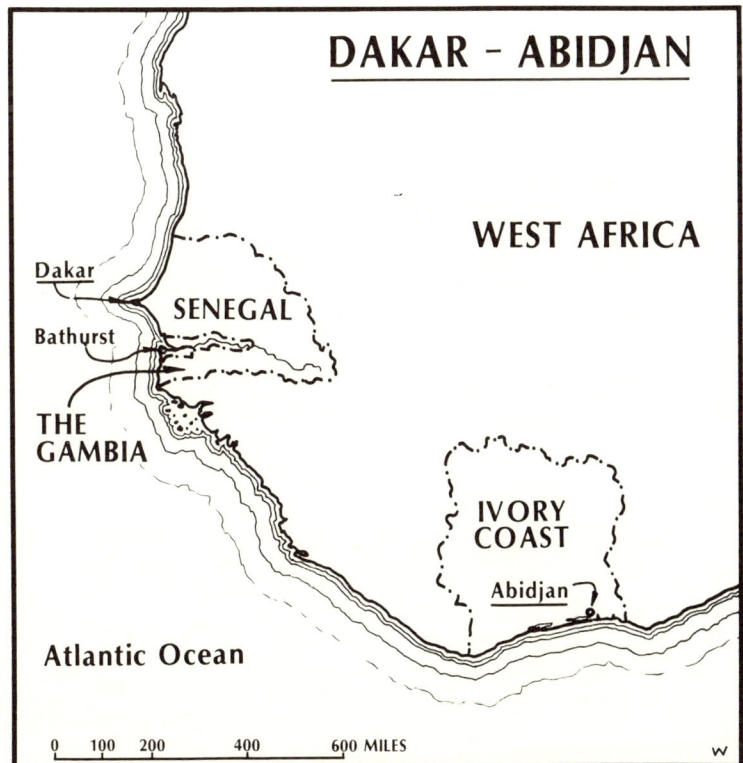

DAKAR - ABIDJAN

WEST AFRICA

Dakar

SENEGAL

Bathurst

THE
GAMBIA

IVORY
COAST

Abidjan

Atlantic Ocean

0   100   200   400   600 MILES

AFRICA

BOSNIA
HERZEGOVINA
(now part of YUGOSLAVIA)

Zadar

Sibenik

Split

Sarajevo

Dubrovnik

MONTENEGRO

DALMATIA

TURKEY

ITALY

Adriatic Sea

0 10 20   40   60   80   100 MILES

EUROPE

Area: 4,916 sq. miles
Pop: 18,720 (1921)
Capital: Zara (Zadar)

Dalmatia is a region on the Adriatic coast of Yugoslavia and includes many islands in the Adriatic Sea. Stamps were issued in 1919-22 during an Italian occupation of the area and also during WWII, while the Germans were occupying Zara.

━━━━━━DANISH WEST INDIES, COLONY OF━━━━━━

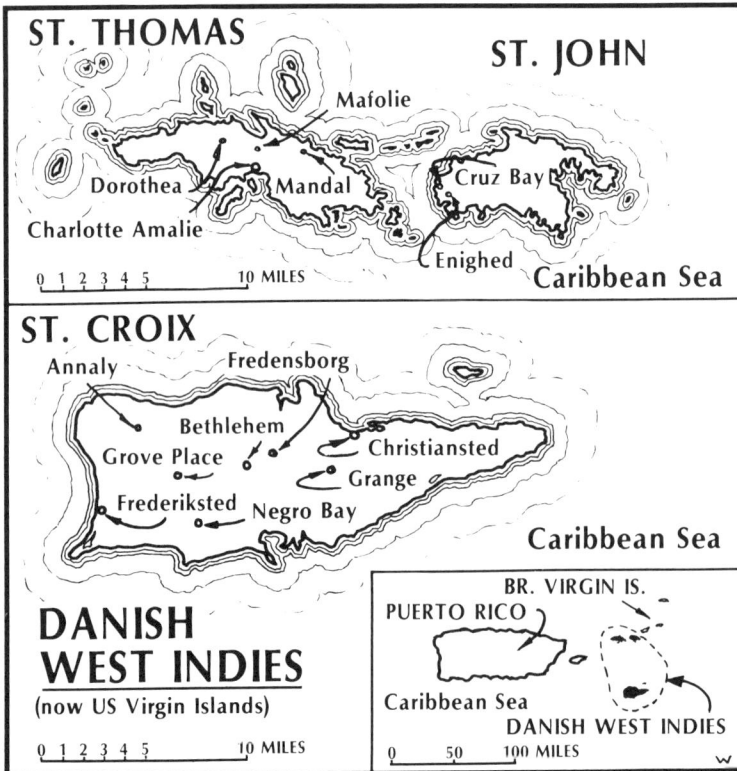

ST. THOMAS

ST. JOHN

Mafolie

Dorothea   Mandal

Cruz Bay

Charlotte Amalie

Enighed

Caribbean Sea

0 1 2 3 4 5   10 MILES

ST. CROIX

Annaly   Fredensborg

Bethlehem

Grove Place   Christiansted

Grange

Frederiksted   Negro Bay

Caribbean Sea

DANISH
WEST INDIES
(now US Virgin Islands)

0 1 2 3 4 5   10 MILES

BR. VIRGIN IS.

PUERTO RICO

Caribbean Sea

DANISH WEST INDIES

0   50   100 MILES

CENTRAL
AMERICA

Area: 132 sq. miles
Pop: 27,085 (1911)
Capital: Charlotte Amalie

The Danish West Indies was a colony of Denmark in the Lesser Antilles of the West Indies. It was bought by the US in 1917 and is now the US Virgin Islands. During the Danish period, stamps were issued beginning in 1855.

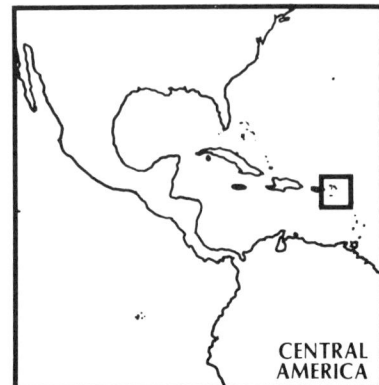

Area: 755 sq. miles
Pop: 407,000 (1939 est.)

A former free city and state on the Baltic coast, Danzig had been part of Germany until WWI, when it was made a free city. In 1939, it was invaded by Germany and absorbed. It was liberated at the end of the war and given to Poland. It is now the Polish city of Gdansk. Stamps were issued during its era as a free city.

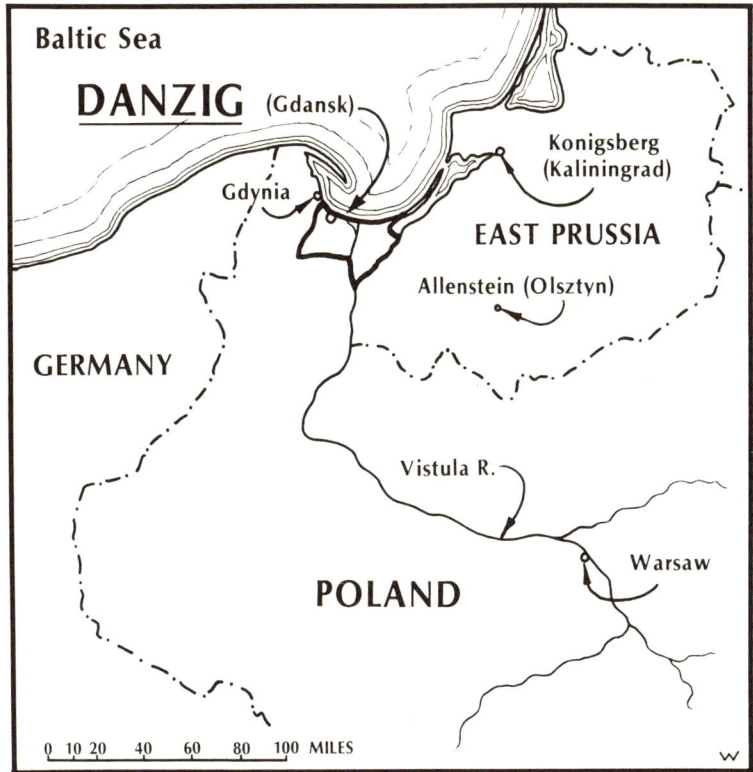

DARDANELLES, REGION OF

The Dardanelles is the name given to the Strait between the Gallipoli Peninsula and Asian Turkey and to a portion of the Turkish mainland, including the city of Canakkale. It was the scene of bitter fighting in WWI. During 1910, Russian stamps were overprinted "DARDANELLES" for use at a Russian post office in the area.

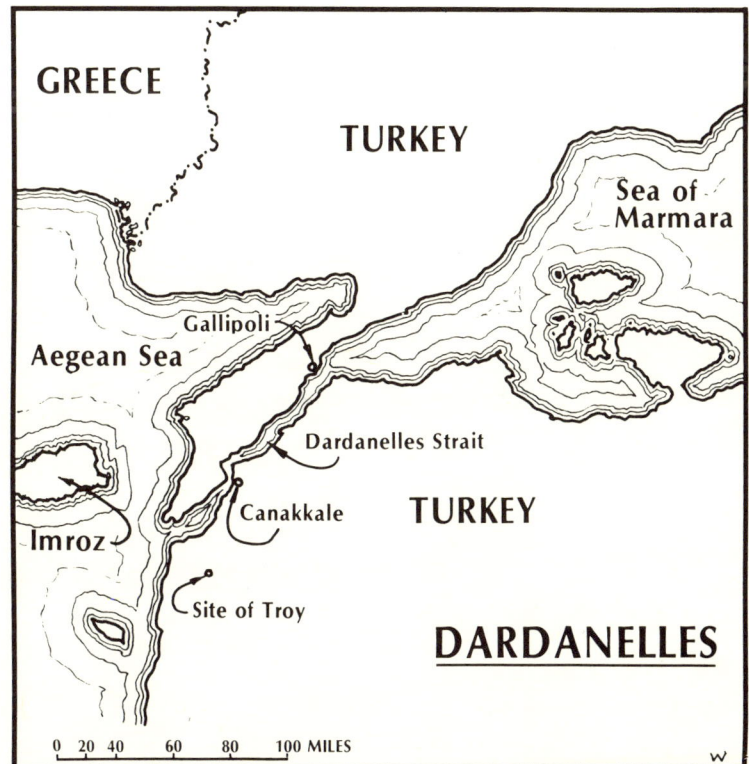

Area: 172 sq. miles
Pop: 75,000 (1900)
     155,122 (1970)

A town and district in eastern Hungary, Debrecen was occupied by Romanian forces at the end of WWI. The occupiers issued a number of stamps during 1919-20.

——— DEDEAGH (ALEXANDROUPOLIS), CITY OF ———

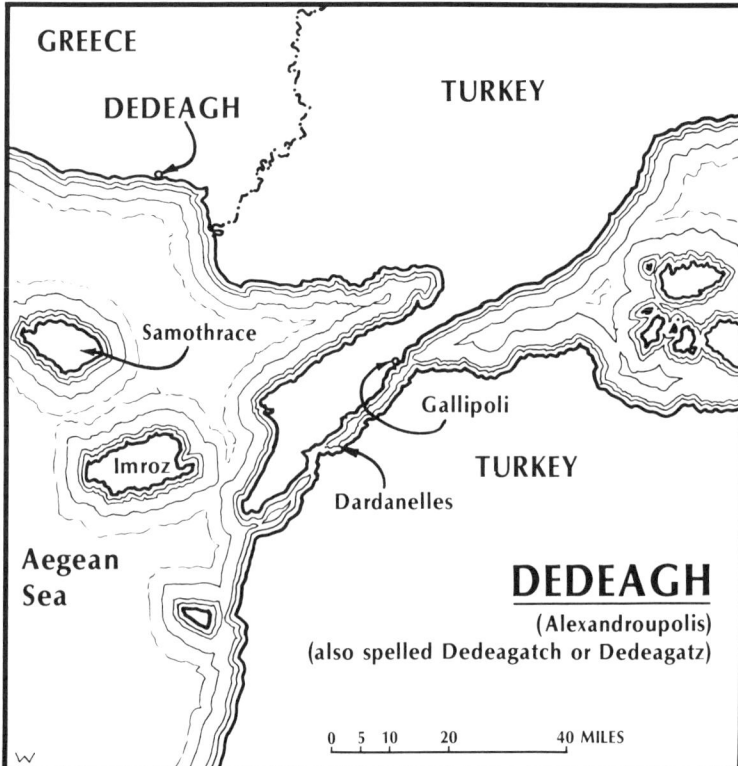

Pop: 3,000 (1900 est.)
     25,124 (1971)

A seaport city and capital of Evros Department, Dedeagh (Dedeagatz or Dedeagatch, now Alexandroupolis) was in Turkish territory until becoming part of Greece. Stamps were issued for a French post office there from 1893 to 1903, and Greece issued stamps for the city in 1913.

Pop: 5,000 (1900 est.)
40,237 (1968)

Diego-Suarez is a harbor and port city located at the northern tip of the island of Madagascar in the Indian Ocean. It was formerly a French naval base and administered as a separate French colony from 1885 to 1896. The town and its fortifications were laid out in the late 19th century by then Colonel Joffre, later to become a top French general of WWI and a Marshal of France.

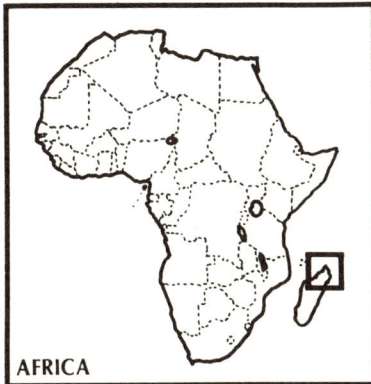

AFRICA

DIEGO-SUAREZ

Indian Ocean

Nossi Be

Mozambique Channel

Ambilobe

Analalava

Antalaha

Maroantsetra

Majunga

Maevatanana

MADAGASCAR

Maintirano

Tamatave

0   50   100 MILES

DOBRUDJA, REGION OF

Area: 8,979 sq. miles

Dobrudja is a province of Romania located between the Danube River and the Black Sea. The chief town is Constanta. The area was occupied by Bulgarian forces during WWI. A portion in the south became Bulgarian after WWII. Stamps were issued by the Bulgarian occupying forces in 1916. They consisted of Cyrillic overprints on Bulgarian stamps including the dates "1916-1917."

EUROPE

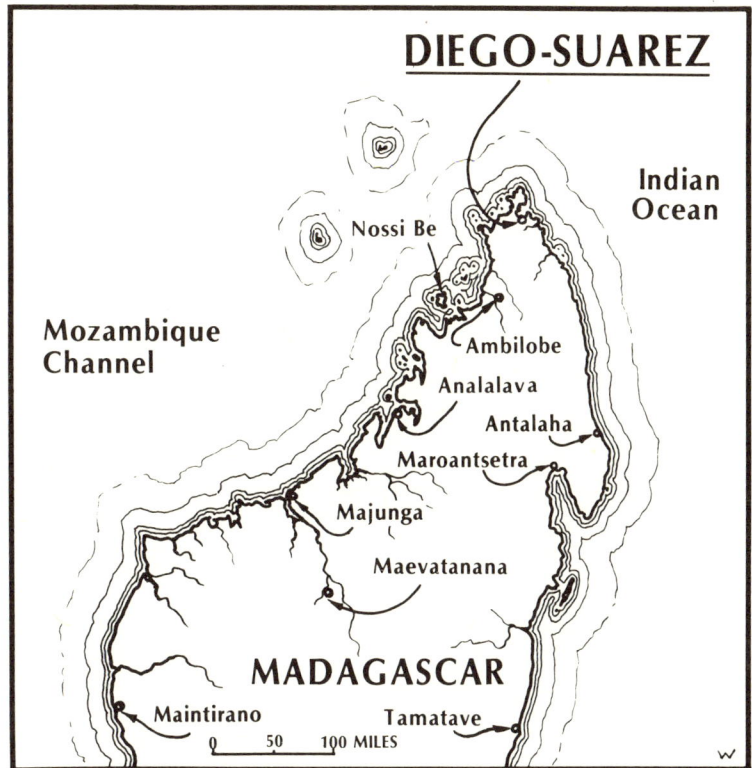

ROMANIA

DOBRUDJA
(Dobrogea)

USSR

Odessa

Galati

Ploiesti

Bucharest

Tulcea

Constanta

Danube River

Black Sea

BULGARIA

Varna

0   20   40   60   80   100 MILES

Area: 1,035 sq. miles
Pop: 140,848 (1936)

The Dodecanese Islands constitute a group in the Aegean Sea off the Turkish coast. They were occupied by Italy during its 1911-1912 war with Turkey and went to Greece at the end of WWII. They are now a department of that country. The following list gives the names used during the period of Italian occupation (with some variations) and the Greek names currently in use: Calchi (now Khalki), Calino or Calimno (now Kalimnos), Caso (now Kasos), Coo or Cos (now Kos), Lero (now Leros), Lisso or Lipso (now Lipsoi), Nisiro (now Nisiros), Patmo (now Patmos), Piscopi (now Tilos), Rhodes or Rhodi (now Rodhos), Scarpanto (now Karpathos), Simi (unchanged), Stampalia (now Astipalaia), and Castelrosso (now Kastellorizon). The latter island joined the group in 1921. The islands are popular with tourists because of their favorable climate and beauty.

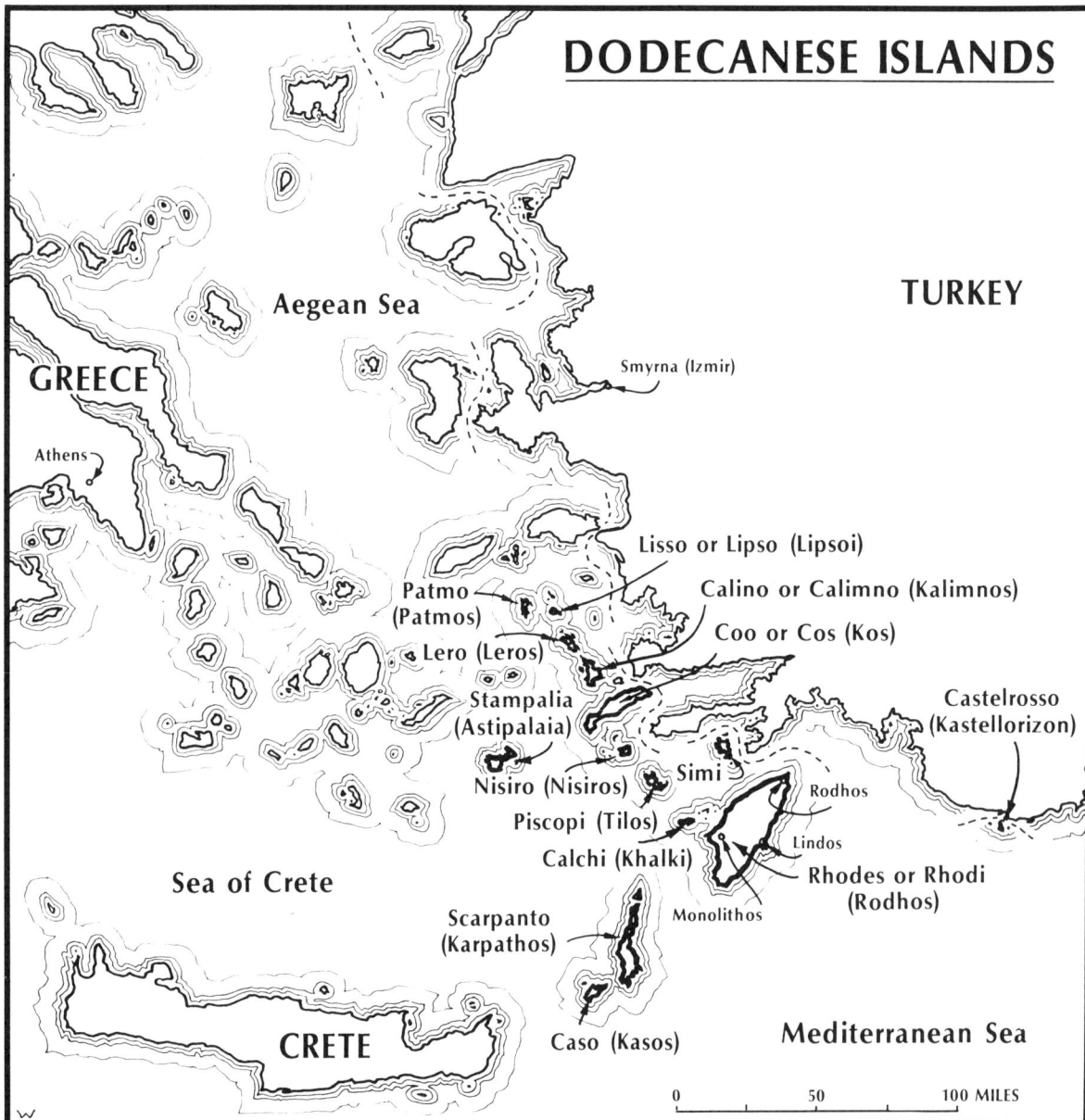

EUROPE

DODECANESE ISLANDS

Aegean Sea

TURKEY

GREECE

Smyrna (Izmir)

Athens

Lisso or Lipso (Lipsoi)

Patmo (Patmos)

Calino or Calimno (Kalimnos)

Coo or Cos (Kos)

Lero (Leros)

Castelrosso (Kastellorizon)

Stampalia (Astipalaia)

Nisiro (Nisiros)

Simi

Piscopi (Tilos)

Rodhos

Calchi (Khalki)

Lindos

Sea of Crete

Rhodes or Rhodi (Rodhos)

Scarpanto (Karpathos)

Monolithos

CRETE

Caso (Kasos)

Mediterranean Sea

0   50   100 MILES

Pop: 130,000 (1978 est.)

Doha is the chief town and capital city of the Persian Gulf state of Qatar. In the 1950s, during the period of British protection of the Persian Gulf states, the British Postal Agencies in Eastern Arabia used their stamps at the Doha post office. The city has grown enormously in recent years as Qatar became a major oil-producing state. During the 1950s its population was recorded as about 10,000.

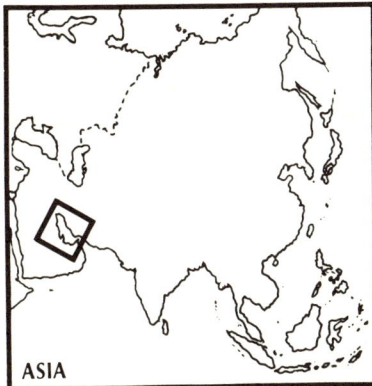

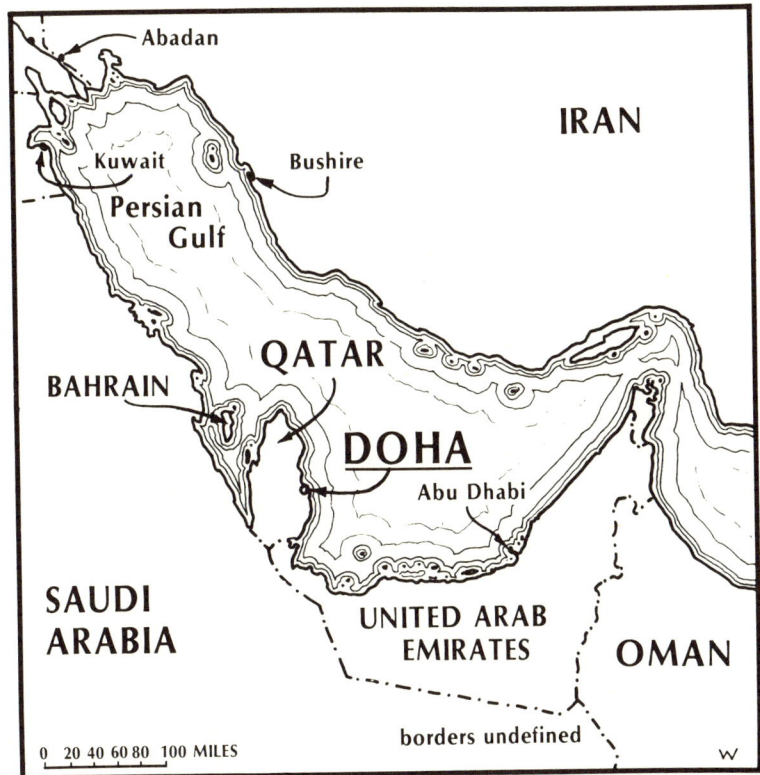

DORPAT

Pop: 87,000 (1969)

Also known as Tartu, Dorpat is a city in what was once the independent country of Estonia. It is now part of the USSR. Stamps were issued by German forces occupying the town during WWI in the form of surcharges on Russian stamps. In WWII the Germans issued specially designed stamps.

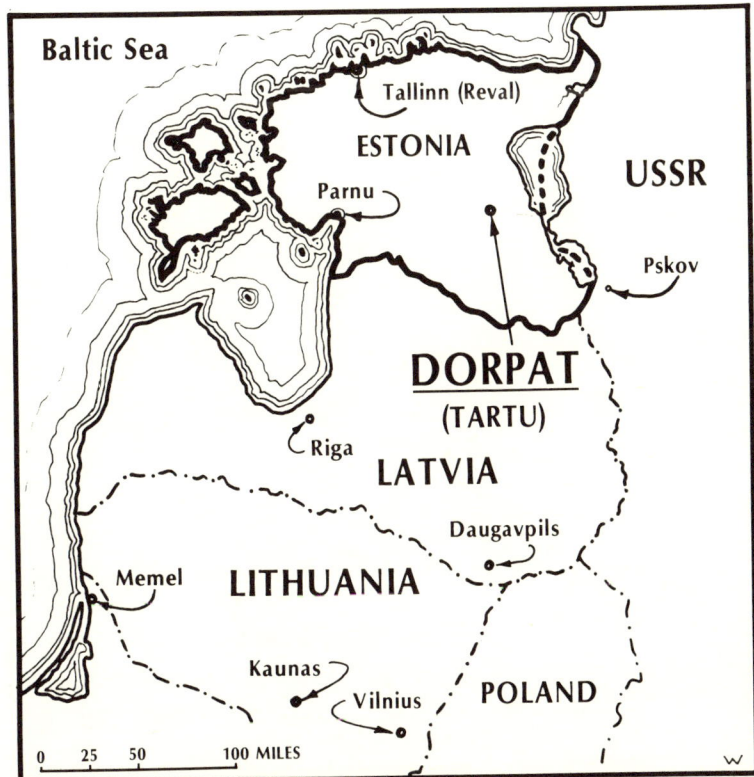

DURAZZO (DURRES), CITY OF

Pop: 53,160 (1967 est.)

Durazzo (now Durres) is a seaport city on the Adriatic coast of Albania. During WWI, the city was occupied by the Italians in 1915 and the Austrians in 1916. Its naval base was destroyed by the Allies. Stamps were issued in 1909-1916 for use at an Italian post office in the city. They are surcharges on stamps of Italy.

EASTERN RUMELIA (SOUTH BULGARIA), REGION OF

Area: 12,585 sq. miles
Pop: 992,386 (1893 est.)
Chief City: Philippopolis

Eastern Rumelia was the name given to an area of the Turkish Empire that acquired autonomous provincial status within the empire in 1878. It became part of Bulgaria as South Bulgaria in 1885, an act that sparked the 1885-86 war with Serbia. Stamps were issued for Eastern Rumelia from 1880 to 1886.

Area: 1,987 sq. miles

A former duchy of Austria-Hungary, Eastern Silesia at the end of WWI was divided between Poland and Czechoslovakia with the new border running through the town of Teschen. Stamps were issued in 1920, during a plebiscite period, but the plebiscite was not held. The stamps consisted of a wide range of Czechoslovak stamps overprinted "SO 1920."

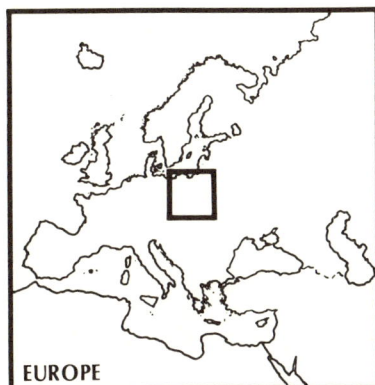

Konigsberg (Kaliningrad)

EAST PRUSSIA

Danzig (Gdansk)

GERMANY

POLAND

Breslau (Wroclaw)

EASTERN SILESIA

SILESIA

Krakow

Teschen (Now divided into Czech Cesky Tesin and Polish Cieszyn)

Brno

Troppau (Ostrava)

CZECHOSLAVAKIA

0 20 40 60 80 100 MILES

EUROPE

EASTERN SZECHWAN, REGION OF

Chief city: Chungking

This region is the eastern portion of the Chinese province of Szechwan. The area gained importance during the period of Japanese invasion of China in the years prior to WWII. The town of Chungking became the capital of China. Stamps were overprinted for use there in the early 1940s during a period of many such regional overprints.

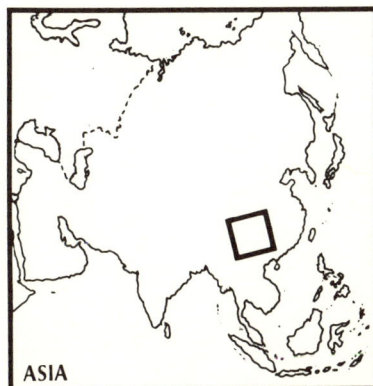

TSINGHAI

KANSU

SHENSI

EASTERN SZECHWAN

Yangtze River

Ch'eng-tu

Chungking (Ch'ung-ch'ing)

HUPEH

HUNAN

YUNNAN

KWEICHOW

0 20 40 60 80 100   150   200   300 MILES

ASIA

An ancient territory located in what is now northern Greece and southern Albania, it was Turkish until, by 1919, Greece had come into possession of the area. The post-WWI settlement put the border of Greece opposite the northern part of the island of Corfu, with the rest of Epirus becoming part of Albania. It was a major battlefield between Greece and Italy during WWII. Stamps were issued in a number of cities in the area prior to WWI.

ERITREA, COLONY OF

Area: 15,755 sq. miles
Pop: 600,575 (1931 est.)
Capital: Asmara

This was an area on the Red Sea that became the Italian colony of Eritrea in 1890 and was used as a base for the Italian invasion of Ethiopia in 1935. Liberated by British forces in 1941, Eritrea was under military administration until becoming federated with Ethiopia in 1952. It became an Ethiopian province in 1962. Recently it has been the site of considerable political unrest.

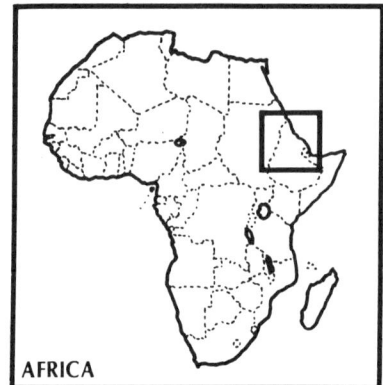

Area: 17,413 sq. miles
Pop: 1,357,000 (1970)
Capital: Tallinn

Now part of the Soviet Union, Estonia was an independent country from 1918 to 1940, when it was annexed to the USSR as the Estonian SSR. The US has never recognized this takeover. Stamps were issued during the period of freedom, and German occupation stamps were used during both WWI and WWII.

EUROPE

─── EUPEN AND MALMEDY ───

Area: 382 sq. miles

This was an area of Germany taken by Belgium at the end of WWI and awarded to that country by the Treaty of Versailles in 1919. The area was occupied by Germany during WWII and liberated Sept. 12, 1944. Belgian stamps were overprinted both jointly for Eupen and Malmedy and separately for each area during 1919-21.

EUROPE

FAR EASTERN REPUBLIC

SIBERIA

Lake Baykal

Irkutsk

Approximate area
of Far Eastern Republic
(borders undefined)

Chita

Sea of Okhotsk

Blagoveshchensk

Khabarovsk

MONGOLIA

MANCHURIA

Vladivostok

0 50 100 200 300 400 500 MILES

ASIA

Area: 2,400,000 sq. miles
Pop: 5,780,000 (1970 est.)
Capital: Chita

This area of eastern Siberia was formed in 1920 based on the town of Chita. The Far Eastern Republic was a short-lived state and soon became part of the new Union of Soviet Socialist Republics. Stamps were issued during 1920-1923.

FERNANDO PO, COLONY OF

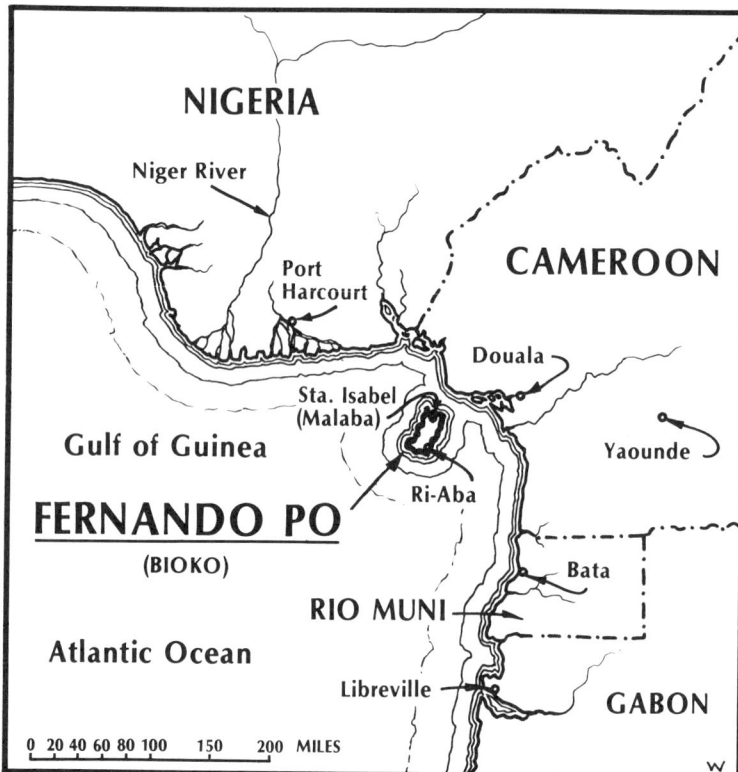

NIGERIA

Niger River

Port
Harcourt

CAMEROON

Douala

Sta. Isabel
(Malaba)

Gulf of Guinea

Yaounde

FERNANDO PO
(BIOKO)

Ri-Aba

Bata

RIO MUNI

Atlantic Ocean

Libreville

GABON

0 20 40 60 80 100   150   200 MILES

AFRICA

Area: 779 sq. miles
Pop: 61,197 (1960)
Capital: Santa Isabel

An island about 60 miles from Douala, Cameroon, Fernando Po was a Portuguese colony and is now part of the Republic of Equatorial Guinea. The town of Santa Isabel is the country's capital city. Stamps were issued from 1868 by the colonial authorities until replaced by those of Equatorial Guinea in 1968.

Area: 27,585 sq. miles
Pop: 1,777,421 (1935 est.)
Capital: Kuala Lumpur

A federation of states on the Malay Peninsula that constituted a British Protectorate, the Federated Malay States comprised the states of Pahang, Perak, Negeri Sembilan, Selangor, and Sungei Ujong. The latter entity had previously become part of Negeri Sembilan. The federation existed from 1895 until the formation of the Federation of Malaya in 1948. The area was occupied by Japan during WWII. It became part of the independent country of Malaysia in 1963. Stamps were issued from 1900 and included the famous "Leaping Tiger" design in use from 1901 to the 1930s. Apart from initial overprints on Negri Sembilan and Perak stamps, the only other stamp design features a group of elephants.

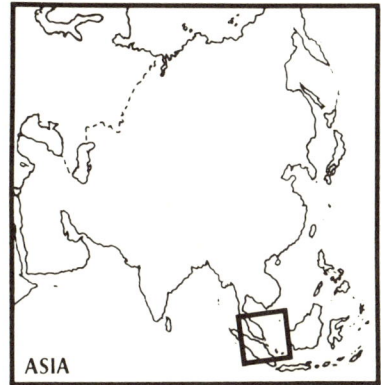

ASIA

FEDERATED MALAY STATES

THAILAND

Alor Setar
KEDAH

Kota Baharu

KELANTAN

PENANG

George Town

PERAK

Kuala Terengganu

TERENGGANU

South China Sea

Strait of Malacca

Ipoh

PAHANG

Kuantan

SELANGOR

Kuala Lumpur

Seremban

SUNGEI UJONG

JOHOR

NEGRI SEMBILAN

MALACCA

Johor Baharu

Singapore

SUMATRA

0 10 20 40 60 80 100 MILES

Map: Fezzan, Libya

TUNISIA

Gulf of Sirte

Tripoli

Bengasi

Ghadames (Ghudamis)

APPROXIMATE AREA
OF **FEZZAN**

LIBYA

Brak (Brach or Birak)

Sebha (Sabhah)

Djerma (Jarmah)

Murzuch (Marzug)

ALGERIA

NIGER

0 25 50 100 200 MILES

CHAD

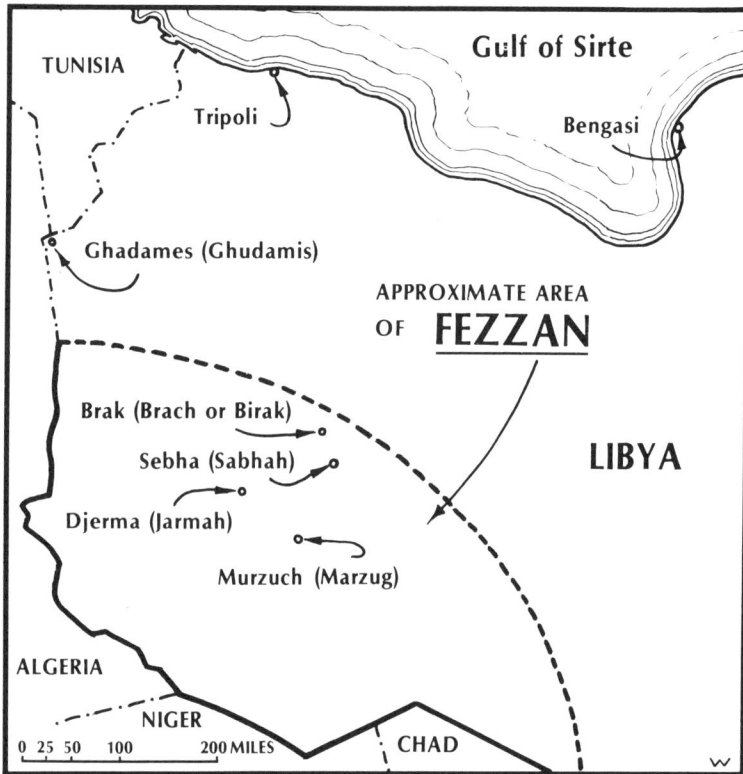

Area: about 213,000 sq. miles
Pop: 78,326 (1964)

Fezzan is an area of Libya. It is located in the southern portion of the country. A region of desert and oases, it was under Turkish control until becoming part of Italian Africa following the 1911-1912 war between the two countries. It was taken by Free French forces in 1942 and was under a military administration until becoming part of the present country of Libya.

AFRICA

FIUME (RIJEKA), FREE CITY OF

Map: Fiume (Rijeka)

AUSTRIA

Italian-Yugoslav border as of 1924

Trento

YUGOSLAVIA

Zagreb

Trieste

FIUME (Rijeka)

Venice

Istria

Susak

Pola

Bologna

Florence

Adriatic Sea

ITALY

0 10 20 40 60 80 100 MILES

Pop: 45,000 (1924 est.)

A seaport town on the Croatian coast of Yugoslavia, Fiume is now known as Rijeka. It had been part of the Austro-Hungarian Empire until the end of WWI, when it was occupied by Italy, which disputed its incorporation into Yugoslavia. Italian irregulars under D'Annunzio took over the town in 1919. The Treaty of Rapallo between Italy and Yugoslavia made it a free city, but despite this agreement, Italy annexed it in 1924.

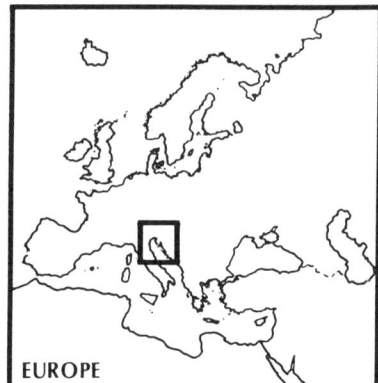

EUROPE

Pop: 900,000 (1970 est.)

Foochow is a seaport on the coast of China about halfway between Shanghai and Hong Kong. Now called Fu-chou, it is the capital of Fukien Province. In the 19th century it became one of the first of the Treaty Ports (q.v.) to be opened to trade with the outside world under the 1842 Treaty of Nanking.

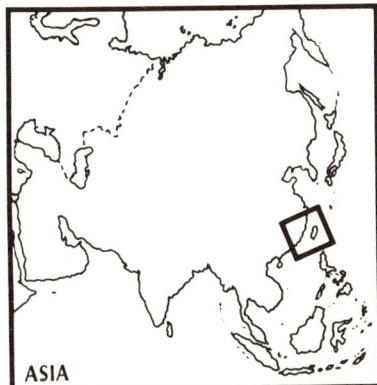

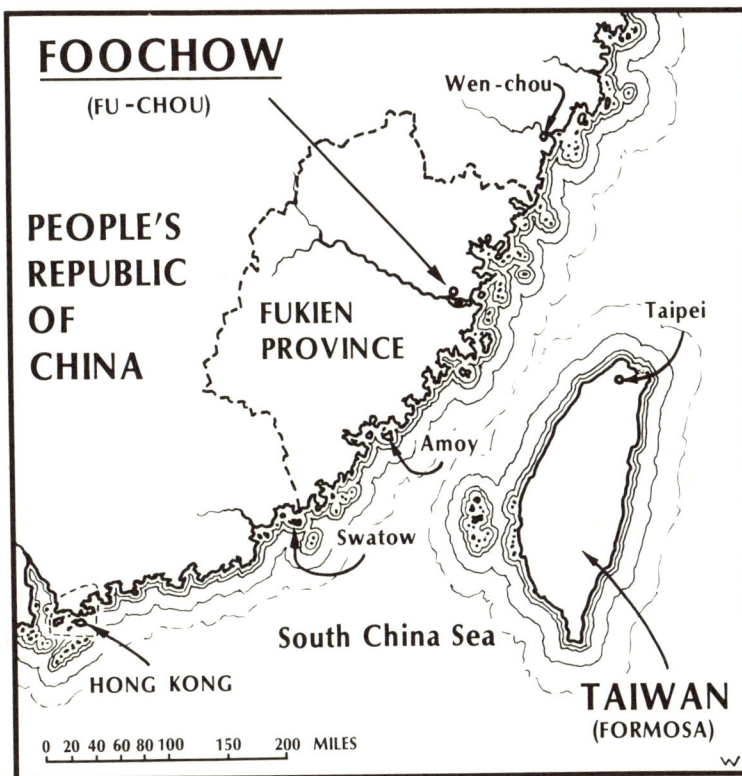

FOOCHOW
(FU-CHOU)

PEOPLE'S REPUBLIC OF CHINA

FUKIEN PROVINCE

Wen-chou

Taipei

Amoy

Swatow

South China Sea

HONG KONG

TAIWAN
(FORMOSA)

0 20 40 60 80 100   150   200 MILES

ASIA

FRENCH EQUATORIAL AFRICA, COLONY OF ————————

Area: 969,112 sq. miles
Pop: 3,127,700 (1934)
Capital: Brazzaville

A former French colony in Central Africa, it was formed in 1936 from Gabon, Middle Congo, Ubangi-Shari, and Chad. In 1958 each of the four became a republic in the French Community. Middle Congo became the People's Republic of the Congo, and Ubangi-Shari is now the Central African Republic. Stamp issues began in 1936 with overprints on stamps of other French colonies.

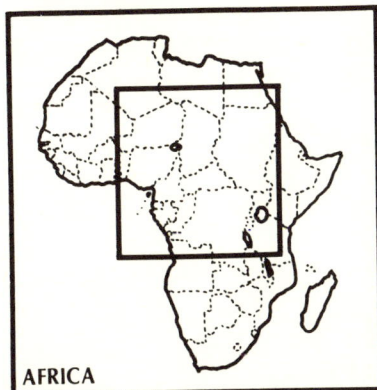

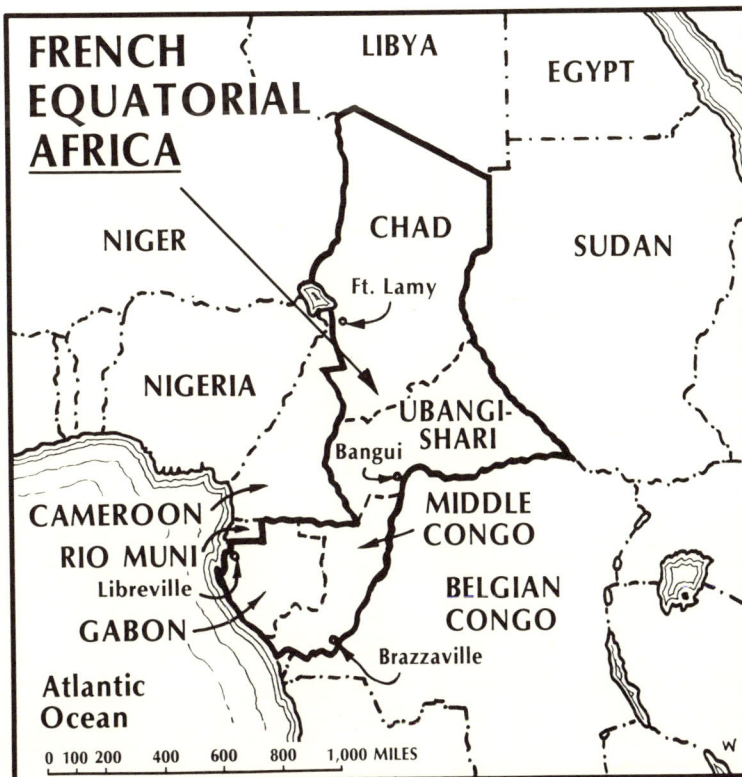

FRENCH EQUATORIAL AFRICA

LIBYA

EGYPT

NIGER

CHAD

SUDAN

Ft. Lamy

NIGERIA

UBANGI-SHARI

Bangui

MIDDLE CONGO

CAMEROON
RIO MUNI

Libreville

BELGIAN CONGO

GABON

Brazzaville

Atlantic Ocean

0 100 200   400   600   800   1,000 MILES

AFRICA

FRENCH GUIANA

Paramaribo

SURINAME

Devil's Island

Cayenne

St. Laurent

Inini

Atlantic
Ocean

BRAZIL

Mouths of
the Amazon

0 20 40 60 80 100   150   200 MILES

SOUTH
AMERICA

Area: 34,749 sq. miles
Pop: 51,000 (1970)
Capital: Cayenne

A former French colony on the north coast of South America, between Suriname and Brazil, French Guiana was the site of Devil's Island, the famous penal colony. It became an overseas department of France in 1946. Stamps were issued from 1886 until 1946. The stamps of France are now used.

———————— FRENCH GUINEA, COLONY OF ————————

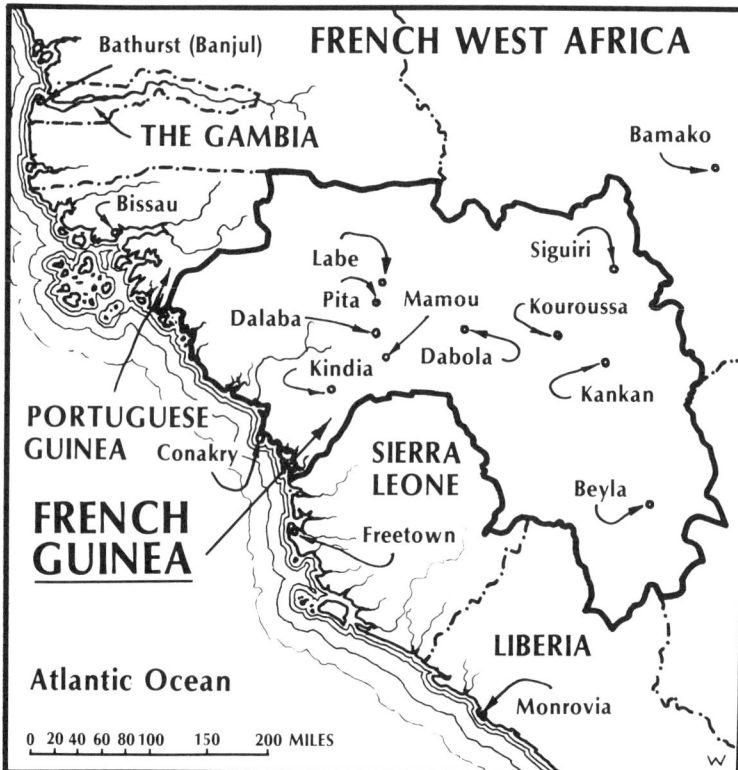

Bathurst (Banjul) **FRENCH WEST AFRICA**

THE GAMBIA

Bamako

Bissau

Labe

Siguiri

Pita

Mamou

Kouroussa

Dalaba

Dabola

Kindia

Kankan

PORTUGUESE
GUINEA   Conakry

**FRENCH
GUINEA**

SIERRA
LEONE

Beyla

Freetown

LIBERIA

Atlantic Ocean

Monrovia

0 20 40 60 80 100   150   200 MILES

AFRICA

Area: 94,925 sq. miles
Pop: 3,920,000 (1970 est.)
Capital: Conakry

A former colony in West Africa, French Guinea is now the Republic of Guinea. Its history as a colony began in 1893, and in 1944 it became a unit of French West Africa until achieving independence in 1958. Stamps were issued from 1893 to 1944, when French West African stamps went into use.

Area: 197 sq. miles
Pop: 323,300 (1941)
Capital: Pondichery

French India consisted of five settlements scattered around the coast of India. They were all that was left of French India after the Napoleonic Wars. Settlements were Chandernagor, Yanaon, Pondichery, Karikal, and Mahe. They were absorbed into the Republic of India between 1949 and 1954.

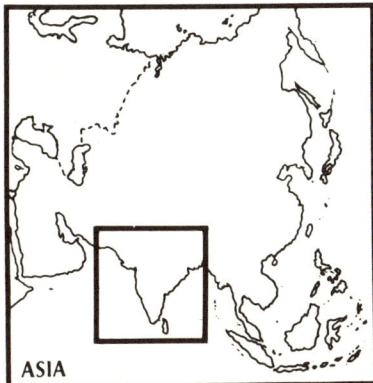

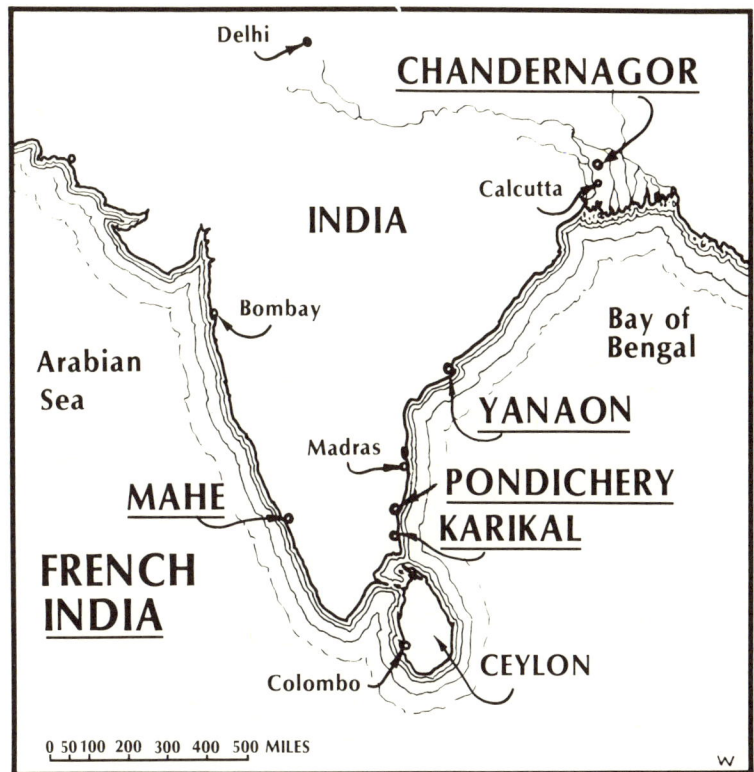

Delhi

CHANDERNAGOR

INDIA

Calcutta

Arabian
Sea

Bombay

Bay of
Bengal

YANAON

Madras

PONDICHERY
KARIKAL

MAHE

FRENCH
INDIA

Colombo

CEYLON

0 50 100 200 300 400 500 MILES

ASIA

FRENCH MOROCCO, PROTECTORATE OF

Area: 153,870 sq. miles
Pop: 6,296,136 (1936)
15,520,000 (1970 as
Kingdom of Morocco)
Capital: Rabat

French influence in Morocco resulted from a 1904 agreement between France and Great Britain, and in 1912 Morocco became a French protectorate. A portion became Spanish Morocco. Both Spanish and French Morocco joined to become independent in 1956 as the Kingdom of Morocco.

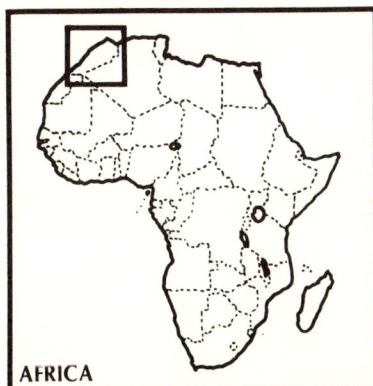

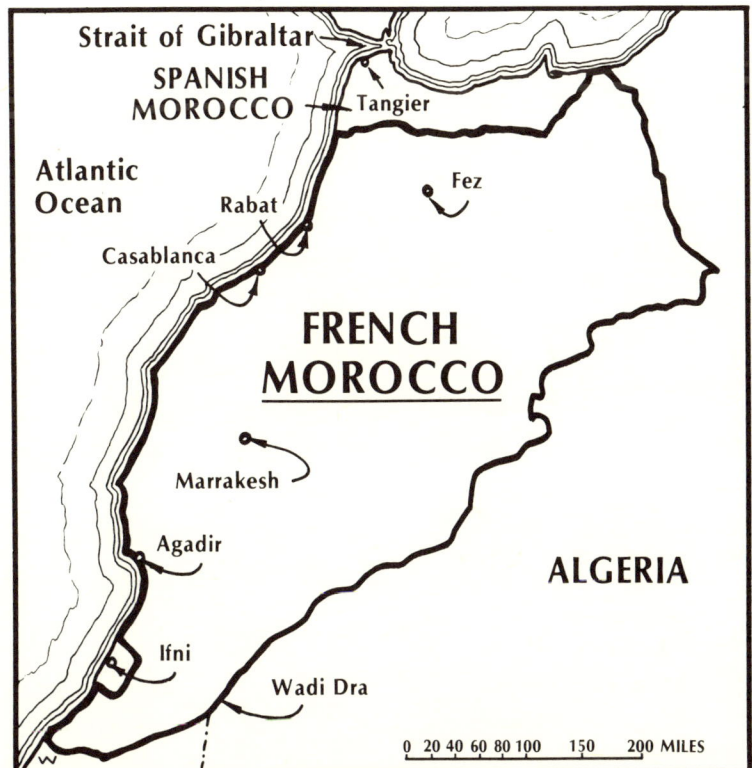

Strait of Gibraltar

SPANISH
MOROCCO

Tangier

Atlantic
Ocean

Fez

Rabat

Casablanca

FRENCH
MOROCCO

Marrakesh

ALGERIA

Agadir

Ifni

Wadi Dra

0 20 40 60 80 100   150   200 MILES

AFRICA

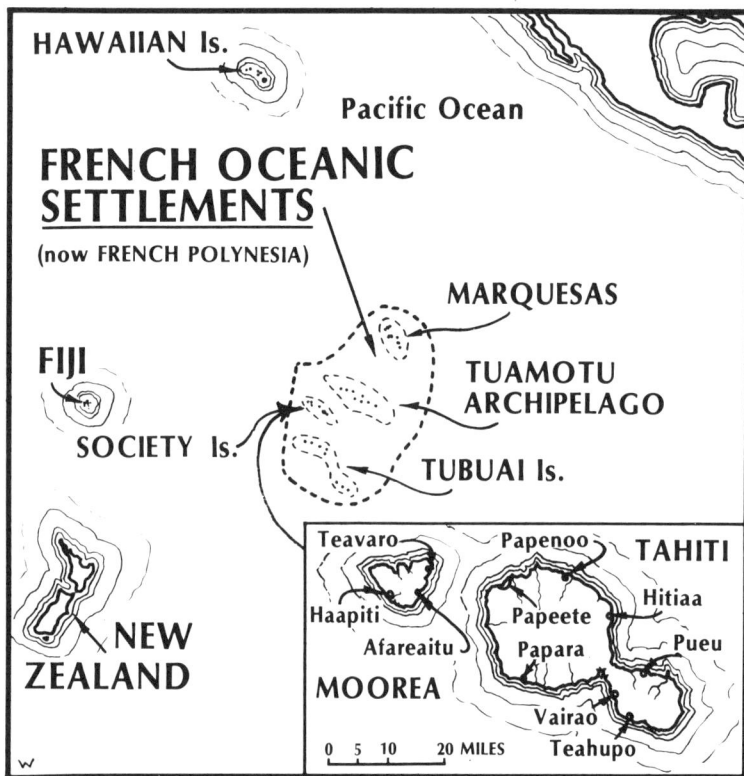

Area: 1,261 sq. miles
Pop: 114,000 (1971 est.)
Capital: Papeete

This French colony was formed in 1903 from a large number of islands covering a wide area of the South Pacific. Included are Tahiti and the other Society Islands, the Marquesas, and the Taumotu Group. Its name was changed to French Polynesia in 1956. The first stamps were issued in 1892.

PACIFIC OCEAN

——— FRENCH SUDAN, COLONY OF ———

Area: 478,652 (approx.)
Pop: 5,031,500 (1970 est.)
Capital: Bamako

A former French colony, in 1899 it was divided among the neighboring French colonies of Dahomey, French Guinea, Ivory Coast, and Senegal and Niger. It was reconstituted in 1921 and became part of French West Africa in 1944. Now it is the independent Republic of Mali.

AFRICA

Area: 1,739,034 sq. miles
Pop: 18,777,163 (est.)
Capital: Dakar

This federation of French colonies in West Africa formed in 1944. It disbanded in 1958 as the individual units achieved independent status within the French Community and later became completely independent. Stamp issues began with surcharges on stamps of Senegal and Mauritania in 1943-44.

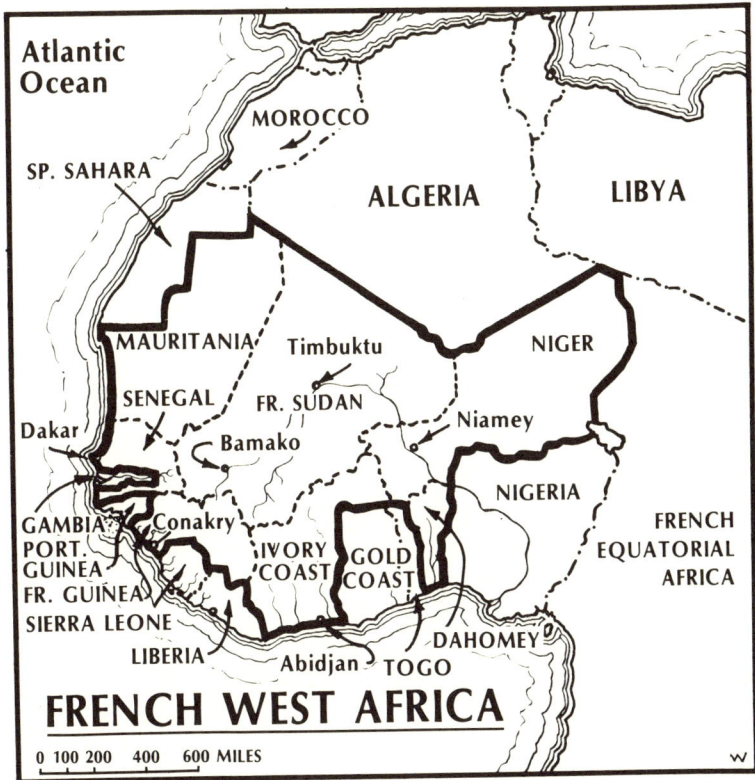

AFRICA

Atlantic Ocean

MOROCCO
SP. SAHARA
ALGERIA
LIBYA
MAURITANIA
Timbuktu
NIGER
SENEGAL
FR. SUDAN
Dakar
Bamako
Niamey
NIGERIA
GAMBIA
PORT. GUINEA
Conakry
IVORY COAST
GOLD COAST
FRENCH EQUATORIAL AFRICA
FR. GUINEA
SIERRA LEONE
LIBERIA
Abidjan
DAHOMEY
TOGO

FRENCH WEST AFRICA

0 100 200 400 600 MILES

FUNCHAL, DISTRICT OF ————

Area: 308 sq. miles
Pop: 150,575 (1900 est.)
   268,700 (1970)
Capital: Funchal

The District of Funchal was located on Madeira in the Atlantic Ocean, which belongs to Portugal. It was a district around the port city of the same name and has long been a popular winter resort. Stamps were issued bearing its name from 1892 to 1905. There were two issues, each bearing a portrait of King Carlos.

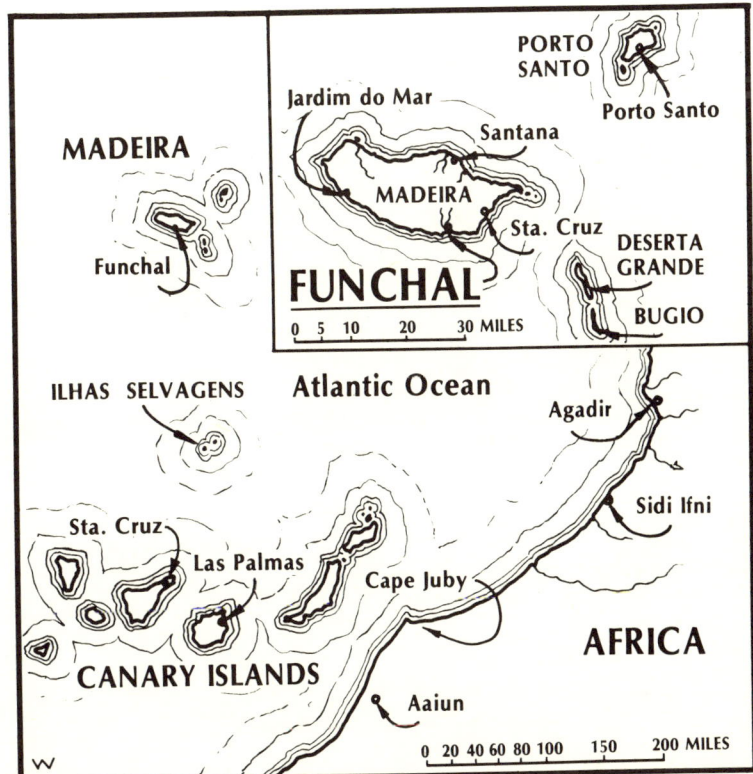

ATLANTIC

PORTO SANTO
MADEIRA
Jardim do Mar
Santana
Porto Santo
MADEIRA
Sta. Cruz
Funchal
DESERTA GRANDE
FUNCHAL
BUGIO

0 5 10 20 30 MILES

ILHAS SELVAGENS
Atlantic Ocean
Agadir
Sta. Cruz
Las Palmas
Cape Juby
Sidi Ifni
CANARY ISLANDS
AFRICA
Aaiun

0 20 40 60 80 100 150 200 MILES

GALAPAGOS

Culpepper (Darwin)
Wenman (Wolf)
Marchena (Bindloe)
Pinta (Abingdon)
Genovesa (Tower)
San Salvador (James)
San Cristobal (Chatham)
Seymour
Isabela (Abermarle)
Baltra
Fernandina (Narborough)
Barrel Mailbox
Espanola (Hood)
Santa Maria (Charles)
Santa Cruz (Indefatigable)

0 20 40 60 80 100 MILES

NORTH AMERICA

ECUADOR

SOUTH AMERICA

GALAPAGOS

Pacific Ocean

SOUTH AMERICA

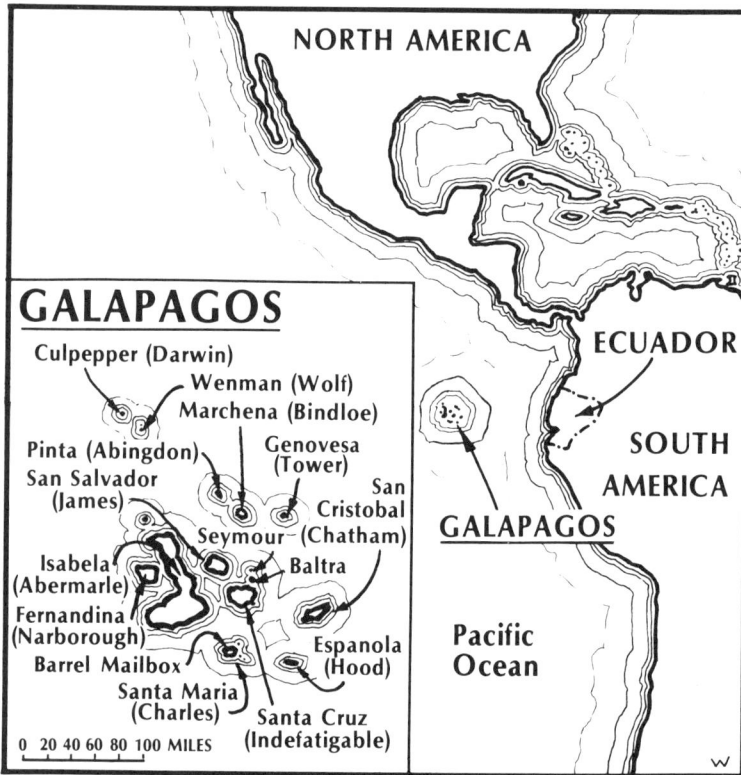

Area: 3,075 sq. miles
Pop: 3,600 (1970 est.)
Capital: San Cristobal

This is an island group in the Pacific Ocean off the coast of Ecuador and constituting a province of that country. The Galapagos are noted for their rich and unusual natural life. Darwin spent some time there during his voyage in HMS *Beagle*. Stamps have been issued bearing the islands' name, although it appears that they were not intended solely for use in the islands.

———————— **GAZA, TERRITORY OF** ————————

Tel-Aviv-Yafo
1949 border
present border
Mediterranean Sea
Jericho
GAZA
Ashdod
Ashquelon
Jerusalem
Amman
Bethlehem
Dead Sea
Khan Yunis
Hebron
GAZA STRIP
Beersheba
El Arish

ISRAEL

EGYPT

JORDAN

SINAI

0 5 10 20 30 40 50 MILES

Gaza is a strip of land some 26 miles long by 4-5 miles wide on the southeastern shore of the Mediterranean Sea around the town of Gaza. Formerly Turkish territory, Gaza was included in the area of Palestine mandated to Britain after WWI. It was under Egyptian control from 1948 to 1967 except for a period from November 1956 to March 1957, when Israel occupied it. Since the 1967 war it has been occupied by Israel.

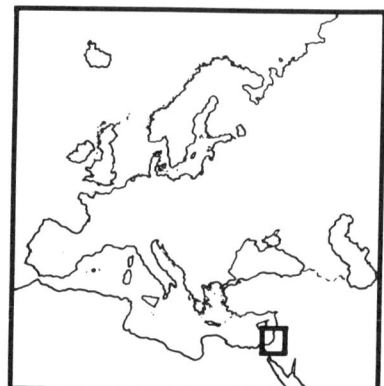

Capital: Warsaw

This was an area of Poland occupied by Germany during both WWI and WWII. A considerable number of special stamps were issued during the longer WWII occupation. At first they were overprints on German stamps, but specially designed stamps were soon released. The area was restored to Poland at war's end.

EUROPE

GENEVA, CANTON OF

Area: 109 sq. miles
Pop: 105,509 (1888)
     331,599 (1970)
Capital: Geneva

Geneva is a canton of Switzerland located in the southwestern portion of the country, around the southern end of Lake Geneva. Stamps were issued by the canton beginning in 1843, prior to the introduction of Swiss federal stamps in 1850.

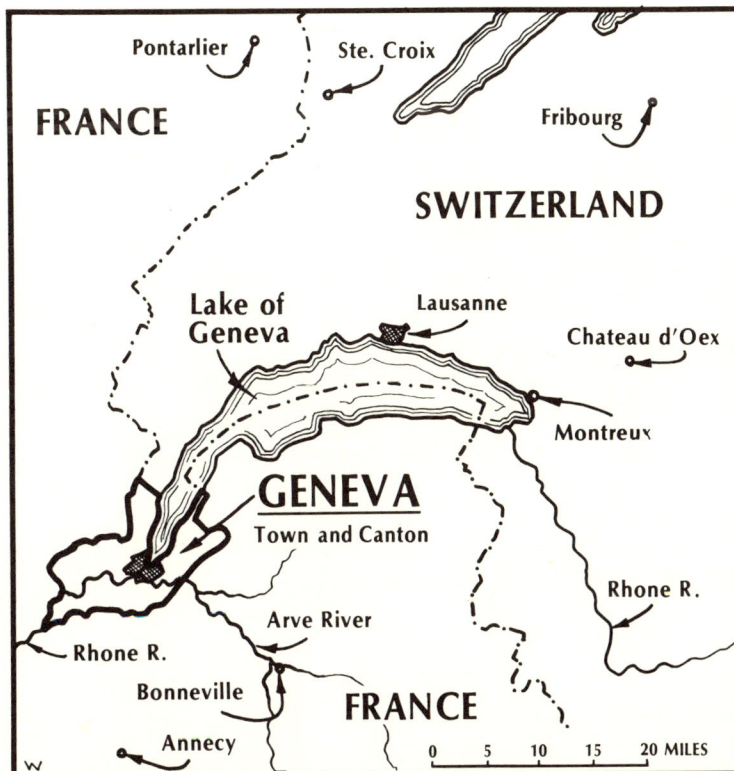

EUROPE

Area: 26,911 sq. miles
Pop: 2,372,403 (1920)
Capital: Tiflis (Tbilisi)

A part of the Russian Empire, Georgia proclaimed itself free following the 1917 Russian Revolution. After a period as part of the Transcaucasian Federation with neighboring Armenia and Azerbaijan, it joined the Transcaucasion SFSR and became part of the USSR. Stamps were issued from 1919 to 1923.

EUROPE

GERMAN EAST AFRICA

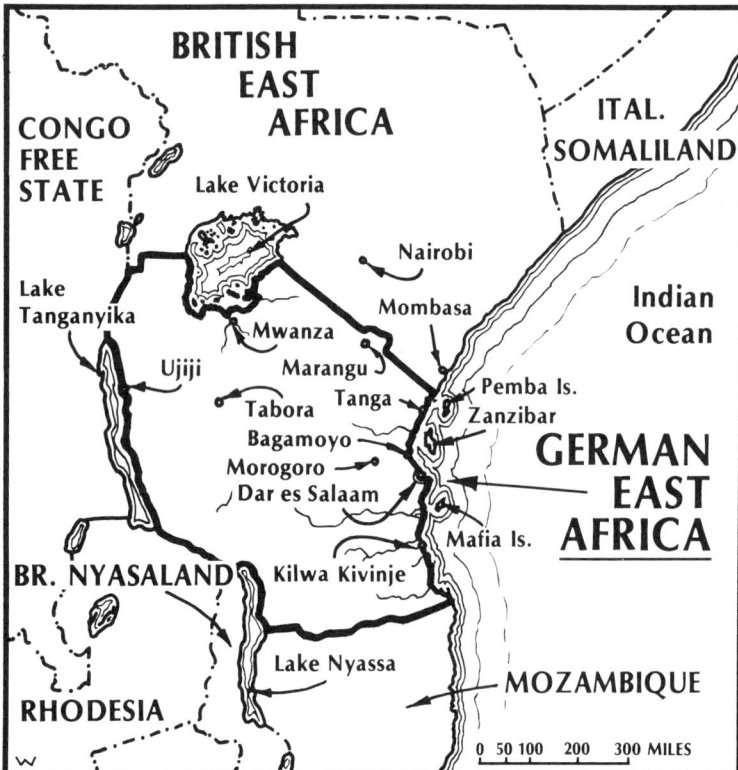

Area: 364,943 sq. miles
Pop: eight million (1900 est.)
Capital: Dar es Salaam

The German East Africa Co. received a charter to the area in 1887, and Germany declared a protectorate over what it named German East Africa in 1891. Following WWI, it was mandated to Britain in 1920 as Tanganyika. Now it is part of the United Republic of Tanzania. Stamps were issued by the Germans beginning in 1893.

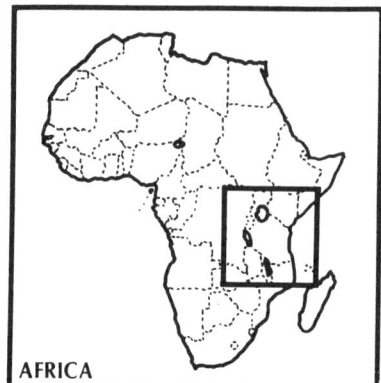

AFRICA

Area: 182,965 sq. miles
Pop: 6,670,000 (1977 est.)
Capital: Yaounde

A German protectorate until WWI, German Kamerun was mandated to Britain and France by the League of Nations in 1922, following its capture by Britain during WWI. German colonial stamps were issued from 1897 until its capture. At first German stamps were overprinted, but later the Kaiser's Yacht key type design was introduced.

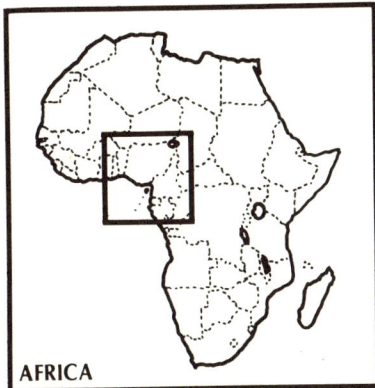

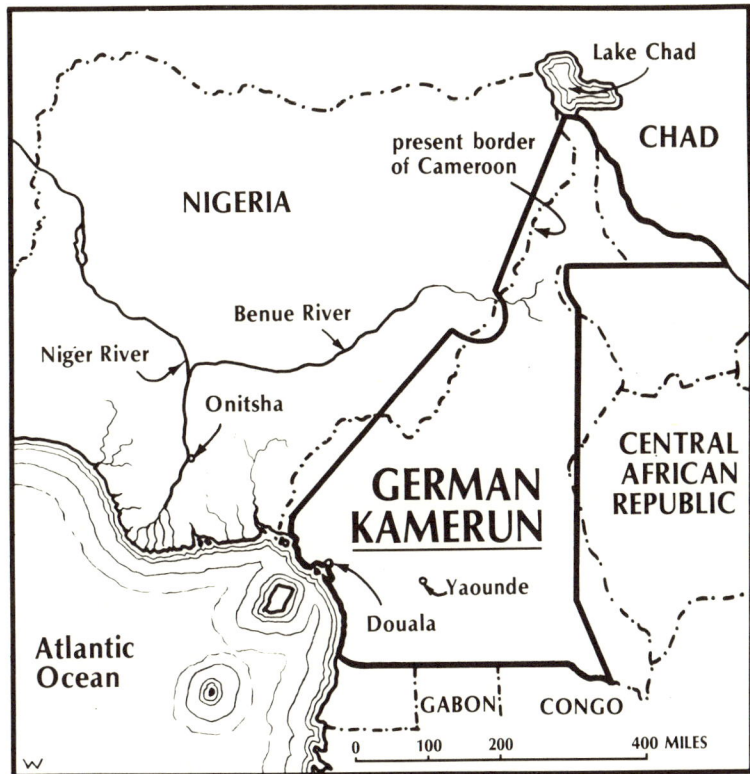

—— GERMAN NEW GUINEA, COLONY OF ——

Area: 93,000 sq. miles
Pop: 601,500 (1913 est.)
Capital: Herbertshohe (Rabaul)

German New Guinea was a protectorate comprising the north part of the eastern portion of the island of New Guinea (called Kaiser Wilhelm Land) and islands in the Bismarck Archipelago. It was occupied by Australian forces in WWI and is now included in Papua New Guinea. German colonial stamps were issued from 1897.

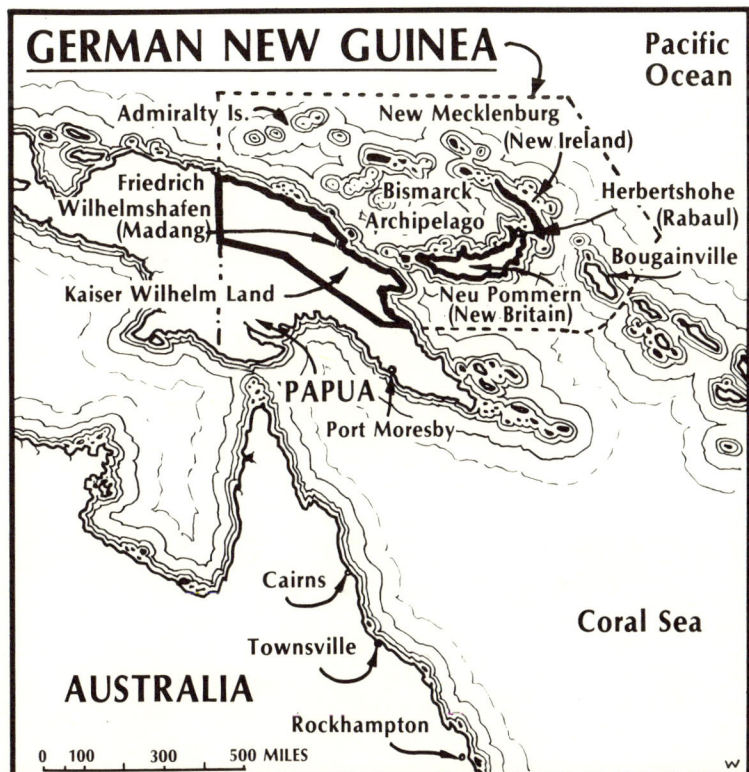

GERMAN SAMOA

NEW HEBRIDES (VANUATU)

US SAMOA

FIJI

NEW CALEDONIA

0 100 200 300 400 500 MILES

SAVAII

APOLIMA

UPOLU

Apia

MANONO

NEW ZEALAND

GERMAN SAMOA

0 10 20   40 MILES

W

PACIFIC OCEAN

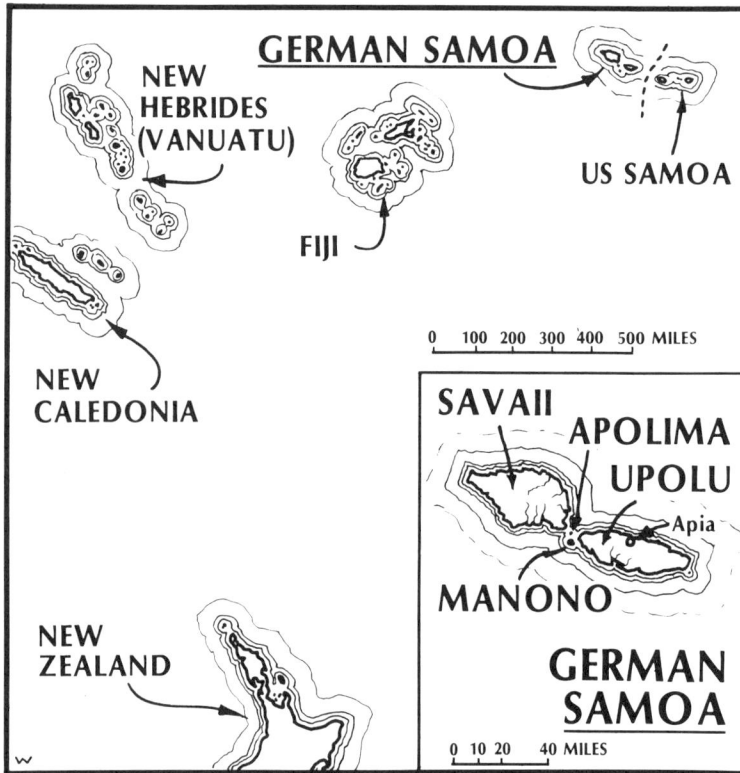

Area: 1,133 sq. miles
Pop: 145,000 (1970 est.)
Capital: Apia

Prior to 1899, Samoa had been administered jointly by Britain, Germany, and the US. In exchange for territory elsewhere, Britain withdrew, and Germany and the US divided the islands between them. The German islands were occupied by New Zealand during WWI and after the war were mandated to that country.

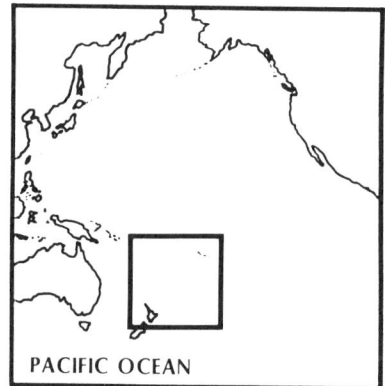

━━━━━━━━ GERMAN SOUTHWEST AFRICA, COLONY OF ━━━━━━━━

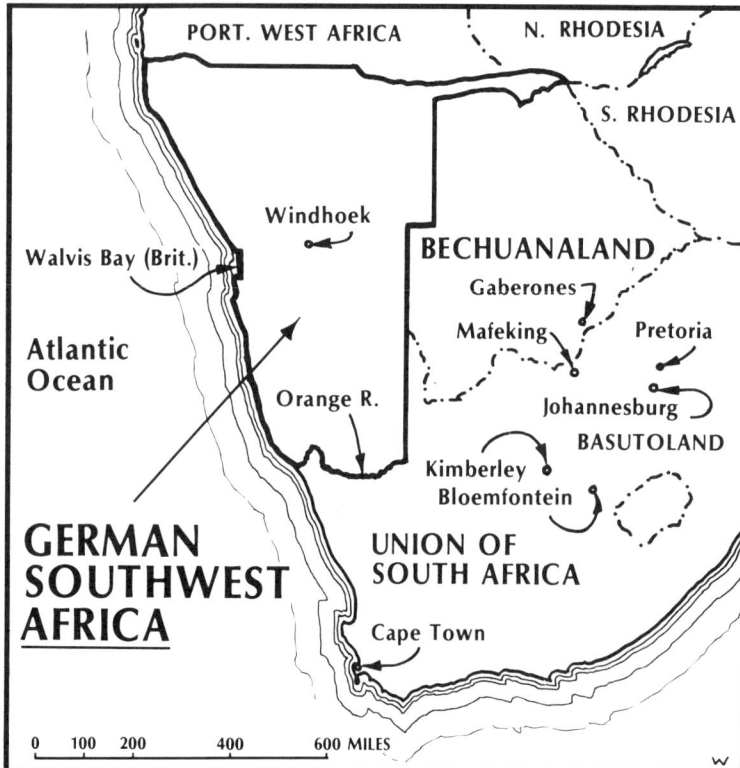

PORT. WEST AFRICA

N. RHODESIA

S. RHODESIA

Windhoek

Walvis Bay (Brit.)

BECHUANALAND

Gaberones

Mafeking

Pretoria

Atlantic Ocean

Orange R.

Johannesburg

BASUTOLAND

Kimberley

Bloemfontein

GERMAN SOUTHWEST AFRICA

UNION OF SOUTH AFRICA

Cape Town

0 100 200   400   600 MILES

W

AFRICA

Area: 322,450 sq. miles
Pop: 200,000 (1900 est.)
Capital: Windhoek

A large German colony, now known as South-West Africa or Namibia, it was occupied by Empire forces during WWI and was mandated to the Union of South Africa in 1920 — a mandate the current Republic of South Africa has refused to give up, despite UN demands. German colonial stamps were issued from 1897.

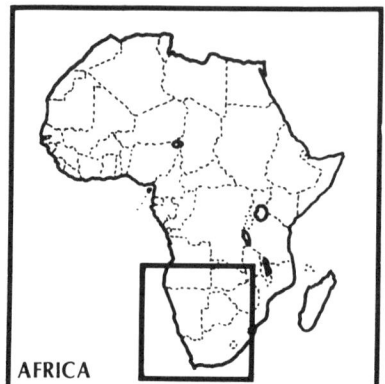

Area: 20,400 sq. miles
Pop: 2,350,000 (1977 est.)
Capital: Lome

Togo was a German colony located between the British Gold Coast and French Dahomey. After WWI and German defeat, it was divided between the British and French and mandated to them by the League of Nations. German colonial stamps were issued from 1897.

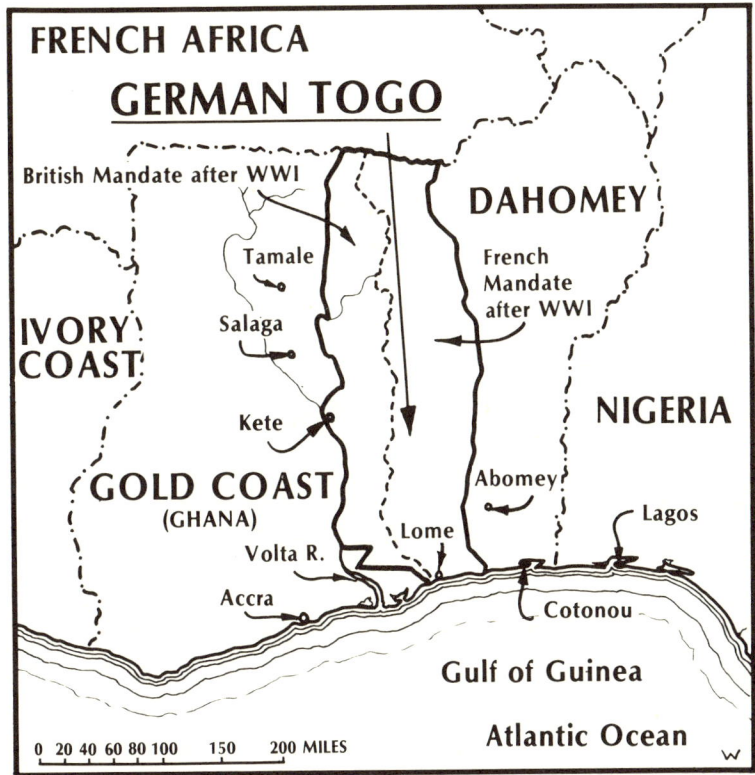

FRENCH AFRICA

GERMAN TOGO

British Mandate after WWI

Tamale

Salaga

IVORY COAST

Kete

GOLD COAST (GHANA)

Volta R.

Accra

DAHOMEY

French Mandate after WWI

NIGERIA

Abomey

Lome

Cotonou

Lagos

Gulf of Guinea

Atlantic Ocean

0 20 40 60 80 100   150   200 MILES

AFRICA

───── GERMANY (NORTH GERMAN CONFEDERATION) ─────

Established in 1868, the North German Confederation was made up of a large number of German states and free cities. The state of Prussia was the dominant partner, and it would be more true to say that the other areas joined Prussia than to say that they federated. Prussian success during the Franco-Prussian War of 1870-71 rendered the later formation of the German Empire under its leadership a great deal easier.

North Sea

DENMARK

SWEDEN

Baltic Sea

Memel

Kiel Canal

Kiel

NETH.

Lubeck

Hamburg   Stettin

Bremen

Berlin

Oder R.

Danzig

Bromberg

Konigsberg

Vistula R.

Warsaw

Cologne

Hanover

Elbe R.

Leipzig

Dresden   Breslau

RUSSIAN POLAND

Mainz

Nuremberg

Mannheim

LORRAINE

Karlsruhe

ALSACE

Stuttgart

Strasbourg

Munich

Vienna

AUSTRIA-HUNGARY

NORTH GERMAN CONFEDERATION
1868-1871

SWITZERLAND

0   50   100   200 MILES

EUROPE

GERMAN EMPIRE

PRIOR TO WORLD WAR I

EUROPE

Area: 208,830 sq. miles
Pop: 56,367,178 (1900 est.)
Capital: Berlin

The German Empire came into being after the Franco-Prussian War, with Bismarck as the first chancellor. A policy of colonial expansion was adopted, and the ludicrous posturing of Kaiser Wilhelm II led the empire into a war that drew in all the major nations as the strings of treaty obligations were pulled tight. The result was a war that Germany could not win.

GERMANY (THE INTER-WAR YEARS)

GERMANY

between World War I
and the Third Reich

EUROPE

Area: 181,738 sq. miles
Pop: 65,804,000 (1935)
Capital: Berlin

The chaos in Germany following WWI almost guaranteed the rise of someone like Hitler. His paranoia led Germany once more into war and an even worse devastation than that following the previous conflict. But more wisdom was shown by the victors, and West Germany at least was rebuilt along democratic lines.

Following WWII, Germany was divided into occupation zones of the major victors. The USSR gained the eastern part of Germany leaving Berlin enclaved. Early in the occupation a number of local issues were released for the various postal districts into which the zone was divided. The map shows those districts. Although Scott does not list these stamps, they are included in the Minkus, Gibbons, and other catalogs.

EUROPE

Baltic Sea

Hamburg

Rostock

MECKLENBURG-WEST POMERANIA

Neustrelitz

Stettin

Schwerin

Elbe R.

BERLIN-BRANDENBURG

EAST GERMANY (SOVIET ZONE)

Hanover

W. GERMANY

BERLIN

Frankfurt

POLAND

Halle

Spremberg

SAXONY

Leipzig

E. SAXONY

Erfurt

Chemnitz

Dresden

THURINGIA

W. SAXONY

0 50 100 200 MILES

W

GHADAMES (GHUDAMIS), TOWN OF

An oasis and town in northwest Libya near the border with Algeria. The area was occupied by Free French forces during WWII and, together with Fezzan (q.v.), was under a military administration until it became part of the newly independent country of Libya. Stamps were issued under French administration and depict a number of views of that remote area.

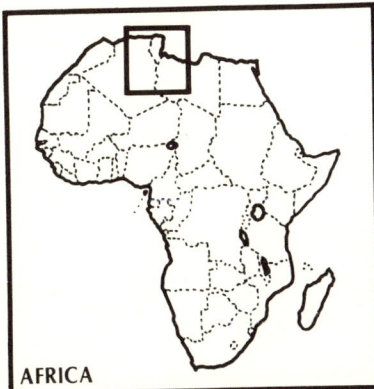

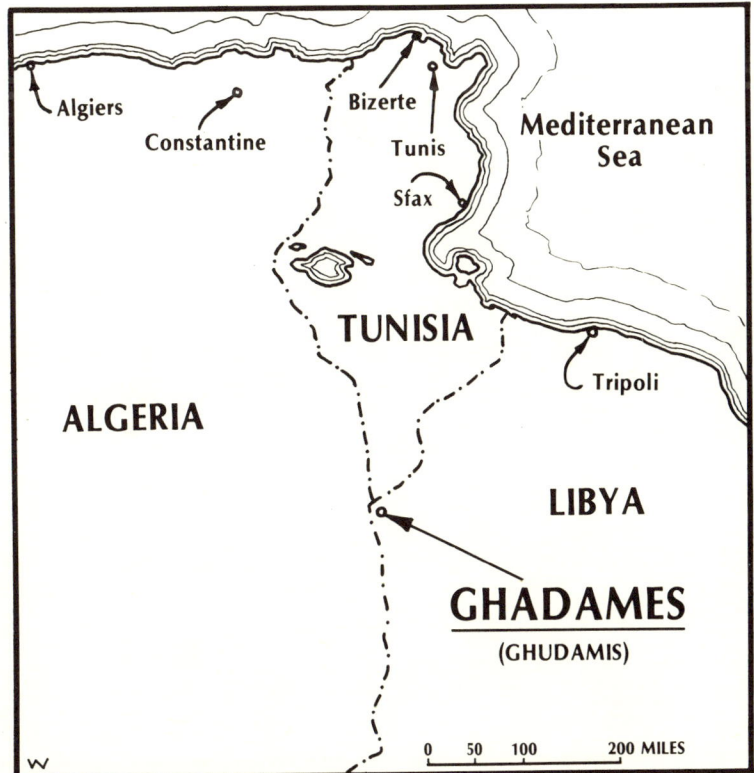

AFRICA

Algiers

Bizerte

Mediterranean Sea

Constantine

Tunis

Sfax

TUNISIA

Tripoli

ALGERIA

LIBYA

GHADAMES
(GHUDAMIS)

0 50 100 200 MILES

W

GILBERT AND ELLICE ISLANDS

(now KIRIBATI and TUVALU)

HAWAII

GILBERT ISLANDS

PHOENIX ISLANDS

NEW GUINEA

Makin
Tarawa
Ocean

Canton

Washington
Fanning

Kingsmill
Group

Christmas

Phoenix
Enderbury

ELLICE ISLANDS

FIJI

Pacific Ocean

AUSTRALIA
Sydney

NEW ZEALAND

0 200 400 600 800 MILES

PACIFIC OCEAN

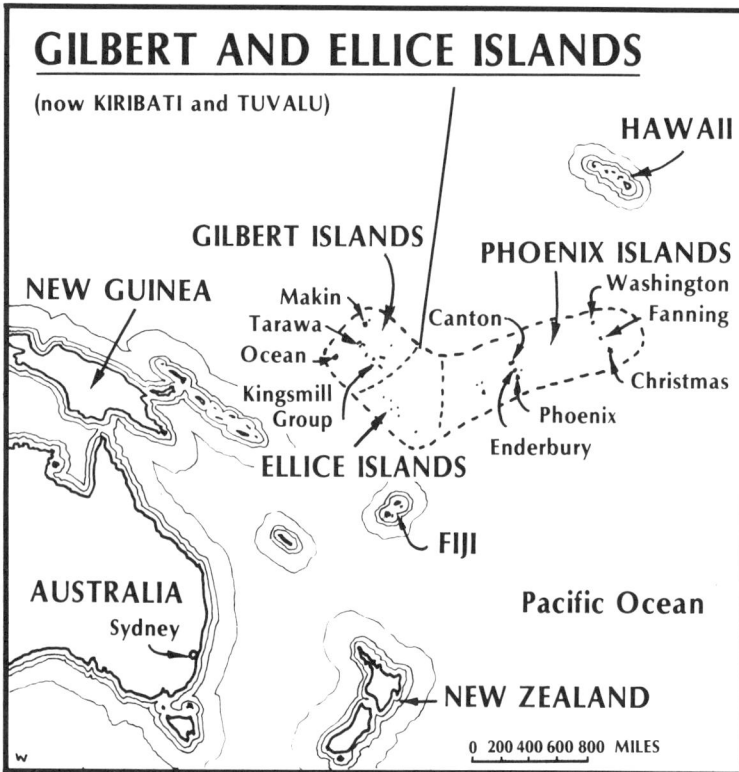

Area: 283 sq. miles
Pop: 56,400 (1970 est.)
Capital: Tarawa

The Gilbert and Ellice groups were combined as a British protectorate in 1892, becoming a colony in 1915. Over the years Fanning, Washington, Ocean, Christmas, and the Phoenix group were added. In 1976, the colony was divided into the Gilbert Islands and Tuvalu. The first stamps, issued in 1911, were overprinted stamps of Fiji.

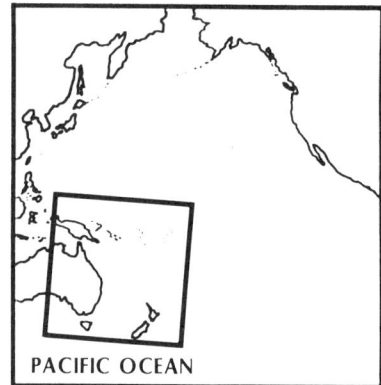

———— GIUMULZINA (KOMOTINI), TOWN OF ————

GIUMULZINA

(also Gumurjina
or Gumuldzhina,
now Komotini)

BULGARIA

Philippopolis
(Plovdiv)

Burgas

Black Sea

Adrianople
(Edirne)

Approximate
area of Thrace

present
borders

TURKEY

Istanbul

GREECE

Dedeagh (Alexandroupolis)

Uskudar

Cavalle
(Kavalla)

Sea of Marmara

Aegean Sea

Canakkale

TURKEY

site of ancient Troy

0 10 20 40 60 80 100 MILES

EUROPE

Pop: 7,000 (1900 est.)
        32,123 (1971)

The town of Giumulzina is now the Greek town of Komotini. It was founded in the Byzantine period, and was located in the province of Thrace in the Turkish Empire. It was also known as Gumurjina and Gumuldzhina. A set of stamps was issued there in 1913, during the period after Greece had occupied the area.

Area: 93,845 sq. miles
Pop: 1,905,000 (1900 est.)
8,545,560 (1970)
Capital: Accra

A former British colony on the coast of West Africa, the Gold Coast became the independent country of Ghana in 1957. Stamps were first issued for the area in 1875, but it was not until 1928 that collectors received a glimpse of the area, with the issue showing Christiansborg Castle.

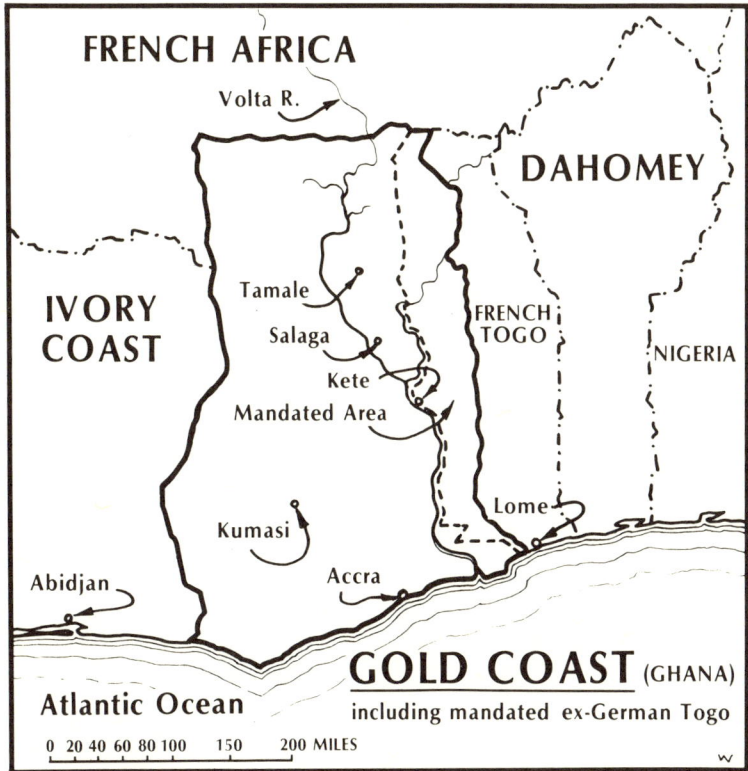

AFRICA

FRENCH AFRICA

Volta R.

DAHOMEY

IVORY COAST

Tamale

Salaga

FRENCH TOGO

NIGERIA

Kete

Mandated Area

Lome

Kumasi

Accra

Abidjan

GOLD COAST (GHANA)

Atlantic Ocean

including mandated ex-German Togo

0 20 40 60 80 100   150   200 MILES

GRANADA, PROVINCE OF

Area: 4,838 sq. miles
Pop: 733,375 (1970)

Granada is a province of Spain in the southern part of the country bordering on the Mediterranean Sea. The capital city of the same name had a 1970 population of 190,429 and is noted for the Alhambra, one of the finest examples of Moorish architecture in the country. Granada's cathedral contains the tombs of King Ferdinand and Queen Isabella.

EUROPE

GRANADA

Baza

Guadix

Granada

SPAIN

Loja

Almeria

Malaga

Motril

Mediterranean Sea

0   10   20   30   40   50 MILES

GRAND COMORO

Indian Ocean

Mitsamiouli

Moroni

Anjouan

Mayotte

Moheli

Diego-Suarez

Nossi-Be

Mozambique Channel

Majunga

MADAGASCAR

0 20 40 60 80 100 MILES

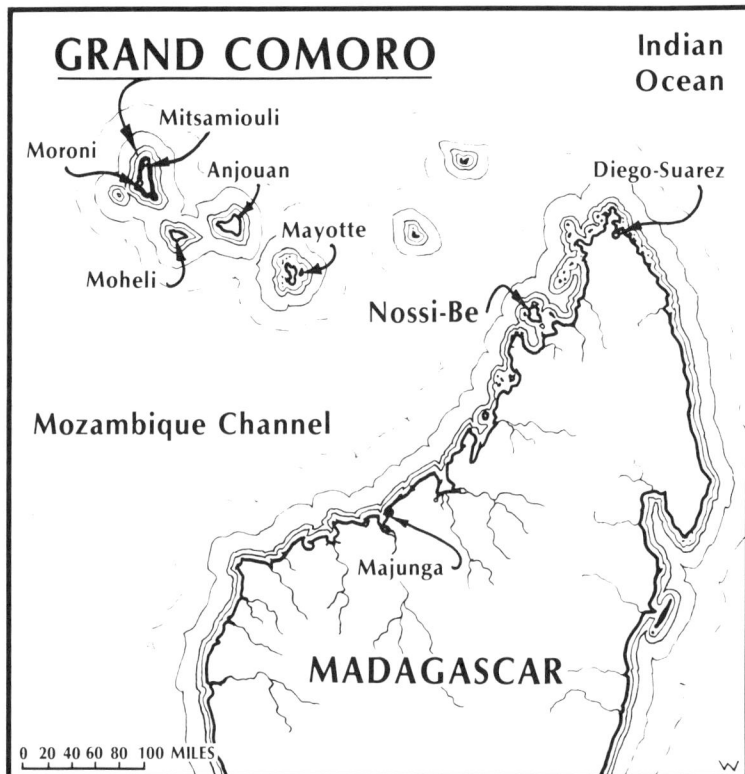

Area: 443 sq. miles
Pop: 132,000 (1970 est.)
Capital: Moroni

An island in the Comoro group in the Mozambique Channel between Madagascar and the African coast, Grand Comoro (Great Comoro) is the largest of the group. Stamps were issued for the island from 1897 to 1912, being superseded by stamps of Madagascar. Now it is part of the Republic of Comoros.

AFRICA

———————— GRIQUALAND WEST, CROWN COLONY OF ————————

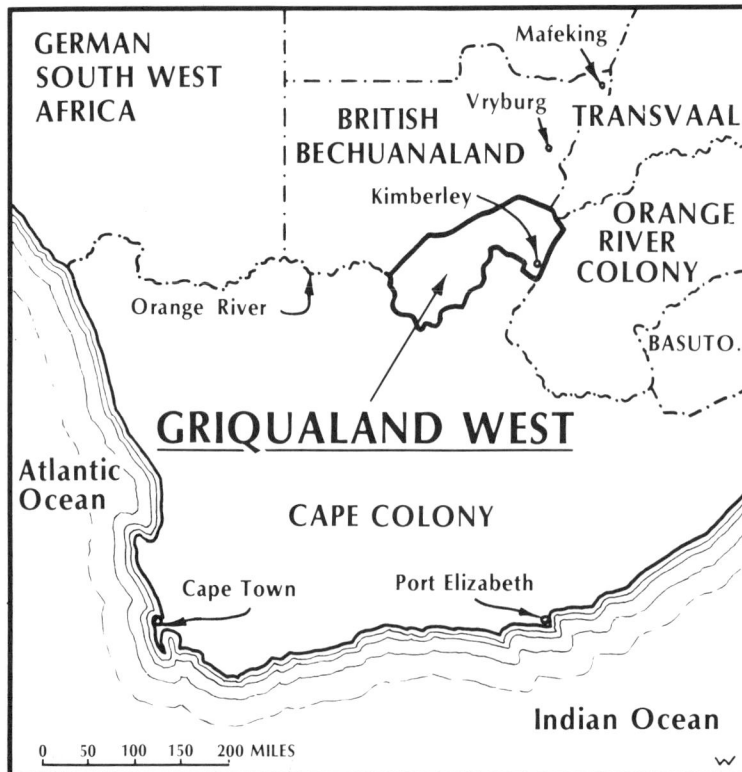

GERMAN SOUTH WEST AFRICA

Mafeking

BRITISH BECHUANALAND

Vryburg

TRANSVAAL

Kimberley

ORANGE RIVER COLONY

Orange River

BASUTO.

GRIQUALAND WEST

Atlantic Ocean

CAPE COLONY

Cape Town

Port Elizabeth

Indian Ocean

0 50 100 150 200 MILES

Area: 15,444 sq. miles
Pop: 83,375 (1891)
Capital: Kimberley

Annexed to Britain in 1871, it was made a crown colony in 1873 until it was merged into the Cape of Good Hope in 1880. Stamps of the Cape of Good Hope were overprinted "G" for use in the colony.

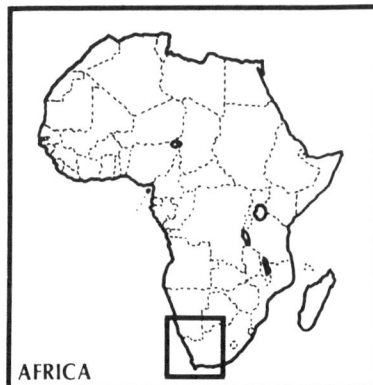

AFRICA

A town and district in Russia prior to WWI, Grodno then became part of Poland during the inter-war years. Occupied and re-occupied by German and Soviet forces, it is now part of the USSR. German occupation stamps were issued in 1916-17; Russian stamps overprinted "Lietuva" appeared in 1919; and Russian occupation stamps were released overprinted "LTSR" in 1940.

LITHUANIA

Memel (Klaipeda)

BALTIC SEA

EAST PRUSSIA

Konigsberg (Kaliningrad)

Kaunas

Vilnius

Danzig (Gdansk)

Minsk

Allenstein (Olsztyn)

GRODNO

Bialystok

Warsaw

present Polish-USSR border

Borders prior to 1939

POLAND

USSR

0 20 40 60 80 100 MILES

EUROPE

GUADALAJARA, CITY OF

Pop: 1,196,218 (1970)

A city in Mexico and capital of the state of Jalisco. It is located near the Santiago River about 290 miles northwest of Mexico City and is an important road and rail center. The city contains a number of historic buildings dating back to the 16th century, shortly after its founding in the early 1530s by Nuno de Guzman. It is named for his birthplace in Spain. Its location was twice moved before 1542.

GUADALAJARA

STATE OF JALISCO

Pto. Vallarta

MEXICO

Pacific Ocean

0 50 100 200 MILES

CENTRAL AMERICA

GUADELOUPE

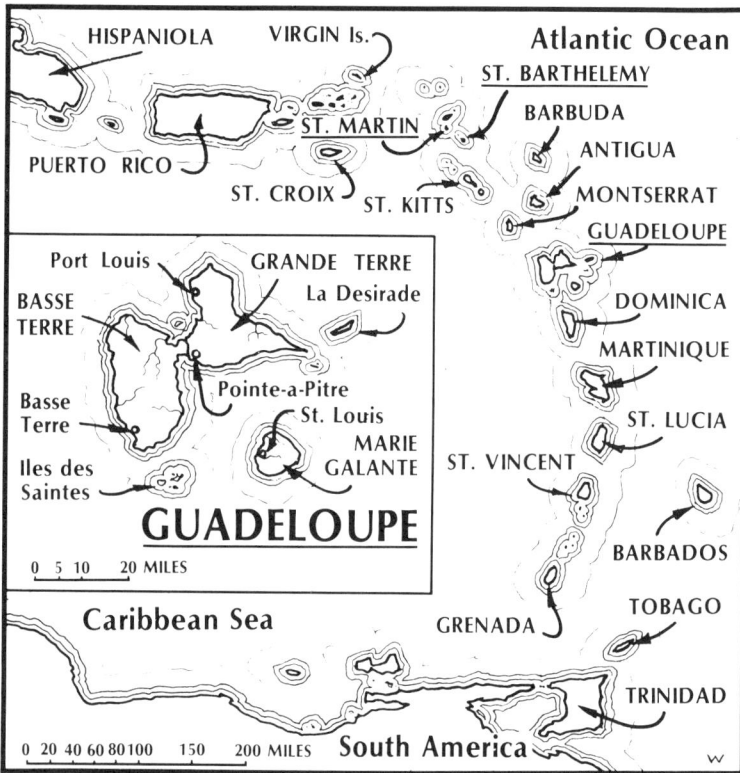

Area: 683 sq. miles
Pop: 327,000 (1970)
Capital: Basse Terre

Guadeloupe is a group of islands in the Lesser Antilles of the West Indies. It is now a department of France. The main islands are Basse Terre and Grande Terre, separated only by a narrow stream. Other dependencies are Marie Galante, Desirade, Iles des Saintes, plus the small island of St. Barthelemy and the northern part of the island of St. Martin.

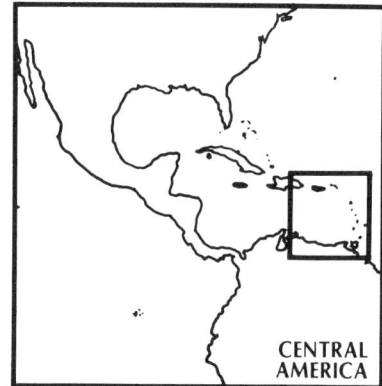

CENTRAL AMERICA

———————— GUAM, US TERRITORY OF ————————

GUAM

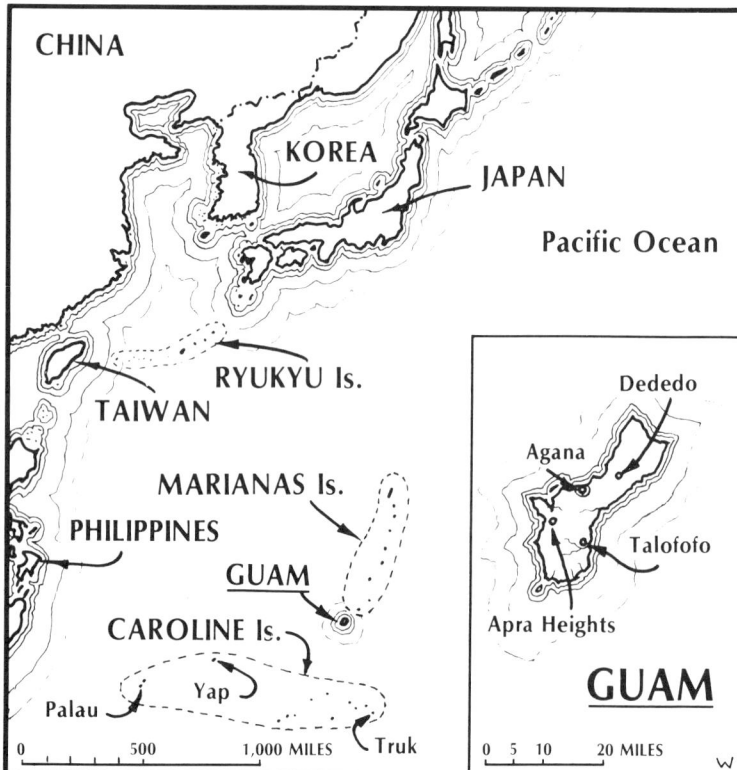

Area: 209 sq. miles
Pop: 22,290 (1940)
    86,926 (1970)
Capital: Agana

An island in the western Pacific Ocean, Guam was a Spanish colony until ceded to the US in 1898 as a result of the Spanish-American War. It has been administered by the US Department of the Interior since 1950.

PACIFIC OCEAN

Area: 4,015 sq. miles
Pop: 188,972 (1970)
Capital: Liberia

A province of Costa Rica, Guanacaste is located in the northwest portion of the country. Stamps were issued from 1885 to 1890. They consisted of Costa Rican stamps overprinted "Guanacaste."

GUAYANA, DISTRICT OF

Guayana was a district of Venezuela based on the city of Ciudad Guayana. The area was thought to be the location of the mythical El Dorado. Stamps were issued there in 1903. Scott notes that they were issued by a group of revolutionaries and had limited local use.

Bay of Biscay

Bordeaux

FRANCE

San Sebastian

Guernica

Biarritz

Pau

Santander

Lourdes

Bilbao

Vitoria

Pamplona

Burgos

GUIPUZCOA

SPAIN

0 20 40 60 80 100 MILES

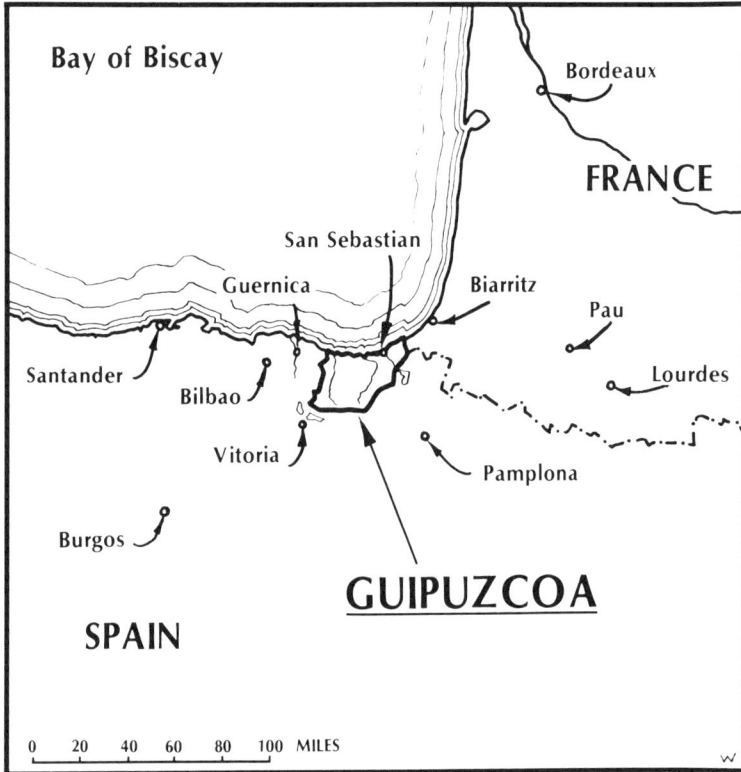

Area: 771 sq. miles
Pop: 631,003 (1970)
Capital: San Sebastian

A province in northern Spain, Guipuzcoa is adjacent to the French border facing on the Bay of Biscay. Stamps were issued in 1937 for use for use on mail from the province during the Spanish Civil War.

EUROPE

———————HADHRAMAUT, AREA OF———————

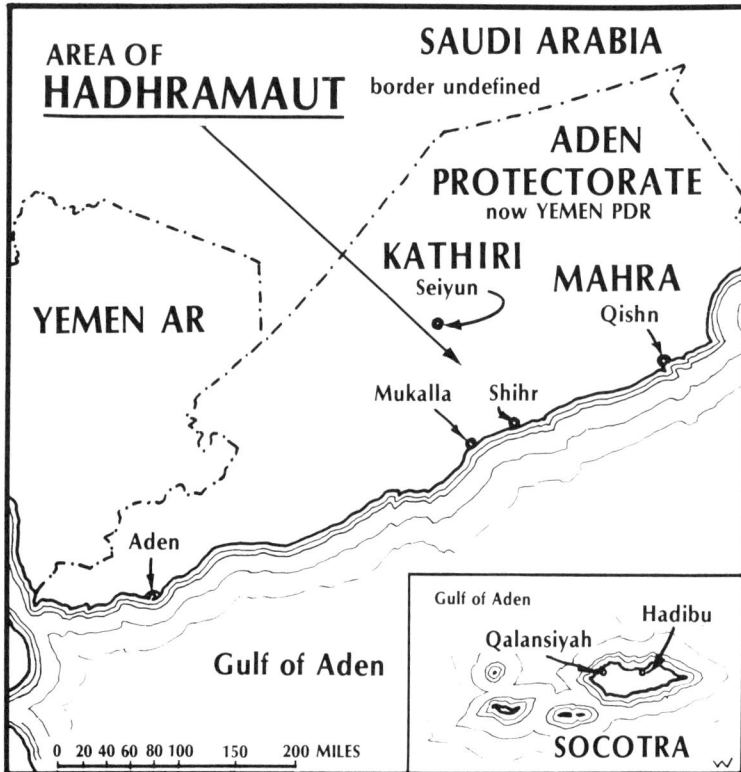

AREA OF
HADHRAMAUT

SAUDI ARABIA

border undefined

ADEN
PROTECTORATE
now YEMEN PDR

KATHIRI
Seiyun

MAHRA
Qishn

YEMEN AR

Mukalla   Shihr

Aden

Gulf of Aden

0 20 40 60 80 100   150   200 MILES

Gulf of Aden

Qalansiyah   Hadibu

SOCOTRA

The Hadhramaut now includes the greater part of the People's Democratic Republic of South Yemen. It was once a British protected area based on the crown colony of Aden and included the stamp-issuing entities of Qu'aiti State in Hadhramaut, the Qu'aiti State of Shihr and Mukalla, the Mahra Sultanate of Qishn and Socotra, and the Kathiri State of Seiyun. The climate is hot, with summer temperatures exceeding 130 degrees F.

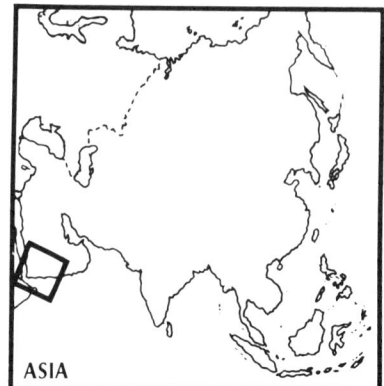

ASIA

Area: 13,124 sq. miles
Pop: 2,800,000 (1953)
Capital: Hai-k'ou

A thickly forested island 15 miles off the southern coast of China, Hainan was included in the Communist South China Liberation Area. Hainan was opened to foreign trade in 1858. The Japanese occupied the island from 1939 to 1945, and it came under the Communists in April 1950.

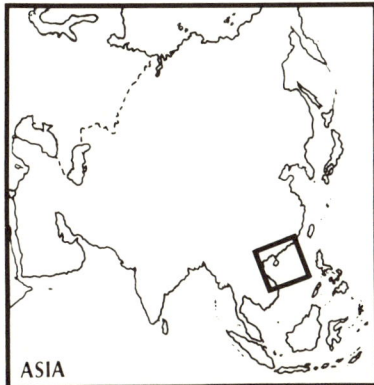

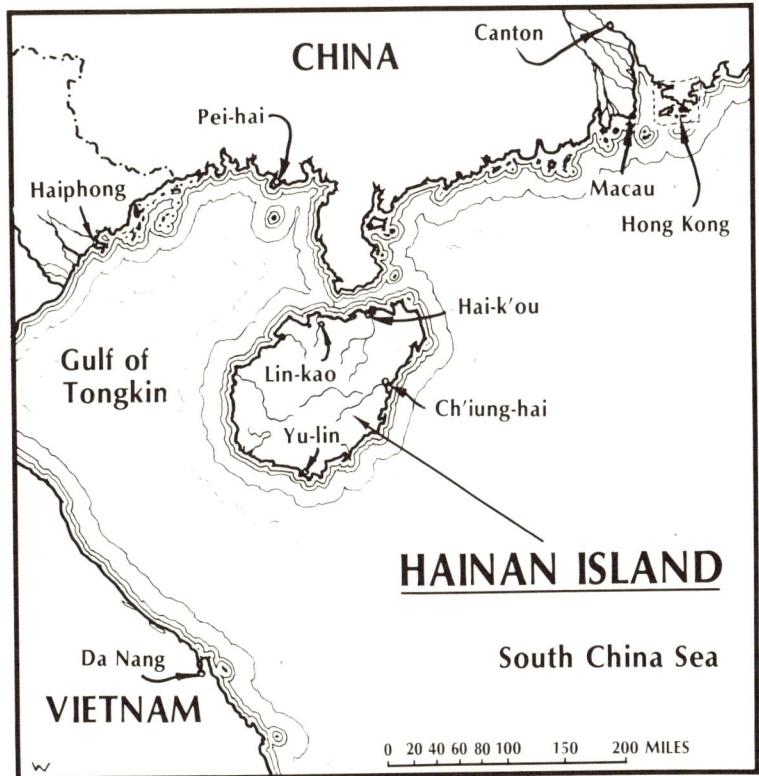

CHINA

Canton

Pei-hai

Haiphong

Macau

Hong Kong

Gulf of Tongkin

Hai-k'ou

Lin-kao

Ch'iung-hai

Yu-lin

HAINAN ISLAND

South China Sea

Da Nang

VIETNAM

0 20 40 60 80 100   150   200 MILES

ASIA

HAMBURG, FREE CITY OF ━━━━━━

Area: 289 sq. miles
Pop: 768,349 (1900)
　　　1,814,100 (1970)

A free city on the Elbe River in Northern Germany, Hamburg had been founded as a fort by Charlemagne between AD 808 and 811. It became an important seaport and trading center and was one of the Hanseatic ports. It was under French rule from 1806 to 1815 and became a member of the North German Confederation, later the German Empire.

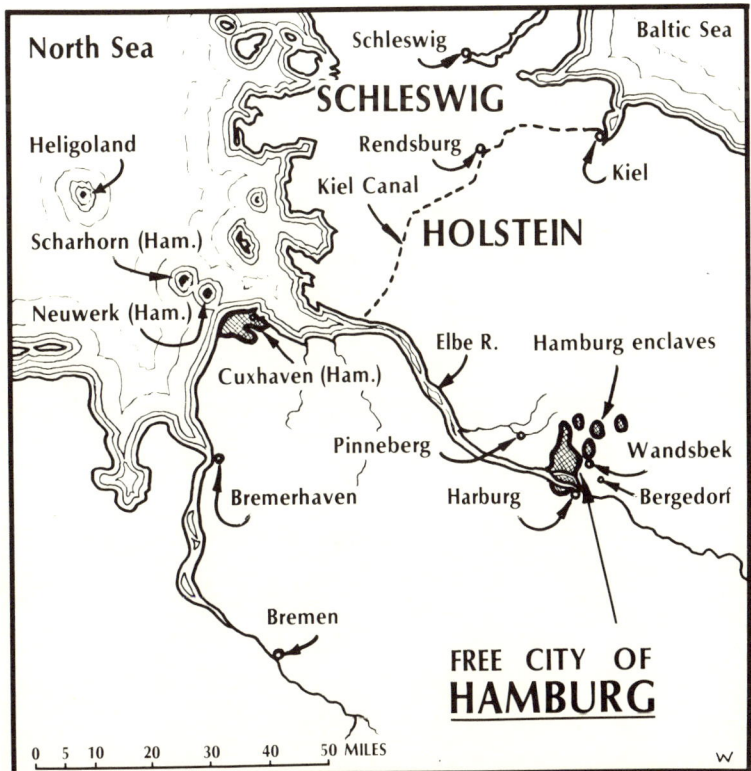

North Sea

Schleswig

Baltic Sea

SCHLESWIG

Heligoland

Rendsburg

Kiel Canal

Kiel

Scharhorn (Ham.)

HOLSTEIN

Neuwerk (Ham.)

Elbe R.

Hamburg enclaves

Cuxhaven (Ham.)

Pinneberg

Wandsbek

Bremerhaven

Harburg

Bergedorf

Bremen

FREE CITY OF
HAMBURG

0 5 10   20   30   40   50 MILES

EUROPE

Area: 14,893 sq. miles
Pop: 2,590,939 (1900)
Capital: Hanover

A former kingdom in north Germany, Hanover was a member of the North German Confederation and became a province of Prussia in 1866. Stamps were issued from 1850 to the union with Prussia. At first featuring the kingdom's coat of arms, stamps later pictured a profile of King George V of Hanover.

HATAY, MANDATE AREA OF

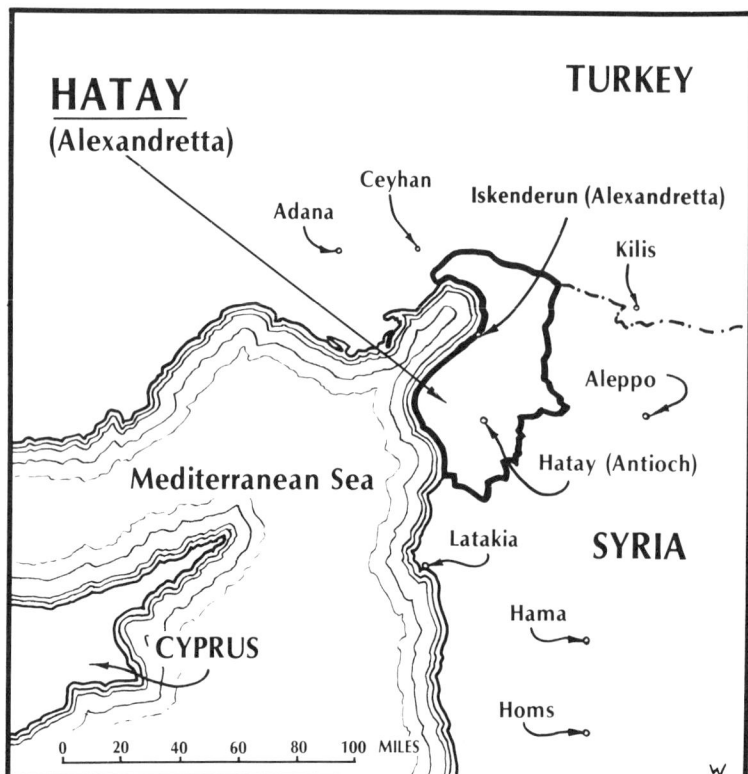

Area: 2,086 sq. miles
Pop: 273,350 (1939)
Capital: Antioch (Antakya)

Formerly the area of Syria under French mandate following WWI, Hatay was known as the Sanjak of Alexandretta. It was named Hatay and transferred to Turkey in 1939 by France. Stamps were issued in 1939 following creation of Hatay and prior to the transfer to Turkey.

Area: 6,450 sq. miles
Pop: 154,000 (1900)
    981,000 (1981)
Capital: Honolulu

An island group in the central Pacific Ocean, now the 50th state in the United States, Hawaii once was an independent kingdom. The islands were annexed to the US in 1898 following four years as a republic. Stamps issued from 1851 to June 13, 1900.

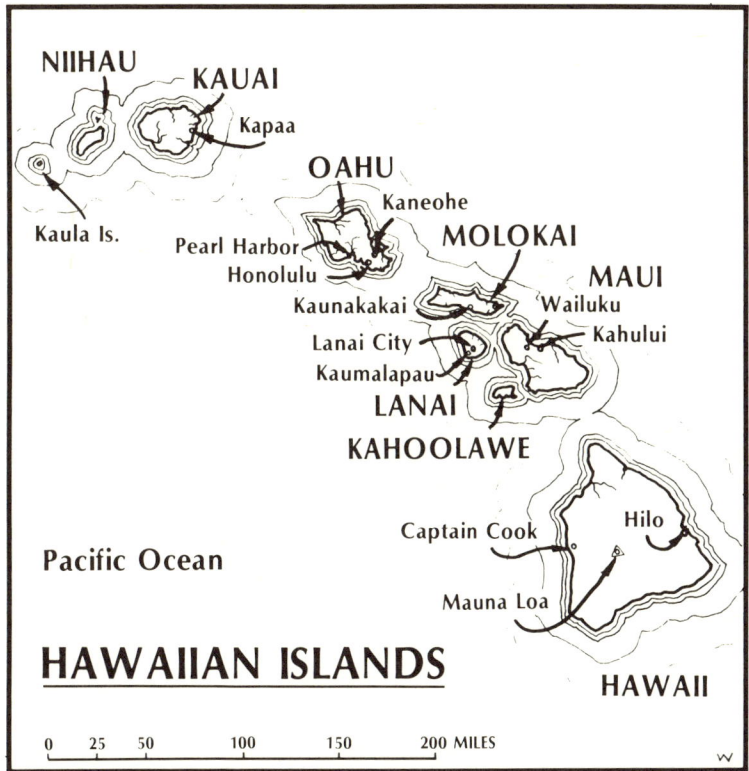

NIIHAU

KAUAI

Kapaa

Kaula Is.

OAHU

Kaneohe

Pearl Harbor

Honolulu

MOLOKAI

MAUI

Wailuku

Kaunakakai

Kahului

Lanai City

Kaumalapau

LANAI

KAHOOLAWE

Captain Cook

Hilo

Pacific Ocean

Mauna Loa

HAWAIIAN ISLANDS

HAWAII

0   25   50   100   150   200 MILES

PACIFIC OCEAN

HEILUNGKIANG-KIRIN, PROVINCES OF

Area: 178,996 sq. miles
    (Heilungkiang)
    72,201 sq. miles (Kirin)
Pop: 21,000 (1967 — Heilungkiang)
    17,000 (1968 — Kirin)
Capital: Harbin (Heilungkiang)
    Kirin (Kirin)

Heilungkiang-Kirin were twin provinces in what was Manchukuo under Japanese occupation. Now the area is part of the People's Republic of China. Stamps were issued there in 1927-29.

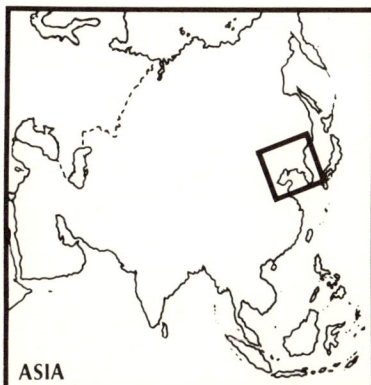

USSR

Tsitsihar

HEILUNGKIANG

MONGOLIA

Harbin

Kirin
(Chi-lin)

Hsingking
(Ch'ang-ch'un)

KIRIN

INNER MONGOLIA

Mukden
(Shen-yang)

Vladivostok

N.
KOREA

Sea of Japan

Peking (Beijing)

CHINA

Seoul
S. KOREA

0 50 100   200   300 MILES

ASIA

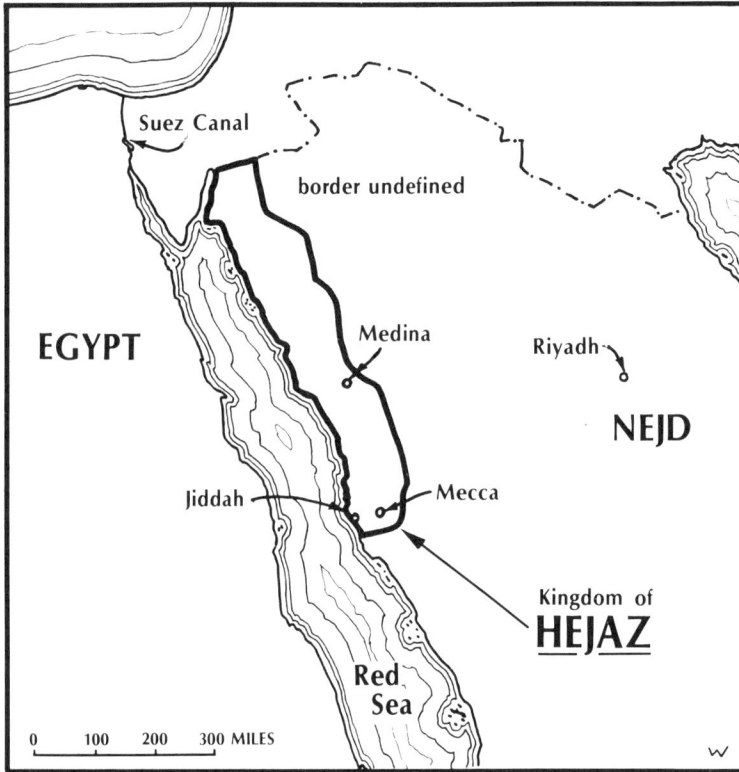

Area: 134,600 sq. miles
Pop: 800,000 (1930 est.)

A former Turkish area in Arabia on the Red Sea, Hejaz became a kingdom in 1916. It was invaded and absorbed by the Sultan of the Nejd in 1926 and became part of the Kingdom of the Hejaz and Nejd. The name was changed to Saudi Arabia in 1932. It contains the Islamic holy city of Mecca. Stamps were issued from 1916 until union with Nejd.

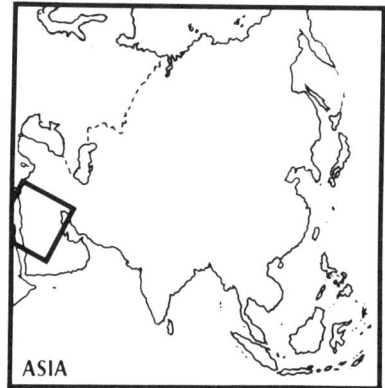

EGYPT

Suez Canal

border undefined

Medina

Riyadh

NEJD

Jiddah

Mecca

Kingdom of
HEJAZ

Red Sea

0   100   200   300 MILES

ASIA

HELIGOLAND, ISLAND OF

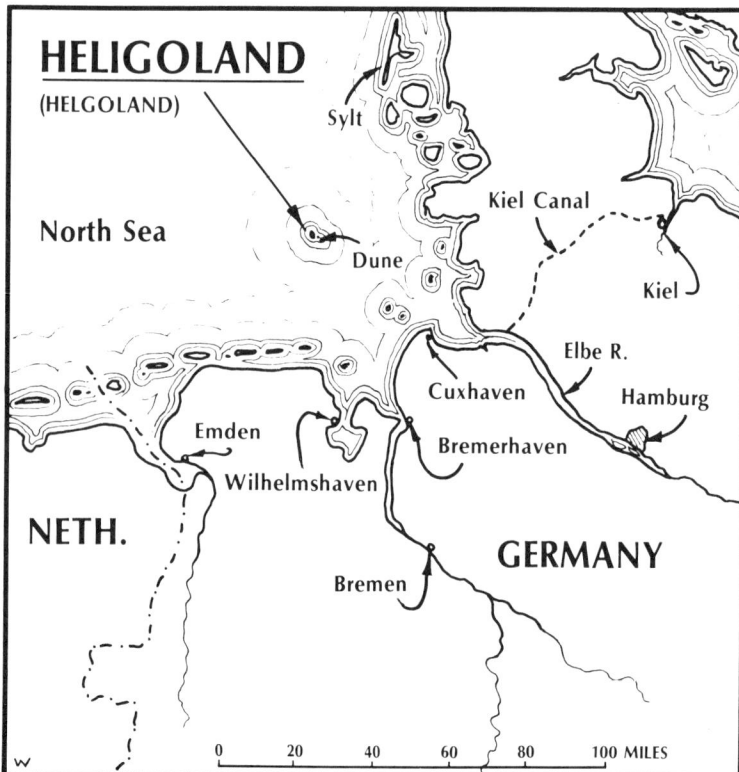

Area: ¼ sq. mile
Pop: 3,200 (1967)

An island in the North Sea, Heligoland was British from 1814 to 1890, when it was ceded to Germany in exchange for territory elsewhere. It was under British control again from 1945 to 1952. Hamburg operated the postal service to June 1866, and its stamps were used. Heligoland issued its own stamps from 1867 to 1890.

HELIGOLAND
(HELGOLAND)

Sylt

North Sea

Dune

Kiel Canal

Kiel

Elbe R.

Cuxhaven

Hamburg

Emden

Bremerhaven

Wilhelmshaven

NETH.

GERMANY

Bremen

0   20   40   60   80   100 MILES

EUROPE

Pop: 483,743 (1979)

Formerly the city of Helsingfors, Helsinki is the capital city of the Republic of Finland. It is located on the Gulf of Finland. The first stamp issue of the new nation of Finland following independence from Russia was released in 1917 and is called the Helsinki Issue.

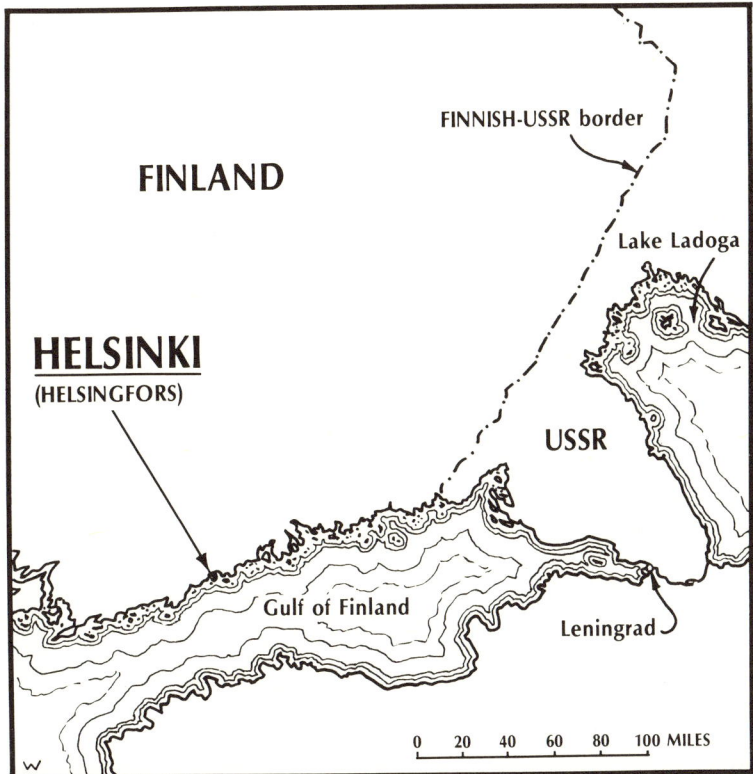

HONAN, PROVINCE OF

Area: 64,479 sq. miles
Pop: 50 million (1968)
Capital: Cheng-chou

Honan is a province in east-central China. Regional overprints had been applied to stamps for use in the area during the 1940s. In 1949, stamps were issued by the Communists for the Central China Liberation Area, of which Honan was a part.

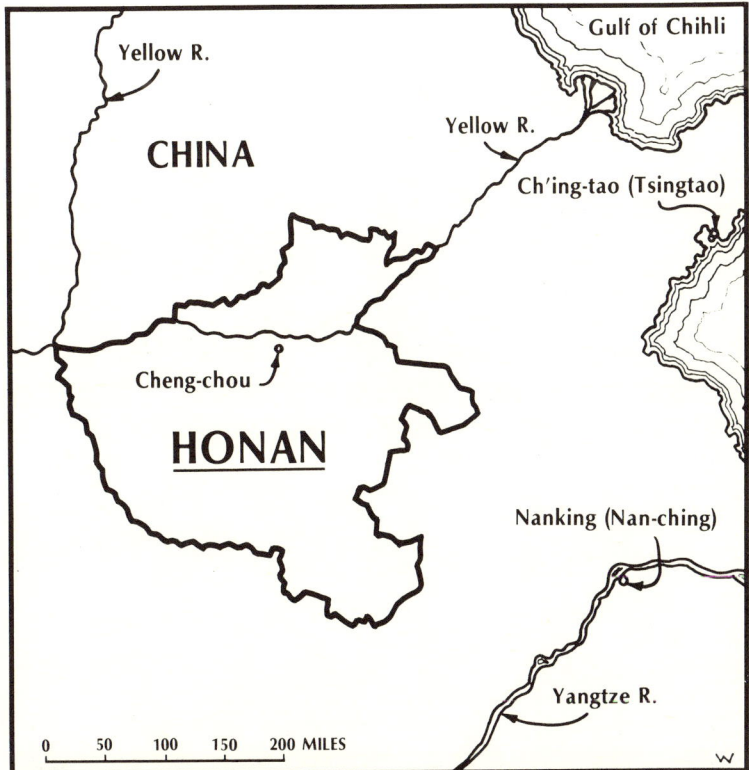

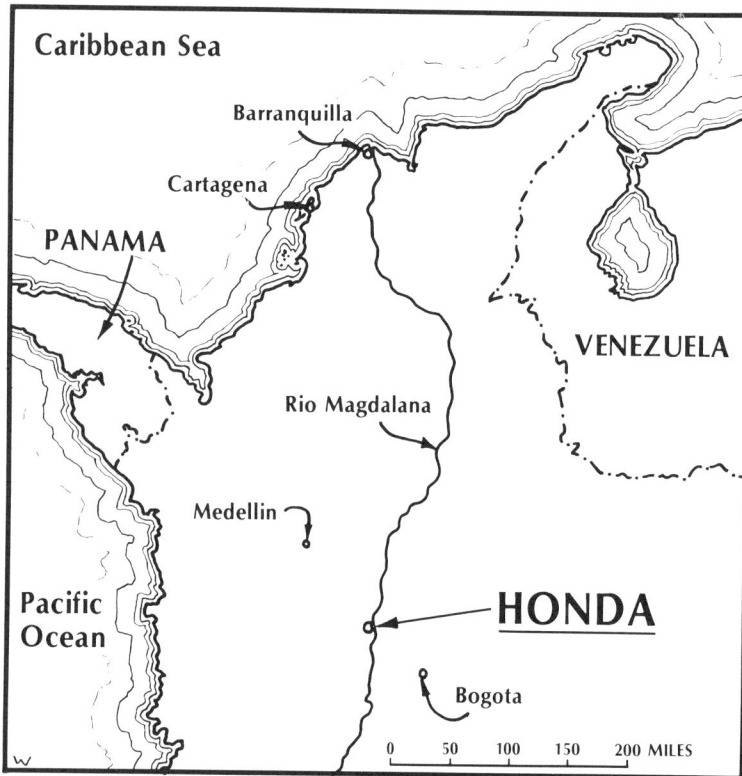

Pop: 22,315 (1968 est.)

Honda is a town in Tolima Department of Colombia, about 50 miles northwest of Bogota. A stamp was issued in 1896 for Tolima that is called the Honda Issue. The town name is included in the overprint inscription.

Caribbean Sea

Barranquilla

Cartagena

PANAMA

VENEZUELA

Rio Magdalana

Medellin

Pacific Ocean

HONDA

Bogota

0 50 100 150 200 MILES

SOUTH AMERICA

━━━━━━━━━HOPEH, PROVINCE OF ━━━━━━━━━

Area: 81,479 sq. miles
Pop: 47 million (1968)

Hopeh is a province in northeast China, bordering on the Gulf of Chihli. Regional overprints were issued in the 1940s. In 1946, stamps were issued by the Communists for the North China Liberation Area, of which Hopeh was a part.

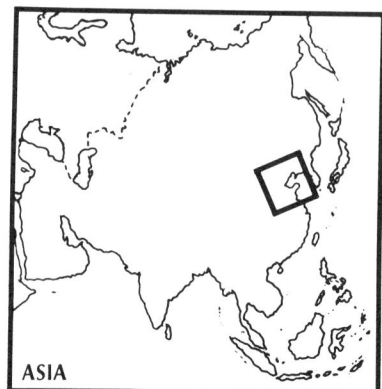

CHINA

Peking (Beijing)

Chin-huang-tao

Chang-chia-kou

Tientsin (T'ien-ching)

Dairen (Ta-lien)

Pao-ting

HOPEH

Gulf of Chihli

Port Arthur (Lu-shun)

Yellow River

Yellow Sea

0 50 100 200 MILES

ASIA

Area: 301 sq. miles
Pop: 43,600 (1970)
Capital: Horta

A district of Portugal in the Azores, Horta includes the islands of Faial, Pico, and Sao Jorge. The Azores are located in the Atlantic Ocean, about 750 miles to the west of Portugal. Stamps were issued inscribed "HORTA" from 1892 to 1905.

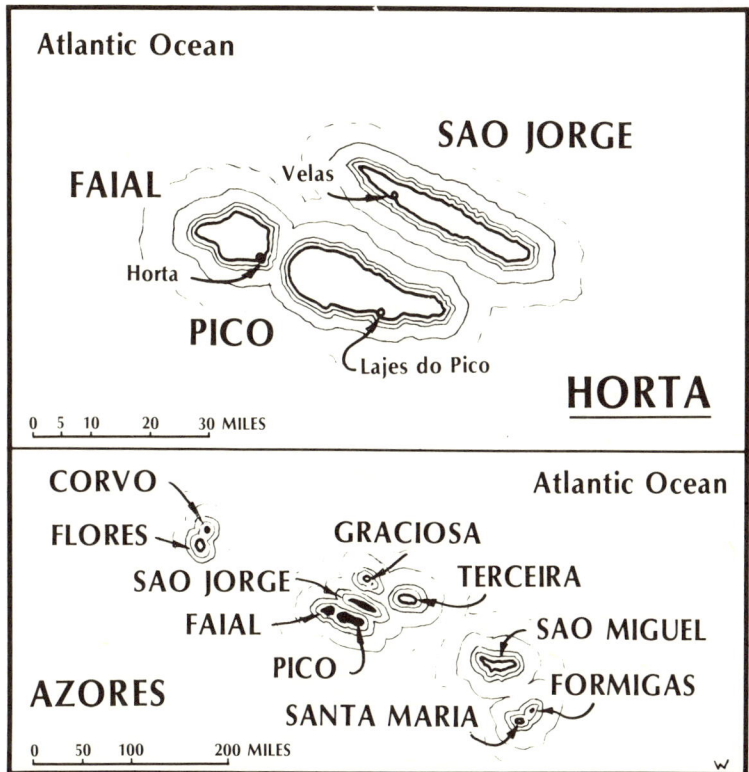

Atlantic Ocean

SAO JORGE

FAIAL

Velas

Horta

PICO

Lajes do Pico

HORTA

0 5 10 20 30 MILES

Atlantic Ocean

CORVO

FLORES

GRACIOSA

SAO JORGE

TERCEIRA

FAIAL

SAO MIGUEL

PICO

FORMIGAS

AZORES

SANTA MARIA

0 50 100 200 MILES

ATLANTIC

━━━━━━━━━━━━━━━━ **HUACHO, TOWN OF** ━━━━━━━━━━━

Pop: 28,700 (1969 est.)

Huacho is a seaport on the coast of Peru about 70 miles to the north of Callao. It is a shipping point for the country's cotton and sugar-growing districts. A provisional stamp issue was released there in 1884, because of a stamp shortage caused by the occupation of Lima and Callao by Chile during the 1879-1884 war with that country.

PERU

BRAZIL

HUACHO

Lima

Callao

Pacific Ocean

Lake Titicaca

SOUTH AMERICA

0 50 100 150 200 MILES

Area: 81,274 sq. miles
Pop: 38 million (1968)
Capital: Ch'ang-sha

Hunan is a province of south-central China. Regional overprints were produced for use in Hunan during the 1940s. In 1949 stamps were issued for the Communist Central Chinese Liberation Area, of which Hunan was part.

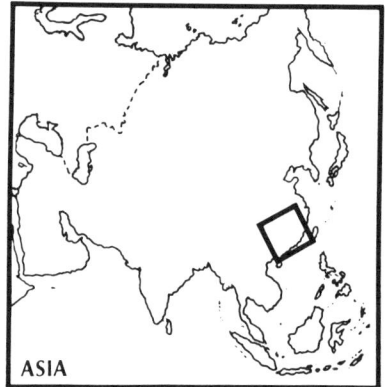

—————— HUPEH, PROVINCE OF ——————

Area: 72,394 sq. miles
Pop: 32 million (1968 est.)
Capital: Wu-han

Hupeh is a province of east-central China. Regional overprints were issued for use in the province during the 1940s. In 1949, stamps were issued for the Communist Central Chinese Liberation Area, of which Hupeh was part.

Area: 99 sq. miles
Pop: 9,600 (1961)

Now known as Ikaria, the island of Icaria is located about 13 miles west southwest of the island of Samos. It is part of the territory known collectively as New Greece. This was territory on the mainland and various islands in the Aegean Sea taken by Greece from Turkey prior to WWI. Stamps were issued during 1912-13 under a Greek military administration.

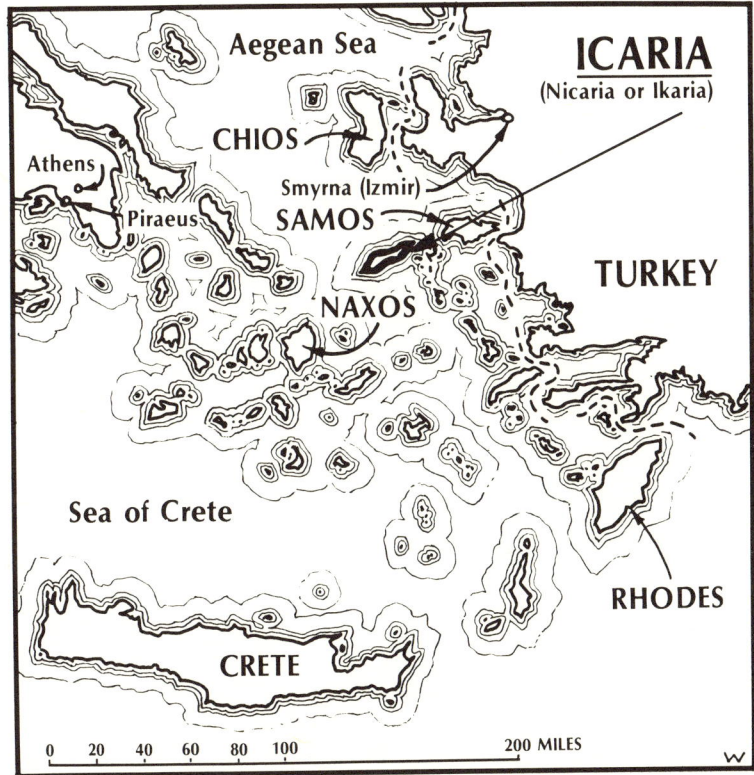

IFNI, COLONY OF

Area: 579 sq. miles
Pop: 50,000 (estimated)
Capital: Sidi Ifni

Ifni was a Spanish colony enclaved on the coast of Morocco. Although Spain owned it from 1860, it was not until 1934 that a Spanish settlement was established. The boundaries were fixed in 1912 under an agreement with France, which controlled Morocco at that time. It was ceded to the Kingdom of Morocco in 1969.

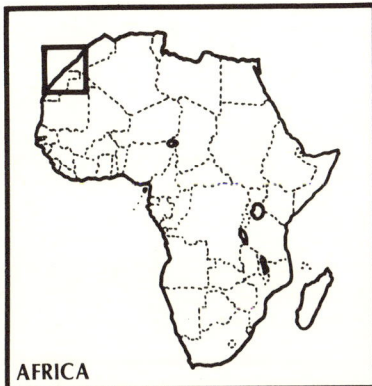

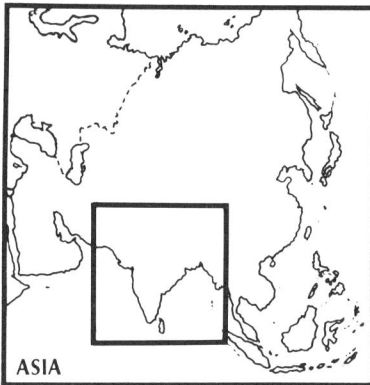

Area: 1,107,968 sq. miles
Pop: 363,100,000 (1934 est.)
Capital: Delhi

The British presence in India came about in the 18th century when the activities of the British East India Company resulted in the acquisition of territory. Having defeated the French, who had colonial aspirations in the area, in 1757, British influence grew as additional territory was gained. By 1887, the areas of India that were not under direct British rule were protected states under native rulers. These were the convention and feudatory states, some of which issued stamps. As the movement for independence grew, the system of government was modified to provide a greater degree of home rule in the areas of direct British control (British India). British rule came to an end with the creation of the Dominions of India and Pakistan in 1947. For information on the convention and feudatory states, see India, Convention States, and India, Feudatory States.

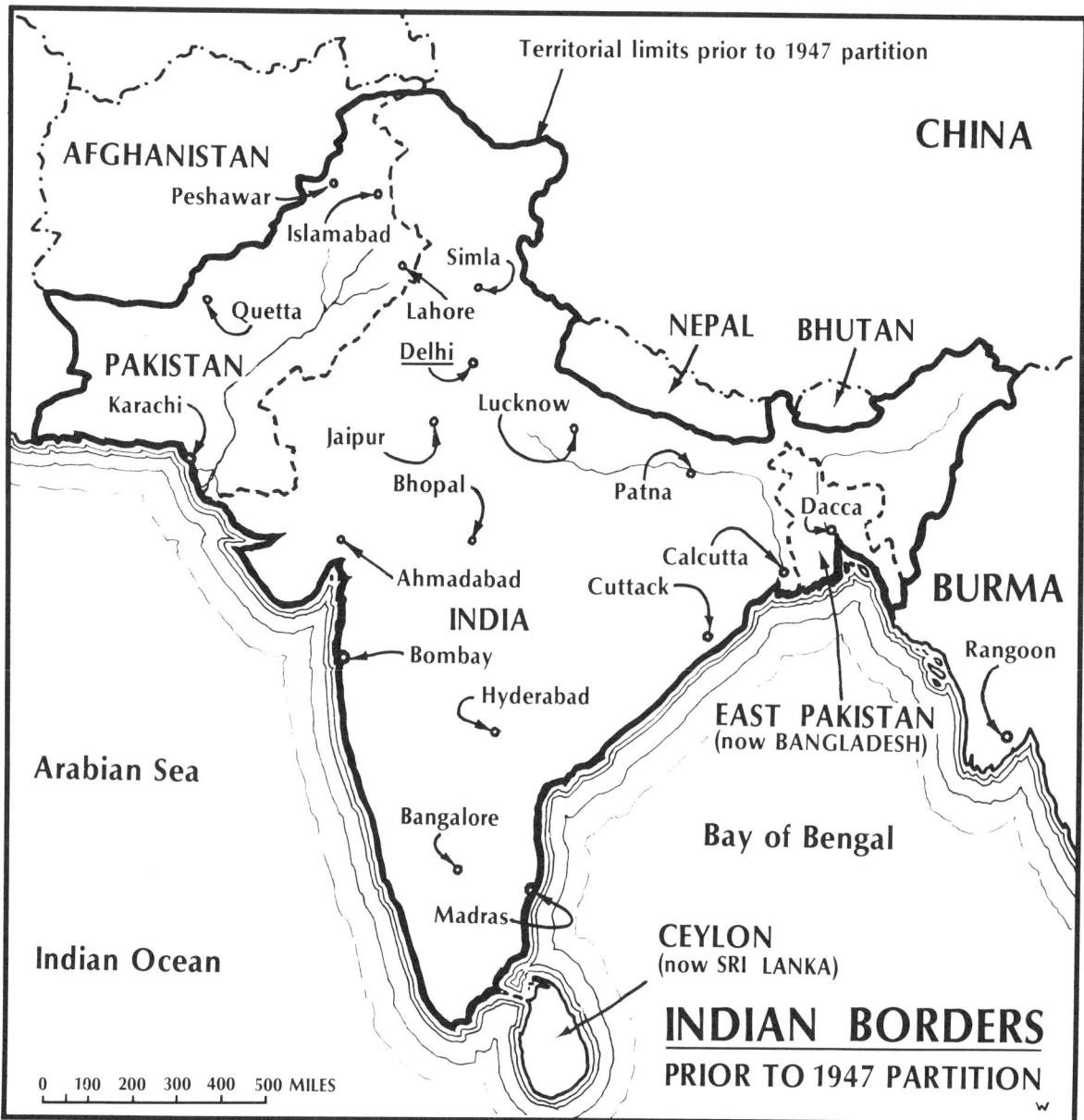

ASIA

Territorial limits prior to 1947 partition

CHINA

AFGHANISTAN

Peshawar

Islamabad

Simla

Quetta

Lahore

NEPAL   BHUTAN

PAKISTAN

Delhi

Karachi

Lucknow

Jaipur

Bhopal

Patna

Dacca

Calcutta

BURMA

Ahmadabad

Cuttack

INDIA

Rangoon

Bombay

Hyderabad

EAST PAKISTAN
(now BANGLADESH)

Arabian Sea

Bangalore

Bay of Bengal

Madras

CEYLON
(now SRI LANKA)

Indian Ocean

INDIAN BORDERS
PRIOR TO 1947 PARTITION

0   100 200 300 400 500 MILES

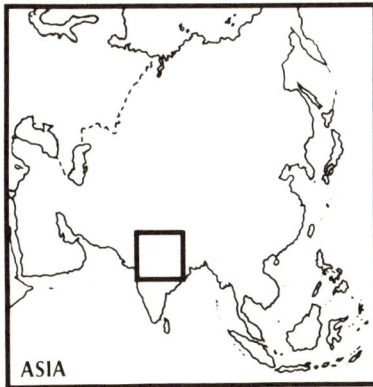

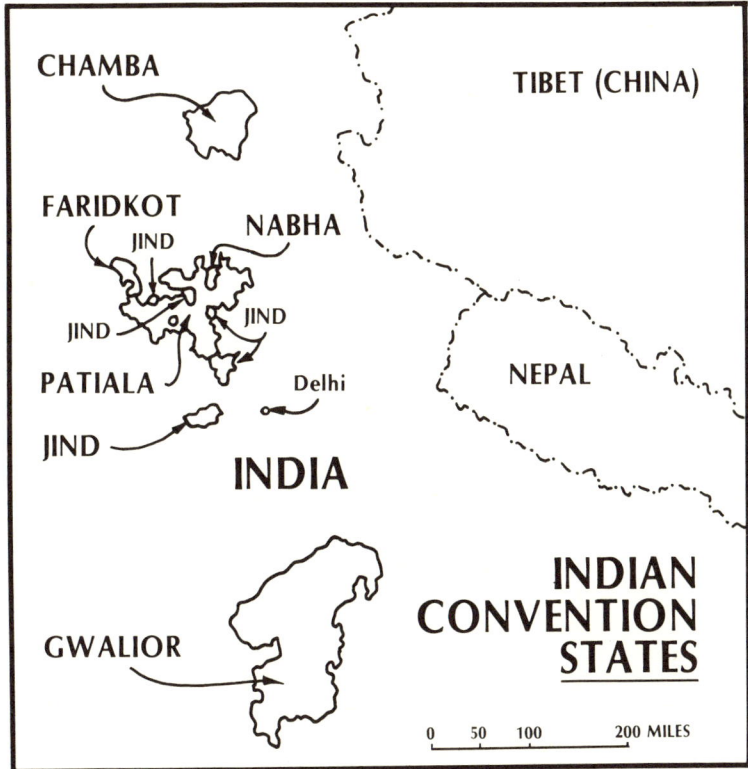

Stamps issued by the various convention states of India were also valid for use throughout the area of British India. The stamp-issuing convention states included Chamba, Faridkot, Gwalior, Jind, Nabha, and Patiala. Faridkot and Jind were previously feudatory states, and are thus also included under Indian Feudatory States.

CHAMBA

Chamba came under British influence about 1846 and was located in the northern part of India to the south of Kashmir. It had an area of 3,131 square miles and a population estimated in 1941 to be about 168,900. Stamps of British India were overprinted for use in Chamba beginning in 1886 and continued until the 1940s.

FARIDKOT

Faridkot became a convention state in 1886, and subsequent stamp issues were overprints on stamps of British India. The state was located in the central Punjab and had an area of about 640 square miles.

GWALIOR

Located in the Central Provinces, Gwalior had an area of 26,367 square miles and a population estimated to be about four million in 1940. Its capital was Lashkar. Stamps of British India were overprinted for use in Gwalior from 1885 until the late 1940s.

JIND

Comprising several enclaves, Jind had an area of about 1,300 square miles and was located in the north Punjab. Its capital was Sangrur. It had been founded by a Sikh raja in 1763 and was loyal to Britain during the Mutiny of 1857. Stamps were those of British India overprinted and were first issued in 1885, continuing until the 1940s.

NABHA

Nabha was one of the Sikh states of the Phulkian group and was formed in the mid-1700s. Its area was 947 square miles and the population estimated at about 340,000 in the 1940s. The capital city was Nabha. Stamps were first issued in 1885 and consisted of overprints on issues of British India. They continued until the 1940s.

PATIALA

Patiala was a Punjab state founded by a Sikh chieftain about 1763. It came under British protection in the early 1800s. Its area was 5,942 square miles, and the population was estimated at close to two million in 1941. The capital was the city of Patiala. Stamps were issued from 1884 and were overprinted on stamps of British India. They continued until the late 1940s.

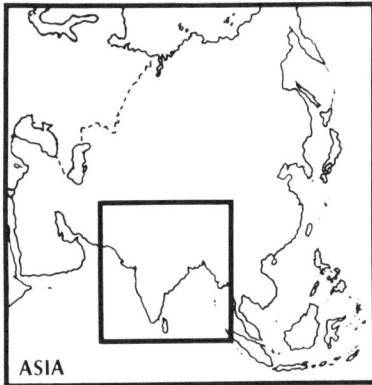

Several of the Indian feudatory states issued their own stamps, and although these are listed in the catalogs, they were, in fact, local issues that were valid only within the particular state issuing them.

ALWAR

Alwar was a princely state founded in 1771. It was based on the city of the same name, located about 98 miles southwest of Delhi. Under British paramountcy, it was controlled by the Jaipur sub-agency of the Rajputana agency. It joined the Matsya union in 1948 and was

merged with Rajasthan in 1949. Its area was 3,241 square miles. Stamps were issued between 1877 and 1902. They depict an Indian dagger.

BAMRA

A small feudatory state located in the Eastern States of Bengal, Bamra was administered by the Orissa State agency. It had an area of about 2,000 square miles and the capital city was Deogarh. Stamps of Bamra were used between 1888 and 1894.

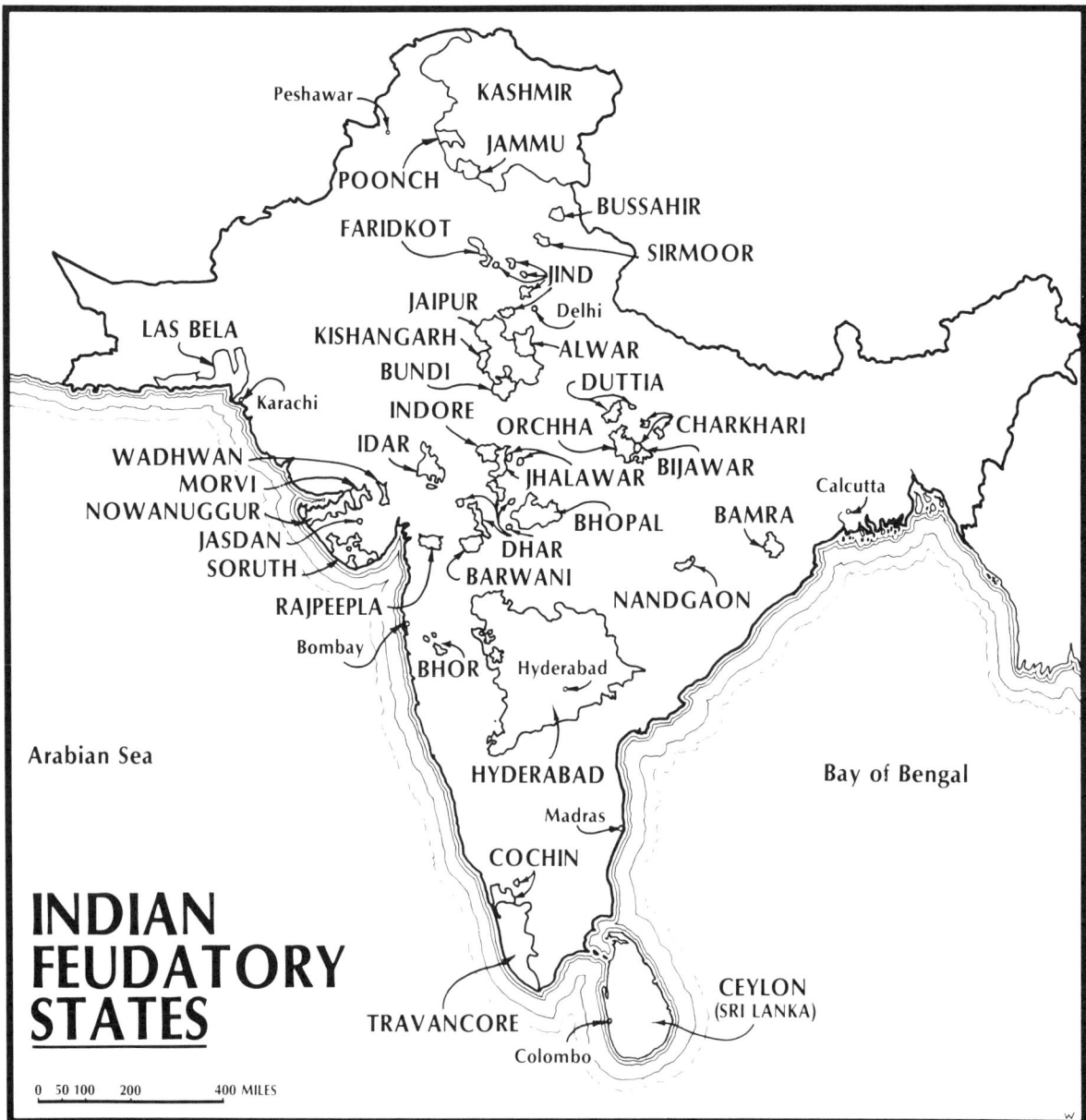

INDIAN FEUDATORY STATES

0 50 100 200   400 MILES

BARWANI

Located about 80 miles southeast of Indore, in west central India, the state of Barwani had an area of 1,175 square miles and a population reported to have been about 150,000. During the period 1921-1948 Barwani used its own stamps. Most were produced in booklet panes of four.

BHOPAL

A princely state formed in 1723 by an Afghan chieftain, Bhopal became a protectorate in British India in 1817. Based on the city of the same name, it was located in the central part of India and had an area of almost 7,000 square miles. Bhopal's own stamps were used from 1876 to 1950, but only Official stamps were issued after 1908.

BHOR

A state of some 900 square miles, Bhor was based on the town of the same name located about 90 miles southeast of Bombay. Three stamps were issued between 1879 and 1901.

BIJAWAR

The town of Bijawar, located about 150 miles southwest of Allahabad, was the capital of Bijawar state, which had an area of about 975 square miles. Stamps were used between 1935 and 1939, but were not withdrawn until 1941.

BUNDI

The 2,150-square-mile state of Bundi was governed from the town of the same name. The state was founded in AD 1342 and came under British protection in 1818. It was subsequently controlled through the Eastern Rajputana sub-agency of Rajputana. Bundi's first stamps were issued in 1894. They were primitive designs featuring a dagger. The final issue came in 1947. From 1948 to 1950, stamps of Rajasthan were used.

BUSSAHIR

Bussahir, or Bashahr, was an Indian feudatory state in the Punjab, located on the lower slopes of the Himalayas at about 32 degrees north and 78 degrees east. The Sutlej River flows through the area from east to west. The rajah of Bussahir ruled under a grant from the East India Company beginning in 1815, according to the 1884 edition of *Chambers Encyclopedia*. Stamps were issued from 1895 to 1901.

CHARKHARI

The state of Charkhari, in the Bundelkhand agency of central India, was located about 125 miles west of Allahabad. It is believed to have had an area of some 900 square miles. Charkhari issued its first stamps in 1894, with the final issue appearing in 1943.

COCHIN

A former princely state on the southwestern coast of India, Cochin had an area of 1,500 square miles and a population reported at 1.4 million at the time it became part of the Republic of India in 1950. Cochin town is a port city located on a narrow tongue of land between the Arabian Sea and a lagoon. Made into a port for ocean-going vessels, it is now a seaport of some importance. The town of Ernakulam is the major trading center, however. Cochin became the earliest European settlement in the sub-continent, when Vasco da Gama established a settlement there in 1502. Subsequently it was owned by the Dutch, with the British gaining final possession in 1795. In 1949, Cochin joined in a federation with Travancore. Cochin's first stamps were issued in 1892 and continued until the merger with Travencore on July 1, 1949.

DHAR

A feudatory state based on the town of the same name about 30 miles west of Indore, Dhar had an area of approximately 2,000 square miles and a population of some 250,000. It used its own stamps from 1887 to 1901.

DUTTIA

A small princely state in central India with an area of about 900 square miles, Duttia's capital city was Datia, which is located about 125 miles southeast of Agra. Stamps were issued by Duttia between 1893 and 1921.

FARIDKOT

The former feudatory state of Faridkot was located in the Punjab agency of India. It had an area of about 640 square miles and was based on the town of the same name. In the mid-1880s it became a convention state, and since it issued stamps as both a feudatory state and a convention state, it gets two listings in the catalogs. As a feudatory state it issued stamps from 1878 to 1886.

HYDERABAD

Hyderabad was a large and important princely state in central India. Its ruler, the Nizam of Hyderabad, was considered to be the world's richest man at the time of the state's annexation to India in 1947. The state's former capital city of Hyderabad possesses many palaces and other fine buildings, attesting to its former glory. It had an area of a little over 82,300 square miles, and its population exceeded 16 million. Stamps were issued from 1869 to 1949.

IDAR

This feudatory state was located in western India, some 320 miles north of Bombay. It had an area of about 1,670 square miles and a population exceeding 260,000. The capital city was Himatnagar. Stamps were issued from 1939 to 1944, but the Idar postal service carried only Official mail, according to Gibbons. All stamps were issued in booklet panes of four, producing stamps with one or more adjacent sides imperf.

INDORE

Formerly known as Holkar State, the feudatory state of Indore was located in central India. According to Schwartzberg's *Historical Atlas of South Asia*, it comprised an area surrounding the capital city of Indore and five nearby enclaves. With an area of almost 10,000 square miles, the state had a population of about 1.5 million. Stamps were first issued in 1886 and continued until stamps of India came into use in the late 1940s.

JAIPUR

A former feudatory state located southwest of Delhi, Jaipur had an area of about 15,500 square miles and a population reported as close to three million. Its capital was the city of Jaipur, located 700 miles northeast of Bombay by rail and 191 miles southwest of Delhi. It is considered to be one of India's most beautiful cities and is known as the Pink City from the prevailing color of its buildings. In 1949, Jaipur joined the states of Bundi and Kishangarh to form Rajasthan. Stamps were issued from 1904 until the formation of Rajasthan.

JAMMU AND KASHMIR

This onetime feudatory state lies in the extreme north of India, where the borders of Afghanistan, China, and Pakistan meet and come very close to the USSR. It is considered to be one of India's most beautiful areas, and the Vale of Kashmir is world famous. The state's population was quoted in 1941 as four million, and the land area was about 86,000 square miles. Since partition, neither India nor Pakistan has been able to agree on the frontier, and Pakistan currently occupies about 32,350 square miles of what was Jammu and Kashmir. The winter capital was the city of Jammu, while Srinagar was tne summer capital. Stamps were issued individually by each state from the mid-1860s, with joint issues appearing in 1878. They became obsolete Nov. 1, 1894.

JASDAN

A small state of some 300 square miles, Jasdan was located on the Kathiawar Peninsula of western India. In 1948, it was incorporated into the state of Saurashtra. Today, much of what was Jasdan is located in the Gir Forest Wildlife Sanctuary, according to Jempson, writing in the January 1982 issue of *Stamps*, a British stamp periodical. The state's population was about 34,000. Jasdan issued only a single stamp in 1942. It was released in booklet panes of four and eight and became obsolete in 1948.

JHALAWAR

A formerly princely state based on the capital city of Jhalrapatan and located about 160 miles south of Jaipur, Jhalawar had an area of 813 square miles and a population estimated at 108,000. Formed in the late 1830s, it was merged into Rajasthan in 1948. The city of Jhalrapatan was also known as Patan or Jhalawar. It is now a trading center of some importance and serves an area producing oilseed and cotton. Two stamps were issued in 1887 and 1890. They became obsolete on Oct. 31, 1900.

JIND

A feudatory state of some 1,300 square miles based on the capital city of Sangrur, Jind became a convention state in the mid-1880s and is thus listed in both sections of the stamp catalogs. Feudatory state stamps were used from 1874 until the convention state stamps went into use.

KISHANGARH

This state was located mostly within the Thar Desert in the Jaipur Residency. The capital city was named Kishangarh and was located to the northwest of the Indian city

of Ajmar. In 1948 the state became part of Rajasthan. Stamps were used from 1899 until the merger.

LAS BELA

A former princely state, Las Bela is now part of the Karachi division of Pakistan. The former capital city is Bela, about 115 miles northwest of Karachi. It had a 1961 population of about 3,100. Las Bela has long been important for its location on the coastal trade route between Sind and Persia. The state had an area of about 7,000 square miles. Its own stamps were used from 1897 to April 1, 1907.

MORVI

Located on the Kathiawar Peninsula, northwest of Bombay, Morvi was a small princely state of about 800 square miles based on the city of the same name. In 1948, it was incorporated into the United States of Saurashtra and subsequently into the Republic of India. It issued its own stamps from April 1, 1931, until Feb. 15, 1948.

NANDGAON

Located in central India, Nandgaon was based on the city of Rajnandgaon. It had an area of about 875 square miles and was within the Chattisgarh States agency, according to the Scott Catalog. First issued in February 1892, its stamps became obsolete Jan. 1, 1895.

NOWANUGGUR

Nowanuggur was a princely state on the Kathiawar Peninsula of western India. Although contemporary sources spell it as Nowanuggur, the city's name has been recorded as Nawanagar and Navanagar and currently it is noted as Jamnagar. The town stands on the south shore of the Gulf of Cutch at the mouth of the Nagna River. It was described in 19th-century references as some four miles in circumference and an important trading center famous for the fine quality of its cloth. Stamps were used from 1877 until Jan. 1, 1895.

ORCHHA

A former state in central India, Orchha had an area of about 2,100 square miles and was based on the city of Tikamgarh. Stamps were used from 1913 until the early 1940s.

POONCH

An Indian state formerly feudatory to Jammu and Kashmir, Poonch had an area of about 1,600 square miles located between the Jammu and Kashmir capital cities of

Srinagar and Jammu. Its capital was the town of Poonch (Punch).

RAJPIPLA

Rajpipla, or Rajpeepla, was a princely state located in the Gujarat States agency to the north of Bombay. Its area was about 1,500 square miles and the population estimated as some 205,000. The capital city was Nandod. It issued three stamps in 1880, which became obsolete in 1886.

SIRMOOR

A former princely state, Sirmoor was located in the Punjab Hill group. It was sometimes known as Nahan, which was the name of its capital city, located about 60 miles south of the town of Simla. Mostly located in the Himalayan foothills, Sirmoor had an area of about 1,100 square miles and a population in 1961 of almost 200,000. Stamps were issued from June 1876 to April 1, 1902.

SORUTH

The name Soruth, according to Gibbons, is a contraction of Saurashtra (see United States of Saurashtra) and originally referred to the entire Kathiawar Peninsula. Philatelically it refers only to a portion including the state of Junagadh or Junagarh. The capital was the city of Junagarh. The state's area was some 3,340 square miles and the population almost 200,000. In 1948, the state joined with the stamp-issuing states of Jasdan, Morvi, Nowanuggur, Wadhwan, and more than 200 other states to form the United States of Saurashtra. It is now part of the Republic of India. Stamps were in use from 1864 until formation of the USS.

TRAVANCORE

A former princely state at the southern tip of India, Travancore came under British protection in 1795. In 1949 it joined with the state of Cochin to form Travancore-Cochin. As a feudatory state, it was part of Madras States agency and had an area of 7,700 square miles and a 1941 population of some six million. Stamps were used from 1888 until June 30, 1949.

WADHWAN

Wadhwan was located in the Kathiawar agency of western India. Its capital was the town of Wadhwan (Surendranager). It had an area of 250 square miles and a population estimated at some 44,260. Stamps were used from 1888 to Jan. 1, 1895.

Area: 272,130 sq. miles
Pop: 18,000 (1900 est)
Capital: Hanoi

French Indo-China consisted of what are now Vietnam, Cambodia, and Laos. The territories making up the colonial area were Annam, Tonkin, Cochin China, Cambodia, and Laos. The area of China leased to France as Kwangchowan was also included for administrative purposes. Occupied by the Japanese during WWII, the area has been in a state of turmoil since then.

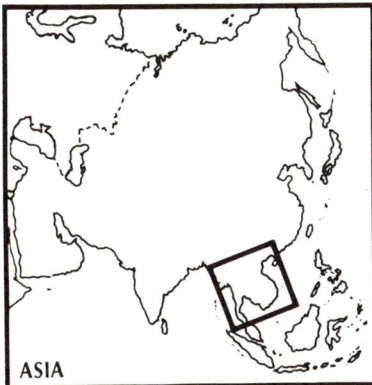

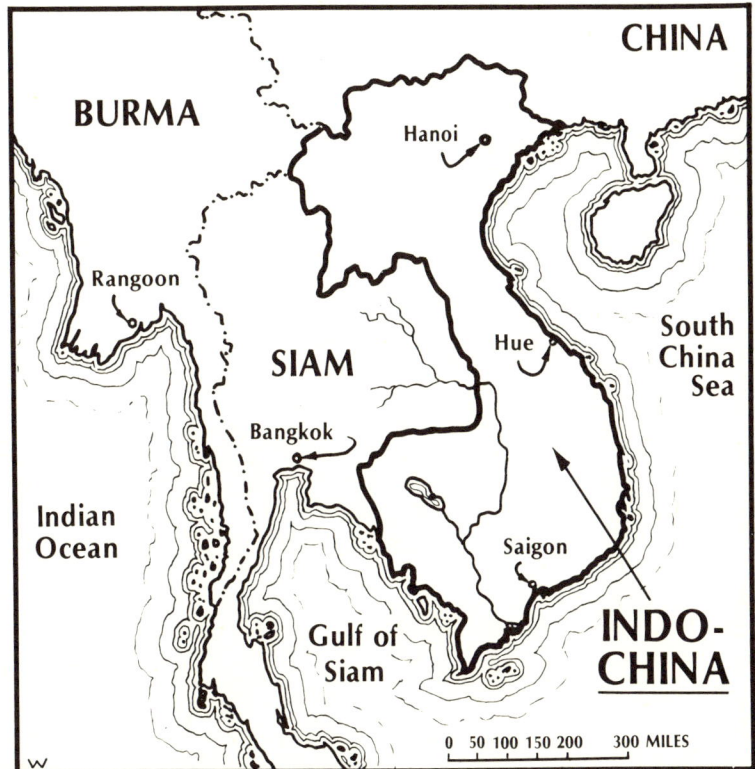

CHINA

BURMA

Hanoi

Rangoon

SIAM

Hue

South China Sea

Bangkok

Indian Ocean

Saigon

Gulf of Siam

INDO-CHINA

0 50 100 150 200   300 MILES

ASIA

INHAMBANE, DISTRICT OF

Area: 26,426 sq. miles
Pop: 745,911 (1970)
Capital: Inhambane

Inhambane is a district of central Mozambique located on the coast and based on the town of the same name. The town, a seaport located on Inhambane Bay, had a 1960 population of about 22,000. As a Portuguese colonial unit apart from Mozambique from 1895 to the end of WWI, Inhambane had its own stamps.

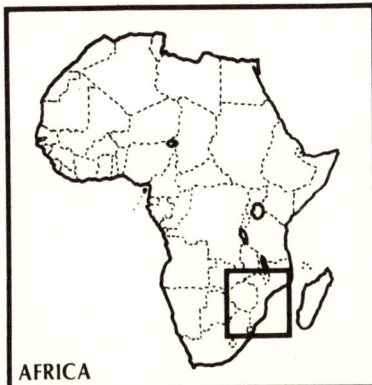

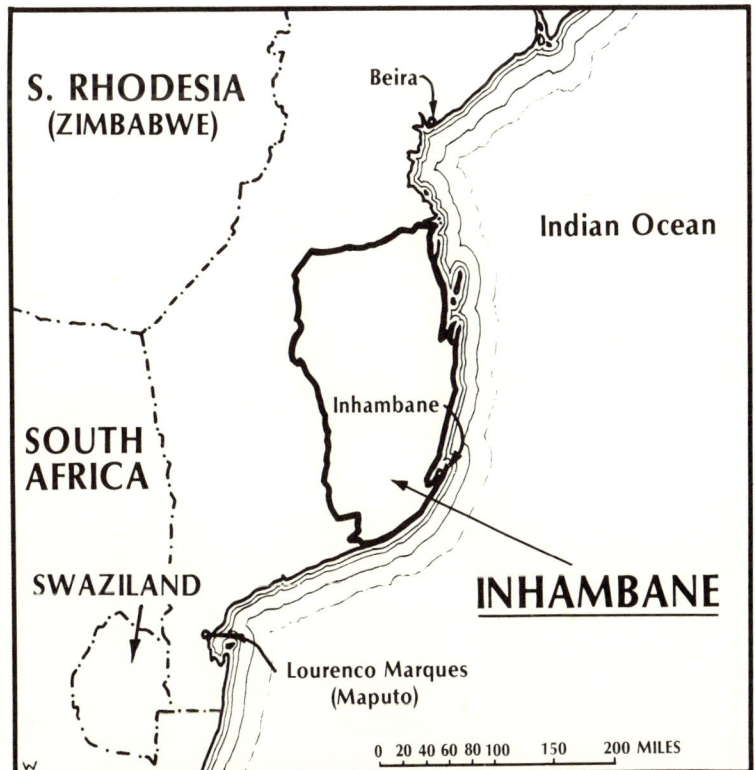

S. RHODESIA (ZIMBABWE)

Beira

Indian Ocean

SOUTH AFRICA

Inhambane

SWAZILAND

INHAMBANE

Lourenco Marques (Maputo)

0 20 40 60 80 100   150   200 MILES

AFRICA

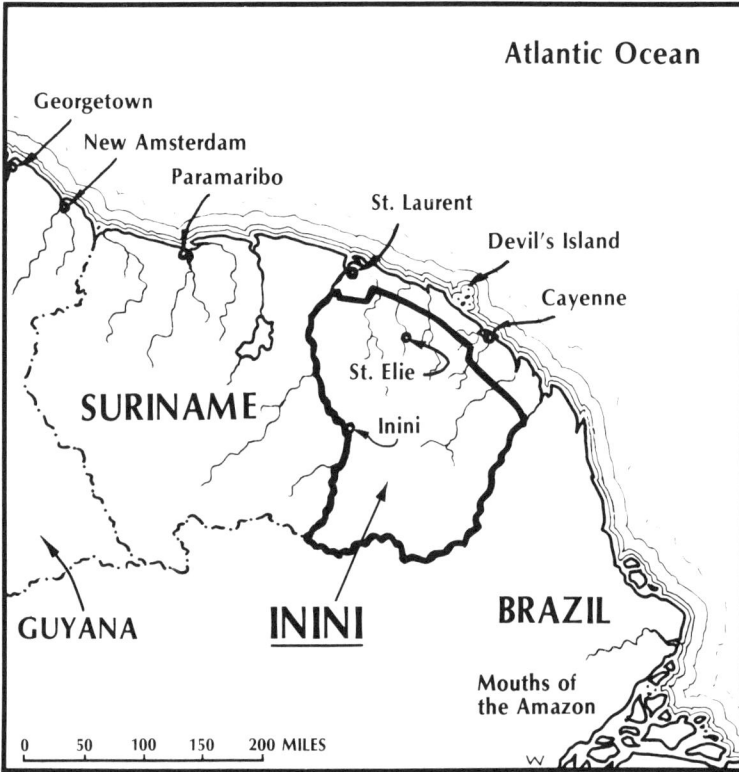

Area: 30,300 sq. miles
Pop: 5,000 (1945 est.)
Capital: St. Elie

The Arrondissement of Inini comprised the greater part of the French colony of French Guiana. It took in all of the interior portion and was mostly dense rain forest with few, if any, roads and a population in keeping with its untrodden depths. Except for flying, the many rivers and streams still provide the easiest mode of travel. Stamps were issued by the French from 1932 until WWII.

─────INNER MONGOLIA (MENG CHIANG)─────

Area: 454,633 sq. miles
Pop: 13 million (1967 est.)
Capital: Huhehot (Hu-ho-hao-t'e)

The area known as Inner Mongolia (Meng Chiang) is currently an autonomous region of the People's Republic of China. Its northern portion is within the Gobi Desert, and parts of its southern border are along the Great Wall of China. Stamps were issued for use there during the 1940s.

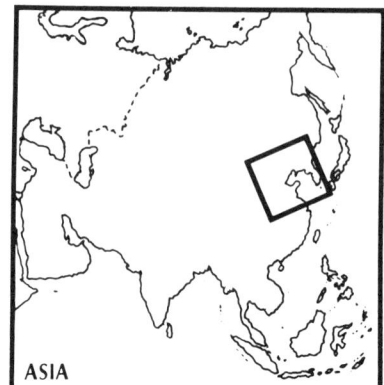

Area: 868 sq. miles
Pop: 183,663 (1971)

The Ionian Islands form a group off the west coast of Greece, except for one off the south coast of that country. They were administered as a protectorate by Britain from 1815 to 1864, when they were granted to Greece. The islands are Corfu, Paxos, Levkas, Ithaca, Cephalonia, Zante, and Cerigo. The map also shows the current Greek names.

EUROPE

ITALY
ALBANIA
CORFU (KERKIRA)
PAXOS
LEVKAS
ITHACA (ITHAKI)
CEPHALONIA (KEFALLINIA)
GREECE
Corinth Canal
ZANTE (ZAKINTHOS)
Ionian Sea
IONIAN ISLANDS
CERIGO (KITHIRA)

0 20 40 60 80 100 MILES

ISTRIA, PENINSULA OF

Area: 1,545 sq. miles

The Istrian Peninsula is located at the head of the Adriatic Sea and is now part of Yugoslavia. The chief town is Pula (Pola), which was once an important naval base of the Austro-Hungarian Empire. The area went to Italy following WWI, and after WWII it was made part of Yugoslavia. Stamps were issued at the end of WWII for the Slovene Coast and Istria, which were in Zone B occupied by Yugoslavia. The stamps were used from 1945 through 1947.

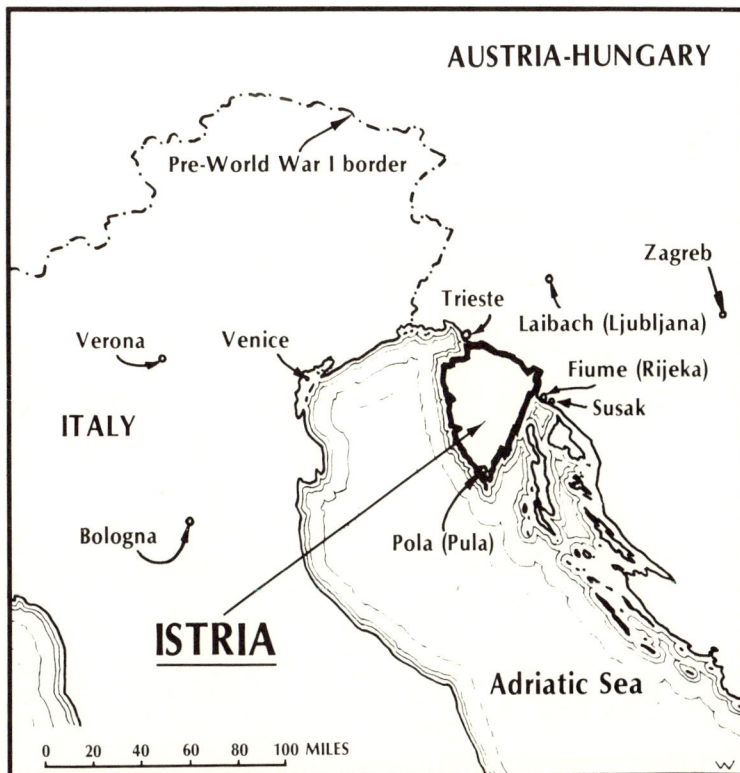

EUROPE

AUSTRIA-HUNGARY
Pre-World War I border
Zagreb
Trieste
Laibach (Ljubljana)
Fiume (Rijeka)
Verona
Venice
Susak
ITALY
Bologna
Pola (Pula)
ISTRIA
Adriatic Sea

0 20 40 60 80 100 MILES

AUSTRIA-HUNGARY
ITALIAN AUSTRIA
areas occupied by Italy following the end of World War I

SWITZERLAND

Trent (Trentino)

Udine

YUGO.

Fiume (Rijeka)

Verona

Trieste

Bologna

Adriatic Sea

ITALY

0 20 40 60 80 100 MILES

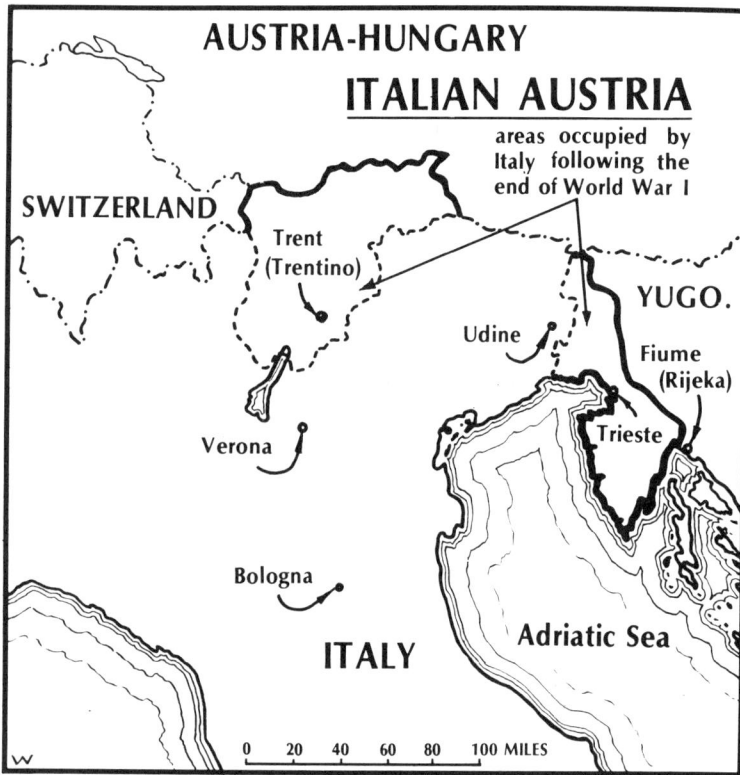

The name Italian Austria was applied to areas of the Austro-Hungarian Empire that were taken by Italy during WWI. The areas included Trentino, the city of Trieste, and the Istrian Peninsula. There had long been a strong movement in Italy for the return of these areas, which had once been Italian and which had a large Italian population. Occupation stamps were issued in 1918-19 by Italian authorities for use in the areas.

EUROPE

————ITALIAN EAST AFRICA, COLONY OF————

SUDAN ITALIAN EAST AFRICA

Red Sea

ARABIA

Massaua

Asmara

Mocha

ERITREA

Aden

Gulf of Aden

Fr. SOMALILAND

Djibouti

Addis Ababa

Br. SOMALILAND

ETHIOPIA

ITALIAN SOMALILAND

KENYA

Mogadishu

Indian Ocean

0 100 200 300 400 500 MILES

Italian East Africa was the name given to the Italian-occupied territories of Eritrea, Ethiopia, and Italian Somaliland. These were made a combined administrative area following the invasion and conquest of Ethiopia prior to WWII. It lasted only a few years, until British forces liberated the area, restored Ethiopia's freedom, retook the British protectorate of Somaliland, and placed Eritrea and Italian Somaliland under military administration.

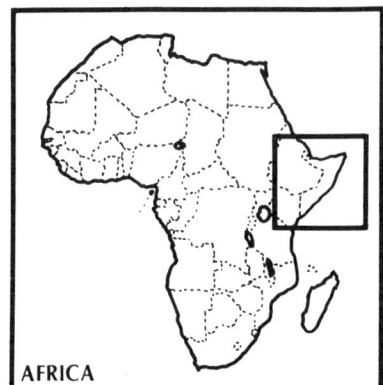

AFRICA

Area: 178,218 sq. miles
Pop: Two million (1931 est.)
Capital: Mogadishu

A former Italian colony in East Africa, Italian Somaliland was part of Italian East Africa until it was taken by British forces during WWII and placed under military administration. After the war, it was placed under Italian administration as a United Nations Trust Territory. In 1960, together with the British Somaliland Protectorate, it became independent as Somalia.

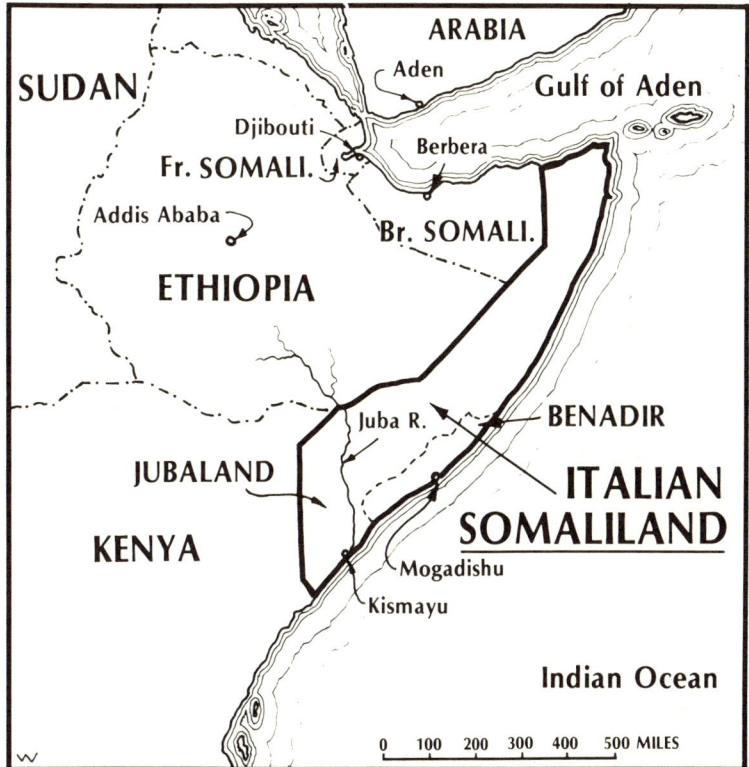

JAFFA, CITY OF

Pop: 23,000 (1900 est.)

Located on the Mediterranean Sea in Israel, the ancient seaport city of Jaffa is now part of the Tel Aviv-Yafo urban complex. Its recorded history goes back many years. It was twice captured by Crusaders, but was lost to Muslims in AD 1196. In 1799, Napoleon took the city, but it was regained by the Turks who held it as part of the Ottoman Empire until WWI, when the British finally liberated it and included it in the Mandate area of Palestine.

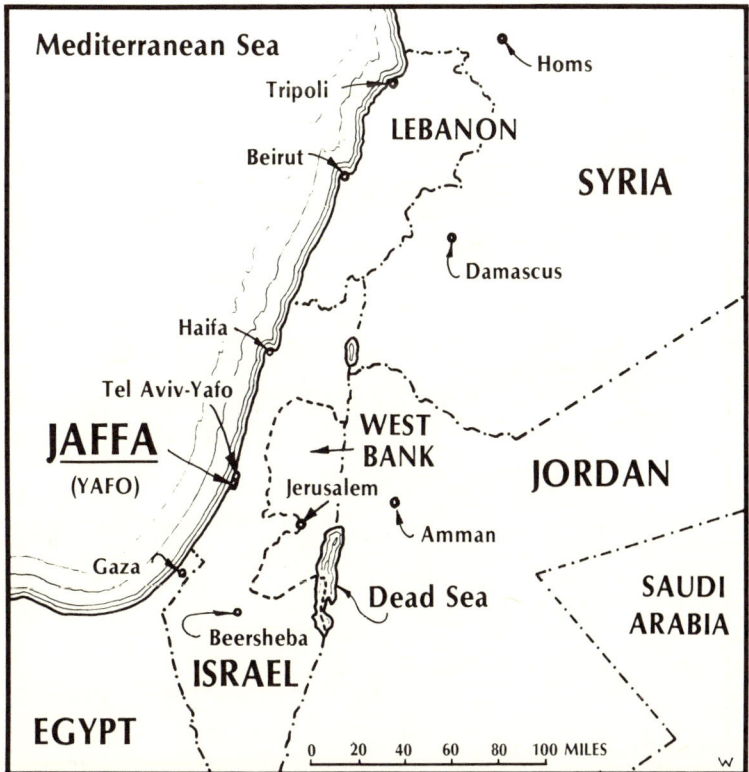

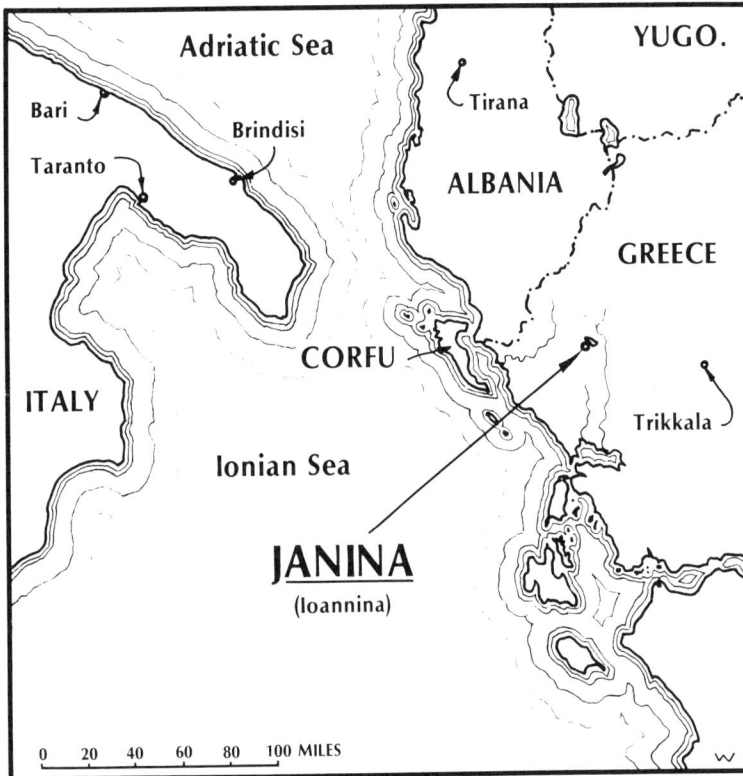

Pop: 20,000 (1900)
38,814 (1971)

Located in northern Greece, the town of Janina is now called Ioannina. It was a Byzantine city until taken by the Turks in 1430. The area was taken by Greece in 1913, and in 1941 the Germans occupied it during their WWII activities. It was liberated in 1944. From 1902 to 1911, Italian stamps were overprinted "JANINA" and surcharged for use at an Italian post office there.

JAVA, ISLAND OF

Area: 50,554 sq. miles
Pop: 26,125,053 (1897)
Capital: Batavia

The island of Java was occupied by the Dutch from the early 1800s and became part of the Dutch Indies. Its chief city was Batavia, now Jakarta, the Indonesian capital. Stamps were issued beginning in 1864 and continued until independence in the late 1940s, with the exception of the period of Japanese occupation in WWII.

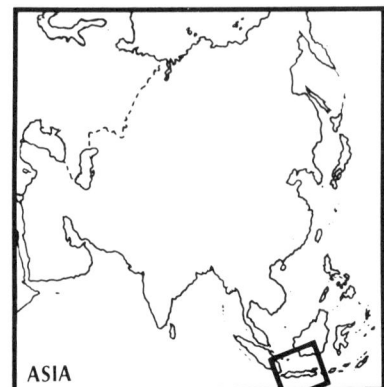

Pop: 40,000 (1900 est.)
376,000 (1978 est.)

A major goal of the medieval Crusaders, the city of Jerusalem was under Muslim domination from the mid-13th century until it was taken by British forces in 1917. It was included in the British mandate area of Palestine and is now the capital city of Israel. Under the Turks, several foreign post offices operated in the city, and the Russians issued stamps overprinted ''Gerusalemme'' in 1909.

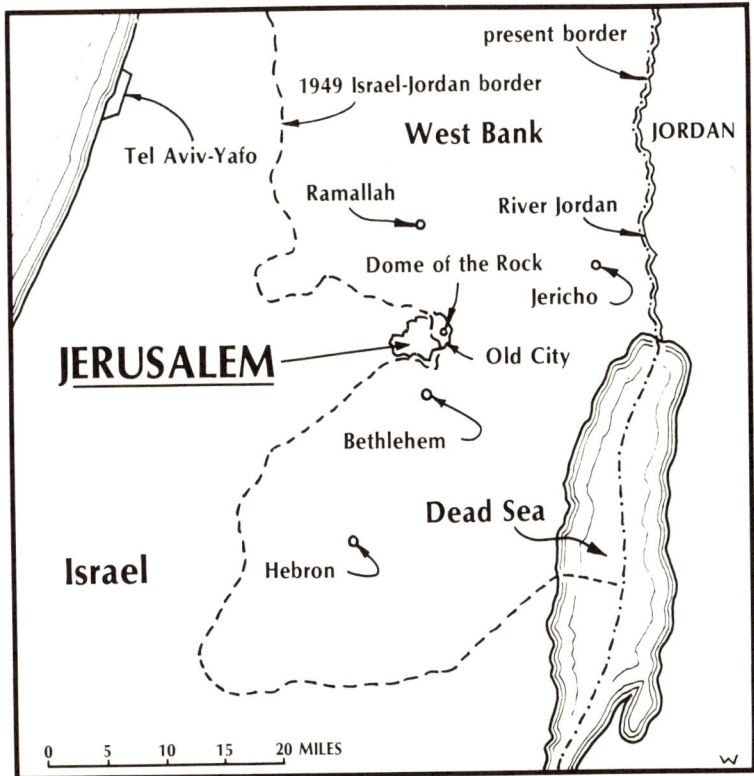

JUAN FERNANDEZ ISLANDS

Area: 79 sq. miles
Pop: 500 (1960)

An island group located about 400 miles off the coast of Chile in the Pacific Ocean, the Juan Fernandez Islands have a claim to fame that far outstrips their actual importance: from October 1704 to February 1709, they were the home of Alexander Selkirk, claimed to be the original of the character in Defoe's famous book *Robinson Crusoe*.

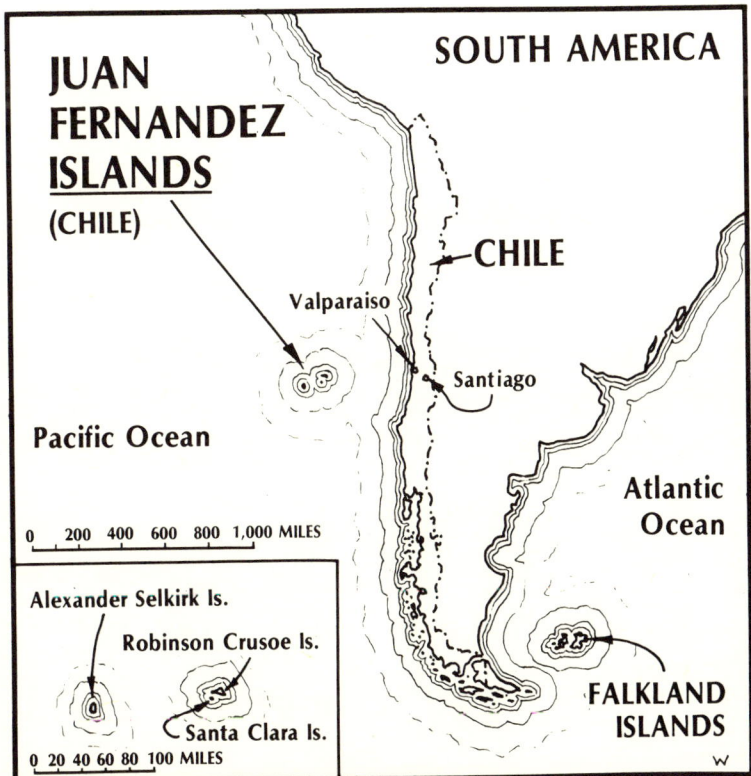

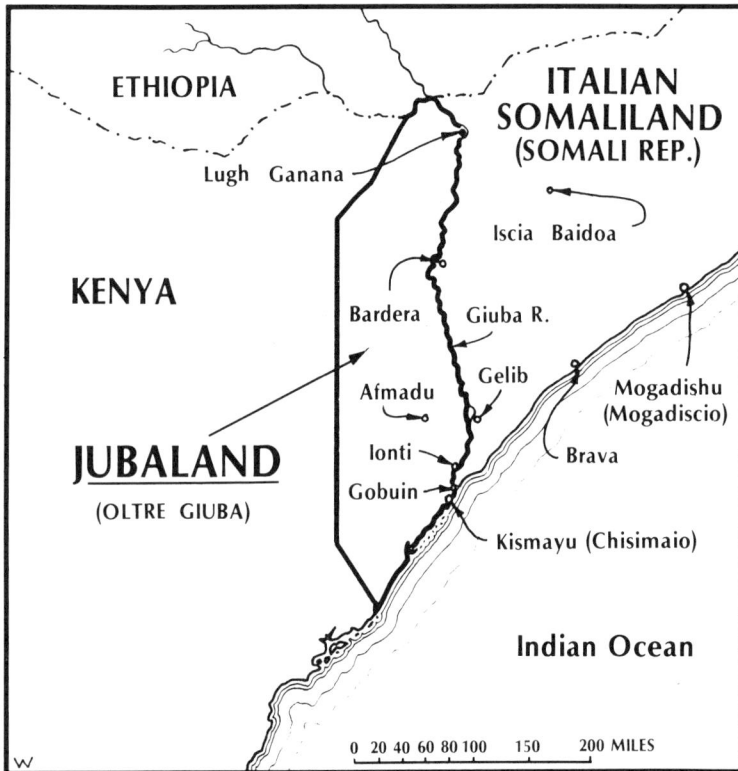

Area: 33,000 sq. miles

An area in East Africa, Jubaland (Italian Oltre Giuba) is located between the Juba River and the border of Kenya. It was included within the borders of Kenya until it was ceded by Great Britain to Italy in 1925. The chief city is Kismayu. In 1926, it was merged into Italian Somaliland and is now part of the Somali Democratic Republic. Stamps were issued for Jubaland by Italy in 1925-26. They are listed by Scott under Oltre Giuba.

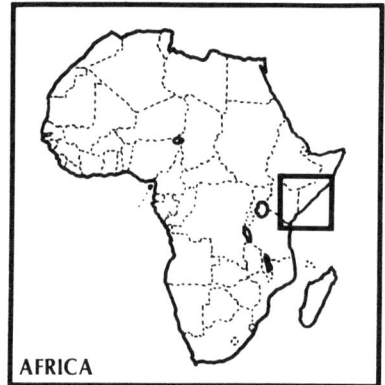

———————————— KANSU, PROVINCE OF ————————————

Area: 137,104 sq. miles
Pop: 13 million (1968 est.)
Capital: Lan-chow

Kansu is a mountainous province of the People's Republic of China. Its valleys form highways, including the ancient Silk Road, by which China traded with India and Persia. For many years part of the Kingdom of Wei, the area came under Kublai Khan in the 13th century. It was made a province of China in 1911. Stamps were overprinted for use in the province during the 1940s.

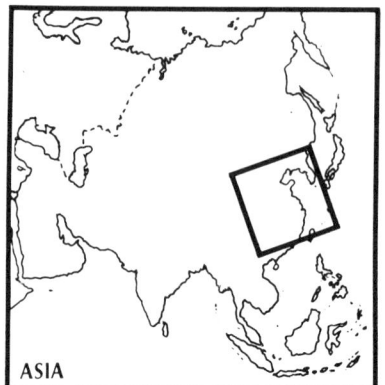

Area: 66,564 sq. miles
Pop: 714,000 (1970 est.)
Capital: Petrovavodsk

Now described as an autonomous republic of the USSR, Karelia was a strong and independent state during the Middle Ages. In 1721 it was annexed by Russia and, except for a brief independence in the early 1920s, has been under Soviet domination ever since. During WWII, the area was fought over and partially occupied by the Finns and Germans.

FINLAND

EASTERN KARELIA

Arkhangelsk

Onega

Pre-WWII border

Maximum Finnish-German advance into Karelia during WWII

Present Finnish-USSR border

WESTERN KARELIA

Petrozavodsk

Salmi

Lake Onega

Vyborg

Olonets

USSR

Leningrad

Lake Ladoga

KARELIA

0 50 100 150 200 MILES

EUROPE

KATANGA, PROVINCE OF

Area: 191,878 sq. miles
Pop: 2,174,400 (1969 est.)
Capital: Lubumbashi

Katanga is a province in the southern part of the African country of Zaire. It seceded in 1960-63, but was reunited with Zaire following United Nations intervention. Stamps were issued during the period of independence, and though the issuing authority was not recognized, the stamps were tolerated in the international mails and are listed in the major catalogs.

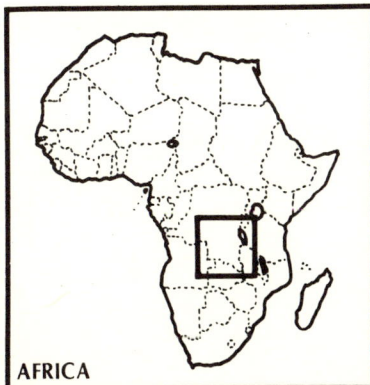

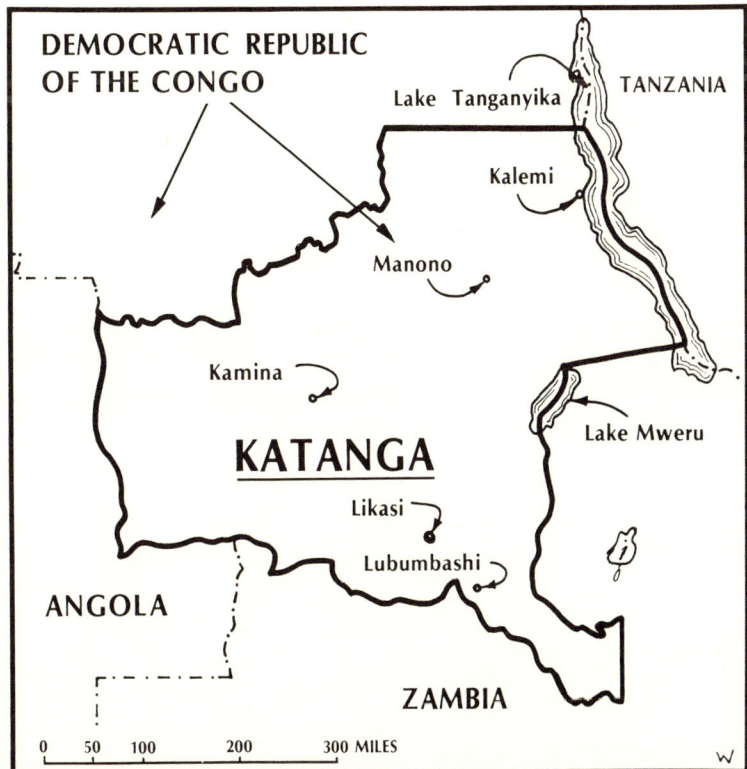

DEMOCRATIC REPUBLIC OF THE CONGO

Lake Tanganyika

TANZANIA

Kalemi

Manono

Kamina

Lake Mweru

KATANGA

ANGOLA

Likasi

Lubumbashi

ZAMBIA

0 50 100 200 300 MILES

AFRICA

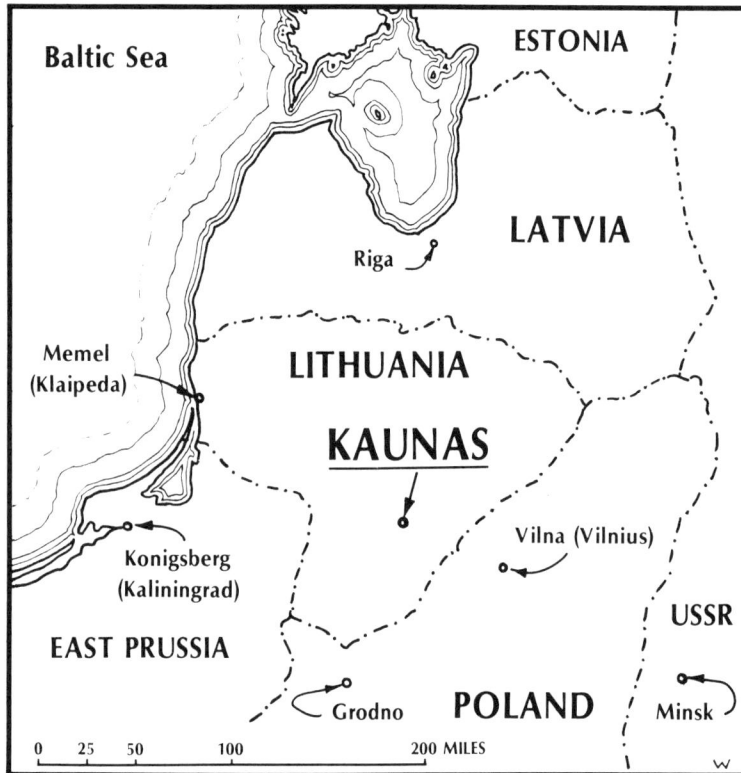

Pop: 284 000 (1967 est.)

A city in the once-independent country of Lithuania, now part of the USSR, Kaunas was the capital of its country following the 1920 Polish taking of Vilnius, the former Lithuanian capital. Several stamp issues are noted as being Kaunas issues, and one used during the Lithuanian occupation of the port of Memel (Klaipeda) is known as a Kaunas printing.

EUROPE

——KENYA, UGANDA, AND TANGANYIKA, PROTECTORATE OF——

Area: 679,800 sq. miles approx.

The African territories of Kenya, Uganda, and Tanganyika were grouped together under British administration. From 1935, they had a common postal system and used stamps inscribed for the three areas. The capital cities were Nairobi (Kenya), Kampala (Uganda), and Dar es Salaam (Tanganyika). Each is now an independent state, with Tanganyika being merged with Zanzibar as Tanzania.

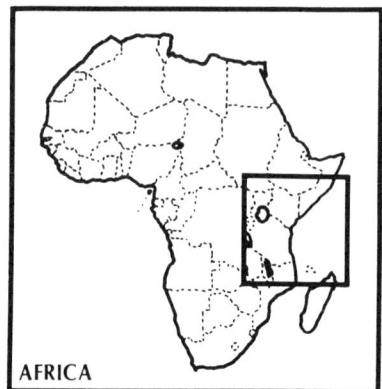

AFRICA

Pop: 25,331 (1965)

Kerassunde (now Giresun) is located on the Black Sea coast of Asian Turkey and is the capital city of the province of the same name. It is the site of a Byzantine fortress. The town is an export center for products of the area, which include nuts, timber, and hides. In 1909, Russia issued stamps overprinted "Kerassunde" for use at a Russian post office operating in the community.

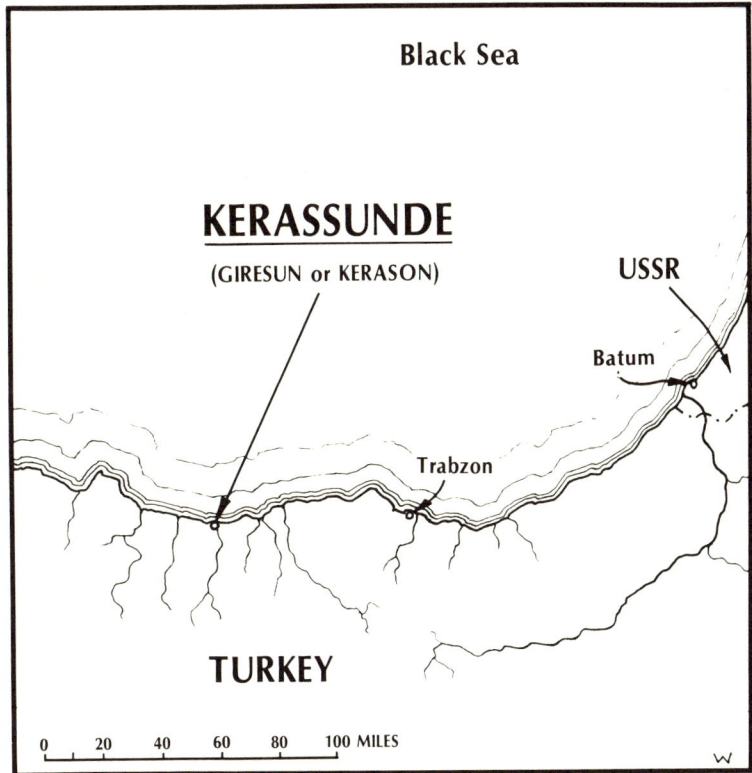

Black Sea

KERASSUNDE

(GIRESUN or KERASON)

USSR

Batum

Trabzon

TURKEY

0   20   40   60   80   100 MILES

KIANGSI, PROVINCE OF

Area: 63,629 sq. miles
Pop: 22 million (1968 est.)

The province of Kiangsi in the People's Republic of China, is not only a fertile one, with large agricultural production, but also has mineral resources, including coal. Some of the finest Chinese porcelain is produced at the city of Ching-te-chen. Kiangsi was part of the Central China Liberation Area prior to the formation of the People's Republic of China in the late 1940s and used the area's stamps.

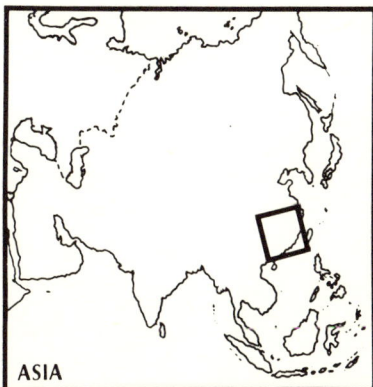

ASIA

Wu-han

Ching-te-chen

Yangtze R.

CHINA

I-ch'un

Shang-jao

Fu-chou

KIANGSI

Kan-chou

Canton

0   50   100   150 MILES

Area: 40,927 sq. miles
Pop: 47 million (1968 est.)
Capital: Nanking

Located on the coast, Kiangsu is one of the smallest but most densely populated of the provinces in the People's Republic of China. The country is flat delta land traversed by the Yangtze River. There are numerous lakes, and the area is a rich agricultural center. It came within the East China Liberation Area, the stamps of which it used beginning in 1949.

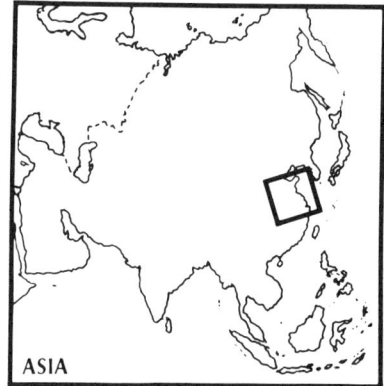

Map labels: Tsingtao (Ching-tao), CHINA, Yellow Sea, Yellow R., Hsu-chou, KIANGSU, Nanking, Wu-hsi, Shanghai, Wu-han, Yangtze R., Su-chou, Hang-chou, 0 50 100 150 200 MILES, ASIA

━━━━━ **KIAUTSCHOU (TSINGTAU), CITY OF** ━━━━━

Area: About 200 sq. miles
Pop: 1.9 million (1970 est.)

A port city on Chia-Chou Bay, Tsingtau (now Tsing-tao) was occupied by Germany in 1897 following the murder of missionaries by the Chinese. The area was leased to Germany in 1898, and a modern city and naval base was built between 1898 and 1914. When war broke out it was taken by British and Japanese forces and retained by the Japanese until 1922.

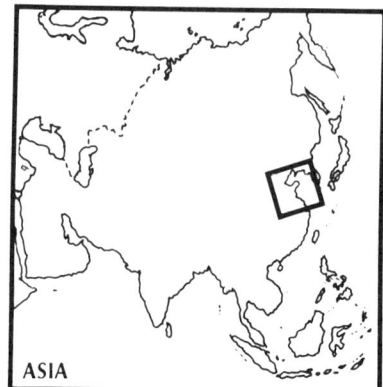

Map labels: Peking (Beijing), KOREA, Tientsin, Gulf of Chihli, Dairen, Port Arthur, Wei-hai-wei, Yellow R., Wei-fang, Yellow Sea, SHANTUNG, CHINA, KIAUTSCHOU (Tsingtau or Chingtao), 0 20 40 60 80 100 150 200 MILES, ASIA

Pop: 38,095 (1965)

A town in Turkey, Kilis is located on the border with Syria about 30 miles north of Aleppo. Following WWI, it was occupied by the French, and a stamp was issued there to meet the needs of a large influx of Armenian refugees fleeing Turkish persecution. The area was returned to Turkish authority in 1923 and today is the center of an agricultural region growing olives and cotton. Silk is also produced there.

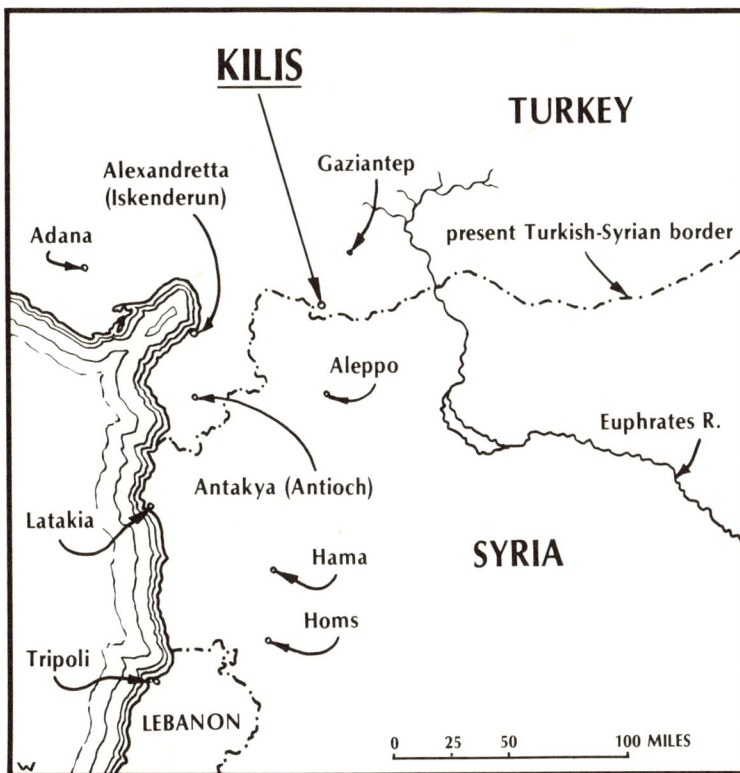

KING EDWARD VII LAND

King Edward VII Land is a peninsula located on the eastern shore of the Ross Sea at the edge of the Antarctic continent. It is at latitude 77 degrees 44 minutes South and longitude 155 degrees West, to the south of New Zealand. The area was claimed for Great Britain in 1902 by Captain Scott and is now within New Zealand's Ross Dependency. In 1908, a quantity of the then-current New Zealand 1d stamp was overprinted "King Edward VII Land" in two lines reading up, and it was taken on the Shackleton expedition to Antarctic region. Gibbons notes two varieties, plus a double-overprint variety, and records only one used example. The issues were made under the authority of the New Zealand Post Office, according to Gibbons, but they appear to have been unnecessary in terms of postal requirements. Their status is the same as similar overprints made for Victoria Land, which were carried on the 1911 Scott expedition. One suspects that they may well have been created to bolster any territorial claims made as a result of the expeditions

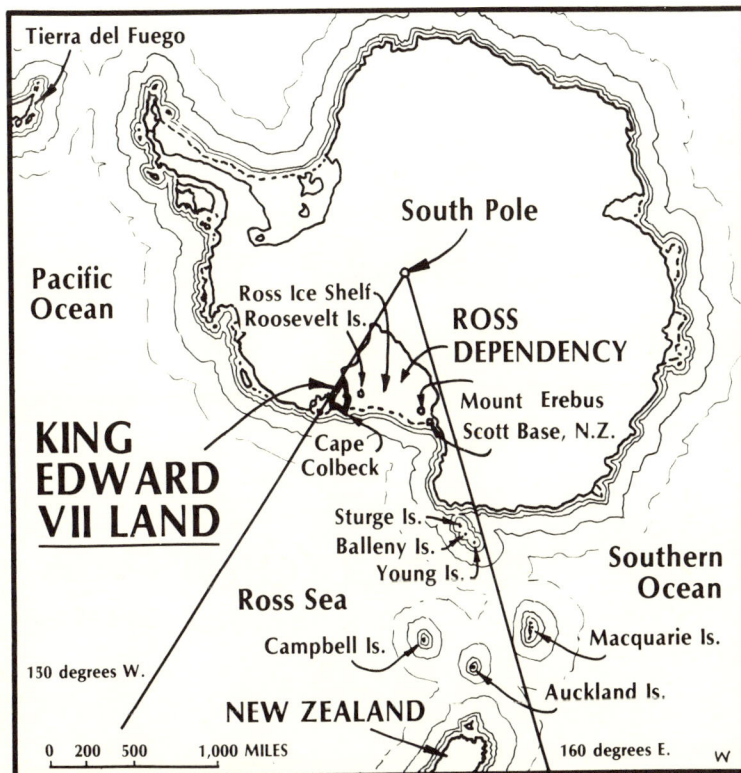

KIONGA (KIONGA TRIANGLE), DISTRICT OF

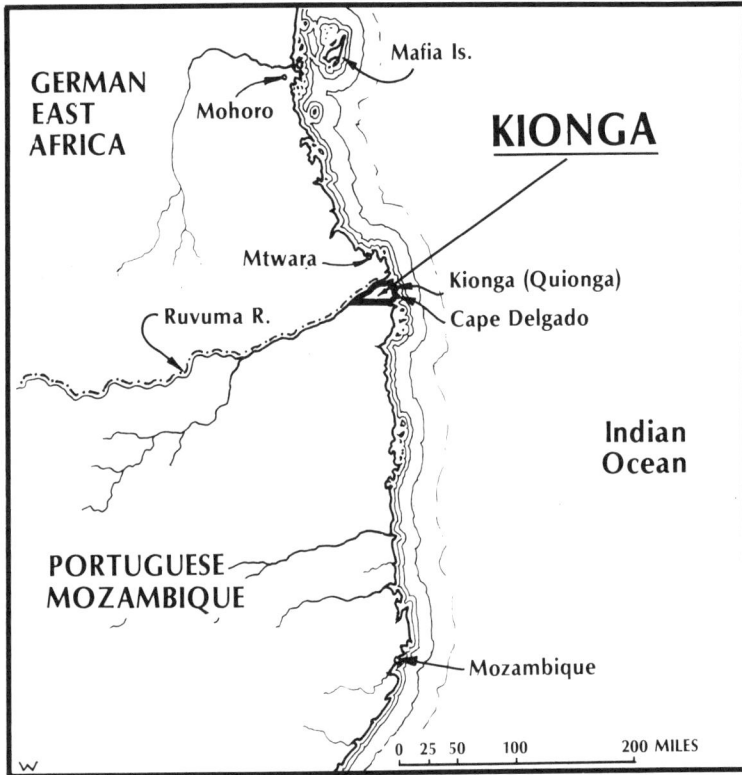

Area: 400 sq. miles

Kionga was a district located on the coast at the southern border of German East Africa to the south of the Ruvuma River. Because of its shape it was known as the Kionga Triangle. During WWI, it was taken by Portugal and made part of its African colony of Mozambique. Prior to its incorporation into Mozambique, an issue of stamps was released by the Portuguese government.

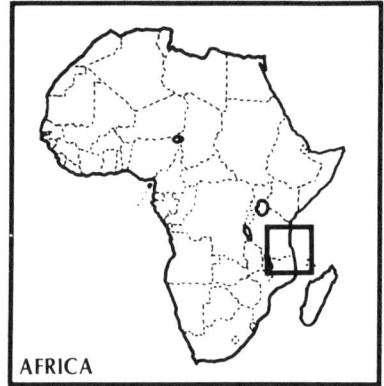

KOUANG TCHEOU-WAN, DISTRICT OF

Area: 325 sq. miles
Capital: Fort Bayard (Chan-chiang)

Kouang Tcheou-wan (or Kwang-chowan) was an area leased by China to France in 1898 for 99 years. It comprised an area on the eastern side of the Liuchow Peninsula, plus two large islands and numerous smaller ones. Occupied by Japan during WWII, it was returned to China by France in 1946.

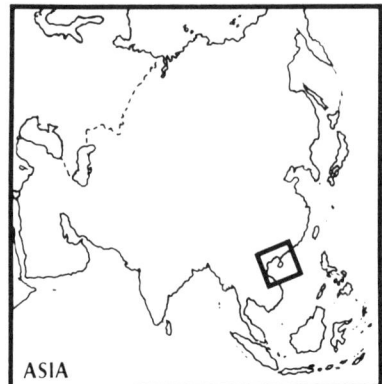

Capital: Ekaterinodar

The District of Kuban was a post-WWI government in that area of Russia located to the east of the Crimea and the Sea of Azov. It has since been divided into Krasnodar Krai and several other autonomous areas. The chief city was Ekaterinodar (now called Krasnodar). Stamps were issued by the Kuban government in 1919, during the chaotic period following WWI.

USSR

Stalingrad (Volgograd)

KUBAN

Don R.

Volga R.

Dneper R.

Rostov

Sea of Azov

Kuban R.

Crimea

Ekaterinodar (Krasnodar)

Yalta

Sevastopol

Black Sea

0 50 100 200 MILES

EUROPE

──────KUNMING (YUNNAN), CITY OF──────

Pop: 50,000 (1896 est.)
1.7 million (1970 est.)

A city in China and capital of Yunnan Province, Kunming is 380 miles southwest of Chungking. It is a trade and transportation center, linked to Hanoi by a railroad built in 1910. During WWII there was a US air base there, and the city was a Chinese military headquarters. Stamps were issued for use at a French post office there during 1903-19.

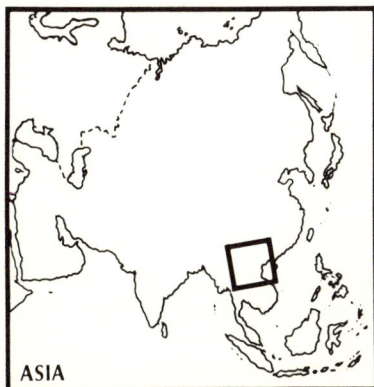

CHINA

KUNMING
(K'un-ming)

BURMA

Haiphong

Hanoi

INDO-CHINA

THAILAND

Gulf of Tonkin

0 50 100 200 MILES

ASIA

KUPA — Area of Croatia occupied by Italy during WWII

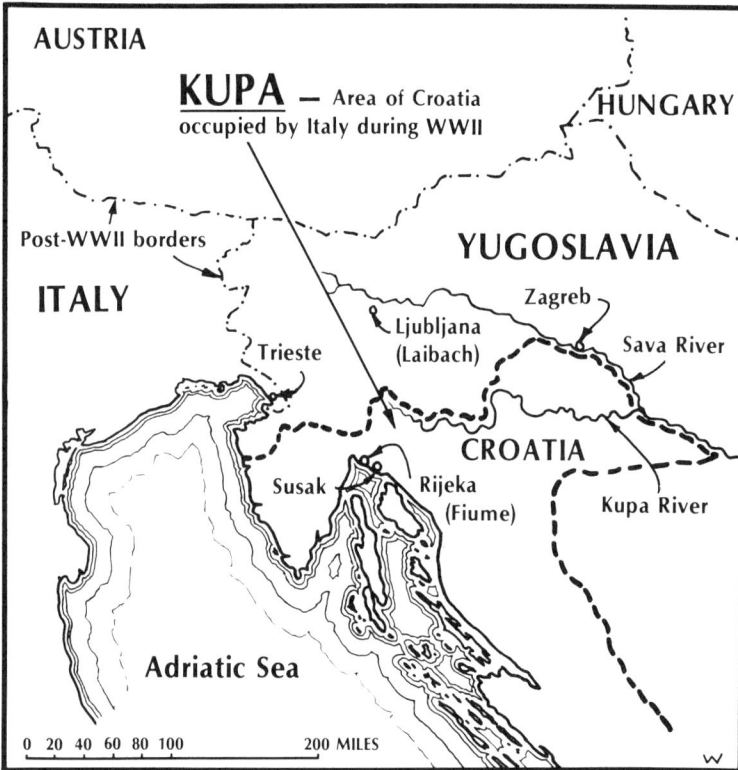

The Kupa area was an undefined part of Croatia in Yugoslavia that included the city of Fiume (Reijeka) and Susak, plus an area along the Kupa River. It was created as an administrative area by the Italians during their occupation in WWII. Stamps were issued in 1941-42 by the occupation authorities for use in the area. They consist of stamps of Yugoslavia overprinted "ZONA/ OCCUPATA/ FIUMANO/ KUPA." Several subsequent stamps were released with additional overprints.

————— KURLAND (COURLAND), DISTRICT OF —————

Russian territory since 1795, Kurland became part of the independent country of Latvia in 1918 and was absorbed by the USSR, when that country invaded and took over the Baltic states. Stamps had been issued for Kurland at Mitau in 1919 by the West Russian Army under Colonel Bermondt-Avalov, according to the Scott catalog. During their WWII occupation, the Germans issued stamps of Germany overprinted "KURLAND."

Area: 85,096 sq. miles
Pop: 24 million (1968 est.)

Kwangsi is an autonomous region in southern China, bordering on the Gulf of Tonkin and Vietnam. It was located in the South China Liberation Area of the Communists prior to the formation of the People's Republic of China and used the stamps issued for the area in 1949-50.

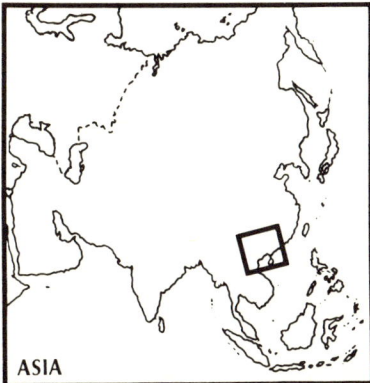

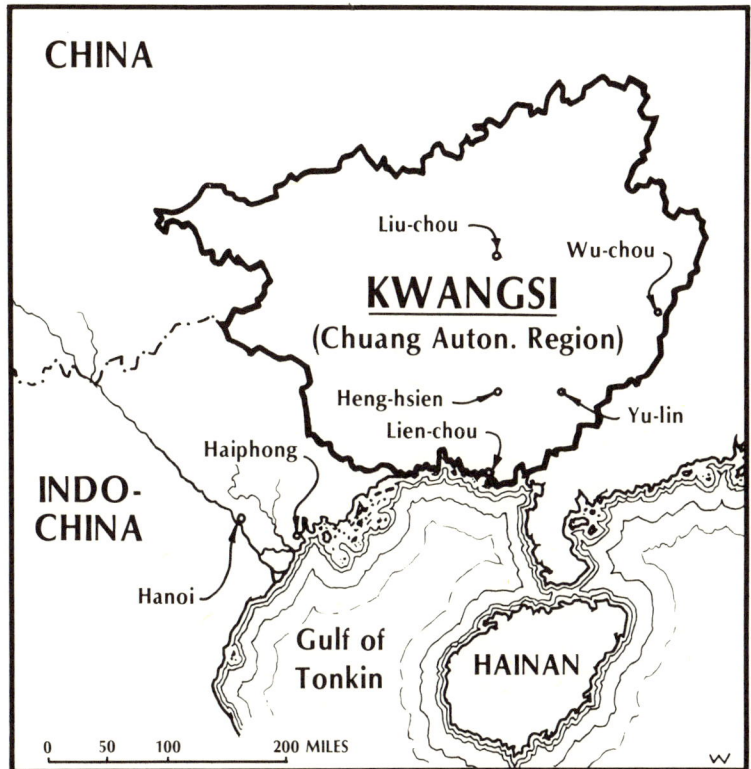

CHINA

Liu-chou
Wu-chou

KWANGSI
(Chuang Auton. Region)

Heng-hsien
Yu-lin
Lien-chou

INDO-CHINA

Haiphong

Hanoi

Gulf of Tonkin

HAINAN

0   50   100   200 MILES

ASIA

──── KWANGTUNG, PROVINCE OF ────

Area: 89,344 sq. miles
Pop: 40 million (1968 est.)
Capital: Canton

Kwangtung is a province in the southern portion of the People's Republic of China. The population was unhappy with imperial rule prior to WWI, and the area was the scene of much unrest, especially during 1911. Later, during WWII, the province was a battleground in the fight between Chinese forces and the invading Japanese.

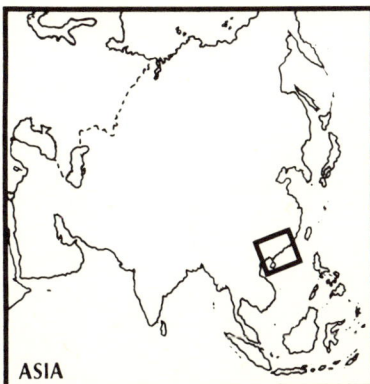

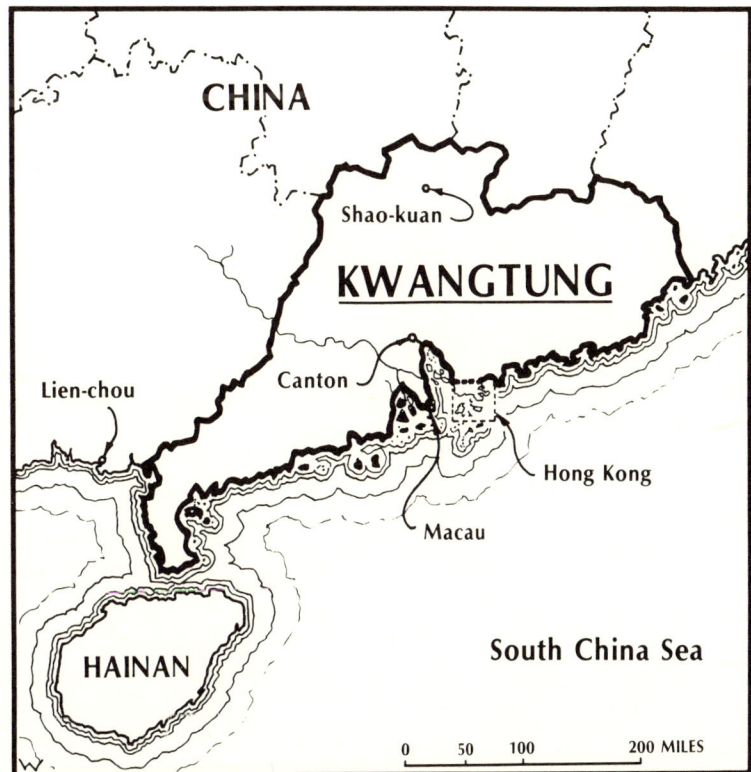

CHINA

Shao-kuan

KWANGTUNG

Lien-chou

Canton

Hong Kong

Macau

HAINAN

South China Sea

0   50   100   200 MILES

ASIA

Area: 67,181 sq. miles
Pop: 17 million (1968 est.)
Capital: Kuei-yang

A province in the southwestern part of the People's Republic of China, Kweichow was the location of important US and Chinese bases during WWII. It was the Southwest China Liberation Area of the Communists prior to the formation of the People's Republic of China and used the stamps that it issued in 1949-50.

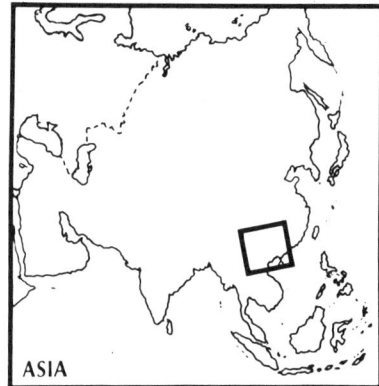

──────── LA AGUERA, COLONY OF ────────

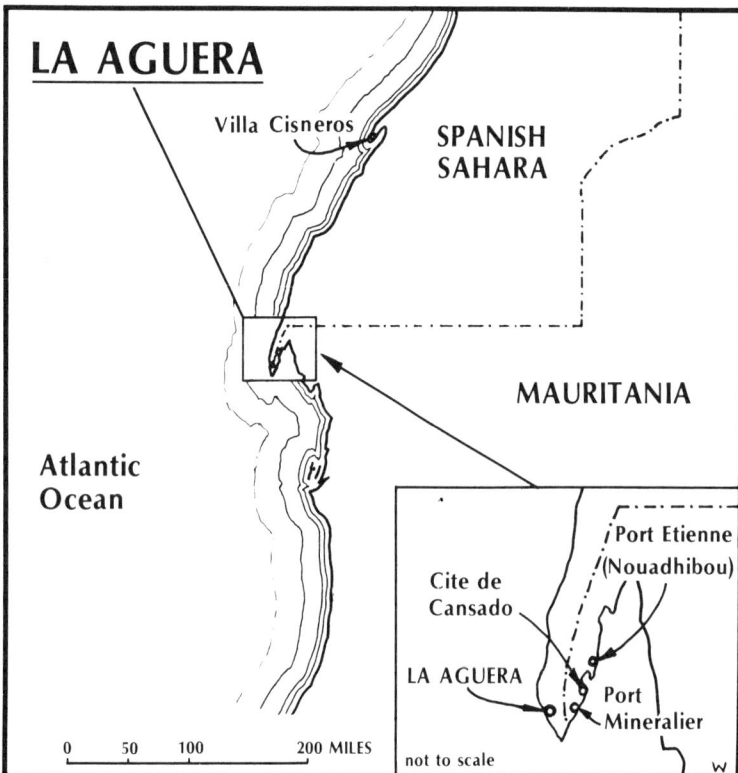

La Aguera was an undefined area on a peninsula located on the northwest coast of Africa in Spanish Sahara. It was a colony of Spain, which issued stamps for the area during 1920-22. The administrative capital was the town of La Aguera at the tip of the peninsula. La Aguera is now within the area believed to be occupied by Morocco. The United Nations does not recognize the Moroccan occupation and refers to the area as Western Sahara.

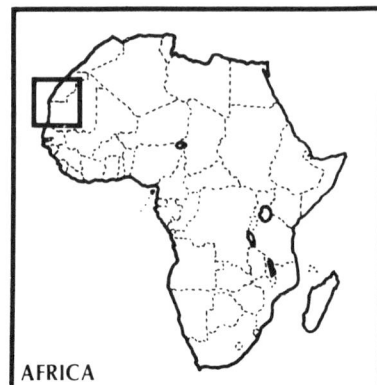

Area: 38 sq. miles
Pop: 5,853 (1891)
    14,904 (1960)

Labuan is a small island off the northwest coast of Borneo. It was made a British crown colony in 1848 and came under the administration of the British North Borneo Company in 1890. In 1906 it was transferred to the Straits Settlements. The island is now part of Malaysia.

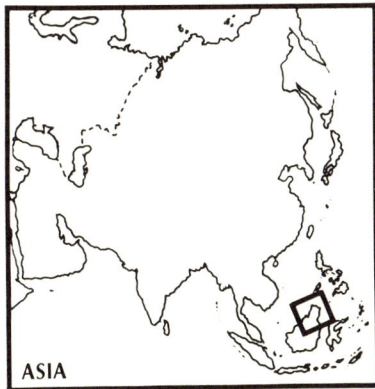

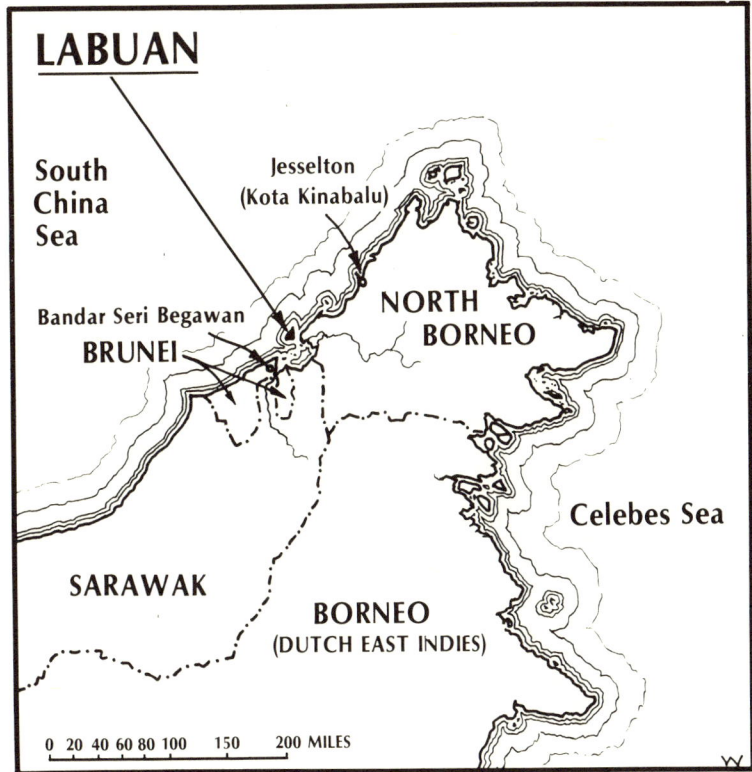

LABUAN

South China Sea

Jesselton (Kota Kinabalu)

Bandar Seri Begawan

BRUNEI

NORTH BORNEO

Celebes Sea

SARAWAK

BORNEO (DUTCH EAST INDIES)

0 20 40 60 80 100   150   200 MILES

ASIA

— LAGOS, COLONY OF —

Area: 3,500 sq. miles approx.
Pop: about 1.5 million (1900)
City Pop: 100,000 (1900 est.)

A former British colony and protectorate, Lagos is now a state of Nigeria, and the city of Lagos is the country's capital. It was merged into Southern Nigeria in 1906, and the stamps it had issued since 1874 came to an end.

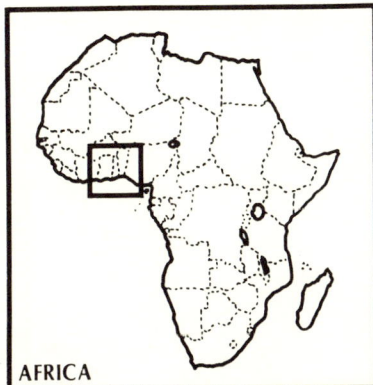

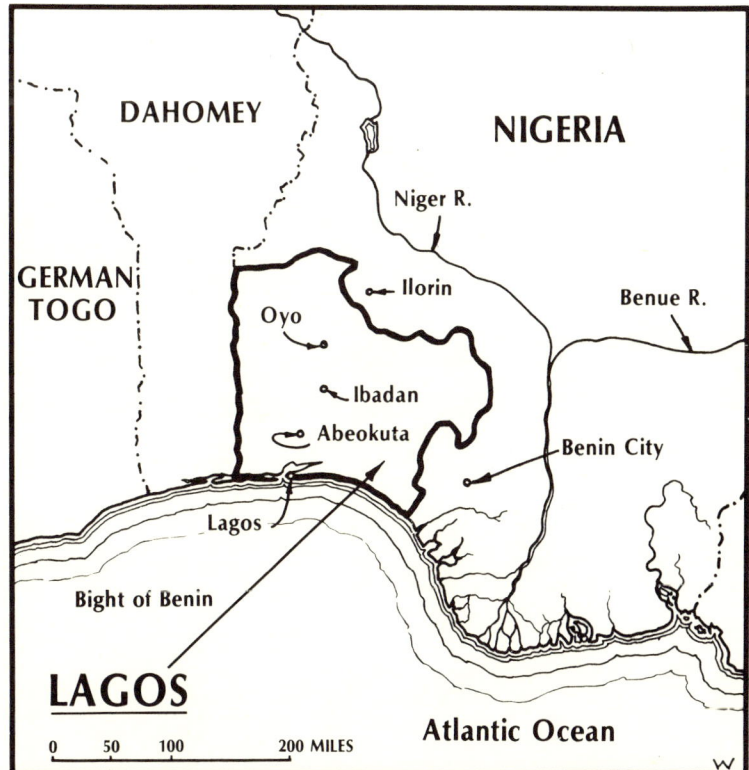

DAHOMEY

NIGERIA

Niger R.

GERMAN TOGO

Ilorin

Oyo

Benue R.

Ibadan

Abeokuta

Benin City

Lagos

LAGOS

Bight of Benin

AFRICA

Atlantic Ocean

0   50   100   200 MILES

Area: 24,595 sq. miles
Pop: 1,995,000 (1939 est.)
  2,365,000 (1970 est.)
Capital: Riga

Formerly the Russian areas of Kurland and Livonia, the independent country of Latvia was formed following WWI, and despite a non-aggression treaty with the USSR, it was occupied and appropriated by that country in 1940. This appropriation has never been recognized by the US.

EUROPE

LEEWARD ISLANDS, COLONY OF

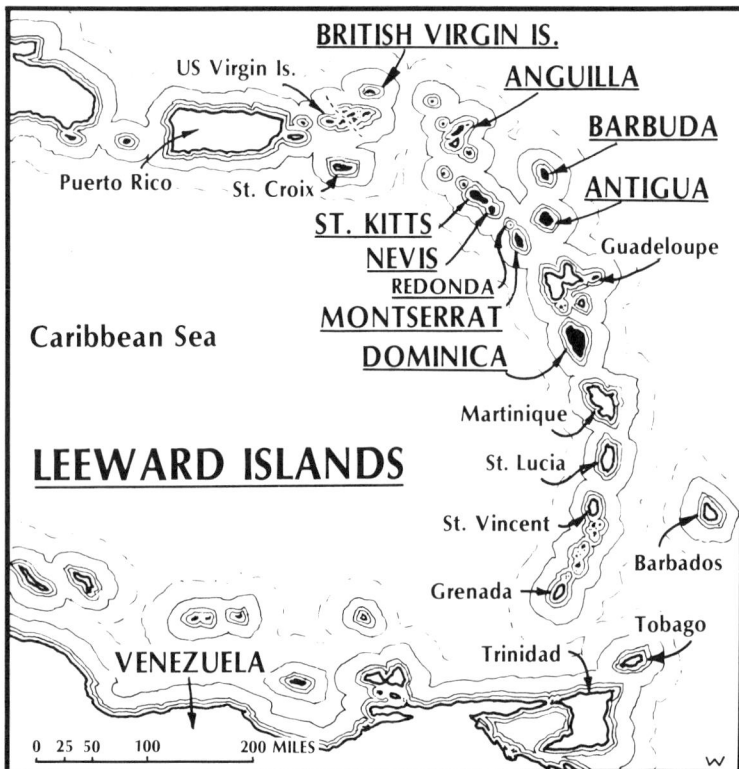

Area: 423 sq. miles (approx.)
Pop: 127,723 (1900)
Capital: St. John's, Antigua

A group of British islands in the Lesser Antilles of the West Indies, the Leeward Islands consisted of Anguilla, Antigua, Barbuda, British Virgin Islands, Dominica (until the end of 1939), Montserrat, Nevis, Redonda, St. Kitts, and Sombrero. Although most of the islands had their own individual stamps, a common key type design was included for the group from 1890 to 1956.

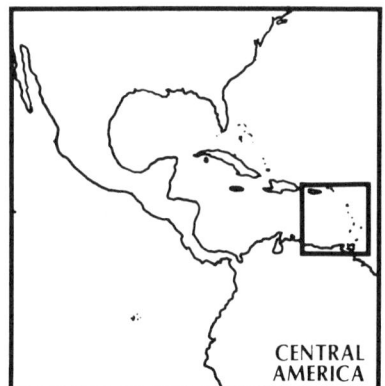

CENTRAL AMERICA

Area: 177 sq. miles
Pop: 21,808 (1961)
Capital: Kastron

Lemnos is a Greek Island in the Aegean Sea off the west coast of Turkey. Mountainous and fertile, the island is a fruit growing area. The island was taken from the Turks by Greek forces during the 1912-1913 war between the two countries. It was a naval base of the Royal Navy during the Dardanelles campaign of WWI.

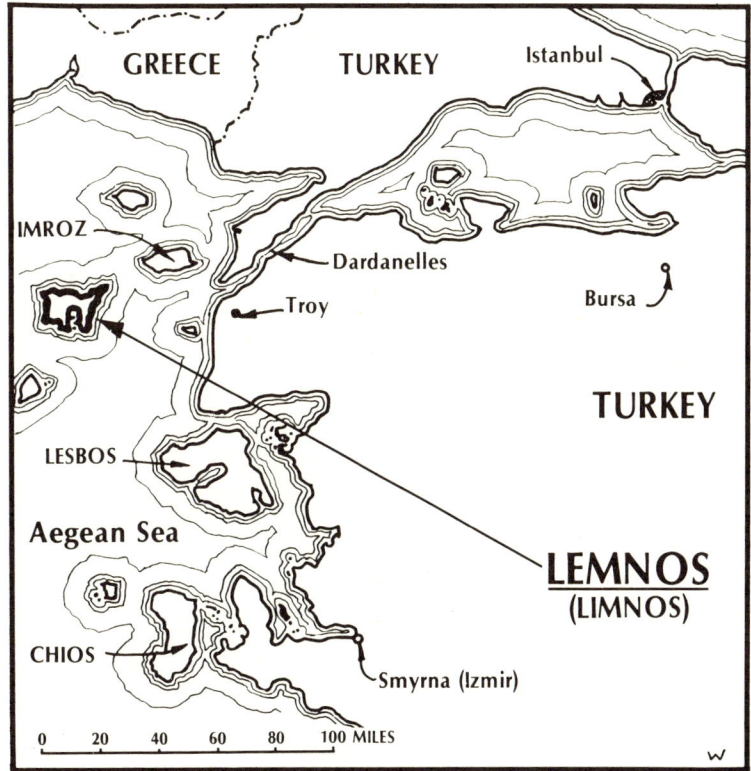

LESBOS (MYTILENE, now LESVOS), ISLAND OF

Area: 630 sq. miles
Pop: 117,371 (1961)
Chief town: Mytilene

An island in the Aegean Sea off the west coast of Turkey, Lesbos is part of Greece. The island has had an eventful past as part of the various empires of the area. From 1462 it was held by the Turks, and it was taken by Greek forces during its war with that country in 1912-1913. Greek occupation stamps were issued at that time.

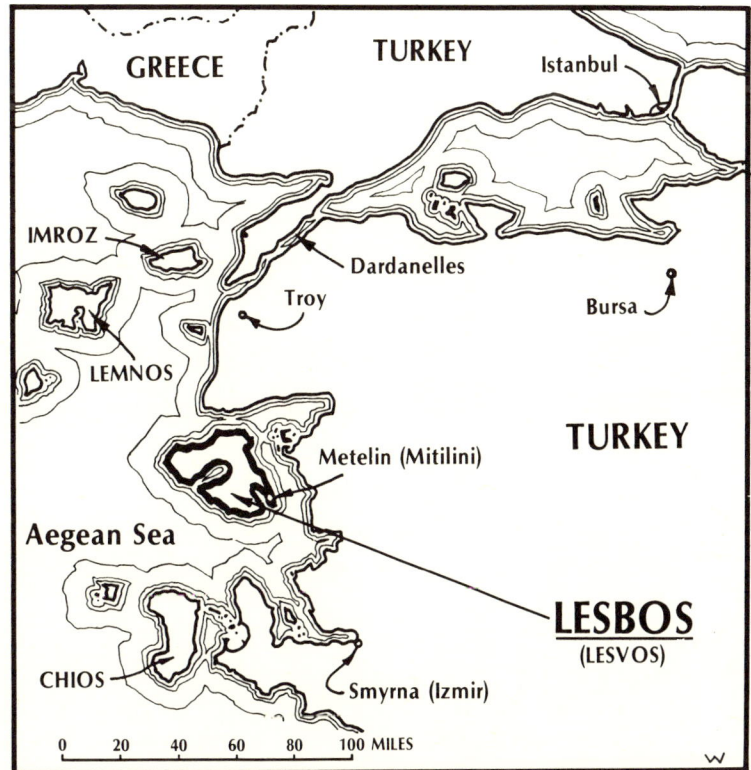

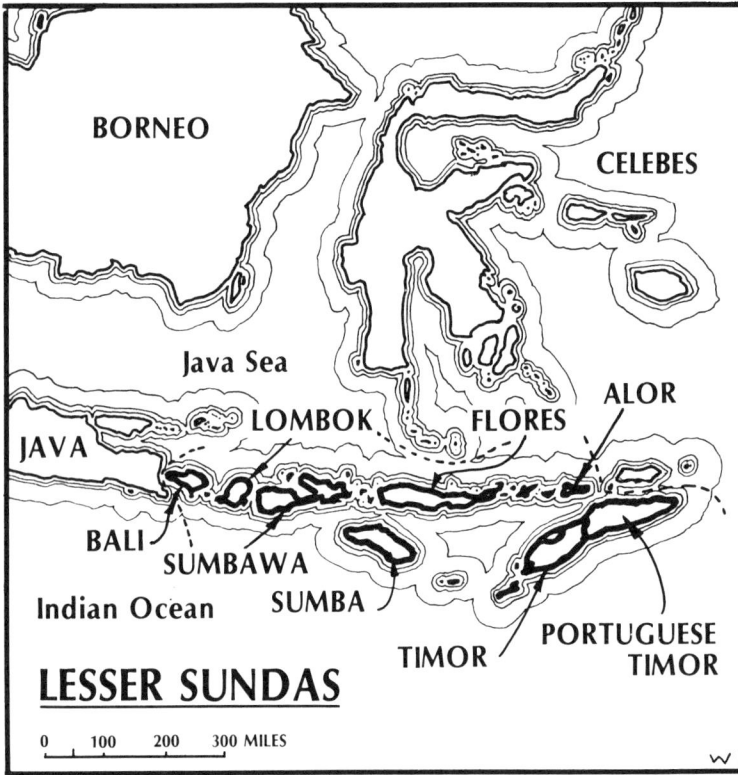

Area: 29,441 sq. miles
Pop: seven million (1970 est.)

The Lesser Sundas is a chain of islands stretching to the east from the island of Bali in Southeast Asia. Included in the chain are Alor and Timor. Once part of the Netherlands East Indies, they are now in the Republic of Indonesia, including what was Portuguese Timor. Stamps were issued for use in the islands in 1943 by the Japanese.

BORNEO

CELEBES

Java Sea

JAVA

LOMBOK

FLORES

ALOR

BALI

SUMBAWA

SUMBA

Indian Ocean

TIMOR

PORTUGUESE TIMOR

LESSER SUNDAS

0   100   200   300 MILES

ASIA

———————— LIMA, CITY OF ————————

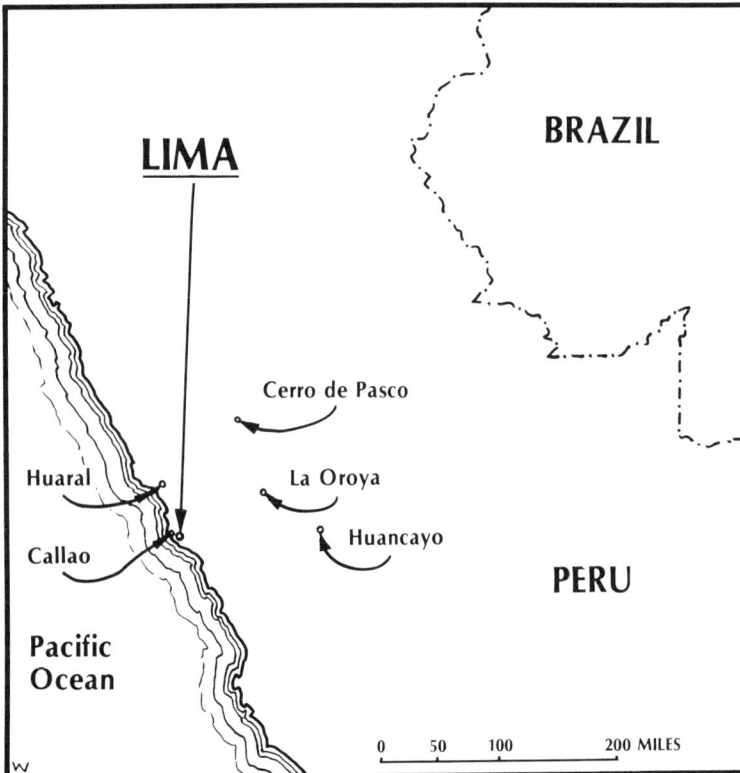

Pop: 2,541,300 (1970 est.)

Founded in 1535 by Pizarro, Lima is the capital city of Peru and of Lima Department. It is the economic and cultural center of the country and is located about eight miles inland from its port of Callao. It has a 16th-century cathedral, and its university, founded in 1551, is the oldest in South America. During the War of the Pacific, 1881-1883, the city was occupied by Chilean forces. In 1881, a series of occupation stamps was issued.

LIMA

BRAZIL

Cerro de Pasco

Huaral

La Oroya

Callao

Huancayo

PERU

Pacific Ocean

0   50   100   200 MILES

SOUTH AMERICA

Area: 25,174 sq. miles
Pop: 3,129,000 (1970)
Capital: Vilinus (later Kaunas)

Acquired by Russia in the 18th century, Lithuania had demanded its freedom in 1905, but did not obtain it until Russia was defeated in WWI. Its capital city of Vilinus was lost in 1920, when Poland took it over. During 1940, the country was occupied and absorbed by the Soviet Union, an act not recognized by the US.

LIVONIA (VIDZEME), AREA OF

Livonia was formerly an area of the Russian Empire that was divided between Latvia and Estonia at the end of WWI, when both countries obtained their freedom. The Latvian portion is now the district of Vidzeme and includes the city of Wenden (now Cesis). The area had been conquered by Sweden in 1629 and was ceded to Russia by that country in 1721. Livonia became part of the Soviet Union during WWII when it invaded the Baltic states.

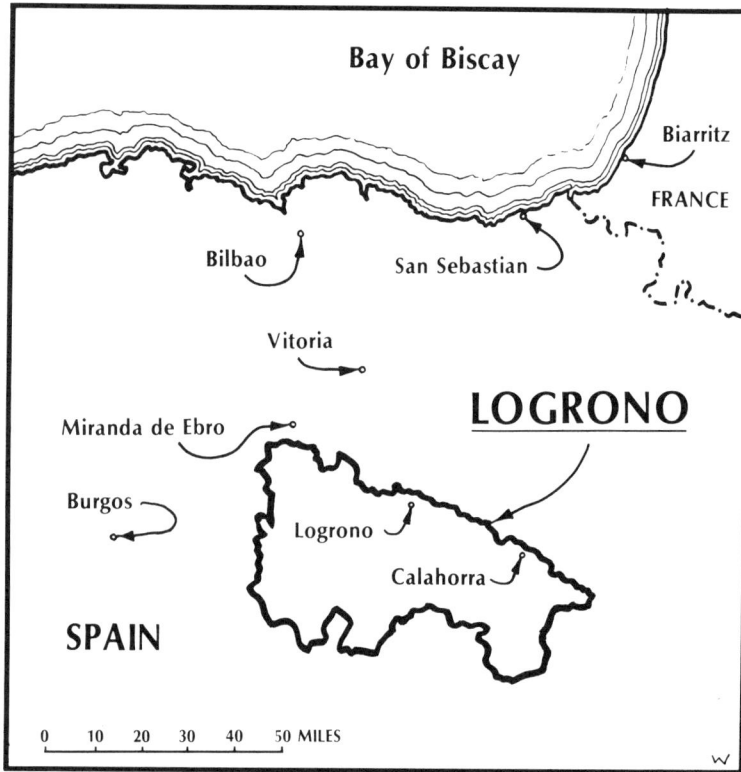

Area: 1,944 sq. miles
Pop: 235,713 (1970)
Capital: Logrono

Logrono is a province in northern Spain with a capital city of the same name. The city is a trading center for an agricultural area, shipping timber, wine, and textiles. It was captured by the Moors in the eighth century and occupied by France from 1808 to 1813.

——————LOMBARDY-VENETIA, KINGDOM OF——————

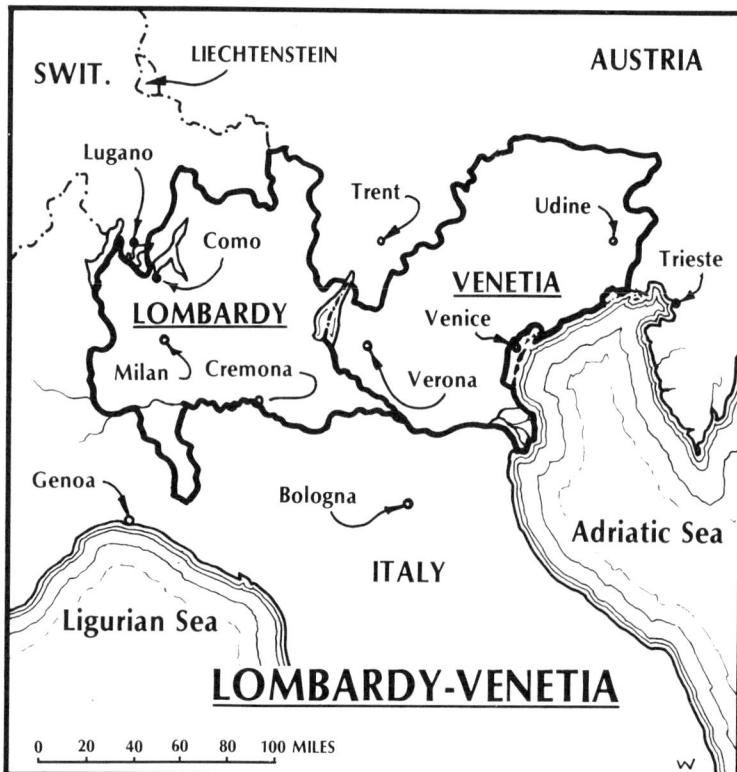

The area of the Kingdom of Lombardy was ceded to Austria by Napoleon in 1815 and became linked with Venetia. After changing hands several times, Lombardy united with the Kingdom of Sardinia in 1859 and became part of the new Kingdom of Italy in 1860, and Venetia was annexed to Italy in 1868. Stamps were issued by the twin areas beginning in 1850.

Long Island is located in the middle of the inlet leading to the Turkish port city of Smyrna (now Izmir). The island is now known as Uzon. It was occupied by British forces for several weeks during WWI, and Turkish revenue stamps were over-printed as occupation stamps. These were followed by a number of primitive typewritten stamps. The stamp-issuing period was from May 7 to 26, 1916.

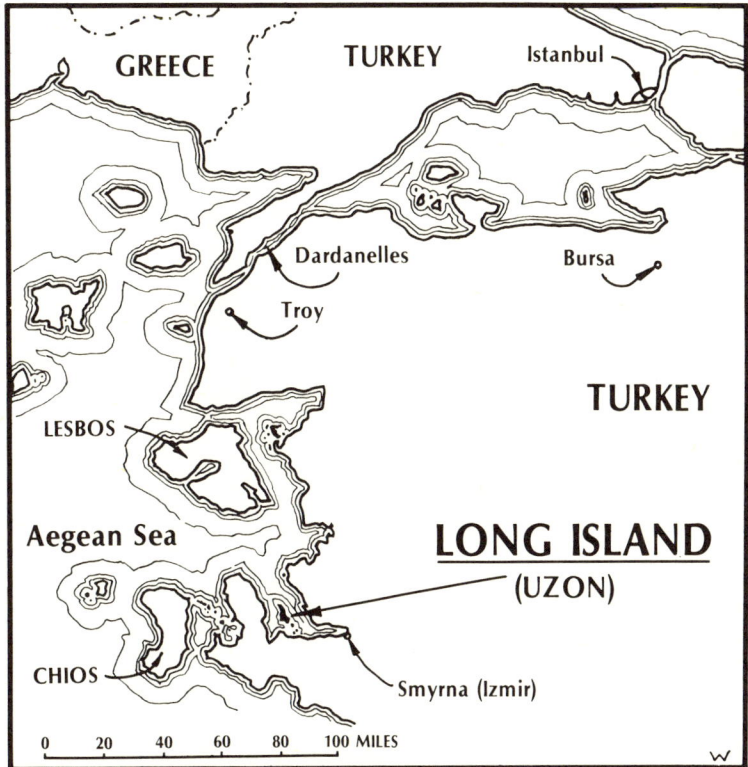

LOURENCO MARQUES, DISTRICT OF

Area: 6,480 sq. miles
Pop: 799,358 (1970)
Capital: Lourenco Marques (Maputo)

The southernmost district in the Portuguese colony of Mozambique, Lourenco Marques is based on the seaport of the same name, which is now called Maputo. The city is the capital of the independent People's Republic of Mozambique. Located on Delagoa Bay, the city has extensive port facilities and is a major export center

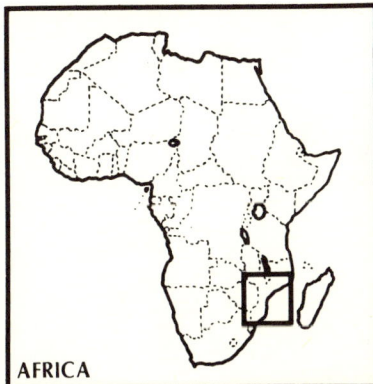

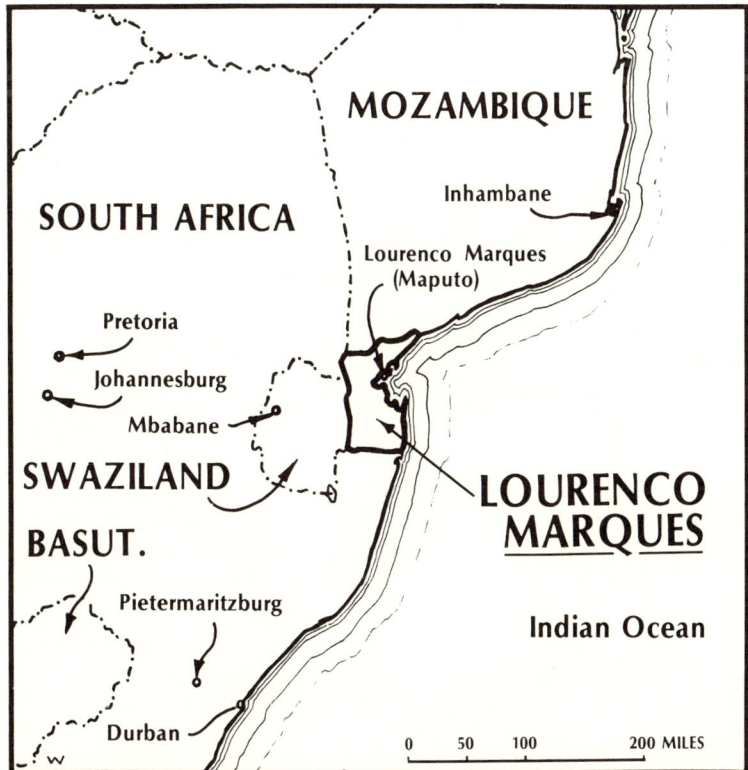

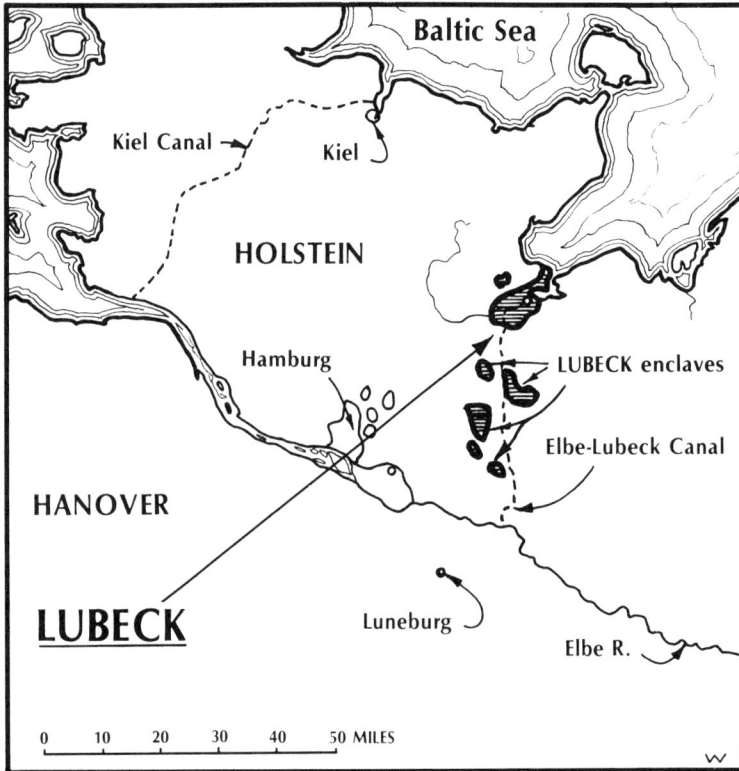

Area: 115 sq. miles
Pop: 96,775 (1900)

A former city and state in northern Germany on the Baltic Sea, Lubeck was the leading port in the Hanseatic League and is now the Federal Republic of Germany's major Baltic seaport. The state included the city of Lubeck and a number of surrounding enclaves. Lubeck joined the North German Confederation when it was formed in 1868.

——————LUBIANA (LJUBLJANA or LAIBACH), CITY OF——————

Pop: 173,570 (1971 est.)

The capital city of Slovenia in Yugoslavia, Lubiana is located on the Sava River, about 75 miles from Zagreb. It is a railroad, industrial, and commercial center that was once the city of Emona, founded in 34 BC by Augustus. It came under the Hapsburgs in 1277 and was the capital of the Illyrian Provinces, later kingdom, from 1809 to 1849.

LUBIANA
(LJUBLJANA or LAIBACH)

During WWII, western Slovenia was province of Lubiana under German and Italian occupation.

Pop: 51,930 (1893 est.)
236,000 (1970)

The Polish city of Lublin was taken by Austro-Hungarian forces during WWI. Following the war it was a city in the new state of Poland. During WWII, it was occupied by the Germans until taken by the Soviet Union in 1944. Stamps were issued there in 1918, prior to the release of general issues for Poland.

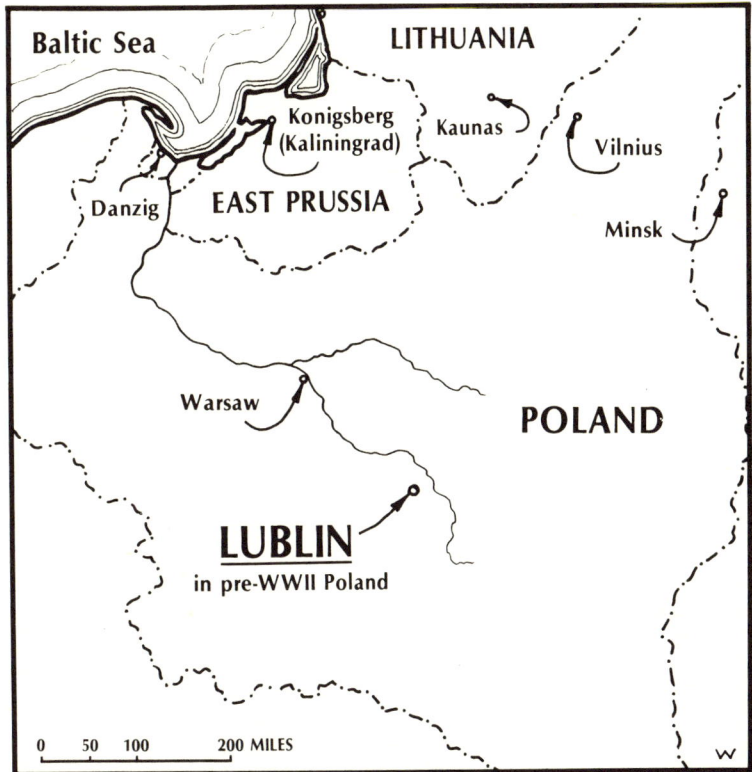

Baltic Sea

LITHUANIA

Konigsberg (Kaliningrad)

Kaunas

Vilnius

EAST PRUSSIA

Danzig

Minsk

Warsaw

POLAND

LUBLIN
in pre-WWII Poland

0 50 100   200 MILES

EUROPE

LYNDENBURG, TOWN OF

Pop: 8,000 (1967 est.)

Lyndenburg is a small town in east-central Transvaal, Republic of South Africa. It had been founded in 1846 by the Boers and was in a district that they proclaimed a republic. It is the center of a sheep-farming district, and platinum is mined nearby. Stamps were issued there in 1900, during the second British occupation of the area.

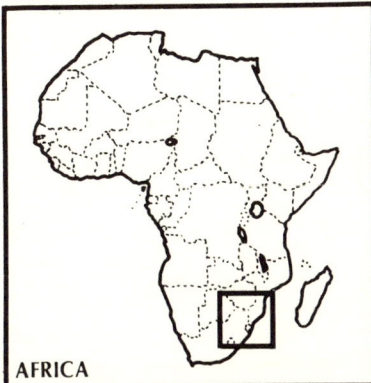

ZIMBABWE

BOTSWANA

MOZAMBIQUE

LYDENBURG

Lourenco Marques (Maputo)

TRANSVAAL

Pretoria

SWAZILAND

Johannesburg

Mbabane

ORANGE FREE STATE

NATAL

0 20 40 60 80 100   200 MILES

Durban

Indian Ocean

AFRICA

Area: About 25,700 sq. miles

Located in the central part of the Balkan Peninsula, Macedonia is an undefined area, parts of which are now in Albania, Bulgaria, Greece, and Yugoslavia. It borders on the Aegean Sea and includes the Greek cities of Salonica (Thessaloniki) and Cavelle (Kavalla). In the late 19th century, rival claims to the area made the "Macedonian Question" a very hot potato indeed and led to the Balkan War of 1912-13.

━━━MADRID, CITY AND PROVINCE OF━━━

Area: 3,087 sq. miles
Pop: Province 3,520,320 (1978)

Madrid is the capital city of Spain and of Madrid Province. It is the transportation center of the country and an important industrial and cultural city. During the Spanish Civil War, it held out against the insurgents until March 1939. A stamp issue released in 1931 is known as the Madrid Issue.

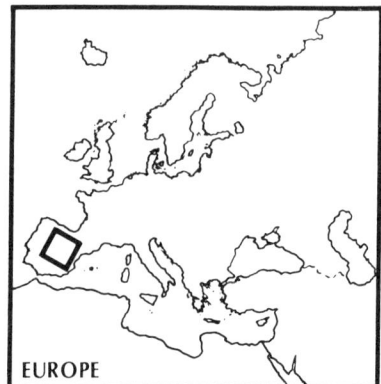

Area: 2,113 sq. miles
Pop: 2,650,000 (1970 est.)
Capital: Pamekasan

An island off the north coast of Java, Madura came under Dutch influence at the beginning of the 18th century and was made a residency of Java in 1885. It is now part of East Java Province in the Republic of Indonesia. In 1908, stamps were overprinted "JAVA" for use in Madura as well as in Java.

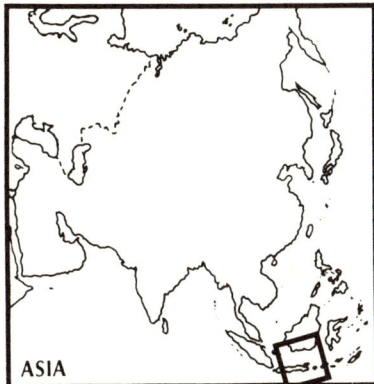

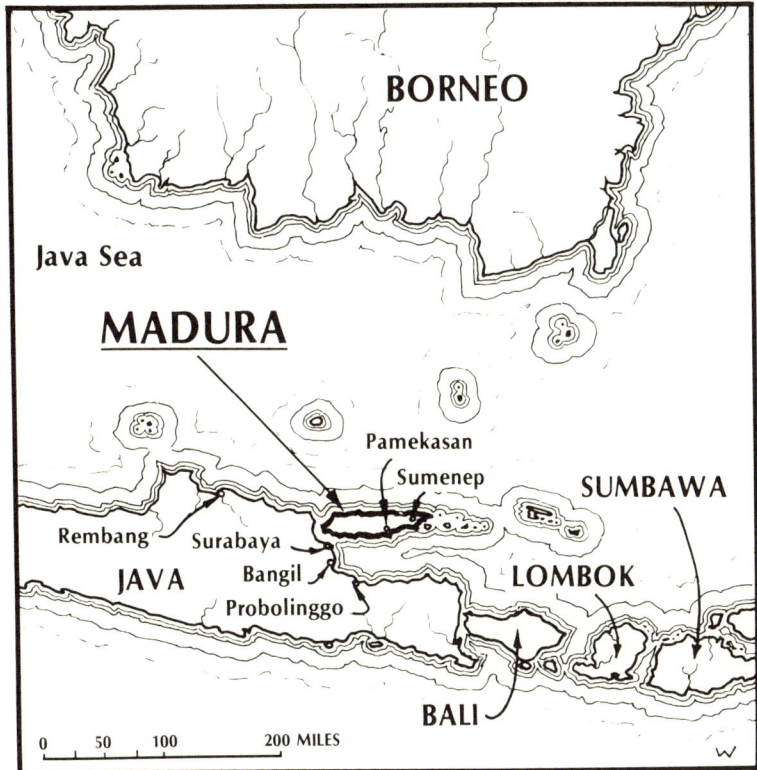

ASIA

BORNEO

Java Sea

MADURA

Pamekasan
Sumenep

SUMBAWA

Rembang
Surabaya
Bangil
Probolinggo

JAVA

LOMBOK

BALI

0   50   100   200 MILES

MAFEKING, TOWN OF

Pop: 6,200 (1967 est.)

Mafeking is a town located in the northern Cape Province of the Republic of South Africa. It became famous because of the 217-day siege of the town during the Boer War at the end of the 19th century. Stamps were issued by the besieged British forces, and included one featuring a portrait of the then-General Robert Baden-Powell.

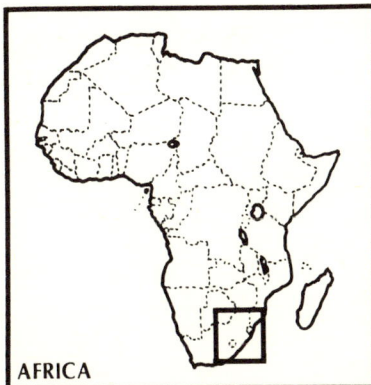

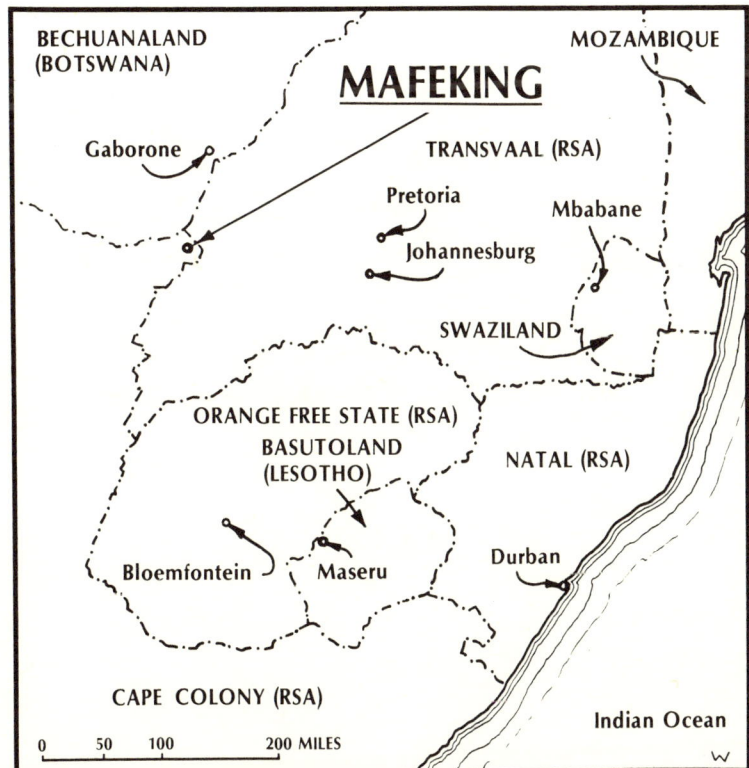

AFRICA

BECHUANALAND
(BOTSWANA)

MOZAMBIQUE

MAFEKING

Gaborone

TRANSVAAL (RSA)

Pretoria

Mbabane

Johannesburg

SWAZILAND

ORANGE FREE STATE (RSA)

BASUTOLAND
(LESOTHO)

NATAL (RSA)

Bloemfontein   Maseru   Durban

CAPE COLONY (RSA)

Indian Ocean

0   50   100   200 MILES

MAFIA ISLAND

Dar-es-Salaam

Zanzibar Is.

GERMAN
EAST
AFRICA
(TANZANIA)

Mafia Channel

Rufiji R.

Indian
Ocean

Kionga triangle

Lake Nyasa

PORTUGUESE MOZAMBIQUE

0 20 40 60 80 100   150   200 MILES

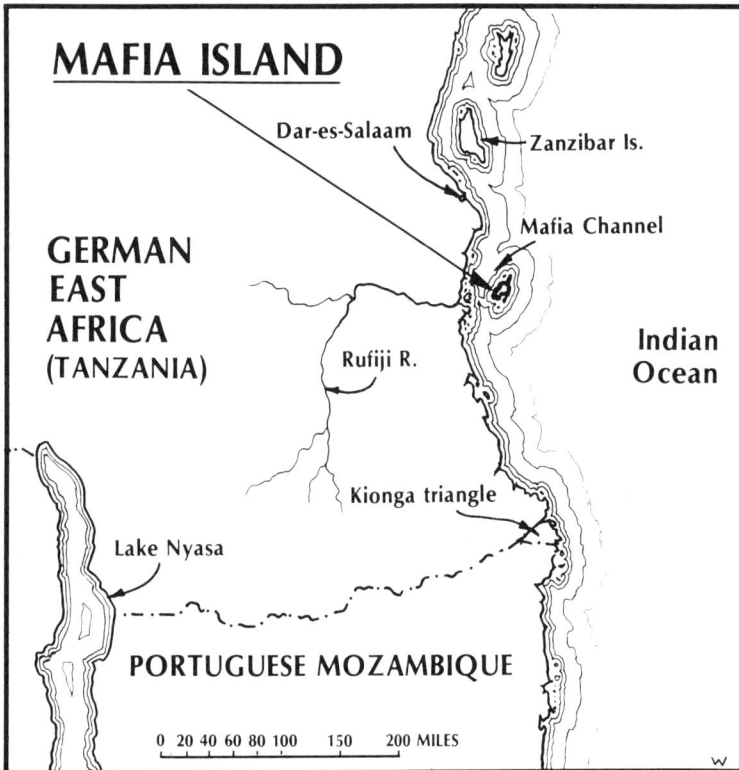

Area: 170 sq. miles
Pop: 15,459 (1967 est.)

Mafia Island is located off the coast
of East Africa and is a part of the
mainland country of Tanzania. It
was occupied by British forces in
December 1914, when the island
was part of German East Africa.
Handstamps were supplied that
were used by the British to overprint the stamps of German East
Africa and, later, stamps of the Indian Expeditionary Forces used in
the operation.

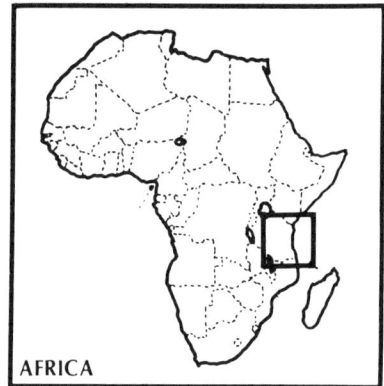

AFRICA

MAGDALENA, DEPARTMENT OF

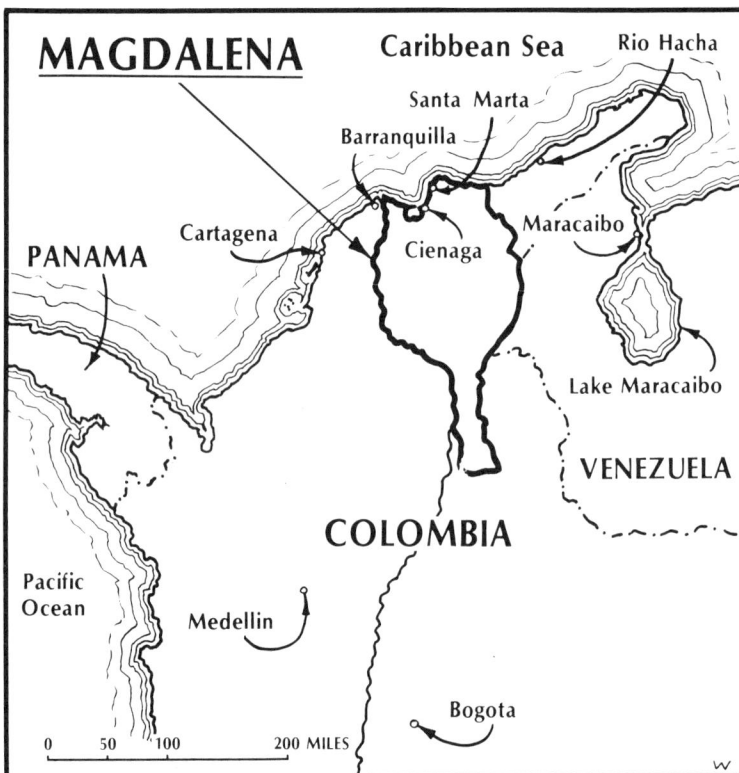

MAGDALENA

Caribbean Sea   Rio Hacha

Santa Marta

Barranquilla

PANAMA

Cartagena

Cienaga

Maracaibo

Lake Maracaibo

VENEZUELA

COLOMBIA

Pacific
Ocean

Medellin

Bogota

0   50   100   200 MILES

Area: 8,843 sq. miles
Pop: 626,989 (1968 est.)
Capital: Santa Marta

A department of the South
American country of Colombia,
Magdalena is located on the Caribbean coast in the northern part of
the country. Catalogs note that
stamps were issued in the department inscribed "No hay estam-
pillas." Scott states that specialists
consider the items to be receipt
labels rather than postage stamps.

SOUTH
AMERICA

Area: 1,405 sq. miles
Pop: 460,030 (1970)
Capital: Palma

Majorca is the largest of the Balearic Islands in the Mediterranean Sea, off the coast of Spain. The island group is a province of that country. A popular tourist center, Majorca has a largely agricultural economy, with many sub-tropical crops being raised.

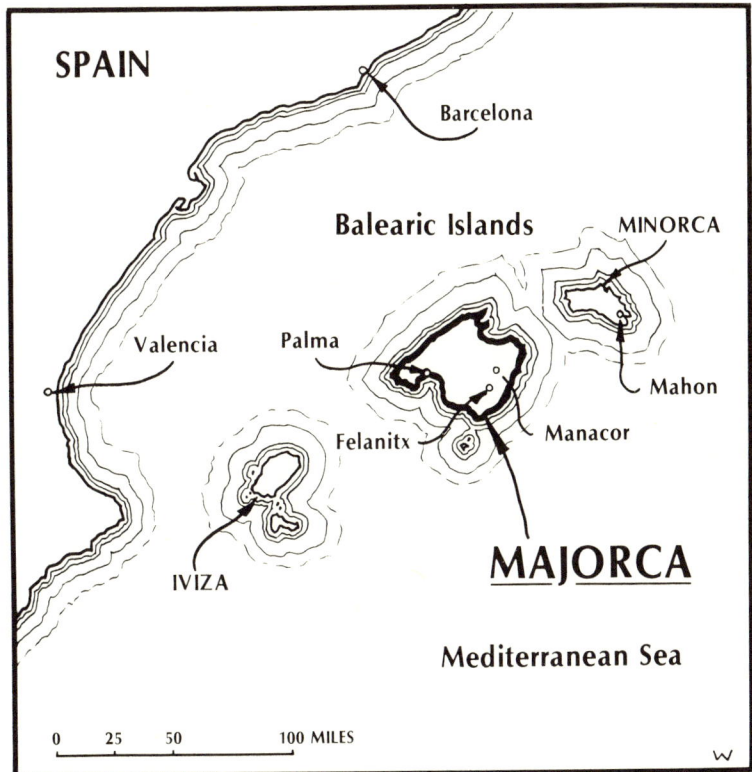

SPAIN

Barcelona

Balearic Islands

MINORCA

Valencia

Palma

Mahon

Felanitx

Manacor

MAJORCA

IVIZA

Mediterranean Sea

0   25   50   100 MILES

EUROPE

MAJUNGA, TOWN OF

Pop: 53,993 (1970 est.)

Majunga is a town located on Bombetoka Bay on the northwest coast of the island of Madagascar. It was used as a base in 1895 for a French expeditionary force that issued stamps in the form of hand-stamped overprints on French stamps. Stamps of Madagascar and Dependencies replaced the initial issue. Today, the town is an important seaport for the shipment of area products.

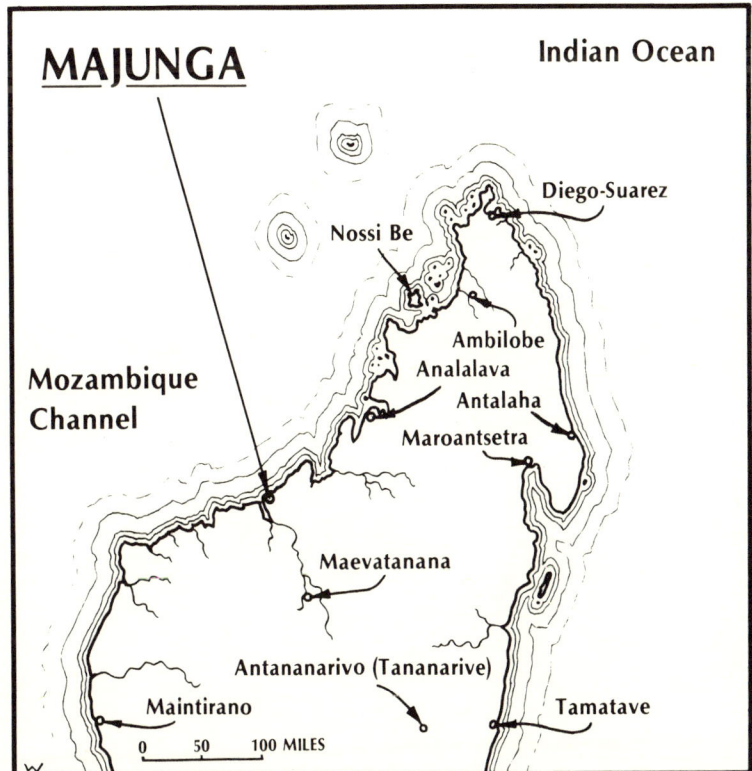

MAJUNGA

Indian Ocean

Diego-Suarez

Nossi Be

Ambilobe
Analalava

Antalaha

Mozambique
Channel

Maroantsetra

Maevatanana

Antananarivo (Tananarive)

Maintirano

Tamatave

0   50   100 MILES

AFRICA

Area: 2,809 sq. miles
Pop: 867,330 (1970)
Capital: Malaga

Malaga is a province, with a capital city of the same name, on the southern coast of Spain. The city of Malaga is located some 66 miles east of Gibraltar. Malaga had been founded in the 12th century by the Phoenicians. It was taken by the Moors in the year AD 711 and reconquered by Ferdinand and Isabella in 1497. It was occupied by the French in 1810-12.

SPAIN

Seville

Antequera

Velez

Ronda

Coin

Estpona

Malaga

Cadiz

MALAGA

Algeciras

Gibraltar

Strait of Gibraltar

Atlantic Ocean

Ceuta

Tangier

Mediterranean Sea

MOROCCO

Tetouan

0 10 20 30 40 50 MILES

EUROPE

━━━━━━━━━━━━━━━ MALI FEDERATION ━━━━━━━━━━━━━━━

Area: 531,000 sq. miles (approx.)
Pop: 5,862,000 (1960 est.)
Capitals: Dakar and Bamako

The French colonies of Senegal and French Sudan became independent in 1958 and on Jan. 17, 1959, joined to become the Federation of Mali. The federation was short-lived and broke up in June 1960. The two countries then became the independent Republic of Senegal and the Republic of Mali (ex-French Sudan).

Atlantic Ocean

MAURITANIA

FR. SUDAN

Timbuktu

Dakar

THE GAMBIA

SENEGAL

Bamako

NIGER

GUINEA BISSAU

GUINEA

UPPER VOLTA

SIERRA LEONE

IVORY COAST

GHANA

MALI FEDERATION
(1959-1960)

LIBERIA

TOGO

DAHOMEY (BENIN)

0 100 200 300 400 500 MILES

AFRICA

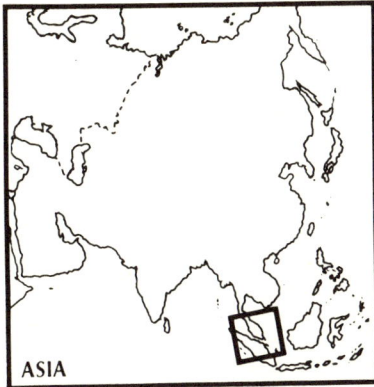

Area: 50,700 sq. miles (approx.)
Pop: 7,140,000 (1960 est.)
Capital: Kuala Lumpur

The Malayan Federation consisted of the former Federated Malay States of Negri Sembilan, Pahang, Perak, and Selangor, plus the unfederated states of Johore, Kedah, Kelantan, Perlis, Trengganu, and the former Straits Settlements of Malacca and Penang. The federation had been set up on April 1, 1946, as the Union of Malaya, changing to the Malayan Federation on Feb. 1, 1948. It became part of Malaysia on Sept. 16, 1963. The Malay Peninsula, on which the states are located, became the world's largest supplier of rubber following its introduction to the area in 1877. About two thirds of the agricultural land was devoted to rubber, and in the late 1960s, some 925,000 tons were produced each year. The federation was also the world's main source of tin and the chief producer of iron in the Far East.

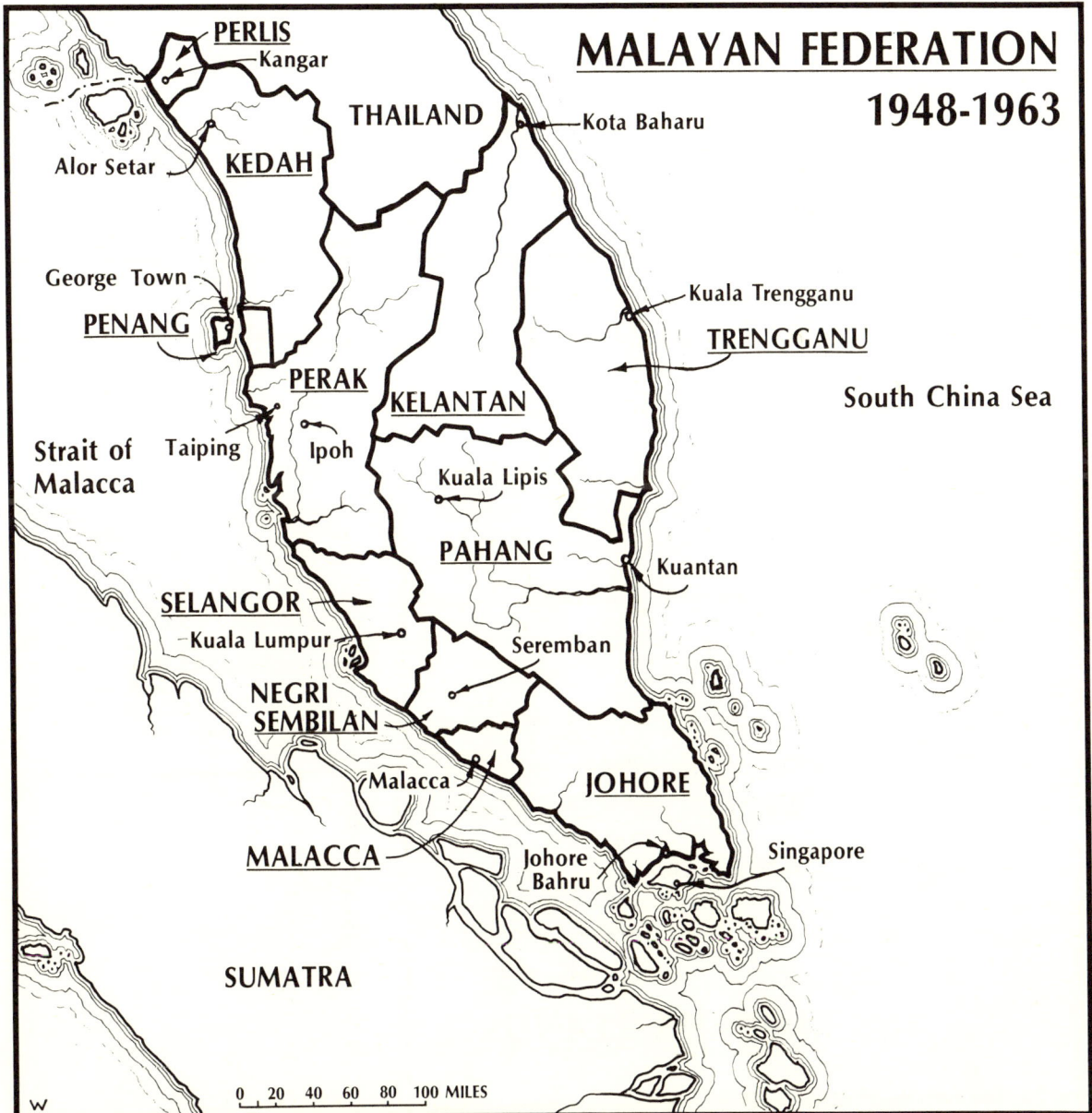

MALAYAN FEDERATION
1948-1963

Area: 482,234 (approx.)
Pop: 34,039,456 (1935 est.)
Capital: Hsinking

Manchukuo was a puppet state set up in northern China by the Japanese in 1932, shortly after they had occupied the area. It was returned to China when Japan was defeated at the end of WWII. Stamps were issued by the Japanese puppet government of Manchukuo from 1932 to 1945.

ASIA

━━━━━━ **MARIANA ISLANDS, COLONY OF** ━━━━━━

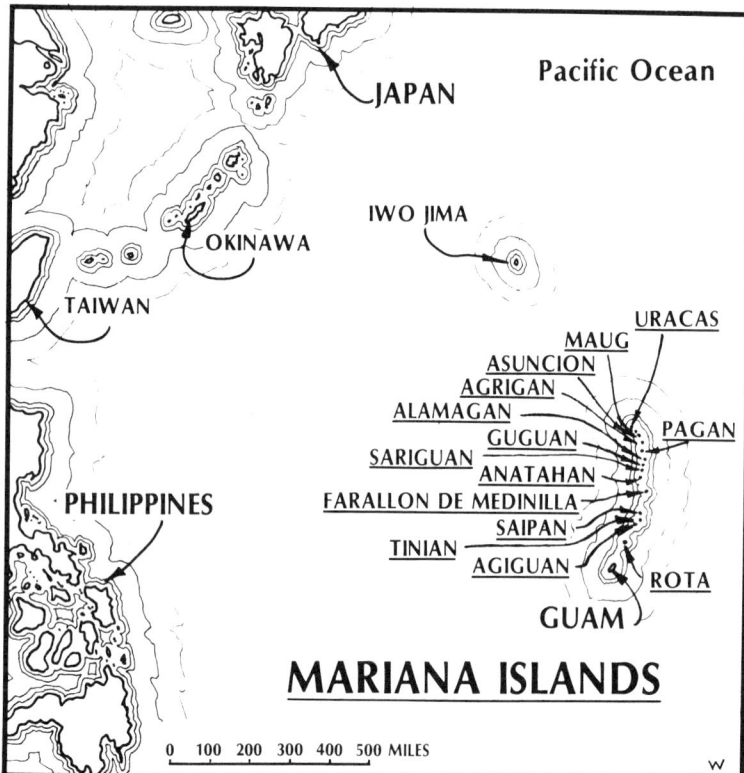

Area: 184 sq. miles
Pop: 10,172 (1903 est.)
Capital: Saipan

The Mariana Islands are in the western Pacific and belonged to Spain until the Spanish-American War of 1898. They were then sold to Germany except for Guam, which went to the US. The islands were occupied by Japan in WWI and mandated to that country in 1919. Liberated from Japan by US forces during WWII, they are now under US administration.

PACIFIC OCEAN

Pop: 23,100 (1970)

The town and district of Marienwerder was located in German East Prussia at the end of WWI. In 1920, a plebiscite was held to determine if it should remain German or become part of Poland. The vote was to remain German. At the end of WWII, the area was assigned to Poland and is now the Polish community of Kwidzyn. Stamps were issued during the plebiscite period.

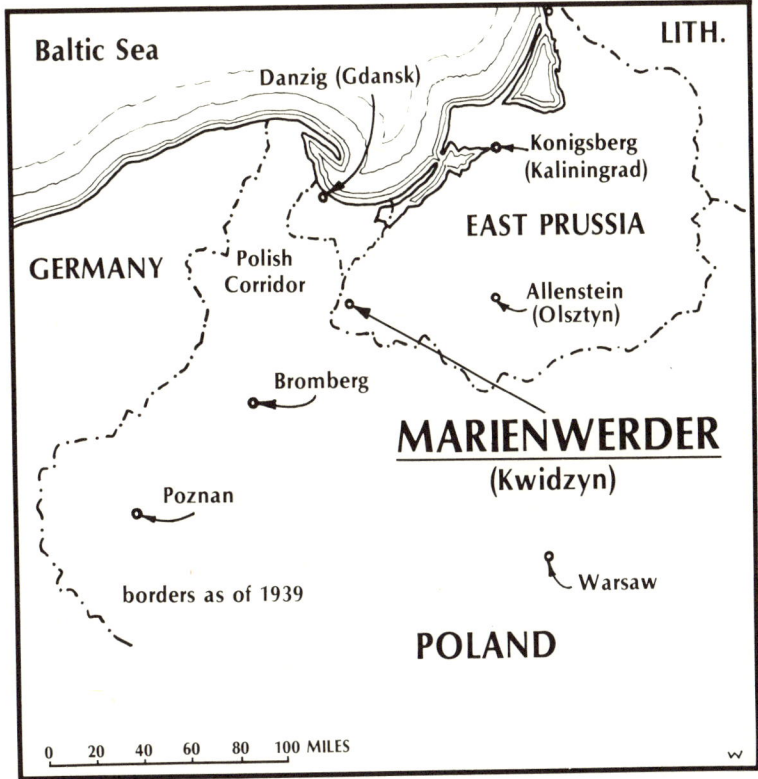

Baltic Sea

LITH.

Danzig (Gdansk)

Konigsberg (Kaliningrad)

EAST PRUSSIA

GERMANY   Polish Corridor

Allenstein (Olsztyn)

Bromberg

MARIENWERDER (Kwidzyn)

Poznan

Warsaw

borders as of 1939

POLAND

0 20 40 60 80 100 MILES

EUROPE

MARSHALL ISLANDS, COLONY OF ———

Land area: 69 sq. miles
Pop: 15,000 (1896 est.)
20,206 (1970 est.)

The Marshall Islands group comprises two chains of islands in the Western Pacific running generally north to south. The islands were a German colony, purchased by that country from Spain in 1899 following the Spanish-American War of 1898. They were mandated to Japan and taken by US forces in WWII.

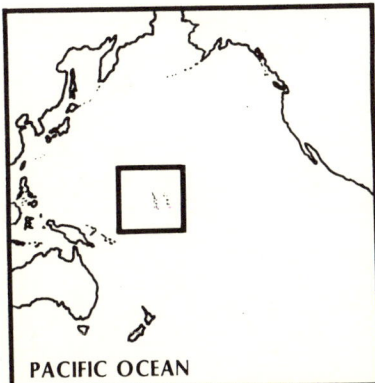

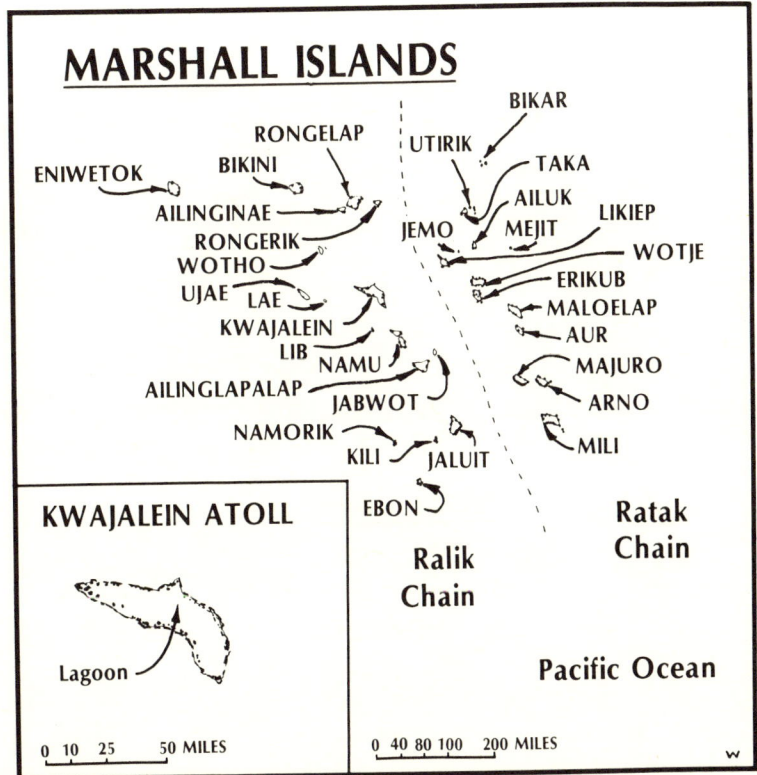

MARSHALL ISLANDS

ENIWETOK

RONGELAP   BIKINI   UTIRIK   BIKAR

AILINGINAE   TAKA

RONGERIK   AILUK

WOTHO   JEMO   MEJIT   LIKIEP

UJAE   LAE   WOTJE

KWAJALEIN   ERIKUB

LIB   MALOELAP

NAMU   AUR

AILINGLAPALAP   JABWOT   MAJURO

ARNO

NAMORIK   MILI

KILI   JALUIT

KWAJALEIN ATOLL   EBON   Ratak Chain

Ralik Chain

Lagoon

Pacific Ocean

0 10 25 50 MILES

0 40 80 100 200 MILES

PACIFIC OCEAN

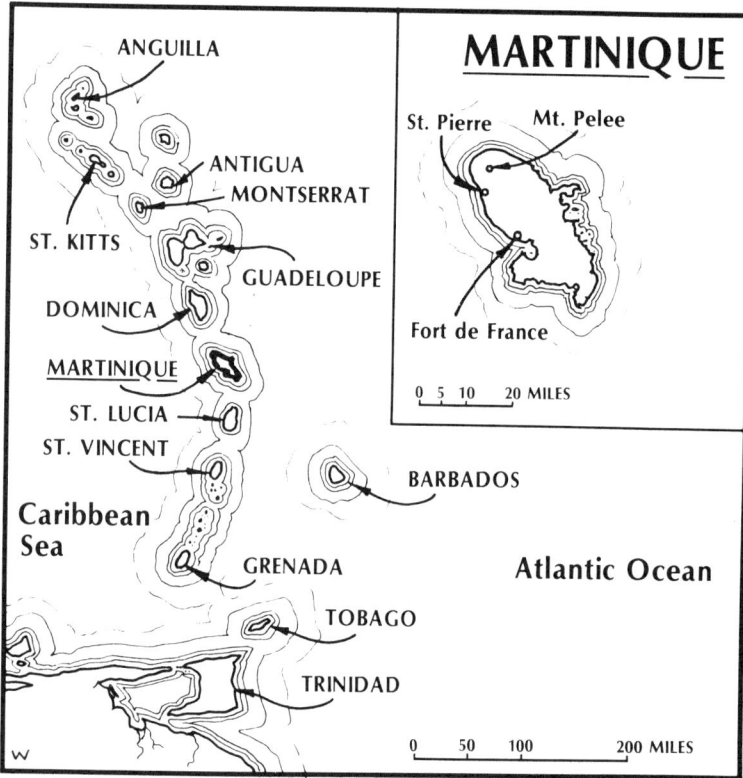

Area: 425 sq. miles
Pop: 246,712 (1936)
　　　310,000 (1979)
Capital: Fort-de-France

An island in the Lesser Antilles of the West Indies, Martinique changed hands between British and French forces a number of times. From the end of the Napoleonic Wars, it was a colony of France, and since 1946 has been a department of that country.

CENTRAL AMERICA

———————— MATURIN, CITY OF ——————————

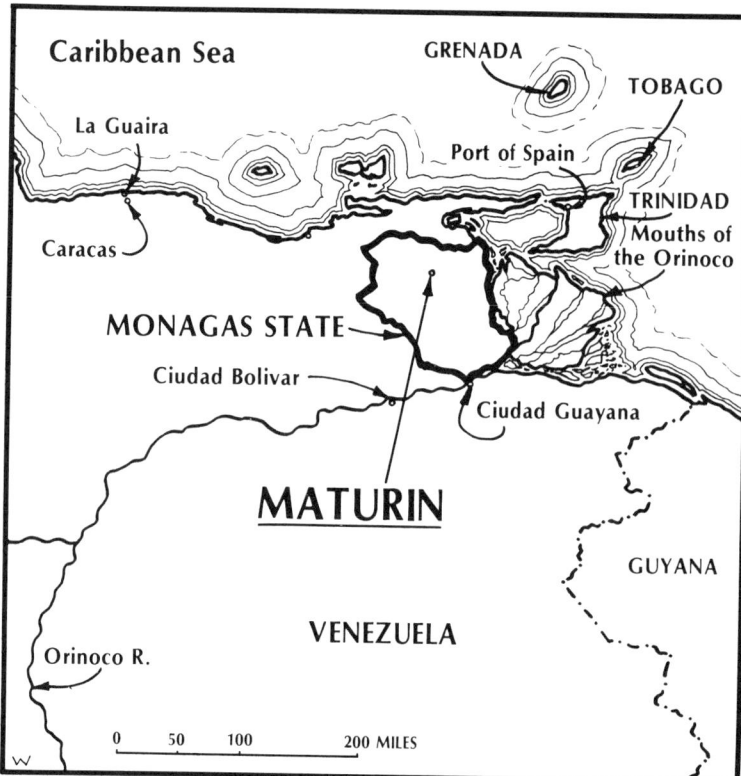

Pop: 14,473 (1891)
　　　97,257 (1970 est.)

A city in the state of Monagas, Venezuela, Maturin is near the mouths of the Orinoco River. During 1902-03, a number of Venezuelan areas issued provisional stamps, and in 1903 several appeared for Maturin in a design depicting the revolutionary steamer *Banrigh*. Later the same year they were re-issued overprinted "CORREOS" (in a semi-circle) and "MATURIN."

SOUTH AMERICA

Area: 144 sq. miles
Pop: 50,400 (1980 est.)
Chief town: Dzaoudzi

Mayotte is an island located in the Mozambique Channel between the island of Madagascar and the African mainland. Once a French colony, it issued its own stamps from 1892 to 1912, and is now a department of France.

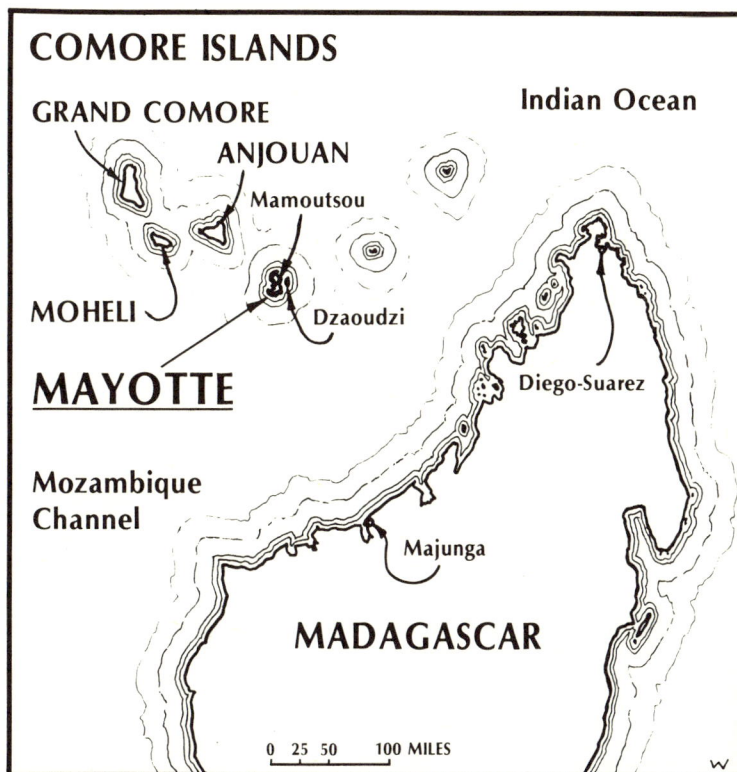

MECKLENBURG SCHWERIN, GRAND DUCHY OF

Area: 5,000 sq. miles (approx.)
Pop: 607,770 (1900)
Capital: Schwerin

A former grand duchy in northern Germany, Mecklenburg Schwerin joined the North German Confederation in 1867 and the German Empire in 1870. It is now within the German Democratic Republic (East Germany). As a grand duchy, it issued its own stamps from 1856 to Jan. 1, 1868.

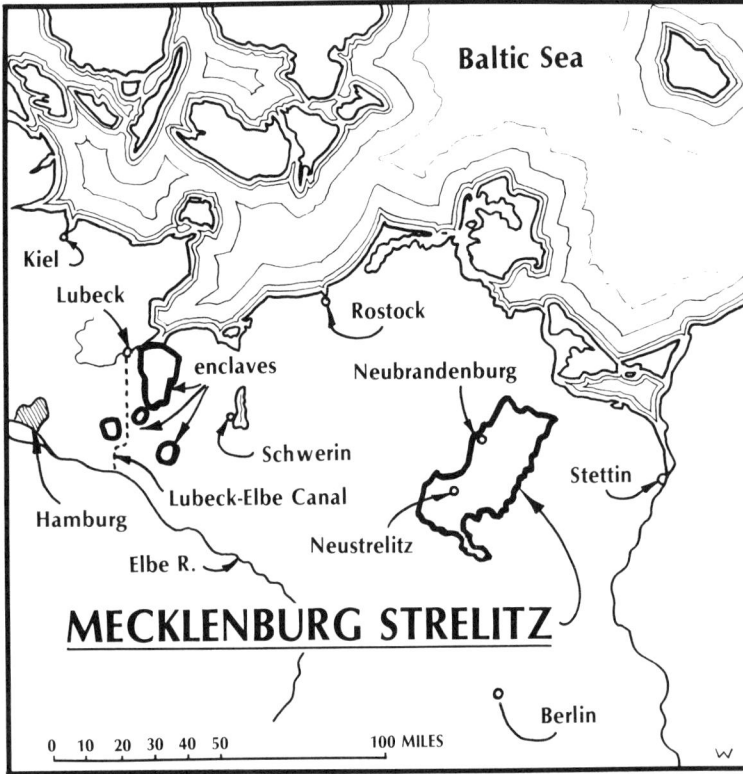

Area: 1,130 sq. miles
Pop: 102,602 (1900)
Capital: Neustrelitz

A former grand duchy in northern Germany, Mecklenburg Strelitz joined the North German Confederation in 1867 and the German Empire in 1870. It is now within the German Democratic Republic (East Germany). As a grand duchy it issued its own stamps from 1864 to Jan. 1, 1868.

EUROPE

—————MEDELLIN, CITY OF—————

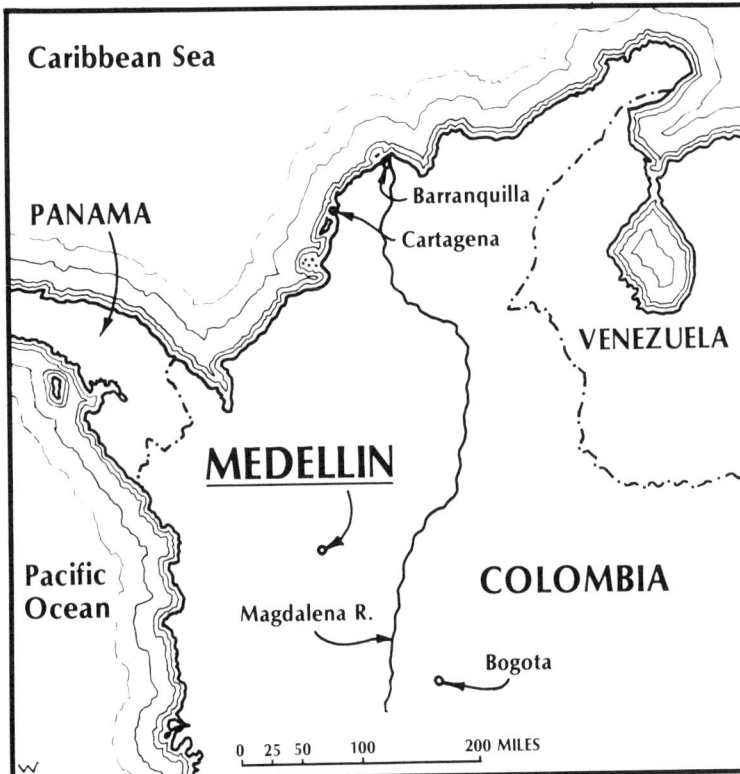

Pop: 50,000 (1886)
1,112,390 (1981 est.)

The city of Medellin is the second largest city of Colombia. It is an industrial, educational, and agricultural center, known for its coffee market. A stamp issue was released in 1888 that is called the Medellin Issue. In 1902, another stamp issue is noted in catalogs as the Medellin Issue. Also noted are local stamps issued for use there.

SOUTH AMERICA

Area: 1,092 sq. miles
Pop: 140,000 (1970)
Capital: Memel (Klaipeda)

An area based on the seaport of Memel (Memelburg, now Klaipeda), it was Prussian territory from the 18th century to WWI. Following the war, it was administered by France under the League of Nations. The Lithuanians seized it in 1923, and it was made part of an autonomous Memel territory until taken by Germany in 1939.

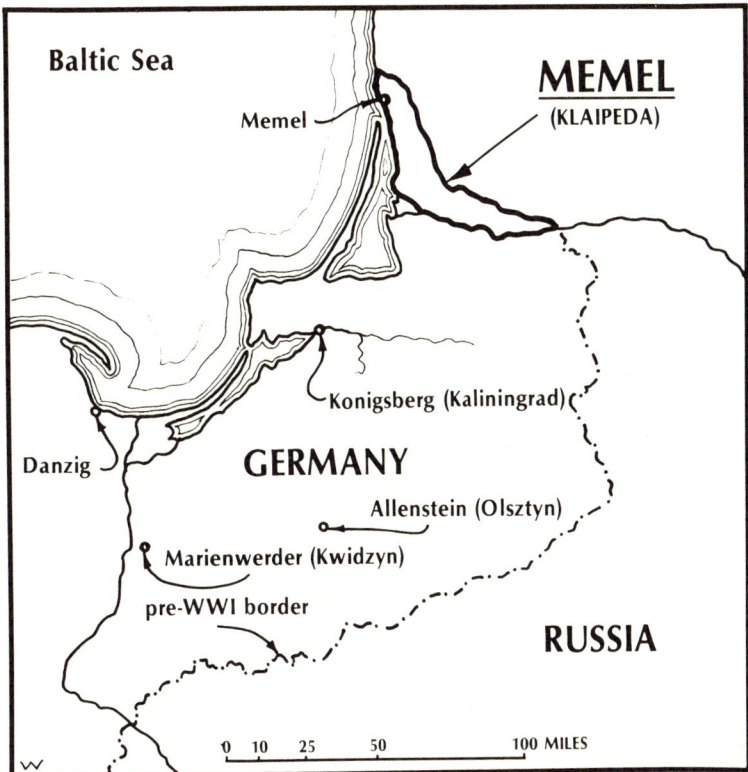

EUROPE

Baltic Sea

MEMEL (KLAIPEDA)

Memel

Konigsberg (Kaliningrad)

Danzig

GERMANY

Allenstein (Olsztyn)

Marienwerder (Kwidzyn)

pre-WWI border

RUSSIA

0 10 25 50 100 MILES

MESOPOTAMIA, AREA OF

Area: indefinite
Major city: Baghdad

Mesopotamia is located in the area of the Tigris and Euphrates Rivers and extends from the mountains of Asia Minor south to the head of the Persian Gulf. It was Turkish territory until taken by British forces during WWI. Mandated to Britain in 1920, it became the Kingdom of Iraq in 1932. It now constitutes the major portion of the Republic of Iraq.

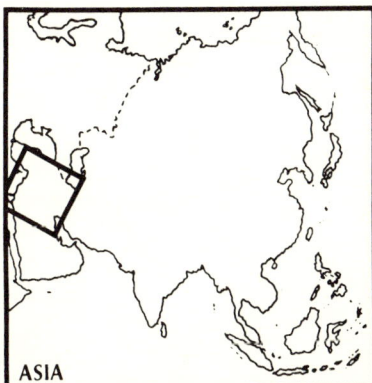

ASIA

TURKEY

USSR

Caspian Sea

Mediterranean Sea

IRAN

Baghdad

IRAQ

Area of **MESOPOTAMIA**

Persian Gulf

Red Sea

ARABIA

0 100 200 300 400 500 MILES

Area: 1,000 sq. miles (approx.)
Pop: 279,254 (1881)
Capital: Modena

Modena was a duchy located in northern Italy. In 1859, the ruler Francis V was toppled, and shortly afterwards the duchy was annexed to the Kingdom of Sardinia, which became the Kingdom of Italy in 1861. Stamps were issued by Modena from 1852 and used until February 1860, when stamps of Sardinia went into use.

━━━━━━━MOHELI, ISLAND OF━━━━━━━

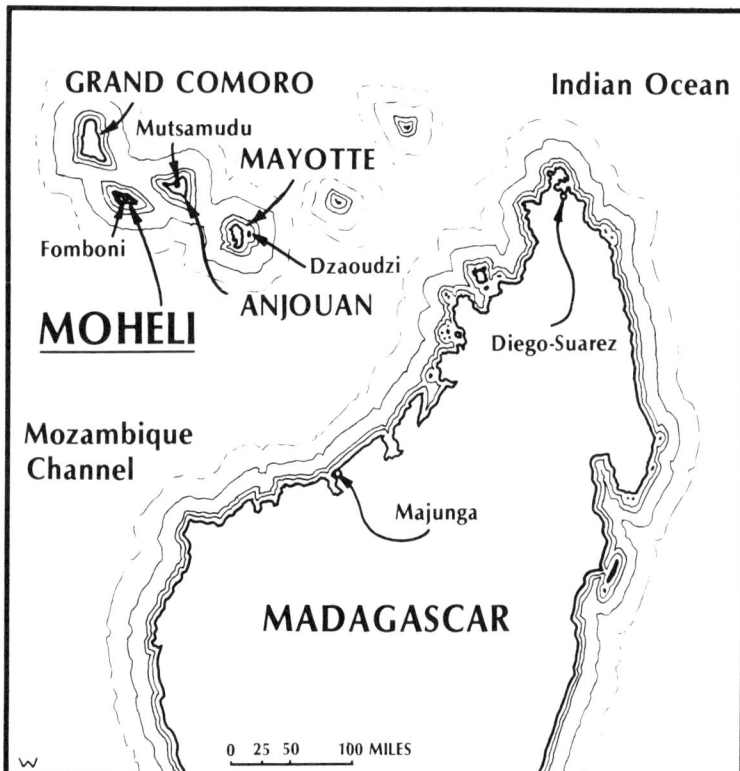

Area: 112 sq. miles
Pop: 12,000 (1970 est.)
Capital: Fomboni

An island in the Mozambique Channel between Madagascar and the African mainland, Moheli was a French colony in the Comoro Islands. It is now part of the Republic of Comoros. Beginning in 1906, stamps in the French colonial Commerce and Navigation key type were issued. These were replaced by the stamps of Madagascar from 1908 until 1950.

Area: 14,690 sq. miles

The Principality of Moldavia was one of the territories that went to make up the present country of Romania. It merged with the Principality of Walachia in 1861 to form the Kingdom of Romania. Stamps were issued from 1858 until 1862, when a joint issue with Walachia was released.

MOLUCCAS, or SPICE ISLANDS

Area: 32,307 sq. miles
Pop: 995,000 (1970 est.)

The Moluccas, or Spice Islands, are located in the East Indies between the islands of Celebes and New Guinea. They were once part of the Dutch East Indies and are now in the Republic of Indonesia. Stamps were issued in 1943 for use in the area by the Japanese occupiers. The stamps were also used in the Lesser Sundas, Celebes, and South Borneo.

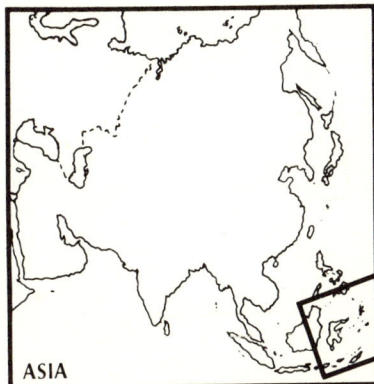

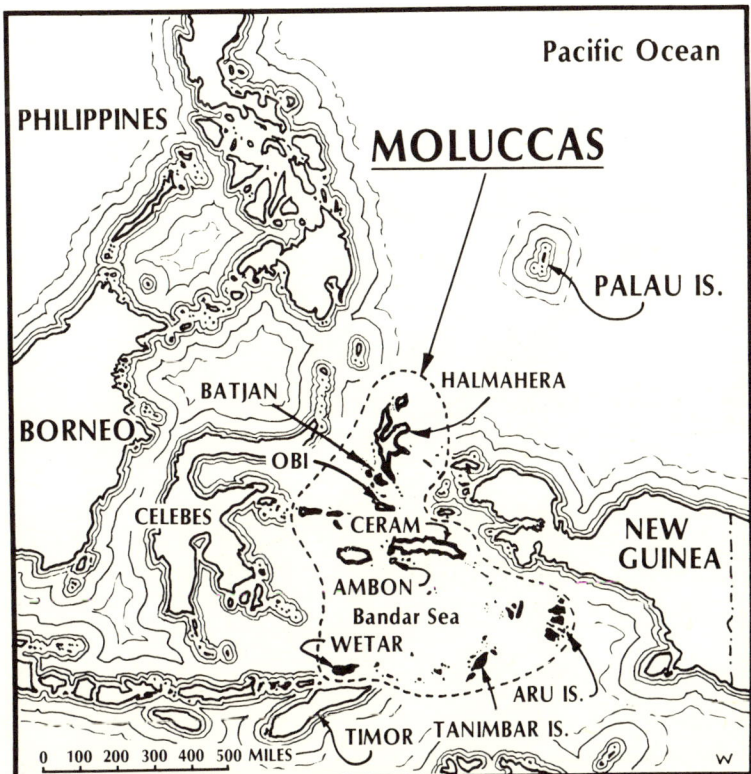

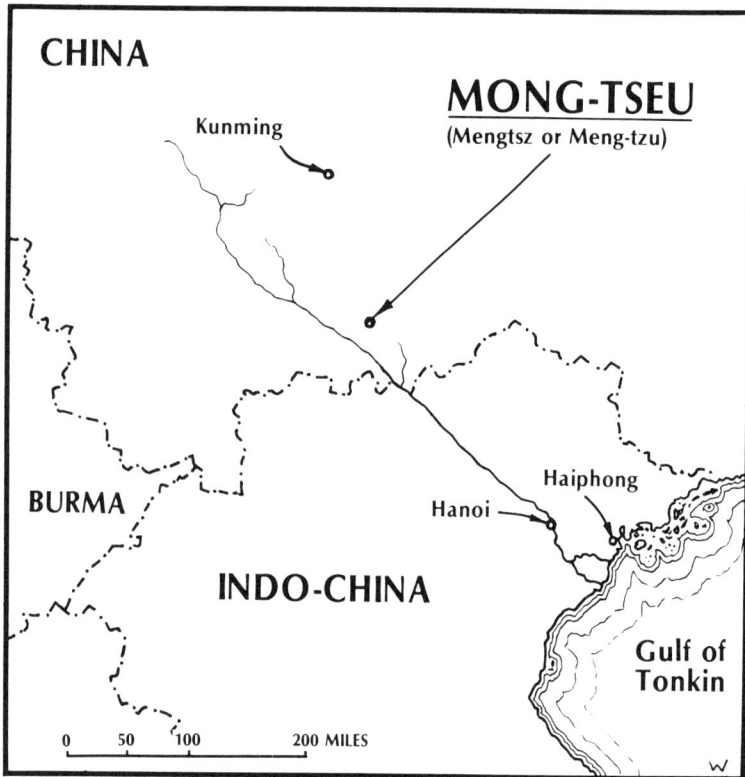

Pop: 12,000 (1898 est.)

A city in China, Mong-tseu (Meng-tzu, or Me gtze), is located in Yunnan Province, not far from the border of Vietnam, and south-southeast of Kunming. It was a Treaty Port (q.v.), and stamps of Indo-China were overprinted "MONGTZE" and "Mong-Tseu" for use at a French post office in the city from 1903 to 1922.

MONROVIA, CITY OF

Pop: 306,000 (1981 est.)

Monrovia is the capital city of the African country of Liberia. In 1893, a series of registration stamps was issued by Liberia inscribed with the names of Monrovia, Buchanan, Grenville (Greenville), Harper, and Robertsport. All are cities located along the coast of the country.

Area: 134 sq. miles
Pop: 1,732 (1970)
Capital: Karyai

A peninsula and mountain, Mont Athos was once part of the Turkish Empire and is now located in northern Greece. From 1869 to 1882, Turkish stamps were overprinted with a variety of devices for use as local stamps at both Constantinople and Mont Athos. In 1909-10, Russian stamps were overprinted "MONT ATHOS" for use at a Russian post office.

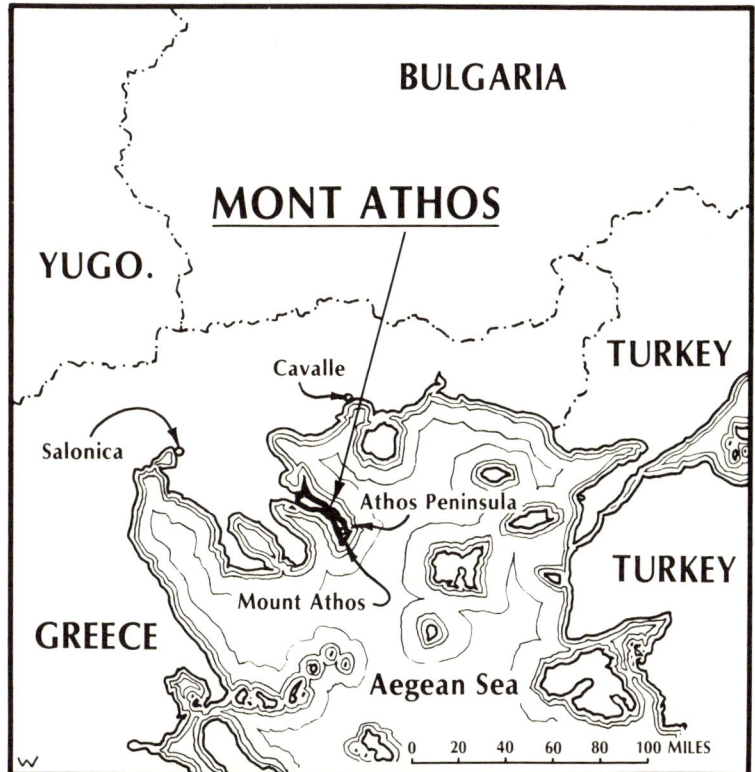

MONTENEGRO, KINGDOM OF

Area: 3,733 sq. miles
Pop: 228,000 (1900)
Capital: Cetinje

A former kingdom, Montenegro is now a constituent republic of Yugoslavia. It never recognized Turkish authority in the Balkans, and at the end of 1876-78 war with that country it obtained complete independence. Following WWI it voted to join with other Balkan areas to form the new country of Yugoslavia.

Pop: 56,955 (1895)
    1.1 million (1978 est.)

Monterrey is the capital of the state of Nuevo Leon in northeast Mexico. An industrial center, it was the scene of a battle during the Mexican War, when US forces under Zachary Taylor took the town. In 1914, rebels overprinted stamps for use from the town. Catalogs note that the local stamps of Monterrey of 1860s vintage are considered to be bogus.

————————————MONTEVIDEO, CITY OF————————

Pop: 238,080 (1892)
    1.5 million (1979 est.)

Montevideo is the capital city of Uruguay and of the department of the same name. It is a seaport and industrial, commercial, and educational center of the country. Settled in 1726 by Spain, it has been occupied over the years by Britain, Argentina, Portugal, and Brazil. Early stamps of Uruguay are inscribed "MONTEVIDEO."

Area: 6,245 sq. miles
Pop: 28,786 (1876)
68,000 (1970 est.)
Capital: Moquegua

A department of Peru, Moquegua is located on the coast at the southern end of the country. Stamps were issued for the area in 1881-85, during a stamp shortage caused by the Chilean occupation of Lima and Callao during the war between the two countries.

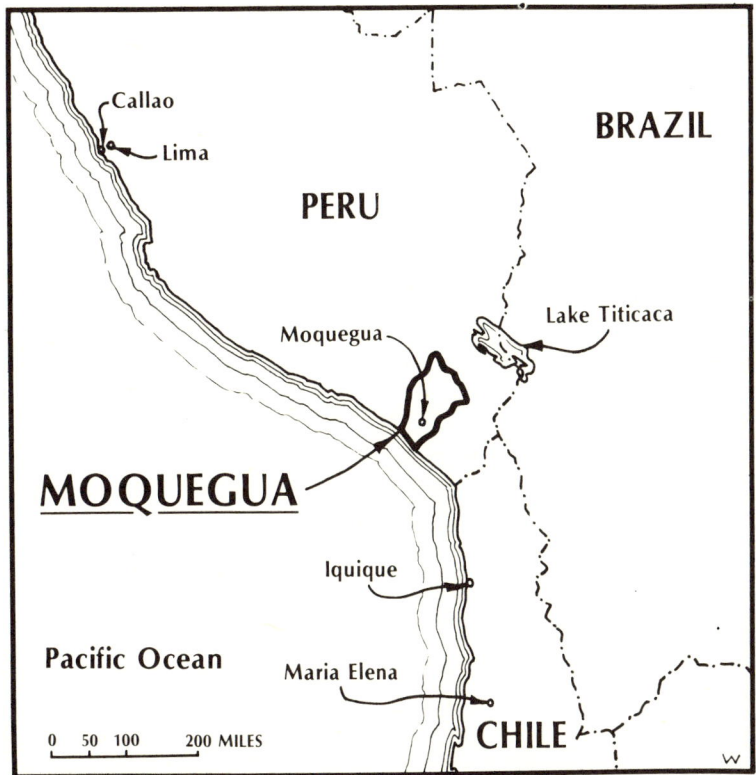

SOUTH AMERICA

Callao · Lima · PERU · BRAZIL · Moquegua · Lake Titicaca · MOQUEGUA · Iquique · Pacific Ocean · Maria Elena · CHILE

0 50 100 200 MILES

MORELIA, CITY OF

Pop: 32,287 (1895)
209,507 (1970)

A city in Mexico, Morelia is the capital of the state of Michoacan. It is the center of an agricultural region. It was founded in 1541 as the town of Valladolid, and became a major center in 1581. It was renamed in 1828 for the revolutionary leader J.M. Morelos y Pavon. Catalogs note that local stamps purporting to be issued there in the 19th century are believed to be bogus.

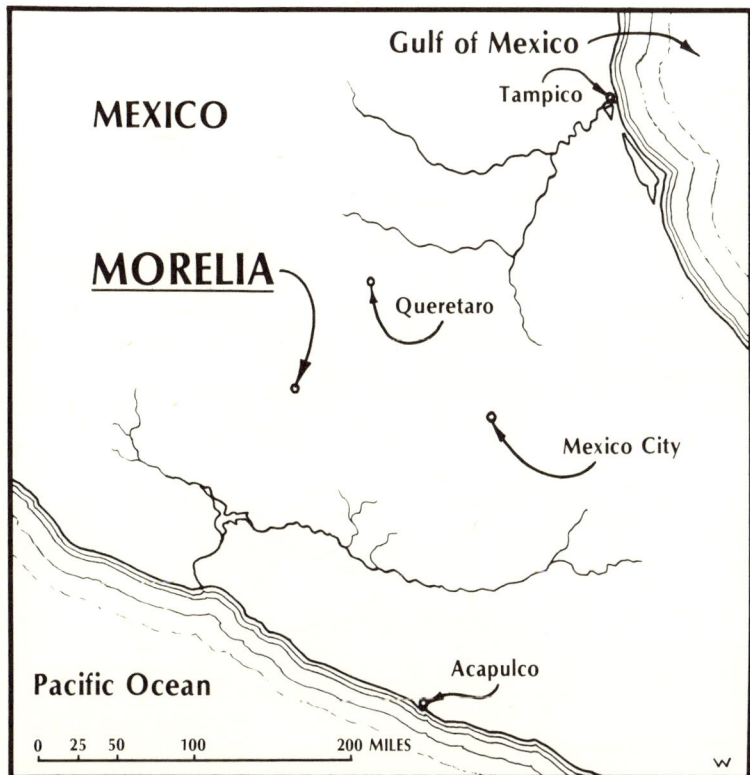

NORTH AMERICA

Gulf of Mexico · Tampico · MEXICO · MORELIA · Queretaro · Mexico City · Pacific Ocean · Acapulco

0 25 50 100 200 MILES

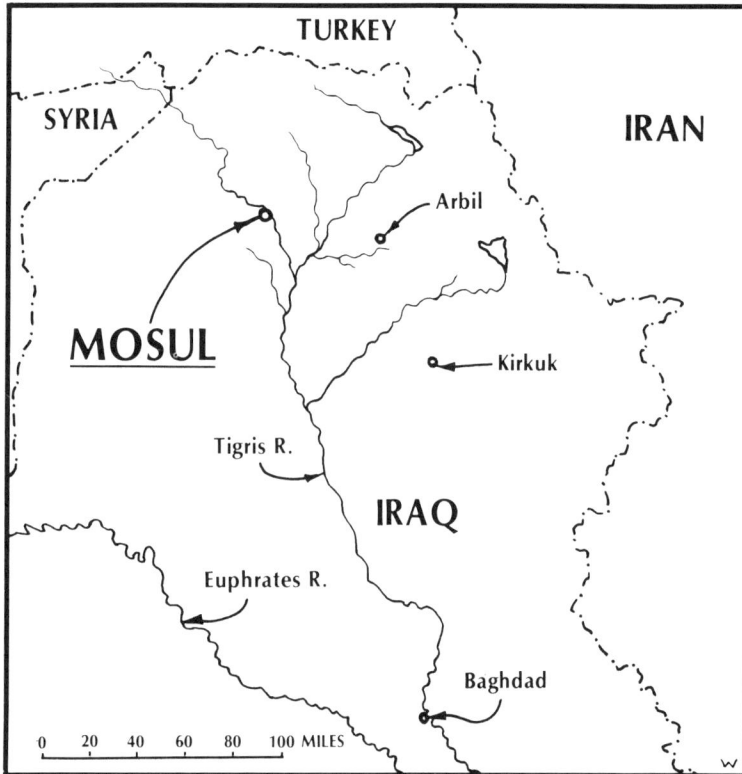

Pop: 57,000 (1900)
243,311 (1965)

Mosul is a city located in Mesopotamia, now the Republic of Iraq. It is on the Tigris River about 220 miles north of Baghdad. The town is across the river from the site of the ancient town of Nineveh. It became part of the Turkish Empire about 1534 and was taken by British forces during their WWI occupation of Mesopotamia. A set of three stamps issued there by the British in 1919 is called the Mosul Issue.

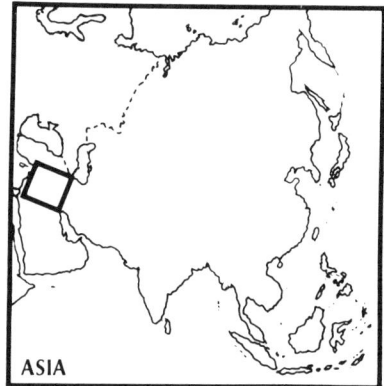

ASIA

━━━━━━━━━━━ MOZAMBIQUE COMPANY ━━━━━━━━━━━

Area: 51,880 sq. miles
Pop: 368,540 (1939 est.)
Capital: Beira

The territory chartered to the Mozambique Company from 1891 to 1941 included the districts of Manica and Sofala in the Portuguese African colony of Mozambique. During the time the company governed the area, it released its own postage stamps beginning in 1892 and continuing until 1941. The stamps were generally colorful and attractive, providing a glimpse of an otherwise little-known area.

AFRICA

Pop: 7,000 (1975 est.)

The town of Muscat was the seat of an independent sheikdom located on the coast of the Gulf of Oman and it is now the capital city of Oman. From 1944 to 1947, stamps of India were overprinted for use at the city, which had an Indian postal administration. From 1947, Pakistan provided a similar service using its stamps. During the period April 1, 1948, to April 29, 1966, stamps of the British Postal Agencies in Eastern Arabia were used.

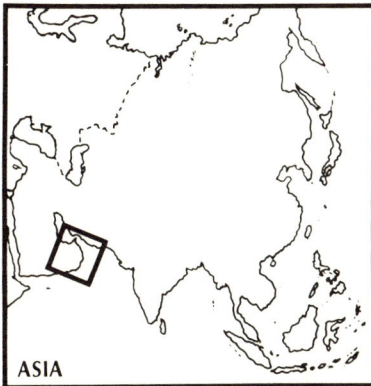

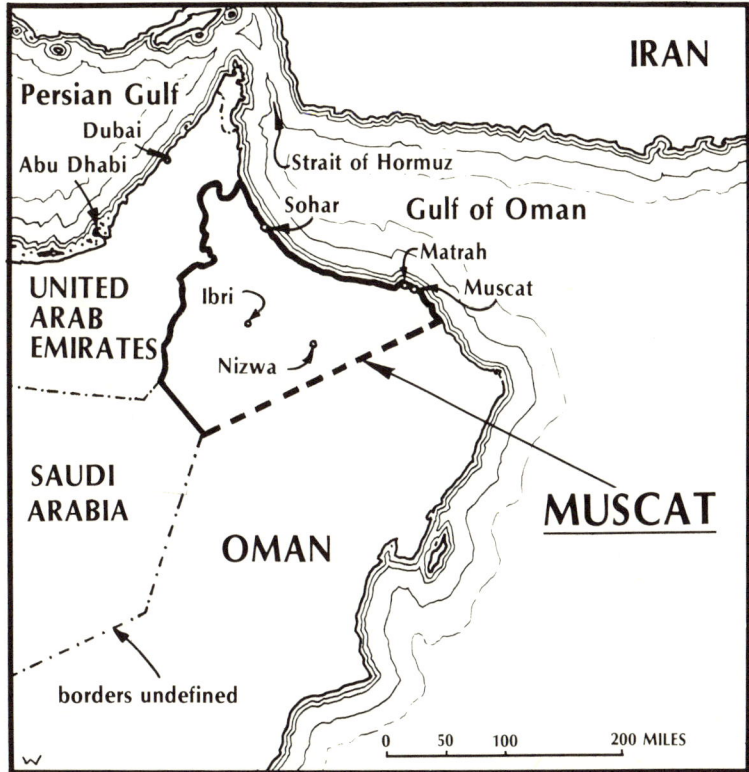

NANKING, CITY OF

Pop: 130,000 (1898 est.)
two million (1970 est.)

A large city on the south bank of the Yangtze River about 200 miles by river above Shanghai, Nanking was the capital of China during 1928-37 and again during 1946-49. Nanking was a Treaty Port (q.v.) from 1858. It is now the capital of Kiangsu Province. A Nanking stamp issue was released in 1912, and stamps were again issued during the WWII period.

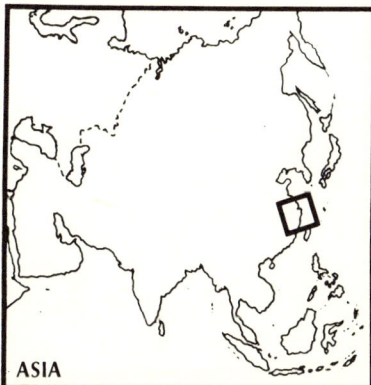

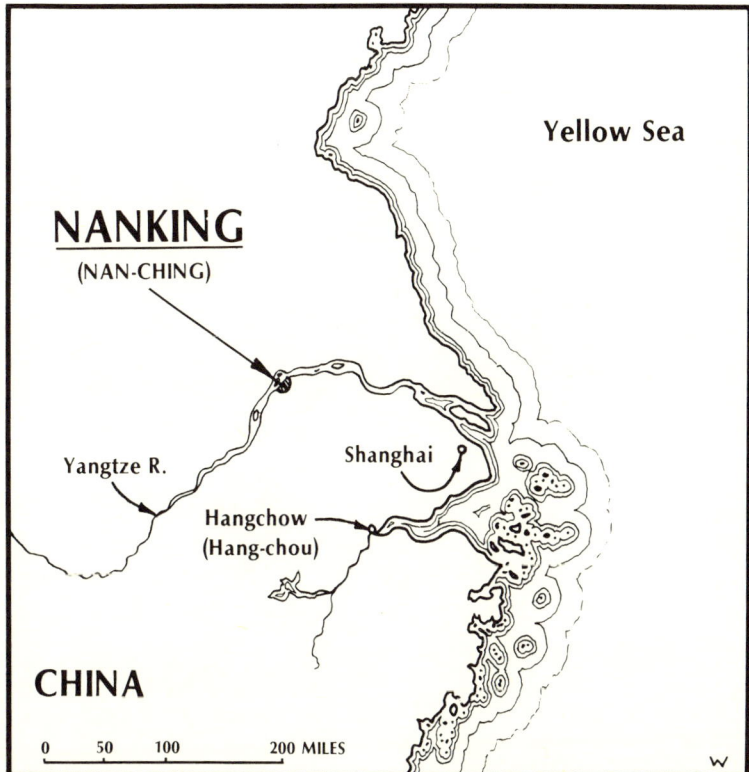

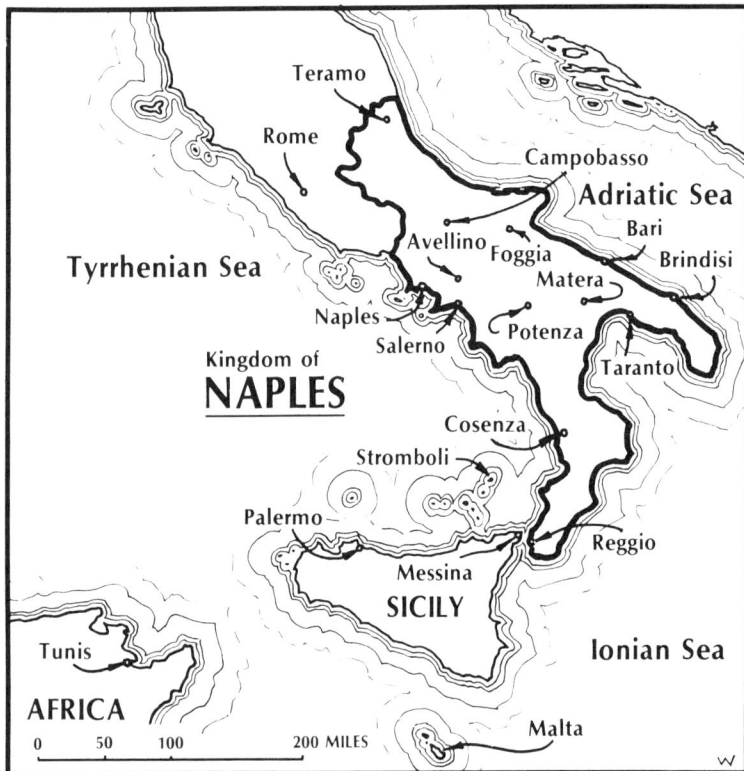

Pop: 1,001,245 (1881)
Capital: Naples

A former kingdom taking up the lower portion of the Italian "boot," the Kingdom of Naples formed part of the kingdom of the Two Sicilies until 1860, when Garibaldi annexed it to the Kingdom of Sardinia. It became part of the Kingdom of Italy shortly thereafter. Stamps were issued during 1858-60 and again in 1861 by the Province of Naples.

━━━━━━━━━━━━━━NATAL, COLONY OF━━━━━━━━━━━━━━

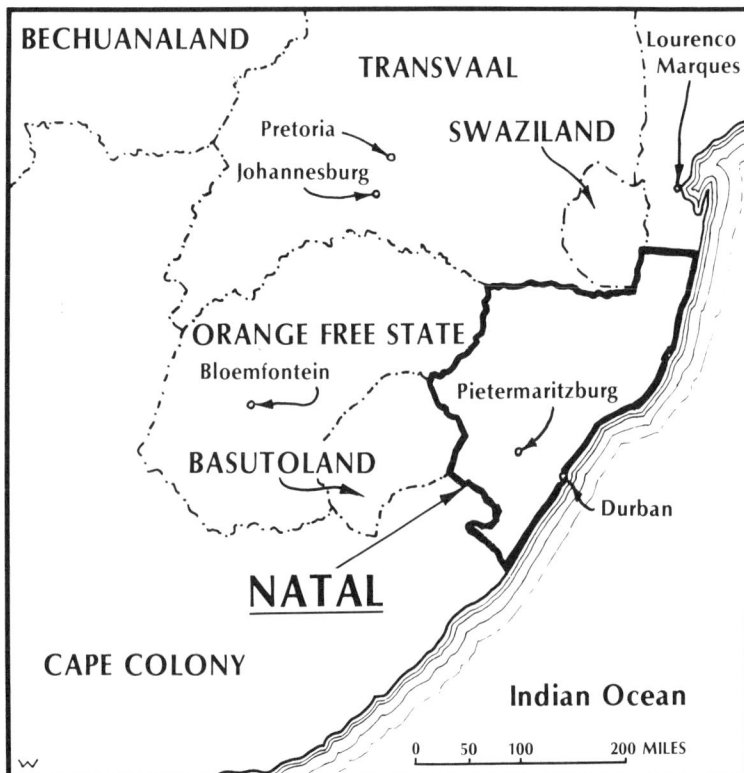

Area: 33,578 sq. miles
Pop: 543,913 (1891)
            3,418,942 (1967 est.)
Capital: Pietermaritzburg

A former British colony in southern Africa, Natal was made a colonial possession in 1843. Except for a period of annexation to the Cape Colony during 1844-56, it remained a colony until it joined the Union of South Africa in 1910. Stamps were issued from 1857 to 1910.

Area: 447,000 sq. miles approx.
Pop: three million (1930 est.)
Capital: Riyadh

Prior to WWI, Nejd was a kingdom under Turkish control, and it gained its freedom at the end of the war. During the early 1920s it was engaged in a war with neighboring Hejaz, which it conquered in 1926 and became the dual Kingdom of the Hejaz and Nejd. In 1932, its name was changed to Saudi Arabia. Stamps were issued from 1916.

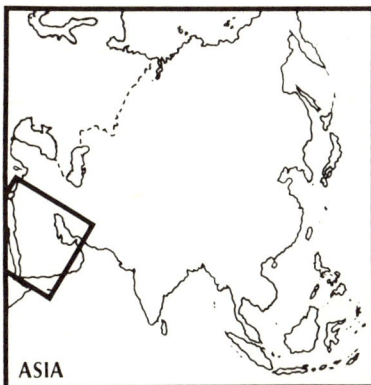

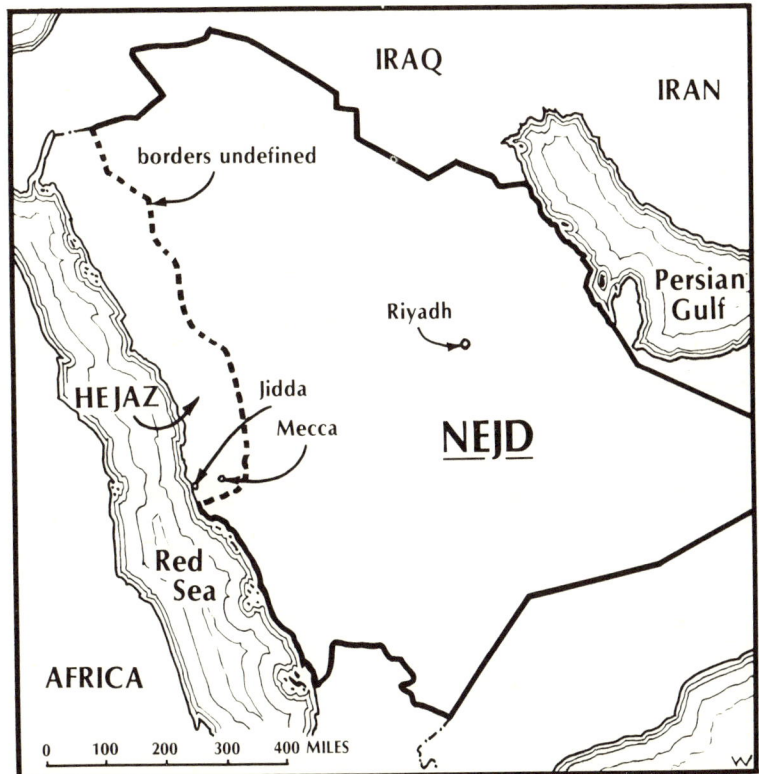

NETHERLANDS NEW GUINEA, COLONY OF

Area: 162,927 sq. miles
Pop: 730,000 (1958 est.)
957,000 (1970 est.)
Capital: Hollandia (Jayapura)

A Dutch colony, Netherlands New Guinea became part of the Republic of Indonesia in 1963, following a period under United Nations administration as West Irian. Stamps were first issued by the Dutch administration in 1950. Prior to that, stamps of the Netherlands Indies were used.

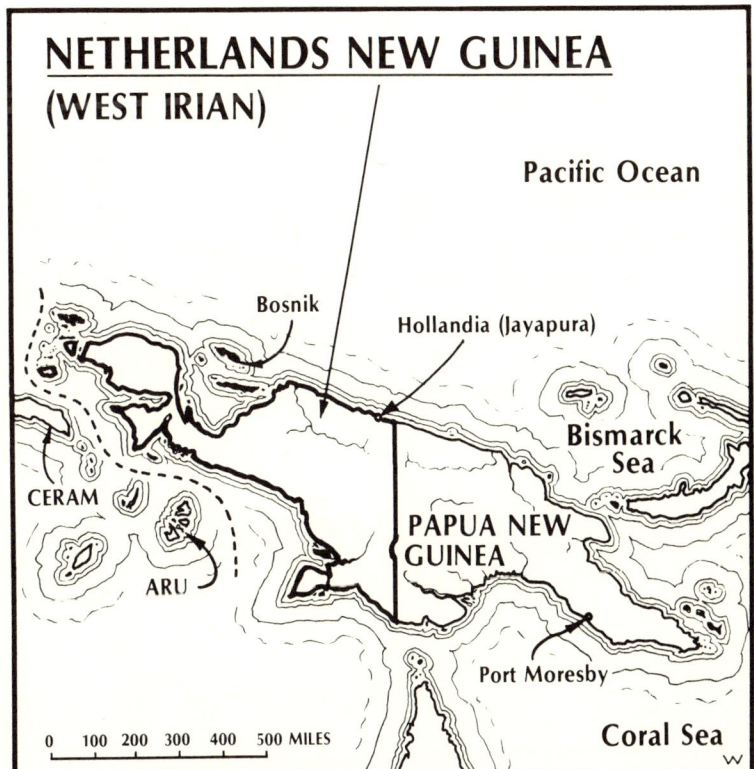

Area: 735,300 sq. miles, approx.
Pop: 76 million (1949 est.)
Capital: Batavia (Jakarta)

Occupying much of the area that is now the Republic of Indonesia, the Netherlands Indies was a prosperous colony comprising a large number of islands in the East Indies. These included Sumatra, Java, the Lesser Sundas, Madura, much of Borneo, Celebes, the Moluccas, and many more smaller islands. The area was originally brought under Dutch influence during 1600-1798 by the Dutch East India Company. The area was under Japanese control during WWII and declared its independence in 1945. This was not recognized by the Dutch, and they attempted to re-establish a colonial government. Nevertheless, the Republic of Indonesia came into being in 1950. Stamps were issued for the Netherlands Indies from 1864 to 1949. Some Japanese occupation issues appeared during the WWII occupation.

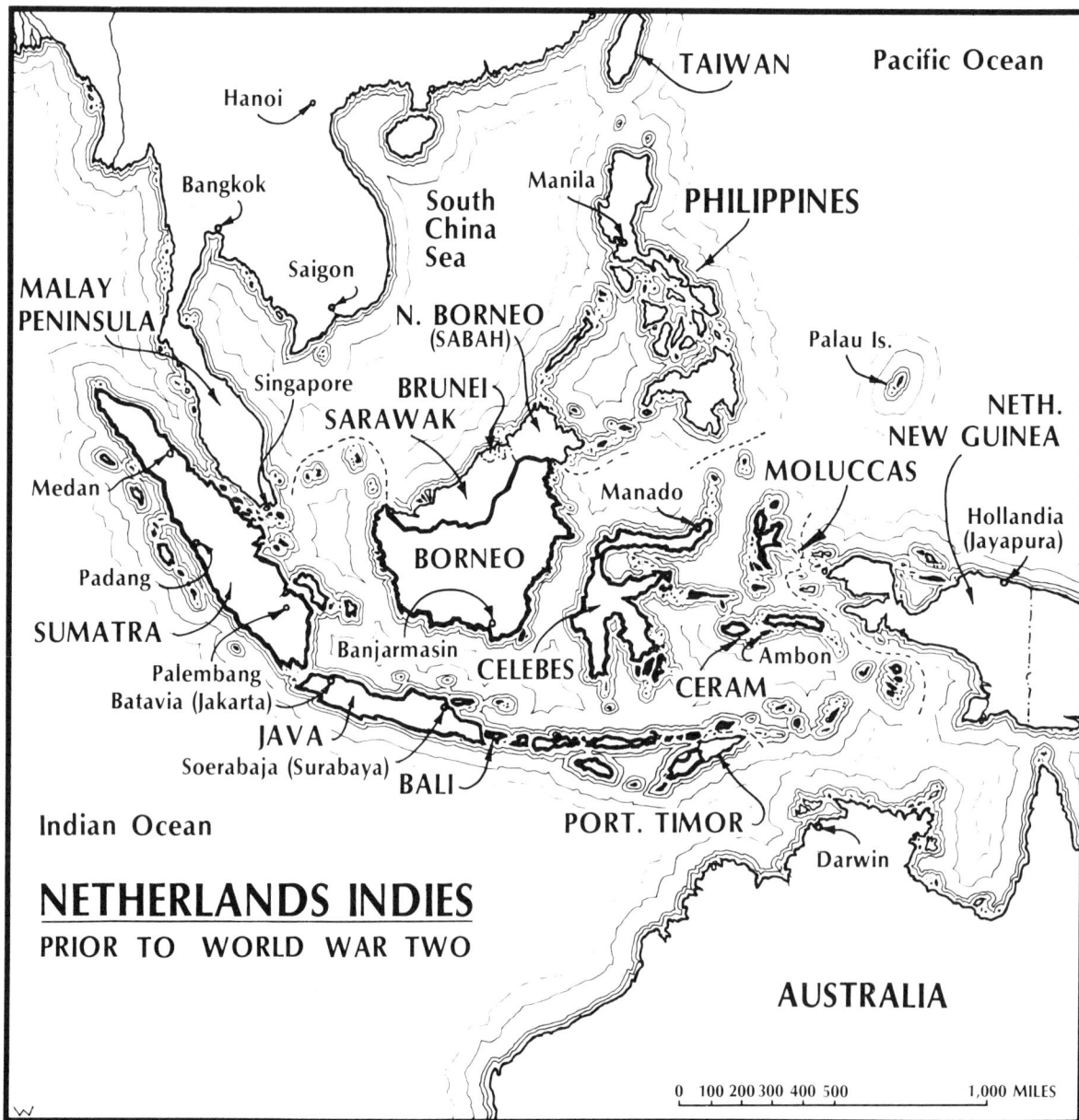

ASIA

TAIWAN   Pacific Ocean

Hanoi

Bangkok

Manila

South China Sea

PHILIPPINES

Saigon

MALAY PENINSULA

N. BORNEO (SABAH)

Palau Is.

Singapore

BRUNEI
SARAWAK

NETH. NEW GUINEA

Medan

MOLUCCAS

Manado

Hollandia (Jayapura)

BORNEO

Padang

SUMATRA

Banjarmasin

Ambon

Palembang
Batavia (Jakarta)

CELEBES

CERAM

JAVA

Soerabaja (Surabaya)

BALI

Indian Ocean

PORT. TIMOR

Darwin

NETHERLANDS INDIES
PRIOR TO WORLD WAR TWO

AUSTRALIA

0 100 200 300 400 500   1,000 MILES

Area: 14,160 sq. miles
Pop: 138,689 (1969 est.)
Capital: Rabaul

Formerly the island of Neu-Pommern, New Britain was part of German New Guinea. During WWI it was taken by Australian forces and re-named. The island became part of the area mandated to Australia after the war. During WWII it was occupied by Japan, and Rabaul was the scene of much action. The area is now part of Papua New Guinea.

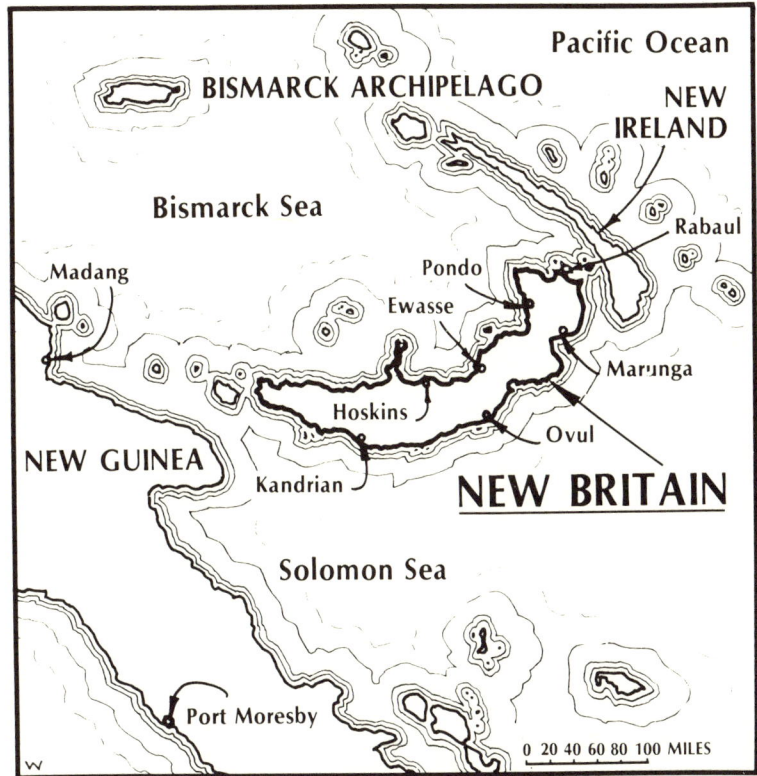

NEW BRUNSWICK, COLONY OF

Area: 28,354 sq. miles
Pop: 331,120 (1901)
        616,788 (1966)
Capital: Fredericton

A former British colony, New Brunswick is located in Eastern Canada and is now a province of that country. Part of the French province of Acadia until 1784, it was incorporated into Nova Scotia before being made a separate colony in 1784. New Brunswick joined Canadian Confederation in 1867. The colony issued its own stamps from 1851 until Confederation.

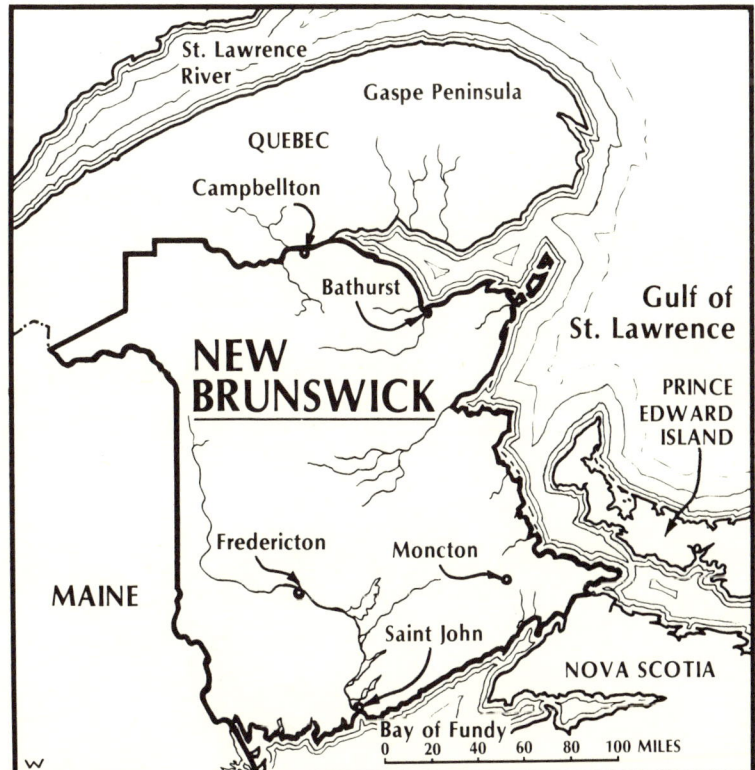

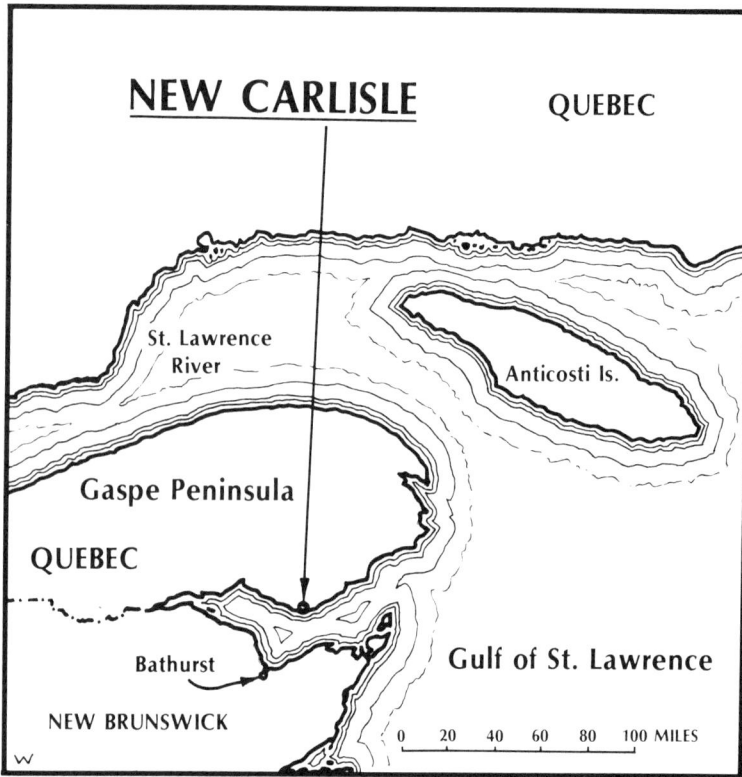

Pop: 6,112 (1970)

An unincorporated area of Bonaventure County in the province of Quebec, Canada, New Carlisle is located on the south side of the Gaspe Peninsula on Chaleur Bay. A postmaster's provisional stamped envelope is listed by Gibbons as the first item of Canada. It is dated April 7, 1851, and the catalog notes that only one is known.

NEWFOUNDLAND, DOMINION OF

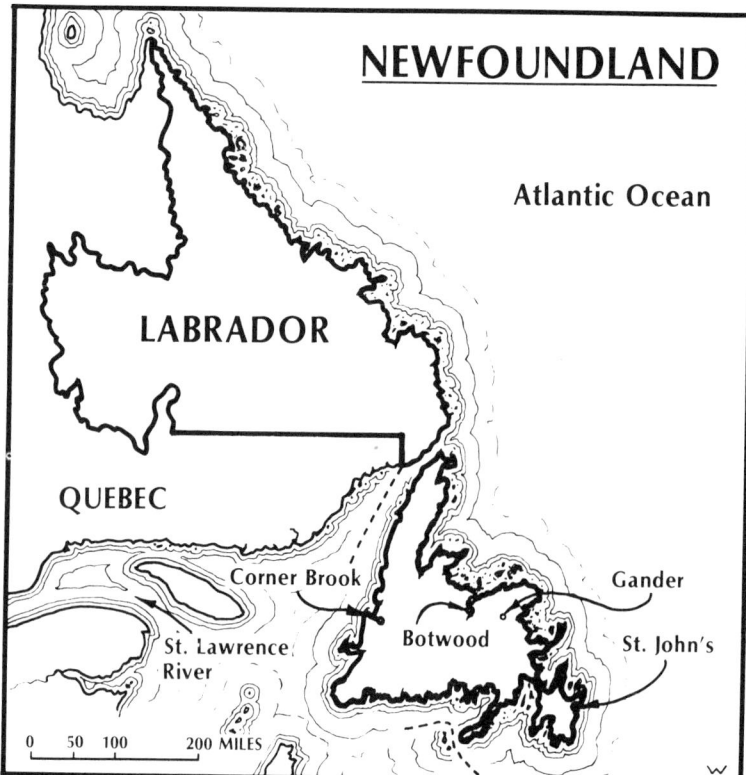

Area: 43,359 sq. miles
Pop: 202,040 (1891)
     485,843 (1966)
Capital: St. John's

The dominion and crown colony (from 1934) of Newfoundland comprised an island off Canada's east coast, plus Labrador on the North American mainland. It joined Canada as the 10th province in 1949. Stamps were issued from 1857 to 1949.

Area: undefined
Pop: not recorded

New Greece was an area taken from Turkey during 1912 by Greece and now constitutes most of the northern part of that country. It included territory in Macedonia, Epirus, and a number of islands in the Aegean Sea. Greece overprinted stamps "Greek Administration" for use in the newly occupied areas.

NEW HEBRIDES, CONDOMINIUM OF

Area: 4,707 sq. miles
Pop: 80,000 (1900 est.)
      112,000 (1979)
Capital: Vila

The New Hebrides group in the South Pacific was governed as a condominium by Britain and France from 1906 until 1980, when it became independent as the Republic of Vanuatu. Stamps were issued beginning in 1908. Generally, they were duplicated, with one having an English inscription and the other being in French.

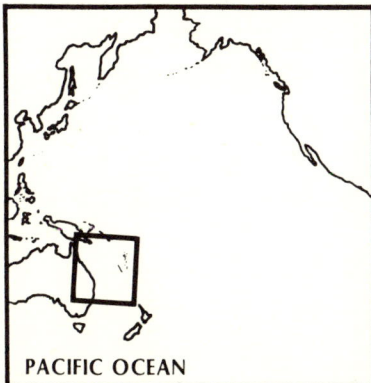

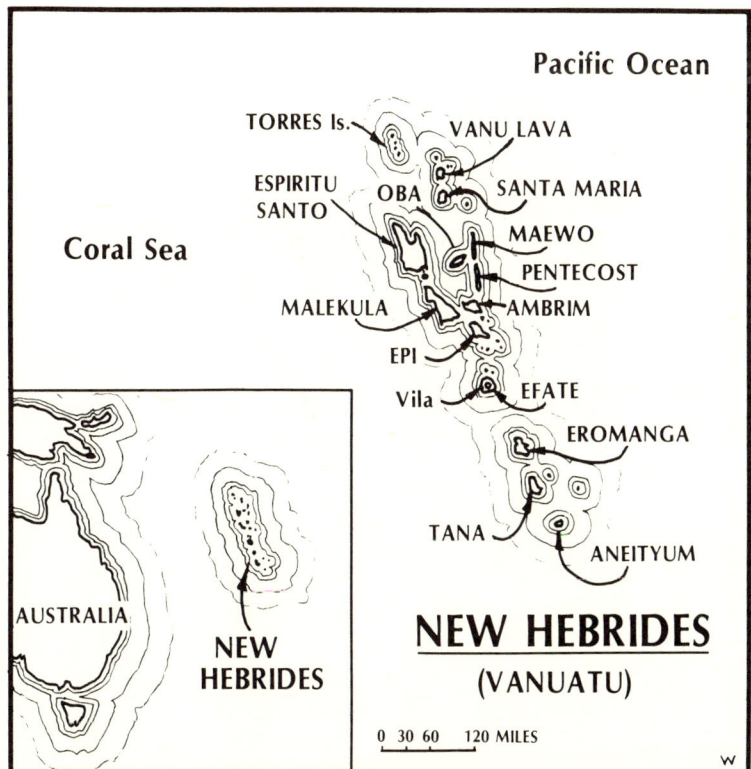

Capital: Vryheid

An area in what is now the South African province of Transvaal, the New Republic existed from 1884 to 1888. It had been established by Boers from Transvaal who gained it from the Zulu people. When the South African colony of Natal annexed Zululand in 1887, it had been excluded from the annexation and later went to Transvaal. Stamps were issued in 1886 and 1887.

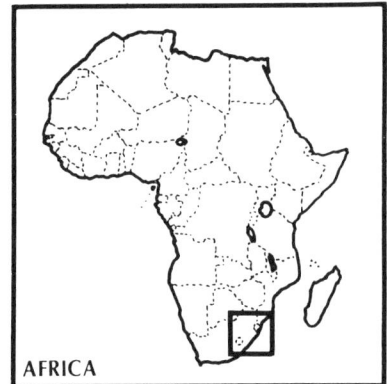

——————— NEW SOUTH WALES, CROWN COLONY OF ———————

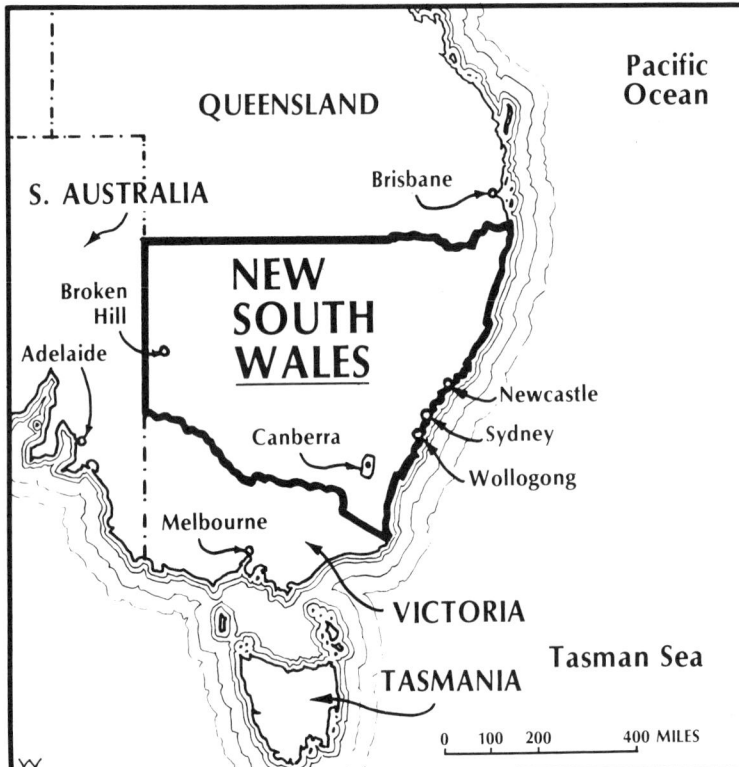

Area: 309,433 sq. miles
Pop: 1,357,050 (1899 est.)
5,078,500 (1980)
Capital: Sydney

A former British colony, New South Wales is now a state in the Commonwealth of Australia. First established at Botany Bay in 1788, the settlement was soon transferred to what is now Sydney. Initially, it included all of Australia except Western Australia. As other colonies were established its area diminished.

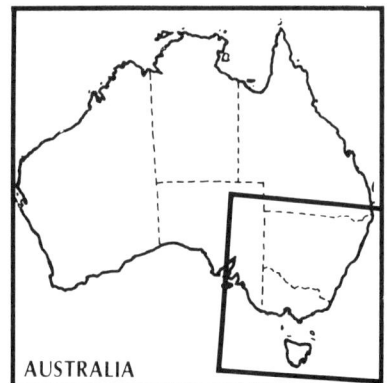

Pop: 32,000 (1967 est.)

The town of Nikolaevsk is located on the north bank of the Amur River in Siberia about 22 miles from its mouth. It was founded in 1850. It is a seaport and transshipment port for ocean and river vessels. A series of stamps was issued there during the chaos of the post-Russian Revolutionary period in 1921, by an anti-Bolshevist, monarchist government that controlled much of Priamur province for a brief time.

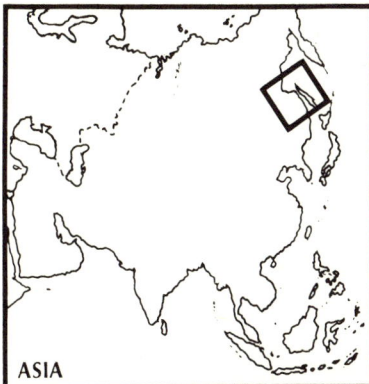

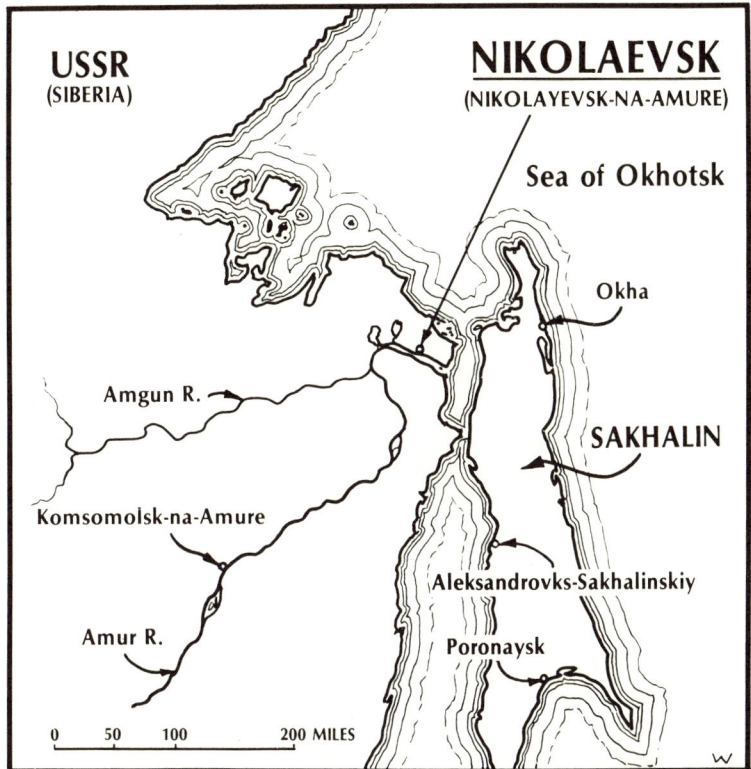

USSR
(SIBERIA)

NIKOLAEVSK
(NIKOLAYEVSK-NA-AMURE)

Sea of Okhotsk

Okha

Amgun R.

Komsomolsk-na-Amure

SAKHALIN

Amur R.

Aleksandrovks-Sakhalinskiy

Poronaysk

0 50 100 200 MILES

ASIA

NINGSIA PROVINCE

Area: 106,115 sq. miles

A former province of China, Ningsia was abolished in 1954 and merged with Kansu. In 1956, much of its area was placed within Inner Mongolia. During the period prior to the establishment of the People's Republic of China, it was part of the Northwest China Liberation Area under Communist control and used its stamps, which were issued from 1945 to 1949.

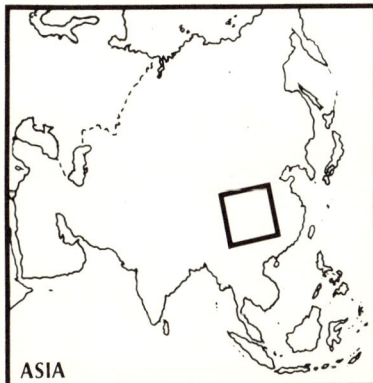

MONGOLIA

INNER MONGOLIA

Shan-pa

NINGSIA

Yellow River

KANSU

Ping-lo

Yin-chuan

CHINA

Wu-chung

SHENSI

TSINGHAI

Ping-liang

Lan-chou

0 50 100 200 MILES

ASIA

NORTH BORNEO
(SABAH)

South China Sea

Kudat

Jesselton (Kota Kinabalu)

LABUAN

BRUNEI

Bandau

Sulu Sea

Sandakan

Meruta

Lahad Datu

SARAWAK

Celebes Sea

NETH. INDIES

0   50   100   200 MILES

ASIA

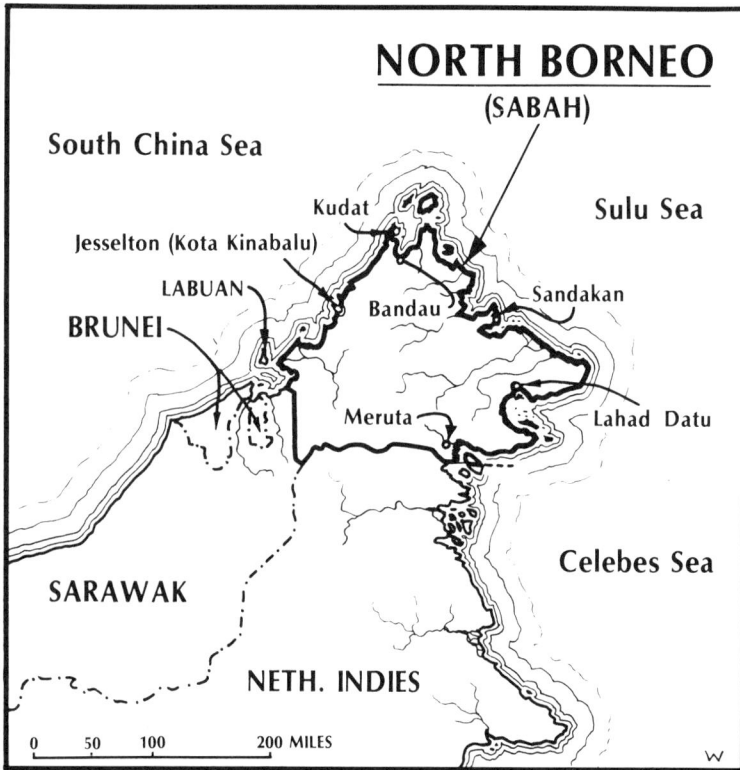

Area: 29,388 sq. miles
Pop: 175,000 (1900 est.)
        270,233 (1931)
Capital: Jesselton

In 1881, the area known as North Borneo on the island of Borneo was granted by British royal charter to the North Borneo Company, which administered the area until 1946, when it became a British colony. It later joined the independent country of Malaysia as Sabah.

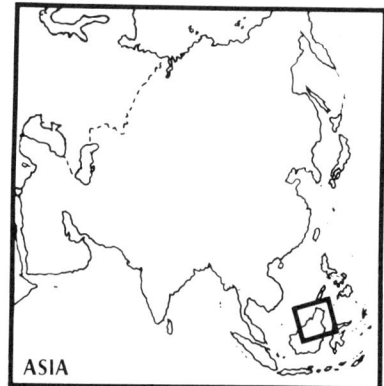

————— NORTHERN NIGERIA, PROTECTORATE OF —————

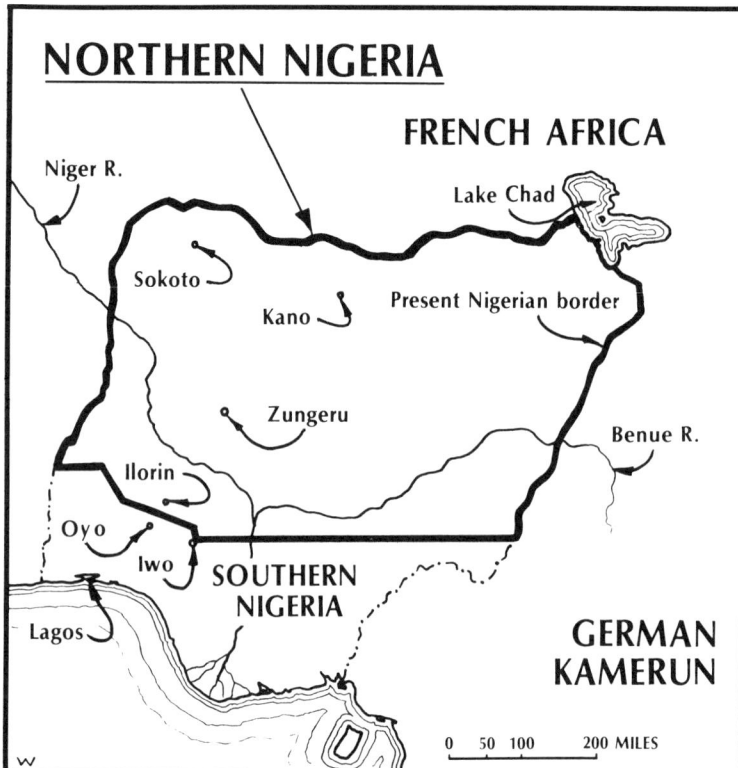

NORTHERN NIGERIA

FRENCH AFRICA

Niger R.

Lake Chad

Sokoto

Kano

Present Nigerian border

Zungeru

Benue R.

Ilorin

Oyo

Iwo

SOUTHERN
NIGERIA

GERMAN
KAMERUN

Lagos

0   50 100   200 MILES

AFRICA

Area: 281,700 sq. miles
Pop: 12 million (approx.)
Capital: Zungeru

A protectorate of Britain, Northern Nigeria was merged with Southern Nigeria in 1914 to form the colony of Nigeria, now the independent Federal Republic of Nigeria. Stamps were issued from 1900 to 1914 and were in the British colonial key type design then current.

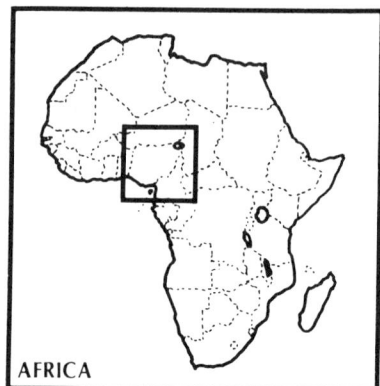

Area: 290,585 sq. miles
Pop: 1.4 million (1938 est.)
4,396,000 (1971 est.)
Capital: Lusaka

From 1889 to 1924, Northern Rhodesia was administered by the British South Africa Company. It was then made a British Protectorate and remained so until joining the Federation of Rhodesia and Nyasaland in 1953. In 1964, it became the Republic of Zambia. Stamps of the British South Africa Co. were used from 1890 to 1924.

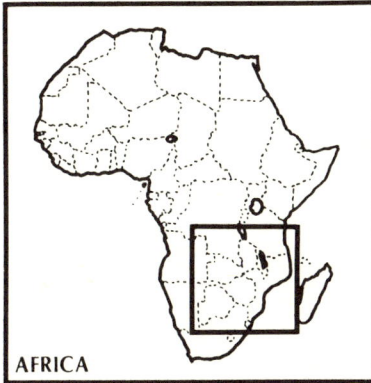

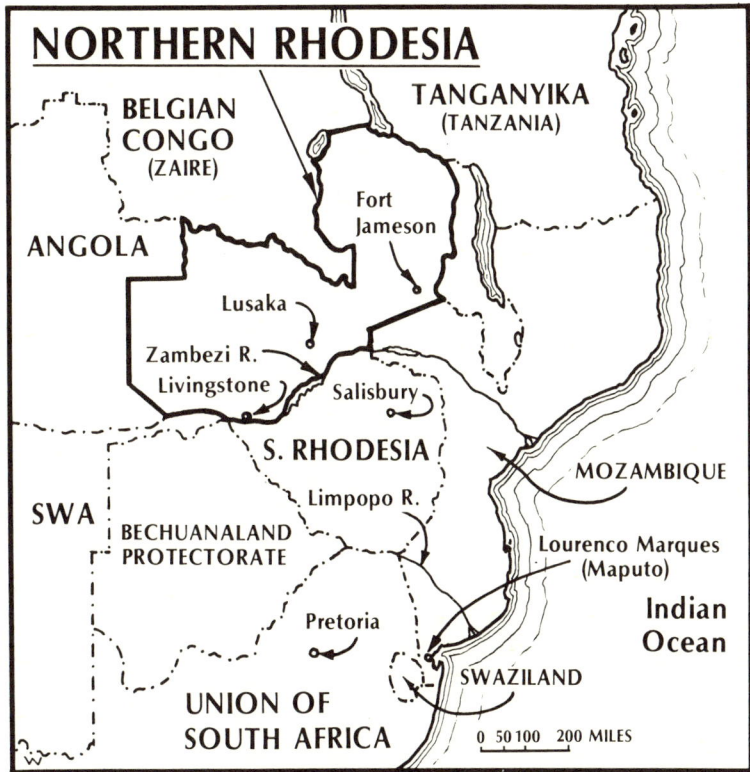

AFRICA

NORTHERN RHODESIA

BELGIAN CONGO (ZAIRE)

TANGANYIKA (TANZANIA)

ANGOLA

Fort Jameson

Lusaka

Zambezi R.

Livingstone

Salisbury

S. RHODESIA

MOZAMBIQUE

SWA

Limpopo R.

BECHUANALAND PROTECTORATE

Lourenco Marques (Maputo)

Indian Ocean

Pretoria

SWAZILAND

UNION OF SOUTH AFRICA

0 50 100 200 MILES

NORTH INGERMANLAND

Area: not recorded

North Ingermanland was a small area located between Lake Ladoga and the Gulf of Finland in the district of Kirjasalo. In 1920 it rebelled against the revolutionary government of Russia then in power. The revolt was quickly suppressed by Russian troops, and the area has been part of the USSR since that time. During its brief freedom, the tiny state released a number of stamps.

EUROPE

NORTH INGERMANLAND

border following World War I

present Finnish-Soviet border

FINLAND

Kirjasalo District (North Ingermanland)

Olonets

Helsinki

Rautu (Sosnovo)

Lake Ladoga

Gulf of Finland

Leningrad

Sestroretsk

USSR

0 20 40 60 80 100 MILES

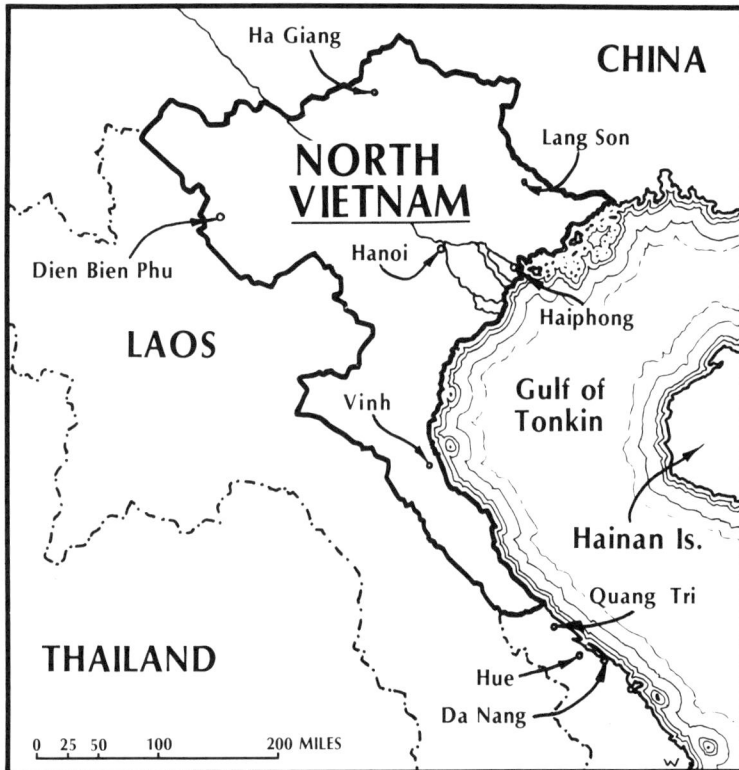

Area: 63,360 sq. miles
Pop: 19.9 million (1970 est.)
Capital: Hanoi

The Communist government set up in North Vietnam (previously part of French Indo-China) was opposed to the non-Communist regime in South Vietnam, and with assistance from other Communist states attempted to wipe out South Vietnam. Despite massive US aid and participation, the entire area was absorbed by the Communists in 1975.

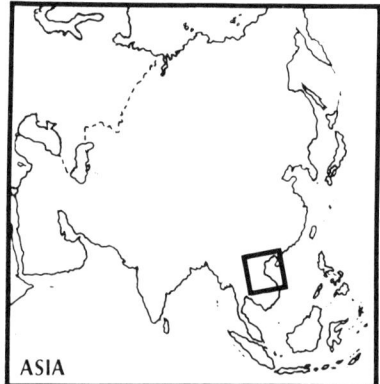

ASIA

——————NORTH WEST PACIFIC ISLANDS——————

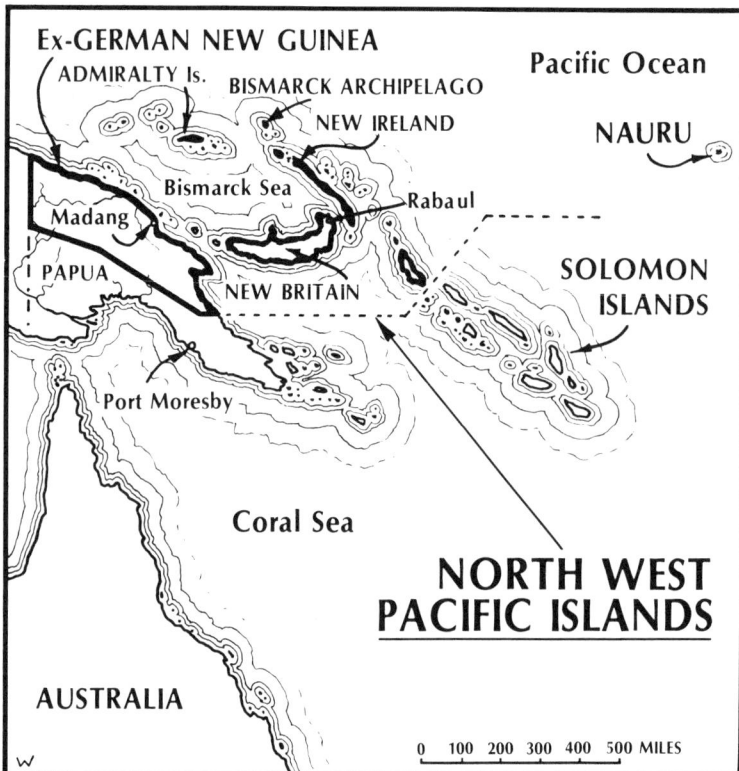

Area: 96,150 sq. miles (approx.)
Pop: 636,000 (1914 est.)

The North West Pacific Islands comprised the former German colonies of German New Guinea and Nauru, which were taken by Australian forces during WWI. They were mandated to Australia by the League of Nations after the war and are now part of Papua New Guinea, except for Nauru, which became an independent republic in 1968.

PACIFIC OCEAN

Area: 129 sq. miles
Pop: 26,462 (1970 est.)
Capital: Hellville

A small island off the northwest coast of Madagascar, the French colony of Nossi Be issued its own stamps from 1889 to 1896, when it was placed under the administration of Madagascar. It is now part of the Democratic Republic of Madagascar.

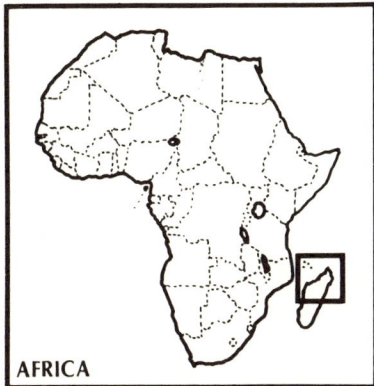

AFRICA

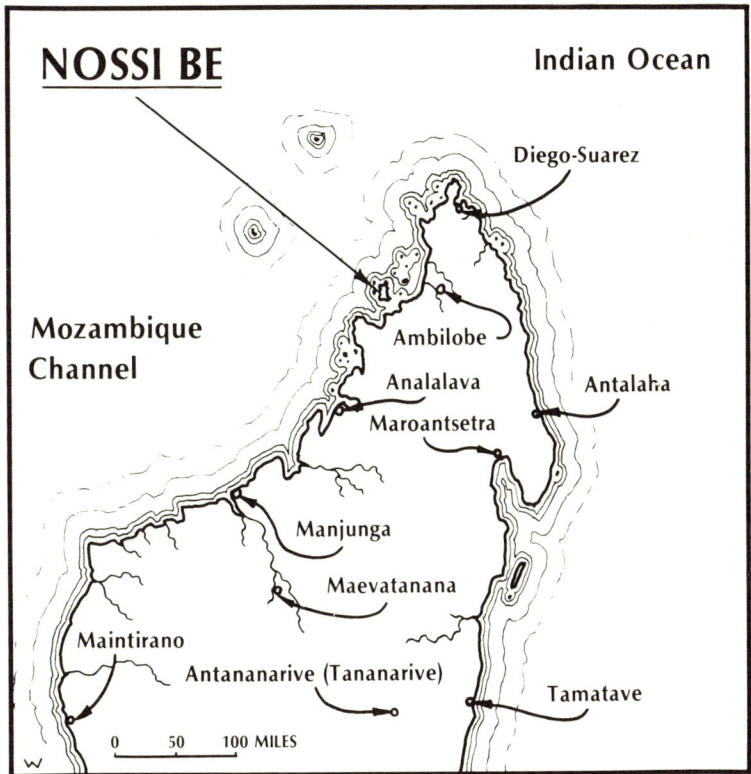

NOVA SCOTIA, COLONY OF

Area: 21,425 sq. miles
Pop: 459,574 (1901)
756,129 (1966)
Capital: Halifax

Nova Scotia was settled in the 18th century by Scots as well as Loyalists from the American colonies. It was split from New Brunswick and made a separate colony in 1784. It entered Canadian Confederation in 1867. Stamps were first issued in 1851 and continued until replaced by those of Canada.

NORTH AMERICA

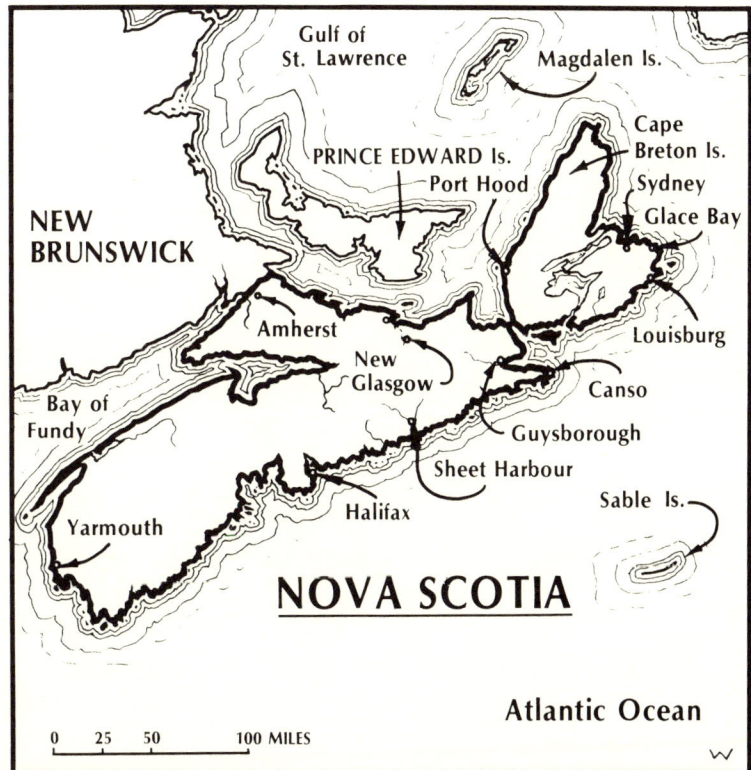

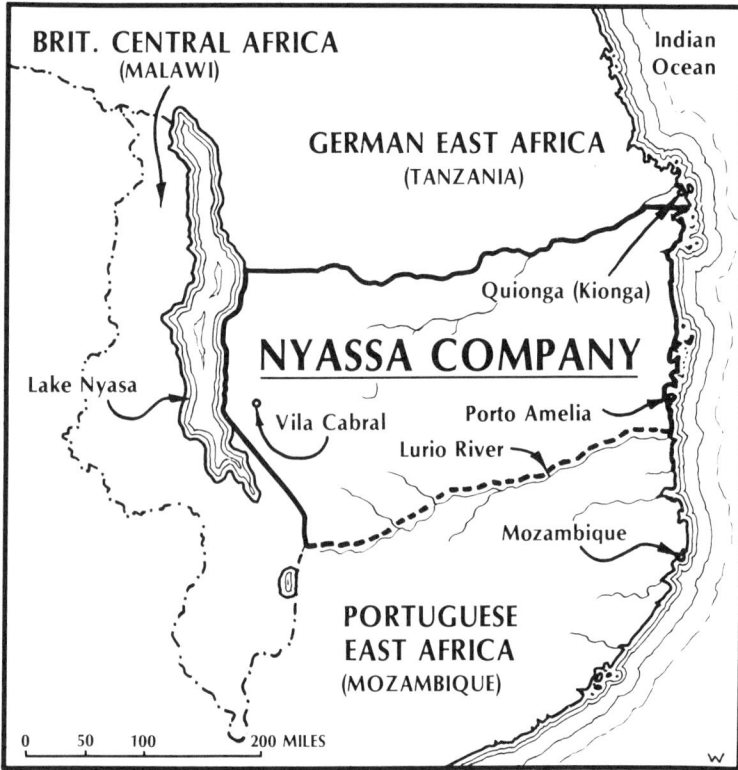

Area: 46,384 sq. miles
Pop: 297,428 (1970)
Capital: Porto Amelia

The Nyassa Company was granted a charter to administer the northern portion of the Portuguese colony of Mozambique in 1894. It administered the area until the charter was revoked in 1929 and colonial government restored. Stamps were issued from 1898 until the area's restoration to colonial government, when the stamps of Mozambique went into use.

OAXACA, STATE OF

Area: 36,820 sq. miles
Pop: 882,529 (1895)
2,011,946 (1970)
Capital: Oaxaca

Oaxaca is a state in the southern portion of Mexico with a capital of the same name. Stamps were issued bearing the state and capital city name during the 1913-16 civil war in that country. Scott notes that the stamps were printed on the back of post office receipt forms.

Pop: 404,651 (1897)
892,000 (1970)

A city in the USSR, Odessa is located on the northwestern shore of the Black Sea. During the chaotic period following the Russian Revolution of 1917, stamps were overprinted with the trident emblem of the Ukraine for use in Odessa. Polish stamps are also reported to have been overprinted with the town name in 1919 for use on mail to that country.

USSR

ODESSA

Nikolajev

CRIMEA

Simferopol

ROMANIA

Sevastopol

Black Sea

Constanta

0 25 50 100 MILES

EUROPE

OIL RIVERS PROTECTORATE

Area: not recorded
Capital: Calabar

The Oil Rivers Protectorate, over the area of the Niger delta, was proclaimed in 1884. It was administered by the Royal Niger Company and became the Niger Coast Protectorate in 1893. From 1891 to 1892 stamps of Great Britain were used, and from 1892 British stamps were overprinted and surcharged. In 1893 special stamps were issued for the Niger Coast Protectorate.

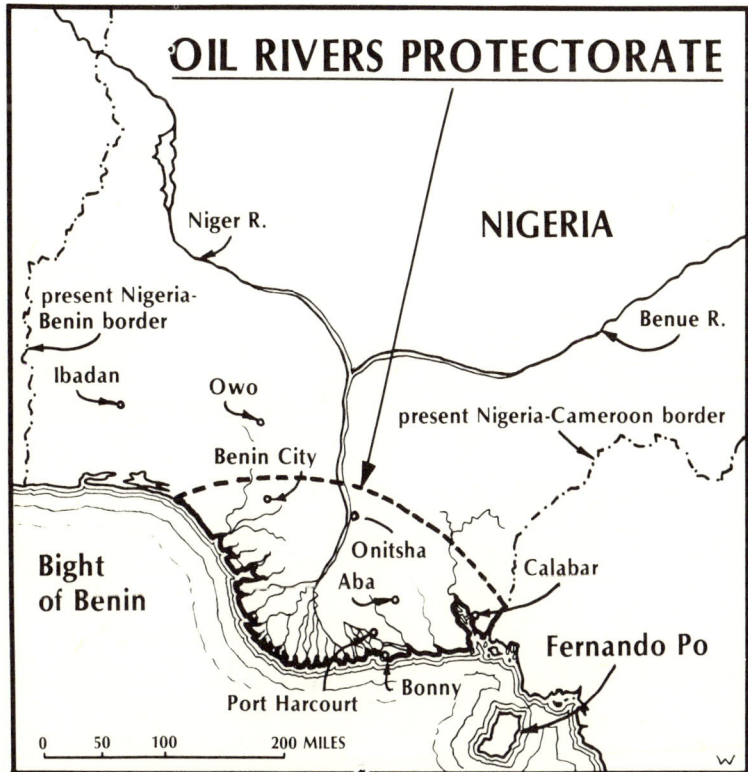

OIL RIVERS PROTECTORATE

Niger R.

NIGERIA

present Nigeria-Benin border

Benue R.

Ibadan

Owo

present Nigeria-Cameroon border

Benin City

Bight
of Benin

Onitsha

Aba

Calabar

Fernando Po

Port Harcourt

Bonny

0 50 100 200 MILES

AFRICA

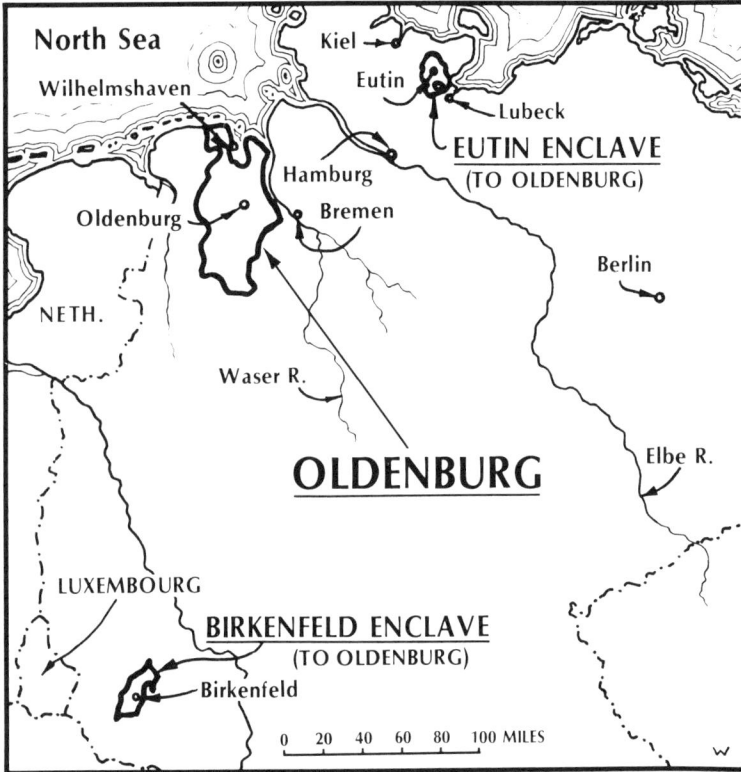

North Sea map

Kiel
Eutin
Lubeck
Wilhelmshaven
EUTIN ENCLAVE
(TO OLDENBURG)
Hamburg
Bremen
Oldenburg
Berlin
NETH.
Waser R.
OLDENBURG
Elbe R.
LUXEMBOURG
BIRKENFELD ENCLAVE
(TO OLDENBURG)
Birkenfeld
0 20 40 60 80 100 MILES

EUROPE

Area: 2,083 sq. miles
Pop: 399,180 (1900)
Capital: Oldenburg

A former grand duchy in northern Germany, Oldenburg was a member of the North German Confederation and became part of the German Empire in 1870. It is now part of the Federal Republic of Germany. Stamps were issued by Oldenburg from 1852 to Jan. 1, 1868.

━━━━━━━ORADEA (NAGYVARAD), CITY OF━━━━━━━

POLAND
USSR
CZECHOSLOVAKIA
present frontiers
Debrecen
Budapest
ORADEA
HUNGARY
Cluj (Kolozsvar)
Szeged
Arad
ROMANIA
Timisoara
YUGOSLAVIA
0 20 40 60 80 100 MILES

EUROPE

Pop: 137,662 (1970)

The city of Oradea is located in Romania. It had been Hungarian until WWI and was occupied by that country again for a period during WWII. Hungarian stamps were overprinted by Romanian occupying forces in 1919 and are noted as the Second Transylvania Issue.

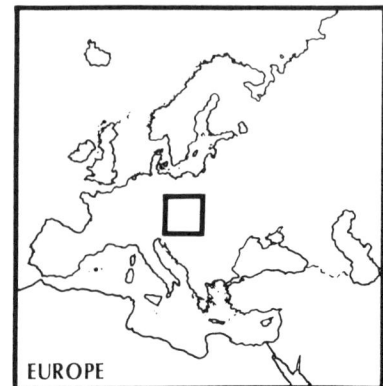

Area: 49,866 sq. miles
Pop: 207,503 (1890)
1,661,756 (1967 est.)
Capital: Bloemfontein

An area to the south of the Transvaal, the Orange Free State was set up as a Boer republic in 1854. It joined the Transvaal in the Boer War against the British and was annexed by Britain as the Orange River Colony in 1900. Now it is part of the Republic of South Africa.

AFRICA

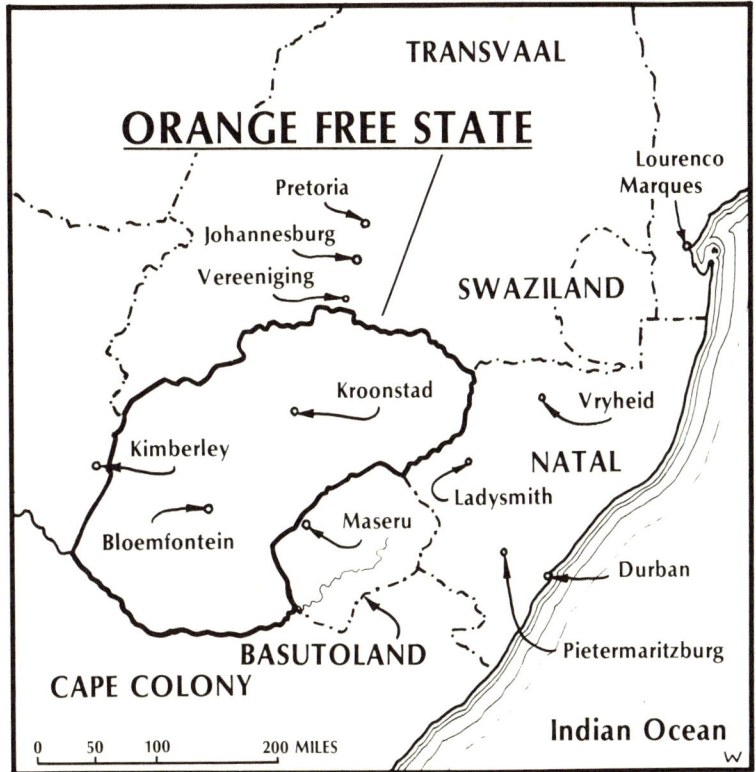

TRANSVAAL

ORANGE FREE STATE

Pretoria
Johannesburg
Vereeniging
Lourenco Marques
SWAZILAND
Kroonstad
Vryheid
Kimberley
NATAL
Ladysmith
Bloemfontein
Maseru
Durban
BASUTOLAND
Pietermaritzburg
CAPE COLONY
Indian Ocean

0   50   100   200 MILES

ORENSE, PROVINCE OF

Area: 2,810 sq. miles
Pop: 413,773 (1970)
Capital: Orense

Orense is a province, with a capital city of the same name, in northern Spain adjacent to the Portuguese border. The capital city is about 250 miles northwest of Madrid. It was destroyed by the Moorish invaders in AD 713 and rebuilt about AD 884. In 1936, during the Spanish Civil War, stamps were issued for use there.

EUROPE

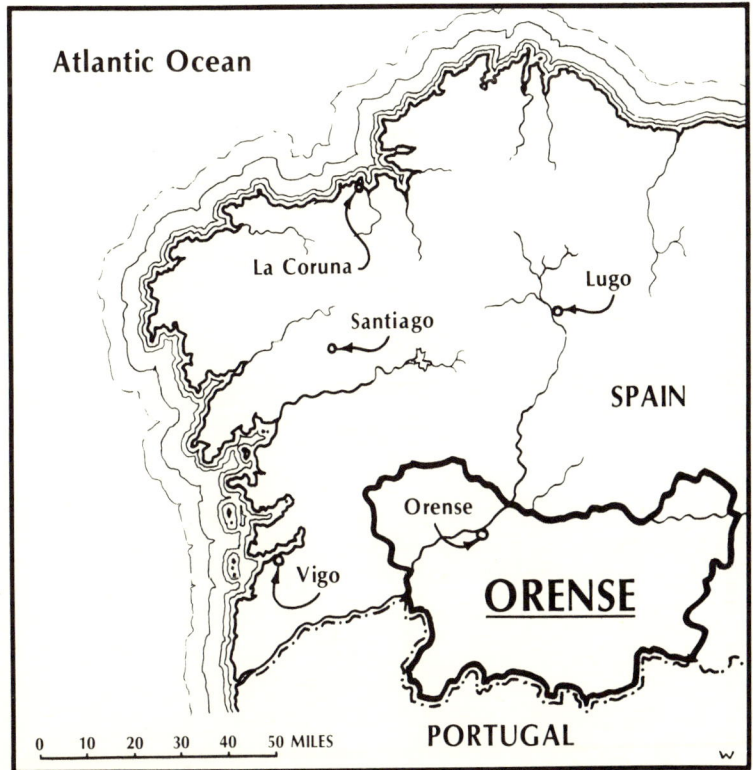

Atlantic Ocean

La Coruna
Lugo
Santiago
SPAIN
Orense
Vigo
ORENSE
PORTUGAL

0   10   20   30   40   50 MILES

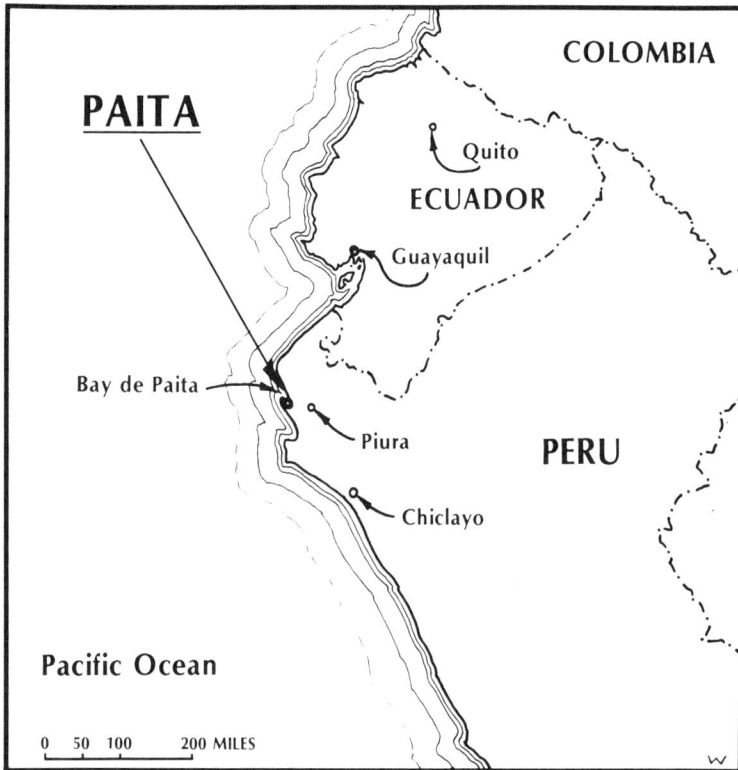

Pop: 9,615 (1970 est.)

A seaport town on the northern coast of Peru, Paita is located in the department of Piura on the Bay de Paita. It is an exporting center for cotton and Panama hats. In 1884, a number of stamps were overprinted with the town's name for use there during a stamp shortage caused by the Chilean occupation of Lima and Calleo in the war between the two countries.

PAKHOI (PEI-HAI), CITY OF

Pop: 20,000 (1898)
175,000 (1970 est.)

Pakhoi is a city in the province of Kwangtung, People's Republic of China, located on the Gulf of Tonkin. It became a Treaty Port (q.v.) in 1877. From 1903 to 1919, stamps of Indo-China were overprinted for use at a French post office that operated there.

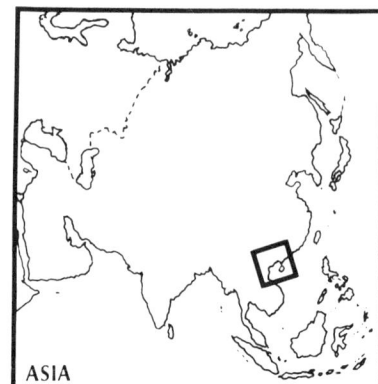

Area: 10,160 sq. miles
Pop: 1,035,821 (1931)
Capital: Jerusalem

Ruled by the Turks from 1516 to 1917, the area of Palestine was taken by British forces under General Allenby during WWI and mandated to Britain by the League of Nations. Increasingly, during and after WWII, conflict between Arab and Jew and Jewish opposition to the British Administration caused great unrest, and the British terminated the mandate in 1948.

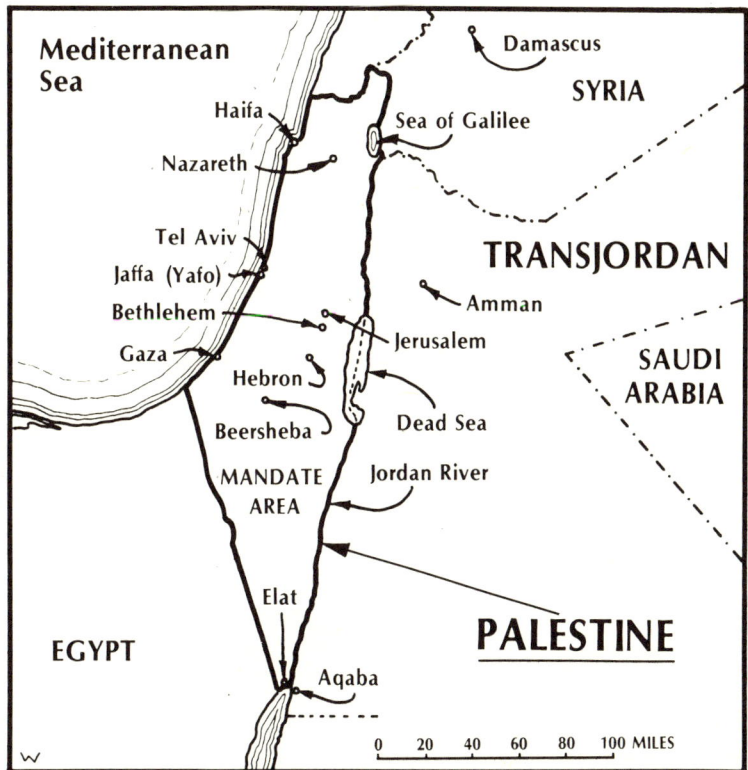

PAPAL STATES (ROMAN STATES)

Area: 16,000 sq. miles (1860)
Pop: 3,125,000 (1853 est.)
Capital: Rome

At one time, the Papal (Roman) States comprised much of central Italy, but with the formation of a unified Kingdom of Italy in 1861, their area was greatly reduced. By 1870 all were absorbed. Stamps of the Papal States were first issued in 1852 and continued until replaced by stamps of Italy as areas were taken into the kingdom.

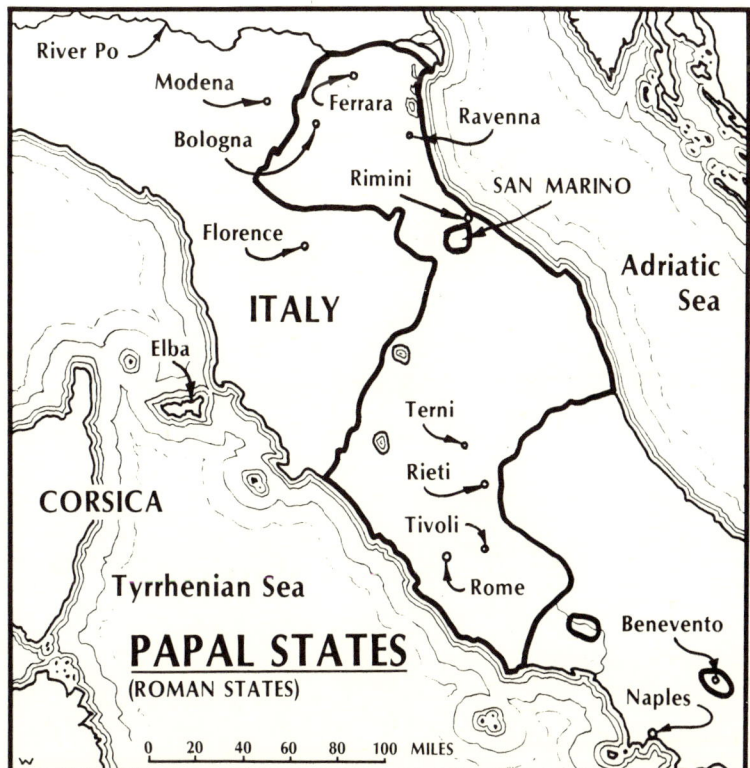

Area: 2,750 sq. miles (approx.)
Pop: 267,306 (1881)
Capital: Parma

The former Duchy of Parma was an area of northern Italy that changed owners many times over the years, finally being annexed to the Kingdom of Sardinia in 1860, which became the Kingdom of Italy a year or so later. Stamps were issued for Parma from 1852 until it joined Sardinia.

————————PASCO, DEPARTMENT OF————————

Area: 8,467 sq. miles
Pop: 188,000 (1971 est.)
Capital: Cerro de Pasco

Pasco is a department located in central Peru. Three stamps were issued there in 1884 during a stamp shortage caused by the Chilean occupation of Lima and Calleo in the war between the two countries. The occupation cut off stamp supplies to the rest of Peru.

Pop: 44,591 (1970)

Patzcuaro is a city located in north central Michoacan State, Mexico, to the west of Mexico City. The city is at an elevation of 6,706 feet. Catalogs note that the provisional stamps supposedly issued there during the revolution to expel the French from Mexico are considered bogus.

PATZCUARO

Tampico

Queretaro

Morelia

Mexico City

Uruapan

Cuernavaca

MEXICO

Acapulco

Pacific Ocean

0 25 50 100 200 MILES

CENTRAL AMERICA

PEKING (BEIJING), DISTRICT OF

Area: 3,386 sq. miles
Pop: 8.5 million (1970 est.)

Peking is the capital city and administrative district of the People's Republic of China and is located in the northern part of the country. It was one of the Chinese Treaty Ports (q.v.), and 1917-19 Italian stamps were overprinted "Pechino" for use at an Italian post office there.

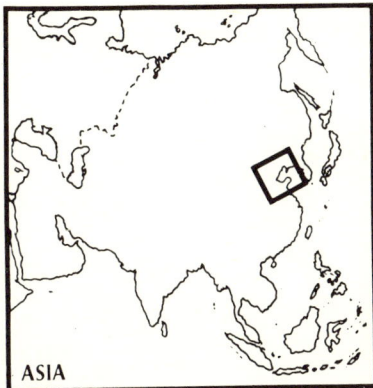

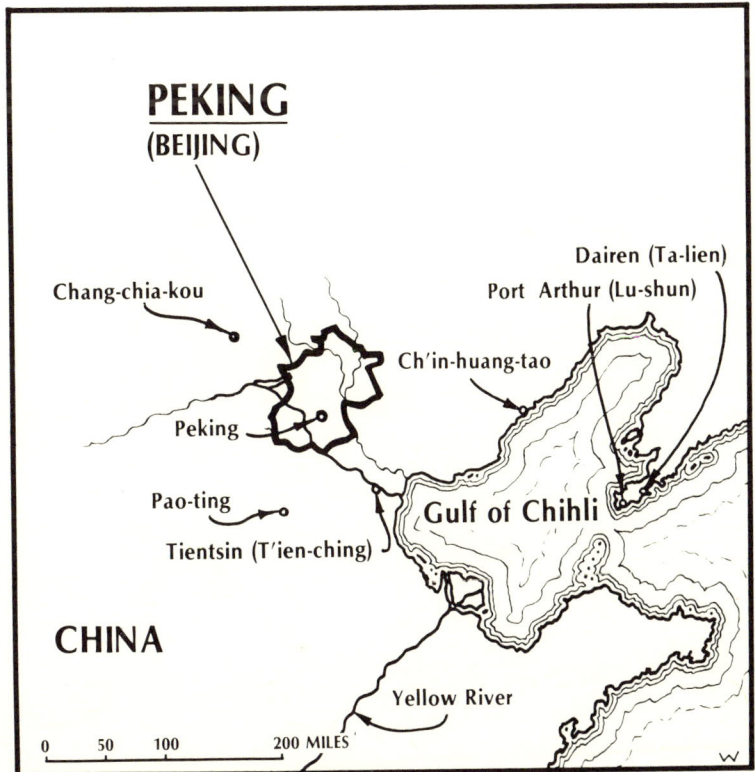

PEKING
(BEIJING)

Chang-chia-kou

Dairen (Ta-lien)

Port Arthur (Lu-shun)

Ch'in-huang-tao

Peking

Pao-ting

Gulf of Chihli

Tientsin (T'ien-ching)

CHINA

Yellow River

0 50 100 200 MILES

ASIA

Area: 628,000 sq. miles
Pop: nine million (1894)
       39.5 million (1981 est.)
Capital: Tehran

The cause of much unrest in western Asia in recent years, Iran, once known as Persia, is a country with an impressive history of conquest and empire. A constitution ending absolute rule was introduced in 1906, and the country officially became Iran in 1935.

——————————PIETERSBURG, TOWN OF——————————

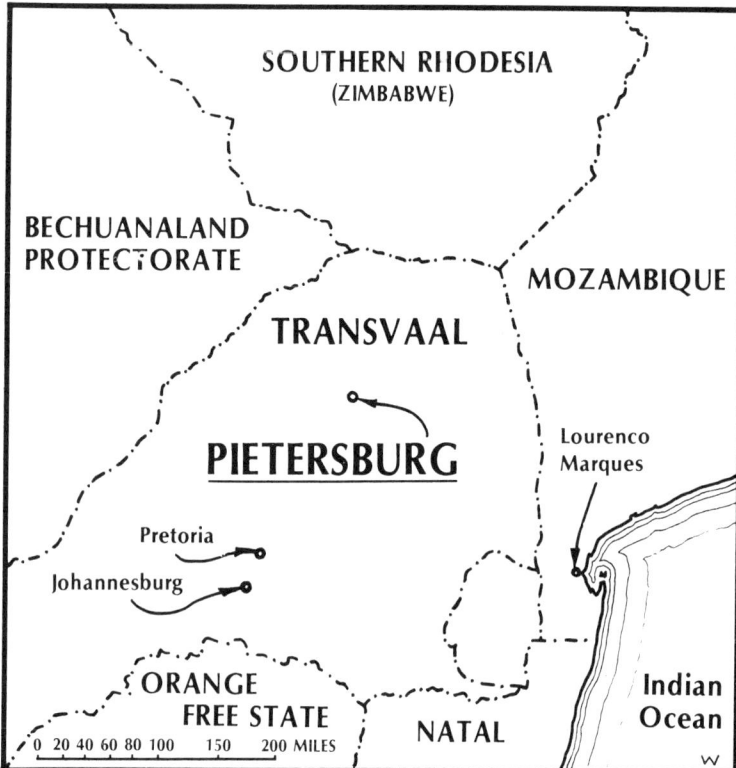

Pop: 35,700 (1967 est.)

A town in north-central Transvaal, in the Republic of South Africa, Pietersburg was, for a time, the Boer headquarters during the Anglo-Boer War. In 1901 a set of stamps was issued for use there. It is known as the Pietersburg Issue.

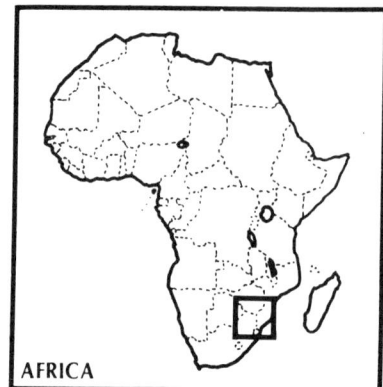

Pop: 27,300 (1970 est.)

The town of Pisco is a seaport located on Pisco Bay in Peru's Ica Department. A provisional stamp was issued there in 1884, because of a stamp shortage caused by the Peruvian war with Chile. Chile had occupied Lima and Callao, cutting off stamp supplies to the rest of the country.

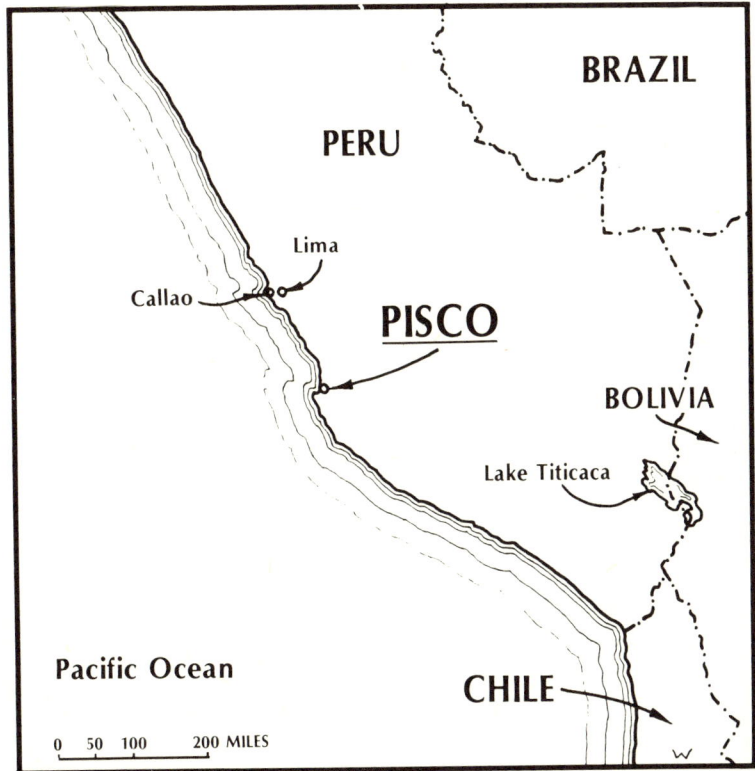

BRAZIL

PERU

Lima

Callao

PISCO

BOLIVIA

Lake Titicaca

Pacific Ocean

CHILE

0 50 100   200 MILES

SOUTH AMERICA

PIURA, DEPARTMENT OF

Area: 12,717 sq. miles
Pop: 922,300 (1970 est.)
Capital: Piura

A department of Peru, Piura is located in the northeastern portion of the country. Provisional stamps were issued there in 1884 during a stamp shortage caused when Chile occupied Lima and Callao in a war between the two countries. This cut off stamp supplies to the rest of Peru.

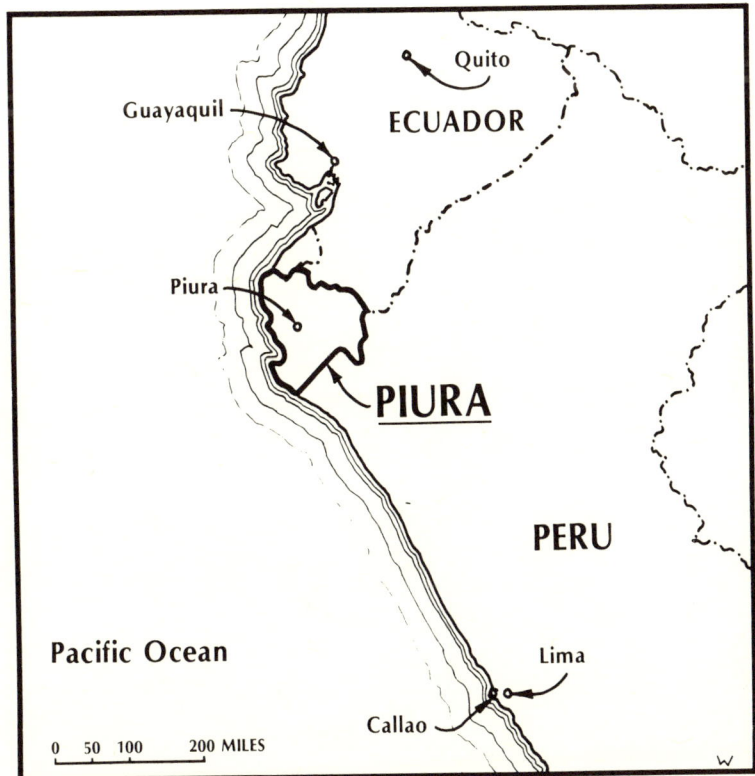

Quito

Guayaquil

ECUADOR

Piura

PIURA

PERU

Pacific Ocean

Lima

Callao

0 50 100   200 MILES

SOUTH AMERICA

SAO MIGUEL

Ribeira
Nordeste
Ponta Delgada
Lagoa
Povoacao
Vila Franca

SANTA MARIA

Administrative District of
PONTA DELGADA

0 5 10 20 30 40 MILES

Vila do Porto

CORVO
AZORES
GRACIOSA
TERCEIRA
FLORES
SAO JORGE
FAIAL
PICO
SAO MIGUEL
SANTA MARIA
FORMIGAS

Atlantic Ocean

0 50 100 150 MILES

ATLANTIC

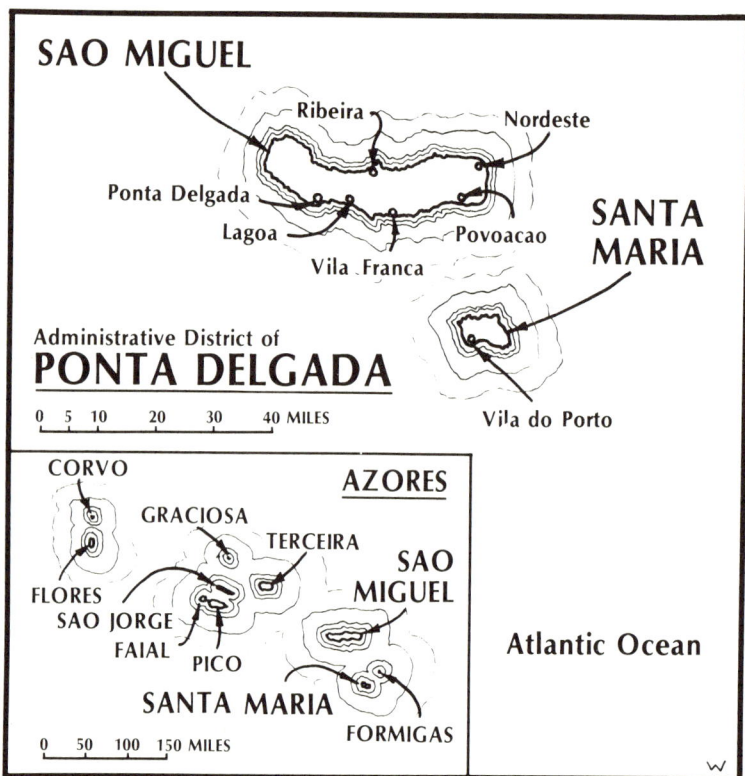

Area: 330 sq. miles
Pop: 186,700 (1970 est.)
Capital: Ponta Delgada

Ponta Delgada is an administrative district in the Azores. It includes the islands of Sao Miguel and Santa Maria. Stamps were issued for the district from 1892 to 1905, when they were replaced by stamps of the Azores.

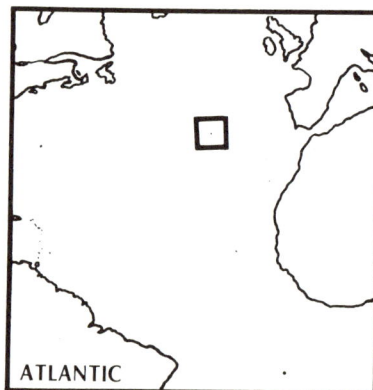

━━━━━━━━━ **PONTEVEDRA, PROVINCE OF** ━━━━━━━━━

Atlantic Ocean

La Coruna

PONTEVEDRA

Santiago

Pontevedra

SPAIN

Vigo

PORTUGAL

0 10 20 30 40 50 MILES

EUROPE

Area: 1,729 sq. miles
Pop: 750,701 (1970)
Capital: Pontevedra

Pontevedra is a province located in northwestern Spain. Stamps were issued there in 1937 by Nationalists during the Spanish Civil War.

Pop: not recorded

Port Lagos is a town located in Greece, on the north shore of the Aegean Sea. A French post office operated there when it was part of the Turkish Empire, and in 1893, French stamps were overprinted for use there.

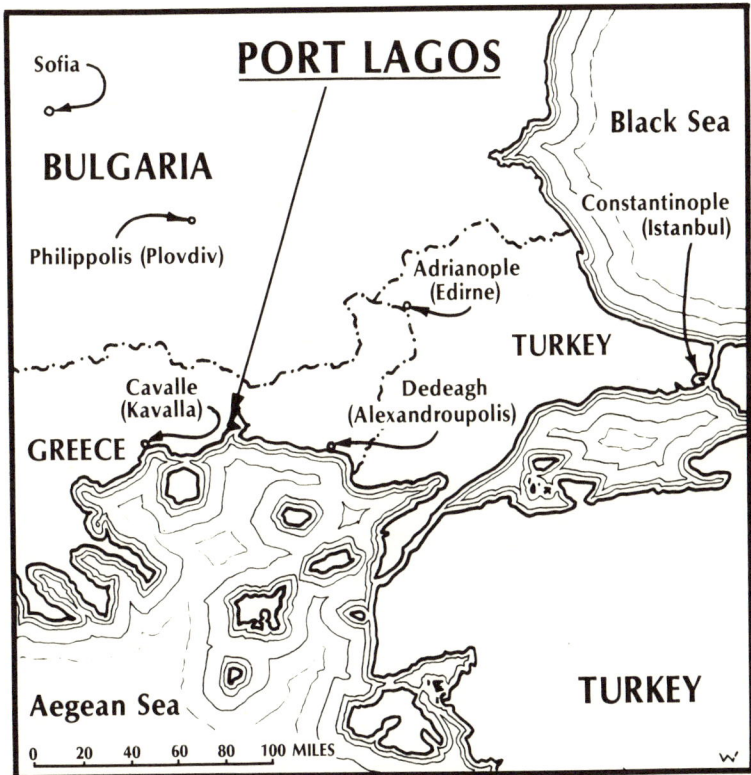

PORT SAID, CITY OF

Pop: 42,095 (1897)
313,000 (1970 est.)

A city in Egypt located at the northern end of the Suez Canal, Port Said was founded in 1859 and became one of the world's most important coaling ports. A French post office operated there, and in 1899-1900 French stamps were overprinted for use there.

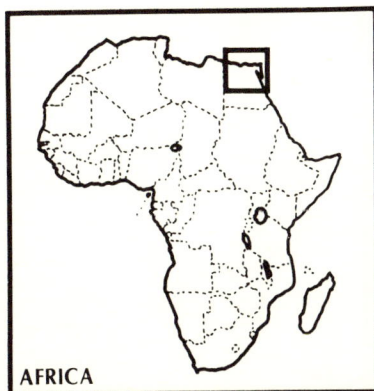

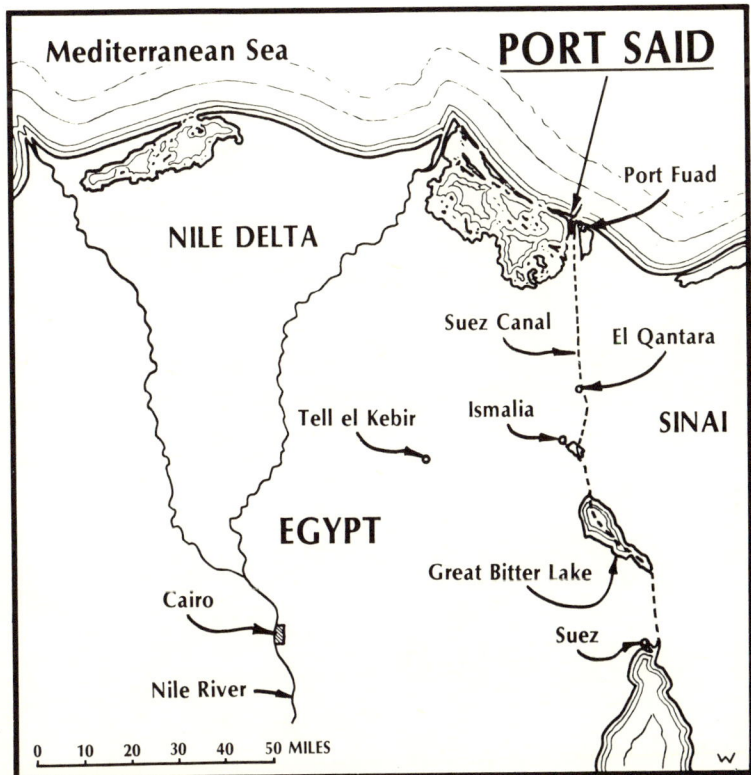

Portuguese Guinea (map)

Atlantic Ocean

MAURITANIA

SENEGAL

Dakar

MALI

Bathurst (Banjul)

THE GAMBIA

Bissau

Bissagos (Bijagos) Is.

GUINEA

PORTUGUESE GUINEA
(GUINEA BISSAU)

Conakry

0 50 100 200 MILES

SIERRA LEONE

W

Area: 13,948 sq. miles
Pop: 351,089 (1940)
         530,000 (1970 est.)
Capital: Bissau

Formerly a Portuguese colony in West Africa, Portuguese Guinea became independent in 1974 as Guinea Bissau. Stamps were first issued in 1881 and followed the general pattern of Portuguese colonial issues until 1974, when issues of the independent nation went into use.

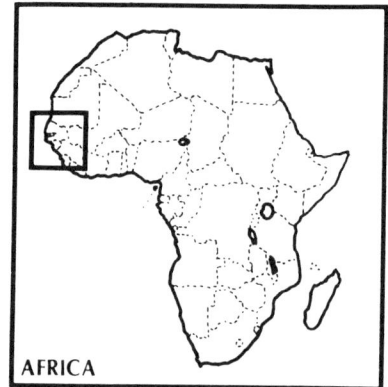

AFRICA

PORTUGUESE INDIA, COLONY OF

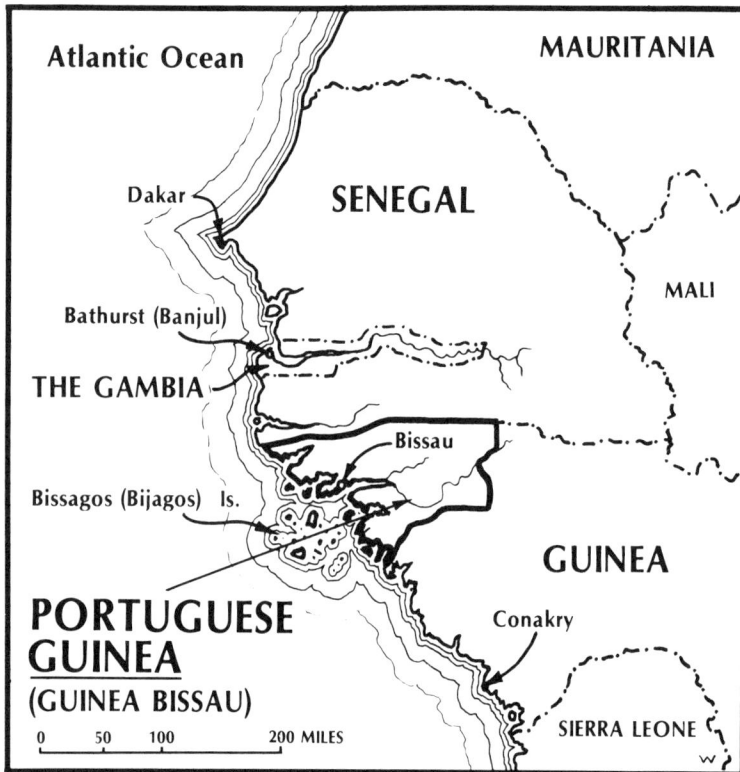

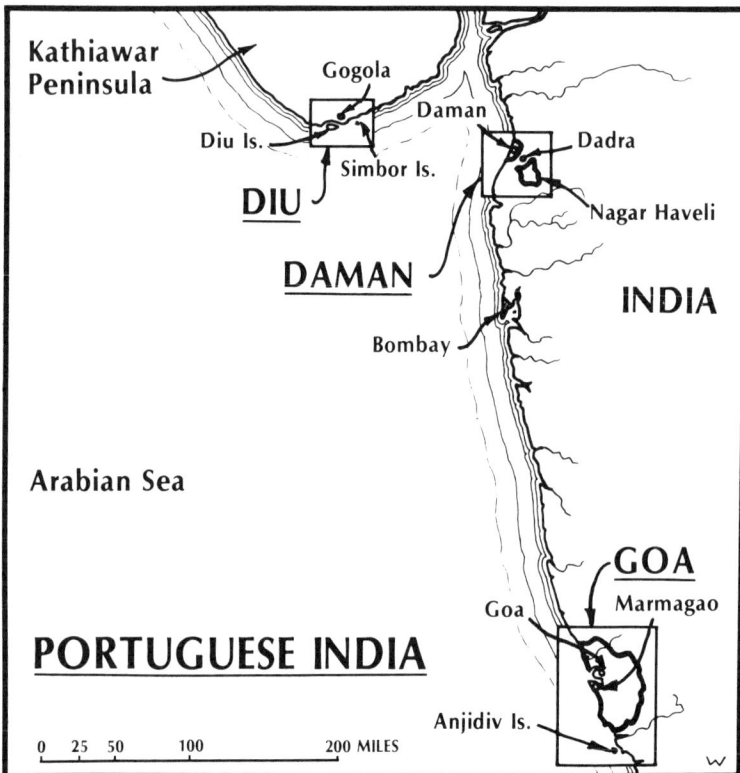

Portuguese India (map)

Kathiawar Peninsula

Gogola

Daman

Diu Is.

Dadra

DIU

Simbor Is.

Nagar Haveli

DAMAN

INDIA

Bombay

Arabian Sea

GOA

Goa

Marmagao

PORTUGUESE INDIA

Anjidiv Is.

0 25 50 100 200 MILES

W

Area: 1,441 sq. miles
Pop: 649,000 (1958 est.)
Capital: Pangim (Goa)

Portuguese India comprised a number of settlements on the west coast of India. On Dec. 18, 1961, they were seized by the Republic of India and made part of that country. Stamps were issued for the colony from 1871 until annexation by India.

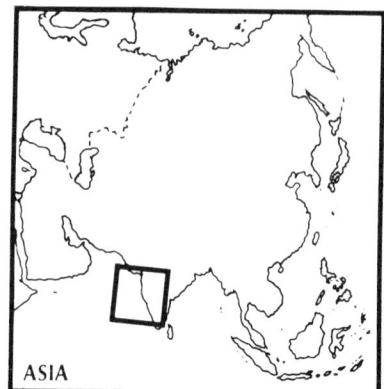

ASIA

Area: 5,763 sq. miles
Pop: 610,541 (1970)
Capital: Dili

Portuguese Timor comprised the eastern portion of the island of Timor in the East Indies, plus the enclave of Ocussi Ambeno on the northern coast of the western part of the island. The colony was occupied by Japan during WWII and annexed to Indonesia May 3, 1976. Portuguese colonial stamps were first issued in 1885.

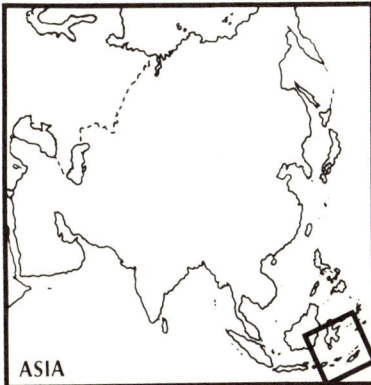

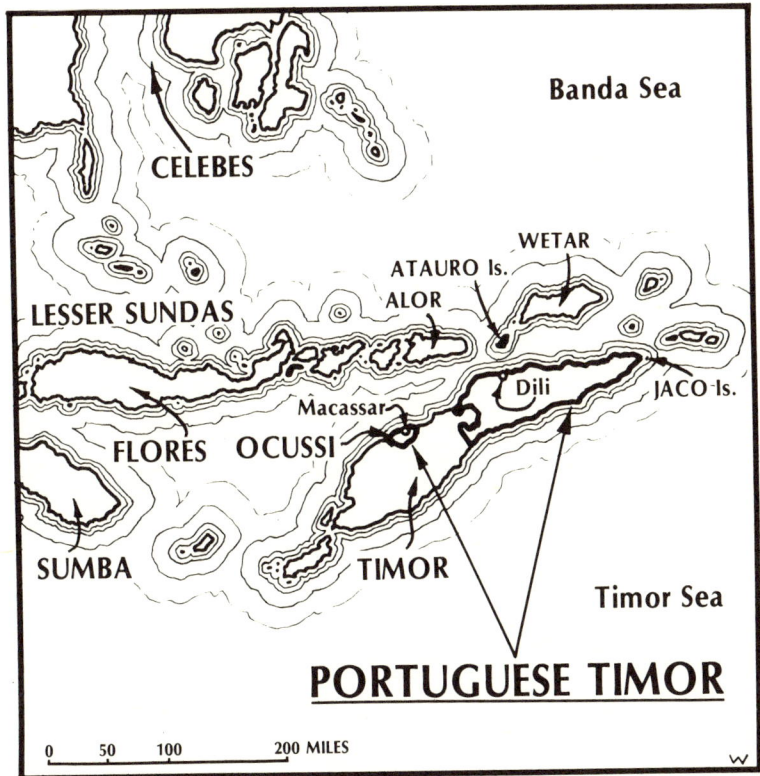

Banda Sea
CELEBES
WETAR
ATAURO Is.
ALOR
LESSER SUNDAS
Dili
JACO Is.
Macassar
FLORES OCUSSI
SUMBA TIMOR
Timor Sea
PORTUGUESE TIMOR
0 50 100   200 MILES
ASIA

POSEN (POZNAN), CITY OF

Pop: 469,000 (1970)

The German city of Posen is now the Polish city of Poznan. It is located on the Warta River, about 160 miles west of Warsaw. The city had been exchanged between Prussia and Poland on several occasions. It had been taken from Germany at the end of WWI and made part of Poland, but was re-occupied by the Germans at the beginning of WWII and suffered great damage.

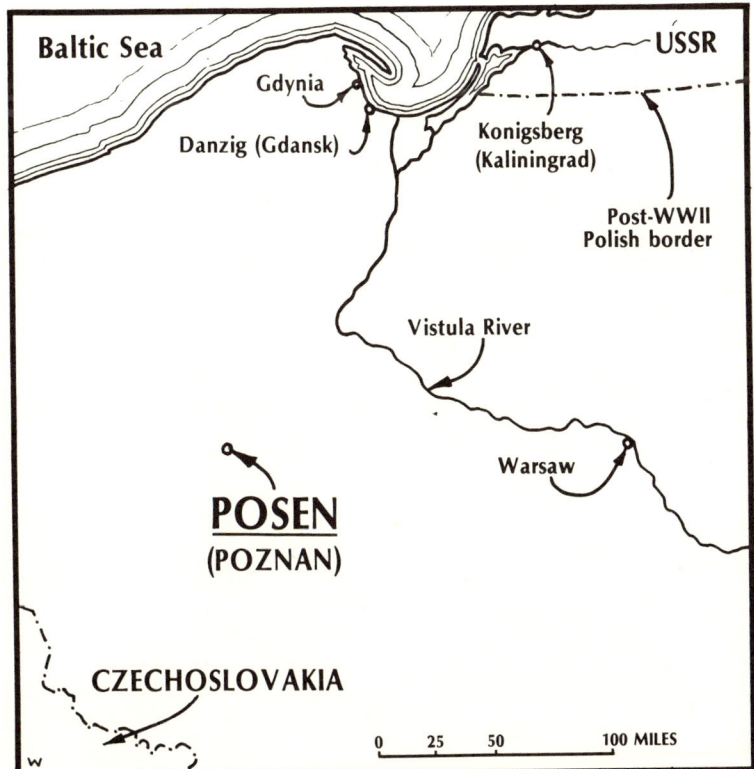

Baltic Sea
USSR
Gdynia
Danzig (Gdansk)
Konigsberg (Kaliningrad)
Post-WWII Polish border
Vistula River
Warsaw
POSEN
(POZNAN)
CZECHOSLOVAKIA
0 25 50   100 MILES
EUROPE

PRIAMUR PROVINCE
(Primor'ye)
and Maritime Area

AMUR

SIBERIA

Amursk

Blagoveshchensk

Khabarovsk

CHINA

Harbin (Ha-erh-pin)

SAKHALIN

Vladivostok

JAPAN

Sea of Japan

0   100   200   300   400   500 MILES

ASIA

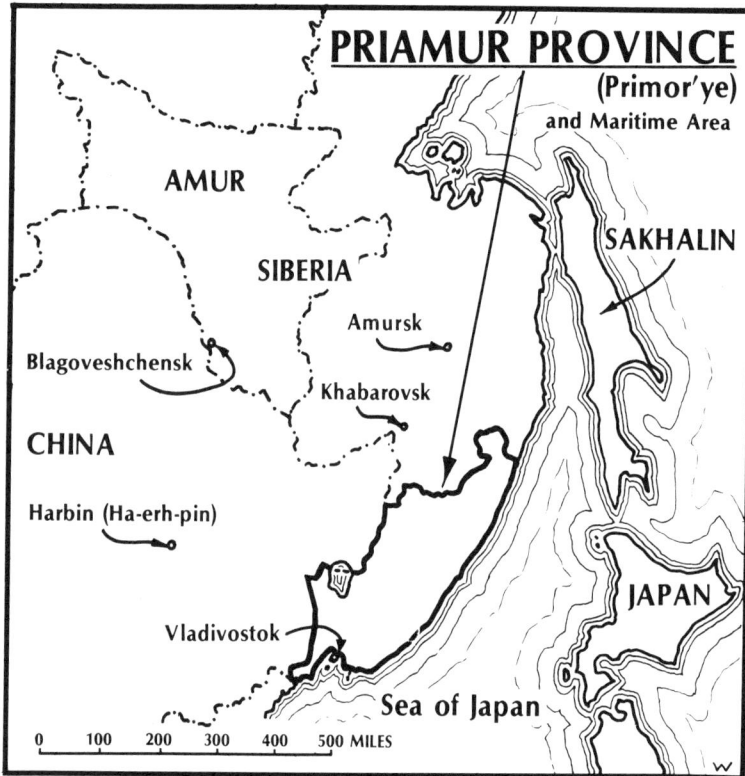

Priamur Province was an area of eastern Siberia in which an anti-Bolshevist government was established in the years following the 1917 Russian Revolution. A number of stamps were issued in 1921-1922, including a commemorative marking the anniversary of the overthrow of the Bolshevists in a celebration that proved somewhat premature, since the revolutionaries soon regained control and the area was taken into the Soviet Union.

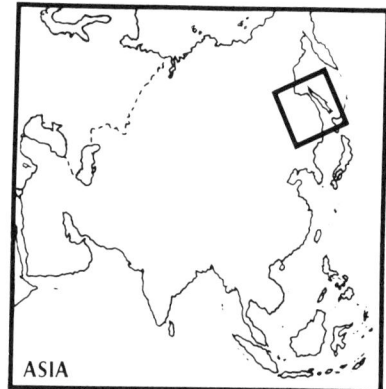

━━━━━━ PRINCE EDWARD ISLAND, COLONY OF ━━━━━━

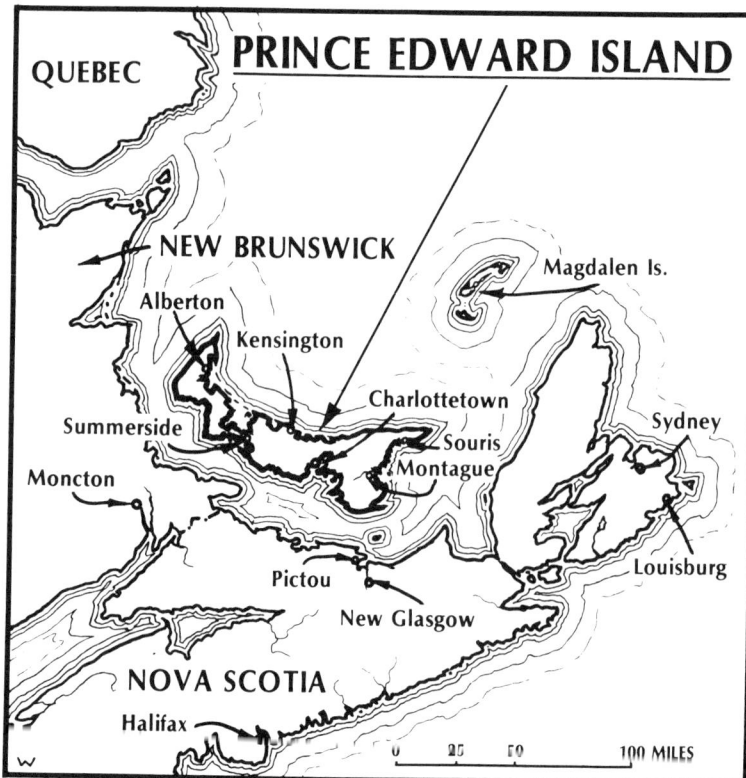

PRINCE EDWARD ISLAND

QUEBEC

NEW BRUNSWICK

Alberton

Kensington

Magdalen Is.

Summerside

Charlottetown

Souris

Montague

Sydney

Moncton

Pictou

New Glasgow

Louisburg

NOVA SCOTIA

Halifax

0   25   50   100 MILES

Area: 2,184 sq. miles
Pop: 103,259 (1901)
        124,900 (1982)
Capital: Charlottetown

A former colony in the Gulf of St. Lawrence, Prince Edward Island became a Canadian province in 1873. It had been British since 1763 when France ceded it to Britain. Stamps were first issued in 1861 and continued until Confederation in 1873.

NORTH AMERICA

Pop: 69,524 (1971)

Pristina is a town located in Macedonia, now the southern part of Yugoslavia. In medieval days it had been the capital of a Serbian Empire. In 1911, Turkey issued a set of stamps overprinted with the names of various cities visited by the Sultan during a journey through Macedonia. One of the cities so honored was Pristina.

PRUSSIA, KINGDOM OF

Area: 134,463 sq. miles
Pop: 34,472,509 (1900)
Capital: Berlin

The Kingdom of Prussia after the mid-19th century was the most powerful of the German states. It was under Prussia's leadership that the North German Confederation was formed in 1868, and later, after its massive victory over France in the Franco-Prussian War of 1870-71, Prussia became the driving force behind the new German Empire.

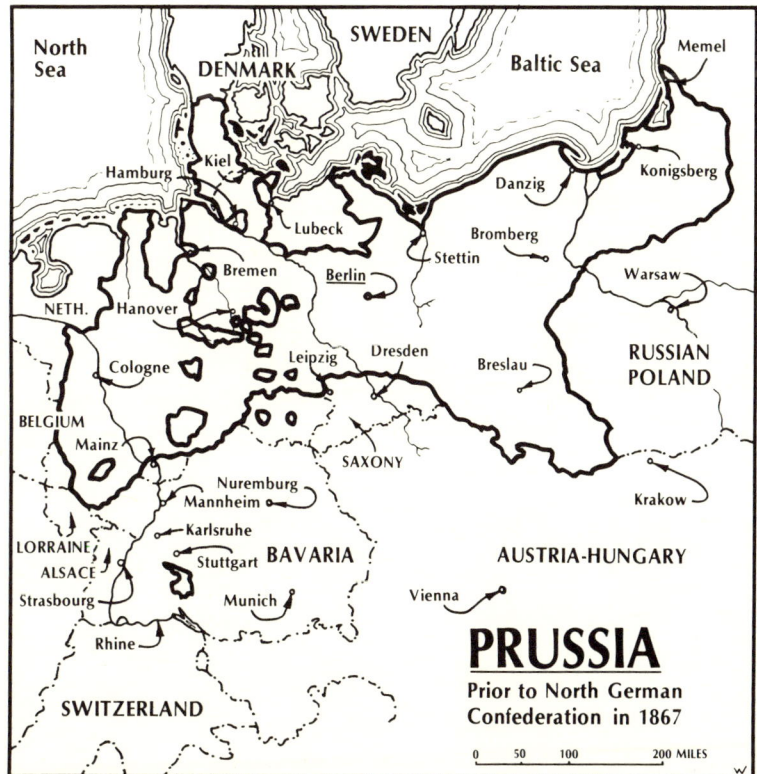

Pop: 221,826 (1978 est.)

A city in the Central part of Cuba and a cattle-raising and agricultural center, Puerto Principe is now named Camaguey. In December 1898, while it was Puerto Principe, local surcharges were created there on Cuban stamps to satisfy a shortage of several denominations.

FLORIDA
Miami
Key West
BAHAMAS
Nassau
Havana
CUBA
Isla de Pinos
CAYMAN ISLANDS
Guantanamo
PUERTO PRINCIPE
(CAMAGUEY) Caribbean Sea
JAMAICA
Kingston
0 50 100 200 MILES

CENTRAL AMERICA

———**PUERTO RICO (PORTO RICO), COMMONWEALTH OF** ———

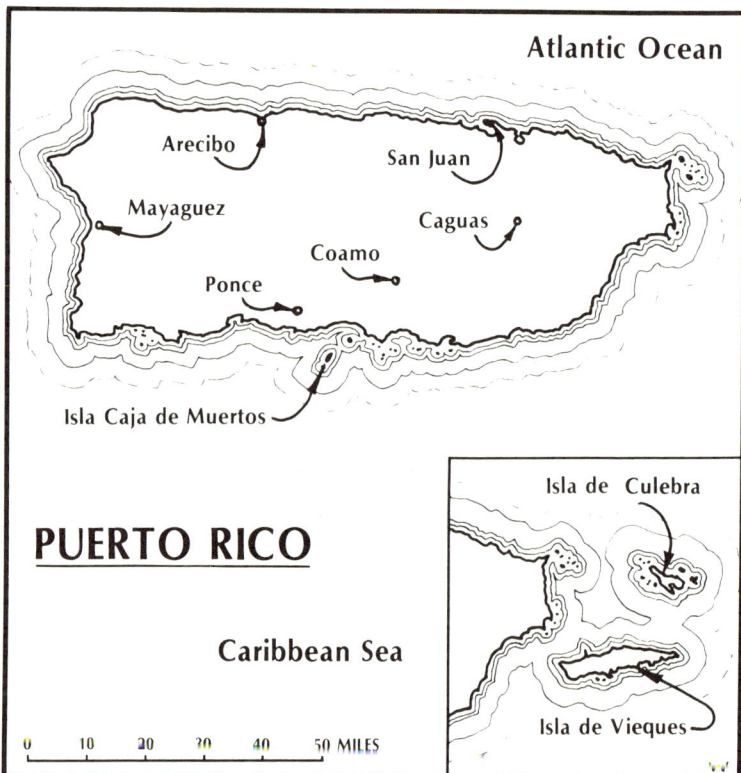

Area: 3,423 sq. miles
Pop: 953,243 (1899)
    3,187,566 (1980)
Capital: San Juan

Located in the Greater Antilles of the West Indies, Puerto Rico was Spanish until it was taken by US forces in 1898. It is currently a commonwealth with autonomy in internal affairs. Stamps were issued under the Spanish administration from 1873 until 1898, when it became a US territory.

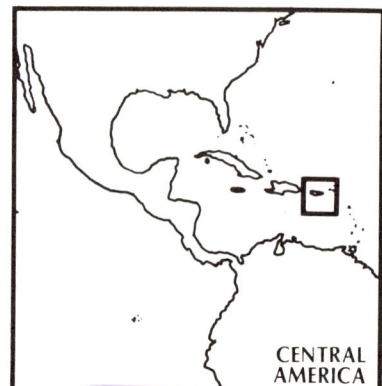

Atlantic Ocean
Arecibo
San Juan
Mayaguez
Caguas
Coamo
Ponce
Isla Caja de Muertos
PUERTO RICO
Caribbean Sea
0 10 20 30 40 50 MILES

Isla de Culebra
Isla de Vieques

CENTRAL AMERICA

Pop: 5,000 (1899 est.)
31,200 (1969 est.)

A town located on the west shore of Lake Titicaca, Puno is at an altitude of 12,641 feet. From 1882 to 1885, several provisional stamps were issued to meet a shortage created by the Chilean occupation of Lima and Callao during a war between the two countries, when stamp supplies were cut off.

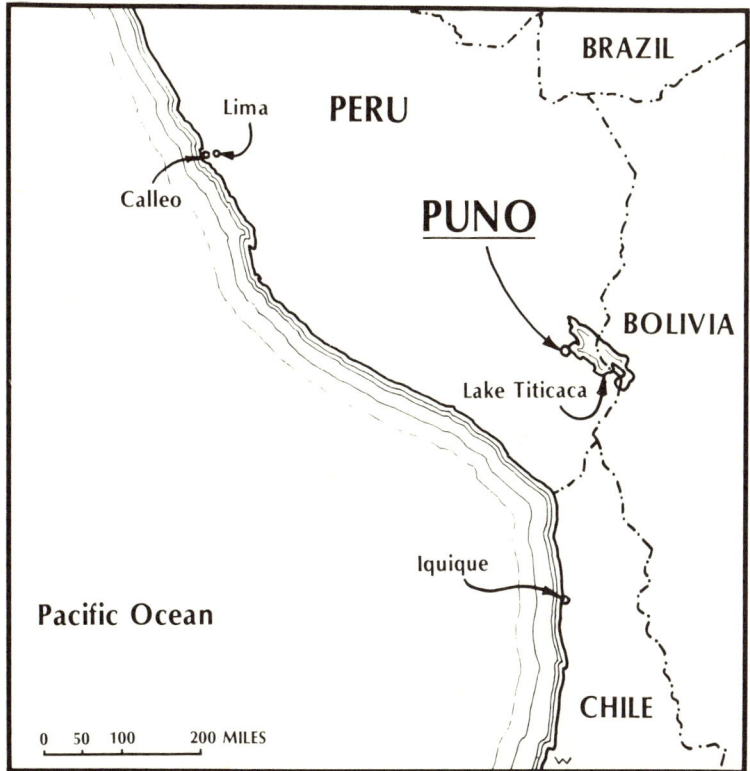

SOUTH AMERICA

BRAZIL
PERU
Lima
Calleo
PUNO
BOLIVIA
Lake Titicaca
Iquique
Pacific Ocean
CHILE
0 50 100   200 MILES

QUEENSLAND, COLONY OF

Area: 667,000 sq. miles
Pop: 492,523 (1899 est.)
2,197,400 (1981)
Capital: Brisbane

The first European settlement in Queensland was a penal settlement at Moreton Bay in 1824. The city of Brisbane was founded in 1842, when the area was opened to free settlers. It became a colony when it was separated from New South Wales in 1859 and a state when it joined the Commonwealth of Australia in 1901.

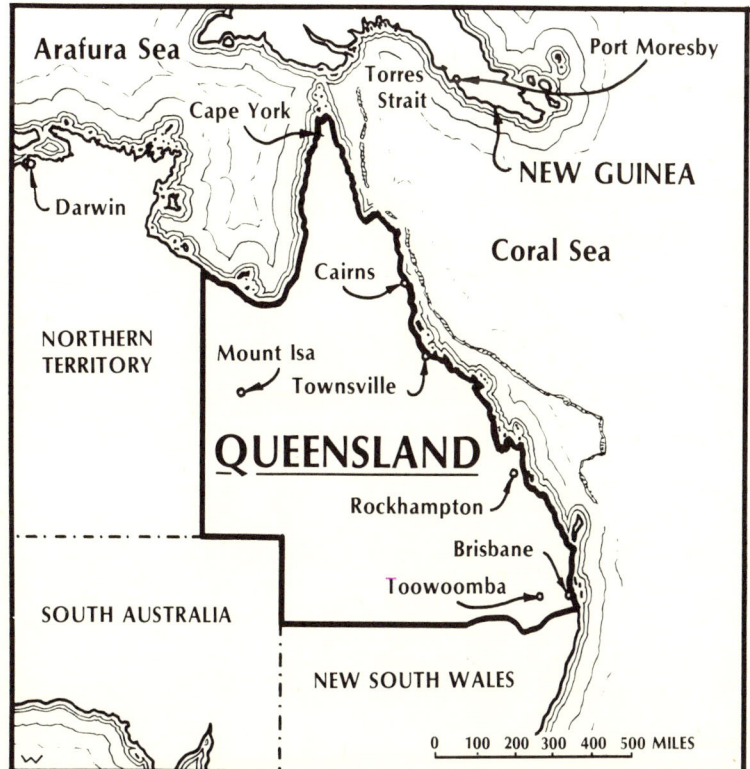

AUSTRALIA

Arafura Sea
Cape York
Torres Strait
Port Moresby
NEW GUINEA
Darwin
Coral Sea
Cairns
NORTHERN TERRITORY
Mount Isa
Townsville
QUEENSLAND
Rockhampton
Brisbane
Toowoomba
SOUTH AUSTRALIA
NEW SOUTH WALES
0 100 200 300 400 500 MILES

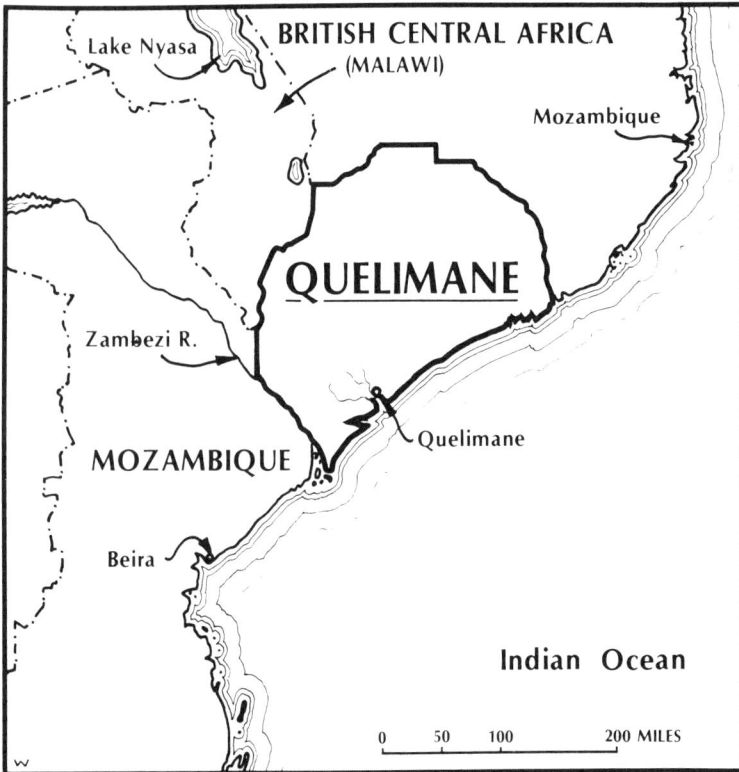

Area: 40,000 sq. miles
Pop: 900,000 (approx.)
Capital: Quelimane

A district of the Portuguese colony of Mozambique based on the seaport town of the same name, Quelimane had its own stamps from 1913 to 1914. The area is now part of the independent country of Mozambique.

——————— RAJASTHAN, GREATER UNION OF ———————

Area: 132,149 sq. miles
Pop: 25,724,142 (1971)
Capital: Jaipur

This union of Indian states was formed in the late 1940s and included the stamp-issuing feudatory states of Bundi, Jaipur, and Kishangarh. Stamp issues consisted of stamps of the various states overprinted. Rajasthan is now a state of the Republic of India located on the border with Pakistan.

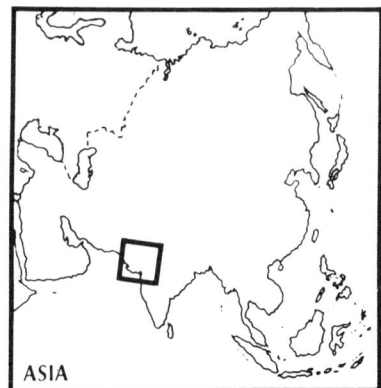

Area: 26 sq. miles
Pop: 10,853 (1968 est.)

The chief island and capital of the Cook Islands, Rarotonga was acquired by Great Britain in 1889 and transferred to New Zealand administration in 1901. From 1919 to 1932, stamps were issued bearing its name. Previously stamps had been inscribed "Cook Islands Federation" and "Cook Islands." Subsequent issues were also inscribed for the Cook Islands.

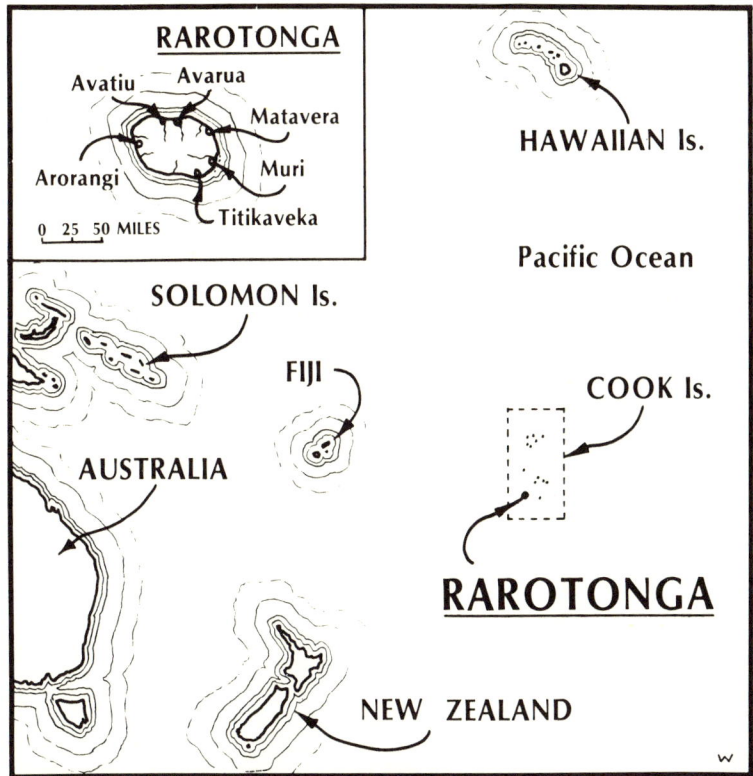

RAROTONGA

Avatiu Avarua
Matavera
Arorangi Muri
Titikaveka
0 25 50 MILES

HAWAIIAN Is.
Pacific Ocean
SOLOMON Is.
FIJI
COOK Is.
AUSTRALIA
RAROTONGA
NEW ZEALAND
PACIFIC OCEAN

RETHYMNON, DISTRICT OF

Area: 578 sq. miles
Pop: 60,856 (1971)
Capital: Rethymnon

Rethymnon is a district of Crete, with its capital city on the island's north coast. It was in the Russian administration area during the 1898-1908 period of joint administration of Crete by Britain, France, Italy, and Russia. Stamps were issued by the Russian authorities in 1899.

Sea of Crete
Canea (Khania)
Rethymnon (Rethimnon)
CRETE
Anoyia
Moundros
Candia (Iraklion)
Timbakion
Gavdhos
RETHYMNON
Mediterranean Sea
0 5 10 20 30 40 50 MILES
EUROPE

Indian Ocean

REUNION

MAURITIUS

MADAGASCAR

REUNION

St. Denis
Ste. Marie
Ste. Suzanne
St. Andre
St. Paul
St. Louis
St. Pierre

0 100 200 400 MILES

0 5 10 20 30 MILES

w

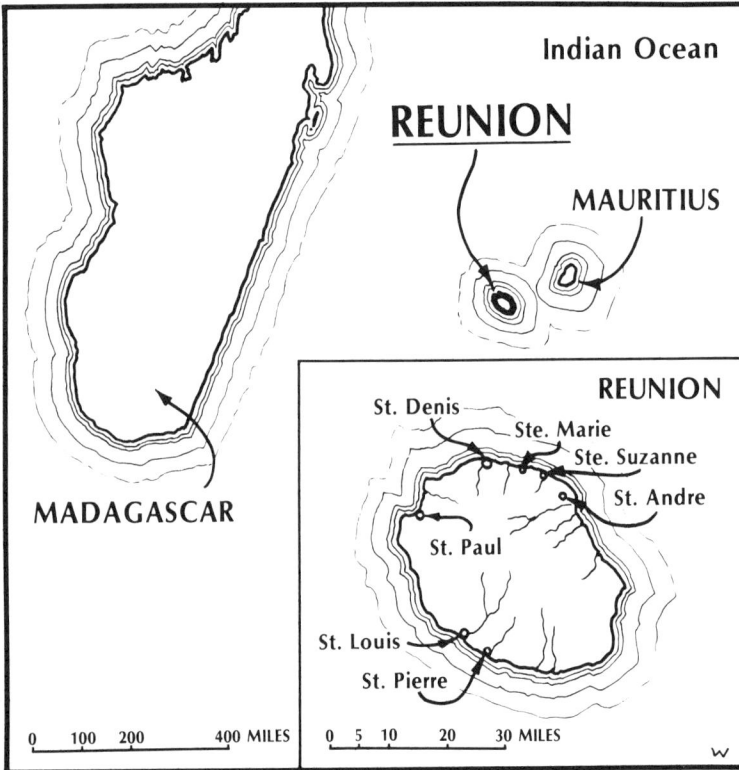

Area: 969 sq. miles
Pop: 171,731 (1892 est.)
535,400 (1981 est.)
Capital: Saint Denis

An island located in the Indian Ocean to the east of Madagascar, Reunion was a French colony until 1947, when it acquired the status of a department of France. Until 1947, it had its own stamps, but subsequent issues were French stamps surcharged for the CFA franc until 1975, when French stamps went into use unsurcharged.

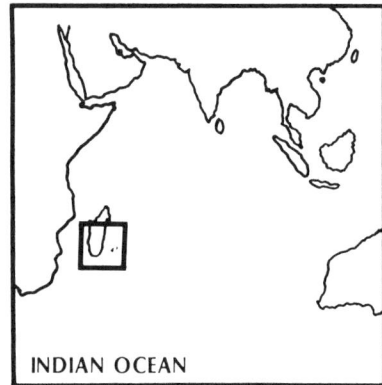

INDIAN OCEAN

———————— RHINELAND PALATINATE ————————

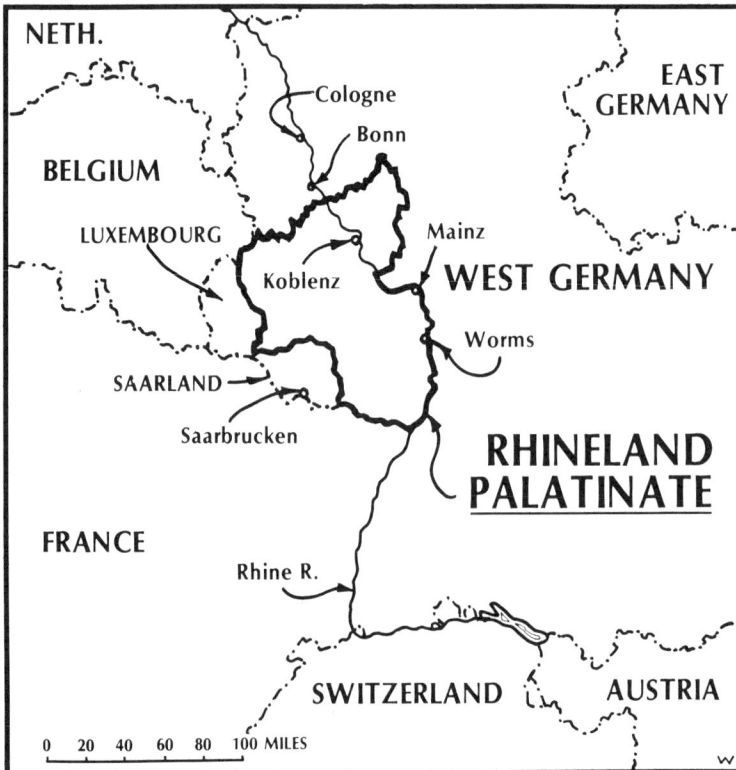

NETH.

Cologne

EAST GERMANY

BELGIUM

Bonn

LUXEMBOURG

Mainz

Koblenz

WEST GERMANY

SAARLAND

Worms

Saarbrucken

RHINELAND PALATINATE

FRANCE

Rhine R.

SWITZERLAND

AUSTRIA

0 20 40 60 80 100 MILES

w

Area: 7,659 sq. miles
Pop: 3,677,000 (1970 est.)
Capital: Mainz

The Rhineland Palatinate is an area of Germany mostly west of the Rhine that was in the French Occupation Zone following WWII. It is now a state of the Federal Republic of Germany. Stamps were issued in 1947-49 under French authority.

EUROPE

Area: 2,279 sq. miles (Riau)
841 sq. miles (Lingga)
Pop: 278,966 (1961-Riau)
not recorded (Lingga)

These twin island groups, off the top of the Malay Peninsula and the east coast of Sumatra, were occupied by Japan during WWII and are now part of Indonesia. Stamps of Indonesia were issued in 1954-64 overprinted "RIAU."

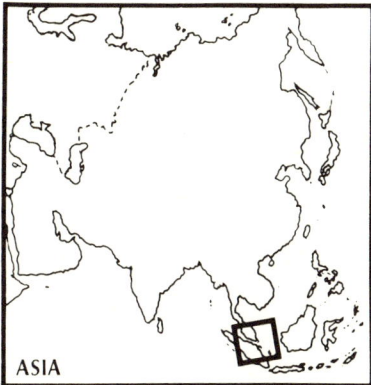

ASIA

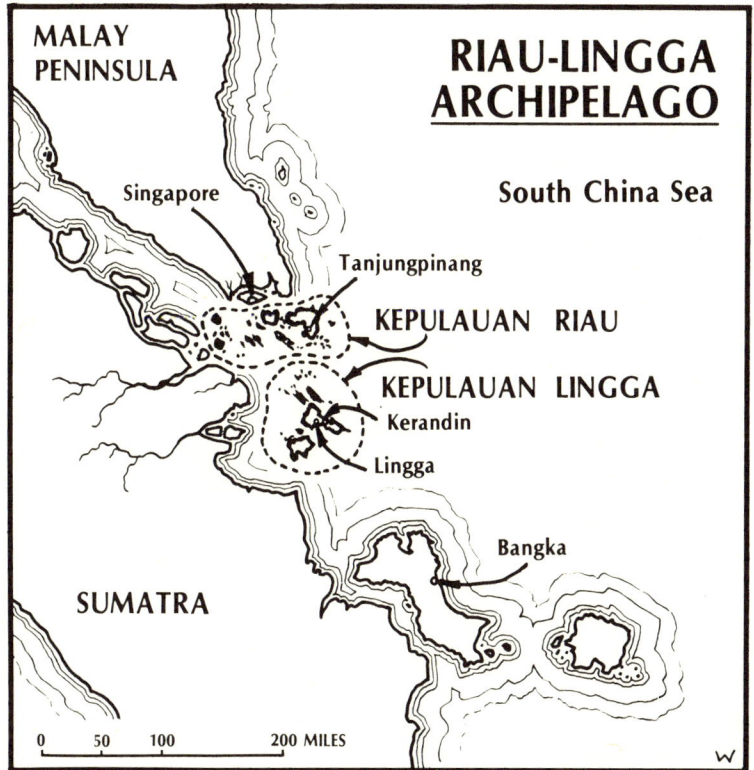

MALAY PENINSULA

RIAU-LINGGA ARCHIPELAGO

South China Sea

Singapore

Tanjungpinang

KEPULAUAN RIAU

KEPULAUAN LINGGA

Kerandin

Lingga

Bangka

SUMATRA

0   50   100   200 MILES

━━━━━RIO MUNI, COLONY OF━━━━━

Area: 10,040 sq. miles
Pop: 203,000 (1968 est.)
Capital: Bata

A former Spanish colony located on the west coast of Africa between Cameroon and Gabon, Rio Muni had used stamps of Spanish Guinea (of which it was part) until 1960, when stamps inscribed "Rio Muni" were introduced. These continued until 1968, when it became part of the Republic of Equatorial Guinea.

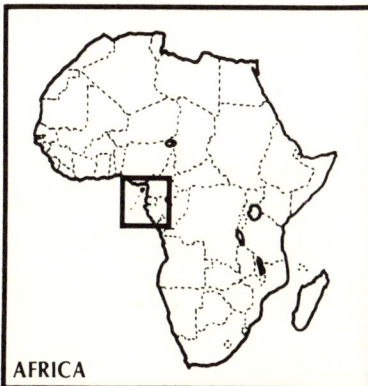

AFRICA

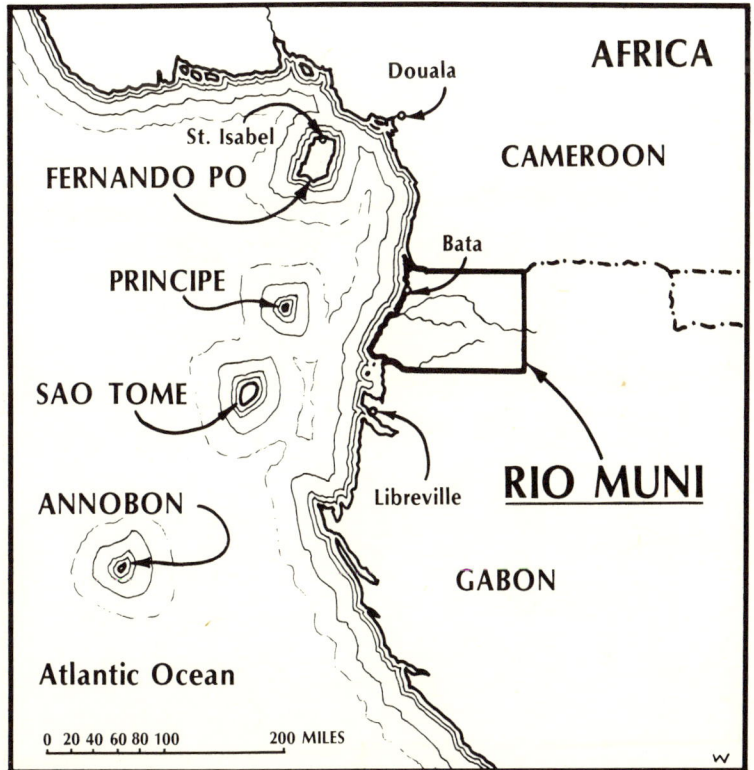

AFRICA

Douala

St. Isabel

FERNANDO PO

CAMEROON

Bata

PRINCIPE

SAO TOME

RIO MUNI

ANNOBON

Libreville

GABON

Atlantic Ocean

0 20 40 60 80 100   200 MILES

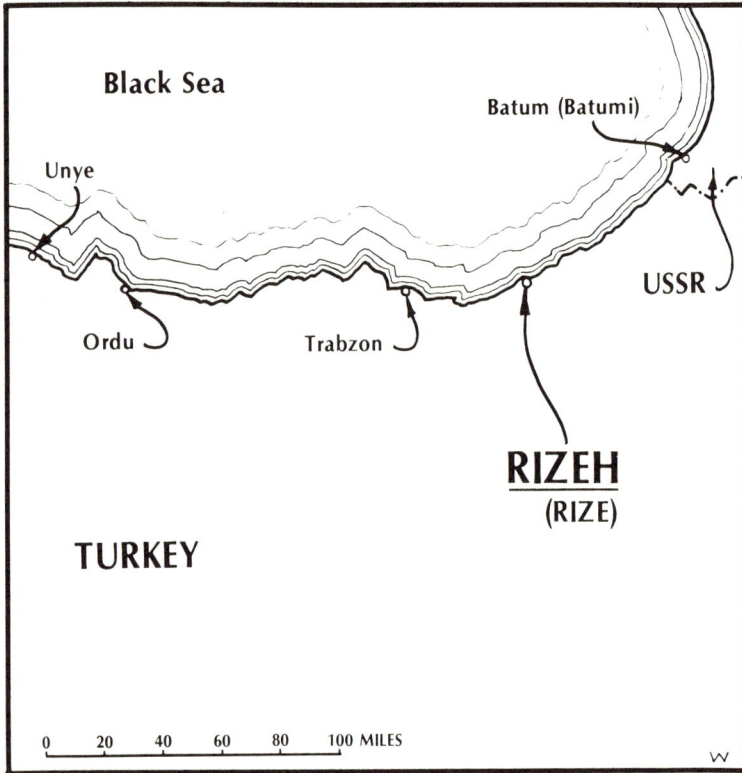

Pop: 26,989 (1965)

The town of Rizeh (now Rize) is located on the Black Sea coast of Asian Turkey not far from the border with the USSR. It is the capital of the Turkish province of the same name. In 1909-10, Russian stamps were overprinted with the town name for use at a Russian post office that operated there.

Black Sea

Batum (Batumi)

Unye

USSR

Ordu

Trabzon

RIZEH
(RIZE)

TURKEY

0 20 40 60 80 100 MILES

———————————— ROMAGNA, STATE OF ————————————

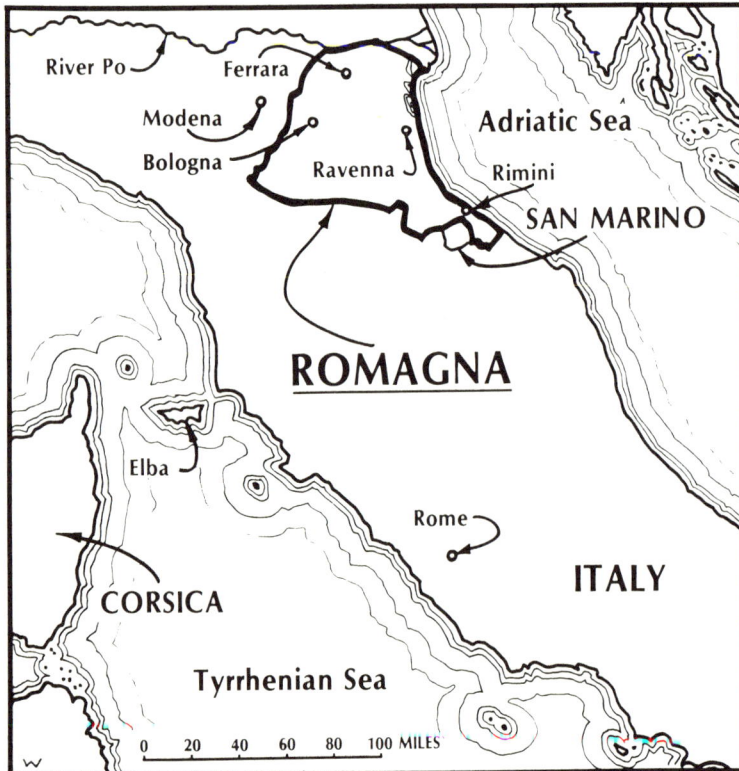

Area: 5,625 sq. miles
Pop: 1,342,000 (1853 est.)
Capital: Ravenna

Comprising the present Italian provinces of Forli, Ravenna, Ferrara, and Bologna, Romagna was annexed to Sardinia in 1860 and became part of the Kingdom of Italy when it was formed. Stamps were issued in 1859 and replaced by those of Sardinia the following year.

River Po

Ferrara

Modena

Bologna

Ravenna

Adriatic Sea

Rimini

SAN MARINO

ROMAGNA

Elba

Rome

ITALY

CORSICA

Tyrrhenian Sea

0 20 40 60 80 100 MILES

EUROPE

Area: 160,000 sq. miles

Ross Dependency includes that area of the Antarctic continent located to the south of latitude 60 degrees South and between longitude 160 degrees East and 150 degrees West. It includes the King Edward VII Peninsula and part of Victoria Land, the Ross Ice Shelf, and the Ross Sea. The Ross Sea once was one of the most important centers of the whaling industry in Antarctic waters. The area was placed under the administration of New Zealand by Great Britain in 1923. Many Antarctic exploratory expeditions have established their bases within the area of Ross Dependency, including those of the Norwegian explorer Roald Amundsen and Admiral Richard E. Byrd. Stamps first were issued for Ross Dependency in 1957. Several have depicted explorers, their ships, and Antarctic scenes.

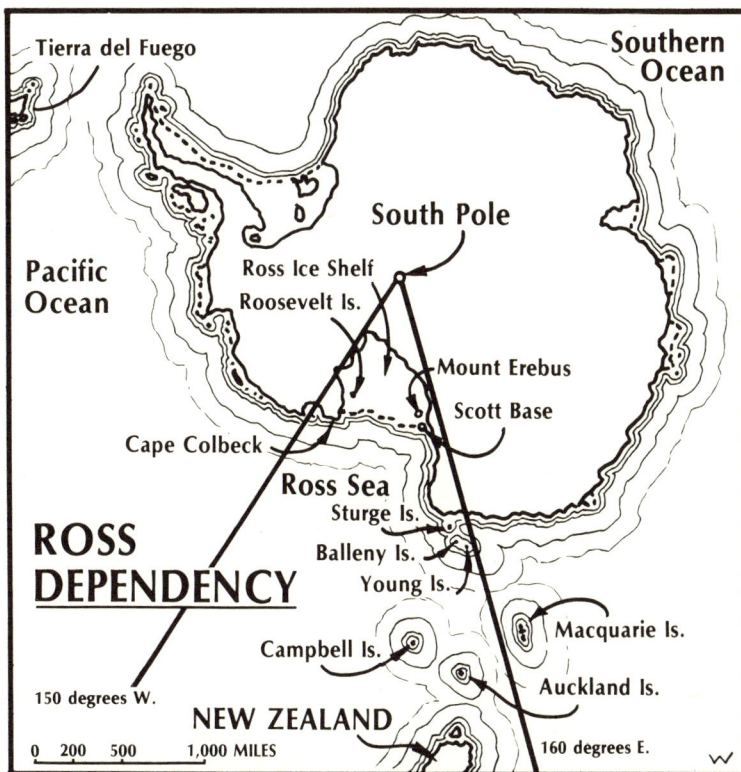

RUANDA-URUNDI, MANDATE OF

Area: 20,916 sq. miles
Pop: 3,378,396 (1944 est.)
     4.7 million (1958 est.)
Capital: Usumbura

The territory of Ruanda-Urundi was part of German East Africa until WWI. It was mandated to Belgium at the end of the war and administered from the Belgian Congo until 1960. In 1962 it was divided into the two independent countries of Rwanda and Burundi. Stamps were issued for Ruanda-Urundi from 1924 until independence.

Area: 8,660,282 sq. miles (1900)
Pop: 128,932,173 (1892)
Capital: St. Petersburg (Leningrad)

A former European and northern Asian empire, Russia is now the main component of the USSR. Except for Finland, it covered a similar area, having sold Alaska to the US in 1867. By the beginning of the 20th century, the facade of the empire was starting to crack, and the defeat by Japan in 1904-05, plus the 1905 revolution attempt, further weakened its structure. In 1914, it perceived that its interests lay with the Allies rather than with the Central Powers, and since it regarded the Turkish Empire as blocking its way to the seas of the world from the Black Sea, it aligned itself against Germany, the Austro-Hungarian Empire, and the tottering Turkish Empire. Unfortunately, Russia was also a spectacularly inept empire by 1914, led by a weak, if well-meaning czar unable to cope with the growing demand by his people for relief from an oppressive regime. Years before, Peter the Great had become czar of Russia in 1682 and was largely responsible for orienting the country towards the West. He did much to transform Russia into a European power. One of Peter's more significant acts was the foundation of St. Petersburg — later Petrograd and now Leningrad — as his "window" on Europe. He made it his capital in 1714. In time, Russia edged its way into Europe as it came to control the Baltic Sea, and in 1721, Peter proclaimed Russia an empire. Weak rulers followed him, until Catherine

RUSSIAN EMPIRE
PRIOR TO WORLD WAR ONE

0   250   500   1,000 MILES

the Great became empress in the latter part of the 18th century. She carried on where Peter had left off. Russian power in Europe grew after the defeat of Napoleon and his retreat from Moscow in 1812. The 19th century saw the expansion of the empire in Asia, although the Crimean War in the 1850s was a disaster. Nevertheless, Russia continued to exert pressure at points of least resistance in an attempt to reach the Persian Gulf and the Pacific. The latter ambition was achieved, but the former continues

to elude the leaders of the Soviet Union, although the current incursion into Afghanistan indicates that the ambition might still remain. Some reforms were made in the 1860s, when local governments were set up to handle local affairs, including mail services and the so-called Zemstov stamp issues. It was a case of "too little and too late" as, in 1881, the czar was assassinated and the final act was set up with the coming to the throne of the ineffectual Czar Nicholas II. Unable to rule properly,

he compensated for his lack of ability with oppression. After military disasters during WWI, the revolution could no longer be contained, and in 1917, the Russian Empire finally came crashing down. The first Russian stamps were issued in 1857, and Russian philately has been varied and full of interest, although it is not widely popular in the West. However, there is an enthusiastic body of collectors of the classic period and the stamps and postal history of the Russian offices abroad are extremely challenging.

RUSSIA IN EUROPE
PRIOR TO THE FIRST WORLD WAR

Map (Transvaal region)

BECHUANALAND

S. RHODESIA

MOZAMBIQUE

TRANSVAAL

RUSTENBURG

Gaborone

Lourenco Marques

Pretoria

SWAZILAND

Mafeking

Mbabane

Johannesburg

ORANGE FREE STATE

Ladysmith

Bloemfontein

NATAL

Indian Ocean

Pietermaritzburg

Maseru

Durban

BASUTO.

0 20 40 60 80 100   150   200 MILES

Pop: 508 (1900)
32,500 (1967 est.)

The town of Rustenburg is in the Transvaal, which is now part of the Republic of South Africa. Located on a branch of the Limpopo River, it is an agricultural center. In 1900, a set of stamps was issued there, and it is known as the Rustenburg Issue.

AFRICA

————————— RYUKYU ISLANDS —————————

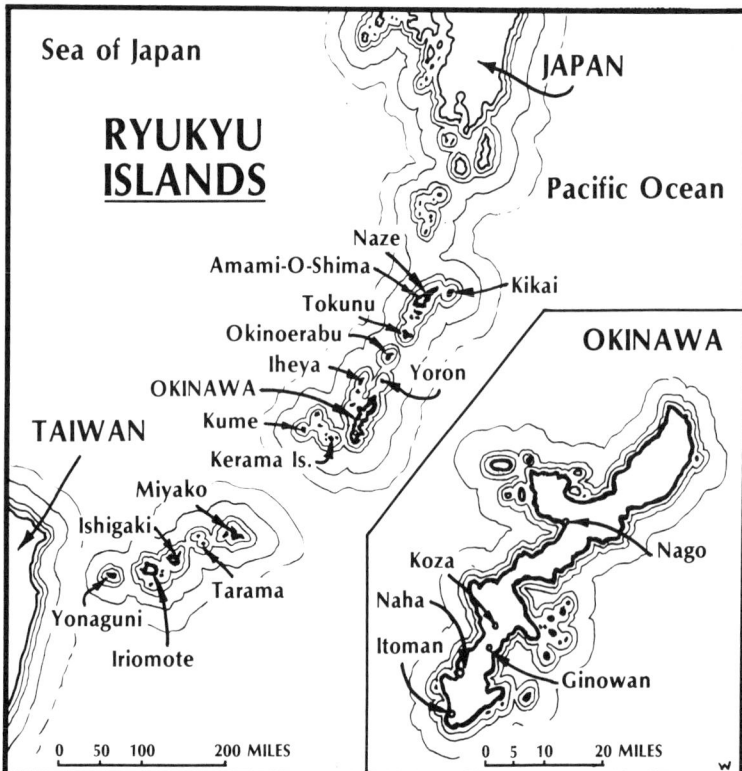

Sea of Japan

JAPAN

RYUKYU ISLANDS

Pacific Ocean

Naze

Amami-O-Shima

Kikai

Tokunu

Okinoerabu

OKINAWA

Iheya

Yoron

OKINAWA

Kume

TAIWAN

Kerama Is.

Miyako

Koza

Nago

Ishigaki

Naha

Tarama

Itoman

Yonaguni

Iriomote

Ginowan

0 50 100   200 MILES

0 5 10   20 MILES

Area: 848 sq. miles
Pop: 945,111 (1970)
Capital: Naha

Once paying tribute to both China and Japan, the Ryukyu Islands were, by 1879, firmly under Japanese control. The islands were placed under a US military government after being taken from Japan during WWII. The Amami group was returned to Japan in 1953, but the rest remained under US administration until 1972, when they, too, went back to Japan.

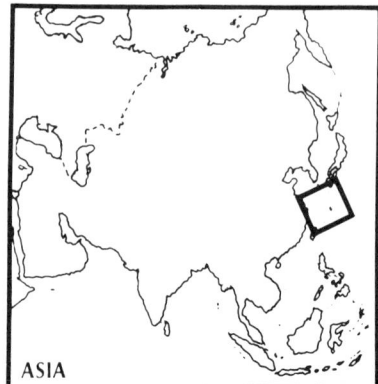

ASIA

Area: 991 sq. miles
Pop: 1,127,000 (1970 est.)
Capital: Saarbrucken

Currently a state of the Federal Republic of Germany (West Germany), the Saar was occupied by France following WWI. Returned to Germany in a 1935 plebiscite, it was part of the occupation zone assigned to France at the end of WWII and was restored to Germany in 1956. Stamps were issued from 1920 to 1935 and again from 1947 to 1959.

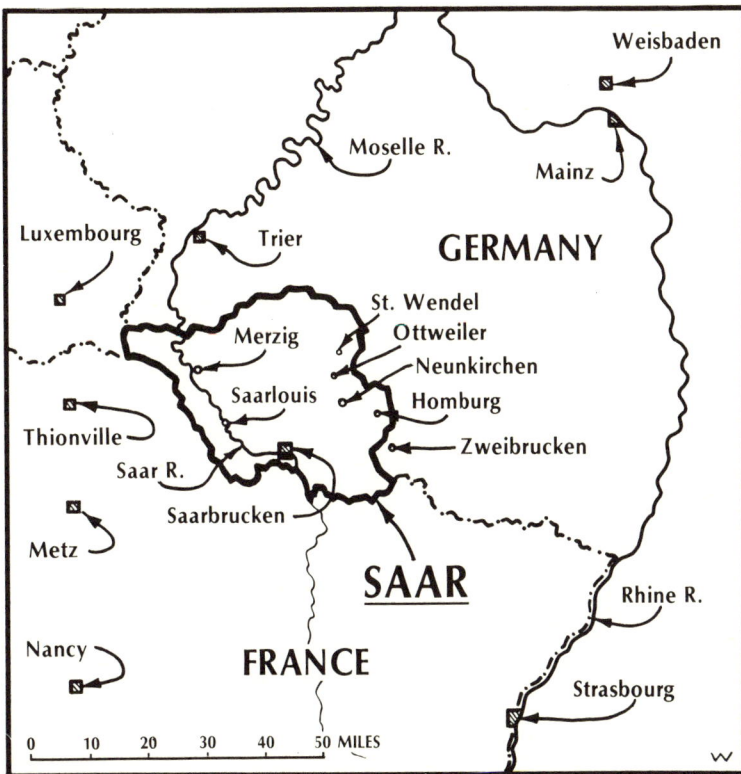

STE. MARIE DE MADAGASCAR, COLONY OF

Area: 65 sq. miles

Ste. Marie de Madagascar is an island off the east coast of Madagascar in the Indian Ocean. It is a former French colony and is now part of the Republic of Madagascar. In 1894 a set of stamps was issued for the island. They were in the French colonial Commerce and Navigation key type. In 1896 they were replaced by the stamps of Madagascar.

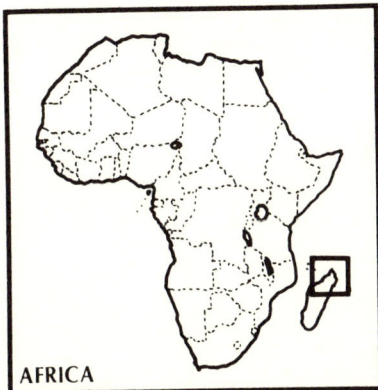

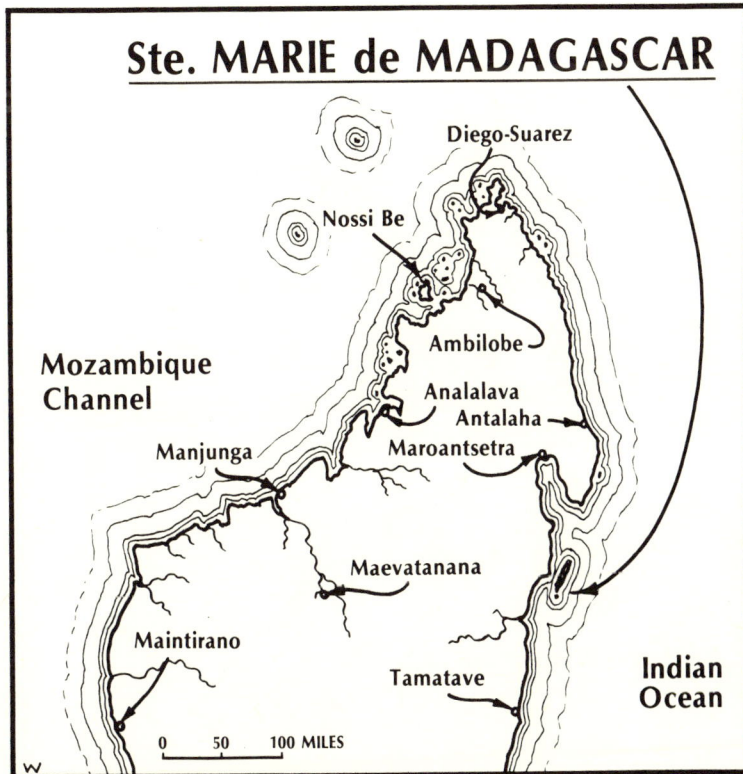

Gulf of
St. Lawrence

NEWFOUNDLAND

Cape Ray

NOVA SCOTIA

Sydney

ST. PIERRE AND MIQUELON

Atlantic Ocean

0   20   40   60   80   100 MILES

W

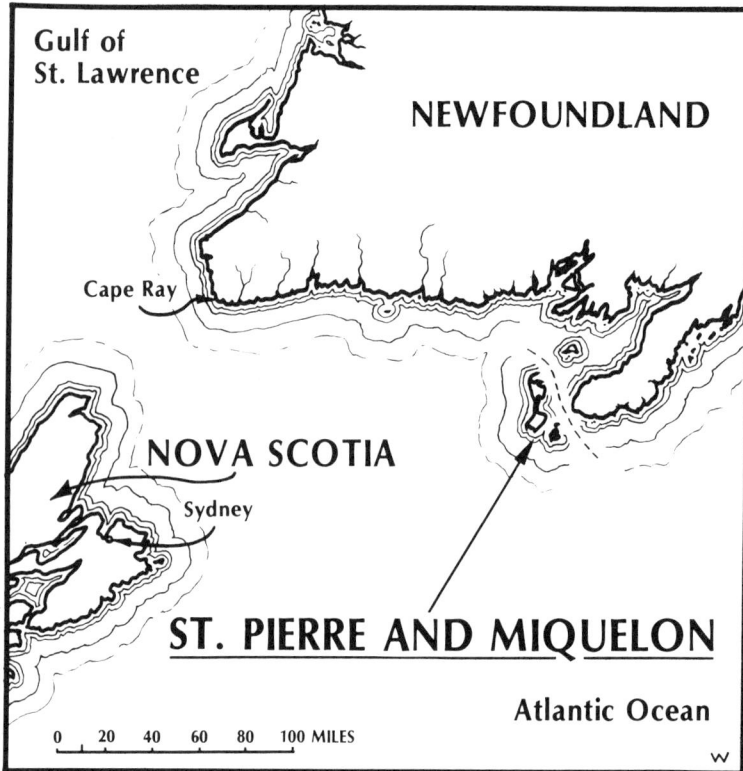

Area: 93 sq. miles
Pop: 4,715 (1936)
        6,300 (1980 est.)
Capital: Saint Pierre

Comprising two adjacent islands, plus several smaller ones, St. Pierre and Miquelon is a cod-fishing center. It was formerly a French colony, but achieved status as a French Overseas Territory in 1949. In 1976 it was made a department of France, and its own stamp issues came to an end. It now uses stamps of France.

NORTH AMERICA

———— ST. THOMAS AND PRINCE ISLANDS ————

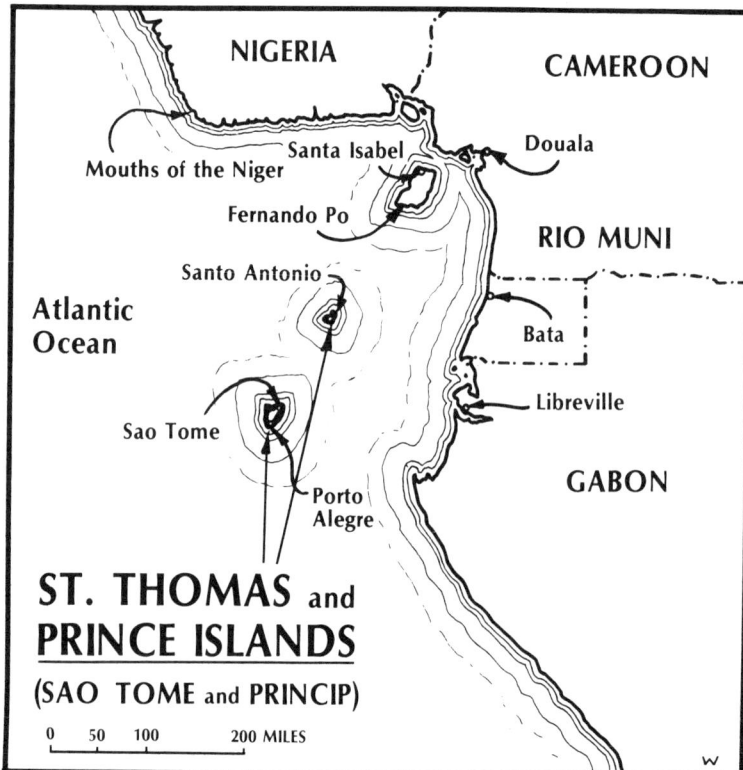

NIGERIA

CAMEROON

Santa Isabel

Douala

Mouths of the Niger

Fernando Po

RIO MUNI

Santo Antonio

Atlantic Ocean

Bata

Libreville

Sao Tome

GABON

Porto Alegre

ST. THOMAS and PRINCE ISLANDS

(SAO TOME and PRINCIP)

0   50   100   200 MILES

W

Area: 372 sq. miles
Pop: 61,000 (1970 est.)
        90,000 (1981 est.)
Capital: Sao Tome

Formerly a Portuguese colony consisting of two islands in the Gulf of Guinea off the coast of Africa, St. Thomas and Prince Islands became a province of Portugal and later an overseas territory. They have been independent since 1975 as the Democratic Republic of Sao Tome and Principe.

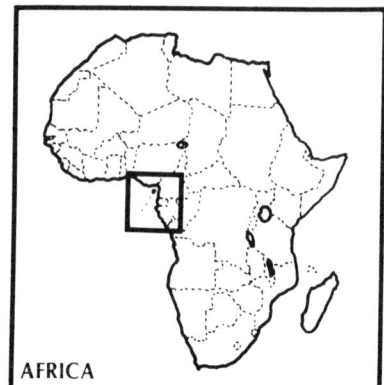

AFRICA

Area: 4,763 sq. miles
Pop: 371,607 (1970)
Capital: Salamanca

A province in the western part of Spain adjacent to the Portuguese border, Salamanca has a capital city of the same name. During the Peninsula War, it was the scene of a British victory by the Duke of Wellington over the French. In 1868-69, a provisional stamp was issued for the city.

SALONICA (THESSALONIKI), CITY OF

Pop: 150,000 (1900 est.)
      339,496 (1971)

A seaport, Salonica (Thessaloniki or Thessalonica) is the capital city of the Greek Department of the same name. It is a railroad center located at the head of the Gulf of Salonica. Founded in 315 BC, it was an important city under the Romans and was part of the Turkish Empire from 1430 to 1912. During WWI, the city was a base for Allied operations, and in WWII it was occupied by the Germans.

SALZBURG

GERMANY

CZECHOSLOVAKIA

Munich

Lake Constance
LIECHTENSTEIN
Bregenz

Salzburg

AUSTRIA

Innsbruck

SWITZ.

TYROL
(TIROL)

ITALY

YUGOSLAVIA

0 20 40 60 80 100 MILES

EUROPE

Area: 2,762 sq. miles
Pop: 399,000 (1971)
Capital: Salzburg

A province of Austria with a capital city of the same name, Salzburg is adjacent to the West German border. In 1945, Allied Military Government stamps were issued for use there during the occupation that followed the end of WWII.

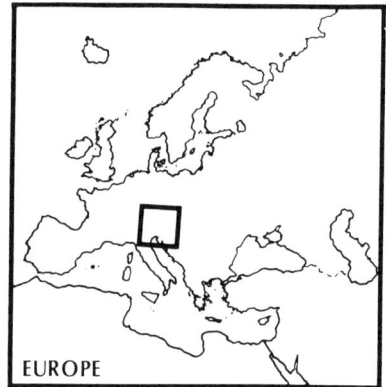

————————————SAMOS, ISLAND OF————————————

LESBOS

Aegean Sea

SAMOS

GREECE

Smyrna

Athens

CHIOS (KHIOS)

TURKEY

Vathi

Sea of Crete

Candia (Iraklion)

RHODES

CRETE

0 20 40 60 80 100 MILES

Area: 184 sq. miles
Pop: 41,124 (1961)
Capital: Vathi (Vathy)

Once Turkish, the Aegean island of Samos has been Greek since 1912, when that country took it as part of New Greece. It was occupied by Axis forces during WWII. Stamps were issued in 1912 by the provisional government following Greek capture of the island.

Area: 24,226 sq. miles
Pop: 1,257,028 (1970)
Capital: San Louis Potosi

An agricultural and mining region, the city of San Louis Potosi was the seat of Juarez's government in 1863. It was here that Madero drew up his social and political program for the Mexican revolution of 1910. In 1914, revolutionary provisional stamps were issued.

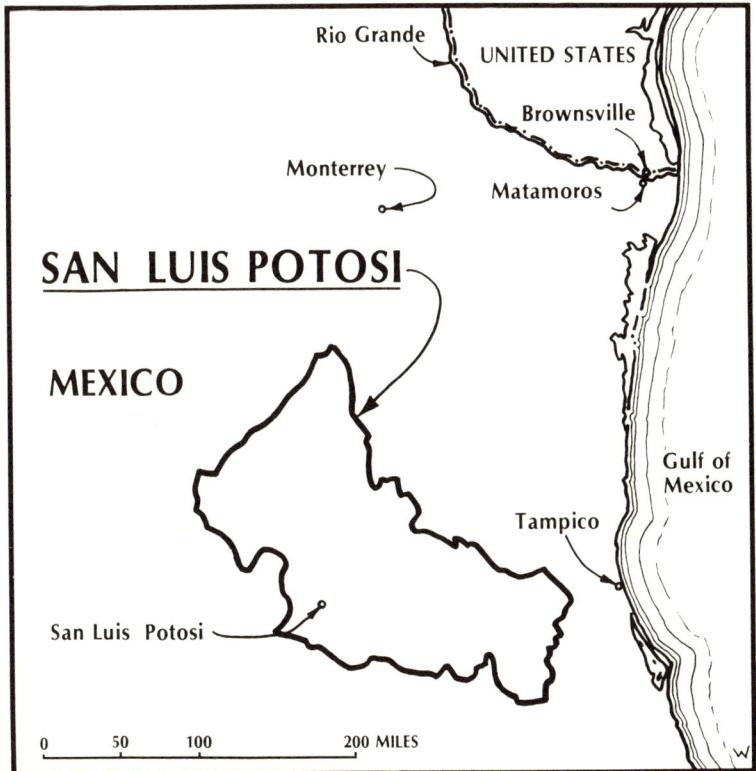

SANTA CRUZ DE TENERIFE

Area: 1,239 sq. miles
Pop: 590,514 (1970)
Capital: Santa Cruz de Tenerife

A province of Spain, Santa Cruz de Tenerife is one of the Canary Islands located off the northwest coast of Africa. During 1936, a set of Spanish stamps was overprinted "Viva Espana/ 18 Julio/ 1936" for use there.

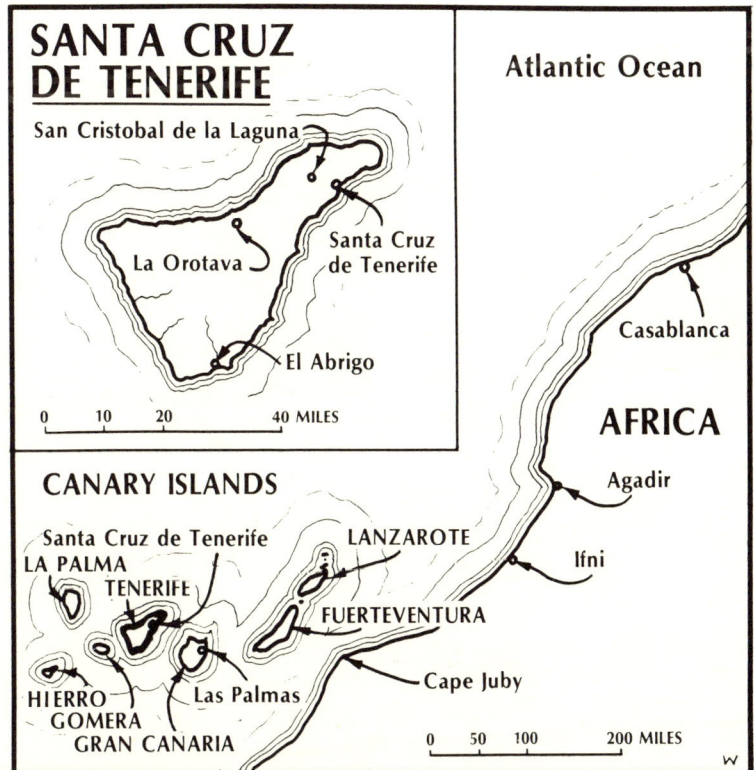

Area: 11,950 sq. miles
Pop: 1,137,000 (1970)
Capital: Bucaramanga

Formerly a state in the United States of Colombia, Santander is now a department of that country. Although the states gave up independence when they federated, most of the stamp-issuing states retained that right. Santander issued stamps from 1884 to 1907.

———————— SARAWAK, STATE OF ————————

Area: 48,342 sq. miles
Pop: 977,103 (1970)
Capital: Kuching

A territory granted to Sir James Brooke by the Sultan of Brunei in 1841, Sarawak continued under the Brooke family as a British protectorate (from 1888) until the Japanese occupation during WWII. After its liberation, it became a crown colony in 1946 and joined Malaysia in 1963.

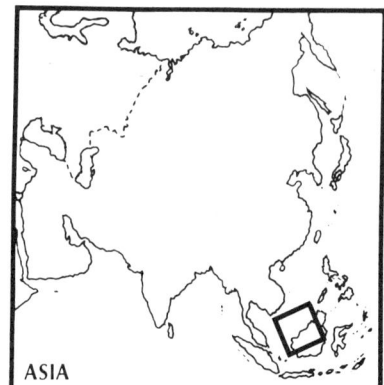

Capital: Turin

By the mid-19th century, the Kingdom of Sardinia had become strong enough to form the nucleus of a united Italian kingdom. It included the Mediterranean island of Sardinia, plus a large area in northern Italy and the territories of Savoy and Nice until 1860, when the latter two were ceded to France. On March 17, 1861, Sardinia became the Kingdom of Italy under Victor Emmanuel II.

SAVOY (to France 1860)

FRANCE

NICE (to France 1860)

Turin

Milan

PIEDMONT

LIGURIA

Genoa

Monaco

Nice

Ligurian Sea

Adriatic Sea

ITALY

Rome

Ajaccio

CORSICA

Tyrrhenian Sea

Sassari

Mediterranean Sea

Nuoro

Cagliari

The **KINGDOM OF SARDINIA**

0   50   100 MILES

EUROPE

SASENO (SAZAN), ISLAND OF

Area: Two square miles

Saseno (now Sazan) is a small island off the coast of Albania at the entrance to the harbor of Vlore. It had been seized by Italy in 1914 and held as a naval base until it was returned to Albania in 1947, following Italian defeat during WWII. Stamps were issued in 1923 for use there and consisted of the overprint "SASENO" on Italian stamps of the 1901-22 issue.

Adriatic Sea

YUGOSLAVIA

Scutari (Shkoder)

SASENO (SAZAN)

Bari

Tirane

Brindisi

ITALY

ALBANIA

Taranto

CORFU

GREECE

Ionian Sea

0   20   40   60   80   100 MILES

EUROPE

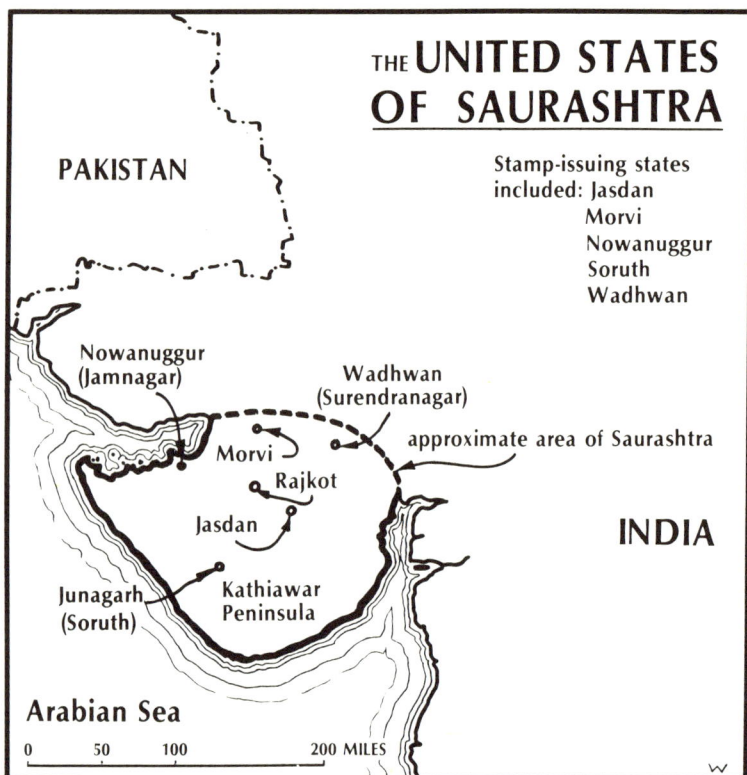

THE UNITED STATES OF SAURASHTRA

Stamp-issuing states
included: Jasdan
Morvi
Nowanuggur
Soruth
Wadhwan

PAKISTAN

Nowanuggur
(Jamnagar)

Wadhwan
(Surendranagar)

approximate area of Saurashtra

Morvi
Rajkot
Jasdan

INDIA

Junagarh
(Soruth)

Kathiawar
Peninsula

Arabian Sea

0   50   100   200 MILES

Area: 31,880 sq. miles
Pop: 2.9 million (1948 est.)
Capital: Junagarh

The United States of Saurashtra was formed in 1948 by a federation of former states on the Kathiawar Peninsula of India. It included the stamp-issuing states of Jasdan, Morvi, Nowanuggur, and Wadhwan, plus 213 other states. In 1956 it became part of Bombay State. Stamps were issued for Saurashtra during 1949.

ASIA

SAXONY, KINGDOM OF

KINGDOM OF SAXONY

Berlin

Magdeburg

PRUSSIA

Elbe River

Halle

Leipzig

Dresden

Chemnitz

BOHEMIA

Prague

BAVARIA

AUSTRIA-HUNGARY

Pilsen (Plzen)

0   25   50   100 MILES

Area: 5,780 sq. miles
Pop: 4,202,216 (1900)
Capital: Dresden

The Kingdom of Saxony joined the North German Confederation in 1868 and became part of the German Empire in 1870. Following WWII it was mostly within the Soviet Zone, now the German Democratic Republic (East Germany). Stamps were issued from 1850 to Jan. 1, 1868.

EUROPE

Area: 6,046 sq. miles
Pop: 2,516,000 (1970 est.)
Capital: Schleswig and Kiel

Comprising twin duchies, Schleswig-Holstein was made part of Prussia in 1866 except for a northern area that went to Denmark in 1864. Following WWI, a plebiscite was held, which resulted in the northern part of Schleswig (Zone 1) going to Denmark, with the area to the south (Zone 2) remaining German.

SCHWEIZER-RENEKE, TOWN OF

Schweizer-Reneke is a small town in the southwestern part of Transvaal, now part of the Republic of South Africa. It lies to the southeast of the town of Vryburg. A stamp issue was released there in 1900, during the war between Great Britain and the Boers. The stamps were those of the Transvaal overprinted "BESIEGED." One-halfpenny and one-penny stamps of the colony of Cape of Good Hope were similarly overprinted.

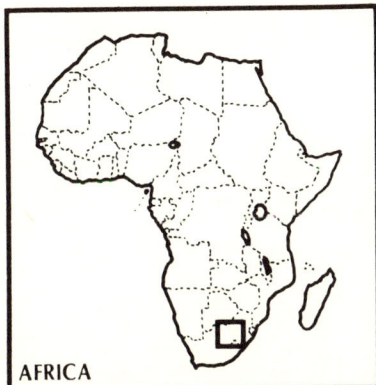

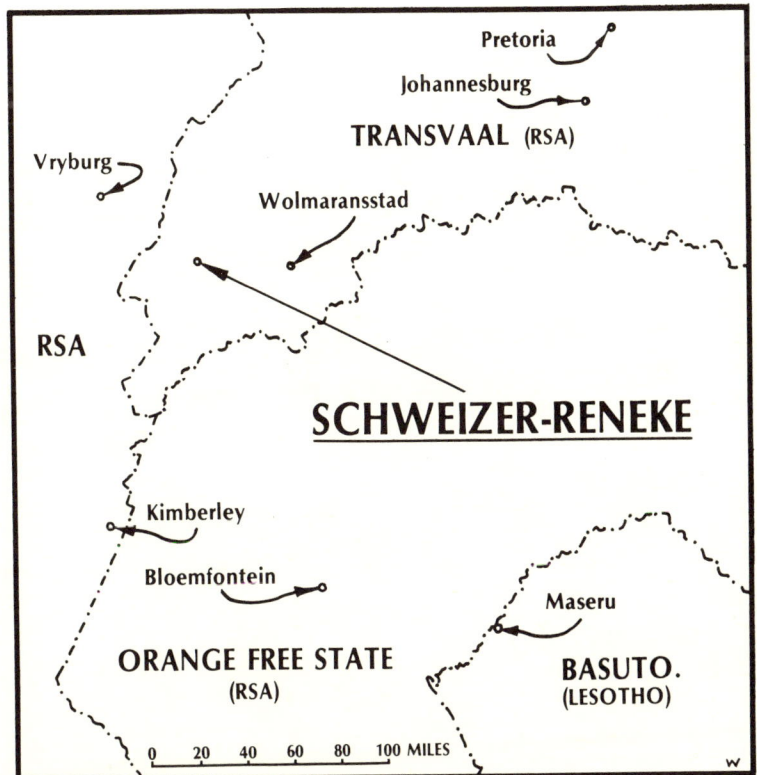

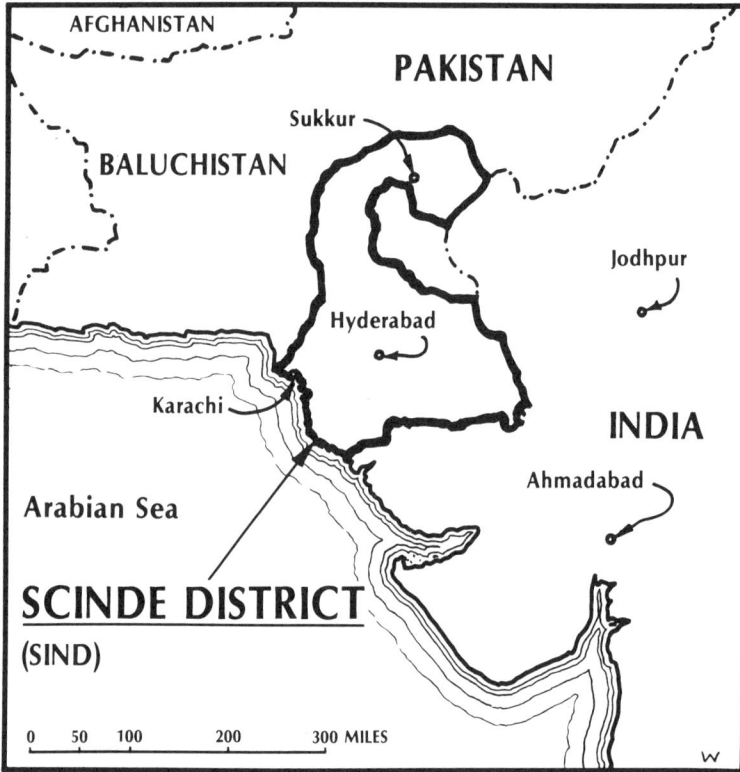

The Scinde District was an area of British India, based on the city of Karachi, in what is now Pakistan. The area had been taken in 1850 by Lord Napier, and the first governor, Sir Bartle Frere, extended an existing runner system of carrying mail and introduced camel riders. On July 1, 1852, stamps were released for use on mail carried on these routes. These were the famous Scinde Dawks, which were produced in three colors and used until October 1854.

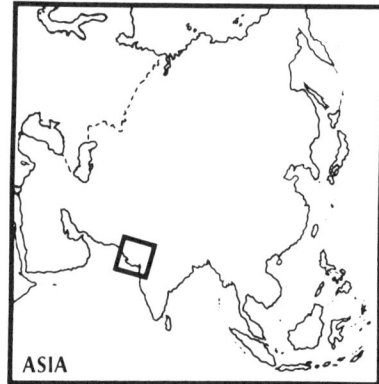

—————— SCUTARI (SHKODER), TOWN OF ——————

Pop: 35,000 (1900 est.)
49,830 (1967 est.)

Scutari, now known as Shkoder, is a town in the northern part of the People's Republic of Albania, near the border with Yugoslavia. A former capital of Albania, it was under Turkish rule from 1479 to 1913 and was a battlefield during WWI. In 1909-10, Italian stamps were overprinted for use from an Italian post office in the town.

Area: 2,682 sq. miles
Pop: 162,770 (1970)
Capital: Segovia

A province of Spain, Segovia is located to the north of Madrid in central Spain. The walled town is about 40 miles from Madrid and contains examples of Roman, Moorish, and Gothic architecture. The French sacked the town in 1808. It is now an industrial center manufacturing chemical products, cement, and fertilizers.

SEGOVIA

Valladolid

Segovia

Avila

SPAIN

Madrid

0 10 20 30 40 50 MILES

EUROPE

—————SERBIA, KINGDOM OF—————

Area: 19,050 sq. miles
Pop: 2,312,484 (1895)
Capital: Belgrade

A kingdom in the Balkans, Serbia was blamed by Austria for the assassination of the Archduke Ferdinand in Sarajevo in 1914. Its ultimatum and declaration of war on Serbia precipitated WWI. After the war, Serbia became one of the states forming the new Kingdom of Yugoslavia.

AUSTRIA-HUNGARY

KINGDOM OF
SERBIA

ROMANIA

Belgrade

Sarajevo

Danube River

Cetinje

BULGARIA

Sofia

MONTENEGRO

Adriatic Sea

TURKEY IN EUROPE

0 20 40 60 80 100 MILES

EUROPE

PORTUGAL

Constantina

Seville Carmona

Marchena

Utrera

Osuna

Montellano

Atlantic
Ocean

SPAIN

SEVILLE

Cadiz

Algeciras

Gibraltar

0 10 20 30 40 50 MILES

W

Area: 5,406 sq. miles
Pop: 1,327,190 (1970)
Capital: Seville

Seville is a province in southern Spain. Its capital city is Seville located on the Guadalquivir River about 62 miles from Cadiz. Stamps were issued in the province in 1936, during the Spanish Civil War. The overprint on stamps of Spain includes the date "JULIO-1936," which marked the beginning of the Franco regime.

EUROPE

———————— SHANGHAI, CITY OF ————————

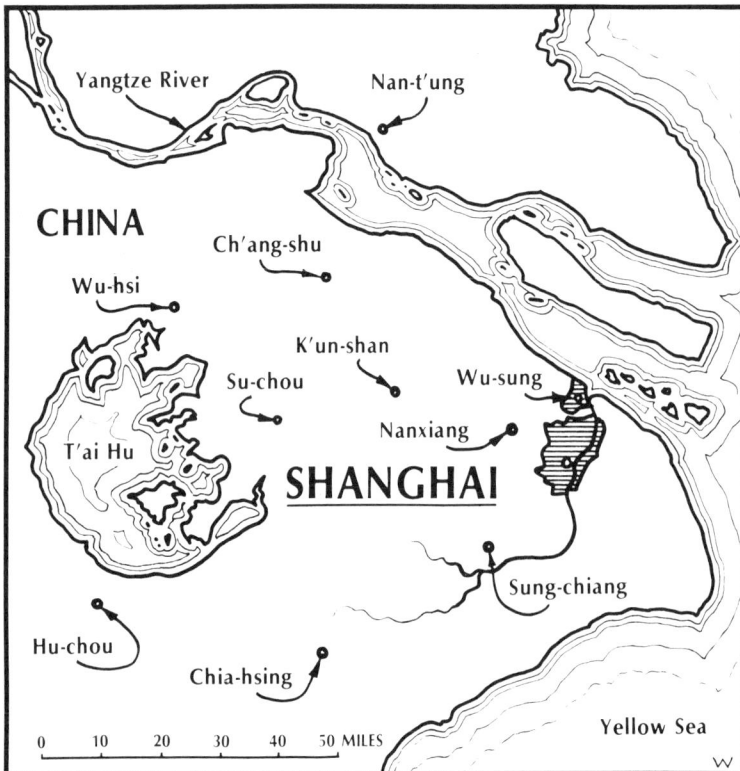

Yangtze River

Nan-t'ung

CHINA

Ch'ang-shu

Wu-hsi

K'un-shan

Su-chou

Wu-sung

Nanxiang

T'ai Hu

SHANGHAI

Sung-chiang

Hu-chou

Chia-hsing

0 10 20 30 40 50 MILES

W

Yellow Sea

Area: 772, sq. miles
Pop: 12 million (1981 est.)

One of the People's Republic of China's major seaports and manufacturing centers, Shanghai constitutes a special administrative unit. In 1842 it became one of the first Treaty Ports (q.v.) and developed rapidly as the foreign concession areas grew.

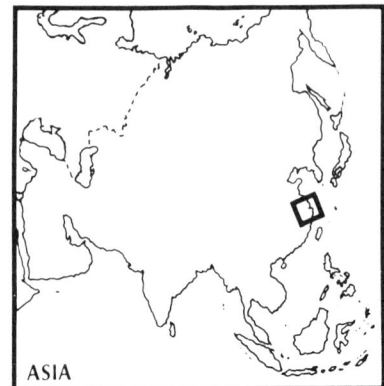

ASIA

Area: 59,189 sq. miles
Pop: 57 million (1967 est.)
Capital: Chi-nan

Shantung is a province of the People's Republic of China. Its eastern part forms a peninsula between the Yellow Sea and the Gulf of Chihli. Stamps issued for North China from 1941 were used in the area, and it later became part of the East China Liberation Area of the Communists, for which stamps were also issued.

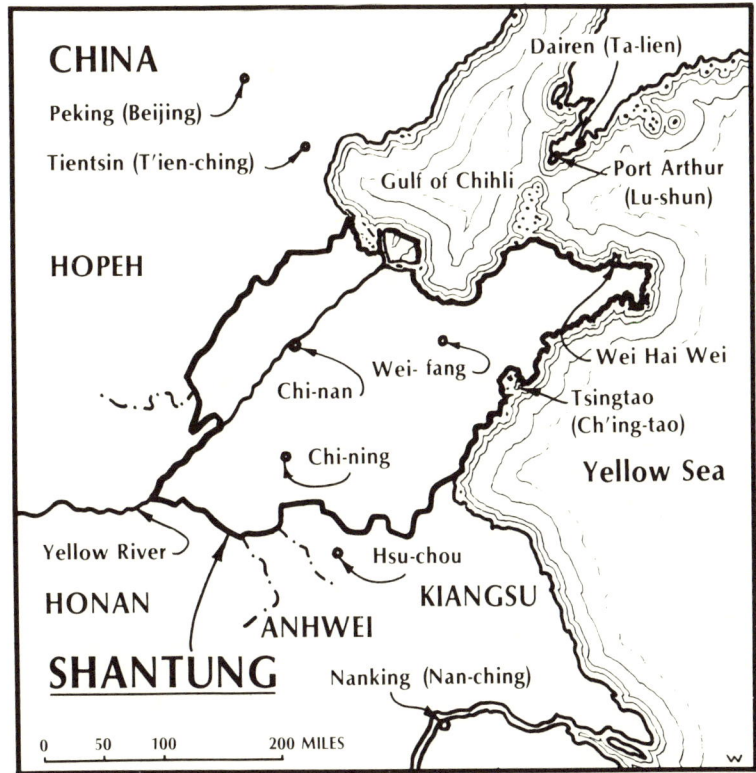

SHANSI, PROVINCE OF

Area: 60,656 sq. miles
Pop: 18 million (1967 est.)
Capital: T'ai-yuan

A province in northeast China, Shansi is located between Inner Mongolia and the plain of North China. The western part was included in the Northwest China Liberation Area of the Communist rebels prior to the formation of the People's Republic of China and used its stamps.

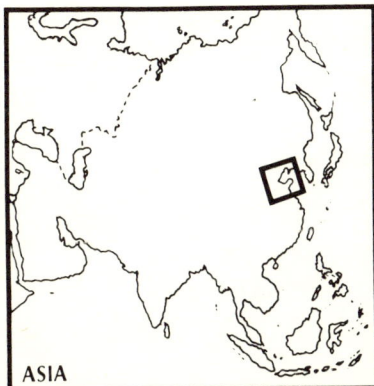

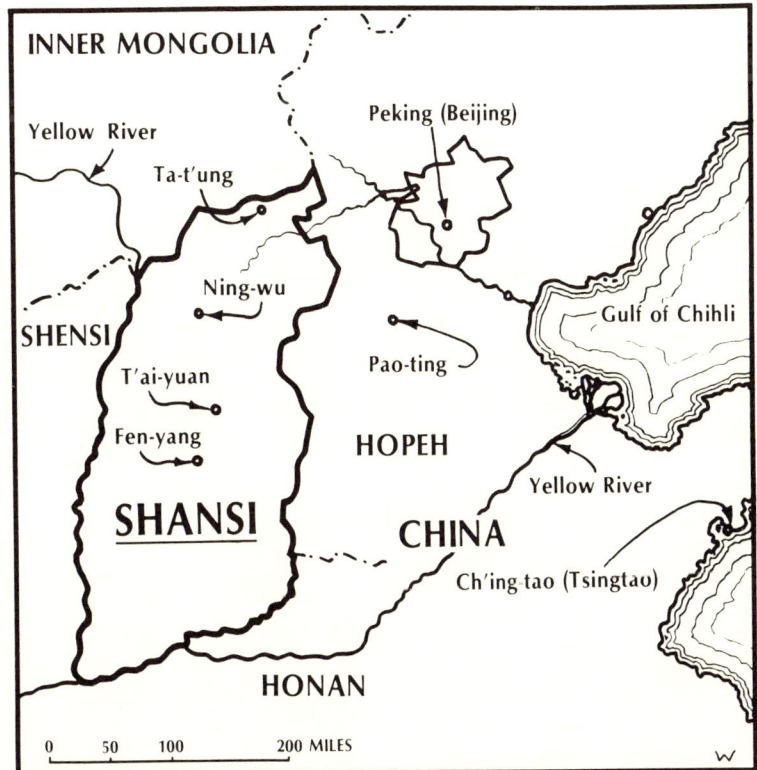

Area: 75,598 sq. miles
Pop: 21 million (1968 est.)
Capital: Hsi-an

Shensi is a province in east central People's Republic of China. Its capital was the chief city of the Chinese Empire for several periods prior to the 12th century. It was also Communist headquarters in the fighting against the Japanese, during their invasion of China from 1937, and later against the Chinese government.

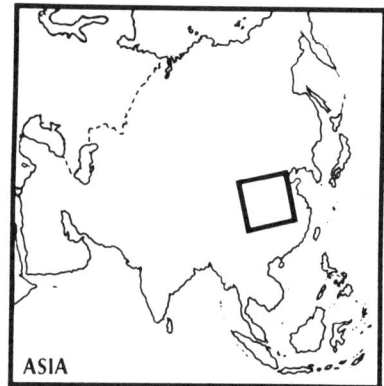

———————————— SICILIES, KINGDOM OF THE TWO ————————————

Capital: Naples

The Kingdom of the Two Sicilies comprised the island of Sicily and the southern portion of what is now the Italian mainland. During its early stamp-issuing history (from 1859), the kingdom was under the rule of the infamous King "Bomba" Ferdinand II, who gained his nickname from his habit of bombarding towns in his kingdom whose inhabitants objected to his oppressive regime.

Sikang was a province of China that was divided in 1955 between Tibet and Szechwan. It is located on the Tibetan plateau, and nearly all of it is above 10,000 feet. Within its area are the headwaters of three great rivers, the Salween, the Mekong, and the Yangtze. While it was part of the Southwest China Liberation Area, the Communist rebels issued stamps for use in the province from 1949.

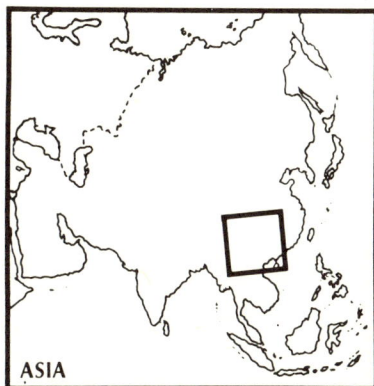

SINAI, PENINSULA OF

Area: 23,442 sq. miles
Pop: 140,000 (1970 est.)
Capital: El Arish

The Sinai Peninsula is an arid region between the Gulf of Suez and the Gulf of Aqaba, with the Mediterranean Sea to the north. It has featured in the various wars between Egypt and Israel. It currently is Egyptian territory. When Turkey ruled the area it issued a set of stamps in 1916, bearing overprints to mark its occupation.

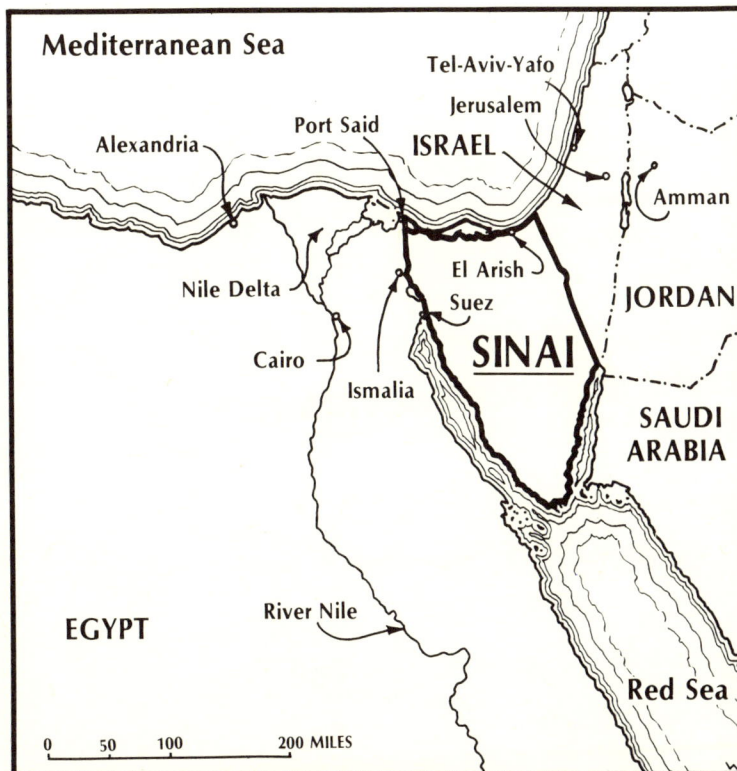

Area: 22,429 sq. miles
Pop: 1,273,228 (1970)
Capital: Culiacan

The Mexican state of Sinaloa is located on the Gulf of California on Mexico's west coast. In 1929, a revolutionary government was set up there, and a set of two stamps was prepared. Scott notes, however, that before they could be placed on sale, government forces moved in and occupied the area.

━━━━━━━━━━━ SINKIANG, AUTONOMOUS REGION OF ━━━━━━━━━━━

Area: 635,829 sq. miles
Pop: eight million (1968 est.)
Capital: Urumchi

Sinkiang is located in the western-most part of the People's Republic of China. It was through this region that the old "Silk Road" ran. This was a route by which China traded with India and Persia. It was under Chinese control from 1872, but was not made a province until 1942. It gained its present status in 1955.

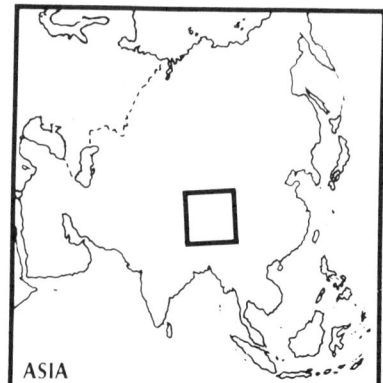

Area: 18,923 sq. miles
Pop: 4,563,460 (1970 est.)
Capital: Bratislava

When the state of Czechoslovakia was formed in 1918, Slovakia became part of the new country. When Germany dismembered the country in 1938, Slovakia broke away and declared its independence, but in 1939, Germany placed it under its "protection." Liberated towards the end of WWII, it became a constituent republic in Czechoslovakia.

SLOVENIA, STATE OF

Area: 7,819 sq. miles
Pop: 1,725,088 (1971)
Capital: Ljubljana

A part of the former Austro-Hungarian Empire, Slovenia was one of the states that joined to form the Kingdom of Yugoslavia following WWI. From 1919 to 1921, prior to the release of Yugoslavian stamps, Slovenia had its own stamps. The first issue was the well-known "Chain-Breakers" design, of which there were many varieties.

Pop: 200,000 (1900 est.)
1.7 million (1979 est.)

Smyrna (now Izmir) is a seaport on the Aegean coast of Asian Turkey. It is the third largest city in Turkey and the country's most important port in Asia. The city has a long history. It was taken by the Romans and became a city in the Byzantine Empire. It was occupied for a time by the Knights of St. John until the Turks took it over in the 15th century. It was occupied by Greek forces from 1919 to 1922.

——————— SONORA, STATE OF ———————

Area: 71,403
Pop: 191,281 (1895)
1,092,458 (1970)
Capital: Hermosillo

Sonora is a state of Mexico located in the northwestern part of the country. Stamps were issued in the state during the 1913-16 civil war. A considerble number of different varieties appeared during that period.

Area: 379,824 sq. miles
Pop: 362,897 (1899 est.)
   1,293,800 (1980)
Capital: Adelaide

South Australia was formed as a British settlement in 1836 and received its first constitution in 1856. The franchise was extended to women in 1894, and they were thus able to vote in the election of 1896. It became a state in the Commonwealth of Australia in 1901.

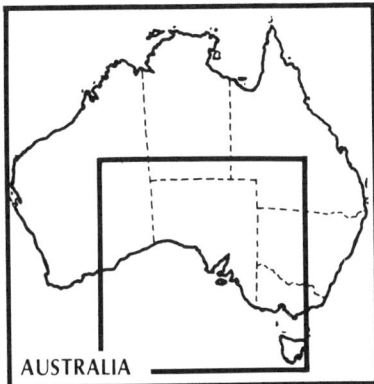

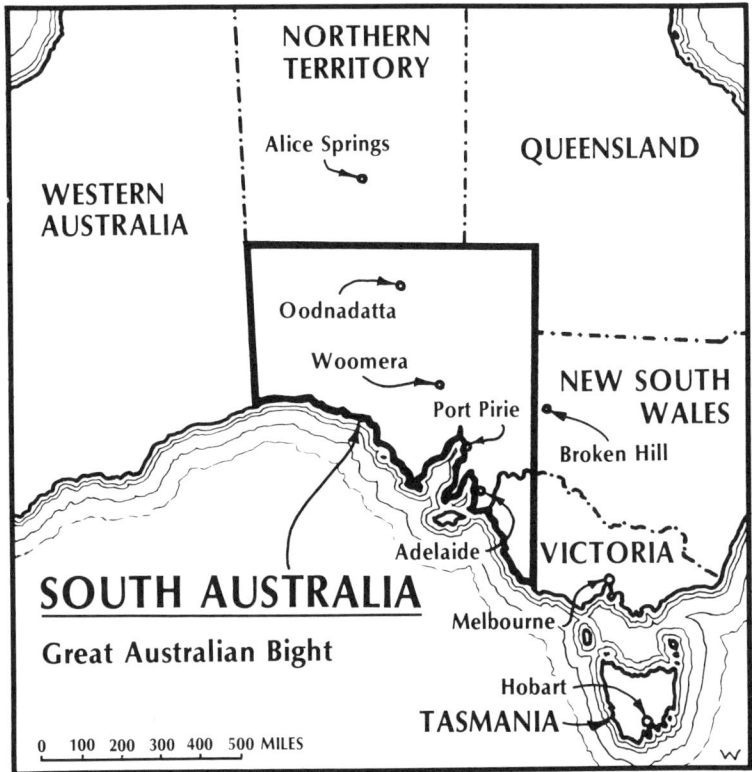

NORTHERN TERRITORY

WESTERN AUSTRALIA

QUEENSLAND

Alice Springs

Oodnadatta

Woomera

Port Pirie

NEW SOUTH WALES

Broken Hill

Adelaide

VICTORIA

SOUTH AUSTRALIA

Great Australian Bight

Melbourne

Hobart

TASMANIA

0 100 200 300 400 500 MILES

AUSTRALIA

───────SOUTHERN CAMEROON, TRUST TERRITORY OF───────

The United Kingdom Trust Territory of Southern Cameroon comprised the southern portion of the area of former German Kamerun that had been mandated to Britain following WWI. The northern part had elected to become part of Nigeria. In 1961, the territory decided to become part of the new United Republic of Cameroon. Stamps of Nigeria were overprinted "CAMEROONS U.K.T.T." for use in the area during 1960-61.

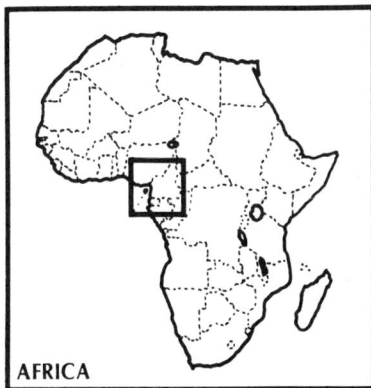

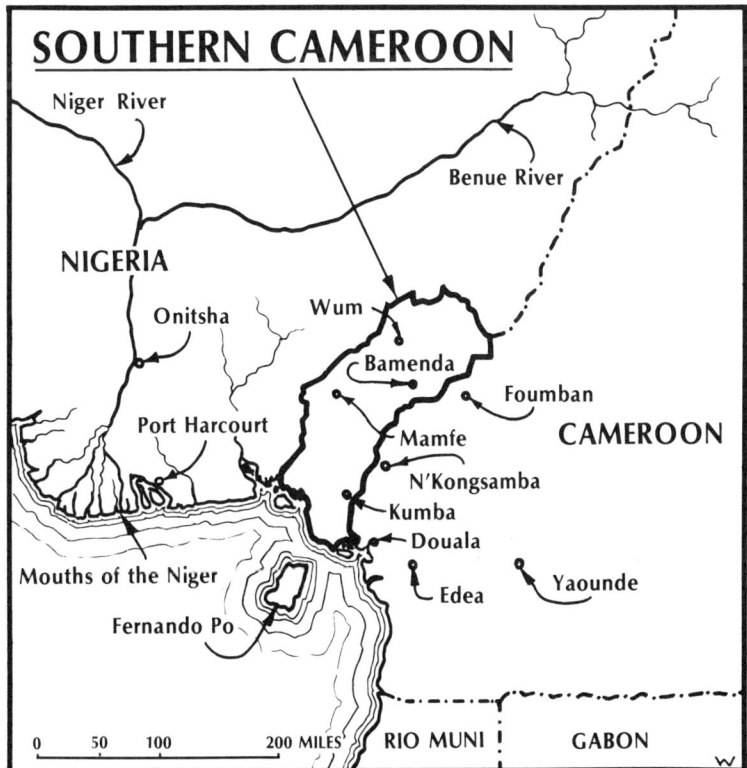

SOUTHERN CAMEROON

Niger River

Benue River

NIGERIA

Onitsha

Wum

Bamenda

Foumban

Port Harcourt

Mamfe

CAMEROON

N'Kongsamba

Kumba

Douala

Mouths of the Niger

Edea

Yaounde

Fernando Po

0 50 100 200 MILES RIO MUNI GABON

AFRICA

SOUTHERN NIGERIA

NORTHERN NIGERIA

Benue River

Niger River

Ilorin

Oyo

Ibadan

Owo

Onitsha

Lagos

Port Harcourt

GERMAN KAMERUN

Bight of Benin

Mouths of the Niger River

0   50   100   200 MILES

AFRICA

Area: 90,900 sq. miles
Pop: eight million (1906 est.)
Capital: Lagos

Formed in 1885, the British colony of Southern Nigeria included the Niger Coast Protectorate plus the colony of Lagos. It then comprised all the southern portion of Nigeria, and in 1914 it merged with Northern Nigeria to become the colony of Nigeria. Stamps were issued from 1901 to 1914.

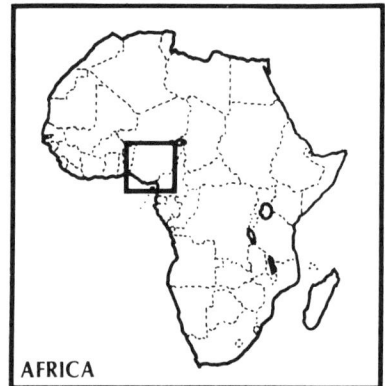

──────────SOUTHERN RHODESIA, COLONY OF──────────

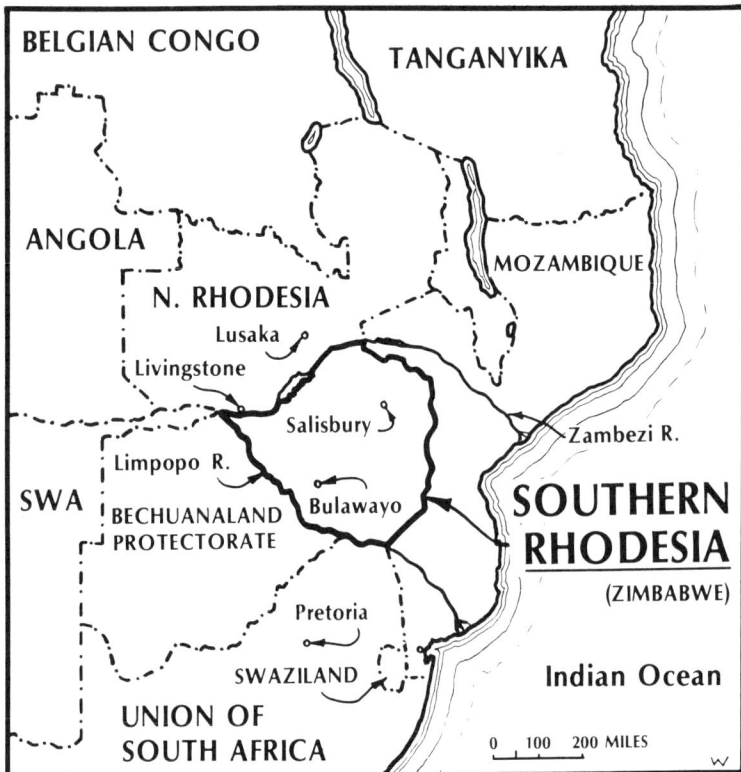

BELGIAN CONGO

TANGANYIKA

ANGOLA

N. RHODESIA

MOZAMBIQUE

Lusaka

Livingstone

Salisbury

Zambezi R.

Limpopo R.

SWA

BECHUANALAND PROTECTORATE

Bulawayo

SOUTHERN RHODESIA

(ZIMBABWE)

Pretoria

Indian Ocean

SWAZILAND

UNION OF SOUTH AFRICA

0   100   200 MILES

AFRICA

Area: 150,820 sq. miles
Pop: 5.4 million (1970 est.)
Capital: Salisbury (Harare)

The colony of Southern Rhodesia was formed in 1923 from territory previously administered by the British South Africa Company. It was part of the Federation of Rhodesia and Nyasaland from 1953 to 1963. In 1965, it declared its independence, an act Britain held to be illegal. On April 17, 1980, the colony became the independent nation of Zimbabwe.

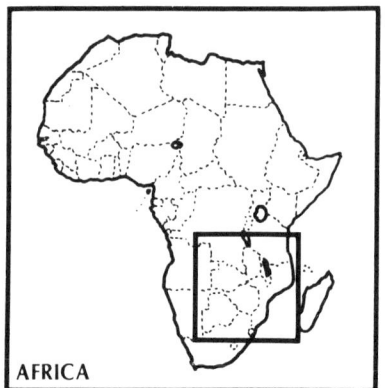

South Kasai was an area in the southern part of Kasai Province in what was then the Congo Democratic Republic (now Zaire), based on the town of Bakwanga. In 1960 the area declared its independence and did not rejoin the Congo until October 1962. Stamps were released during the independent period, although not all catalogs recognize them. Gibbons lists a total of nine and notes that others were prepared but not sent to the area.

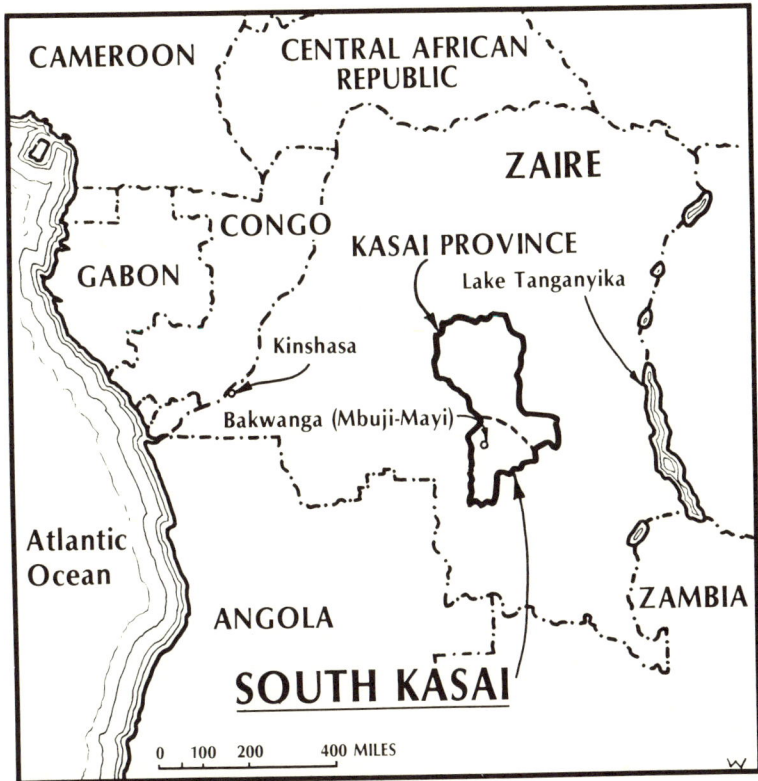

SOUTH VIETNAM, REPUBLIC OF

Area: 67,108 sq. miles
Pop: 18,332,000 (1970 est.)
Capital: Saigon

The Republic of Vietnam was established in 1955 in the southern portion of Vietnam. A hostile Communist regime was in power in the northern region, and the boundary was along the 17th parallel. Communist pressure on the south grew, and despite massive US aid, the entire area was overrun. South Vietnam ceased to exist in April 1975. Stamps were issued from 1955 to 1975.

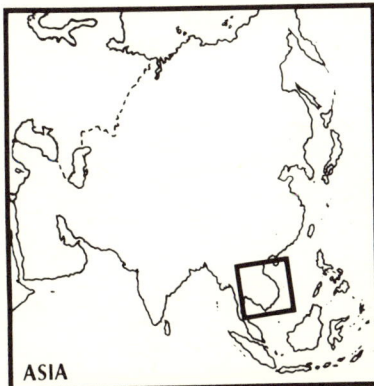

Area: 18,000 sq. miles (approx.)
Pop: one million (approx. 1950)
Capital: Tetuan

Spanish Morocco was established in 1912, with French permission and British approval, in the northern part of Morocco. Under an agreement with Britain it had become an area of French influence. The colony joined French Morocco to become independent in 1956.

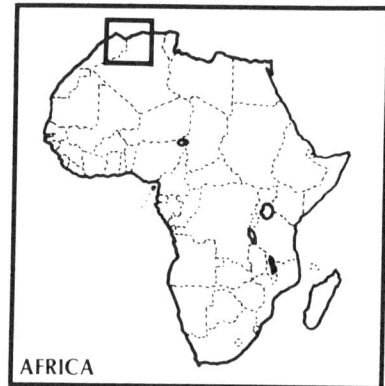

——————— SPANISH SAHARA, COLONY OF ———————

Area: 102,703 sq. miles
Pop: 76,425 (1970)
Capital: Aaiun

Proclaimed in 1884, Spanish Sahara became an overseas territory in 1958. It included the area of Rio de Oro and Cape Juby. The area was relinquished by Spain in 1976 and divided between Morocco and Mauritania. Mauritania subsequently turned over its portion to Morocco. The UN does not recognize Moroccan authority and refers to the area as Western Sahara.

Area: 5,000 sq. miles (approx.)
Capital: Vryburg

The Republic of Stellaland was established in 1884 by the Boers of South Africa. It was an attempt to annex territory belonging to the Bechuana People. The state was dis-established by the British and became part of British Bechuanaland in 1885. Stamps were issued in 1884-85.

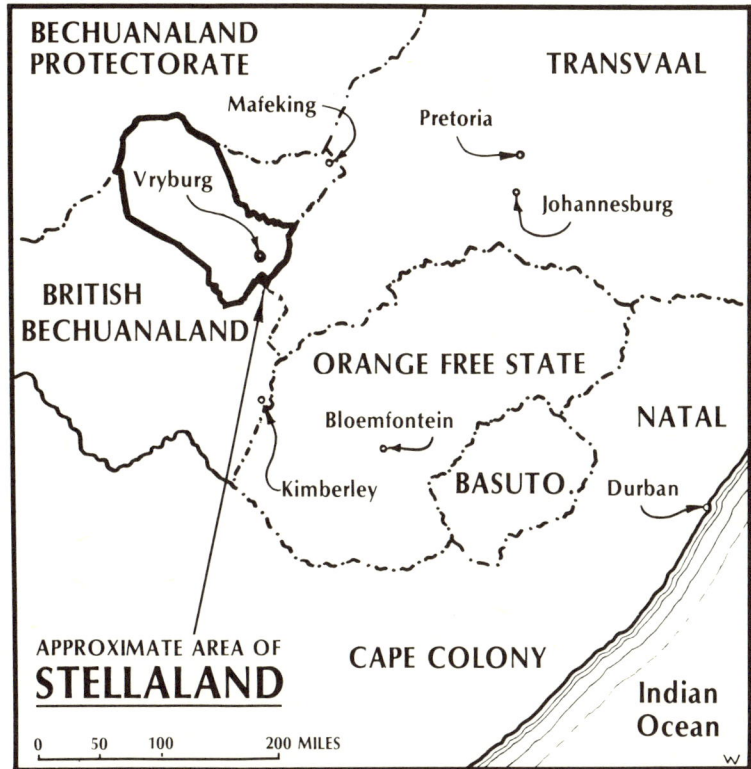

AFRICA

BECHUANALAND PROTECTORATE

TRANSVAAL

Mafeking

Pretoria

Vryburg

Johannesburg

BRITISH BECHUANALAND

ORANGE FREE STATE

Bloemfontein

NATAL

Kimberley

BASUTO.

Durban

APPROXIMATE AREA OF
STELLALAND

CAPE COLONY

Indian Ocean

0 50 100 200 MILES

STRAITS SETTLEMENTS, CROWN COLONY OF

Area: 1,355 sq. miles
Pop: 1,119,186 (1935)
Capital: Singapore

The Crown Colony of the Straits Settlements was formed in 1867. It comprised Malacca, Penang with Province Wellesley, and Singapore on the Malay Peninsula, plus Christmas Island in the Indian Ocean, Cocos (Keeling) Islands, and Labuan (from 1906). The colony was disbanded in 1946. Stamps were issued beginning in 1867.

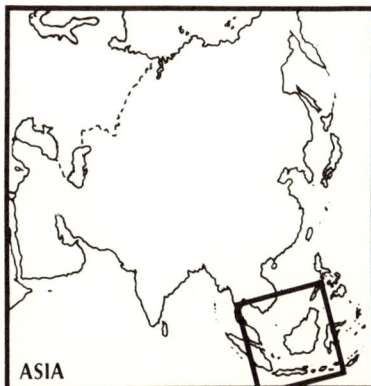

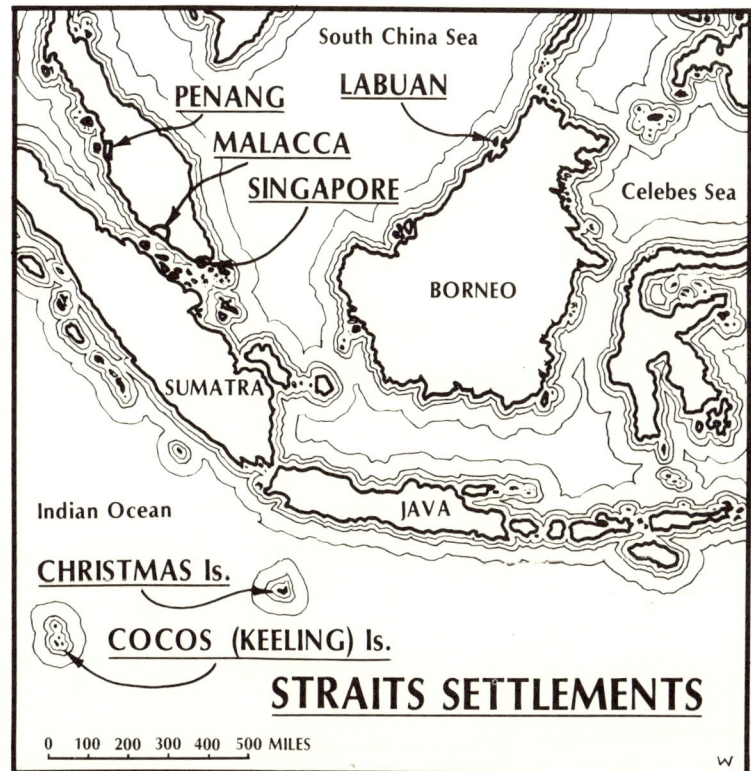

ASIA

South China Sea

PENANG

LABUAN

MALACCA

SINGAPORE

Celebes Sea

SUMATRA

BORNEO

Indian Ocean

JAVA

CHRISTMAS Is.

COCOS (KEELING) Is.

STRAITS SETTLEMENTS

0 100 200 300 400 500 MILES

Area: 6,326 sq. miles
Pop: 1,191,000 (1971)
Capital: Graz

Styria is a province of Austria, located in the central part of the country. It is a mountainous area containing the rivers Mur, Murz, and Enns. Major cities are Graz, Knittelfeld, and Bruck. Its southern border lies on the Austrian frontier with Yugoslavia. Stamps were issued in 1945, under the Allied military administration.

———— SUDETENLAND OF CZECHOSLOVAKIA ————

Area: 8,719 sq. miles

The Sudetenland was the name applied to areas of Czechoslovakia where there were German-speaking inhabitants. Germany seized the Sudetenland in September 1938, an act permitted by Britain and France in a vain attempt to appease German expansionist aims. The area was restored to Czechoslovakia at the end of WWII. Czech stamps were overprinted for use in some Sudetenland cities prior to the German takeover.

Area: 112,493 sq. miles
Capital: Hu-ho-hao-t'e

Suiyuan is a former province of China incorporated into the area of Inner Mongolia. It was located to the west of Peking. The province was in the Communist North China Liberation Area and used the stamps issued for that area beginning in 1946.

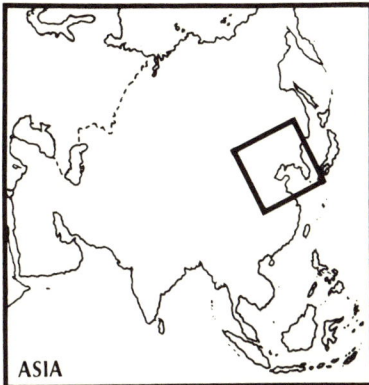

USSR

Irkutsk
Chita

Ulan Bator

MONGOLIA

Peking (Beijing)

Kweuhsui (Hu-ho-hao-t'e)

KOREA

SUIYUAN

Shanghai
Yellow Sea

CHINA

0 100 200 300 400 500 MILES

ASIA

SUMATRA, ISLAND OF

Area: 182,561 sq. miles
Pop: 19,840,000 (1970 est.)

Sumatra is a large island that forms the western part of the Republic of Indonesia. It was formerly in the Netherlands Indies and was invaded and occupied by the Japanese during WWII. Stamps were issued by Japanese authorities for use on the island during the occupation.

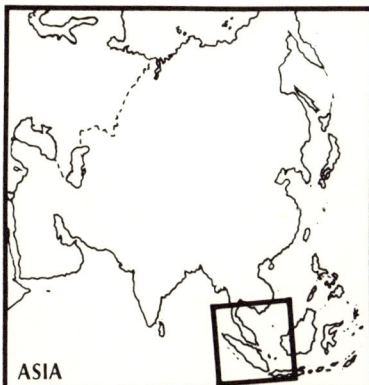

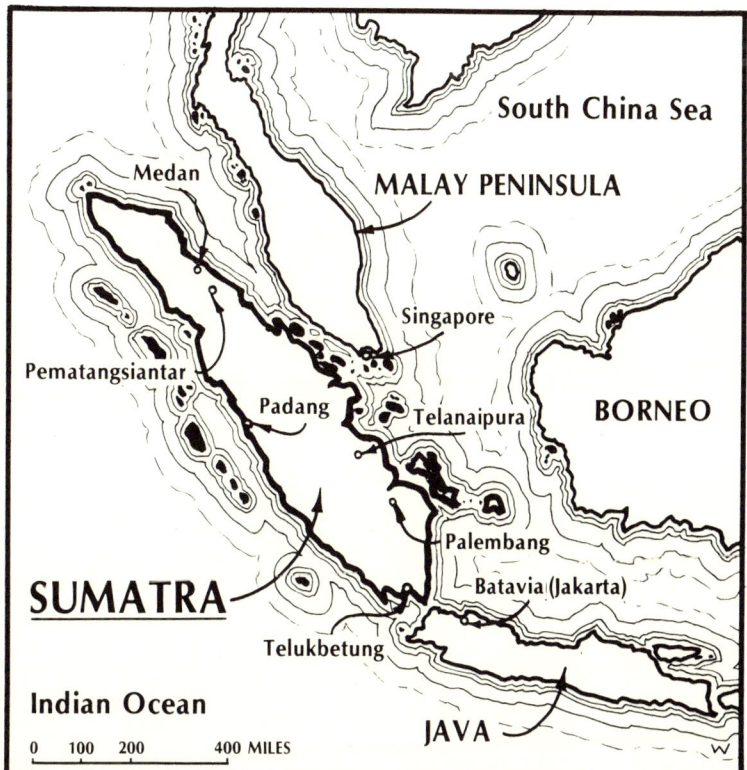

South China Sea

Medan

MALAY PENINSULA

Singapore

Pematangsiantar

BORNEO

Padang

Telanaipura

Palembang

SUMATRA

Batavia (Jakarta)

Telukbetung

Indian Ocean

JAVA

0 100 200 400 MILES

ASIA

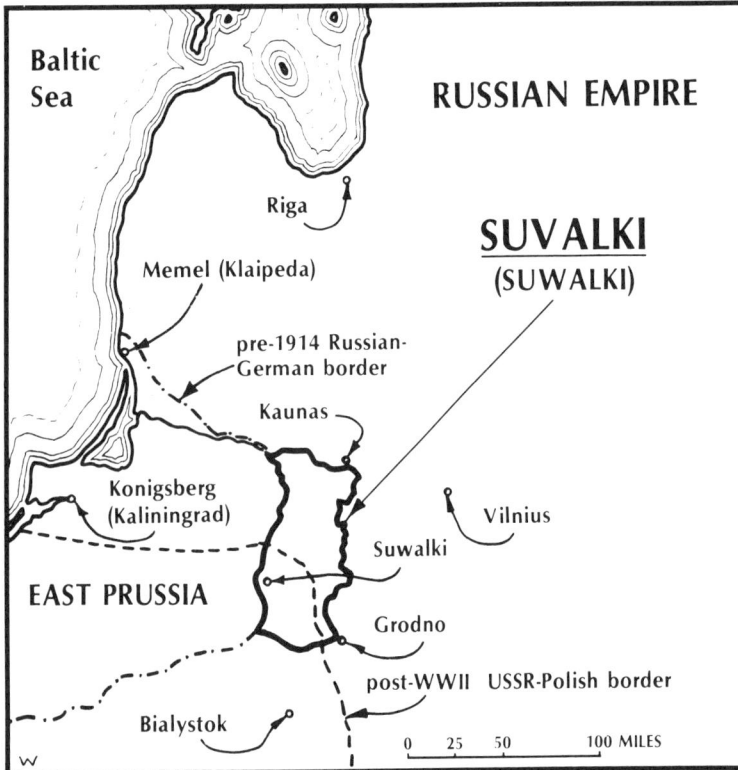

Pop: 604,973 (1897)

A former province of the Russian Empire bordering on German East Prussia, Suvalki was divided at the end of WWI, with the northern part going to Lithuania and the southern portion becoming part of Poland. The area is currently divided between Poland and the USSR. Stamps were issued for the area in 1940 and consisted of Lithuanian stamps overprinted "LTSR" by Soviet occupying forces.

SZECHWAN, PROVINCE OF

Area: 219,691 sq. miles
Pop: 70 million (1968 est.)
Capital: Ch'eng-tu

Following the outbreak of war with Japan in 1937, as that country began its invasion of China, the Chinese government moved to Chungking in Szechwan Province. In 1933 and in 1949, regional overprints and surcharges were issued for use in the western portion of the province.

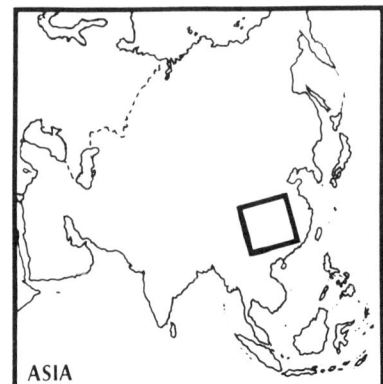

Pop: 118,490 (1970)

A city in southern Hungary, near the Yugoslav border, Szeged is a port on the Tisza River. Stamps were issued there in 1919 by the "Hungarian National Government," an anti-Bolshevist government that opposed the regime then in power in Hungary.

Map: SZEGED, Hungary, with Budapest, Tisza River, Danube River, Yugoslavia, Belgrade, Romania, Arad, Timisoara, Kolozsvar (Cluj), Czechoslovakia, USSR, post-WWII borders. EUROPE inset.

TACNA, DEPARTMENT OF

Area: 5,701 sq. miles
Pop: 90,600 (1969 est.)
Capital: Tacna

Tacna is a province located in the extreme south of Peru. It was partially occupied by Chile from 1884. A plebiscite was held prior to 1930, when the region was divided between the two countries. Stamps were issued in 1925-28 by Peru to help defray the plebiscite costs.

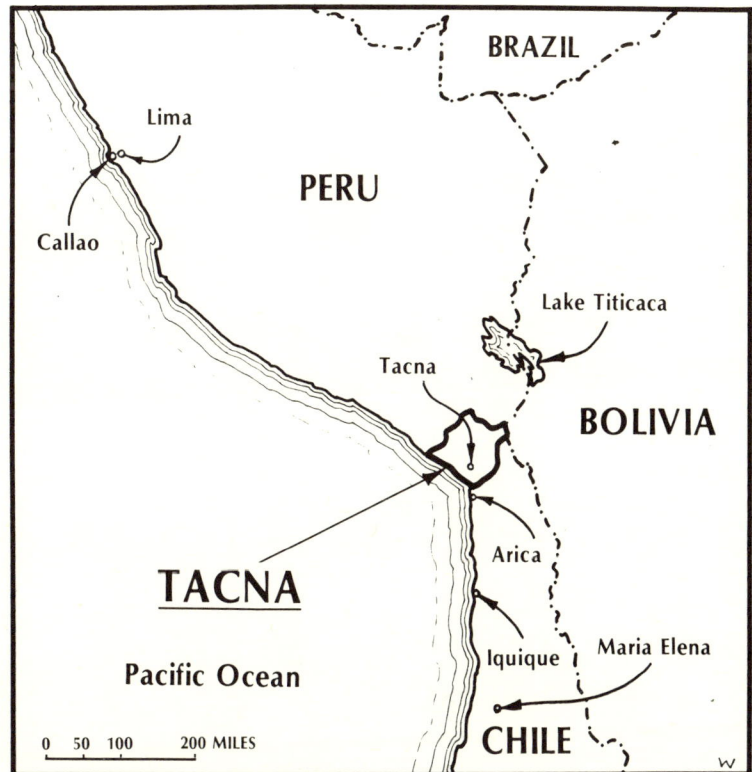

Map: TACNA, Peru, with Lima, Callao, Lake Titicaca, Bolivia, Arica, Iquique, Maria Elena, Chile, Pacific Ocean, Brazil. SOUTH AMERICA inset.

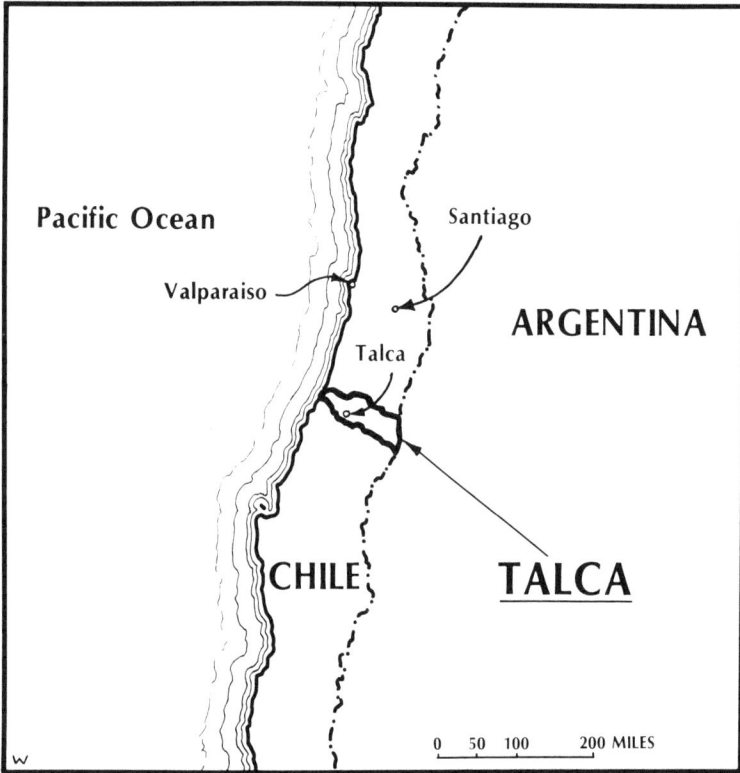

Pop: 80,777 (1966 est.)

The capital city of a province of the same name in central Chile, Talca is a commercial and railroad center. In 1942, a 10c postal tax stamp was sold in the city for the purpose of raising funds to pay for the city's bicentennial celebration. It was inscribed "Bicentenario de Talca."

Pacific Ocean

Santiago

Valparaiso

ARGENTINA

Talca

CHILE

TALCA

0   50 100   200 MILES

SOUTH AMERICA

——————TANGIER, INTERNATIONAL ZONE——————

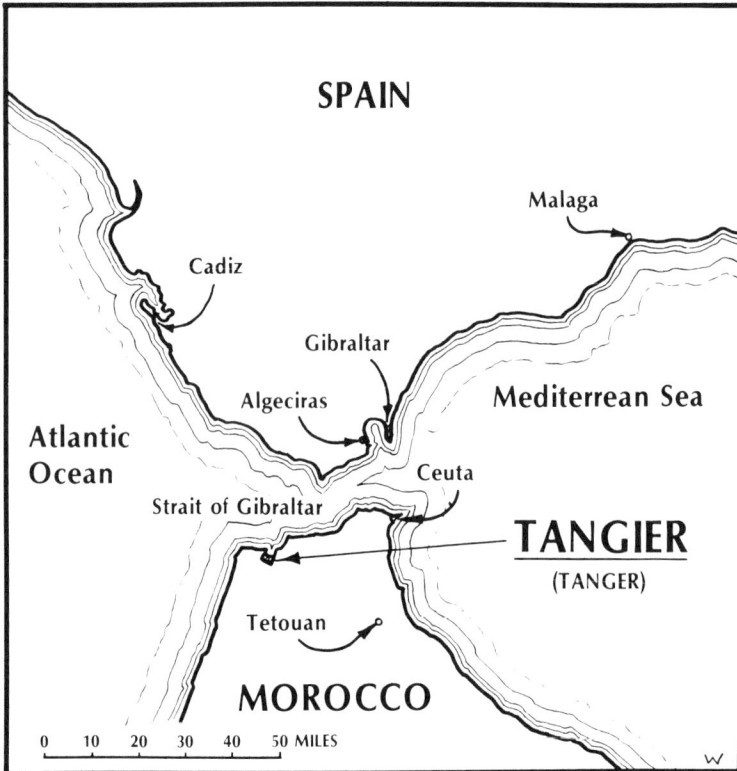

Area: 225 sq. miles
Pop: 102,306 (1940)

The International Zone of Tangier was established in 1923-24 by agreement among Britain, France, and Spain. It provided for permanent neutralization of the area and government by an international commission. The zone was administered by Spain during the WWII period and abolished in 1956. Stamps were issued for use in the zone by Britain, France, and Spain.

SPAIN

Malaga

Cadiz

Gibraltar

Mediterrean Sea

Algeciras

Atlantic Ocean

Ceuta

Strait of Gibraltar

TANGIER
(TANGER)

Tetouan

MOROCCO

0 10 20 30 40 50 MILES

AFRICA

Area: 65,380 sq. miles
Pop: 231,000 (1970)
Capital: Kyzyl

Until 1911, Tannu Tuva was part of Mongolia. It was nominally independent from 1911 to 1914, then under Russian protection until 1917, when it came under Chinese rule. It was independent from 1921 until 1944, when the Soviet Union took it. Stamps were released from 1926, and a number of issues appeared through the 1930s.

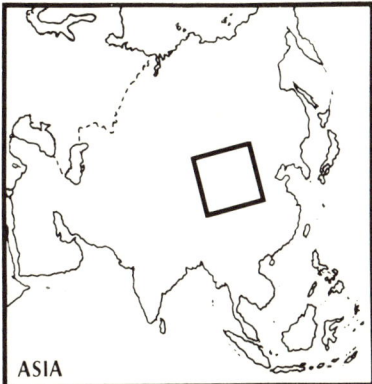

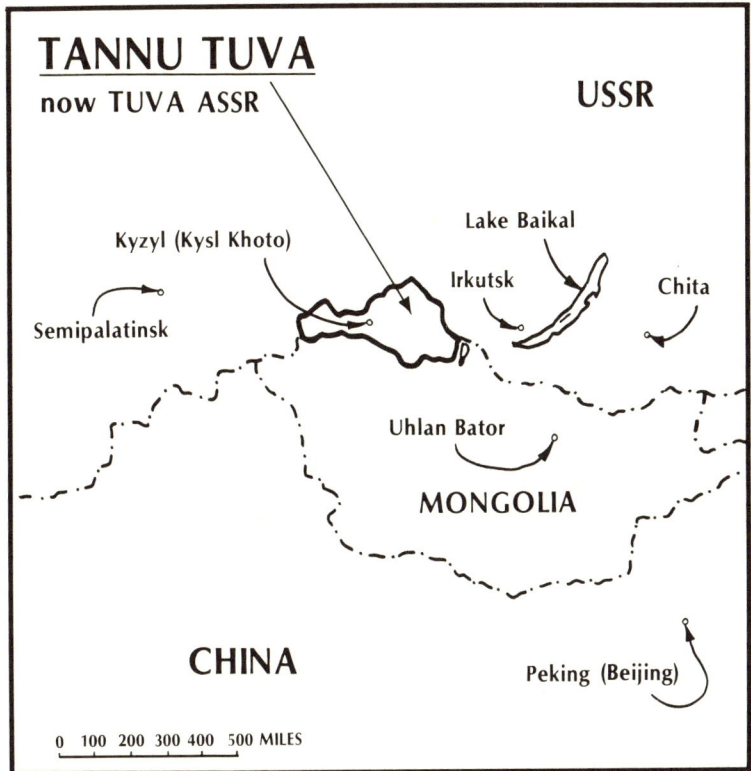

TANNU TUVA
now TUVA ASSR
USSR

Kyzyl (Kysl Khoto)

Lake Baikal

Irkutsk

Chita

Semipalatinsk

Uhlan Bator

MONGOLIA

CHINA

Peking (Beijing)

0 100 200 300 400 500 MILES

ASIA

TASMANIA, COLONY OF

Area: 26,383 sq. miles
Pop: 177,340 (1899 est.)
Capital: Hobart

Named Tasmania in 1853, the island located to the south of Australia had been called Van Diemen's Land since it was discovered by Tasman in 1652. Taken by Great Britain in 1803, it was used as a penal colony. Stamps were first used in 1853, and the colony became one of the states of the Commonwealth of Australia in 1901.

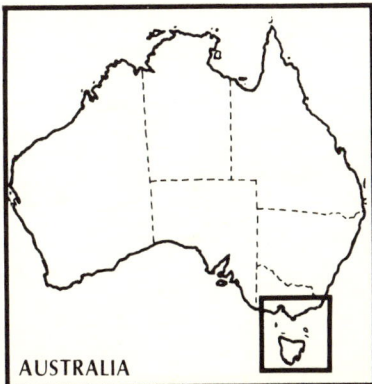

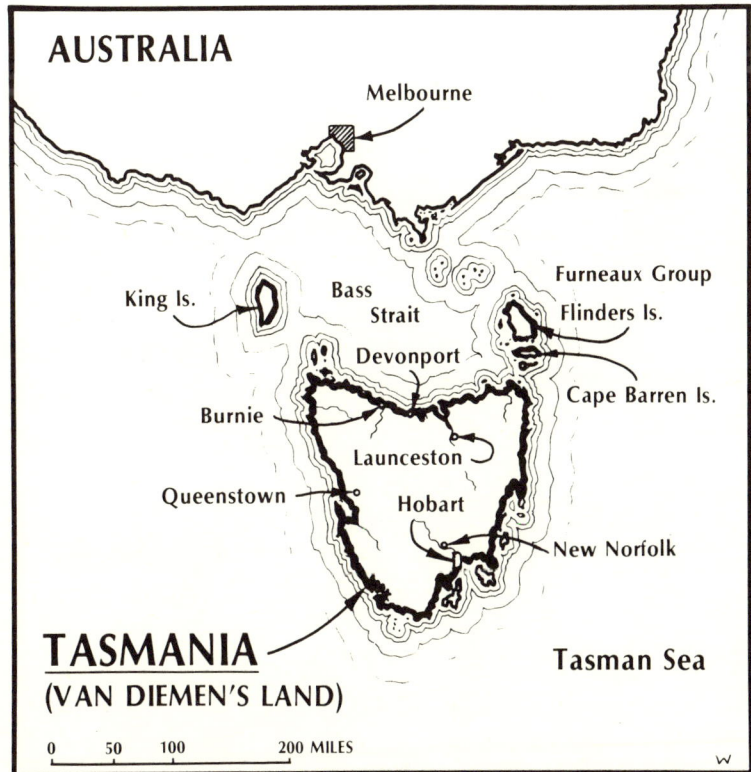

AUSTRALIA

Melbourne

King Is.

Bass
Strait

Furneaux Group

Flinders Is.

Devonport

Cape Barren Is.

Burnie

Launceston

Queenstown

Hobart

New Norfolk

TASMANIA
(VAN DIEMEN'S LAND)

Tasman Sea

0 50 100 200 MILES

AUSTRALIA

Pop: 218,510 (1969 est.)

Tegucigalpa is the capital city of the Central American country of Honduras. It is one of the few world capitals that does not possess a railroad link with other parts of the country. Founded as a gold and silver-mining center about 1579, it has been the Honduran capital since 1880. An 1877 stamp issue is known as the Tegucigalpa Issue.

TEMESVAR (TIMISOARA), CITY OF

Pop: 192,616 (1970 est.)

Temesvar, now Timisoara, is a Romanian city located near the border with Hungary and Yugoslavia. It was once part of the Austro-Hungarian Empire. During WWI it was occupied by Serbian forces, but at the end of the war, the occupation was taken over by Romania. Stamps were issued by both administrations.

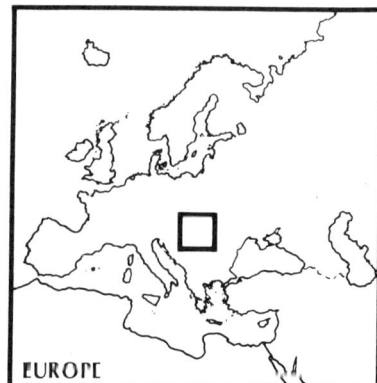

Area: 5,715 sq. miles
Pop: 170,284 (1970)
Capital: Teruel

Teruel is a province of Spain located in the eastern portion of the country. In 1868-69, a set of provisional stamps was released for use in the province. They comprise stamps of Spain handstamped "HPN" in black. Considering the prices given to them in the catalogs, it is not surprising that counterfeits exist.

EUROPE

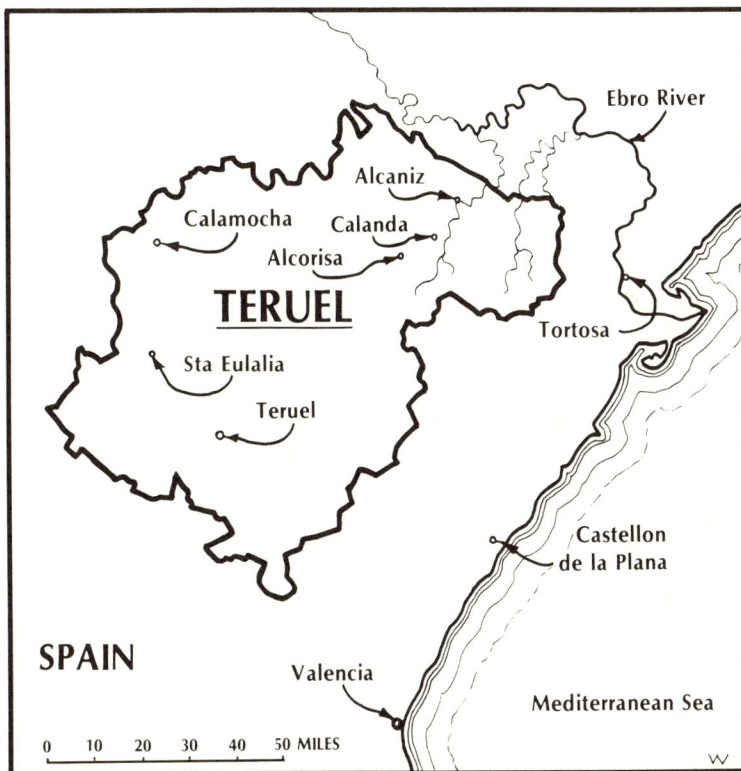

SPAIN

Ebro River
Alcaniz
Calamocha
Calanda
Alcorisa
TERUEL
Tortosa
Sta Eulalia
Teruel
Castellon de la Plana
Valencia
Mediterranean Sea

0 10 20 30 40 50 MILES

Area: 38,886 sq. miles
Pop: 492,233 (1970)
Capital: Tete

A district in the western part of the former Portuguese colony of Mozambique, now the People's Republic of Mozambique, Tete had its own stamps during 1913-14. The first were overprints and surcharges on Portuguese colonial stamps, but in 1914 an issue of the Ceres key type inscribed for Tete was released. It was replaced by stamps of the colony of Mozambique.

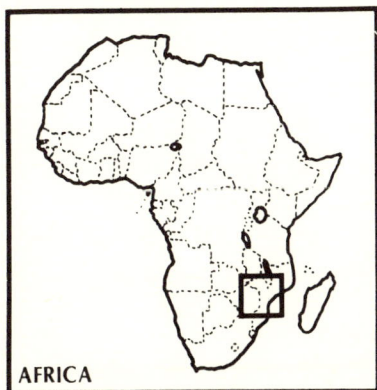

AFRICA

BELGIAN CONGO (ZAIRE)
MOZAMBIQUE
Vila Coutinho
Fingoe
Zumbo
Furancungo
TETE
Br. CENTRAL AFRICA (MALAWI)
Zomba
Blantyre
Quelimane
Sena
S. RHODESIA (ZIMBABWE)
Zambeze River
Beira
Indian Ocean

0 50 100 200 MILES

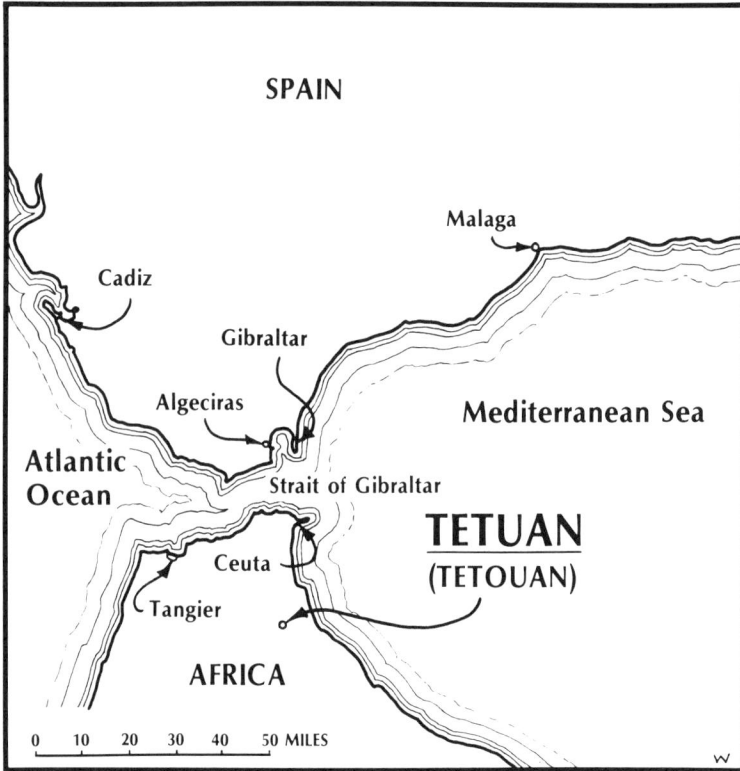

Pop: 101,352 (1960)

Tetuan, now Tetouan, was the capital city of Spanish Morocco and is now a city in the Kingdom of Morocco. It is about 25 miles to the south of Cueta. During 1908, two issues of stamps of the Spanish Offices in Morocco were hand-stamped with "TETUAN" for use from that city.

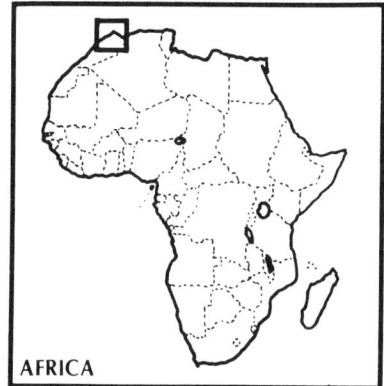

———————THESSALY, REGION OF———————

Area: 5,382 sq. miles
Pop: 659,243 (1971)
Chief town: Larisa

A region in Greece, Thessaly was ceded to that country by Turkey in 1881. It is an area that has played a prominent role in classical Greek history and was the scene of several great battles. During its 1897-98 war with Greece, Turkey issued a set of distinctive eight-sided stamps for use by its troops then in the area.

The House of Thurn and Taxis was an organization that operated postal services under monopolies granted by rulers of the various European states it served. From the 1500s to 1867, it ran a mail service that at its height served most of Europe. It employed 20,000 people and had offices in most European cities. A yellow trumpet on the front and back of a messenger's jacket was a familiar sight on European highways. As states developed their own government organizations, they grew more inclined to want their own postal services also, and so the network of Thurn and Taxis services was gradually eroded. The Napoleonic Wars caused complications in communications and further stimulated feelings of nationalism. After those wars, Thurn and Taxis was never to fully recover its previous scope. In 1852, it released its first adhesive postage stamps. They were divided into two issues, one with denominations expressed in silbergroschen (groschen) and thalers for use in northern states, and the other in kreuzer and gulden for use in southern areas. On the map, areas numbered 1, 3, 9, 10, 11, 12, 15, 16, and 18 were northern areas; the remainder used stamps for the southern group. In 1867, the few remaining services were sold to

EUROPE

Prussia, and the name disappeared from the mail routes of Europe.

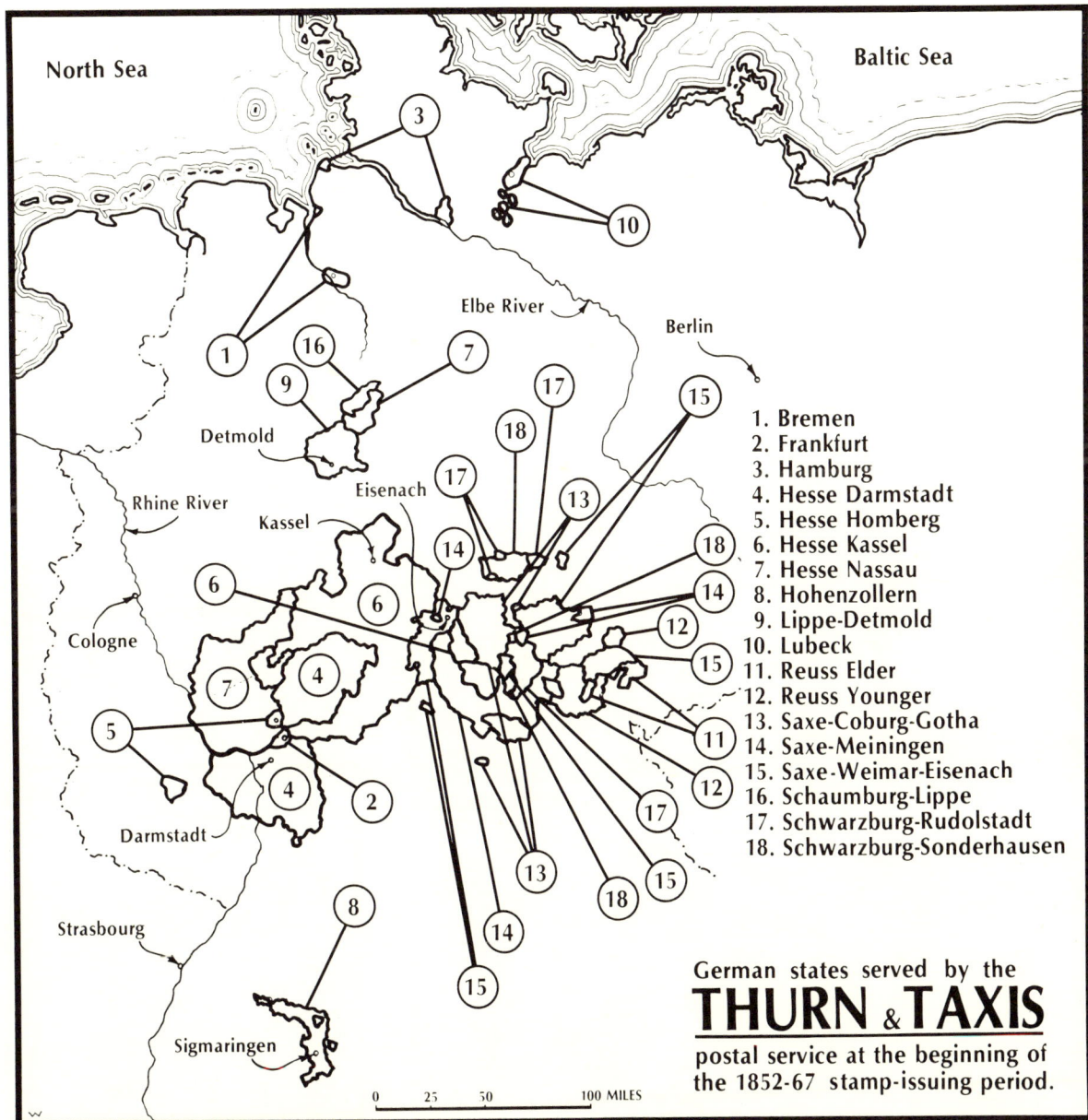

North Sea

Baltic Sea

Elbe River

Berlin

Detmold

Rhine River

Eisenach

Kassel

Cologne

Darmstadt

Strasbourg

Sigmaringen

1. Bremen
2. Frankfurt
3. Hamburg
4. Hesse Darmstadt
5. Hesse Homberg
6. Hesse Kassel
7. Hesse Nassau
8. Hohenzollern
9. Lippe-Detmold
10. Lubeck
11. Reuss Elder
12. Reuss Younger
13. Saxe-Coburg-Gotha
14. Saxe-Meiningen
15. Saxe-Weimar-Eisenach
16. Schaumburg-Lippe
17. Schwarzburg-Rudolstadt
18. Schwarzburg-Sonderhausen

German states served by the

THURN & TAXIS

postal service at the beginning of the 1852-67 stamp-issuing period.

0   25   50   100 MILES

Area: 471,660 sq. miles
Pop: 1.4 million (1968 est.)
Capital: Lhasa

A remote state in Asia, Tibet was occupied in 1950 by Communist Chinese forces and, while nominally autonomous, is firmly within the People's Republic of China. Beginning in 1912, Tibet had its own local stamps. Mail to points outside Tibet had to bear stamps of a neighboring country, usually India.

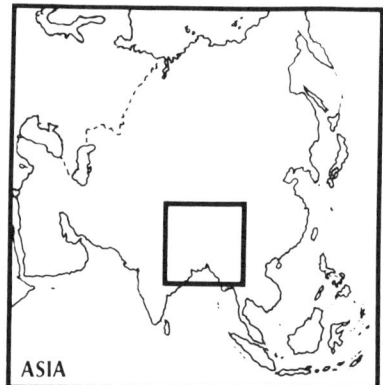

TIENTSIN, CITY OF

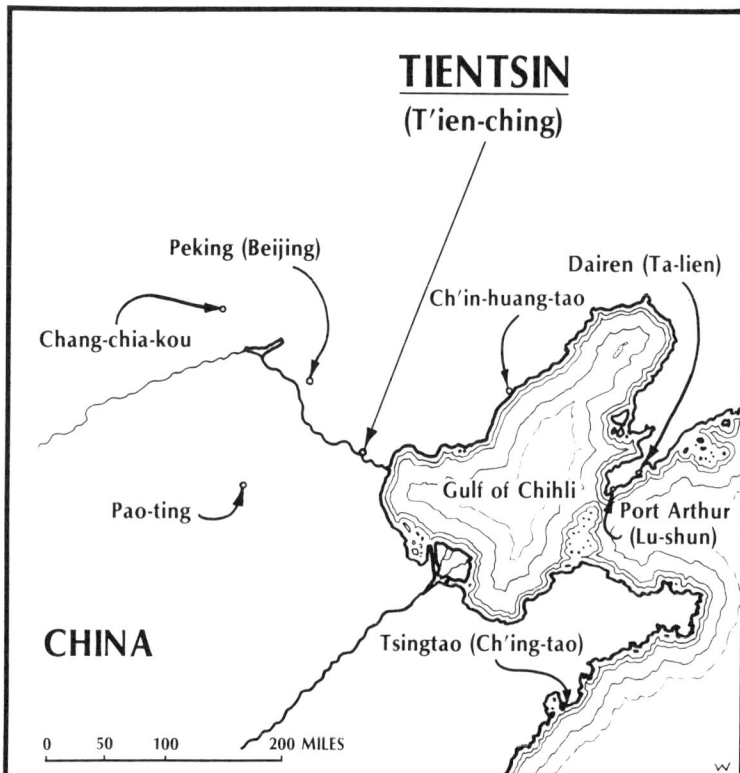

Pop: 4.5 million (1970 est.)

The city of Tientsin (T'ien-ching) is a major seaport and industrial center about 80 miles from Peking in the People's Republic of China. It was one of the Treaty Ports (q.v.) and the scene of heavy fighting during the Boxer Rebellion of 1900. In the early 1900s, German stamps were overprinted "CHINA" for use there. Italy's stamps were overprinted "Tientsin" and surcharged for use from its post office there from 1917 to 1921.

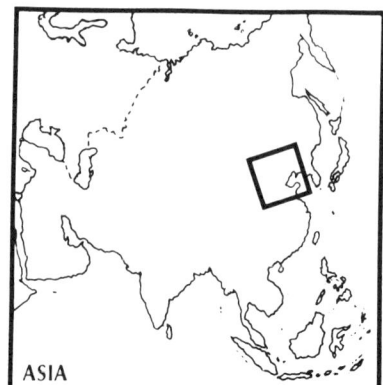

Tlacotalpan is a small town located in the Mexican state of Veracruz on the Gulf of Mexico. In 1856 a local stamp was issued there. The Gibbons catalog describes it as a monogram "I.M.C." in fancy script capitals on a black rectangle in a shaded oval with a pen surcharge "Habilitado ½" at the foot of the stamp.

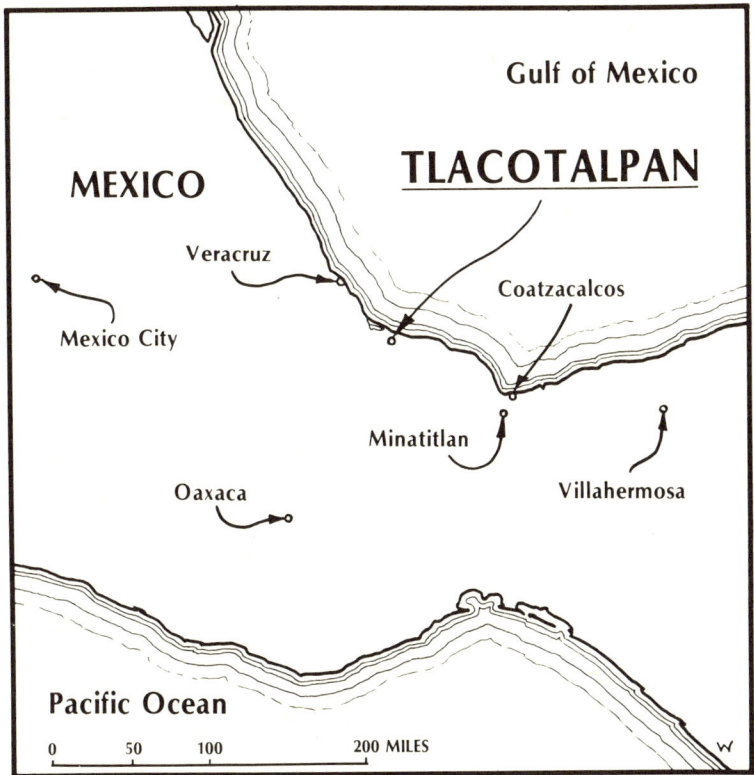

Gulf of Mexico

MEXICO

TLACOTALPAN

Veracruz

Coatzacalcos

Mexico City

Minatitlan

Villahermosa

Oaxaca

Pacific Ocean

0   50   100   200 MILES

NORTH AMERICA

── TOBAGO, COLONY OF ──────────

Area: 116 sq. miles
Pop: 39,280 (1970)
Capital: Scarborough

An island in the Lesser Antilles of the West Indies, Tobago is located northeast of Trinidad. It currently forms part of the independent Republic of Trinidad and Tobago. English since 1814, it had previously changed hands several times between English, Dutch, and French forces. It was united with Trinidad in 1898.

Caribbean Sea

GRENADA   **TOBAGO**

Port of Spain

TRINIDAD

Caracas

mouths of the Orinoco

VENEZUELA

Ciudad Guayana

Ciudad Bolivar

Orinoco River

Parlatuvier

Plymouth   Castara

Buccoo Reef

Little Tobago
Roxborough
Pembroke

airport

Scarborough   **TOBAGO**

0   50   100   200 MILES   0   5   10   20 MILES

SOUTH AMERICA

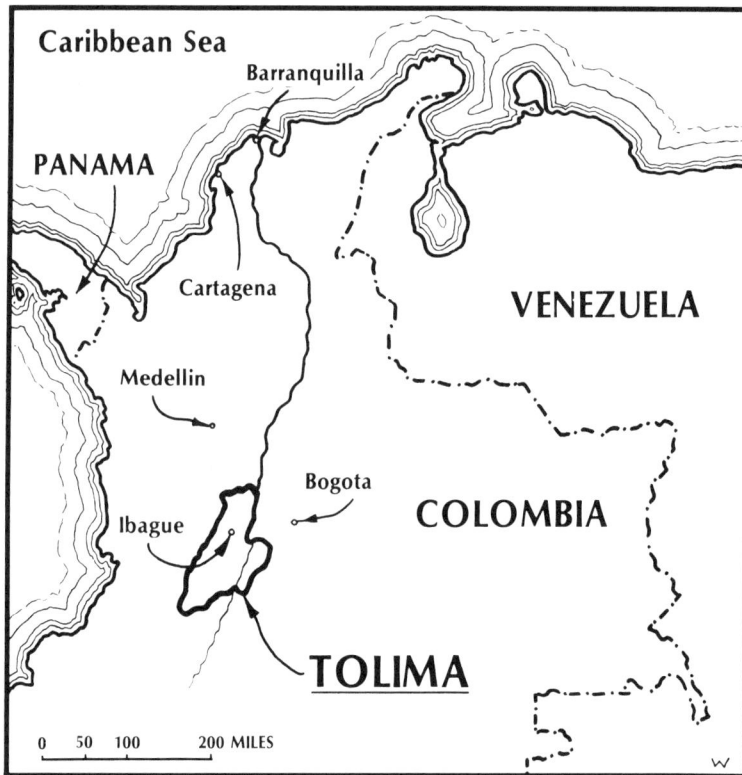

Area: 9,006 sq. miles
Pop: 879,751 (1968 est.)
Capital: Ibague

Originally one of the states of the Granadine Confederation that joined to form the country of Colombia in 1886, Tolima issued its own stamps from 1870 to 1904, when stamps of Colombia went into use.

———————TRANSJORDAN, MANDATE OF———————

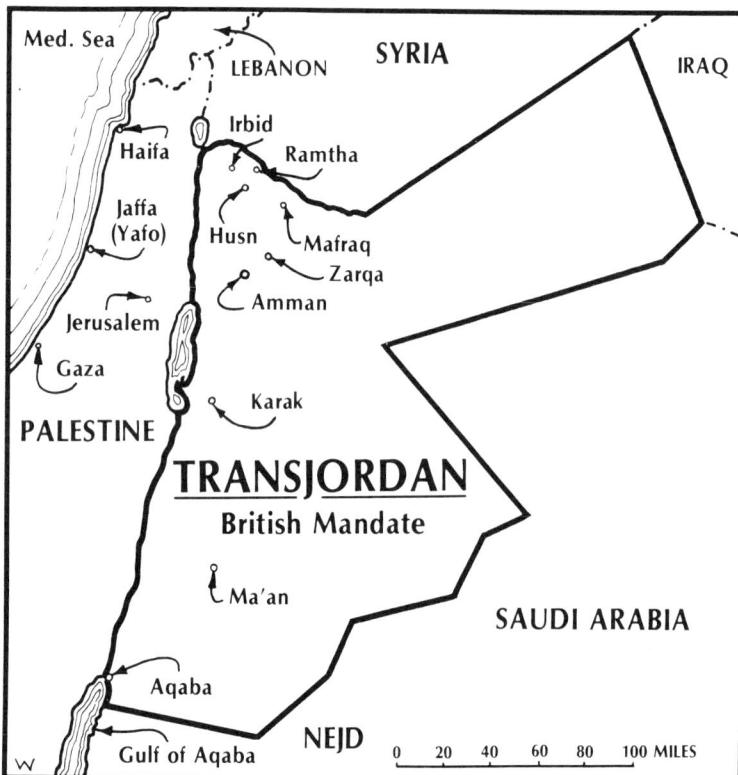

Area: 37,737 sq. miles
(includes West Bank)
Pop: 2,348,000 (1970 est.
including West Bank)
Capital: Amman

A mandate area, Transjordan was created from ex-Turkish territory taken by British forces during WWI. In 1923, it was made an independent state under British protection. Stamps were first issued in 1920 during the mandate period.

TRANSVAAL (SOUTH AFRICAN REPUBLIC)

Area: 109,621 sq. miles
Pop: 1,094,156 (1898)
Capital: Pretoria

The first settlement in the Transvaal was by Boers in 1838. The South African Republic was formed in 1856. It was annexed by Britain in 1877-81, but independence was again granted. It became a British crown colony in 1900 and joined the Union of South Africa in 1910. It is now part of the Republic of South Africa.

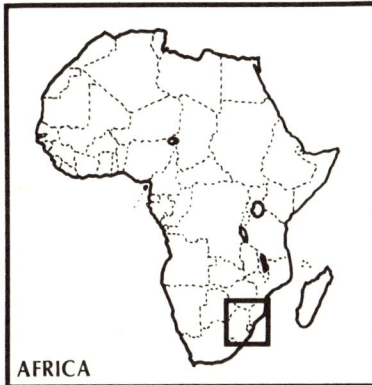

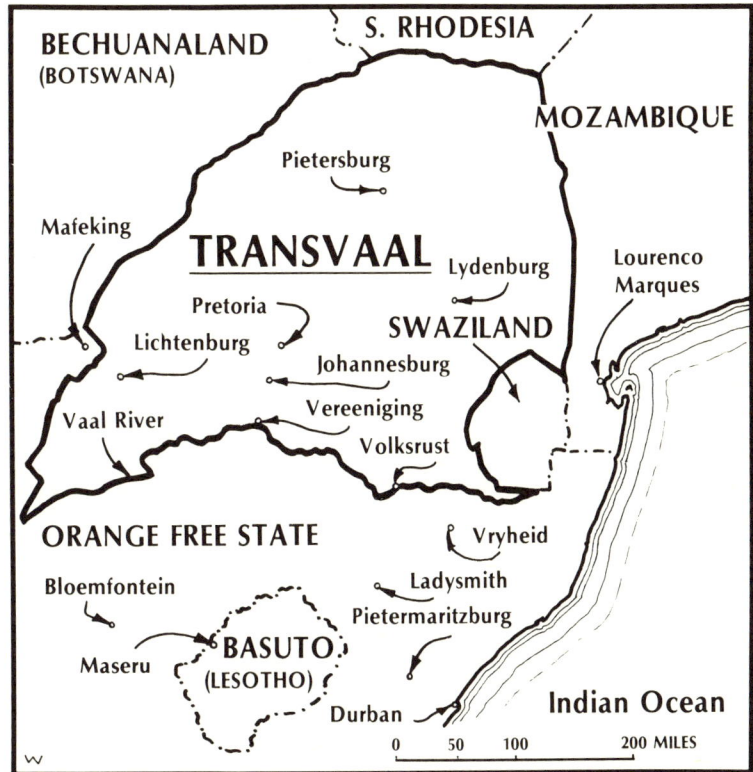

TRANSYLVANIA

Area: 21,297 sq. miles
Pop: 2,247,049 (1890)
Chief town: Klausenburg (Cluj)

Transylvania was located within the Austro-Hungarian Empire until it was taken by Romania during WWI. It remains part of that country. A portion was occupied by Hungary during WWII but was restored at the end of the war. A number of occupation overprints on Hungarian stamps were made in 1919 by Romanian occupying forces.

ASIA

The so-called Treaty Ports were cities in China and Japan at which foreign nations had special status, including the right to operate their own post offices. The British offices were under the British Post Office in London until Jan. 1, 1868, after which they were administered from Hong Kong. Eventually, Germany, France, Italy, Japan, Russia, and the US had postal facilities at various Treaty Ports. In 1917, stamps of Hong Kong were overprinted "CHINA" for use at the Treaty Ports. The British offices in Treaty Ports were closed in 1922. US stamps were overprinted "SHANGHAI" and surcharged for use at the US postal agency in that city from 1919 to 1922. Germany overprinted its stamps "CHINA"; Italy overprinted its stamps "TIENTSIN" and "PECHINO" (Peking) for use at those places; and Japan overprinted stamps in Japanese for Treaty Port use. Russia also overprinted stamps beginning in 1899. Foreign activities at Treaty Ports were related to commercial trade and since businessmen required fast and reliable communications, postal facilities were of prime importance.

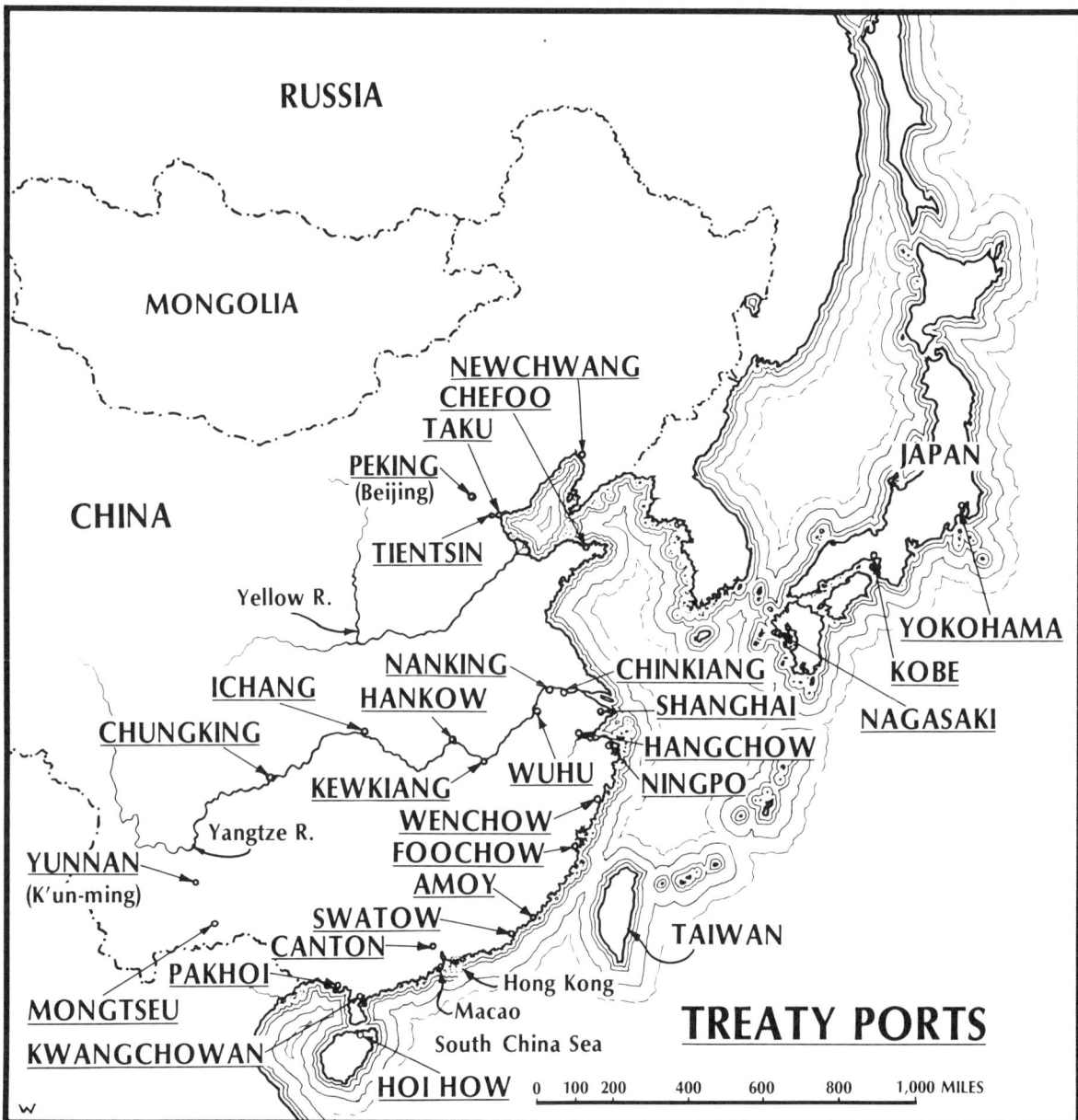

RUSSIA

MONGOLIA

CHINA

NEWCHWANG
CHEFOO
TAKU
PEKING (Beijing)
TIENTSIN

Yellow R.

JAPAN

YOKOHAMA
KOBE
NAGASAKI

ICHANG
NANKING
HANKOW
CHUNGKING
KEWKIANG
Yangtze R.
WUHU
CHINKIANG
SHANGHAI
HANGCHOW
NINGPO
WENCHOW
FOOCHOW
AMOY
YUNNAN (K'un-ming)
SWATOW
CANTON
PAKHOI
MONGTSEU
KWANGCHOWAN
Hong Kong
Macao
South China Sea
TAIWAN

HOI HOW

TREATY PORTS

0 100 200 400 600 800 1,000 MILES

Pop: 65,516 (1965)

Trebizond is a Turkish city on the Black Sea coast. It is an ancient town founded in the seventh century BC, and for a long time was a terminus of trade routes to Persia. It was the capital city of the Greek Empire of Trebizond from 1204 to 1478. In 1909-10, Russia overprinted stamps "TREBIZONDE" for use at Russian post offices in the city.

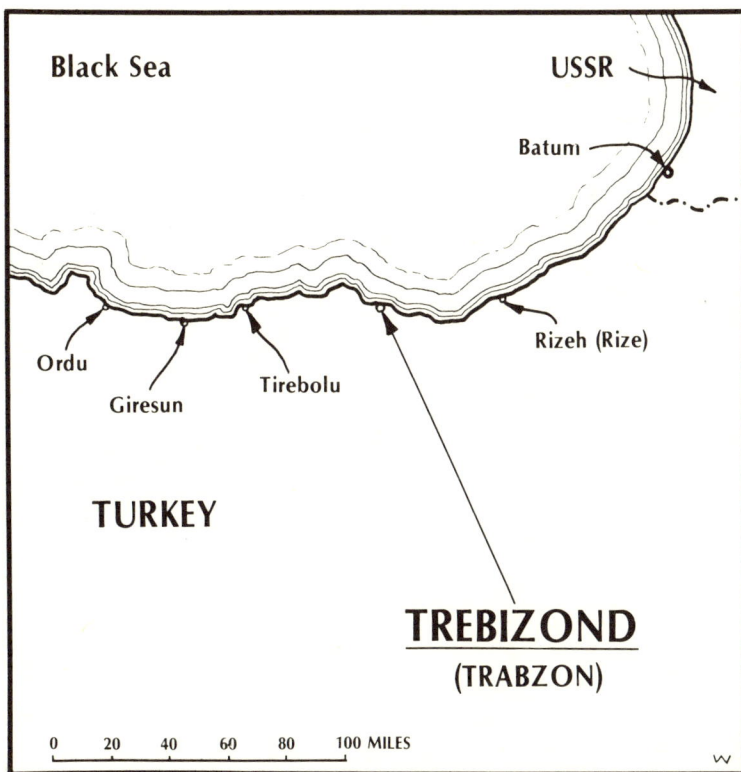

Black Sea

USSR

Batum

Ordu

Giresun

Tirebolu

Rizeh (Rize)

TURKEY

TREBIZOND
(TRABZON)

0 20 40 60 80 100 MILES

TRIESTE, CITY OF

Pop: 279,376 (1968 est.)

A city at the head of the Adriatic Sea, Trieste has had an eventful history. It came under the Austro-Hungarian Empire in 1867 and was ceded to Italy as a result of WWI. After WWII, it was in the occupation Zone A (91 sq. miles) of the British and US governments. The city was returned to Italy in 1954. Stamps were issued beginning in 1947 with the "A.M.G./ F.T.T." occupation overprints on Italian stamps.

AUSTRIA

ITALY

post-WWII border

pre-WWII border

Udine

Vittorio

Gorizia

YUGO.

Treviso

Koper

Izola

Venice

Piran

TRIESTE

Adriatic Sea

ISTRIA

0 10 20 30 40 50 MILES

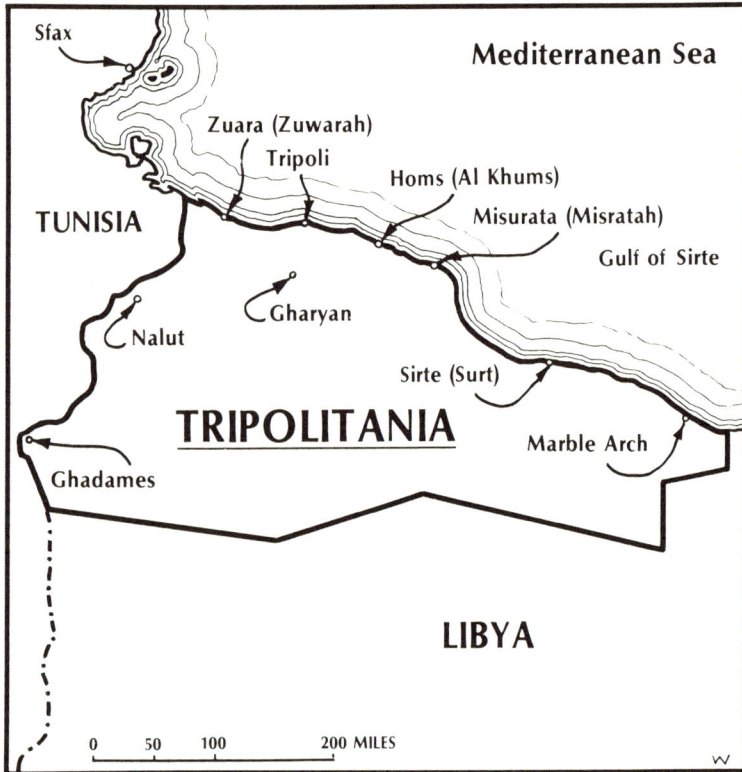

Area: 73,803 sq. miles
Pop: 344,000 (1971 est. urban area)
Capital: Tripoli

Tripolitania was an Italian colony in North Africa based on the town of Tripoli. Together with Cyrenaica, Fezzan, and some smaller areas, it now forms the Socialist People's Libyan Arab Jamahiriya. Stamps were issued for Tripolitania beginning in 1923, although Italy had overprinted stamps for use at its post office at Tripoli from 1901, before it took the area from Turkey in its 1911-12 war with that country.

Sfax

Mediterranean Sea

Zuara (Zuwarah)
Tripoli
Homs (Al Khums)
Misurata (Misratah)
Gulf of Sirte

TUNISIA

Gharyan

Nalut

Sirte (Surt)

TRIPOLITANIA

Marble Arch

Ghadames

LIBYA

0   50   100   200 MILES

AFRICA

————————————— TSINGHAI, PROVINCE OF —————————————

Area: 278,378 sq. miles
Pop: two million (1967 est.)
Capital: Hsi-ning

A province located in west central China, Tsinghai is, for the most part, above 10,000 feet in elevation. The Yellow River has its source in the area, winding through great gorges in the eastern part of the province. The province was in the Northwest China Liberation Area of the Communists prior to the formation of the People's Republic of China in 1949.

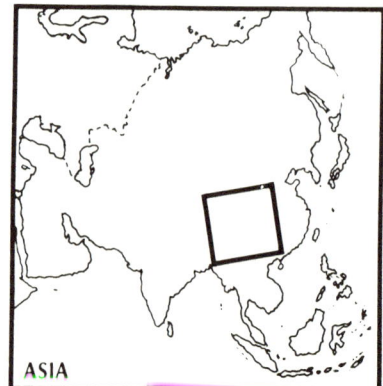

USSR

Ulan Bator

MONGOLIA

TSINGHAI

Sining (Hsi-ning)

CHINA

Lapulengsze

Lan Chow (Lan-chou)

Djou Dum (Cheng-to)

Yangtze River

Chungking (Ch'ung-ch'ing)

0 100 200 300 400 500 MILES

ASIA

Area: 30,000 sq. miles
Pop: 179,138 (1968)
Capital: Dubai

The Trucial States comprised a federation of seven sheikdoms located mostly on the south coast of the Persian Gulf, formed Jan. 7, 1961. It lasted for two and a half years until they went their separate ways to re-form on Dec. 2, 1971, as the present United Arab Emirates. The seven Trucial States are Abu Dhabi, Ajman, Dubai, Fujeira, Sharjah, Ras al Khaima, and Umm al Qiwain. Following the 19th-century treaties signed with Great Britain ending piracy in the area, which prompted the name of "Trucial Coast," the sheikdoms were under the protection of Britain. One set of 11 stamps was released during the Trucial State federation, and they were used only from Dubai. It was after they separated that the flood of agency-inspired stickers began that was to make the term "sand-dune states" one of philatelic disgust.

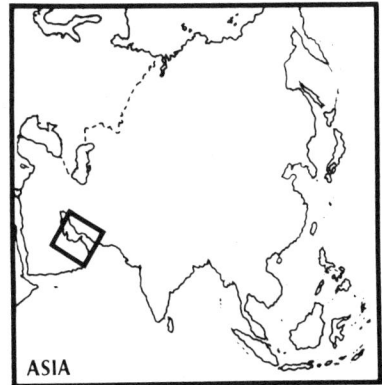

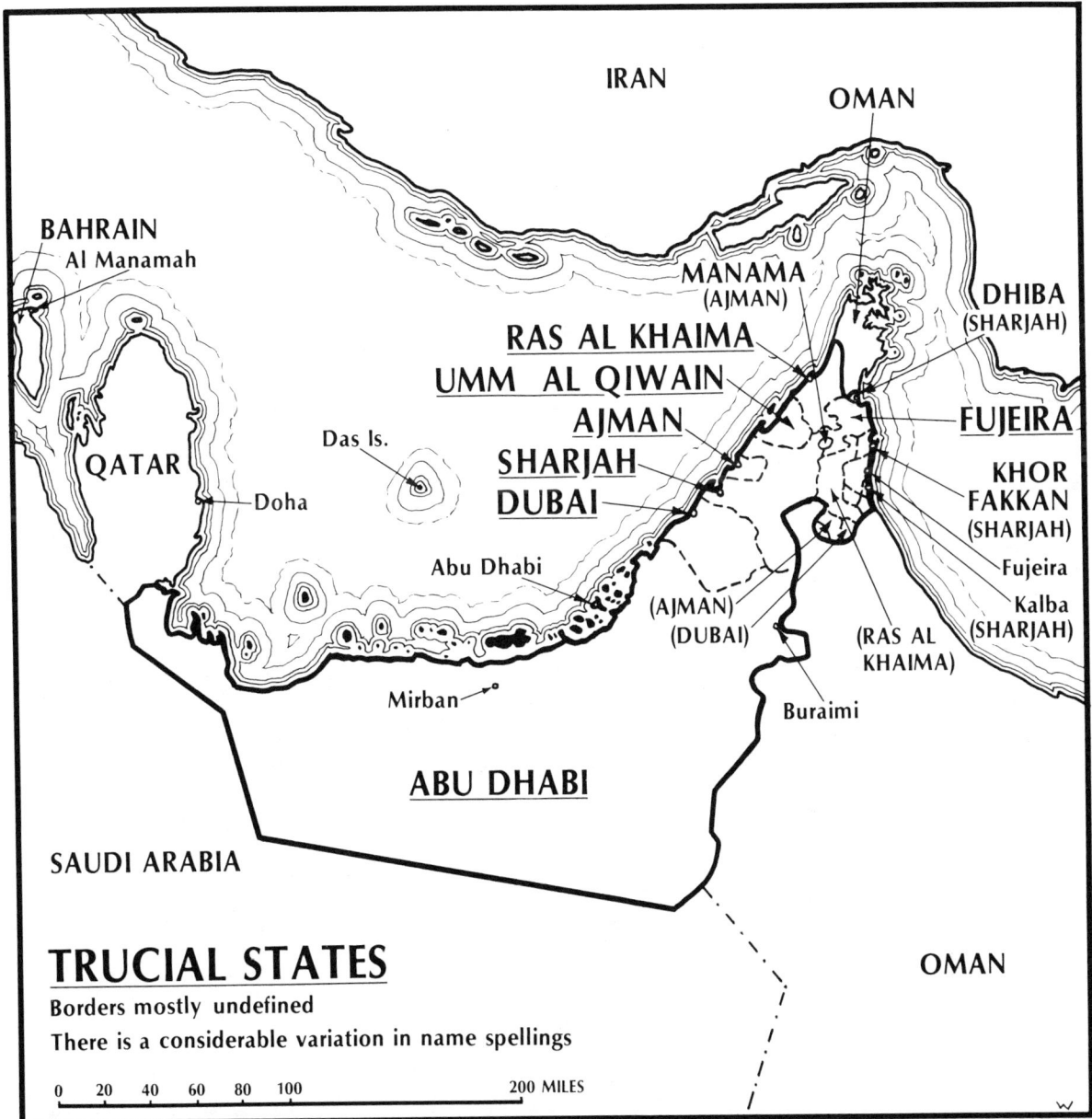

ASIA

IRAN

OMAN

BAHRAIN
Al Manamah

MANAMA
(AJMAN)

DHIBA
(SHARJAH)

RAS AL KHAIMA

UMM AL QIWAIN

AJMAN

FUJEIRA

Das Is.

QATAR

SHARJAH

KHOR
FAKKAN
(SHARJAH)

DUBAI

Doha

Abu Dhabi

Fujeira

(AJMAN)
(DUBAI)

Kalba
(SHARJAH)

(RAS AL
KHAIMA)

Mirban

Buraimi

ABU DHABI

SAUDI ARABIA

OMAN

TRUCIAL STATES

Borders mostly undefined

There is a considerable variation in name spellings

0 20 40 60 80 100   200 MILES

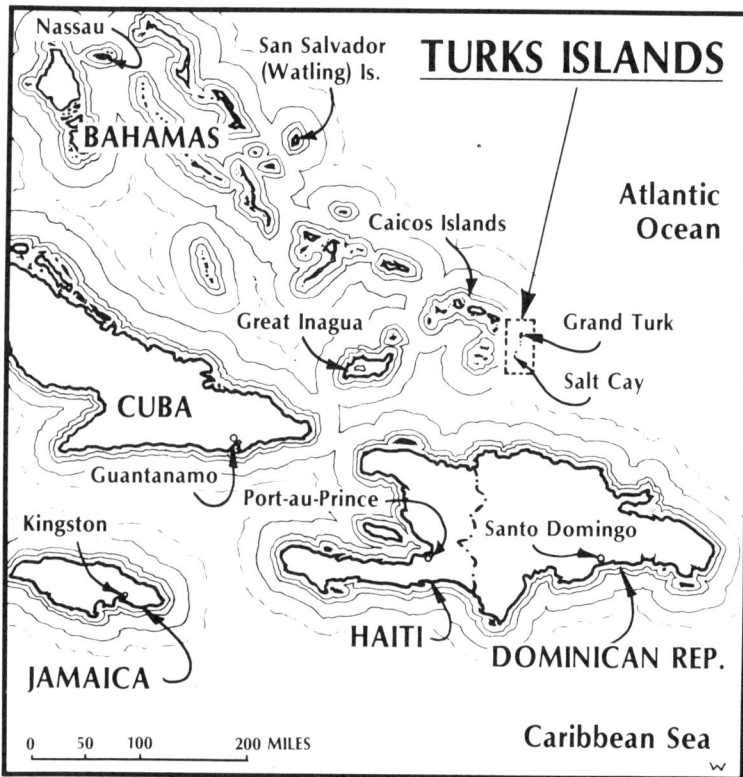

Capital: Grand Turk

The Turks Islands consist of the islands of Grand Turk and Salt Cay and are now part of the British Turks and Caicos Islands colony, located north of Hispaniola in the Atlantic Ocean. The area and population of the Turks Islands are not recorded, but the total area of the Turks and Caicos Islands is 166 square miles and and its 1970 estimated population about 5,675.

TUSCANY, GRAND DUCHY OF

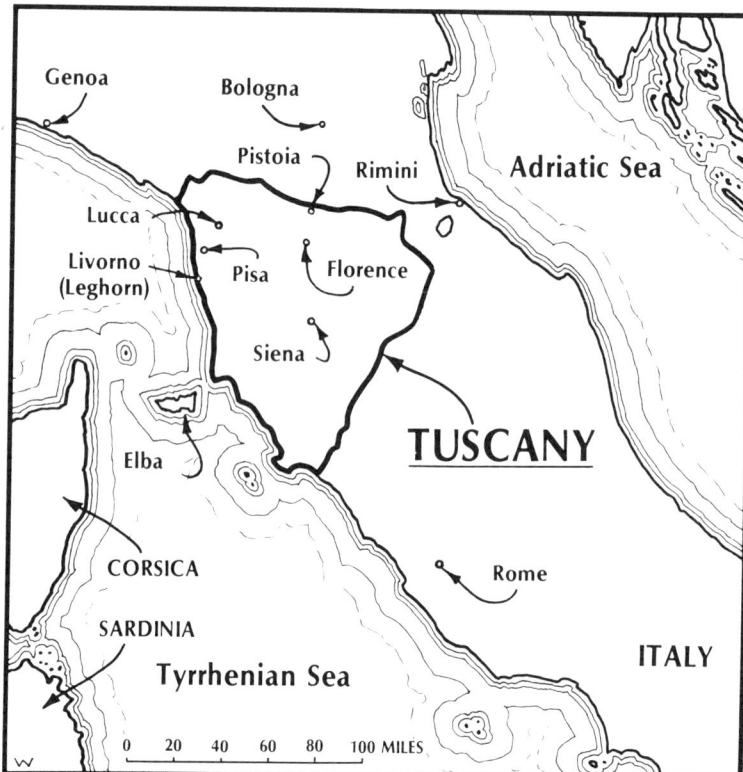

Area: 8,875 sq. miles
Pop: 2,208,869 (1881)
        3,434,618 (1968 est.)
Capital: Florence

The Grand Duchy of Tuscany was located on the west coast of the Italian peninsula opposite the island of Corsica. It was annexed to the Kingdom of Sardinia shortly before it became the unified Kingdom of Italy in 1861. The area suffered great damage during WWII and in floods in 1966. It is now an autonomous region of Italy.

Area: 171,000 sq. miles (approx.)
Pop: 47,136,000 (1970)
Capital: Kiev

Formerly a part of the Russian Empire, following the 1917 Russian Revolution, the Ukraine enjoyed a brief period of independence before being made part of the USSR in 1923. Stamps were issued during the period of freedom in 1918-1923. At first, the trident overprint was applied to Russian stamps in a large variety of forms. Later, specially designed stamps were issued.

──────UMM SAID, CITY OF──────

Umm Said is a city in the State of Qatar, located on the eastern side of the peninsula that forms Qatar and which juts into the Persian Gulf from the Arabian shore. From February 1956 to March 31, 1957, British stamps surcharged originally for use in Muscat were used at the British-run post office there. The Gibbons catalog lists them under issues of the British Postal Agencies in Eastern Arabia, and Scott puts them under Oman (Muscat and Oman).

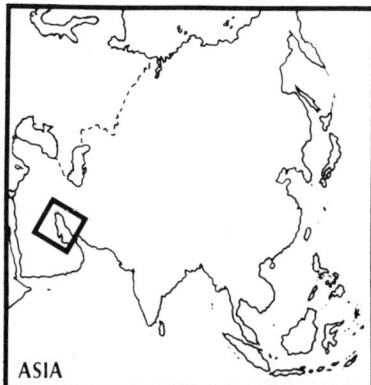

The United Arab Republic was a short-lived union between Egypt and Syria, plus, briefly, the Yemen Arab Republic. It was formed in 1958 and dissolved in 1961. During the period of Yemen Arab Republic's membership it was known as the United Arab States. The union resulted in some stamps of similar design but differing in the currency in which the denominations were expressed.

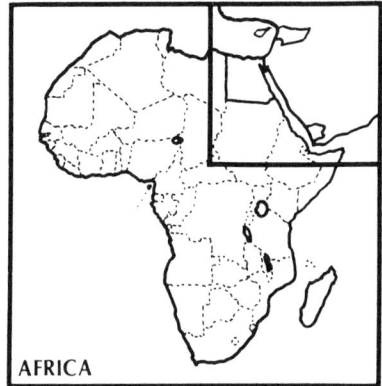

TURKEY

SYRIA

Med. Sea

IRAQ

Cairo

Damascus

Persian Gulf

EGYPT

ARABIA

YEMEN AR

AFRICA

Red Sea

San'a

UNITED ARAB REPUBLIC

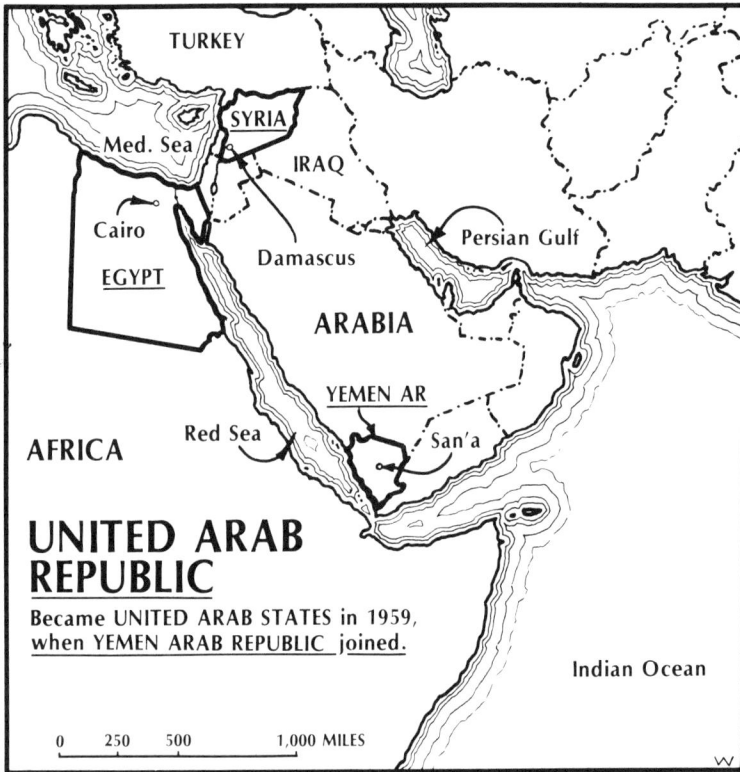

Became UNITED ARAB STATES in 1959, when YEMEN ARAB REPUBLIC joined.

Indian Ocean

0   250   500   1,000 MILES

AFRICA

══════════════ UPPER AUSTRIA, STATE OF ══════════════

Area: 4,625 sq. miles
Pop: 1,244,000 (1971)
Capital: Linz

A state of Austria, Upper Austria lies between Lower Austria and the Federal Republic of Germany, bordering on Czechoslovakia to the north. In 1945, it was one of the areas for which Britain and the US jointly issued Allied Military Government (AMG) stamps. They feature a posthorn design and are inscribed "OSTERREICH."

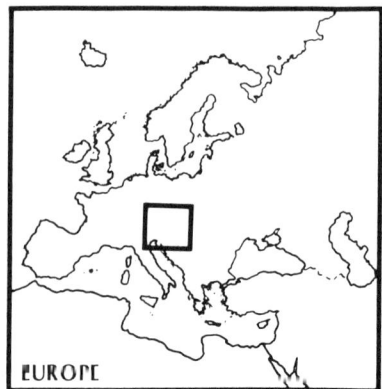

Prague

CZECHOSLOVAKIA

UPPER AUSTRIA

VIENNA

GERMANY

Vienna

Bratislava

Linz

Steyr

Wiener Neustadt

Danube R.

LOWER AUSTRIA

AUSTRIA

HUNGARY

YUGOSLAVIA

0   20   40   60   80   100 MILES

EUROPE

The area of Upper Silesia had been Prussian since it was seized from Austria in 1742. Following Germany's defeat in WWI, a plebiscite was held there to determine its future. Since the plebiscite result was inconclusive, it was divided by the League of Nations between Poland and Germany. Stamps were issued during 1920-22 while the disposition of the territory was being decided. They are inscribed "COMMISSION DE GOUVERNEMENT HAUTE SILESIE."

━━━━━━━━━━━━━USKUB, (SKOPJE), CITY OF━━━━━━━━━

Pop: 28,000 (1900 est.)
312,091 (1971)

The city of Uskub (now Skopje) is the capital of Yugoslavian Macedonia and is located in the southern part of the country, about 200 miles from Belgrade. It is an important road junction and industrial center and was the capital of medieval Serbia. It was Turkish from 1392 to 1913.

UNITED STATES

CANADA
Boscawen, N.H.
Brattleboro, Vt.
Providence, R.I.

Millbury, Mass.

St. Louis, Mo.

Lockport, N.Y.
New York, N.Y.
Alexandria, Va.

New Haven, Conn.

Baltimore, Md.
Annapolis, Md.

Tuscumbia, Ala.

Atlantic Ocean

US POSTMASTERS' PROVISIONALS

Towns for which stamps were issued prior to 1847 issue.

0 50 100 200   400 MILES

NORTH AMERICA

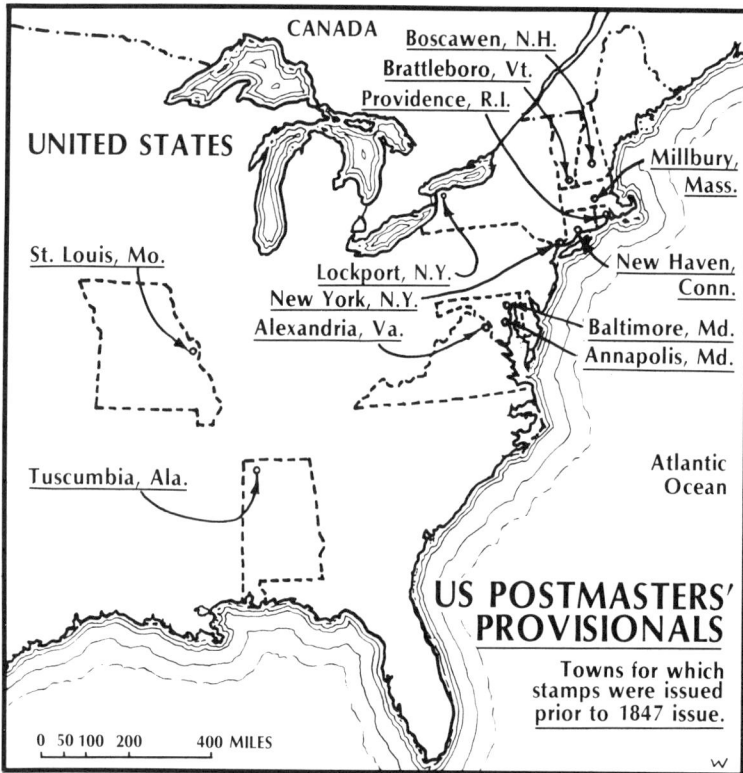

Provisional postage stamps were issued in a number of United States cities between 1845, when uniform postal rates were established by Congress, and 1847, when United States postage stamps appeared. The first postmasters' provisional stamp was issued in July 1845 by New York Postmaster Robert H. Morris, and other postmasters followed his example. The map indicates the cities in which such stamps were issued. Not all were adhesives, and some were hand-stamped directly into envelopes.

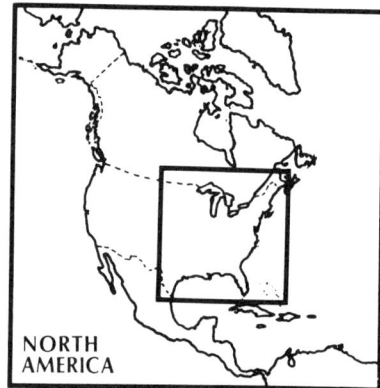

━━━━━━ **VALONA (VLORE), CITY OF** ━━━━━━

YUGOSLAVIA
Cetinje

Adriatic Sea

Bari

Tirane

Brindisi

ITALY

ALBANIA

GREECE

Taranto

VALONA (VLORE)

CORFU

Ionian Sea

0   20   40   60   80   100 MILES

EUROPE

Pop: 50,351 (1967 est.)

The capital of Vlore Province in Albania, the city of Vlore (Italian, "Valona") is a seaport on the Bay of Vlore. Under Turkish rule from 1464 to 1912, it was the place at which Albanian independence was proclaimed Nov. 28, 1912. It was occupied by Italian forces during WWI and again in WWII. Italian stamps were overprinted for use at an Italian post office in the city from 1909.

VALLADOLID, PROVINCE OF

Area: 3,166 sq. miles
Pop: 412,572 (1970)
Capital: Valladolid

Valladolid is a province in north-central Spain near the Portuguese border, based on the capital city of the same name. In 1868-69, provisional stamps were created there by handstamping regular issues of Spain. The overprint reads "HABILITADO/ POR LA/ NACION."

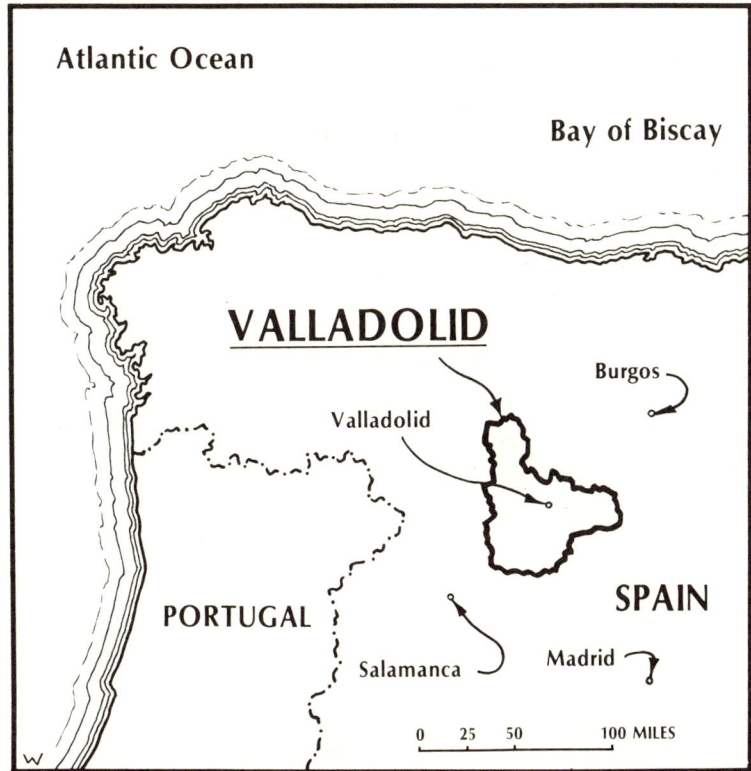

VANCOUVER ISLAND, COLONY OF

Area: 12,408 sq. miles
Pop: 36,767 (1891)
Capital: Victoria

A large island off the west coast of Canada, Vancouver Island was made a British crown colony in 1849 and united with the colony of British Columbia in 1866. Stamps for Vancouver Island were issued Sept. 19, 1865, and following the 1866 merger with British Columbia, stamps of each were used in both areas.

Pop: 44,316 (1970 est.)

Located in Finland, on the Gulf of Bothnia, Vasa (now Vaasa) was founded in 1606. It is a city of some importance and the capital of the province of the same name. In 1918, a set of Finnish stamps was printed there and is noted by Scott as the Vasa Issue.

VEGLIA (KRK), ISLAND OF

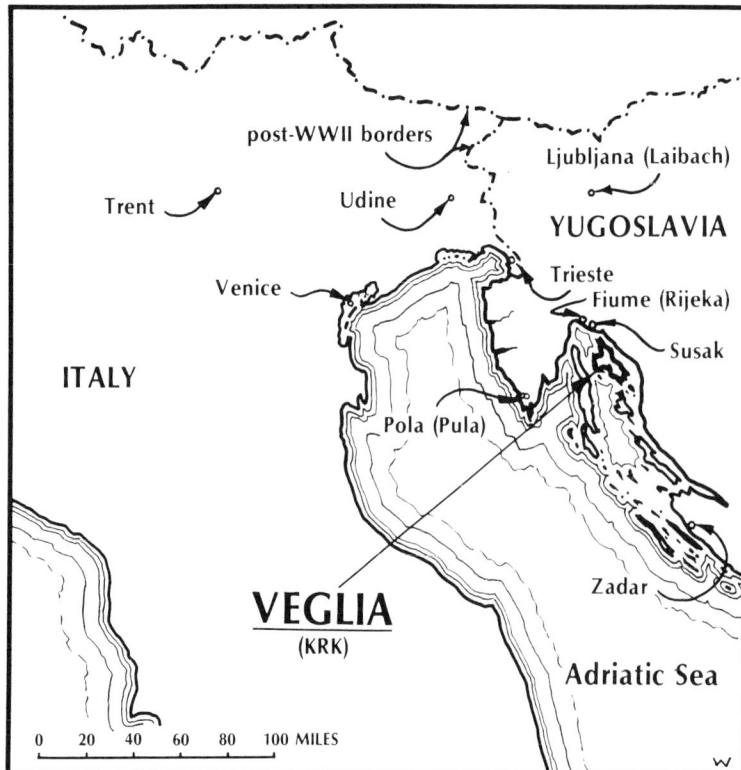

Area: 157 sq. miles
Pop: 19,871 (1900 est.)
     14,548 (1961)
Capital: Krk

An island off the coast of Croatia, Veglia was formerly part of the Austro-Hungarian Empire. It is now Yugoslavian. During the period of occupation by the Italian adventurer D'Annunzio following WWI, stamps of Fiume were overprinted for use on the island. Shortly thereafter it was handed over to the new Kingdom of Yugoslavia.

Area: 3,457 sq. miles
Pop: 977,257 (1936)
Capital: Trieste

A department of Italy up to WWII, Venezia Giulia included an area along the Italian-Yugoslav border, the cities of Trieste and Fiume, the Istrian Peninsula, several islands, and Zara (Zadar) to the south. Following WWI, Italy overprinted Austrian stamps to mark its acquisition of Venezia Giulia. At the end of WWII, the Allies occupied it and issued Italian stamps overprinted "A.M.G./V.G."

GERMANY AUSTRIA

VENEZIA GIULIA Graz

Innsbruck

Trent

Udine Ljubljana (Laibach)

Gorizia Fiume (Rijeka)

Venice Karlovac

Trieste

Susak

ITALY YUGOSLAVIA

Pola (Pula)

Adriatic Sea

0 20 40 60 80 100 MILES

EUROPE

VICTORIA, COLONY OF

Area: 87,884 sq. miles
Pop: 1,176,854 (1899 est.)
3,853,500 (1980)
Capital: Melbourne

A former British colony, Victoria was first settled in 1835. It received colony status in 1851 and became a state in the Commonwealth of Australia in 1901. It experienced a great surge in population as a result of the Ballarat gold discovery in 1851.

S. AUSTRALIA NEW SOUTH WALES

Wagga Wagga

Shepparton Wangaratta

Horsham Bendigo

VICTORIA

Ballarat Melbourne

Tasman Sea

King Is. Bass Strait

Furneaux Group

TASMANIA

0 50 100 200 MILES

AUSTRALIA

Victoria Land is an undefined area of the Antarctic continent, located partially in the Ross Dependency administered by New Zealand. It was formerly known as South Victoria Land, according to some authorities. The area is mountainous and includes peaks up to about 13,000 feet. Evidence of volcanic activity has been found in the northern part of Victoria Land. New Zealand stamps were overprinted "VICTORIA/ LAND" in two lines for the 1911 Scott expedition to the Antarctic region. They were the ½ d green and 1d carmine of the 1909 issue. Gibbons notes that although they were made under the authority of the New Zealand Post Office, there was little need for them. It is stated, however, that they did frank correspondence. In New Zealand, the stamps were sold to the public at a small premium.

——————VLADIVOSTOK, CITY OF——————

Pop: 13,050 (1900 est.)
442,000 (1970)

The major city of the USSR on that country's east coast, Vladivostok is a seaport at the tip of a peninsula jutting into a bay on the Sea of Japan, near the borders with the People's Republic of China and North Korea. It is the eastern terminus of the Trans-Siberian Railway and the base of the Soviet Pacific fleet.

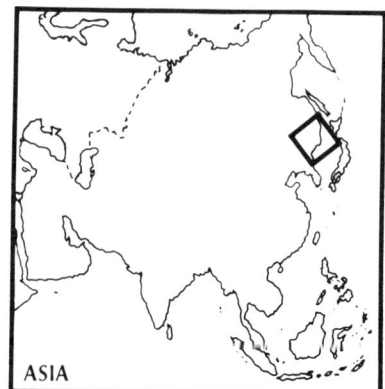

Pop: 17,100 (1967 est.)

A town in the northern part of Cape Colony, South Africa, Vryburg is about 125 miles north of Kimberley. It was the capital of the Boer Republic of Stellaland during its 1882-85 existence. Stamps were issued in the town while it was under Boer occupation during the Boer War. They took the form of stamps of the Cape of Good Hope overprinted "Z.A.R." and surcharged.

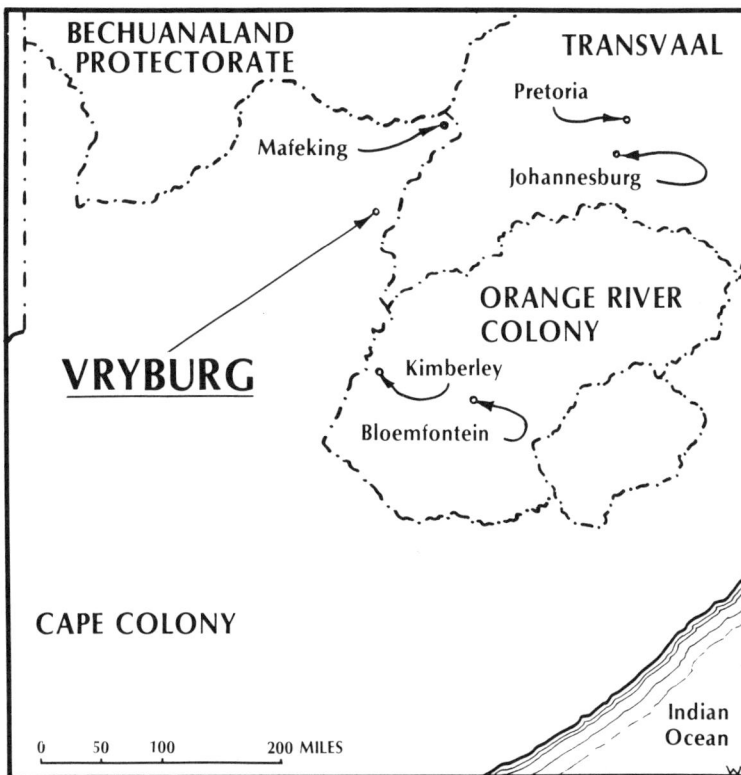

BECHUANALAND PROTECTORATE

TRANSVAAL

Pretoria

Mafeking

Johannesburg

VRYBURG

ORANGE RIVER COLONY

Kimberley

Bloemfontein

CAPE COLONY

0   50   100   200 MILES

Indian Ocean

AFRICA

── WALACHIA, PRINCIPALITY OF ──────────────

Area: 29,575 sq. miles

The Principality of Walachia forms a large part of what is now the Eastern European country of Romania. It united with the neighboring Principality of Moldavia in 1859 to establish the Kingdom of Romania. Stamps were issued for Moldavia-Walachia beginning in 1862.

BUKOWINA

RUSSIA

Bakau (Bacau)

MOLDAVIA

AUSTRIA-HUNGARY

Galatz (Galati)

Rimnicu Sarat

Tirgochil (Tirgu Jiu)

Buseo (Buzeu)

Pitesti

WALACHIA

Crajova (Craiova)

Bucharest

Danube R.

DOBRUDJA

BULGARIA

0   25   50   100 MILES

EUROPE

Map

Dairen (Ta-lien)

Port Arthur (Lu-shun)

Peking (Beijing)

Tientsin (T'ien-ching)

Gulf of Chihli

Yellow River

Wei-fang

CHINA

Tsingtao (Ch'ing-tao)

WEI-HAI-WEI

Yellow Sea

0   50   100   200 MILES

ASIA

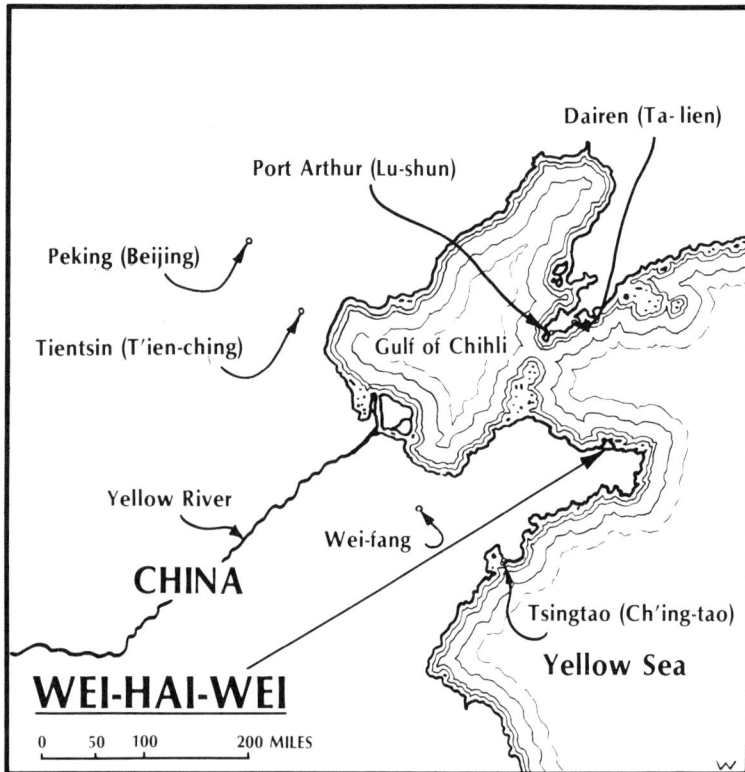

A seaport, in a district of the same name, on the north coast of the Shantung Peninsula, Wei-Hai-Wei was leased to Great Britain by China in 1898 and used as a naval base to counter similar German bases on the northern Chinese coast. It was returned to China in 1930. The Japanese occupied it from 1938 to 1945, and it is now a naval base of the People's Republic of China. During the British period, Wei-Hai-Wei had two post offices, Port Edward and Liu Kung Tau.

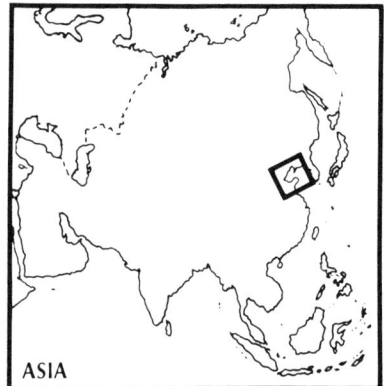

━━━━━━ **WESTERN AUSTRALIA, COLONY OF** ━━━━━━

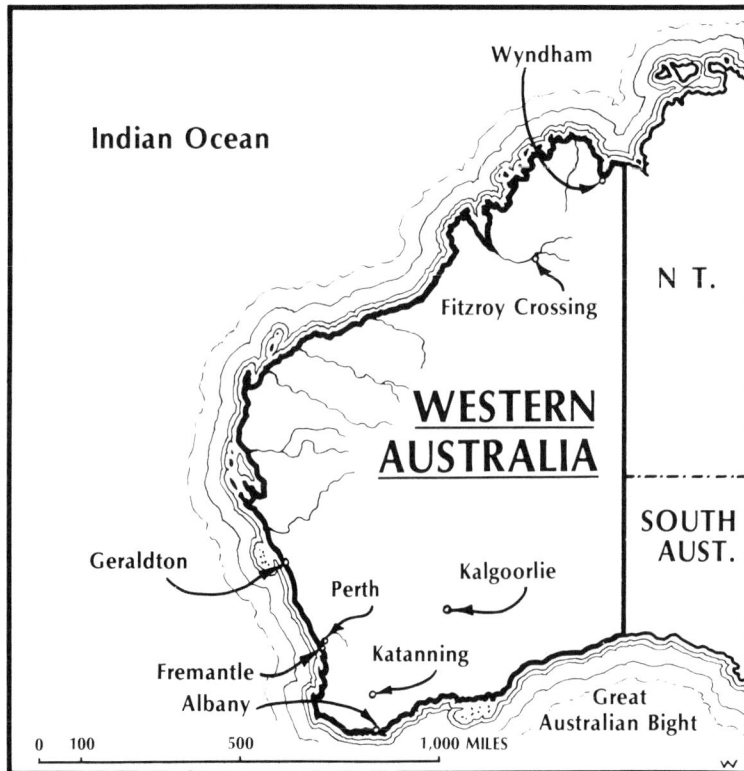

Wyndham

Indian Ocean

Fitzroy Crossing

N T.

WESTERN AUSTRALIA

Geraldton

Kalgoorlie

Perth

SOUTH AUST.

Fremantle

Katanning

Albany

Great Australian Bight

0   100   500   1,000 MILES

AUSTRALIA

Area: 975,920 sq. miles
Pop: 168,480 (1899 est.)
          980,000 (1970 est.)
Capital: Perth

George Vancouver took formal possession of this area for England in 1791, and the first settlement was established in 1829 as the Swan River Settlement. Western Australia became a colony in 1886 and joined the Commonwealth of Australia in 1901. Stamps were first issued in 1854.

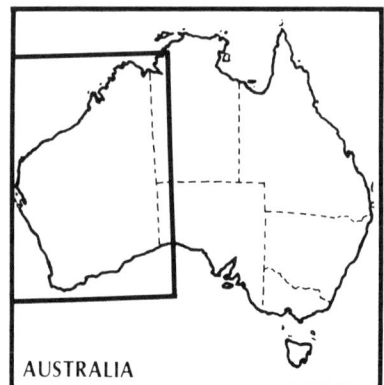

Chief town: Lemberg (L'vov)

Western Ukraine was a short-lived republic formed in 1918 from eastern Galicia and part of Bukowina, which had been provinces of the Austro-Hungarian Empire. Later that same year, Romania annexed the Bukowina portion, and in 1919 Poland took the rest. The entire area was taken by the USSR during WWII and remains within that country.

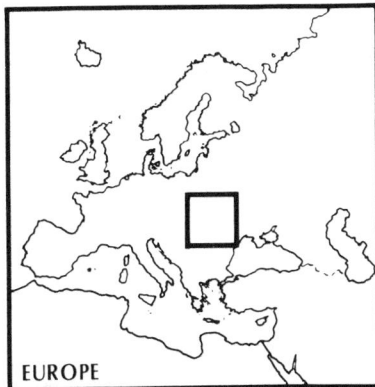

EUROPE

APPROXIMATE AREA OF
WESTERN UKRAINE

pre-WWI border of Austria-Hungary

GALICIA

**RUSSIA
(USSR)**

Lemberg (L'vov)

Przemysl

Stanislav (Ivano-Frankovsk)

Kolomyya

Czernowitz

present border of Ukraine

Debrecen

BUKOWINA

TRANSYLVANIA

Jassy (Iasi)

0   25   50   100   200 MILES

WOLMARANSSTAD, TOWN OF

Wolmaransstad is a town located in the southern portion of the Transvaal and is now part of the Republic of South Africa. Tension between the Boer settlers and the British had been growing during the periods of varying status of the Transvaal, until the Boer War broke out in 1899. During the war, stamps of the Boer South African Republic established in the Transvaal were overprinted in various towns. Stamps were overprinted "Cancelled/ V.R.I." by the British at Wolmaransstad during 1900.

AFRICA

WOLMARANSSTAD

TRANSVAAL

Mafeking

Pretoria

SWAZILAND

Johannesburg

**ORANGE
FREE STATE**

NATAL

Bloemfontein

Ladysmith

Kimberley

Maseru

BASUTO.

Durban

Pietermaritzburg

Indian Ocean

0   50   100   200 MILES

THE KINGDOM OF
WURTTEMBERG

HESSE

Rhine River

Wurzburg

Heidelberg

BAVARIA

Karlsruhe

Heilbronn

Strasbourg

Danube R.

Stuttgart

Ulm

Augsburg

Freiburg

HOHENZOLLERN

BADEN

Ravensburg

Lake Constance

SWITZERLAND

0   50   100   200 MILES

W

Area: 7,528 sq. miles
Pop: 2,169,480 (1900)
Capital: Stuttgart

A constitutional monarchy from 1819 to 1918, Wurttemberg became a member of the North German Confederation and later, of the German Empire. It is now part of Baden-Wurttemberg in the Federal Republic of Germany. Stamps were first issued by Wurttemberg in 1851, and it retained its postal autonomy until 1902. Official stamps were used until 1923.

EUROPE

━━━━━━ YCA (ICA), DEPARTMENT OF ━━━━━━

BRAZIL

PERU

Lima

Callao

Pisco

Yca (Ica)

Lake Titicaca

YCA
(ICA)

Pacific Ocean

CHILE

0   50   100   200 MILES

W

Area: 8,205 sq. miles
Pop: 60,111 (1876)
           349,800 (1969 est.)
Capital: Yca (Ica)

Yca, now Ica, is a department of Peru located on the coast south of Lima. Provisional stamps were issued there in 1884. These had been made necessary because of the Chilean occupation of Lima and Callao during the late-19th-century war between the two countries.

SOUTH AMERICA

Area: 16,749 sq. miles
Pop: 297,507 (1895)
774,011 (1970)
Capital: Merida

A state of Mexico, Yucatan is located in the northern part of the Yucatan Peninsula. A richly historical area, it was the seat of the ancient Mayan civilization and, later, of the Toltecs. In 1924, the local authorities issued two stamps, a 5c and a 10c. These exist both perf and imperf.

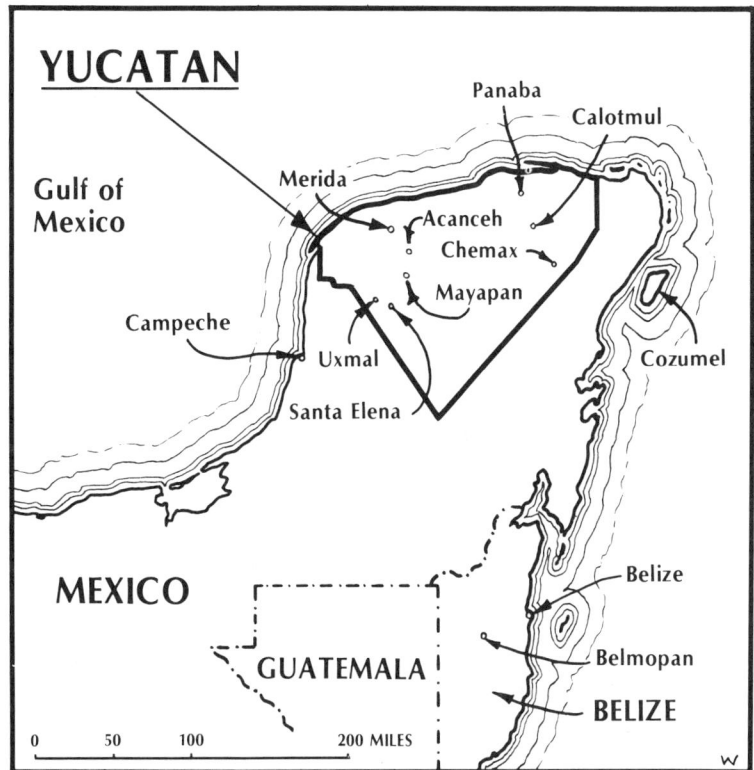

YUCATAN

Gulf of Mexico

Panaba
Calotmul
Merida
Acanceh
Chemax
Mayapan
Campeche
Uxmal
Santa Elena
Cozumel

NORTH AMERICA

MEXICO

GUATEMALA

Belize
Belmopan
BELIZE

0   50   100   200 MILES

YUNNAN, PROVINCE OF

Area: 168,417 sq. miles
Pop: 23 million (1968 est.)
Capital: K'un-ming

Yunnan is a mountainous province in southwest China. In 1926, a stamp issue was released there. It consisted of Chinese stamps overprinted "For exclusive use in Province of Yunnan" in Chinese characters. This was to prevent the use of the depreciated currency of Yunnan to buy stamps for use elsewhere in China.

SZECHWAN

Chao-t'ung

KWEICHOW

Pao-shan

Tung-ch'uan

K'un-ming

KWANGSI

YUNNAN

Meng-tzu

INDO-CHINA
(VIETNAM)

BURMA

Hanoi

ASIA

0   50   100   200 MILES

ZACATECAS

Mazatlan

Zacatecas

Islas Marias

Pacific Ocean

Guadalajara

MEXICO

0   50   100   200 MILES

Area: 28,973 sq. miles
Pop: 452,720 (1895)
      949,663 (1970)
Capital: Zacatecas

Zacatecas is a state in west central Mexico. During the 1913-15 revolutionary period, provisional stamps were created in many areas of the country, and in 1914, two issues were released in Zacatecas. They consisted of overprints on the stamps of Mexico.

NORTH AMERICA

ZANZIBAR, PROTECTORATE OF

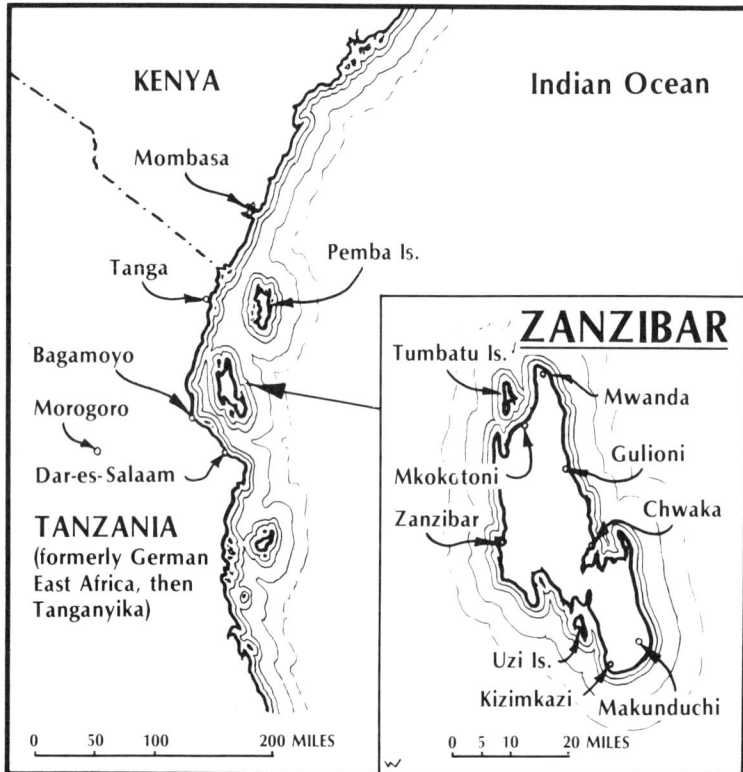

KENYA

Indian Ocean

Mombasa

Pemba Is.

Tanga

Bagamoyo

Morogoro

Dar-es-Salaam

TANZANIA
(formerly German East Africa, then Tanganyika)

0   50   100   200 MILES

ZANZIBAR

Tumbatu Is.

Mwanda

Gulioni

Mkokotoni

Zanzibar

Chwaka

Uzi Is.

Kizimkazi

Makunduchi

0   5   10   20 MILES

Area: 1,020 sq. miles
Pop: 150,000 (1900 est.)
      475,655 (1978)
Capital: Zanzibar

A former sultanate, now part of Tanzania, Zanzibar consisted of Zanzibar Island, Pemba Island, and a number of smaller islands. Zanzibar became a British protectorate in 1890 and an independent sultanate in 1963, prior to merging with Tanganyika to form Tanzania.

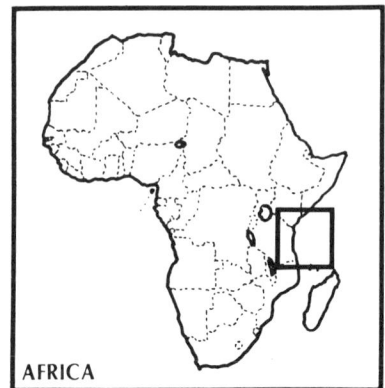

AFRICA

Pop: 31,000 (1965 est.)

The town, of Zara, now Zadar, in a district of the same name, is located on the coast of Yugoslavia, about 70 miles north of Split. Part of the Austro-Hungarian Empire until WWI, it was ceded to Italy by the 1920 Treaty of Rapallo and made a free port in 1923. During WWII, it was occupied by the German's and various Italian stamps were overprinted for use there.

ZARAGOZA, PROVINCE OF

Area: 6,639 sq. miles
Pop: 760,186 (1970)
Capital: Zaragoza

Zaragoza is a province of Spain located in the northeastern part of the country. Its capital city was an important center under the Romans and was later taken by the Moors. It was the capital of Aragon until the 15th century. In 1937, during the Spanish Civil War, the Nationalist authorities issued stamps there.

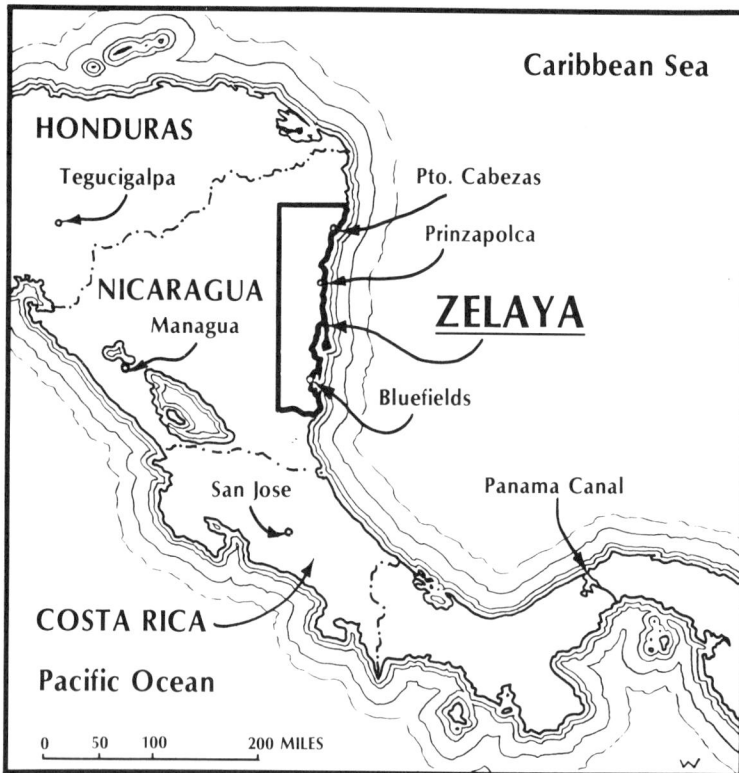

Current area: 22,816 sq. miles
Pop: 105,823 (1970 est.)
Capital: Bluefields

Zelaya is a province on the Caribbean coast of Nicaragua. Beginning in 1904, Nicaraguan stamps were overprinted "B" and "Dpto Zelaya." These stamps were made necessary because silver currency was used in the province, while the rest of the country, except Cabo Gracias a Dios (q.v.), used paper money.

━━━━━━━━━━━━ZULULAND, COLONY OF━━━━━━━━━━━━

Area: 10,362 sq. miles
Pop: 166,367 (1895 est.)
      570,160 (1960)
Capital: Eshowe

Zululand came under British control in 1887 and was made part of the colony of Natal in 1897. Now in the Republic of South Africa.

Stamps were first issued in 1888 and consisted of stamps of Great Britain overprinted "ZULULAND." Key type stamps inscribed for the colony were issued in 1894.

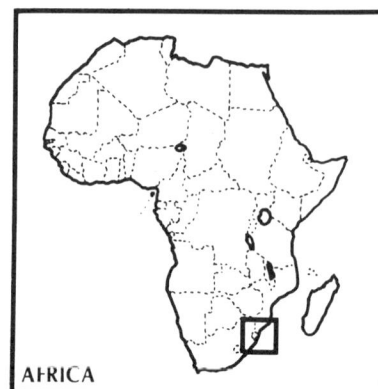

Area: 668 sq. miles
Pop: 337,183 (1888)
1,107,788 (1970)
Capital: Zurich

A canton of Switzerland, Zurich is based on the town of the same name at the northern end of Lake Zurich.

Beginning in 1843, it issued its own stamps, which were among the earliest to be issued. However, the fact that they were cantonal, rather than national, removes them from lists of the first national postage stamps.

350

British Guiana and Guyana

Danzig and Gdansk, Poland

Aden and Yemen PDR

Ceylon and Sri Lanka

Timor and Indonesia

Russia and the USSR

Persia and Iran

Then and now...

These pairs of stamps reflect the political changes that have taken place around the world. The first stamp is from a past entity now served by the second stamp.

Rio Muni and Equatorial Guinea

Basutoland and Lesotho

Section Three

Stamp-issuing areas of today

There is no escaping the world of today: we live in it, affect it, and are affected by it whether we wish it or not. Thus, a knowledge of its politics and geography is at once interesting and valuable in increasing our understanding.

To watch the passing parade via stamps is to become familiar with society's successes and its failures. It might even help us to determine the direction of the parade!

The maps in this section will show you the location of today's stamp-issuing areas, and you will be able to see the proximity of one to another. In addition to the larger maps locating all of these areas, there are a number of maps spotlighting many of the smaller and lesser-known countries, some of which may well be destined to play significant roles in tomorrow's world.

Many of these countries are new to independence; through the stamps they issue, we can watch their development, and from their philatelic policies, determine their philosophies.

The challenge of perceiving those philosophies is not great today, since the postage stamp is more than ever both a weapon of political propaganda and a means of enriching the coffers of a country. By the subject matter a country selects for portrayal and the means by which its stamps are merchandised, we can, without too much difficulty, "read" the message it sends.

If the appeal of today's philately is great, so are the rewards as we thread our way through the great mass of available material. For, in so doing, we are compiling the story of our own time.

Africa

Once a continent of colonies, Africa was for years known as the Dark Continent. Some of its early settlements were truly "the white man's grave," and it was an area to which colonial administrators went to assume "the white man's burden."

Today, Africa is a continent on the move. Its many divisions are colonies no longer, and it is a diverse group of nations moving toward a dream of technological advancement and self-sufficiency.

Some of its elements are already a long way down the road to that dream; others are in a condition of economic poverty and political unrest. A few seem out of step with everyone and appear to delight in maintaining a condition of unrest among their neighbors.

In short, Africa is a continent still in transition, with its greatest development still to come and the dream of its peoples yet to be fulfilled.

To follow the philately of Africa is to chart its progress to what must someday make it an area of great influence in the world.

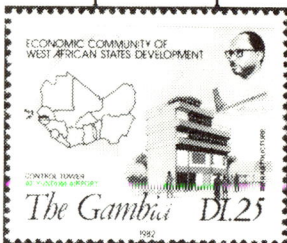

353

Stamp-issuing countries of Africa

1. Algeria
2. Angola
3. Ascension
4. Benin
5. Botswana
6. Burundi
7. Cameroon
8. Cape Verde
9. Central African Rep.
10. Chad
11. Comoros
12. Congo
13. Djibouti
14. Egypt
15. Equatorial Guinea

16. Ethiopia
17. Gabon
18. Gambia
19. Ghana
20. Guinea
21. Guinea-Bissau
22. Ivory Coast
23. Kenya
24. Lesotho
25. Liberia
26. Libya
27. Madagascar
28. Madeira
29. Malawi
30. Mali

31. Mauritius
32. Mauritania
33. Morocco
34. Mozambique
35. Niger
36. Namibia (SWA)
37. Nigeria
38. Rwanda
39. St. Helena
40. Sao Tome & Princip
41. Senegal
42. Seychelles
43. Sierra Leone
44. Somali Republic

45. South Africa
46. Sudan
47. Swaziland
48. Tanzania
49. Togo
50. Tristan da Cunha
51. Tunisia
52. Uganda
53. Upper Volta
54. Western Sahara
55. Zaire
56. Zambia
57. Zil Elwagne Sesel
58. Zimbabwe

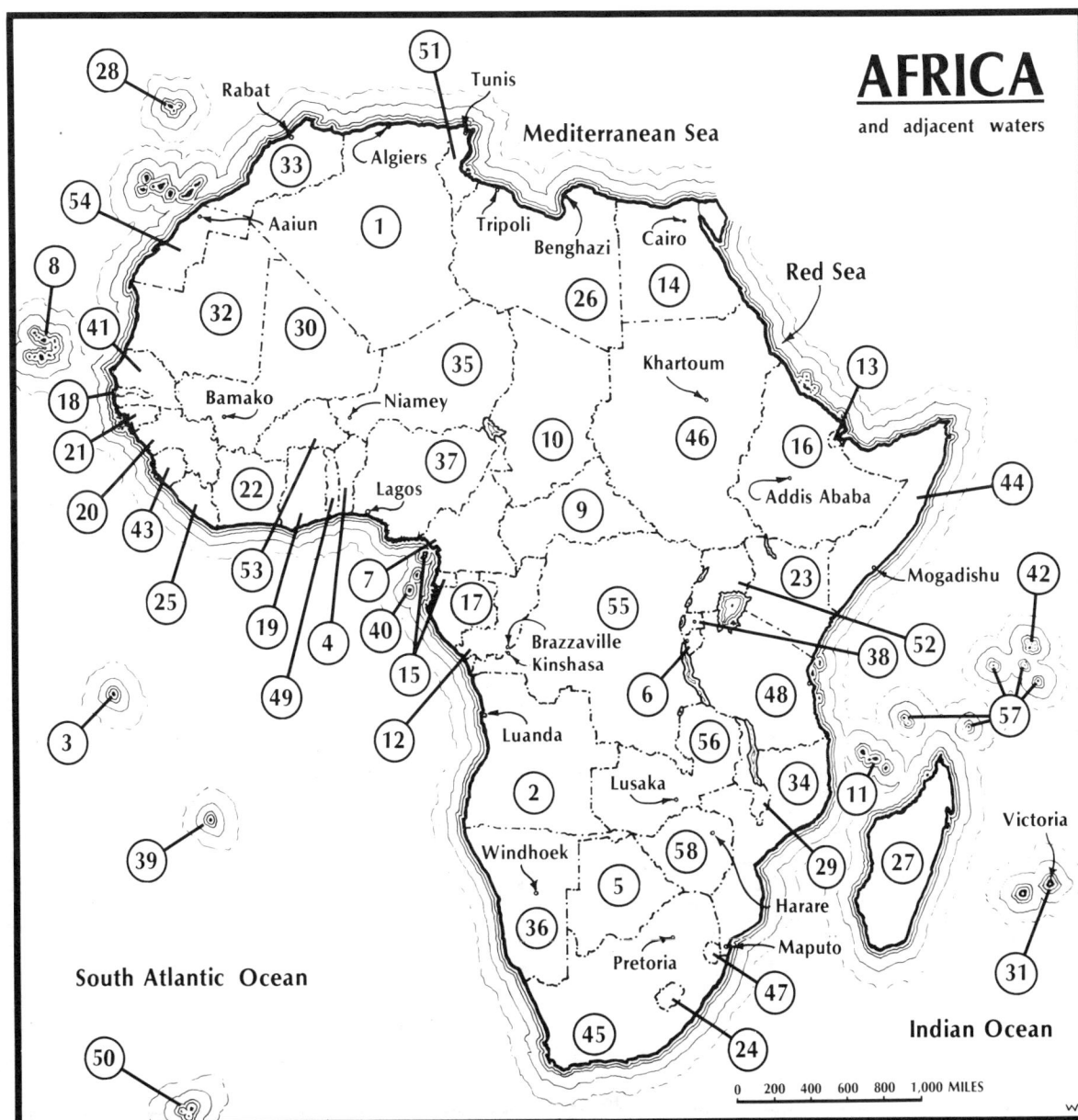

AFRICA and adjacent waters

354

ASCENSION ISLAND ————

Area: 34 sq. miles
Pop: 1,363 (1968 est.)
Chief town: Georgetown

The British island of Ascension in the South Atlantic has a position that has given it an importance far beyond its size and resources. During WWII it was a staging and refueling point on the air route from North America to the war zones in the Middle and Far East.

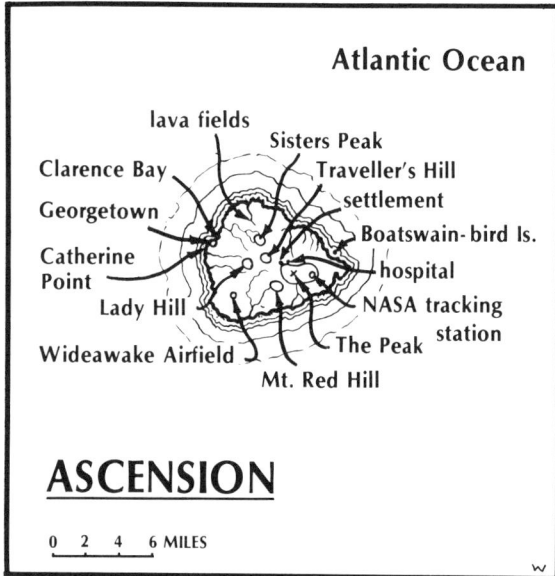

ASCENSION

0   2   4   6 MILES

GAMBIA, REPUBLIC OF THE ——

Area: 4,003 sq. miles
Pop: 374,770 (1971 est.)
Capital: Banjul (Bathurst)

This narrow strip of a country in West Africa is surrounded by the Republic of Senegal, except for a short stretch of coastline. It has a width of about six miles on either side of the Gambia River and runs for some 200 miles inland.

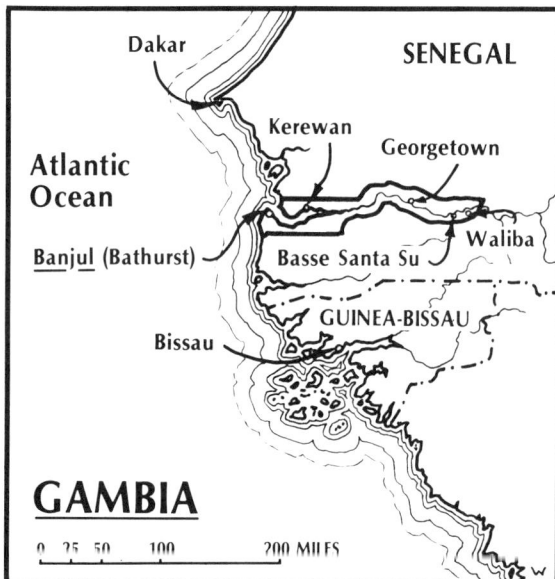

GAMBIA

0   25   50   100   200 MILES

CAPE VERDE, REPUBLIC OF——

Area: 1,557 sq. miles
Pop: 246,000 (1970 est.)
Capital: Praia

Once a colony of Portugal, this group of volcanic islands became independent on July 5, 1975. It was discovered in 1456 by Ca Da Mosto, a Venetian in the service of Prince Henry of Portugal, and in 1495 was made a part of the royal domain.

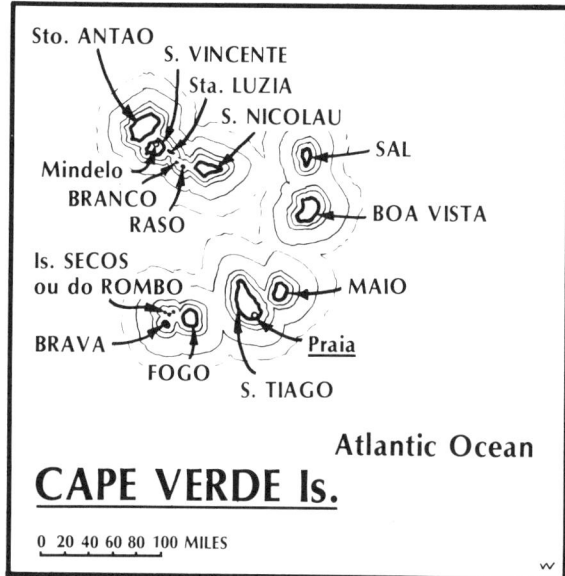

CAPE VERDE Is.

Atlantic Ocean

0 20 40 60 80 100 MILES

MADEIRA——

Area: 308 sq. miles
Pop: 268,700 (1970 est.)
Capital: Funchal

The islands of Madeira and Porto Santo, plus several barren islets, together form the Funchal District of Portugal. The islands were discovered in 1420, and a settlement was founded at Funchal in 1421.

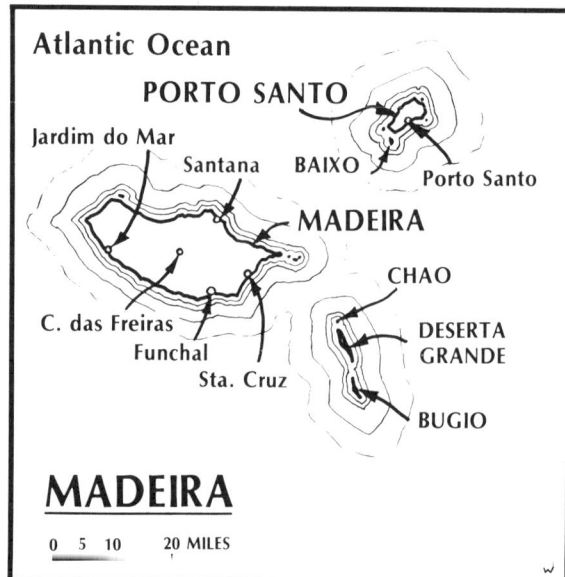

MADEIRA

0   5   10   20 MILES

MAURITIUS, ISLAND OF ——————

Area: 787 sq. miles
Pop: 970,000 (1981 est.)
Capital: Port Louis

In the minds of stamp collectors the ex-British colony of Mauritius will always be famous for its first two stamps, known as the "Post Office" Mauritius because of the inscription. The island was discovered by the Portuguese in 1505.

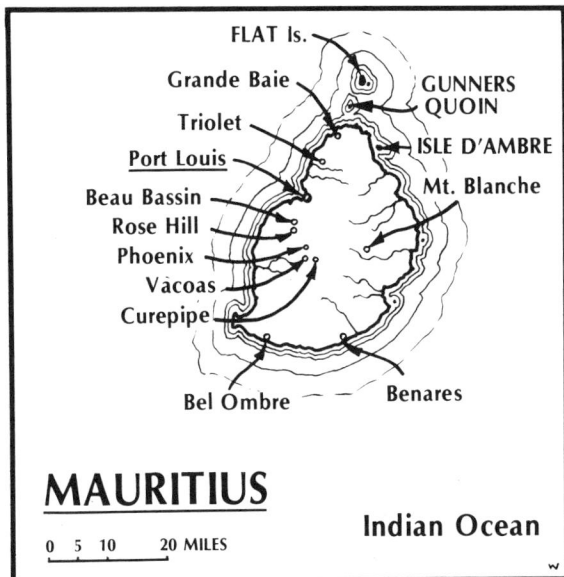

MAURITIUS

Indian Ocean

0 5 10   20 MILES

ST. HELENA ——————————

Area: 47 sq. miles
Pop: 4,829 (1969 est.)
Capital: Jamestown

St. Helena gained fame as the place to which Napoleon was exiled after he was finally defeated in 1815. He lived there until his death in 1821. During the Boer War, a detention camp housed Boer prisoners.

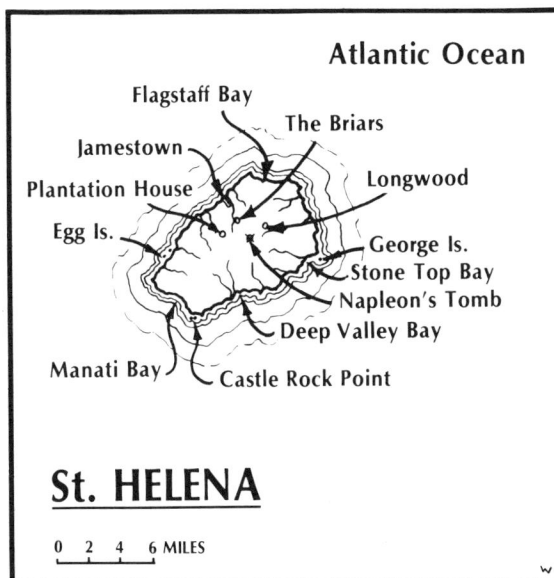

St. HELENA

Atlantic Ocean

0 2 4   6 MILES

SEYCHELLES, REPUBLIC OF ——————

Area: 171 sq. miles
Pop: 70,000 (1980 est.)
Capital: Victoria

First claimed by the French in 1744, the Seychelles were taken by the British in 1794. Made a dependency of Mauritius in 1810, the islands became a crown colony in 1903. In June 1976, the island group became a republic within the British Commonwealth.

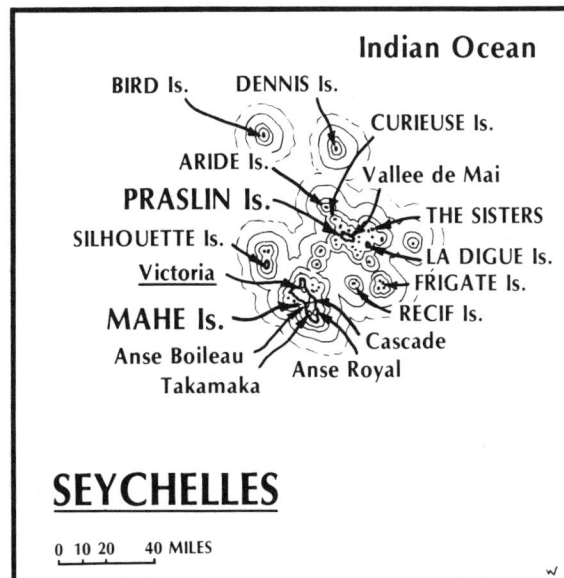

SEYCHELLES

Indian Ocean

0 10 20   40 MILES

SIERRA LEONE, REPUBLIC OF ——————

Area: 27,699 sq. miles
Pop: 3,470,000 (1981 est.)
Capital: Freetown

Freetown was founded in 1788 as a settlement for freed slaves, and it became a British colony in 1808. The interior was acquired by treaty with France in 1895 and made a protectorate in 1896. Independence was granted in 1961.

SIERRA LEONE

Atlantic Ocean

0 25 50   100   200 MILES

SOUTH AFRICA AND HOMELANDS

Area: 435,868 sq. miles
Pop: 29 million (1981 est.)
Capitals: Cape Town (legislative)
  Pretoria (administrative)
  Bloemfontein (judicial).

The Cape of Good Hope was first settled by the Dutch in the 17th century. It was taken by the British in 1808, and the Dutch gradually expanded northward. The history of South Africa is complex, and there was much fighting between the original inhabitants and the European intruders. Following the Boer War of 1899-1902 between the Boers and the British, the area was finally brought together, and the various colonies that had been established in the area merged to form the Union of South Africa. The republic was formed in 1961, when South Africa withdrew from the Commonwealth. Since independence, the policy of discrimination against the enormous number of black South Africans has tarnished the country's image. In recent years the government has created a number of what it calls "homelands" for the black population. The first of these areas was Transkei in 1976, followed by Bophuthatswana in 1977 and Venda in 1979. Ciskei is the most recent.

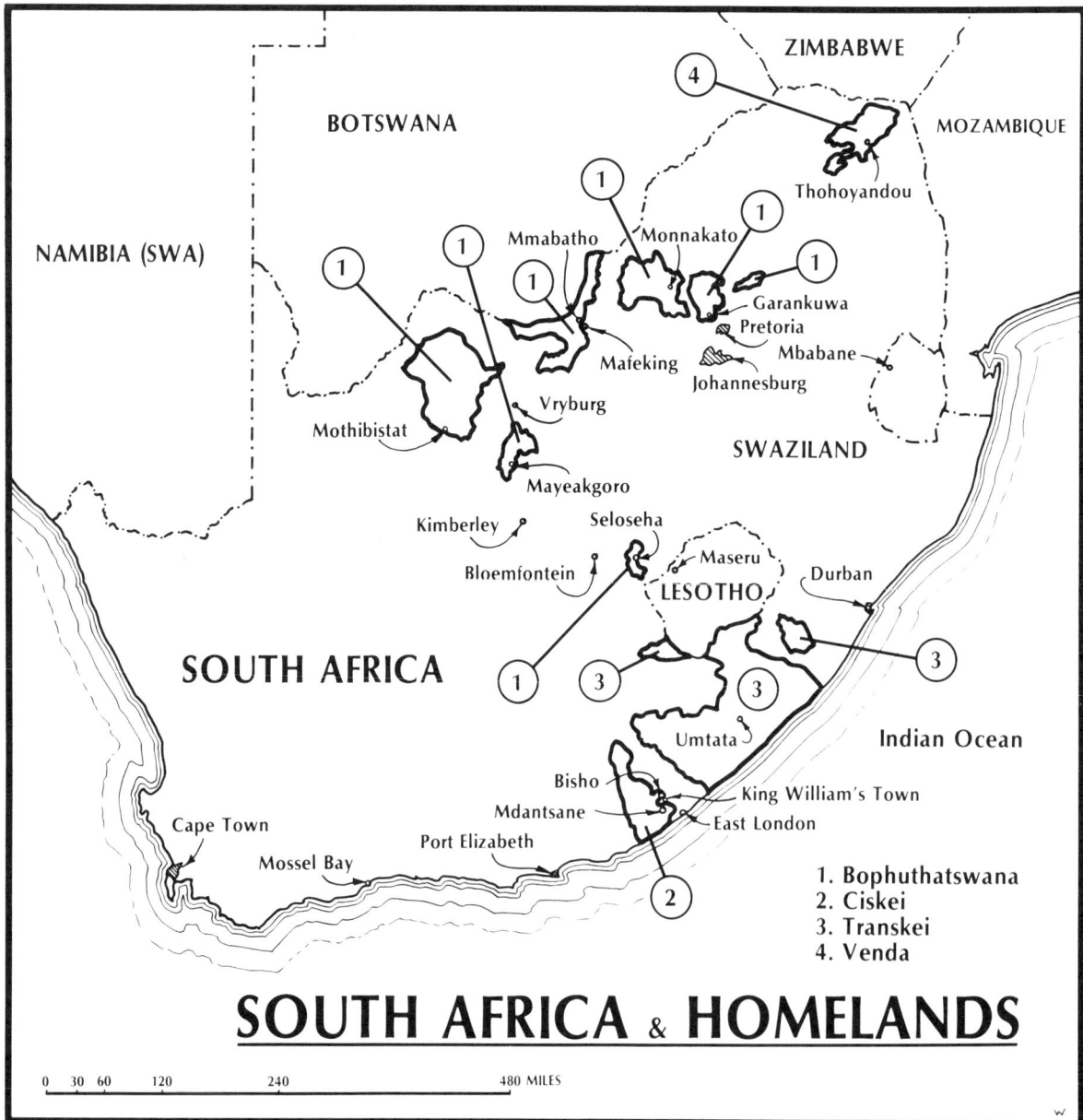

ZIMBABWE

MOZAMBIQUE

BOTSWANA

④

Thohoyandou

① Monnakato

NAMIBIA (SWA)

① Mmabatho

①

①

Garankuwa

Pretoria

Mbabane

Mafeking

Johannesburg

Vryburg

Mothibistat

SWAZILAND

Mayeakgoro

Kimberley

Seloseha

Maseru

Durban

Bloemfontein

LESOTHO

SOUTH AFRICA

①

③

③

③

Umtata

Indian Ocean

Bisho

King William's Town

Mdantsane

East London

Cape Town

Port Elizabeth

Mossel Bay

②

1. Bophuthatswana
2. Ciskei
3. Transkei
4. Venda

SOUTH AFRICA & HOMELANDS

0 30 60 120   240   480 MILES

W

SWAZILAND, KINGDOM OF

Area: 6,704 sq. miles
Pop: 570,000 (1981 est.)
Capital: Mbabane

One of Africa's last ruling dynasties, the royal house of Swaziland can be traced back some 400 years. Its autonomy was guaranteed by Britain, which assumed responsibility for the country in 1903. Independence came in 1968.

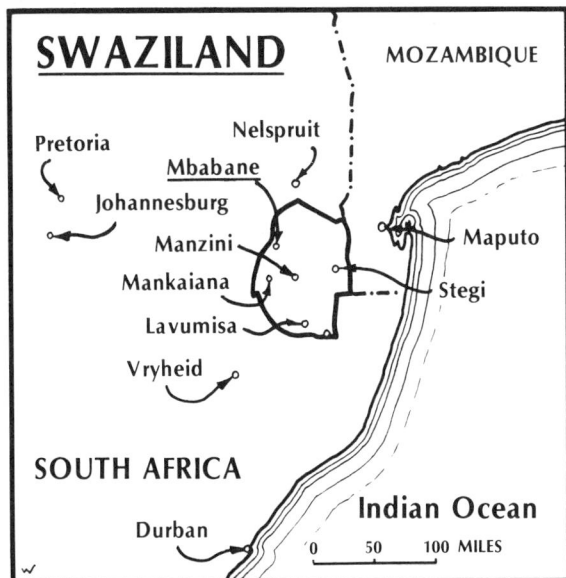

TUNISIA, REPUBLIC OF

Area: 63,378 sq. miles
Pop: 6,600,000 (1981 est.)
Capital: Tunis

The site of the ancient city of Carthage and a former Barbary state under the Turkish Empire, Tunisia has had an eventful history. It became a French protectorate in 1881, and obtained independence in 1956.

TRISTAN DA CUNHA

Area: 52 sq. miles
Pop: 271 (1968)
Highest point: 6,760 feet

The island group forming the South Atlantic settlement of Tristan da Cunha is composed of Tristan da Cunha, Inaccessible, Nightingale, Stoltenhoff, and Middle Islands, with Gough Island some distance to the south.

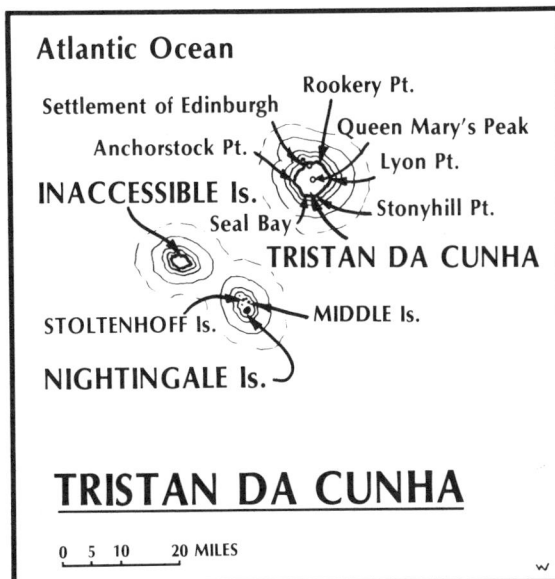

ZIL ELWAGNE SESEL

Pop: about 3,000

Zil Elwagne Sesel (formerly Zil Eloigne Sesel) encompasses some 25 islands of the Seychelles group located to the south of the main islands. It includes the three groups of Amirante, Farquhar, and Aldabra, plus Coetivy Island. In 1980, the Seychelles postal authorities announced that these islands would constitute a postal entity with its own postage stamps.

Antarctica

Although the antarctic continent has segments claimed by various nations, a 1959 treaty established the entire continent as a demilitarized zone, and the United States recognizes no claim of sovereignty, either for itself or any other state.

It is an area of about 5.5 million square miles with an ice cap having an average thickness of one mile. The highest point is the Vinson Massif at 16,860 feet.

Nations making territorial claims in the area include Argentina, Australia, Chile, France, Great Britain, New Zealand, and Norway.

Areas administered by Australia, France, Great Britain, and New Zealand have released stamps, which are regarded more as evidence of political claim rather than serving any real postal purpose.

The South Pole was first reached by Roald Amundsen on Dec. 17, 1911.

Stamp-issuing areas of Antarctica

1. Australian Antarctic Territory
2. British Antarctic Territory
3. French Southern and Antarctic Territory
4. Ross Dependency
5. South Georgia with So. Sandwich Islands forms Falkland Islands Dependencies

Australian Antarctic Territory is located south of latitude 60 degrees South and between 160 degrees E. longitude and 45 degrees E. longitude except for the Adelie Land area.

British Antarctic Territory comprises area south of latitude 60 degrees South and between 80 degrees W. longitude and 20 degrees W. longitude. It is about 652,000 sq. miles in area and is administered from the Falkland Islands.

French Southern and Antarctic Territory incudes Adelie Land in Antarctica plus the Indian Ocean islands of Amsterdam, St. Paul, Kerguelen Islands, and Crozet Islands. Established in 1955, it is a French Overseas Territory.

Ross Dependency is administered by New Zealand and consists of antarctic land south of latitude 60 degrees South and between 160 degrees E. longitude and 150 degrees W. longitude, plus Balleny Island, Coulman Island, Ross Island, Scott Island, King Edward VII Peninsula, and part of Victoria Land. It has an area 160,000 sq. miles of land and 130,000 sq. miles of ice shelf.

South Georgia is a British island in the South Atlantic. It is currently administered together with the South Sandwich Islands as the Falkland Islands Dependencies. South Georgia has an area of 1,450 sq. miles and a 1964 population of 499. Its highest point is 9,625 feet. The island was claimed for Britain by Capt. Cook during his 1772-75 voyage.

Asia and the Far East

Asia and the Far East represent an area of our world rich in ancient cultures. From humid, steamy India and southeast Asia to the windswept and bleak space of northern China, we can trace man's earliest days.

Asia today is a mixture of the ancient and the modern — a mixture that often produces a bubbling pot of strife for her peoples. The pressures of modern life and the starkness of imposed political philosophies sit ill on the civilized heritage of so many Asians. When combined with the natural pressure of a mushrooming population, the result is often unrest, famine, and misery.

But despite the problems of the present, the face of its rich cultural heritage shines through to give hope for the future and serve as a reminder that as the culture of European colonialism ran its course, with the best features being retained and the rest abandoned, so perhaps will periods of political tyranny also be weathered.

Asia, more than most areas, reflects its culture, pride, and problems on its postage stamps, and through them we can watch and hope.

Stamp-issuing countries of Asia

1. Bangladesh
2. Bhutan
3. Brunei
4. Burma
5. Cambodia
6. China, People's Republic of
7. China (Taiwan)
8. Christmas Island
9. Cocos (Keeling) Islands
10. Hong Kong
11. India
12. Indonesia
13. Japan
14. Korea, North
15. Korea, South
16. Laos
17. Macao
18. Malaysia
19. Maldive Islands
20. Mongolia
21. Nepal
22. Philippines
23. Singapore
24. Sri Lanka
25. Thailand
26. USSR in Asia
27. Vietnam

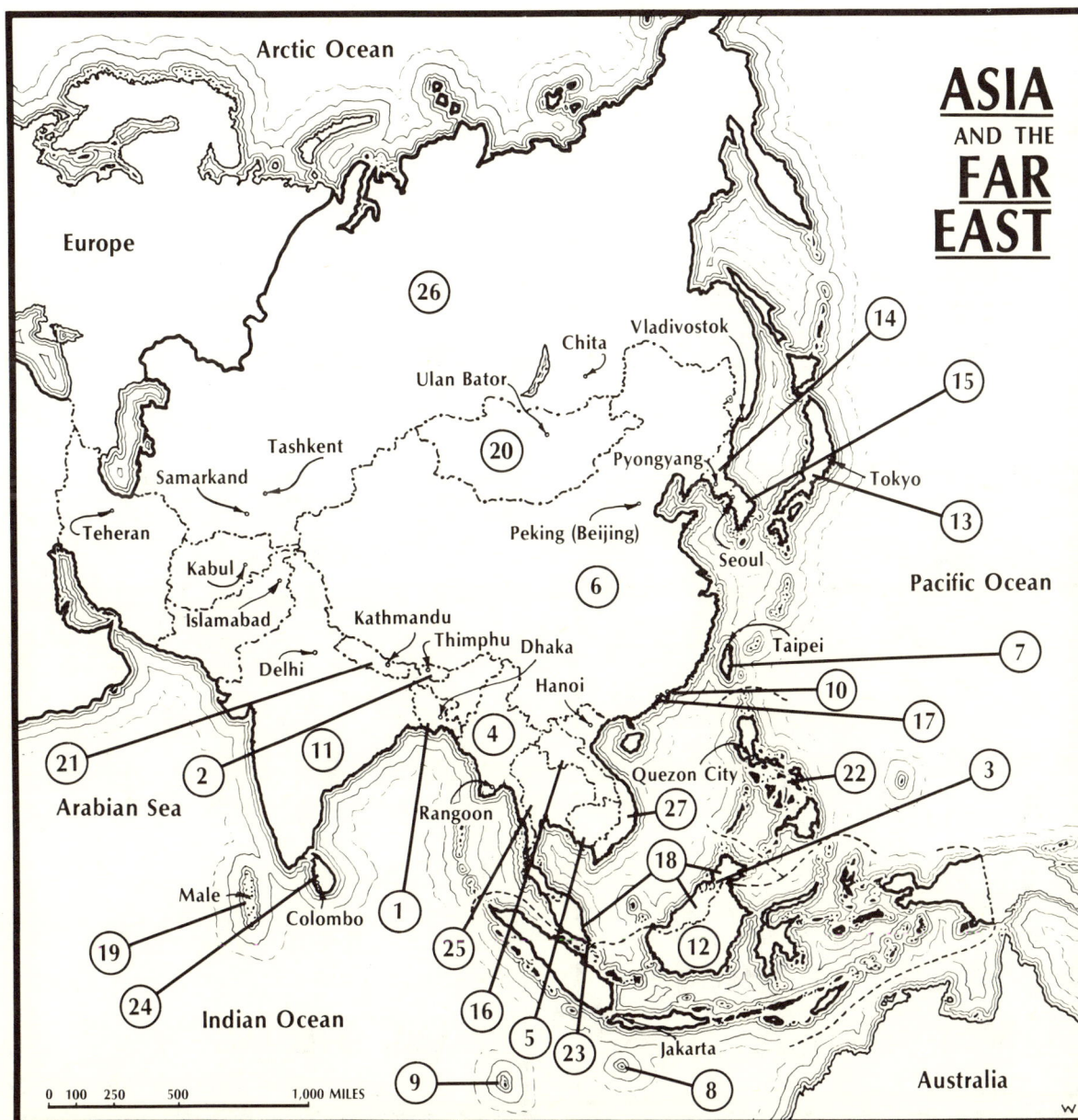

ASIA AND THE FAR EAST

362

BHUTAN, KINGDOM OF

Area: 17,800 sq. miles
Pop: 1.4 million (1981 est.)
Capital: Thimbu

The Himalayan Kingdom of Bhutan came under Chinese influence about 1720, with British contacts beginning around 1772. Britain assumed responsibility for external affairs in 1902. In recent years India has advised the government.

COCOS (KEELING) ISLANDS

Area: 5.5 sq. miles   **Pop:** 487 (1980)
A group of small islands to the south of Sumatra administered by Australia.

CHRISTMAS ISLAND

Area: 52 sq. miles   **Pop:** 3,094 (1978)
Located 230 miles south of Java, Christmas Island was transferred to Australia in 1958.

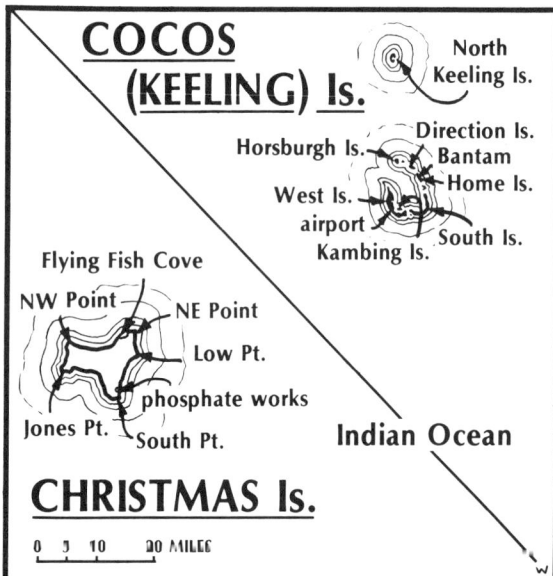

BRUNEI, STATE OF

Area: 2,226 sq. miles
Pop: 213,000 (1980 est.)
Capital: Bandar Seri Begawan

A sultanate under British protection, Brunei is in two parts, both surrounded by Malaysia. The area was visited by Magellan in 1521 and taken by Spain in 1580. It later became a haven for pirates. Brunei signed a treaty of protection with Britain in 1846.

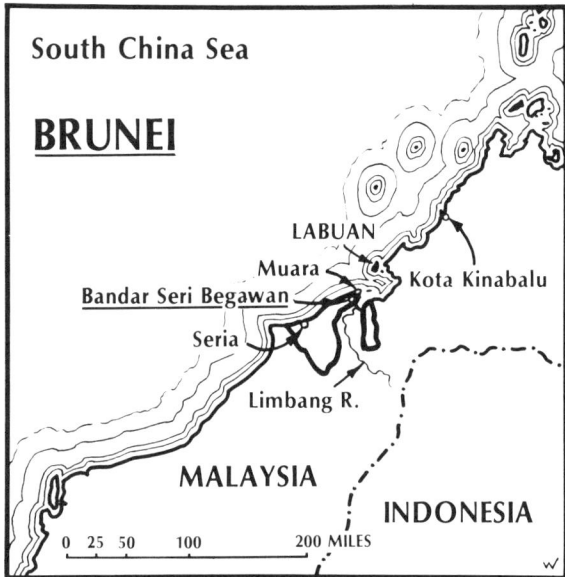

HONG KONG

Area: 398 sq. miles
Pop: 5,108,000 (1981 est.)
Capital: Victoria

Britain's lease on much of the mainland and some islands constituting Hong Kong expires in 1997. It is currently a major commercial center, a transshipment port, a manufacturing center, and a naval base.

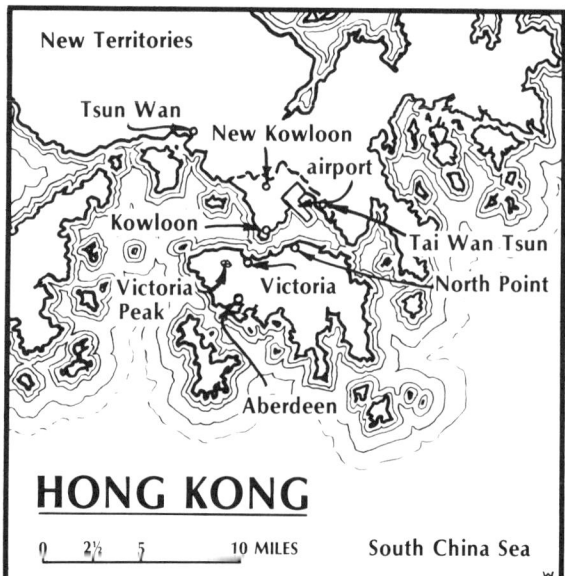

MACAO

Area: six sq. miles
Pop: 276,700 (1981 est.)

Like nearby Hong Kong, Macao is one of those rare places in today's world — an outpost of a once powerful empire. It is Portugal's sole remaining Far East possession and is about 40 miles to the west of Hong Kong. It consists of a small peninsula holding most of the population, plus two small islands.

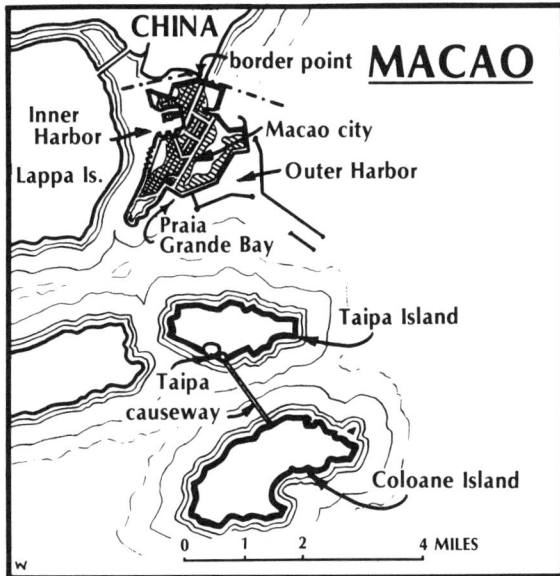

MALDIVE ISLANDS

Area: 115 sq. miles
Pop: 150,000 (1980 est.)
Capital: Male

This Indian Ocean group of islands consists of 19 atolls made up of 1,087 islands, only 203 of which are inhabited. None is more than five square miles in area, and there are no hills. Fish processing and tourism are mainstays of the economy.

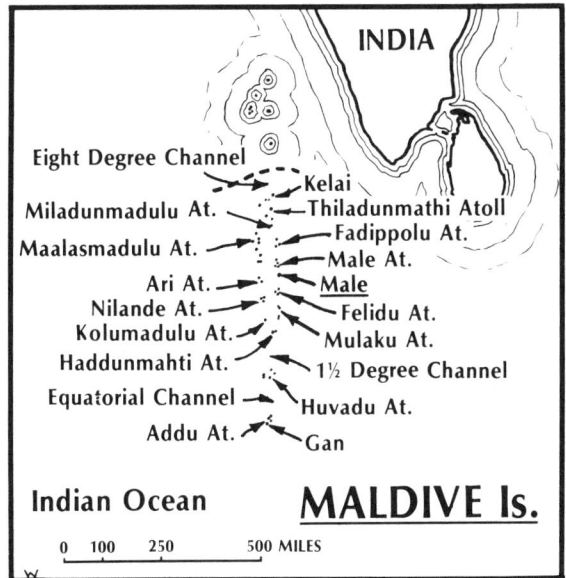

NEPAL, KINGDOM OF

Area: 56,136 sq. miles
Pop: 15.3 million (1981 est.)
Capital: Katmandu (Kathmandu)

Originally a group of principalities, Nepal became dominated by the Gurkhas, who gained a reputation in the British Army as fearless fighters. Closed to the rest of the world for centuries, the country can now be reached by road or air from India.

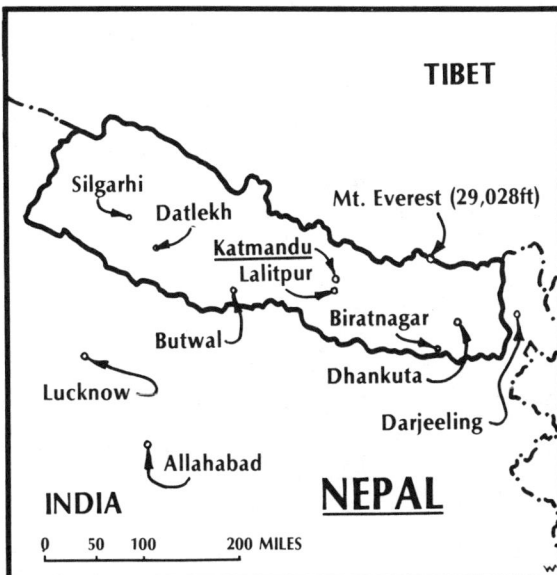

SINGAPORE, REPUBLIC OF

Area: 239 sq. miles
Pop: 2.5 million (1981 est.)
Capital: Singapore

Like Hong Kong, Singapore is a seaport and commercial center of growing importance and is the world's fourth largest port. It was founded in 1819 by Sir Thomas Stamford Raffles and was a British colony until becoming independent in 1959.

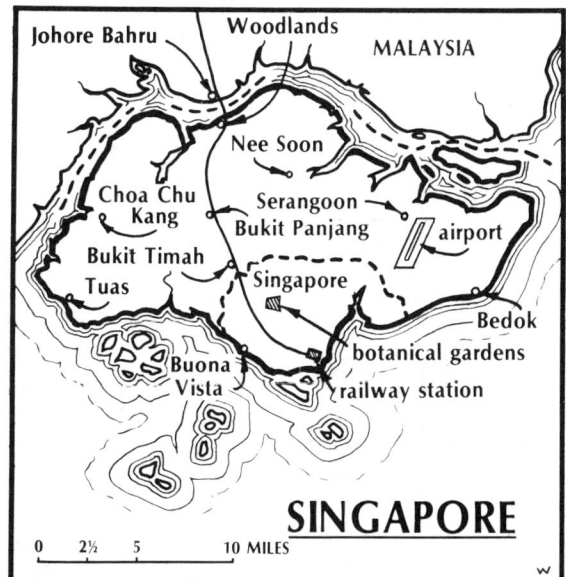

Asia, Southwest

Although belonging in Asia proper, the southwest portion of that continent possesses an importance out of all proportion to its size.

Not only an area currently crucial to the welfare and peace of the world, it is also the birthplace of both Christianity and Islam. Thus, much of the world's religion and culture can be traced directly to Southwest Asia, or the Middle East, as it is commonly called.

Today, "trouble in the Middle East" means the same to us as did the phrase "trouble in the Balkans" to a previous generation.

It is a flashpoint and will remain so until Arab and Jew, and Arab and Arab, find a way to live together in peace.

The area has received much pubicity in recent years, and the chain of events that led us to wait for hours to buy a few gallons of gasoline during the early 1970s began there.

From both a cultural and economic standpoint, Southwest Asia holds the key that can open either the door to peace or the one leading to disaster.

Stamp-issuing countries of Southwest Asia

1. Afghanistan
2. Bahrain
3. Iran
4. Iraq
5. Israel
6. Jordan
7. Kuwait
8. Lebanon
9. Oman
10. Pakistan
11. Qatar
12. Saudi Arabia
13. Syria
14. Turkey
15. United Arab Emirates
16. Yemen Arab Republic
17. Yemen, PDR

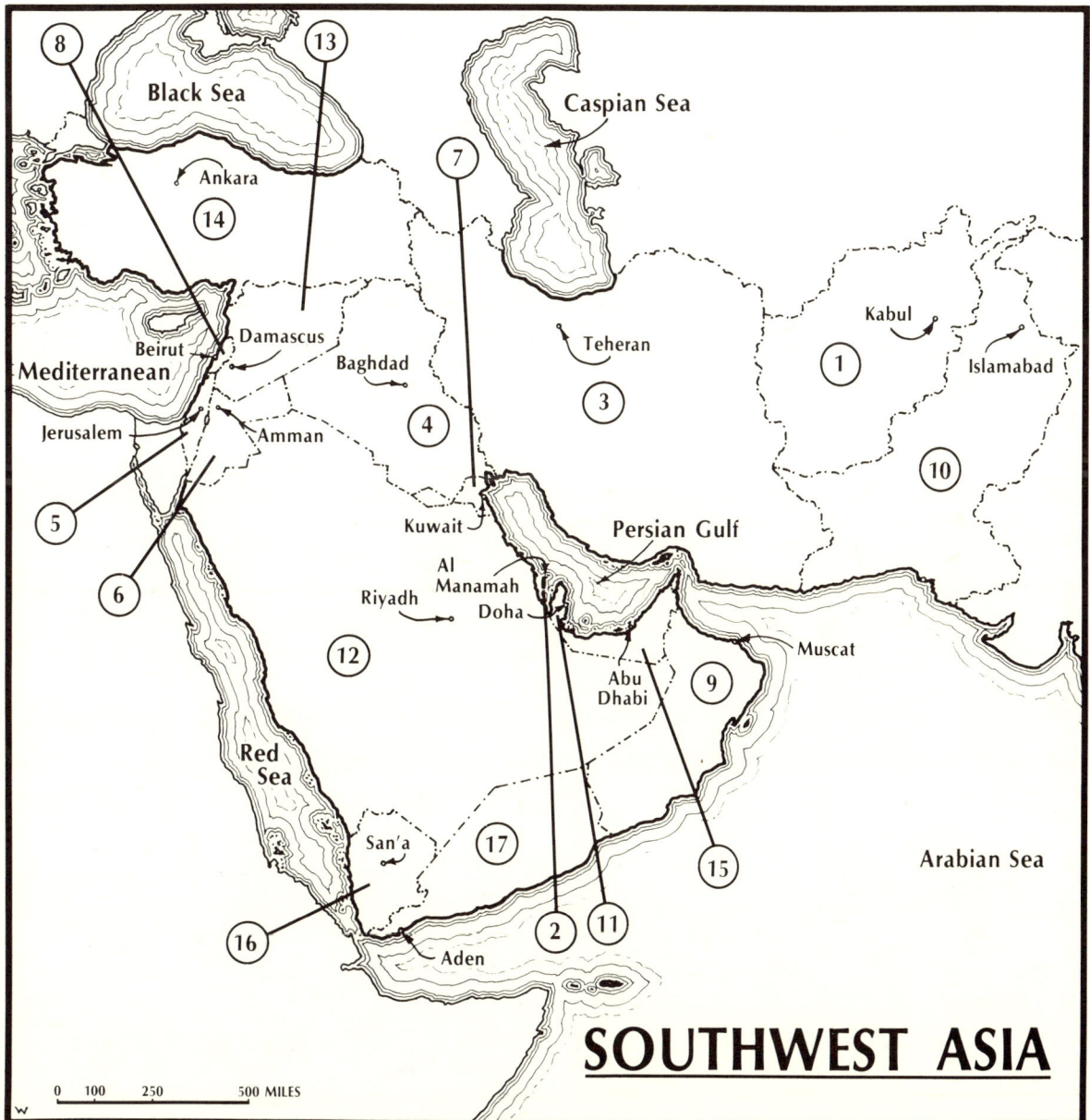

Black Sea
Ankara
14

Caspian Sea

Mediterranean
Beirut
Damascus
Baghdad
Teheran
Kabul
Islamabad
1
10

Jerusalem
Amman
Kuwait
Persian Gulf
3
4

Al Manamah
Doha
Riyadh
12
Abu Dhabi
Muscat
9

Red Sea
San'a
17
15

16
Aden
2 11

Arabian Sea

SOUTHWEST ASIA

0 100 250 500 MILES

BAHRAIN, STATE OF

Area: 258 sq. miles
Pop: 360,00 (1981)
Capital: Al Manamah (Manama)

Bahrain was under British protection from 1861 until it achieved independence in 1971. It is an island in the Persian Gulf, to the west of the Qatar Peninsula. Plans for a causeway linking it with Saudi Arabia on the Arabian mainland are reported.

LEBANON, REPUBLIC OF

Area: 3,950 sq. miles
Pop: 3 million (1981 est.)
Capital: Beirut

Formerly part of the Turkish Empire, Lebanon was mandated to France after WWI and became independent after WWII. It currently is occupied by Syrian and Israeli forces. A multinational peace-keeping force is trying to maintain order.

KUWAIT, STATE OF

Area: 6,532 sq. miles
Pop: 1.5 million (1981 est.)
Capital: Kuwait

Located at the head of the Persian Gulf, Kuwait is flat, arid, and extremely hot. During the summer, temperatures reach 130 degrees F., and rainfall is about four inches a year. From 1899 until independence in 1961, Britain protected Kuwait.

YEMEN ARAB REPUBLIC

Area: 77,200 sq. miles
Pop: 5.3 million (1981 est.)
Capital: San'a

After many years under Turkish domination, North Yemen (now the Yemen AR) gained its independence in 1918, but it remained poor and in recent years has been wracked by revolution and civil war, a condition rendered worse by a long period of drought.

Australasia and the Pacific Ocean

Australasia and the Pacific Ocean encompasses an enormous area. It includes the island continent of Australia, the twin islands of New Zealand, and the world's largest ocean, with its thousands of scattered atolls and islands.

From bustling Sydney to remote Pitcairn, it is an area of dramatic contrasts.

The major lands are still new in terms of our society. Without modern travel facilities, many of the remote areas, where the ties with yesterday are more evident, would be difficult to reach.

The dream of one's own palm-fringed island set like a gem in a blue-green lagoon becomes more real in the South Pacific, and for those who must stay home, the dream can be visualized on the many stamps of the area.

Nature lovers need not feel neglected, since much of Australia's strange fauna can be admired via its stamps, as can the tropic beauty of the whole area's flora.

Stamp-issuing countries of Australia & Pacific

1. Aitutaki
2. Australia
3. Cook Islands
4. Fiji
5. French Polynesia
6. Kiribati
7. Nauru
8. New Caledonia
9. New Zealand
10. Niuafo'ou
11. Niue
12. Norfolk Island
13. Palau
14. Papua New Guinea
15. Penrhyn
16. Pitcairn Islands
17. Samoa
18. Solomon Islands
19. Tokelau Islands
20. Tonga
21. Tuvalu
22. Vanuatu
23. Wallis and Futuna

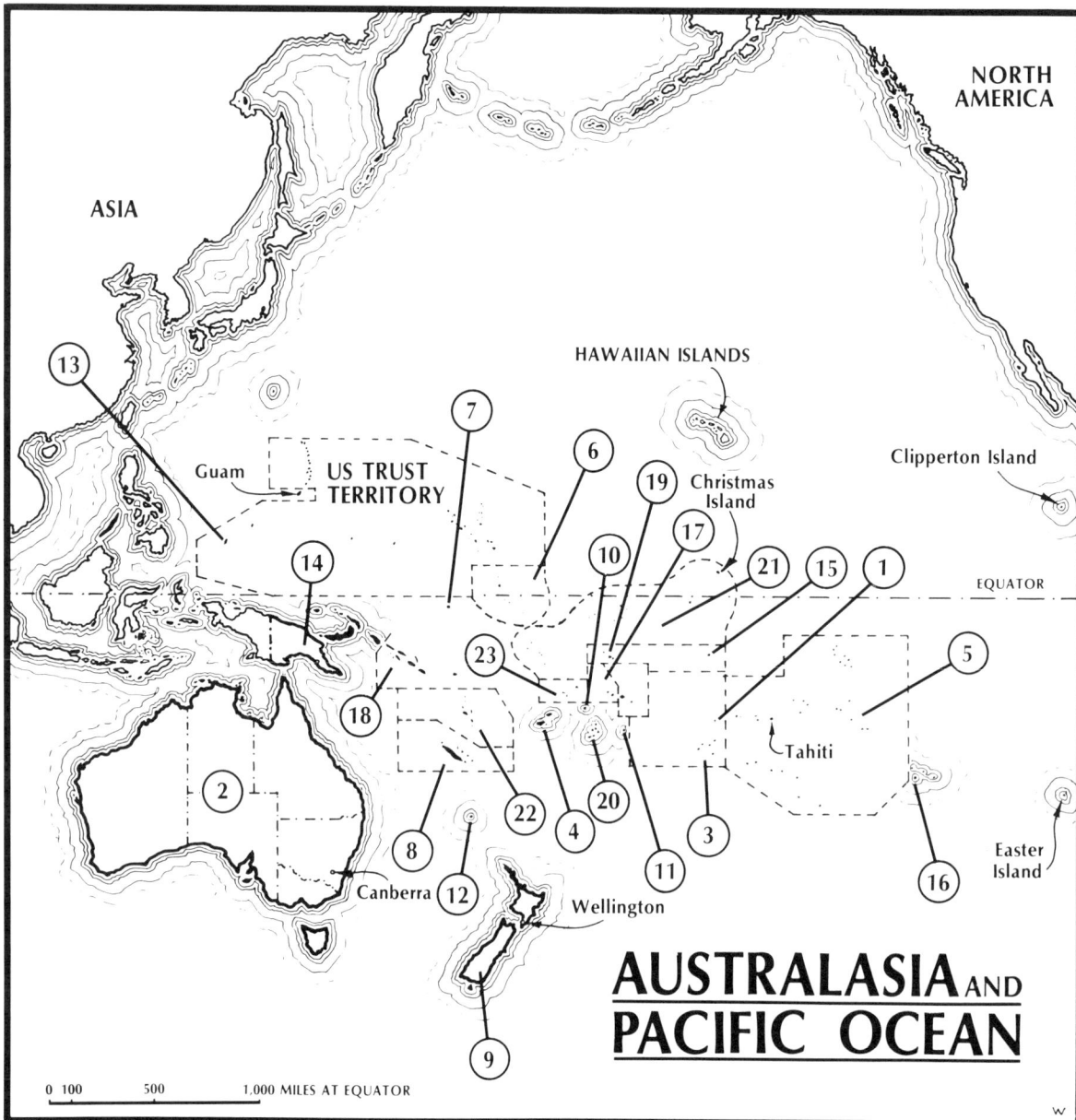

AUSTRALASIA AND PACIFIC OCEAN

NEW CALEDONIA

Area: 8,548 sq. miles   **Pop:** 139,600 (1980 est.)
Acquired by France in 1853, the island group is now a French overseas territory.

NAURU, REPUBLIC OF

Area: eight sq. miles   **Pop:** 8,000 (1981)
Discovered in 1798, Nauru was annexed to the German Empire in 1886. It became independent in 1968.

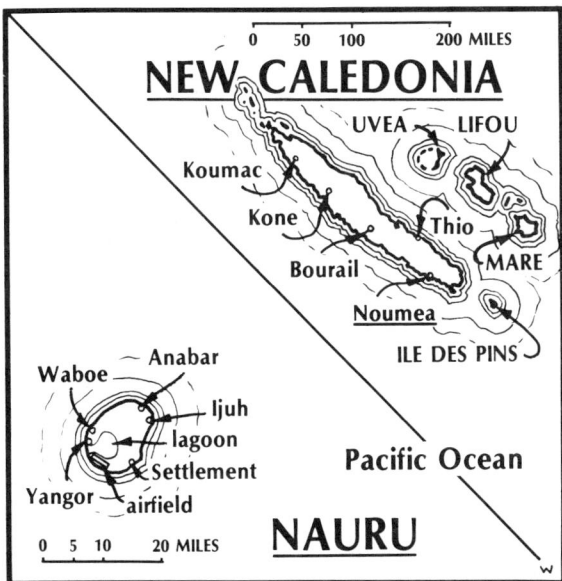

PALAU, REPUBLIC OF

Area: 179 sq. miles
Pop: 12,525 (1970 est.)
Chief town: Koror

Located in the US Trust Territory of the Pacific Islands, Palau is planning to have internal self-government in "Free Association with the US." The US will remain responsible for defense and foreign affairs.

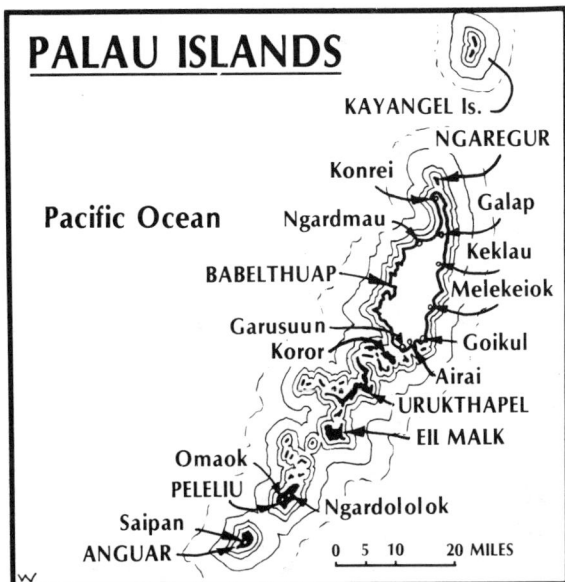

NIUE, DEPENDENCY OF

Area: 100 sq. miles   **Pop:** 3,400 (1981 est.)
Niue is an island dependency of New Zealand, which is responsible for its defense and foreign affairs.

NORFOLK ISLAND

Area: 13.5 sq. miles   **Pop:** 1,900 (1978)
Discovered by Capt. Cook in 1774, it is administered by Australia, which granted limited home rule in 1978.

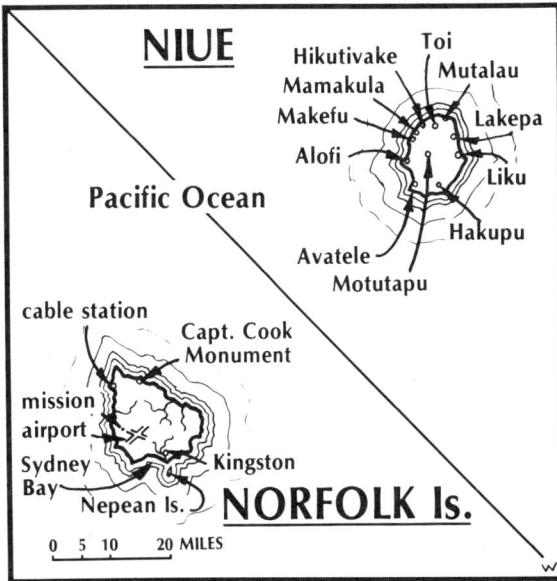

SOLOMON ISLANDS

Area: 10,640 sq. miles
Pop: 240,000 (1981 est.)
Capital: Honiara

The first European sighting of the Solomons was in 1567, by Alvaro de Mendana. The islands were made a protectorate by Britain in 1893, with Germany getting the northern islands of Choiseul and Santa Isabel, which are now in Papua New Guinea.

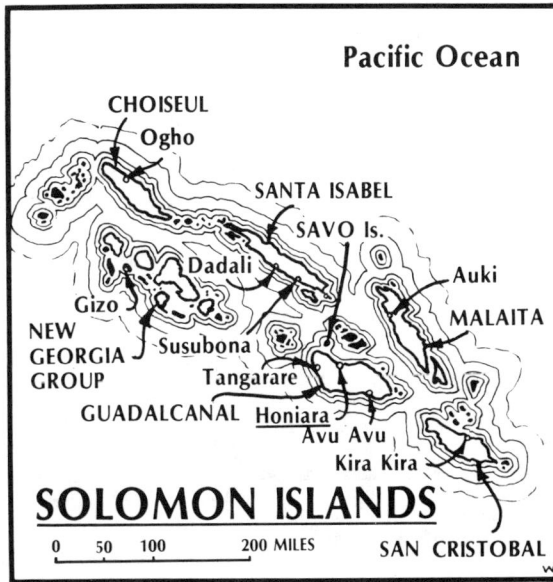

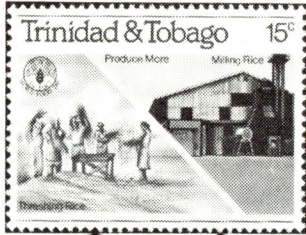

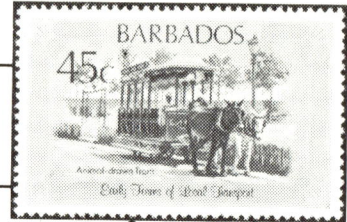

Eastern Caribbean

The main feature of the eastern Caribbean area is the Lesser Antilles, that chain of island pearls that curves from Puerto Rico to South America at Trinidad.

In addition, I have included the Greater Antilles countries of Haiti, the Dominican Republic, and Puerto Rico, plus the Netherlands Antilles off the coast of Venezuela and the Turks and Caicos Islands to the north.

The Lesser Antilles includes the two groupings known as the Leeward and Windward Islands. These are the islands that were pawns in the 18th-century wars between Britain and France and which changed hands so often during those turbulent times.

The recorded history of the eastern Caribbean islands reaches from the voyages of Columbus, who was the first European to sight many of them, to the present-day tourists, who delight in their spectacular scenery and balmy climate.

Fortunately, it is not only those lucky enough to visit these treasure islands who may enjoy them — stamp collectors may "island hop" through their albums whenever they wish. Now, if only our stamps could also transmit the scent of tropic flowers borne on a soft evening breeze, or the sound of trade winds rustling the palms along a white, sandy beach!

Stamp-issuing countries of eastern Caribbean

1. Anguilla
2. Antigua
3. Aruba (Neth. Antilles)
4. Barbados
5. Barbuda (Antigua)
6. Bonaire (Neth. Antilles)
7. Curacao (Neth. Antilles)
8. Dominica
9. Dominican Republic
10. Grenada
11. Grenada Grenadines
12. Guadeloupe
13. Haiti
14. Martinique
15. Montserrat
16. Nevis

17. Puerto Rico
18. Redonda (Antigua)
19. Saba (Neth. Antilles)
20. St. Barthelemy (Guadeloupe)
21. St. Kitts
22. St. Lucia
23. St. Martin (Guadeloupe)
24. St. Vincent
25. St. Vincent Grenadines
26. Sint Eustatius (Neth. Antilles)
27. Sint Maarten (Neth. Antilles)
28. Trinidad and Tobago
29. Turks and Caicos Islands
30. Virgin Islands, British
31. Virgin Islands, US

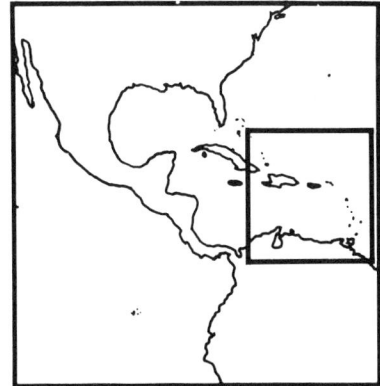

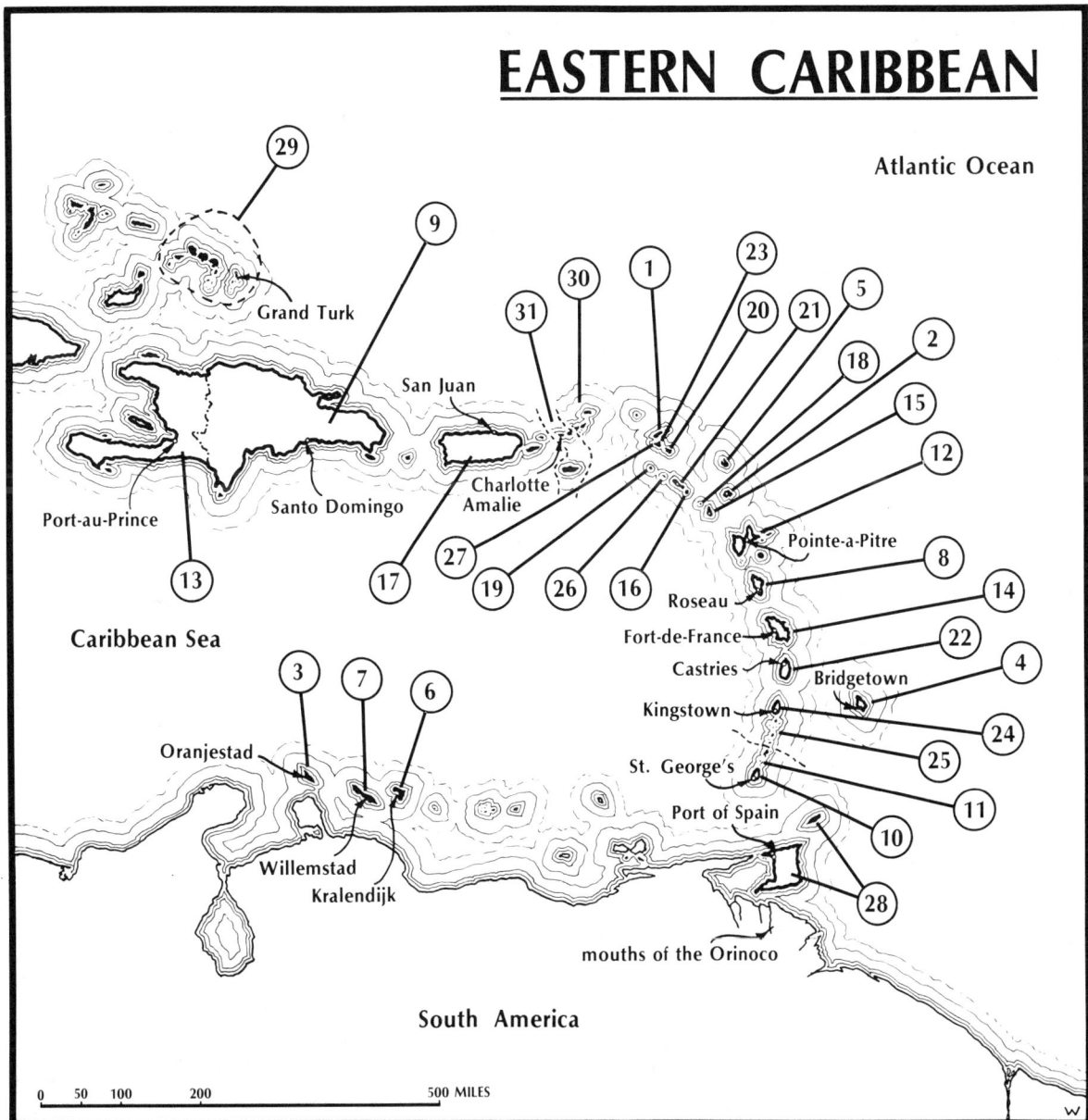

EASTERN CARIBBEAN

ANTIGUA AND BARBUDA

Area: 171 sq. miles
Pop: 76,000 (1981 est.)
Capital: St. John's

A British colony from 1632, Antigua (pronounced Anteega), with its dependency of Barbuda and half-square-mile islet of Redonda, is part of the Leeward Islands group. Antigua became independent Nov. 1, 1981.

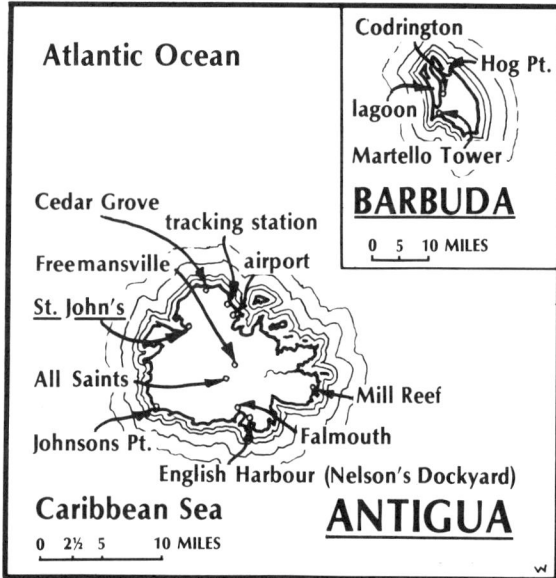

Codrington
Hog Pt.
lagoon
Martello Tower
BARBUDA
0 5 10 MILES

Atlantic Ocean

Cedar Grove
tracking station
Freemansville
airport
St. John's
All Saints
Johnsons Pt.
Mill Reef
Falmouth
English Harbour (Nelson's Dockyard)
Caribbean Sea
ANTIGUA
0 2½ 5 10 MILES

BARBADOS

Area: 166 sq. miles
Pop: 290,000 (1981 est.)
Capital: Bridgetown

An island located slightly to the east of the chain of the Lesser Antilles, Barbados was upwind from the other islands and thus escaped occupation and re-occupation during the Franco-British wars. It was first settled in 1626 and became independent in 1966.

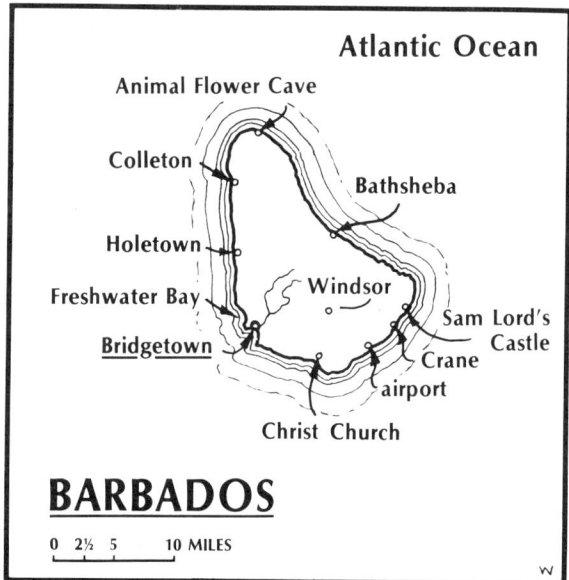

Atlantic Ocean

Animal Flower Cave
Colleton
Bathsheba
Holetown
Freshwater Bay
Windsor
Bridgetown
Sam Lord's Castle
Crane
airport
Christ Church
BARBADOS
0 2½ 5 10 MILES

BRITISH VIRGIN ISLANDS

Area: 59 sq. miles
Pop: 10,484 (1970)
Capital: Roadtown

Discovered and named by Columbus in 1493, the British Virgin Islands are part of the British Leeward Island group. They consist of about 30 islands. The islands produce fruit and tobacco, although the main industry nowadays is tourism.

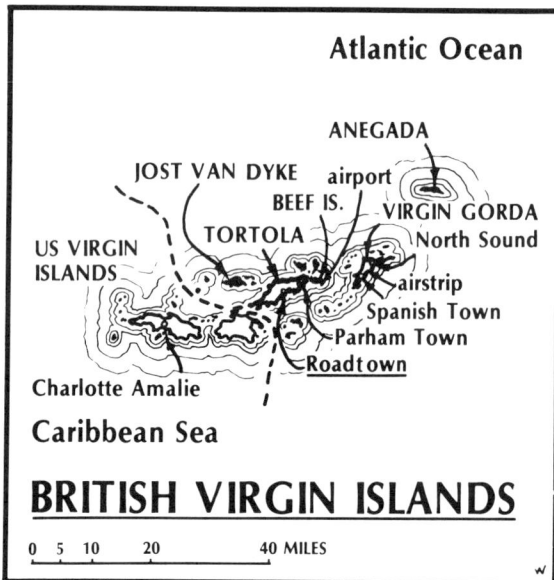

Atlantic Ocean

ANEGADA
JOST VAN DYKE
airport
BEEF IS.
VIRGIN GORDA
TORTOLA
North Sound
US VIRGIN ISLANDS
airstrip
Spanish Town
Parham Town
Roadtown
Charlotte Amalie
Caribbean Sea
BRITISH VIRGIN ISLANDS
0 5 10 20 40 MILES

DOMINICA

Area: 290 sq. miles
Pop: 80,000 (1981 est.)
Capital: Roseau

Dominica (pronounced Dom-in-eeca) became independent in 1978. It had been a British colony from 1805. The island changed hands between the French and British several times during the Napoleonic wars.

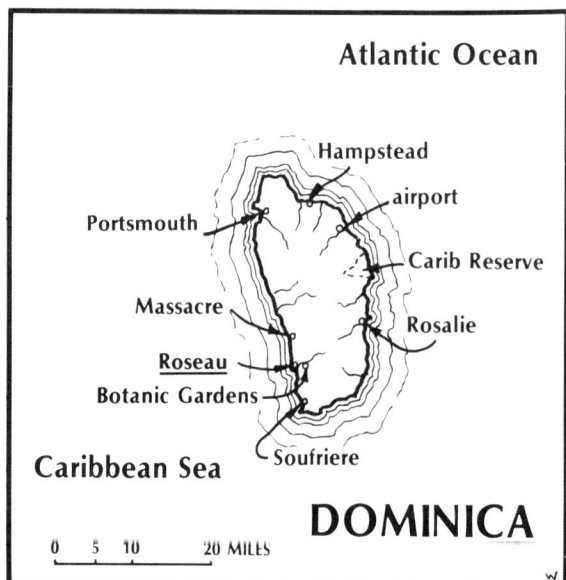

Atlantic Ocean

Hampstead
Portsmouth
airport
Carib Reserve
Massacre
Rosalie
Roseau
Botanic Gardens
Soufriere
Caribbean Sea
DOMINICA
0 5 10 20 MILES

DOMINICAN REPUBLIC ──────

Area: 18,704 sq. miles
Pop: 5.9 million (1981 est.)
Capital: Santo Domingo

The Dominican Republic shares the Greater Antilles island of Hispaniola with the Republic of Haiti and occupies the eastern two-thirds of the island. Santo Domingo was founded in 1496 and is the oldest European settlement in the hemisphere.

HAITI, REPUBLIC OF ──────

Area: 10,714 sq. miles
Pop: six million (1981 est.)
Capital: Port au Prince

Discovered by Columbus in 1492, Haiti was occupied by France from 1677, gaining its independence early in the 19th century following a slave revolt. It has had a stormy political life. The US sent in the Marines in 1915, and administered the country until 1934.

GRENADA, STATE OF ──────

Area: 133 sq. miles
Pop: 108,000 (1980 est.)
Capital: St. George's

Southernmost of the Windward Islands and about 90 miles north of Trinidad, Grenada is known as the Spice Island for its chief crops, which include nutmeg and mace, as well as cocoa, limes, and bananas. Grenada was British from 1784 until 1974.

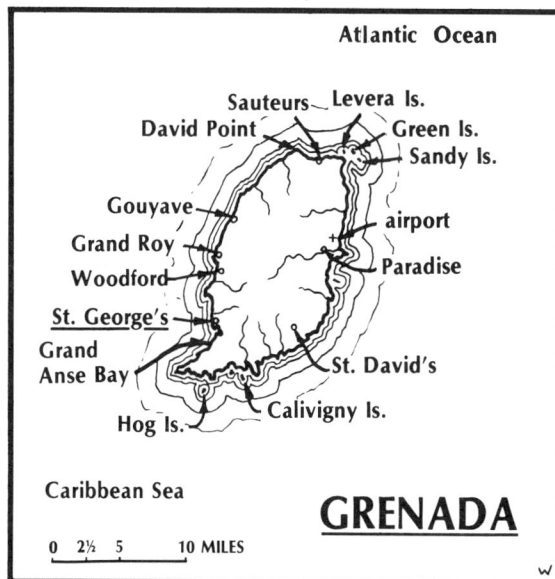

MONTSERRAT, COLONY OF ──────

Area: 40 sq. miles
Pop: 12,302 (1970)
Capital: Plymouth

Located in the Leeward Island group of the Lesser Antilles, Montserrat was discovered by Columbus in 1493. It became a British settlement in 1632, but was occupied on several occasions by the French. It is of volcanic origin.

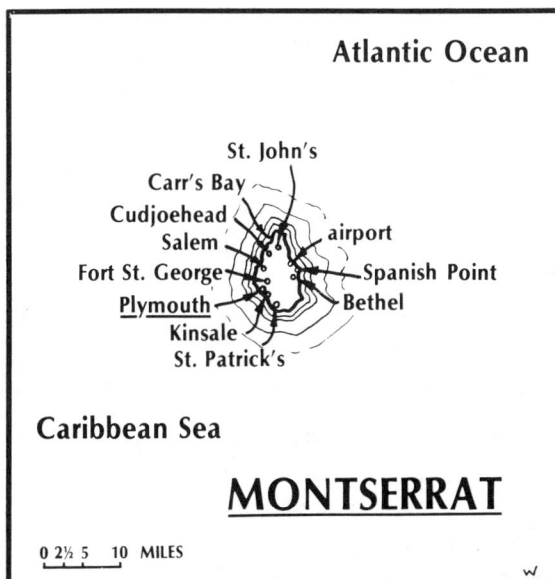

Area: 385 sq. miles
Pop: 246,500 (1979 est.)
Capital: Willemstad

The Netherlands Antilles consists of two widely separated groups of Caribbean islands. In the south, off the coast of Venezuela, are Curacao, Aruba, and Bonaire; to the north are Sint Eustatius, Sint Maarten, and Saba.

ARUBA

Area: 74 sq. miles
Pop: 59,813 (1969 est.)
Chief town: Oranjestad

Aruba is a barren island but has important oil refineries, which process oil from Venezuela.

BONAIRE

Area: 111 sq. miles
Pop: 8,099 (1969 est.)
Chief Town: Kralendijk

Bonaire is located about 30 miles east of Curacao.

CURACAO

Area: 171 sq. miles
Pop: 143,778 (1969 est.)
Capital: Willemstad

Oil refining and tourism are the two main industries of this generally flat island.

SABA

Area: five sq. miles
Pop: 972 (1969 est.)
Chief town: Bottom

Saba consists of the tip of an extinct volcano, with the settlement of Bottom being located partway down to the floor of the crater.

SINT EUSTATIUS

Area: 11 sq. miles
Pop: 1,341 (1969)
Chief town: Oranjestad

Settled by France in 1625, it became Dutch in 1632 and is now one of the northern group of islands forming the Netherlands Antilles.

SINT MAARTIN

Area: 13 sq. miles
Pop: 6,081 (1969 est.)
Chief town: Philipsburg

This part of the Netherlands Antilles consists of the southern portion of the island of St. Martin, with the rest of the island being part of the French department of Guadeloupe. The island has been divided in this fashion since 1648.

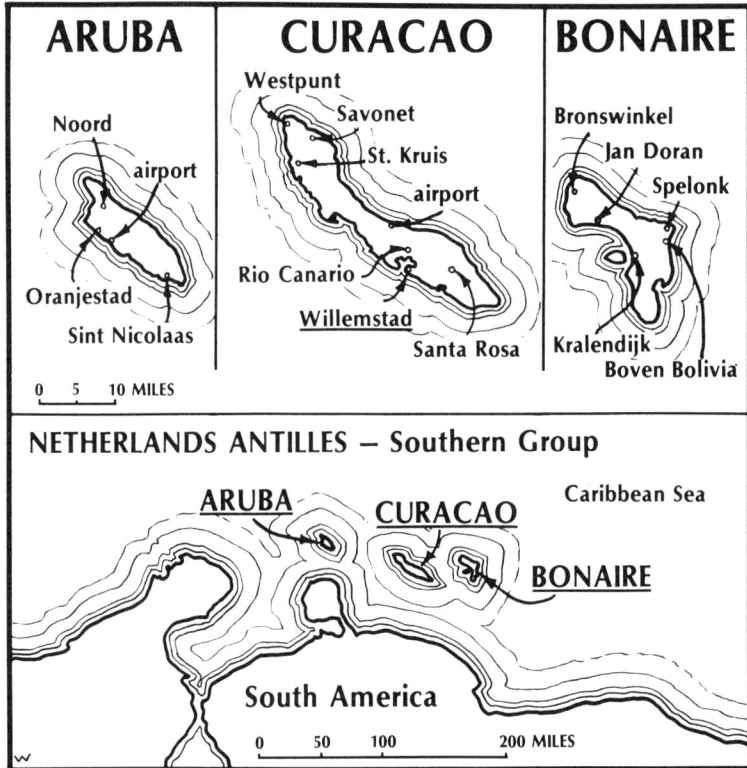

ARUBA

Noord

airport

Oranjestad

Sint Nicolaas

0   5   10 MILES

CURACAO

Westpunt

Savonet

St. Kruis

airport

Rio Canario

Willemstad

Santa Rosa

BONAIRE

Bronswinkel

Jan Doran

Spelonk

Kralendijk

Boven Bolivia

NETHERLANDS ANTILLES — Southern Group

ARUBA   CURACAO   Caribbean Sea

BONAIRE

South America

0   50   100   200 MILES

Quartier d'Orleans

Marigot (to France)

airport

Philipsburg

ST. MAARTIN

0 2½ 5 MILES

Tumble Down Dick Bay

airport

Oranjestad

ST. EUSTATIUS

0   2½   5 MILES

airport

Hellsgate

Windwardside

The Bottom

SABA

0   1½   3 MILES

NETHERLANDS ANTILLES — Northern Group

Atlantic Ocean

PUERTO RICO — VIRGIN IS.

ANGUILLA

ST. MAARTIN

BARBUDA

ST. KITTS

SABA

ST. EUSTATIUS

ANTIGUA

Caribbean Sea

NEVIS

GUADELOUPE

0   50   100   200 MILES

ST. KITTS-NEVIS

Area: 118 sq. miles
Pop: 58,000 (1980 est.)

These two members of the Leeward Islands have associated-state status with Great Britain.

ANGUILLA: With an area of 35 sq. miles and a population of about 6,000, Anguilla broke away from St. Kitts-Nevis in 1967.

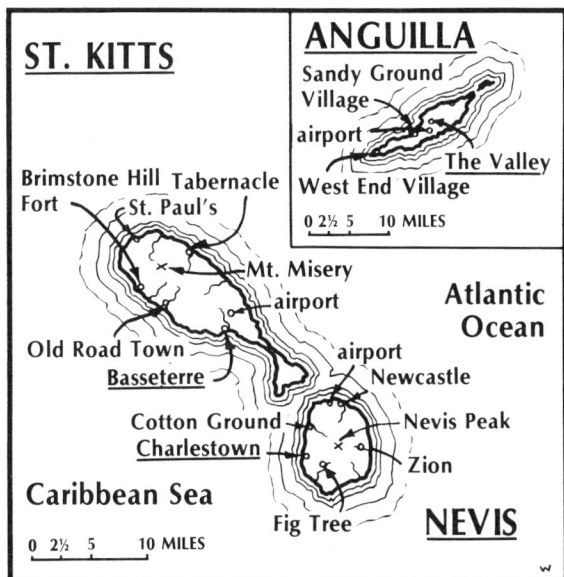

ST. LUCIA

Area: 238 sq. miles
Pop: 124,000 (1981 est.)
Capital: Castries

Located in the Windward Islands, St. Lucia has had a stormy history. Its native Carib inhabitants stoutly resisted attempts by Europeans to settle the island. Following a treaty with the Indians, the island changed hands between England and France a number of times.

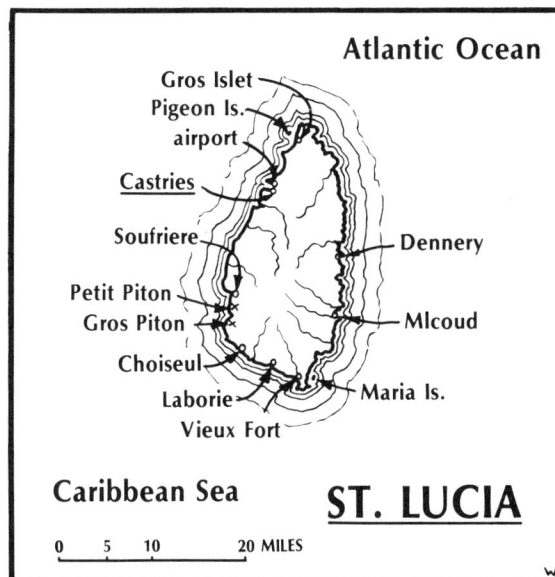

GRENADINES OF ST. VINCENT AND GRENADA

Area: 17 sq. miles (St. Vincent)
   13 sq. miles (Grenada)
Pop: 5,068 (1960 - St. Vincent)
   8,179 (1968 est. - Grenada)

The Grenadines is a 60-mile chain of some 600 islands between St. Vincent to the north and Grenada to the south. They are divided between the two islands. The chief islands in the St. Vincent group are Bequia, Mustique, Canouan, Mayreau, and Union. The main island in the Grenada group is Carriacou, the largest of the Grenadines. Although the tiny islands grow limes and cattle is raised, it is as a resort area that they are best known. Stamps have been issued for both groups of Grenadines since the latter part of 1973. Unfortunately, stamp issues have been far more prolific than postal requirements would justify. However, with 183 stamps listed by Gibbons to the latter part of 1980, St. Vincent is much more restrained than Grenada with its 423 stamps released during the same period. The current (1984) Scott catalog does not list stamps of either of the Grenadine groups.

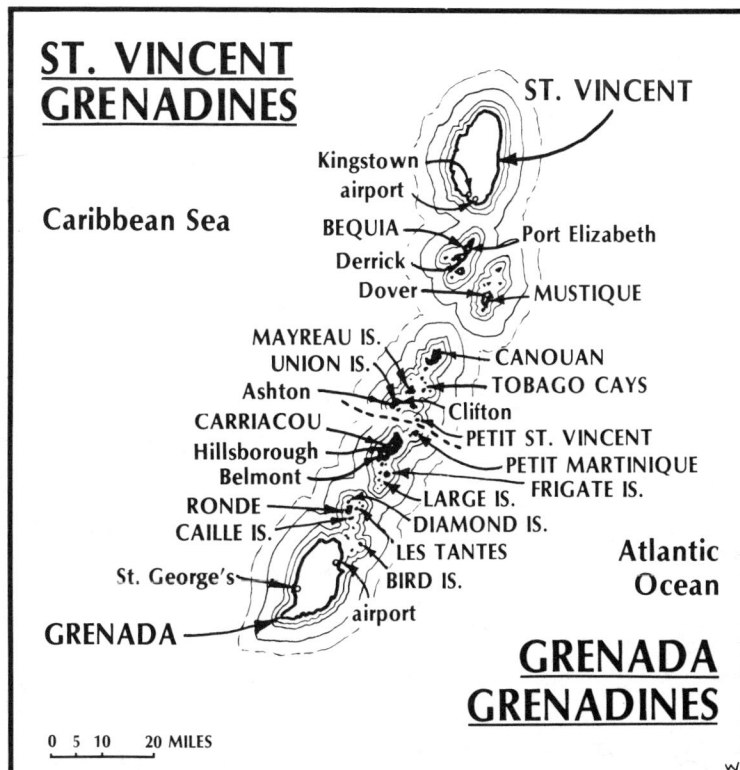

ST. VINCENT——————————————

Area: 150 sq. miles (including Grenadines)
Pop: 120,000 (1980 est.)
Capital: Kingstown

The island of St. Vincent was discovered by Columbus, who landed there on St. Vincent's Day in 1498. The British and French fought over its possession, with Britain retaining it since the 1783 Treaty of Versailles.

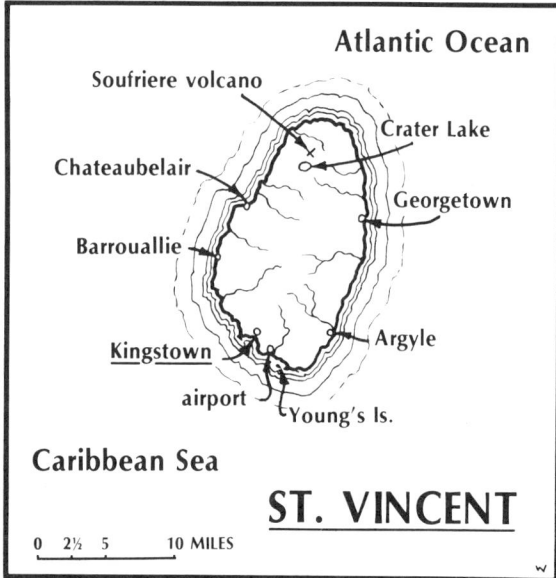

TURKS AND CAICOS ISLANDS—

Area: 166 sq. miles
Pop: 7,000 (1980)
Capital: Grand Turk

The Turks and Caicos, like the Bahamas, are not technically Caribbean islands, although they are usually included in that grouping. They lie to the north of the Greater Antilles, in the Atlantic.

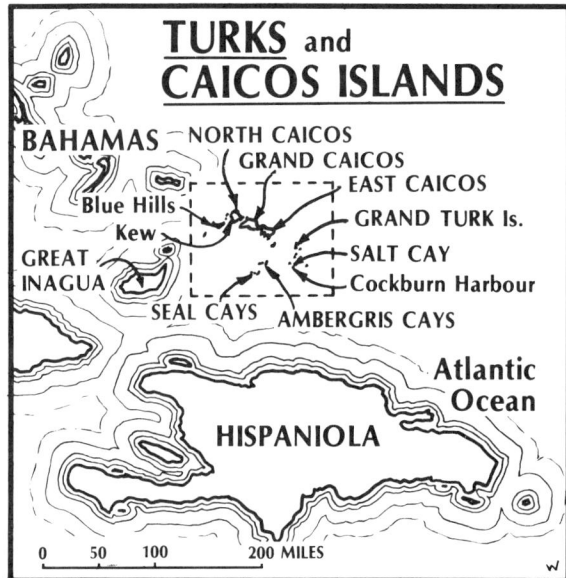

——————TRINIDAD AND TOBAGO, REPUBLIC OF——————

Area: 1,980 sq. miles
Pop: 1.2 million (1981 est.)
Capital: Port of Spain

One of the most highly developed and prosperous Caribbean countries, with one of the area's most stable governments, Trinidad and Tobago is an important crossroads of the Caribbean. It was sighted by Columbus in 1498 and was British from 1802 until granted independence in 1962. It became a republic in 1976. As in most transportation centers, Trinidad's people include many varied races and nationalities, and its society is vibrant, as anyone who has been there during Carnival can testify! In contrast, Tobago, off to the northeast, is a quiet, charming island, well suited to those who wish to get away from it all. Trinidad is roughly square with mountains along the north coast and a fertile central and southern area. Many crops are grown, and the island is famous for its rum, a byproduct of the large sugar production. Trinidad's famous Pitch Lake, on the southern peninsula, has provided paving material for roads around the world.

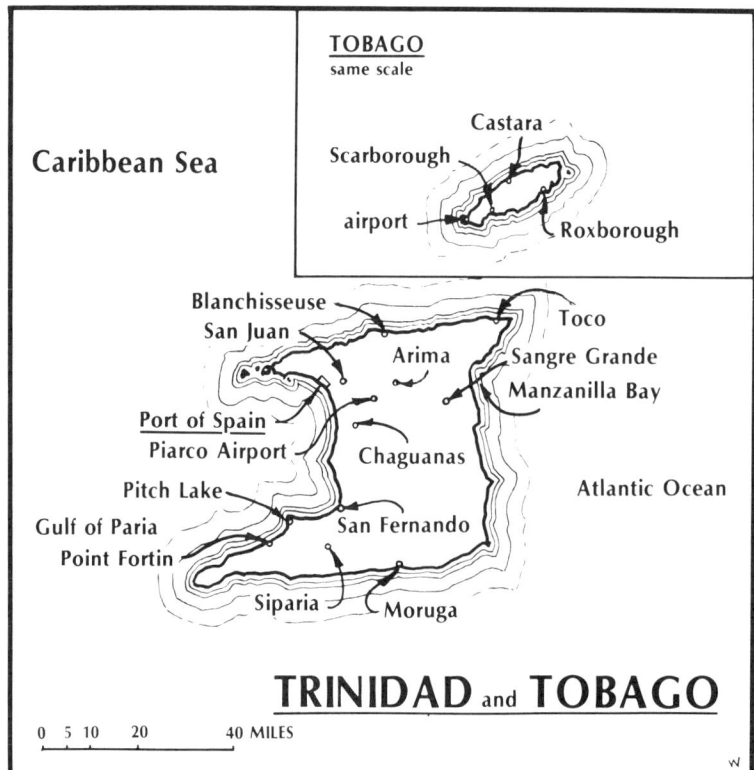

Western Caribbean and Central America

Visions of treasure-laden galleons taking the loot of the Americas back to Spain, and stories of Drake and the Spanish Main — these color our view of the western Caribbean and Central America.

The area's past lives on in such places as historic Cartagena and the strip of Panama, across which the treasure of Peru was hauled and where Cortez stood silent on that peak in Darien.

But, while the beauty and sunny climate are unchanged and the tourists swarm to Jamaica and the resorts of Yucatan, there is also strife and misery. Sad little El Salvador is currently wracked by death and terror, and the clash of ideologies may well spread to areas yet untouched.

Doubtless, current events will take their place in history alongside stories of Spanish dominion and revolutions long past. In the context of the centuries, they may rate but a page or two. Meanwhile, the free world watches with concern and sympathy.

With some exceptions, the philately of the area has not been widely popular, and that is a pity, since there is much of interest here. The collector who would venture off the freeways of our hobby will be well rewarded.

——Stamp-issuing countries of Central America & W. Caribbean——

1. Belize
2. Cayman Islands
3. Costa Rica
4. Cuba
5. El Salvador

6. Guatemala
7. Honduras
8. Jamaica
9. Nicaragua
10. Panama

CENTRAL
AMERICA

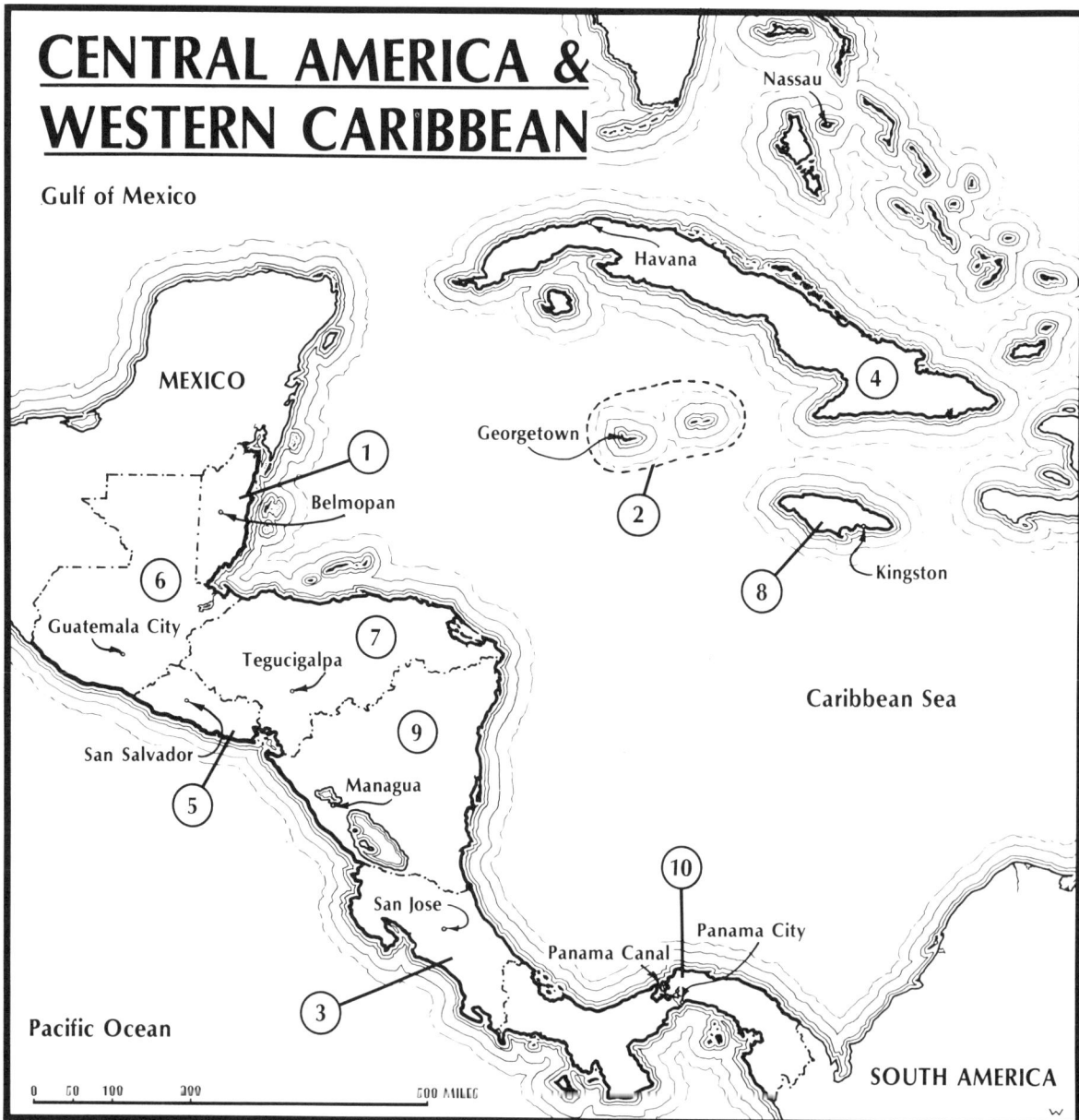

CENTRAL AMERICA &
WESTERN CARIBBEAN

Gulf of Mexico

Nassau

Havana

MEXICO

Georgetown

Belmopan

Guatemala City

Tegucigalpa

San Salvador

Managua

San Jose

Kingston

Caribbean Sea

Panama Canal
Panama City

Pacific Ocean

SOUTH AMERICA

0 50 100 200   500 MILES

CAYMAN ISLANDS, DEPENDENCY OF

Area: 93 sq. miles
Pop: 17,000 (1980)
Capital: Georgetown

The three Cayman Islands of Grand Cayman, Little Cayman, and Cayman Brac were discovered by Columbus in 1503, but were not inhabited until about 1734 when English settlers arrived from Jamaica. Most of the population is concentrated on Grand Cayman, which is about 190 miles from Jamaica. Previously governed from Jamaica, the islands are now a dependency of Great Britain. Turtles are important to the islands' economy, and the original name given to the islands by Columbus was Las Tortugas. In recent years the Caymans have become a popular tourist resort, and Georgetown is also an international banking center. The only other town on Grand Cayman is Boddentown. The two smaller islands are about 60 and 90 miles to the east northeast.

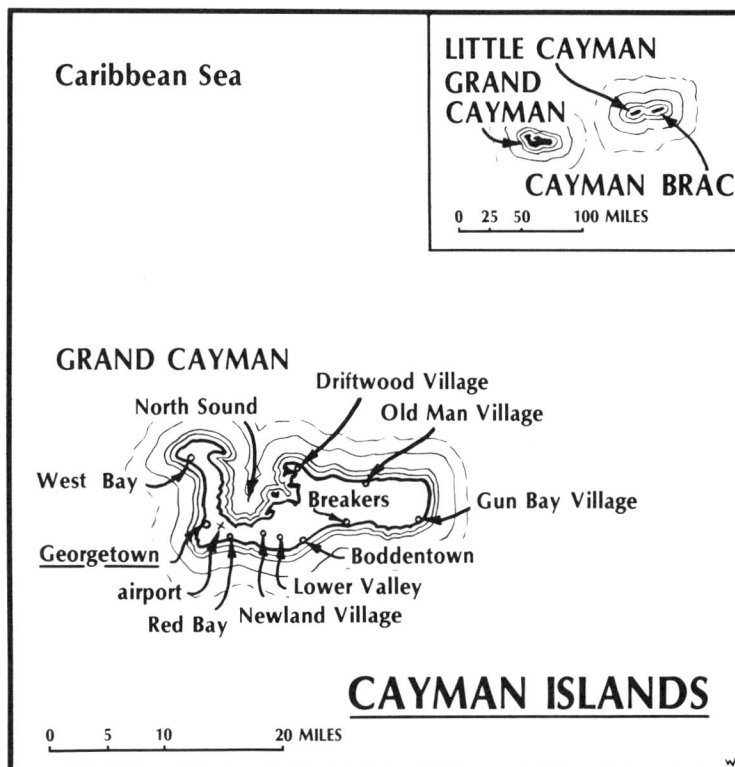

COSTA RICA, REPUBLIC OF

Area: 19,653 sq. miles
Pop: 2.3 million (1981 est.)
Capital: San Jose

Discovered by Columbus in 1502 on his last voyage, the region of Costa Rica (Spanish, meaning "Rich Coast") was conquered by Spain by 1530 and became a Spanish province in 1540. Together with other Central American countries, Costa Rica revolted against Spain in 1821 and became independent. The republic was declared in 1848 after brief periods as part of the Mexican Empire (1822-23) and of the United Provinces of Central America (1823-38). Costa Rica is Central America's most developed, peaceful, and prosperous country. Apart from some political unrest in 1949, the country has preserved its free political institutions. In recent years, there have been economic problems, and the inflation rate rose to 40 percent. Despite this, the people enjoy a relatively high standard of living and social services, especially when compared with neighboring countries.

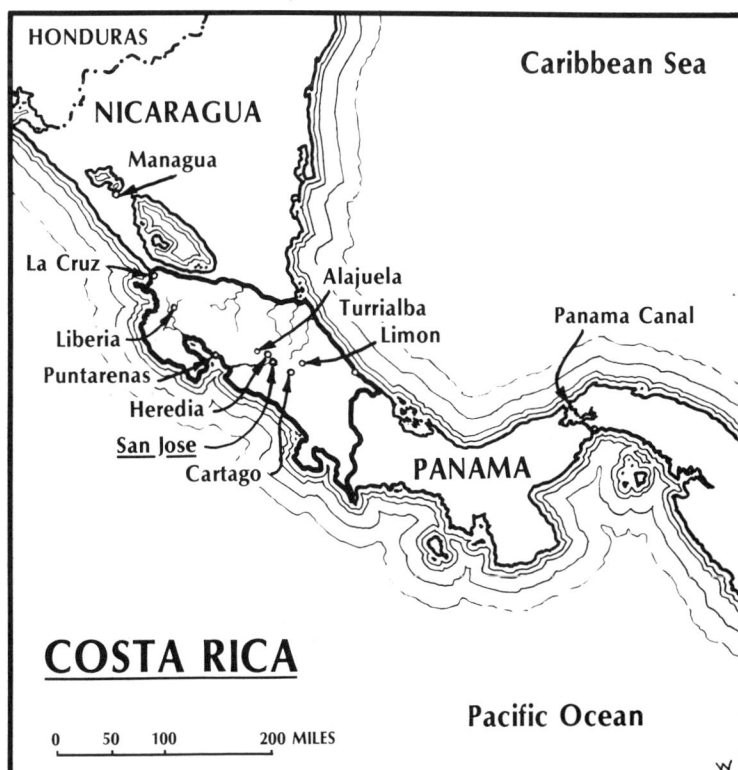

380

EL SALVADOR, REPUBLIC OF

Area: 8,124 sq. miles
Pop: five million (1981 est.)
Capital: San Salvador

The area of El Salvador was included in the Spanish captaincy general of Quatemala but became independent of that country in 1821. It was a member of the United Provinces of Central America from 1823 to 1829. El Salvador's political history has been one of revolutions and coups. Today it is wracked by civil war as leftist terrorists attempt to take control of the country. The country's economy is largely based on coffee, although other crops are grown. It is the smallest and most densely populated of the Central American countries, with a 170-mile Pacific coastline. The climate is tropical on the coast and moderated by altitude in the interior. El Salvador was one of the four countries to sign an agreement with Nicholas Seebeck for free stamps in exchange for Seebeck's right to make and sell reprints to collectors.

JAMAICA, STATE OF

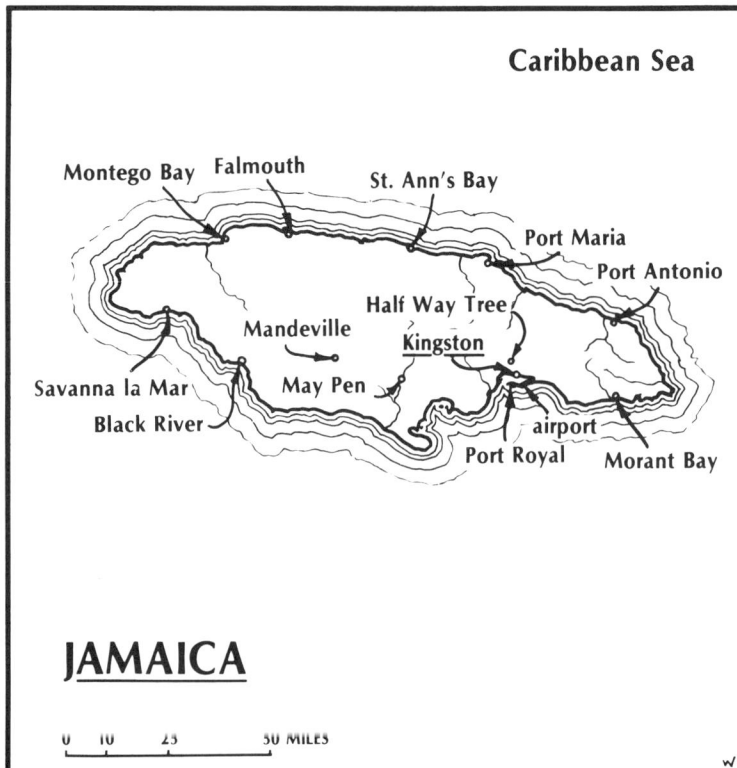

Area: 4,244 sq. miles
Pop: 2.3 million (1981 est.)
Capital: Kingston

Jamaica was visited by Columbus in 1494 and ruled by Spain until taken by Britain in 1655. The colony became an independent member of the British Commonwealth in 1962. The main products are bauxite, sugar, bananas, coffee, and cocoa, although the tourist industry is also an important source of income. The island has been a victim of major earthquakes. The thriving city and center of the slave trade, Port Royal, was destroyed during the 17th century, and the city of Kingston was built to replace it. In its turn, Kingston suffered heavy damage during a 1907 earthquake. During WWII, several areas were leased to the US as part of a deal for 50 old destroyers desperately needed by a hard-pressed Britain. Jamaica's first stamps were released in 1860, and since 1900 there has been a flow of stamps, some extremely attractive, showing various aspects of the island's geography, history, and culture.

Europe

Europe is the cultural cradle of many of us, whether we be first-generation immigrants or of that select group whose ancestors arrived on the *Mayflower*.

Its cultures have spread around the world, first by colonial means and later by immigrants, as thousands sought a new life, sometimes to escape religious or political persecution or just to get away from their overcrowded homelands.

As the birthplace of the industrial revolution in the 19th century, Europe became an area of teeming, polluted cities, dirty factories, and slum dwellings, as the wages and security offered drew thousands from the rural areas.

The new technology also created European war machines that put horrible weapons into the hands of rulers, still feudal in their thinking, who were eager to conquer and subdue their neighbors. Thus Europe became a cradle for both war and culture. The two world wars had their origins in the center of Europe as men became mad with the power that technology had provided.

Today, Europe is relatively peaceful, its peoples exhausted by conflict, and the flashpoints of war lie elsewhere.

Stamp-issuing countries of Europe

1. Aland Islands
2. Albania
3. Alderney
4. Andorra
5. Austria
6. Azores
7. Belgium
8. Berlin, West
9. Bulgaria
10. Cyprus
11. Czechoslovakia
12. Denmark

13. England
14. Faroe Islands
15. Finland
16. France
17. Germany, East
18. Germany, West
19. Gibraltar
20. Greece
21. Greenland
22. Guernsey
23. Hungary
24. Iceland

25. Ireland
26. Isle of Man
27. Italy
28. Jersey
29. Liechtenstein
30. Luxembourg
31. Malta
32. Monaco
33. Netherlands
34. Northern Ireland
35. Norway
36. Poland

37. Portugal
38. Romania
39. San Marino
40. Scotland
41. Spain
42. Sweden
43. Switzerland
44. USSR
45. Vatican City
46. Wales
47. Yugoslavia

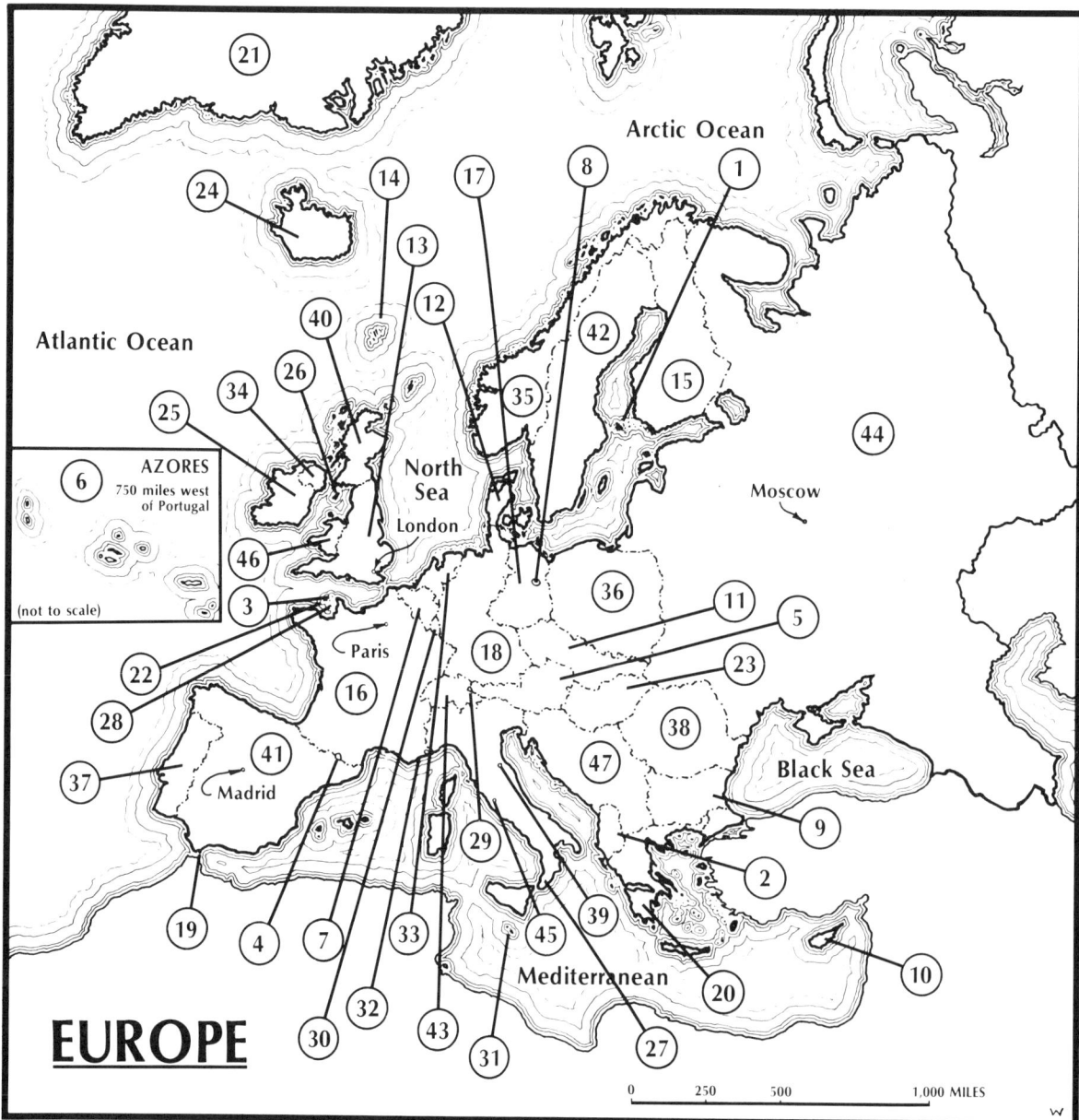

EUROPE

ALAND ISLANDS, PROVINCE OF

Area: 581 sq. miles
Pop: 20,494 (1970)
Capital: Mariehamn

The Aland Islands are a province of Finland and are located at the entrance to the Gulf of Bothnia between Finland and Sweden. About 80 of the 300 islands are inhabited. The islands were colonized by Sweden in the 12th century. They were seized by Peter the Great following his defeat of the Swedish fleet in 1714, but were returned to Sweden in 1721. In 1809, together with the rest of Finland, they were handed over to Russia. When Finland gained its freedom in 1917, the Aland Islands remained part of that country. The General Directorate of Posts and Telecommunications of Finland announced that the Aland Islands would have stamp issues beginning in 1984. The stamps were to be valid only in the Aland Islands, although Finnish stamps will also be sold for postal use there.

ANDORRA, PRINCIPALITY OF

Area: 188 sq. miles
Pop: 36,000 (1981 est.)
Capital: Andorra la Vella

The Principality of Andorra is located high in the Pyrenees Mountains on the border between France and Spain. It is a co-principality with joint sovereignty vested in the President of France and the Bishop of Urgel in Spain. The principality consists of narrow valleys and high mountain peaks, the highest of which is Pics d'Etats at 10,295 feet. There are highway connections with France and Spain. In the valleys, there is good pasture on which sheep and cattle are raised. Some tobacco and fruit are grown, but the main sources of income are tourism and the principality's "free port" status. Smuggling is also said to be a lucrative profession! The principality's status dates from the year 1278, when it came under the joint suzerainty of the French counts of Foix and the Spanish Bishop of Urgel. The French rights passed to King Henry IV in 1589 and eventually to the President of France.

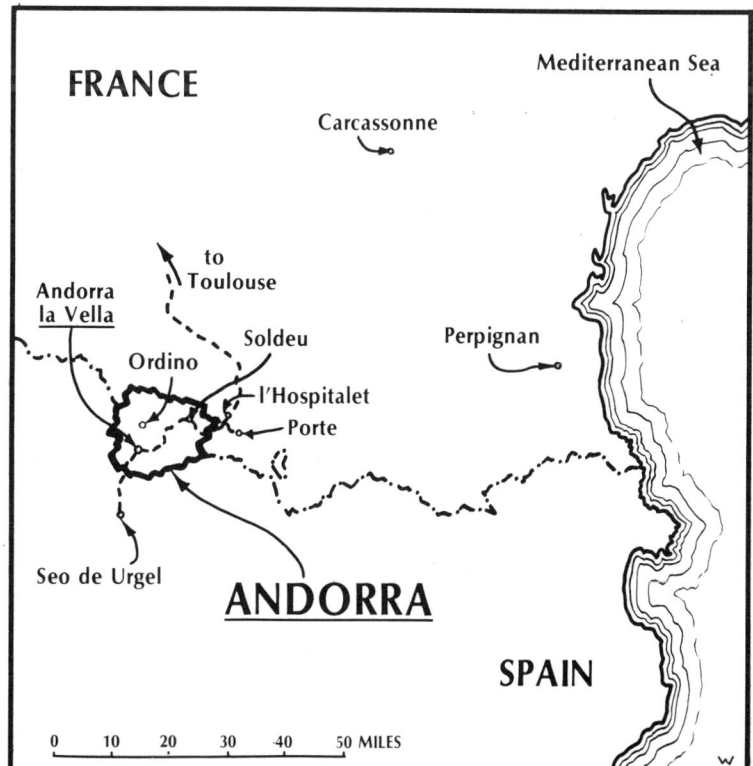

BERLIN, WEST

FRENCH ZONE

EAST GERMANY

Tegel Airport

Wedding

Tiergarten

BERLIN WALL

Charlottenburg

BRITISH ZONE

SOVIET ZONE

Spandau

Hitler's
Bunker site

Gatow

Wannsee

Lichtenberg

Grunewald
Forest

EAST BERLIN

Potsdam

Dahlem

Havel

AMERICAN
ZONE

Checkpoint Charlie

Tempelhof Airport

city limits

WEST BERLIN

0 2   5   10 MILES

Area: 185 sq. miles
Pop: 2,130,900 (1970 est.)

West Berlin comprises the post-WWII occupation zones of Britain, France, and the US. It is completely enclaved in the German Democratic Republic (East Germany), of which the Soviet zone of the city is the capital. Prior to the end of WWII, Berlin was the capital of Germany and one of the world's major cities. During WWII, it was heavily damaged by British and US bombing and, towards the end of the war, by Soviet forces, which occupied the city in the closing days of the war in April-May 1945. In 1948-49, the Soviet Union unsuccessfully tried to force its former allies out of the city by establishing a blockade of road and rail traffic from West Germany into the British, French, and US zones. An enormous airlift operation was mounted to supply the city and succeeded in keeping it out of Soviet hands. When it was obvious that the blockade had failed, it was lifted.

CYPRUS, REPUBLIC OF

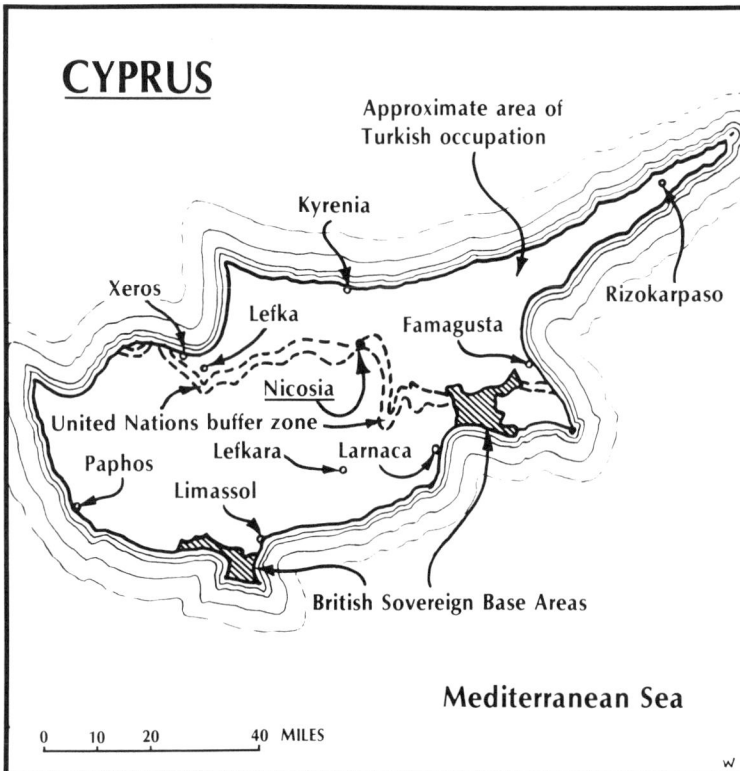

CYPRUS

Approximate area of
Turkish occupation

Kyrenia

Rizokarpaso

Xeros

Lefka

Famagusta

Nicosia

United Nations buffer zone

Lefkara

Larnaca

Paphos

Limassol

British Sovereign Base Areas

Mediterranean Sea

0   10   20   40 MILES

Area: 3,572 sq. miles
Pop: 630,000 (1981 est.)
Capital: Nicosia

Formerly part of the Roman and Byzantine empires, Cyprus was captured by King Richard I of England during the Third Crusade. Its modern history begins in 1878, when Turkey asked Britain to assume responsibility for administering the island. It was annexed to Britain at the outbreak of WWI against the Turkish Empire and became a crown colony in 1925. It was granted independence in 1960, and since then there has been strife between the Greek segment of the population and the Turkish. The UN has maintained a peace-keeping force on the island since 1964. In 1974, Turkey invaded Cyprus and currently occupies the northern 40 percent of the island. The first stamps of Cyprus were released in 1880 and consisted of British' stamps overprinted "CYPRUS."

ENGLISH CHANNEL ISLANDS

Area: 30 sq. miles (Guernsey
and dependencies)
45 sq. miles (Jersey)
Pop: 53,734 (Guernsey 1971 est.)
72,629 (Jersey)
Capitals: St. Peter Port (Guernsey)
St. Helier (Jersey)

The English Channel Islands are the sole remaining parts of the Dukedom of Normandy, an extensive area of France that was once a British possession. They are located a few miles off the French coast. Christianity came to the area in the sixth century AD. In the 10th century, the islands became the property of the Duke of Normandy. Following the conquest of England by the Normans, who became its rulers, the Dukedom of Normandy became part of the English kingdom. The island group now consists of two political entities, the Bailiwick of Guernsey and the Bailiwick of Jersey. They were the only parts of Great Britain to be invaded and occupied by the Germans during WWII. It was during the occupation that the first stamps were issued for the Channel Islands. The Baliwick of Guernsey consists of the islands of Guernsey, Alderney, Brechou, Herm, Jethou, and Sark. The so-called "island" of Lithou (Lihou) is actually only an island at high tide. At other times it is part of Guernsey.

Alderney

Alderney is a three-square-mile island at the north of the group, about eight miles from the French coast. Its chief town is St. Anne. The island now issues its own stamps under an agreement with the Guernsey Post Office.

Brechou

Brechou is an island of 74 acres located to the west of Sark.

Guernsey

Guernsey, with an area of 24.5 square miles, is the largest island in the Bailiwick of Guernsey. It is 16 miles to the northwest of Jersey and about 28 miles west of the French coast. There are low beaches to the north and rocky cliffs along the southern shore. Victor Hugo lived at the capital city of St. Peter Port for 15 years. Raising cattle, vegetables, and providing a haven for tourists seeking the mild climate are the main occupations.

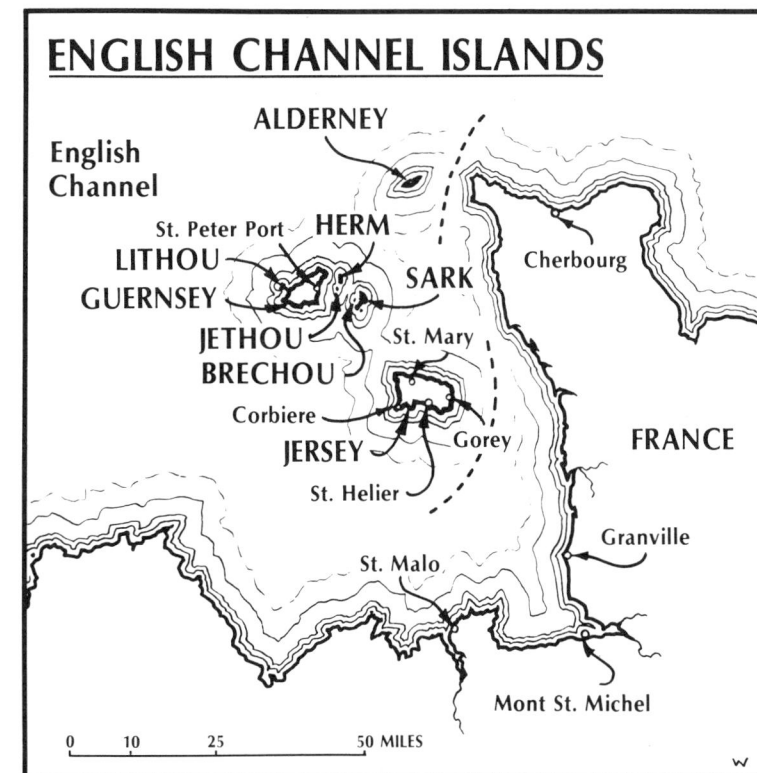

Herm

Herm is about three miles to the east of Guernsey and has an area of one-half square mile.

Jethou

Jethou is an island with an area of 44 acres, to the south of Herm. It is reported to be uninhabited.

Sark

The island of Sark is composed of Little Sark and Great Sark, which are joined by an isthmus. It has an area of two square miles and a population of about 600. It is seven miles to the east of Guernsey.

Jersey

Jersey is the largest of all the English Channel Islands, with an area of 45 square miles. It is also the most southerly of the group. Like Guernsey, it depends for its income on dairy farming, vegetable raising, and tourism. The Jersey cow, like the Guernsey, is world famous for the quality of its milk. The breed is closely guarded, and no cattle imports are permitted. Even Jersey cows that have been exported are not allowed to return. The mild climate makes Jersey a popular vacation resort and permits the raising of early vegetables for the British market. In the past, local carriage labels have been issued for some of the islands, and the reader is referred to the British Offshore Islands in the section devoted to local issues.

FAROE ISLANDS

FAROE ISLANDS

North Atlantic

KALSOY, KUNOY, EYSTURDY, VIDOY, STREYMOY, Vestmanhavn, Hattervig, VAGAR, SVINOY, Myggenaes, BORDOY, Klaksvig, Thorshavn, Hvidenaes, SANDOY, Husevig, SUDUROY, Lobra

0 10 20 30 40 50 MILES

Area: 540 sq. miles
Pop: 43,300 (1980)
Capital: Thorshavn

The Faroes group consists of 22 islands, of which 17 are inhabited. The group is located in the North Atlantic about 200 miles northwest of the Shetland Islands. It is a self-governing unit within the Kingdom of Denmark. The islands are tips of the submarine mountain range that runs from Scotland to Greenland. The climate is influenced by the Gulf Stream, and there are large amounts of fog and rain. The people are of Viking descent, and their parliament was founded more than 1,000 years ago. There are six political parties ranging from left to right, with opinions varying from those seeking closer ties with Denmark to those wanting complete independence. Sheep raising is important to the economy, but it is fishing that supports the Faroes. In 1940, Great Britain assumed responsibility for the protection of the islands while Denmark was under German occupation.

GIBRALTAR

GIBRALTAR

Neutral Zone, border, airfield, North Mole, town, harbor, Catalan Bay, water catchments, South Mole, Bay of Algeciras, The Rock, Rosia Bay, Windmill Hill Flats, summit (1,398ft), Little Bay, Europa Point, Mediterranean

0 ½ 1 2 MILES

Area: 2.25 sq. miles
Pop: 29,000 (1980)

Gibraltar is a British naval and air base located on a peninsula jutting south from the mainland of Spain on the Strait of Gibraltar between Europe and Africa. It thus guards the eastern entrance to the Mediterranean Sea and has been British since 1704. It is dominated by the massive 1,396-foot high rock. Most of the population is concentrated in Gibraltar town. Gibraltar was captured by the Moors under Tarik ibn-Zaid and named Jabal al-Tarik, from which its present name has derived. It came into the possession of Spain in 1462 and was taken in 1704 by the British during the War of the Spanish Succession. The French and Spanish unsuccessfully laid siege to Gibraltar in 1779-83. Spain has made claim to it and in recent years closed the border across the narrow isthmus that connects it to the mainland.

ISLE OF MAN

Area: 227 sq. miles
Pop: 64,000 (1980 est.)
Capital: Douglas

The Isle of Man is a popular vacation island located in the middle of the Irish Sea between England, Scotland, Ireland, and Wales. The mild climate permits the growth of some sub-tropical plants, and much of the island is taken up with agriculture. The island came under Scandinavian rule from the ninth to 13th centuries, when it was ceded to Scotland. It was granted to England in 1346 and has remained English, while retaining much of its Scandinavian culture. There has been considerable mining of the island's mineral resources, and other occupations include fishing, dairy farming, and the raising of flowers and vegetable crops. The shoreline generally has tall cliffs indented with bays, and the island's highest point is Snaefell at 2,034 feet.

LIECHTENSTEIN, PRINCIPALITY OF

Area: 62 sq. miles
Pop: 30,000 (1980 est.)
Capital: Vaduz

The tiny Principality of Liechtenstein is located on the east bank of the Rhine between Switzerland and Austria. There is a narrow strip of flat land along the river, with the rest being mountainous. Some peaks reach to more than 8,000 feet. The principality became sovereign under Austrian protection in 1866 and was a member of the Austrian Customs Union until the end of WWI, when it entered the Swiss customs union. Because of low taxes, many foreign corporations have headquarters in Liechtenstein, and foreign workers constitute a third of the total population. Wine, fruit, and corn are grown, and there is considerable dairy farming. Light industry is also well established, and textiles and pharmaceutical products are made.

LUXEMBOURG, GRAND DUCHY OF

BELGIUM

Clervaux

GERMANY

Bastogne

Wiltz

Diekirch

Ettelbruck

Mersch

Arlon

Capellen

Grevenmacher

Luxembourg

Remich

Bettembourg

Differdange

Esch

Dudelange

LUXEMBOURG

FRANCE

0 5 10 15 20 MILES

Area: 1,000 sq. miles
Pop: 360,000 (1981 est.)
Capital: Luxembourg

Luxembourg was noted as a county of the Holy Roman Empire in the 10th century. It became a duchy in 1354, although it has been under the control of Spain, Austria, and France. It was part of the Kingdom of the Netherlands from 1815 to1830, but when Belgium revolted and declared its independence, the western part of the duchy was given to the new country. The rest remained a grand duchy linked to the Netherlands. Its neutrality and independence were guaranteed in the late 1860s, but that did not prevent Germany from invading and occupying the duchy in both WWI and WWII. Since the end of WWII, Luxembourg has given up its traditional neutrality and is now a member of NATO (since 1949) and of the European Common Market (since 1958). There is a large steel industry in Luxembourg, and wheat, potatoes, and wine are other products. Textiles and chemicals are manufactured.

MALTA

Victoria (Rabat) **GOZO**

Xaghra

Nadur

COMINO

Xewkija

St. Paul's Bay

Birkirkara

Sliema

MALTA

Mosta

Mdina

Floriana

Valletta

Rabat

Cospicua

Zebbug

Zabbar

Qormi

Paola

Siggiewi

Luqa

Zejtun

Hamrun

int. airport

MALTA

Mediterranean Sea

0 2½ 5 10 MILES

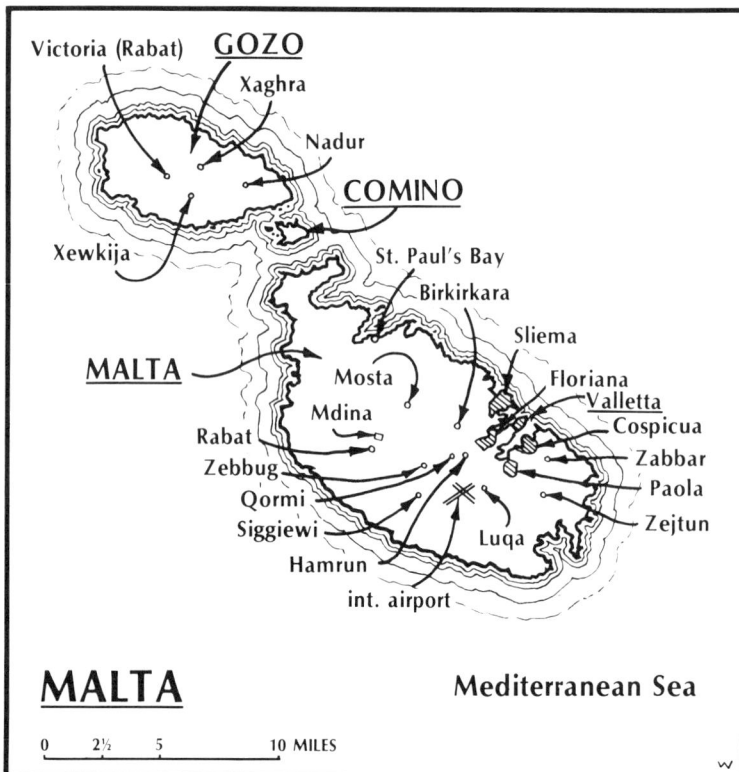

Area: 124 sq. miles
Pop: 350,000 (1981 est.)
Capital: Valletta

Malta consists of the islands of Malta, Gozo, and Comino. It is located to the south of Sicily in the central Mediterranean. First recorded as a Phoenician trading settlement, the islands have had a long and eventful history. About 218 BC they became part of the Roman Empire, and in AD 60, St. Paul was wrecked there at St. Paul's Bay. During the period of the Byzantine Empire, Malta came under Arab occupation. That left a strong imprint on the island's culture. Norman adventurers drove the Arabs out in AD 1090. In 1533, the islands were ceded to the Knights of St. John of Jerusalem, and Malta was their kingdom for 275 years, until they surrendered to Napoleon. With British help, the inhabitants drove out the French in 1800. In 1814, the islanders decided to place themselves under British protection as part of the British Empire.

MONACO, PRINCIPALITY OF

Area: 0.73 sq. miles
Pop: 30,000 (1980 est.)
Capital: Monaco-Ville

Tiny Monaco, enclaved on the Mediterranean coast of France, has been independent for 300 years. It has been ruled by the House of Grimaldi since AD 1297, except for a period during the 18th-century French Revolution. It was under the protection of the Kingdom of Sardinia from 1815 to 1860, and since then, of France. The mainstay of the principality is tourism, with significant contributions coming from the Casino and the sale of postage stamps to collectors, although stamp-issuing policies are no longer considered as excessive as they once were. In recent years, there has been considerable economic and real estate development, and the principality's area has been increased by landfills. Monaco's Oceanographic Museum is well known and is under the direction of Jacques Coustou. Forty-eight governments maintain consulates in Monaco.

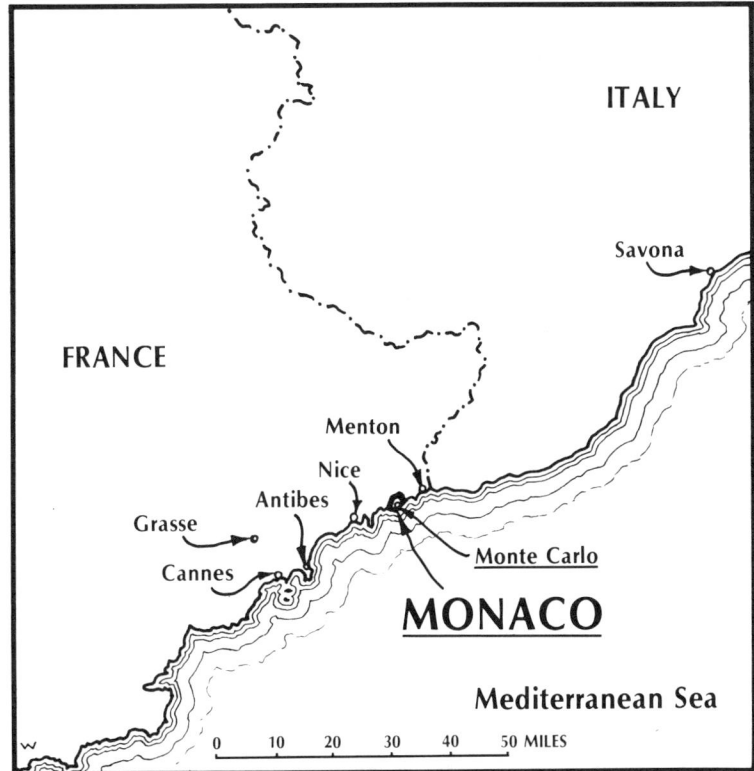

ITALY

Savona

FRANCE

Menton

Nice

Antibes

Grasse

Monte Carlo

Cannes

MONACO

Mediterranean Sea

0 10 20 30 40 50 MILES

NORTHERN IRELAND

Area: 5,463 sq. miles
Pop: 1,540,000 (1978 est.)
Capital: Belfast

Strife-torn and wracked by religious conflict, Northern Ireland consists of six of the nine counties of Ulster at the northeastern tip of Ireland. In 1920, as a mainly protestant area, it chose to remain British when the rest of Ireland opted for separation. As part of the United Kingdom, Northern Ireland has 12 members in the British parliament. It is by far the most prosperous and economically developed area of Ireland. It has resisted the republic's invitations to merge, and internal unrest continues as the Catholic minority battles what it regards as second-class status in a Protestant society. During the past 12 years, more than 2,000 persons have been killed in terrorist acts both in Northern Ireland and in England itself.

Londonderry

Portrush

NORTHERN IRELAND

Belfast

Armagh

Sligo

Irish Sea

Galway

Dublin

Atlantic Ocean

REPUBLIC OF IRELAND

Limerick

Waterford

Cork

0 20 40 60 80 100 MILES

390

SAN MARINO, MOST SERENE REPUBLIC OF

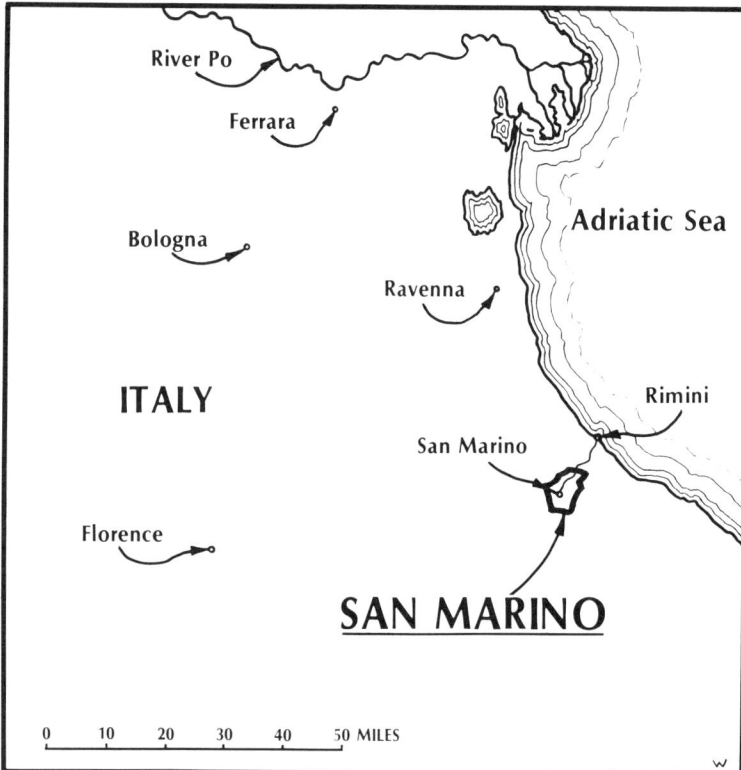

Area: 24 sq. miles
Pop: 21,537 (1980 est.)

San Marino is a republic located in north central Italy some 12 miles from the coastal town of Rimini and entirely surrounded by that country. It is claimed that the republic is the oldest state in Europe and to have been founded in the forth century by a Christian stonecutter named Marinus as a refuge against religious persecution. A monastery is recorded there in the ninth century. A community grew around it, and over the years it has resisted all assaults on its independence from Casare Borgia to Napoleon and Mussolini. In 1862, San Marino signed a treaty of friendship with Italy, and that has been periodically renewed. Farming and livestock-raising, plus some light industry and cheesemaking, are the main income producers, although many collectors would have said that postage stamps are pretty high on the list.

SCOTLAND

Area: 3,405 sq. miles
Pop: 5,195,600 (1977 est.)
Capital: Edinburgh

Scotland is a kingdom now united with England, Wales, and Northern Ireland as the United Kingdom. It is located at the northern tip of the island containing England and Wales, and includes many offshore islands. To the south, between the Firth of Forth (with Edinburgh) and the Firth of Clyde (with Glasgow), is the Lowlands; to the north is the Highlands. Three-quarters of the population and most of the industry are located in the Lowlands. Glasgow is the major industrial and shipbuilding center of the UK. Scotland was called Caledonia by the Romans, and they waged war against the Pict and Celtic tribes along the northern border of the Roman Empire. The Kingdom of Scotland was founded in AD 1018, but it was not until 1603, when King James VI of Scotland came to the throne of England as James I, that the two countries became united.

SWITZERLAND (SWISS CONFEDERATION)

Area: 15,941 sq. miles
Pop: 6,343,000 (1981 est.)
Capital: Bern

Switzerland is located in the alpine region of central Europe bordering on Austria, France, Germany, Italy, and Liechtenstein.

Properly called the Swiss Confederation, it is composed of 20 full cantons and six half cantons.

The area was inhabited in ancient times by the Celtic Helvetii, from which the Latin name of Helvetia is derived.

The invading Romans led by Julius Caesar conquered the area in 58 BC and made it the province of Helvetia in the Roman Empire. Following the collapse of the Roman Empire, the area was subjected to numerous invasions until by the sixth century AD it was controlled by the Franks.

From the year 1033 it was part of the Holy Roman Empire. By the end of the 13th century, the first cantons had been formed and the seeds of political unity sown. By the 16th century, the confederation was a military power of the first rank, and it was not until the defeat by France in 1515 at the battle of Marignano that an agreement was made that the Swiss would not serve in any war against France. This agreement became known as the Perpetual Peace. Since that time, Switzerland has been involved in no wars outside its borders, and a policy of armed and strict neutrality has been maintained.

The activities of Calvin at Geneva and Zwingli in Zurich made Switzerland a center of the Reformation during the 16th century.

Following a period of French occupation after the French Revolution, Swiss independence was restored in 1815 when Swiss neutrality was guaranteed, and the country generally assumed its present form.

The industrial revolution was greeted by the Swiss with mixed feelings, and railway development

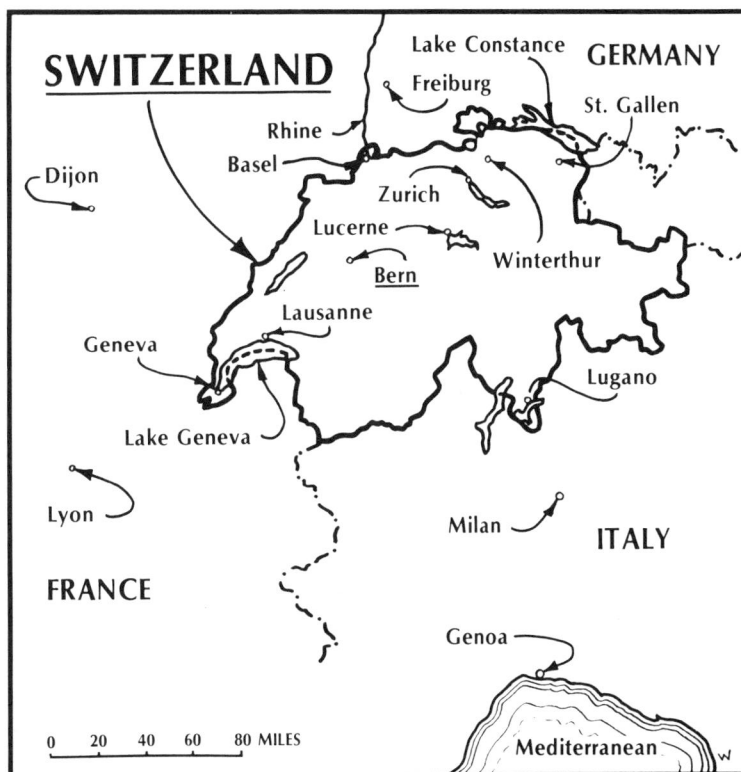

in particular was not initially welcomed. It was the great hydroelectric resources that enabled the Swiss to develop relatively unpolluting industry, and Swiss watches and optical equipment became world famous.

The building of a rail network, despite the forbidding terrain, rendered possible a great tourist industry as the scenic wonders of the country became popular with visitors. Swiss hotels are noted for their quality, and hotel management has become a Swiss tradition. It is also an international banking center.

Switzerland managed to escape the devastation suffered by the rest of Europe during WWI and WWII by maintaining its neutrality. However, it would doubtless have fought strongly to defend itself had Germany attempted an invasion as it did of other small countries on its

borders. After WWI, the Swiss city of Geneva became the home of the League of Nations, and since then the country has continued to provide facilities for many international organizations, including the United Nations and its international agencies.

Geographically, Switzerland is more than half covered by two mountain ranges, the Jura on the French border and the Alps. The population is largely concentrated in the plateau area between the mountain ranges. It is a place of rolling foothills with forested areas and dotted with villages and towns.

The philately of Switzerland is both popular and varied. In addition to Swiss stamps, there are those of the international organizations and agencies based in the country, plus such sidelines as the Soldiers' stamps, the Hotel Posts, and Railway stamps.

VATICAN CITY, STATE OF

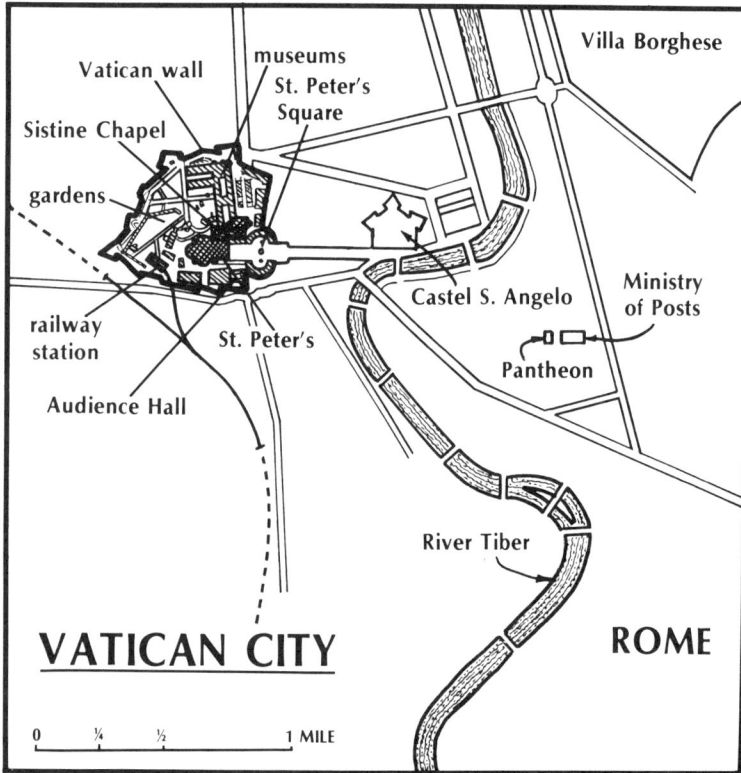

Area: 109 acres
Pop: 1,000 (1979 est.)

The Vatican City is located in the Italian capital city of Rome. For many years, popes had exercised temporal sovereignty over large areas of Italy (the so-called Papal States), which at one time amounted to 16,000 square miles, with a population of more than three million. When the territory was incorporated into the Kingdom of Italy, the pope's sovereignty was restricted to the palaces of the Vatican and the villa of Castel Gandolfo. The independence of the Vatican was established by a treaty of Feb. 11, 1929. The treaty was made part of the Constitution of Italy in 1947. The Vatican City includes St. Peter's, the Vatican Palace and Museum, and neighboring buildings and gardens. Eighty-four nations maintain diplomatic representation in the Vatican, although the United States does not have an official ambassador.

WALES, PRINCIPALITY OF

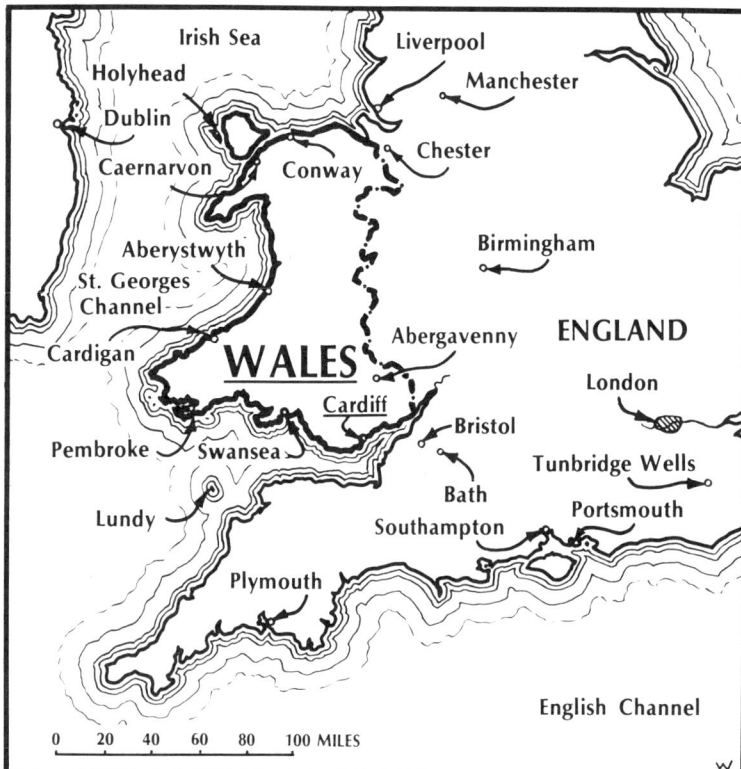

Area: 8,016 sq. miles
Pop: 2,768,200 (1977 est.)
Capital: Cardiff

Wales is administered with England as a single unit. In the dawning of recorded history, Anglo-Saxon invaders drove the Celtic peoples west from England into the mountains of what is now Wales. They were termed by the newcomers Waelise (Welsh, or foreign). In their mountainous region they developed a distinct society and culture. In AD 1283, the ruling house of Gwynedd made war on England but was defeated. As a gesture of friendship, the son of Edward I of England was made the first Prince of Wales in 1301. This is a tradition that continues, and the eldest son of the British monarch is invested as Prince of Wales. The current prince is Prince Charles. The language of Wales is spoken by less than 20 percent of the population; about 30,000 people speak it exclusively.

North America

The vast mainland of North America now contains only the three stamp-issuing countries of Canada, Mexico, and the United States.

In the past, there have been many entities with their own stamps, including the British colonies that confederated to form Canada, the US towns where postmasters' provisional stamps were used, the Confederate States during the Civil War, and a number of states and cities of Mexico that issued stamps during periods of political turmoil.

Today, however, the collector can collect the history and culture of this enormous region by taking only the stamps of those three countries, all of which are relatively conservative in their stamp-issuing policies — although by no means as conservative as in years gone by.

It has become traditional in philatelic circles to include within the North American region the Bahama Islands and Bermuda, and I have continued that tradition, since their histories are so closely linked with that of the North American mainland.

Stamp-issuing countries of North America

1. Bermuda
2. Bahamas
3. Canada
4. Mexico
5. United States

BAHAMAS, COMMONWEALTH OF

Area: 5,353 sq. miles
Pop: 260,000 (1981 est.)
Capital: Nassau

The Commonwealth of the Bahamas consists of nearly 700 islands, 30 of which are inhabited, and more than 2,000 islets spread over a strip running northwest to southeast off the coast of Florida and north of Cuba. It was on the Bahama island of San Salvador (Watling Island) that Columbus first set foot in the New World. The year was 1492, and the islands' only residents were the Arawak Indians. British settlers began to arrive in 1647, and the islands became a British colony in 1783. Independence within the Commonwealth was granted July 10, 1973. Today the islands are a haven for North Americans fleeing the rigors of a northern winter or harried businessmen seeking a tropic beach on which to relax. In addition to the tourist business, which employs 66 percent of the workforce, the islands are a center of international banking.

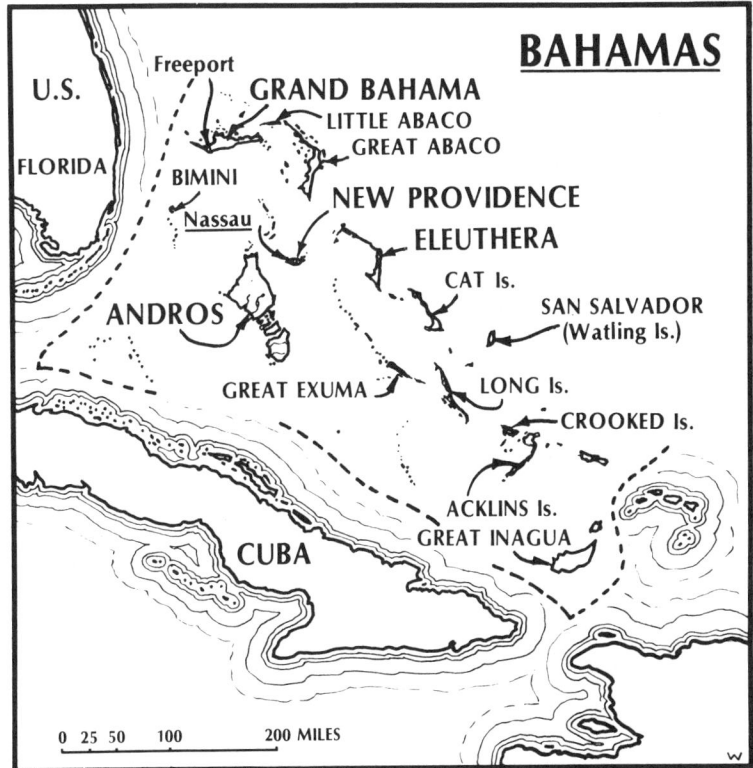

BERMUDA, COLONY OF

Area: 21 sq. miles
Pop: 54,893 (1980)
Capital: Hamilton

The Bermuda Islands group comprises a total of 360 small islands, only 20 of which are inhabited. The group is located about 580 miles to the east of the North Carolina coast. Bermuda was discovered in 1503 by a Spanish explorer named Juan de Bermudez, who was shipwrecked there and for whom the islands are named. In 1609, Sir George Somers and a group of colonists bound for North America were also wrecked and stranded there for 10 months. In 1612, based on the reports of Somers, another group landed and founded the town of St.George, now the oldest continuous English-speaking settlement in the New World. Until the late 1940s, a railway ran from Hamilton to St. George and provided a very scenic journey along the coast and past fields of Easter lilies, which when in bloom are a spectacular sight.

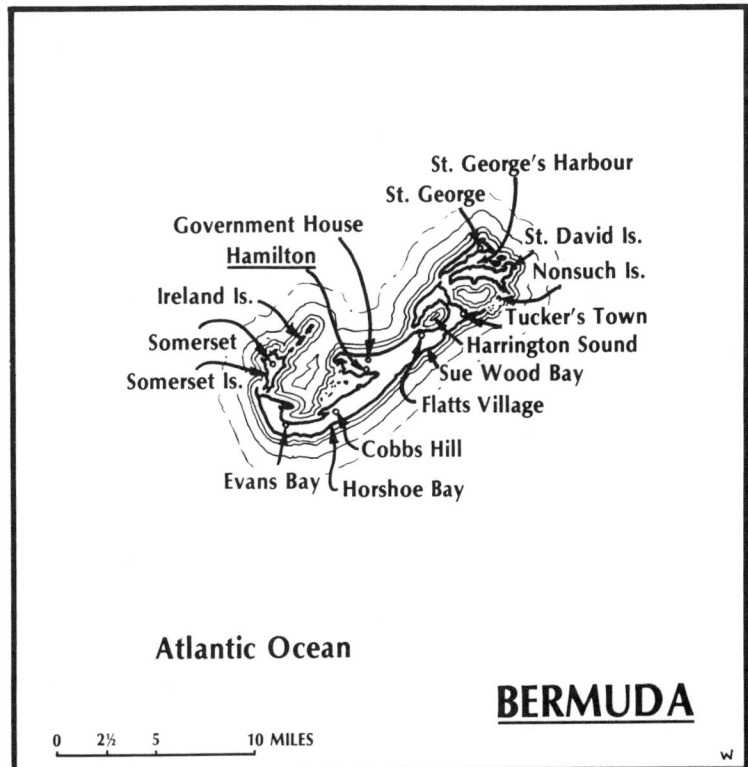

South America

The story of South America has largely been one of early colonial exploitation, bloody struggles for independence, and a post-independence history of revolutions and coups.

There have been relatively few periods of real stability in South America. Yet, in contrast to Africa, the continent shook off its bonds of colonialism at a remarkably early date, and many of its countries have been independent since the first part of the 19th century.

The three Guianas on the continent's northern coast were the last to lose colonial status, and one, French Guiana, has been made part of its European parent.

Only one area, and that not part of South America but included here for convenience, remains a colony — the Falkland Islands.

The Falkland islanders made their desires clear during the 1982 attempted takeover by Argentina, when they opted for continued colonial status rather than risk the perils of an Argentine economy gone mad.

The philately of South America is far more interesting than the slight attention shown by collectors would indicate. Most of its countries have a varied philatelic history that would generously repay the adventurous collector.

Stamp-issuing countries of South America

1. Argentina
2. Bolivia
3. Brazil
4. Chile
5. Colombia
6. Ecuador
7. Falkland Islands
8. French Guiana
9. Guyana
10. Paraguay
11. Peru
12. Suriname
13. Uruguay
14. Venezuela

SOUTH AMERICA

ECUADOR, REPUBLIC OF———

Area: 113,424 sq. miles
Pop: 8,350,000 (1981 est.)
Capital: Quito

The northern Inca Empire occupied the region now known as Ecuador. It was conquered by Spain in 1533. After about 300 years as an exploited colonial possession, it gained its freedom in the 1820s and for a short while was part of the state of Greater Colombia.

FALKLAND ISLANDS———

Area: 4,700 sq. miles
Pop: 1,800 (1980 est.)
Capital: Stanley

There are about 200 islands in the Falklands group, although there are only two main islands: West Falkland and East Falkland on which the capital and only major town is located. The islands have been in continuous British possession since 1833.

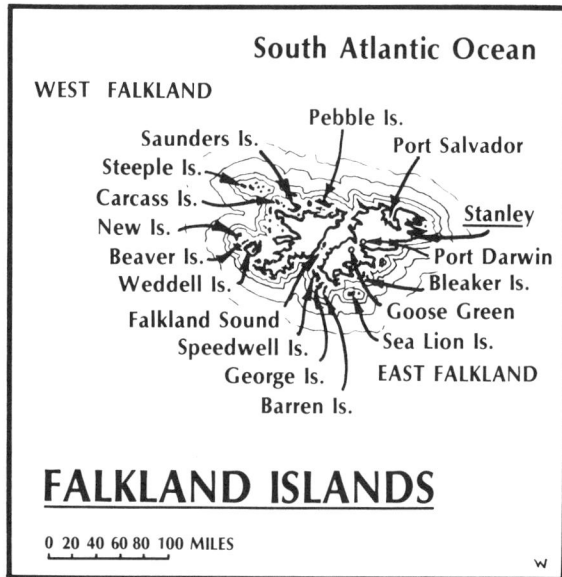

SURINAME———

Area: 70,060 sq. miles
Pop: 420,000 (1981 est.)
Capital: Paramaribo

Suriname became a colony of the Netherlands in 1667, when it was acquired from Britain in exchange for what is now New York City. In 1954, the colony was raised to a level of equality with the Netherlands and the Netherlands Antilles. Independence came in 1975.

URUGUAY———

Area: 68,037 sq. miles
Pop: 2,910,000 (1981 est.)
Capital: Montevideo

Spain started to settle the area of Uruguay in 1624. Rebels began to fight for independence in 1810, and the republic was proclaimed Aug. 25, 1825. The country's standard of living was one of the highest on the continent, until inflation and recession hit in 1981.

Section Four
Local Posts

A local post is generally a private operation that serves a specific, restricted area.

When stamps are issued for such a service, they are valid only to frank mail carried on the service and have no national or international validity.

Regulations require that such local stamps be placed on the back of items of mail, with the official national postage stamps being applied in the usual manner and in addition to any local stamps.

As might be expected with such privately produced material, there is much that has been created to sell to collectors or tourists, and some, indeed, serves no postal function at all.

National postal strikes have prompted the release of many privately produced local post stamps, some of which have actually been used on private delivery services that flourished during the strike period.

Because of their unofficial nature, very few local post stamps have gained catalog recognition.

The posts featured in this section are only a few of those that have existed or that exist in the name of a specific geographic area.

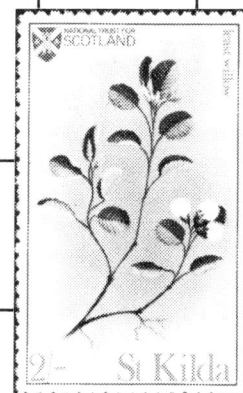

399

LOCAL POSTS IN AUSTRALIA

Noted below are four areas of Australia in which local posts were operating at the time of writing. There have been many such operations, with varying degrees of postal necessity. As with such operations elsewhere, some appear to exist mainly as tourist or publicity gimmicks, others are used to perform a genuine postal service, and many fall somewhere in between.

BUMBUNGA, PROVINCE OF

The so-called Province of Bumbunga consists of an eight-acre strawberry farm located at Bumbunga in South Australia, to the northeast of Adelaide. A patriotic Englishman named Alex Brackstone, who owns the farm, is said to have been concerned at the lack of royalist sentiment in Australia and set himself up as governor of his own state as a bulwark against what he perceived as galloping republicanism. Stamps have been issued for the province. All of them depict members of the British royal family. The stickers are used on mail sent to the nearest Australian post office, where Australian stamps are required for onward transmission.

HUTT RIVER PROVINCE

The Hutt River Province was established in 1970 by a wheat farmer named Leonard George Casley, following a dispute with the Australian government over wheat quotas. The farm is located in Western Australia, near Northampton, to the north of Perth. In 1980 Casley upgraded his province to a kingdom and now calls himself King Leonard. Local stamps were issued beginning in 1973, and since then there has been a flow of stickers inscribed for the "kingdom." They are used by the large numbers of tourists attracted by the "secession" of the farm from Australia. The labels are applied to the back of mail carried to the nearest Australian post office,

where Australian stamps are required.

MAGNETIC ISLAND

Magnetic Island is located off the coast of Queensland, near Townsville. For many years, Hayles Magnetic Island Pty Ltd. has operated a ferry service between Townsville and the island. Since 1920, local stamps have been used to frank packages carried to the island. According to Hornadge (*Local Stamps of Australia*), the labels are not used on items carried from the island to Townsville. Unlike many local posts, this operation caters neither to the stamp collector nor the tourist, and the labels are strictly utilitarian items used to perform a genuine parcel service for residents of the island.

RAINBOW CREEK, STATE OF

The State of Rainbow Creek is located near the town of Cowwarr east of Melbourne in the Australian state of Victoria. It came into being in 1979 as a result of a dispute between area farmers and the government over flood control and land erosion. The "state" is located on land owned by Thomas Barnes, who proclaimed himself governor. A few months after "secession," Barnes issued local stamps for his domain. Since then, a number of issues commemorating various events have been released. As with other local issues, the labels of Rainbow Creek are valid only to carry mail to the nearest Australian post office and must be applied to the back of mail items.

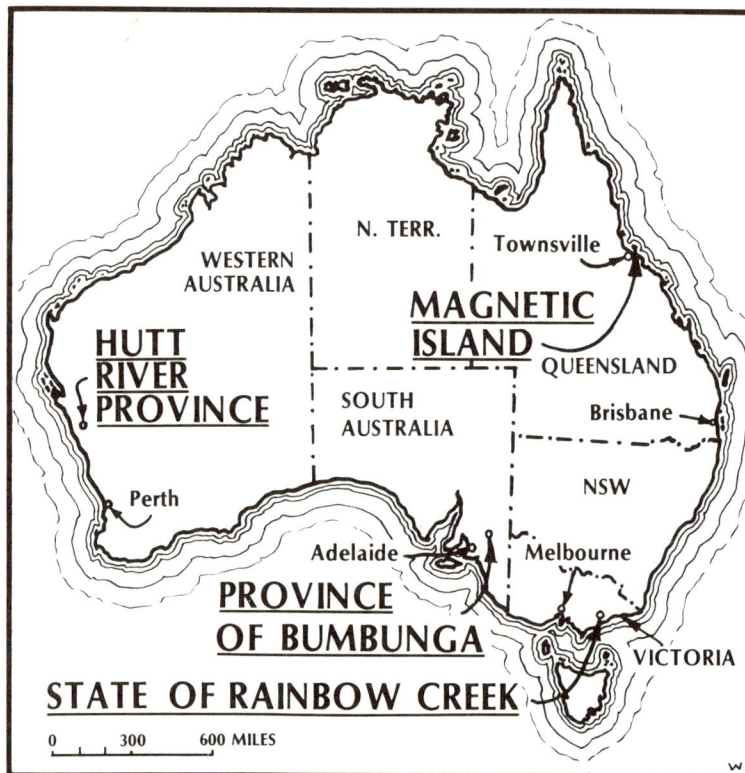

BRITISH OFFSHORE ISLANDS

1. Alderney
2. Bardsey
3. Bernera
4. Brecqhou
5. Caldey
6. Calf of Man
7. Canna
8. Davaar
9. Eynhallow
10. Gairsay

11. Gugh
12. Herm
13. Heston (Hestan)
14. Hilbre
15. Incholm
16. Jethou
17. Lihou
18. Lundy
19. Pabay
20. St. Kilda

21. Sanda
22. Sark
23. Shuna
24. Soay
25. Staffa
26. Steepholm
27. Stroma
28. Summer Isles (Tanera More)

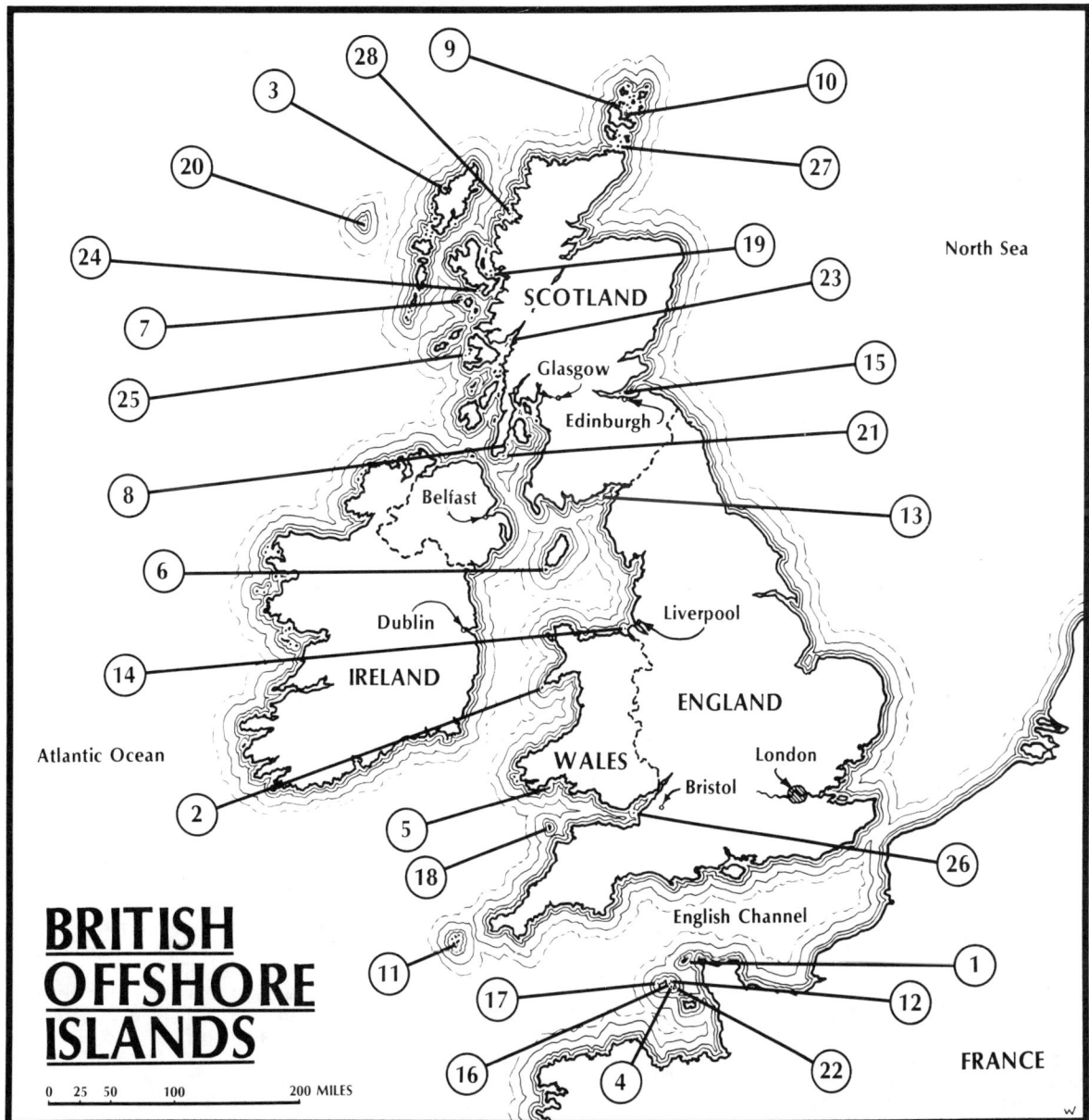

BRITISH OFFSHORE ISLANDS

0 25 50 100   200 MILES

BRITISH OFFSHORE ISLANDS

Numerous islands around the coast of the British Isles have issued stamps known as local carriage labels. These range from islands that have a need for some means of franking mail to the mainland where it can be deposited into the British mail system, to other, sometimes uninhabited rocks for which frequent and colorful issues of stickers are created solely for the purpose of selling them to collectors in the guise of postage stamps. When properly used, these local carriage labels are placed on the back of a letter in addition to the normally applied official British postage stamps.

ALDERNEY

Alderney is one of the English Channel Islands and is a dependency of Guernsey. Although it now has its own official postage stamps, it once had local labels bearing its name. These were intended only to frank packages carried between the island and Guernsey by the Commodore Shipping Co. Some were overprinted to frank letters during the British postal strike of 1971.

BARDSEY

Bardsey is an island off the coast of Wales. Labels bearing its name are described by Gibbons as being essentially tourist souvenirs, and no local post is known to have operated.

BERNERA

Bernera is an island in the Hebrides off the west coast of Scotland. Labels bearing its name are also described by Gibbons as tourist souvenirs.

BRECQHOU (BRECHOU)

Brecqhou is a privately owned island in the English Channel Islands. There is no public access to Brecqhou, and thus the labels inscribed with its name must be considered as produced only for sale to collectors. It is located off the west coast of Sark.

CALDEY

Caldey is an island off the south coast of Wales. Gibbons notes that no local post has existed and that the labels are in the nature of tourist souvenirs.

CALF OF MAN

The Calf of Man is a nature reserve located off the southern tip of the Isle of Man in the Irish Sea. In 1945, the British Post Office discontinued the mail service it had operated between the island and the Isle of Man, and with the Manx Museum and National Trust acting as agents, local carriage labels were introduced in 1962. Between then and 1972, when they were discontinued, almost 400 different were issued.

CANNA

Canna is an island off the west coast of Scotland. Since there is a British post office on the island, labels bearing its name have no postal validity whatsoever. They are properly charity seals, since their purpose was claimed to be to raise funds for the Shipwrecked Mariners' Society.

DAVAAR

Located at the entrance to Campbeltown Loch in Argyllahire, Scotland, Davaar has a lighthouse and a reported population of six. There is some tourist traffic, and mail is carried to the mainland weekly, weather permitting. Hundreds of varied stickers have been created, most obviously with an eye to philatelic sales.

EYNHALLOW

Eynhallow is an island in the Orkney group, to the north of Scotland. Gibbons notes that there is no evidence of any local post service being provided, despite the release during the 1970s of numerous labels.

GAIRSAY

Also located in the Orkneys, Gairsay too is not known to have provided any local mail service, according to Gibbons.

GUGH

Gugh is a small island in the Scilly Islands about 30 miles off Land's End. As Duke of Cornwall, Prince Charles is the landlord. The island is visited by tourists from other of the Scilly Islands, and mail is carried to the nearest British post office on St. Agnes.

HERM

An island off the coast of Guernsey in the English Channel Islands, Herm is one mile long by half a mile wide. A small permanent population is multiplied by visitors from March to October. The island is leased from Guernsey, of which it is a part, and a number of local labels have been issued to frank mail carried to the post office on Guernsey.

HESTON (HESTAN)

Heston (Hestan) is a small island located off the coast of Wigtownshire, Scotland. Gibbons reports that no known local mail service has ever been operated to justify any labels bearing its name.

HILBRE

Hilbre is an island off the Cheshire coast near Liverpool. Gibbons notes that there is no evidence of any local post service on the island.

INCHOLM

An island off the north shore of the Firth of Forth, near Edinburgh. Gibbons notes that no evidence of any local post is known to exist.

JETHOU

Located in the English Channel Islands, Jethou is off the coast of Herm. It is about one and a half miles in circumference and has about 20 acres of flat plateau.

LIHOU

Lithou is an island only at high tide. At other times it is accessible from Guernsey in the English Channel Islands, of which it is a part.

LUNDY

The island of Lundy in the Bristol Channel, off the north coast of Devon, has used local carriage labels to convey mail to the nearest British post office on the mainland since the late 1920s, following a disagreement between the owner and the British Post Office. Denominations of its labels are expressed in puffins, named for the many birds of that species that live on the island. See also under Lundy.

PABAY

Located about two miles off Broadford on the Isle of Skye, Scotland, Pabay (or Pabbay) has an area of one square mile. There are some year-round residents, and it is visited by tourists in the summer.

ST. KILDA

This is the most remote of all the British offshore islands. It is out in the Atlantic about 100 miles from the coast of Scotland and 50 miles west of the Outer Hebrides. The island had a British post office until 1930. Subsequently, the Royal Air Force and the British Army have both operated mail service for servicemen and the civilian population. Gibbons notes that, despite the existence of labels, there is no evidence of any local post service being provided.

SANDA

Located off the coast of Scotland, south of Campbeltown, Sanda has a small permanent population. Mail is reported to be conveyed to the mainland by a boatman hired by the owner.

SARK

Like its companion English Channel island of Alderney, Sark has been served by the Commodore Shipping Co. and labels inscribed "GUERNSEY — SARK" were used to frank packages carried to Guernsey by the shipping line.

SHUNA

Shuna is an island off the coast of Scotland near Oban. The year-round population is said to number five to 10, with some summer visitors.

SOAY

Soay is an island located at the entrance to Loch Scavaig off the island of Skye. There was a British post office there until the mid-1950s. The British Stamp Trade Standing Committee has declared labels bearing the name of Soay to be bogus.

STAFFA

Staffa's main claim to fame is as the location for Fingal's Cave, which inspired Mendelssohn's Fingal's Cave Overture, following an 1829 visit by the composer to the island. A second claim to fame for Staffa is the enormous number of labels released since 1969 in all manner of strange forms and with every imaginable theme. Gibbons notes that these are essentially tourist souvenir items, since "no local post in the true sense of the term is operated."

STEEPHOLM

Steepholm (or Steep Holm) is a small island off the resort town of Weston Super Mare in Somerset. Gibbons notes that labels bearing its name are essentially tourist souvenir items, since "no local post in the true sense of the term is operated."

STROMA

A small island off the northernmost tip of Scotland in the Pentland Firth between Scotland and the Orkney Islands, Stroma is believed to have no permanent population. Gibbons notes that there is no evidence of any local post service being operated there.

SUMMER ISLES (TANERA MORE)

The island of Tanera More is located off the Western Ross coast of Scotland. It is claimed to be inhabited, and a considerable number of tourists is said to visit during the summer. It is reported that mail is transported to the mainland three times a week. The first local carriage labels were issued in 1970.

These stamps were issued by the island of Lundy to mark the 40th anniversary of the island's first stamps. They depict sea-borne links with the outside world, fishing, oldtime transportation on Lundy, and a more recent air service to the mainland.

404

CAMPIONE D'ITALIA

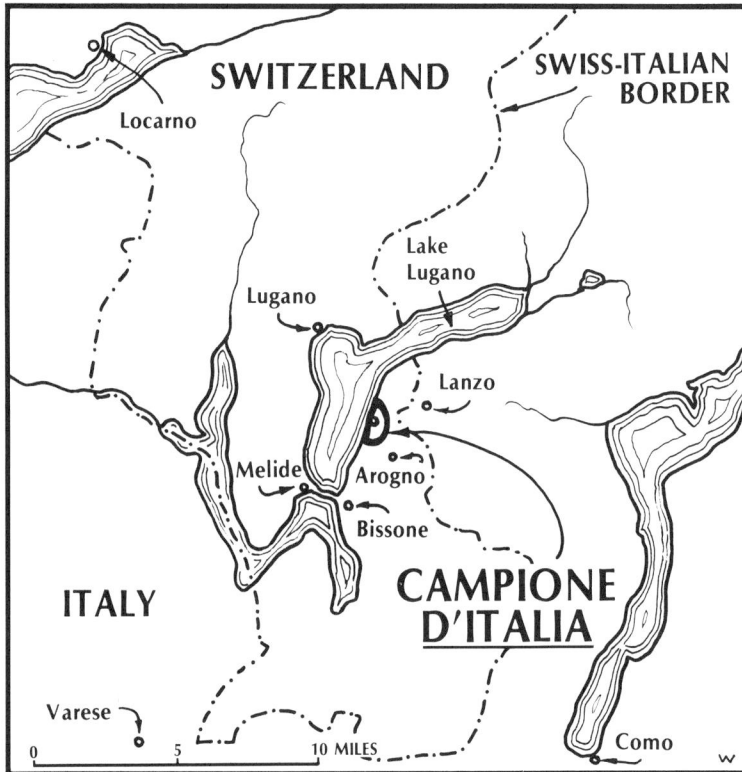

Campione D'Italia is a tiny enclave of Italy within the territory of Switzerland. It is located on the eastern shore of Lake Lugano. During WWII, it sided with the anti-Fascist government of Italy that had surrendered to the Allies after deposing Mussolini. It was cut off by the German puppet government in northern Italy called the Italian Socialist Republic. During this period stamps were issued, which were valid only within the enclave and to carry mail to Switzerland. Swiss stamps were used for international mail.

CHRISTMAS ISLAND (PACIFIC)

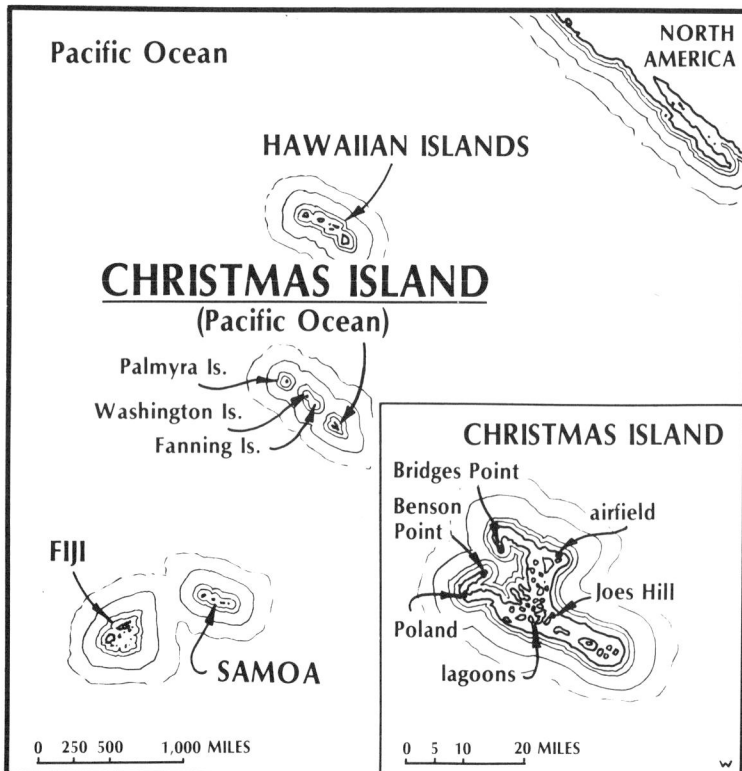

Atoll: 234 sq. miles
Land area: 94 sq. miles
Pop: 477 (1963)

Formerly included in the Ellice Island group, Christmas Island in the Pacific Ocean is now part of Kiribati. During the inter-war years there was no post office, and the Central Pacific Coconut Plantation Ltd. issued a local stamp depicting its schooner *Ysabel*. The vessel is reported to have carried mail franked with the stamps to the nearest port with postal facilities.

405

CLIPPERTON ISLAND

Area: two sq. miles
Pop: none

Once Mexican but currently French, Clipperton Island is some 670 miles off the Pacific coast of Mexico. It is named for John Clipperton, an English pirate who used it as a base. During the mid-19th century, the Oceanic Phosphate Co. of San Francisco began exporting the island's guano deposits. During this period, the firm prepared local stamps to frank mail between the company's offices in San Francisco and the island.

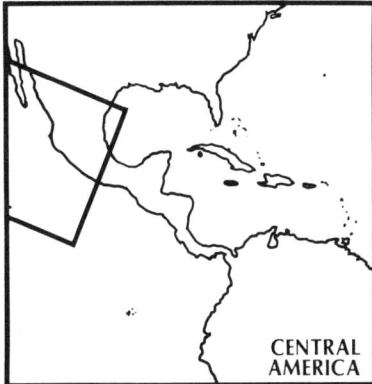

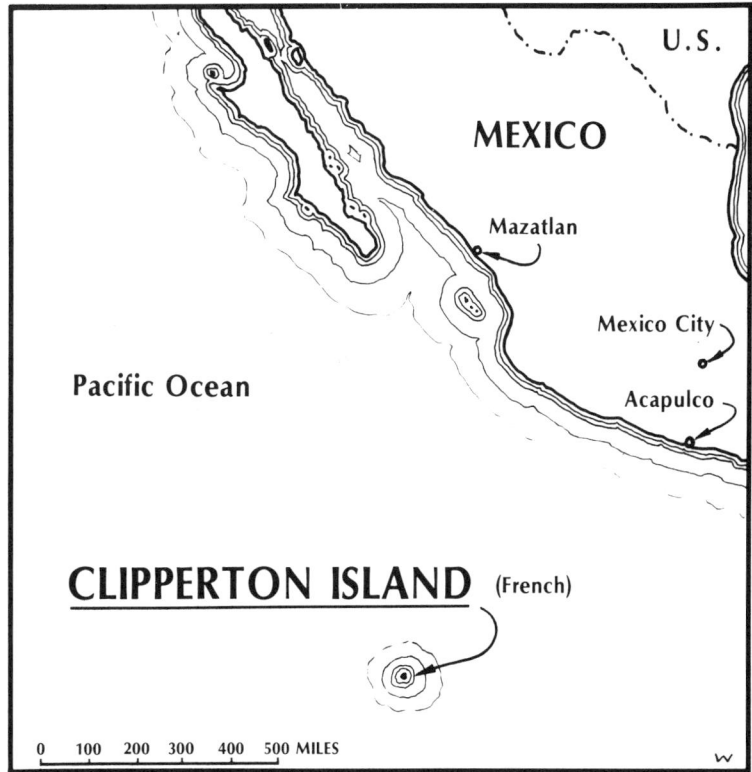

CENTRAL AMERICA

U.S.

MEXICO

Mazatlan

Mexico City

Acapulco

Pacific Ocean

CLIPPERTON ISLAND (French)

0   100   200   300   400   500 MILES

KAULBACH ISLAND

Kaulbach Island is located off the Atlantic coast of Nova Scotia, Canada. It is in Mahone Bay about a mile off the village of Indian Point and about six miles southwest of the town of Chester, according to Lorne Bentham, *Stamp Collector's* Canadian columnist. The island's name is said to be derived from that of an early settler. For several years, the island's owner has created local post stamps used to frank mail to the nearest Canadian post office on the mainland.

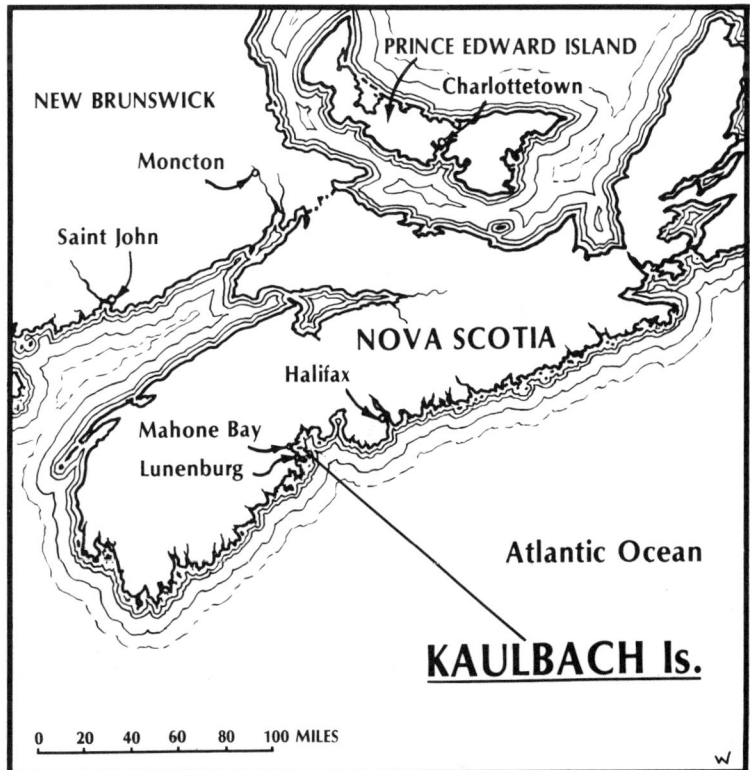

NORTH AMERICA

NEW BRUNSWICK

PRINCE EDWARD ISLAND
Charlottetown

Moncton

Saint John

NOVA SCOTIA

Halifax

Mahone Bay
Lunenburg

Atlantic Ocean

KAULBACH Is.

0   20   40   60   80   100 MILES

LUNDY ISLAND

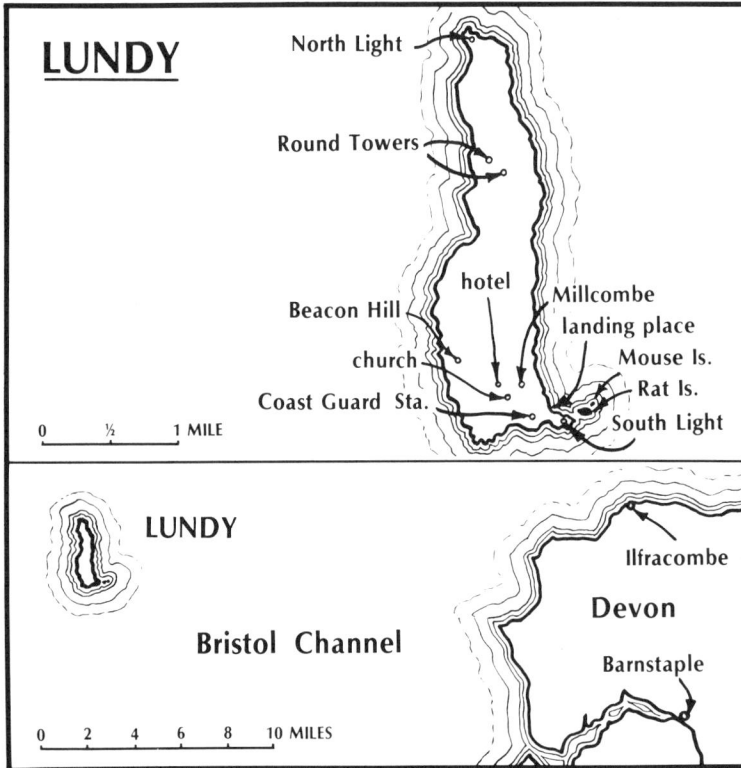

LUNDY

North Light
Round Towers
hotel
Beacon Hill
Millcombe
landing place
church
Mouse Is.
Coast Guard Sta.
Rat Is.
South Light

0   ½   1 MILE

LUNDY

Ilfracombe

Devon

Bristol Channel

Barnstaple

0   2   4   6   8   10 MILES

Area: 2 sq. miles
Pop: about 20

The island of Lundy, in the Bristol Channel off the northern coast of Devon, is well known to collectors for the local stamps bearing its name that have been issued since 1929. They came about following a dispute between the island's owner and British postal authorities that closed the post office there. The island was once the haunt of pirates and smugglers.

EUROPE

MANIZALES, CITY OF

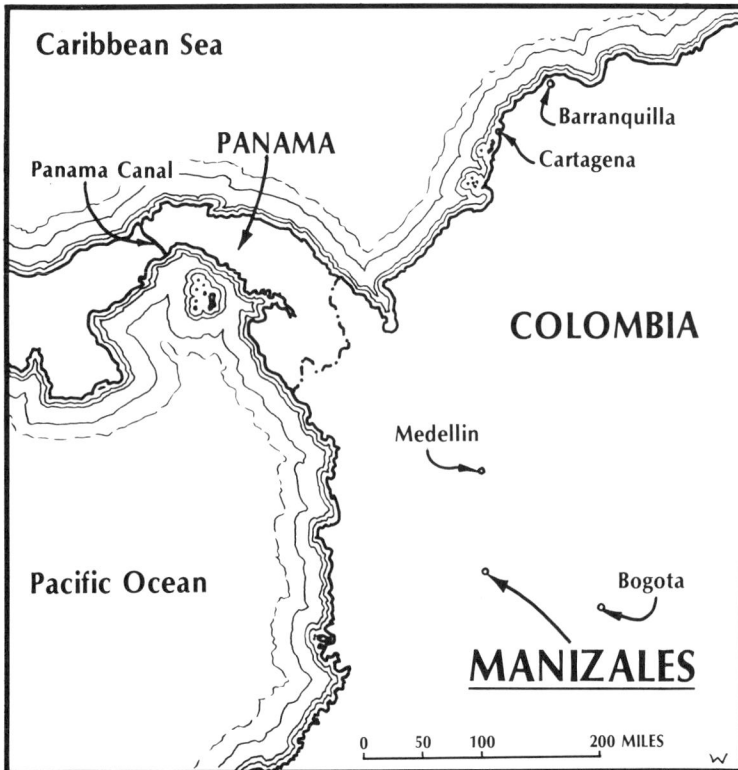

Caribbean Sea

PANAMA

Panama Canal

Barranquilla

Cartagena

COLOMBIA

Medellin

Pacific Ocean

Bogota

MANIZALES

0   50   100   200 MILES

Pop: 219,496 (1968 est.)

The city of Manizales is located in the western part of Colombia, about 110 miles west of Bogota, in the Department of Caldas. It is an important coffee-growing center and is in the Cordillera Central of the Andes at an altitude of 7,000 feet. During the 19th century a number of stamps were issued. According to the Scott and Gibbons catalogs, they were created for a private local post.

SOUTH AMERICA

NAGALAND

Area: 6,366 sq. miles
Pop: 515,561 (1971)
Capital: Kohima

Nagaland is a state of the Republic of India, located in the northeastern part of the country on the Burmese frontier. A segment of the population wishes to be independent of India, and attempts at secession have been made. The so-called "stamps" of Nagaland have confused collectors for several years. They appear to be politically motivated and serve no postal purpose.

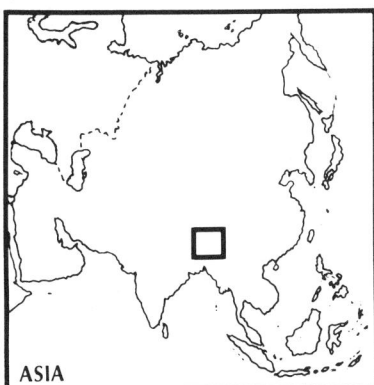

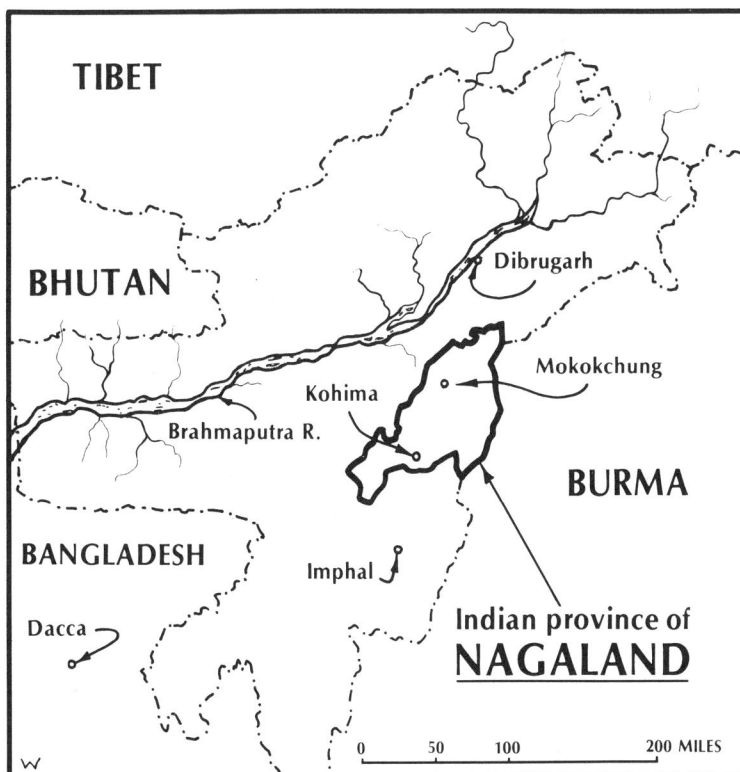

RATTLESNAKE ISLAND

Rattlesnake Island, Ohio, is a small islet in Lake Erie. It is to the west of Middle Bass Island. There is a resort on the island, and a passenger service was operated to the island from Port Clinton using an old Ford Trimotor aircraft. Several years ago, local stamps were created to carry mail on the aircraft from the island to the US post office on the mainland. US postal authorities forbade them on the grounds that they might be mistaken for US postage stamps. The operators then issued local stamps in triangular format.

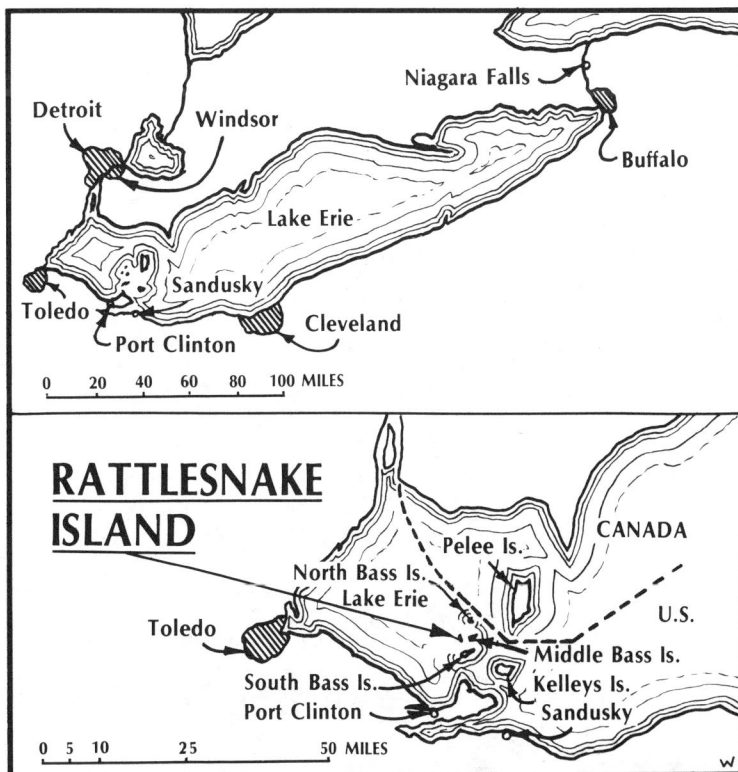

SOUTH MOLUCCAS

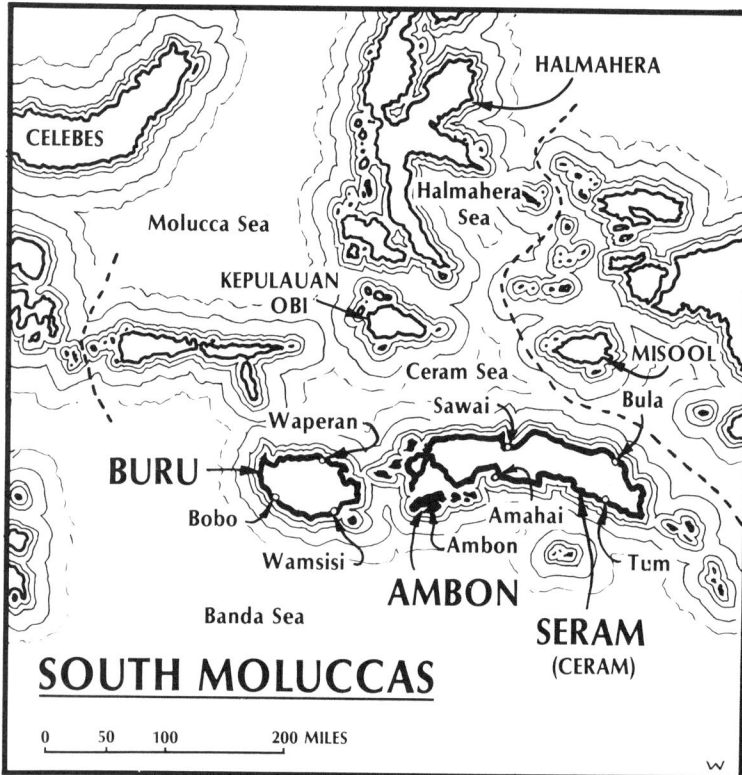

The South Moluccas island group is located to the west of New Guinea. It is part of the Republic of Indonesia. The main islands are Ambon, Buru, and Seram. In 1950, the inhabitants revolted against the Indonesian government and set up their own state. Indonesian and Netherlands Indies stamps were overprinted "REPUBLIK MALUKU SELATAN," followed by specially printed stamps for the new, if unofficial, state. There is doubt that many were used.

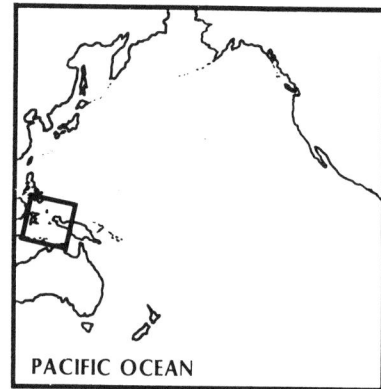

CELEBES

HALMAHERA

Molucca Sea

Halmahera Sea

KEPULAUAN OBI

Ceram Sea

MISOOL

Bula

Sawai

Waperan

BURU

Bobo

Amahai

Ambon

Wamsisi

Tum

AMBON

Banda Sea

SERAM (CERAM)

SOUTH MOLUCCAS

0   50   100   200 MILES

PACIFIC OCEAN

TIERRA DEL FUEGO

Area: 18,530 sq. miles
Pop: 15,658 (Argentine portion 1970)

Tierra del Fuego (Land of Fire) is a large island at the southern tip of South America. It is divided from north to south, with Chile owning the western half and Argentina the eastern portion. In 1890, a Romanian named Julio Popper obtained a concession to mine gold in the Argentine portion, and to establish his authority over the inhabitants, he issued a single postage stamp in January 1891.

ARGENTINA

Atlantic Ocean

Rio Gallegos

CHILE

Strait of Magellan

Rio Grande
ARGENTINA

Ushuaia

CHILE

Pto Williams

Punta Arenas

Staten Island

CHILE and ARGENTINA

Drake Passage

Cape Horn

Pacific Ocean

TIERRA DEL FUEGO

0   50   100   200 MILES

SOUTH AMERICA

TRINIDAD

Area: about 10 sq. miles

The small and rocky island of Trinidad in the Atlantic off the coast of Brazil is owned by that country, although it was claimed for Great Britain in 1700 by Alexander Dalrymple. Another claimant was the self-styled Baron James Harden-Hickey. He set himself up as "king" of his "Principality" of Trinidad, which he had visited briefly during a voyage around Cape Horn to the Orient.

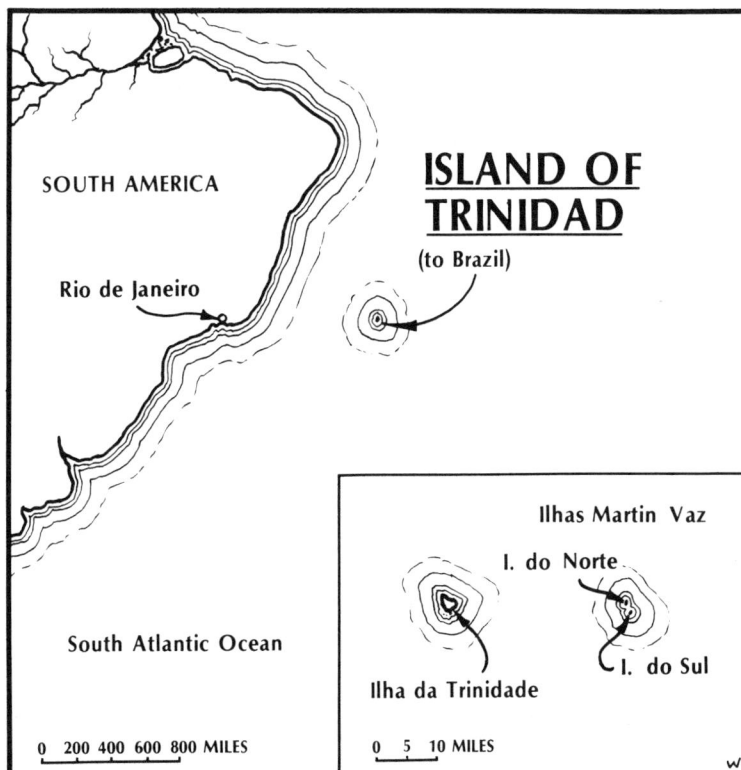

SOUTH AMERICA

ISLAND OF TRINIDAD
(to Brazil)

SOUTH AMERICA

Rio de Janeiro

South Atlantic Ocean

0 200 400 600 800 MILES

Ilhas Martin Vaz

I. do Norte

Ilha da Trinidade

I. do Sul

0   5   10 MILES

New names for old

The following is a worldwide, cross-referenced, alphabetical listing of cities and towns that have had one or more name changes during the past 140 years, or that have a local spelling less familiar to English-speaking collectors.

Each locality is listed under all of its variations; that means that any variation you check will bring you to the appropriate place.

The list will help you to identify place names in old cancelations from localities that no longer exist under those names and thus cannot be found in current reference sources.

As an added convenience, the place name currently in use is shown in capital letters, and the country in which it is now located is given at the end of each entry.

Where both names are in capitals, it indicates either that one is a local spelling and the other the English-language version, or that both names appear to be currently in use.

-A-

AACHEN (Aix-la-Chapelle), Federal Republic of Germany.
Abercorn (MBALA), Zambia.
Abo (TURKU), Finland.
ACHALPUR (Ellichpur), India.
Acre (AKKO), Israel.
ADANA (Seyhan), Turkey.
AD DAWHAH (DOHA), Qatar.
Adrianople (EDIRNE), Turkey.
Affreville (KHEMIS MIL), Algeria.
Agram (ZAGREB), Yugoslavia.
Aix-la-Chapelle (AACHEN), Federal Republic of Germany.
AKKO (Acre), Israel.
Akyab (SITTWE), Burma.
ALEPPO (HALEB), Syria.
Alexandretta (ISKENDERUN), Turkey.
ALEXANDRIA (EL ISKANDARIYA), Egypt.
ALEXANDROUPOLIS (Dedeagh), Greece.
ALGER (ALGIERS or EL DJEZAIR), Algeria.
ALGIERS (ALGER OR EL DJEZAIR), Algeria.
AL KHUMS (HOMS), Libya.
AL KUWAYT (KUWAIT), Kuwait.
AL MADINAH (MEDINA), Saudi Arabia.
AL MANAMAH (MANAMA), Bahrain.
AL MUKHA (MOCHA), Yemen Arab Republic.
Allenstein (OLSZTYN), Poland.
AMOY (HSIA-MEN), Republic of China.
Angora (ANKARA), Turkey.
Angram (ZAGREB), Yugoslavia.
ANKARA (Angora), Turkey.
ANNABA (Bone), Algeria.
ANTAKYA (Antioch or Hatay), Turkey.
Antananarivo (TANANARIVE), Madagascar.
ANTWERP (ANVERS), Belgium.
Antioch (ANTAKYA or Hatay), Turkey.
ANVERS (ANTWERP), Belgium.
Argyrokastron (GJIROKASTER), Albania.
Asmara (ASMERA), Ethiopia-Eritrea.
ASMERA (Asmara), Ethiopia-Eritrea.
ATHENS (ATHINAI), Greece.
ATHINAI (ATHENS), Greece.

-B-

Bahia (SALVADOR), Brazil.
BANGHAZI (BENGHAZI or Bengasi), Libya.
BANGKOK (KRUNG THEP), Thailand.
BANJUL (Bathurst), The Gambia.
Baroda (VADODARA), India.

BASEL (BASLE), Switzerland.
BASLE (BASEL), Switzerland.
Batavia (JAKARTA), Indonesia.
Bathurst (BANJUL), The Gambia.
BEIJING (PEKING or Pei-ching), People's Republic of China.
BEIRUT (Beyrouth), Lebanon.
Bengasi (BENGHAZI or BANGHAZI), Libya.
BENGHAZI (Bengasi or BANGHAZI), Libya.
BEOGRAD (BELGRADE), Yugoslavia.
BELGRADE (BEOGRAD), Yugoslavia.
Beyrouth (BEIRUT), Lebanon.
BITOLA (Monastir), Yugoslavia.
Bjorneborg (PORI), Finland.
Bone (ANNABA), Algeria.
BRATISLAVA (Pressburg), Czechoslovakia.
BRAUNSCHWEIG (BRUNSWICK), Federal Republic of Germany.
Breslau (WROCLAW), Poland.
BRNO (Brunn), Czechoslovakia.
Broken Hill (KABWE), Zambia.
Bromberg (BYDGOSZCZ), Poland.
BRUGES (BRUGGE), Belgium.
BRUGGE (BRUGES), Belgium.
Brunn (BRNO), Czechoslovakia.
BRUNSWICK (BRAUNSCHWEIG), Federal Republic of Germany.
BRUSSELS (BRUXELLES), Belgium.
BRUXELLES (BRUSSELS), Belgium.
BUCHAREST (BUCURESTI), Romania.
BUCURESTI (BUCHAREST), Romania.
Budweis (CESKE BUDEJOVICE), Czechoslovakia.
BUSHEHR (Bushire), Iran.
Bushire (BUSHEHR), Iran.
BYDGOSZCZ (Bromberg), Poland.
Bytown (OTTAWA), Canada.

-C-

CAIRO (EL QAHIRA), Egypt.
Candia (IRAKLION), Crete.
Canea (KHANIA), Crete.
CANTON (KUANG-CHOU), People's Republic of China.
CAPE TOWN (KAAPSTAD), Republic of South Africa.
CASABLANCA (DAR EL BEIDA), Morocco.
Cattaro (KOTOR), Yugoslavia.
Cavalle (KAVALLA), Greece.
CAWNPORE (KANPUR), India.
CESKE BUDEJOVICE (Budweis), Czechoslovakia.
CETINJE (Cettinge), Yugoslavia.

Cettinge (CETINJE), Yugoslavia.
Chemnitz (KARL MARX STADT), German
  Democratic Republic.
CHERNOVTSY (Czernowitz), USSR.
CH'I-CH'I-HA-ERH (Tsitsihar), People's Republic of
  China.
CHI-LIN (Kirin), People's Republic of China.
Chimarra (HIMARE), Albania.
CHIN-MEN (QUEMOY), Republic of China, Taiwan.
CHIPATA (Fort Jameson), Zambia.
CHISIMAIO (Kismayu), Somali Republic.
Chkalov (ORENBURG), USSR.
CH'UNG-CH'ING (Chungking), People's Republic of
  China.
Chungking (CH'UNG-CH'ING), People's Republic of
  China.
Ciudad Trujillo (SANTO DOMINGO), Dominican
  Republic.
CLUJ (Kolozsvar or Klausenburg), Romania.
COBH (Queenstown), Ireland.
COLOGNE (KOLN), Federal Republic of Germany.
Constance (KONSTANZ), Federal Republic of
  Germany.
Constantinople (ISTANBUL), Turkey.
COPENHAGEN (KOBENHAVN), Denmark.
CORFU (KERKIRA), Greece.
Cracow (KRAKOW), Poland.
Czernowitz (CHERNOVTSY), USSR.

-D-

Dacca (DHAKA), Bangladesh.
Dairen (LU-TA or TA-LIEN), People's Republic of
  China.
DA NANG (Tourane), Vietnam.
Danzig (GDANSK), Poland.
DAR EL BEIDA (CASABLANCA), Morocco.
DARNAH (Derna), Libya.
DAUGAVPILS (Dunaburg), USSR.
Dedeagh (ALEXANDROUPOLIS), Greece.
Derna (DARNAH), Libya.
DHAKA (Dacca), Bangladesh.
DOHA (AD DAWHAH), Qatar.
Dorpat (TARTU), Estonia — now USSR.
DUBROVNIK (Ragusa), Yugoslavia.
Dunaburg (DAUGAVPILS), USSR.
Durazzo (DURRES), Albania.
DURRES (Durazzo), Albania.

-E-

EDIRNE (Adrianople), Turkey.
Ekaterinodar (KRASNODAR), USSR.
EL DJEZAIR (ALGIERS or ALGER), Algeria.
EL ISKANDARIYA (ALEXANDRIA), Egypt.
Ellichpur (ACHALPUR), India.
EL QAHIRA (CAIRO), Egypt.

-F-

FIRENZE (FLORENCE), Italy.
Fiume (RIJEKA), Yugoslavia.
FLORENCE (FIRENZE), Italy.
Foochow (FU-CHOU), People's Republic of China.
Fort Jameson (CHIPATA), Zambia.
Fort Lamy (N'DJAMENE), Chad.
FREDERIKSHAB (Pamiut), Greenland.
Friedrich Wilhelmshafen (MADANG), Papua New
  Guinea.
FU-CHOU (Foochow), People's Republic of China.
Funfkirchen (PECS), Hungary.

-G-

GALATI (Galatz), Romania.

Galatz (GALATI), Romania.
Gallipoli (GELIBOLU), Turkey.
GAND (GHENT or GENT), Belgium.
GDANSK (Danzig), Poland.
GENT (GHENT or GAND), Belgium.
GELIBOLU (Gallipoli), Turkey.
GENOA (GENOVA), Italy.
GENOVA (GENOA), Italy.
Ghadames (GHUDAMIS), Libya.
GHENT (GENT or GAND), Belgium.
GHUDAMIS (Ghadames), Libya.
GIRESUN (Kerassunde or Kerason), Turkey.
GJIROKASTER (Argyrokastron), Albania.
GORKIY (Nizhniy Novgorod), USSR.
GOTEBORG (Gothenburg), Sweden.
Gothenburg (GOTEBORG), Sweden.
Gratz (GRAZ), Austria.
GRAZ (Gratz), Austria.

-H-

HABANA (HAVANA), Cuba.
HAERHPIN (Harbin), People's Republic of China.
Hague, The (s'GRAVENHAGE), The Netherlands.
HAI-K'OU (Hoihow), People's Republic of China.
HALEB (ALEPPO), Syria.
Hankow (WUHAN), People's Republic of China.
HARARE (Salisbury), Zimbabwe.
Harbin (HAERHPIN), People's Republic of China.
Hatay (ANTAKYA or Antioch), Turkey.
HAVANA (HABANA), Cuba.
Herbertshohe (RABAUL), Papua New Guinea.
Helsingfors (HELSINKI), Finland.
HELSINKI (Helsingfors), Finland.
HIMARE (Chimarra, Khimara, or Chimara), Albania.
HO CHI MINH CITY (Saigon), Vietnam.
Hoihow (HAI-K'OU), People's Republic of China.
Hollandia (JAYAPURA or Sukarnapura), Indonesia.
HOLSTEINSBORG (Sisimiut), Greenland.
HOMS (AL KHUMS), Libya.
HSIA-MEN (AMOY), Republic of China.

-I-

IASI (Jassy), Romania.
IRAKLION (Candia), Crete.
ISKENDERUN (ALEXANDRETTA), Turkey.
ISTANBUL (Constantinople), Turkey.
IVANO FRANKOVSK (Stanislav), USSR.
IZMIR (Smyrna), Turkey.

-J-

Jaffa (YAFO), Israel.
JAKARTA (Batavia), Indonesia.
JAKOBSTAD (Pietarsaari), Finland.
Jassy (IASI), Romania.
JAYAPURA (HOLLANDIA or Sukarnapura),
  Indonesia.
Jedda (JIDDAH), Saudi Arabia.
Jesselton (KOTA KINABALU), Malaysia.
JIDDAH (Jedda), Saudi Arabia.

-K-

KAAPSTAD (CAPE TOWN), Republic of South
  Africa.
KABWE (Broken Hill), Zambia.
KALININGRAD (Konigsberg), USSR.
KANPUR (CAWNPORE), India.
KARL MARX STADT (Chemnitz), German
  Democratic Republic.
KAUNAS (Kovno), USSR.
KAVALLA (Cavelle), Greece.

Kerassunde (GIRESUN or Kerason), Turkey.
Kerason (GIRESUN or Kerassunde), Turkey.
KERKIRA (CORFU), Greece.
KHANIA (Canea), Crete.
KHEMIS MIL (Affreville), Algeria.
Khimara (HIMARE), Albania.
KIEV (KIYEV), USSR.
KINSHASA (Leopoldville), Zaire.
Kirin (CH'I-LIN), People's Republic of China.
KISANGANI (Stanleyville), Zaire.
Kismayu (CHISIMAIO), Somali Republic.
KIYEV (KIEV), USSR.
KLAIPEDA (Memel), USSR.
Klausenburg (CLUJ or Kolozsvar), Romania.
KOBENHAVN (COPENHAGEN), Denmark.
KOLN (COLOGNE), Federal Republic of Germany.
Kolozsvar (CLUJ or Klausenburg), Romania.
Konigsberg (KALININGRAD), USSR.
KONSTANZ (Constance), Federal Republic of
  Germany.
KORCE (Koritsa), Albania.
Koritsa (KORCE), Albania.
KOTA KINABALU (Jesselton), Malaysia.
KOTOR (Cattaro), Yugoslavia.
Kovno (KAUNAS), USSR.
KRAKOW (Cracow), Poland.
KRASNODAR (Ekaterinodar), USSR.
KRISTIANIA (OSLO), Norway.
KRUNG THEP (BANGKOK), Thailand.
KUANG-CHOU (CANTON), People's Republic of
  China.
K'UN-MING (Yunnan), People's Republic of China.
KUWAIT (AL KUWAYT), Kuwait.
KWIDZYN (Marienwerder), Poland.

-L-

Laibach (LJUBLJANA), Yugoslavia.
LA-SA (LHASA), Tibet in People's Republic of China.
Leghorn (LIVORNO), Italy.
LEGNICA (Liesnitz), Poland.
Lemberg (L'VOV), Poland.
LENINGRAD (St. Petersburg), USSR.
Leopoldville (KINSHASA), Zaire.
LHASA (LA-SA), Tibet in People's Republic of China.
Liesnitz (LEGNICA), Poland.
LISBOA (LISBON), Portugal.
LISBON (LISBOA), Portugal.
LIVORNO (Leghorn), Italy.
LOANDA (LUANDA), Angola.
LJUBLJANA (Laibach), Yugoslavia.
Lourenco Marques (MAPUTO), Mozambique.
LUANDA (LOANDA), Angola.
LUCERNE (LUZERN), Switzerland.
Lugansk (VOROSHILOVGRAD), USSR.
LU-SHUN (Port Arthur), People's Republic of China.
LU-TA (TA-LIEN or Dairen), People's Republic of
  China.
L'VOV (Lemberg), USSR.
LUZERN (LUCERNE), Switzerland.

-M-

Maarianhamina (MARIEHAMN), Aland Islands,
  Finland.
MADANG (Friedrich Wilhelmshafen), Papua New
  Guinea.
Mahrisch Ostrau (OSTRAVA), Czechoslovakia.
Makassar (UJUNG PANDANG), Indonesia.
MAKKAH (MECCA), Saudi Arabia.
MALABA (Sta. Isabel), Equatorial Guinea.
MANAMA (AL MANAMAH), Bahrain.
Manitsoq (SUKKERTOPPEN), Greenland.
MAPUTO (Lourenco Marques), Mozambique.

MARIEHAMN (Maarianhamina), Aland Is., Finland.
Marienwerder (KWIDZYN), Poland.
MASQAT (MUSCAT), Oman.
MBALA (Abercorn), Zambia.
MECCA (MAKKAH), Saudi Arabia.
MEDINA (AL MADINAH), Saudi Arabia.
Memel (KLAIPEDA), USSR.
MOCHA (AL MUKHA), Yemen Arab Republic.
MOGADISCIO (Mogadishu), Somali Republic.
Mogadishu (MOGADISCIO), Somali Republic.
Molotov (PERM), USSR.
Monastir (BITOLA), Yugoslavia.
MOSCOW (MOSKVA), USSR.
MOSKVA (MOSCOW), USSR.
Mukden (SHEN-YANG), People's Republic of China.
MUNCHEN (MUNICH), Federal Republic of Germany.
MUNICH (MUNCHEN), Federal Republic of Germany.
MUSCAT (MASQAT), Oman.

-N-

NAPLES (NAPOLI), Italy.
NAPOLI (NAPLES), Italy.
N'DJAMENE (Fort Lamy), Chad.
New Amsterdam (NEW YORK, N.Y.), United States.
NEW YORK, N.Y. (New Amsterdam), United States.
Nizhniy Novgorod (GORKIY), USSR.
NUREMBERG (NURNBERG), Federal Republic of
  Germany.
NURNBERG (NUREMBERG), Federal Republic of
  Germany.

-O-

Oldenburg (SOPRON), Hungary.
OLSZTYN (Allenstein), Poland.
OPORTO (PORTO), Portugal.
ORAN (OUAHRAN), Algeria.
ORENBURG (Chkalov), USSR.
OSLO (Kristiania), Norway.
OSTRAVA (Mahrisch Ostrau), Czechoslovakia.
OTTAWA (Bytown), Canada.
OUAHRAN (ORAN), Algeria.
OULU (Uleaborg), Finland.

-P-

Pakhoi (PEI HAI), People's Republic of China.
Pamiut (FREDERIKSHAB), Greenland.
PECS (Funfkirchen), Hungary.
Pei-ching (BEIJING or Peking), People's Republic of
  China.
PEI HAI (Pakoi), People's Republic of China.
PEKING (BEIJING or Pei-ching), People's Republic of
  China.
PERM (Molotov), USSR.
Pernambuco (RECIFE), Brazil.
Philippeville (SKIKDA), Algeria.
Philippopolis (PLOVDIV), Bulgaria.
Pietarsaari (JAKOBSTAD), Finland.
Pilsen (PLZEN), Czechoslovakia.
PIRAEUS (PIRAIEVS), Greece.
PIRAIEVS (PIRAEUS), Greece.
PLOVDIV (Philippopolis), Bulgaria.
PLZEN (Pilsen), Czechoslovakia.
Pola (PULA), Yugoslavia.
POONA (PUNE), India.
PORI (Bjorneborg), Finland.
Port Arthur (LU-SHUN), People's Republic of China.
PORTO (OPORTO), Portugal.
Posen (POZNAN), Poland.
POZNAN (Posen), Poland.
PRAGUE (PRAHA), Czechoslovakia.
PRAHA (PRAGUE), Czechoslovakia.

Pressburg (BRATISLAVA), Czechoslovakia.
PULA (Pola), Yugoslavia.
PUNE (POONA), India.

-Q-

Queenstown (COBH), Ireland.
QUEMOY (CHIN-MEN), Republic of China, Taiwan.

-R-

Rabul (Herbertshohe), Papua New Guinea.
Ragusa (DUBROVNIK), Yugoslavia.
Ratisbon (REGENSBURG), Federal Republic of
  Germany.
RECIFE (Pernambuco), Brazil.
REGENSBURG (Ratisbon), Federal Republic of
  Germany.
Reval (TALLINN), USSR.
RHODES (RODHOS), Rhodes.
RIJEKA (Fiume), Yugoslavia.
RODHOS (RHODES), Rhodes.
Ruschuk (RUSE), Bulgaria.
RUSE (Ruschuk), Bulgaria.

-S-

SAIDA (Sidon), Lebanon.
Saigon (HO CHI MINH CITY), Vietnam.
St. Petersburg (LENINGRAD), USSR.
Salisbury (HARARE), Zimbabwe.
Salonica (THESSALONIKI), Greece.
SALVADOR (Bahia), Brazil.
Sta. Isabel (MALABA), Equatorial Guinea.
SANTO DOMINGO (Ciudad Trujillo), Dominican
  Republic.
SARAGOSSA (ZARAGOZA), Spain.
Scutari (SHKODER), Albania.
SEOUL (SOUL), South Korea.
Seyhan (ADANA), Turkey.
s'GRAVENHAGE (The Hague), The Netherlands.
SHEN-YANG (Mukden), People's Republic of China.
SHKODER (Scutari), Albania.
Sidon (SAIDA), Lebanon.
SIRACUSA (SYRACUSE), Italy.
Sisimiut (HOLSTEINSBORG), Greenland.
SITTWE (Akyab), Burma.
SKIKDA (Philippeville), Algeria.
SKOPJE (Uskub), Yugoslavia.
Smyrna (IZMIR), Turkey.
SOFIA (SOFIYA), Bulgaria.
SOFIYA (SOFIA), Bulgaria.
SOPRON (Oldenburg), Hungary.
SOUL (SEOUL), South Korea.
Sour (TYR or TYRE), Lebanon.
SOVETSK (Tilsit), USSR.
Spalato (SPLIT), Yugoslavia.
SPLIT (Spalato), Yugoslavia.
Stalingrad (VOLGOGRAD), USSR.
Stanislav (IVANO-FRANKOVSK), USSR.
Stanleyville (KISANGANI), Zaire.
Stettin (SZCZECIN), Poland.
STRASBOURG (Strassburg), France.
Strassburg (STRASBOURG), France.
Stuhlweissenburg (SZEKESFEHERVAR), Hungary.
Sukarnapura (JAYAPURA or Hollandia), Indonesia.
SUKKERTOPPEN (Manitsoq), Greenland.
SYRACUSE (SIRACUSA), Italy.
SZCZECIN (Stettin), Poland.
SZEKESFEHERVAR (Stuhlweissenburg), Hungary.

-T-

Tammersfors (TAMPERE), Finland.
TAMPERE (Tammersfors), Finland.

TANANARIVE (Antananarivo), Madagascar.
TANGER (TANGIER), Morocco.
TANGIER (TANGER), Morocco.
TARFAYA (Villa Bens), Morocco.
TARTU (Dorpat), Estonia — now USSR.
Tashi Chho (THIMBU), Bhutan.
TBILISI (Tiflis), USSR.
Temesvar (TIMISOARA), Romania.
Tetuan (TETOUAN), Morocco.
TETOUAN (Tetuan), Morocco.
THESSALONIKI (Salonica), Greece.
THIMBU (Tashi Chho), Bhutan.
Tiflis (TBILISI), USSR.
Tilsit (SOVETSK), USSR.
Timbuktu (TOMBOUCTOU), Mali.
TIMISOARA (Temesvar), Romania.
Tobruch (TOBRUQ or TOBRUK), Libya.
TOBRUK (TOBRUQ or Tobruch), Libya.
TOBRUQ (TOBRUK or Tobruch), Libya.
TOMBOUCTOU (Timbuktu), Mali.
TORINO (TURIN), Italy.
Tourane (DA NANG), Vietnam.
TRENT (Trient), Italy.
TREVES (TRIER), Federal Republic of Germany.
TRIER (TREVES), Federal Republic of Germany.
Trient (TRENT), Italy.
Tsitsihar (CH'I-CH'I-HA-ERH), People's Republic of
  China.
TURIN (TORINO), Italy.
TURKU (Abo), Finland.
TYR (TYRE or Sour), Lebanon.
Tzaritzin (Stalingrad or VOLGOGRAD), USSR.

-U-

UJUNG PANDANG (Makassar), Indonesia.
ULAANBAATAR (Urga or ULAN BATOR), Mongolia.
ULAN BATOR (Urga or ULAANBAATAR), Mongolia.
Uleaborg (OULU), Finland.
Urga (ULAANBAATAR or ULAN BATOR), Mongolia.
Uskub (SKOPJE), Yugoslavia.

-V-

VADODARA (Baroda), India.
VENEZIA (VENICE), Italy.
VENICE (VENEZIA), Italy.
VIENNA (WIEN), Austria.
Villa Bens (TARFAYA), Morocco.
VOLGOGRAD (Tzaritzin or Stalingrad), USSR.
VOROSHILOVGRAD (Lugansk), USSR.

-W-

Walfisch Bay (WALVIS BAY), Namibia or South-
  West Africa.
WALVIS BAY (Walfisch Bay), Namibia or South-
  West Africa.
WARSAW (WARSZAWA), Poland.
WARSZAWA (WARSAW), Poland.
WIEN (VIENNA), Austria.
WROCLAW (Breslau), Poland.
WUHAN (Hankow), People's Republic of China.

-Y-

YAFO (Jaffa), Israel.
Yunnan (K'UN-MING), People's Republic of China.

-Z-

ZADAR (Zara), Yugoslavia.
ZAGREB (Angram), Yugoslavia.
Zara (ZADAR), Yugoslavia.
ZARAGOZA (Saragossa), Spain.

References

Atlases

Aldine University Atlas, First Edition. Aldine Publishing Co., Chicago, 1969.

Atlas of European History, Oxford University Press, New York, 1957.

Atlas of India, Sir W.W. Hunter, W.&A.K. Johnston, London, 1894.

Atlas of the World and Gazetteer, Funk & Wagnalls Co., 1924.

Atlas of the World, Literary Digest, Funk & Wagnalls Co., 1927.

Atlas of the World, Literary Digest, Funk & Wagnalls Co., 1931.

Atlas of World History, Rand McNally & Co., Chicago, 1957.

Britannica Atlas, Encyclopedia Britannica, Inc., Chicago, 1947.

Britannica Atlas, Encyclopedia Britannica, Inc., Chicago, 1970.

Century Atlas of the World, Times Co., New York, 1906.

Columbia Standard Atlas of the World, Consolidated Book Publishers, Chicago, 1958.

Cosmopolitan World Atlas, Rand McNally & Co., Chicago, 1949.

Cram's Superior Family Atlas of the World, George F. Cram, Chicago, 1903.

Frye's Complete Geography, Ginn & Co., The Athenaeum Press, Boston, 1901.

German Area Map Set, Germany Philatelic Society, Inc., Box 563, Westminster, MD 21157.

Goode's World Atlas, 15th Edition, Rand McNally & Co., Chicago, 1980.

Great World Atlas, Reader's Digest Association, New York, 1963.

Hammond's Comprehensive Atlas of the World, C.S. Hammond & Co., New York, 1916.

Harper's Geography, Harper & Brothers, New York, 1879.

Historical Atlas of South Asia, Schwartzberg. No information.

Historical Atlas of the Indian Peninsula, C. Collin Davies, 1949.

Imperial Atlas of the World, Rand McNally & Co., Chicago, 1909.

Medallion World Atlas, Hamond Inc., Maplewood, N.J., 1971.

Modern Atlas of the World, C.S. Hammond & Co., New York, 1923.

National Geographic Society maps, National Geographic Society, Washington, D.C.

New Encyclopedia Atlas P.F. Collier & Son, New York, 1907.

New Encyclopedia Atlas, P.F. Collier & Son, New York, 1912.

New International Atlas, J.W. Clement Co., Matthews-Northrup Div., New York, 1938.

New Reference Atlas of the World, C.S. Hammond & Co., New York, 1929.

New Standard Atlas of the World, Rand McNally & Co., Chicago, 1890.

New World Atlas, Educational Book Club, Inc., Des Moines, Iowa, 1963.

Oxford Atlas, Oxford University Press, London, 1970.

Oxford Home Atlas of the World, Oxford University Press, London, 1960.

Road Atlas of Britain and Ireland, Wm. Collins Sons, Glasgow, 1980.

Schonberg's Atlas of the World, Schonberg & Co., New York, 1867.

Times Atlas of the World, Comprehensive Edition, Quadrangle/The New York Times Book Co., New York, 1975.

World Atlas and Gazetteer, P.F. Collier & Son, New York, 1942.

World Atlas, Classics Edition, C.S. Hammond & Co., Maplewood, N.J., 1957.

World Atlas, Encyclopedia Britannica, Inc., Chicago, 1947.

World Atlas, Premier Edition, Rand McNally & Co., Chicago, 1935.

World Atlas, Rand McNally & Co., Chicago, 1952.

World Atlas, Rand McNally & Co., Chicago, 1955.

General References

Chambers' Encyclopedia, Belford, Clarke & Co., Chicago, 1884.

Edwards, C.B., Instant World Facts, Tutor Press, Toronto, Canada, 1980.

Encyclopedia Britannica, 200th Anniversary Edition, 1970.

Encyclopedia of World Travel, Second Edition, Doubleday & Co., New York, 1973.

Etherton, Col. P.T. and Vernon Barlow, Lundy — The Tempestuous Isle, Lutterworth Press, London, 1954.

Hawthorn, A.J., Countries of the World, Coles Publishing Co., Toronto, Canada, 1981.

History of the Second World War, Sir Basil Liddell Hart, editor, Marshall Cavendish USA Ltd., 1973.

History of the World War, Funk &

Wagnalls Co., New York, 1920.

Morris, Richard B. and Graham W. Irwin, Encyclopedia of the Modern World, Harper & Row, New York, 1970.

Robson, R.W., Pacific Islands Handbook, MacMillan Co., New York, 1944.

Standard Reference Encyclopedia, Funk & Wagnalls Co., 1970.

Status of the World's Nations, US Department of State, Bureau of Intelligence and Research, 1978.

Topographical Dictionary of Great Britain and Ireland, Chapman and Hall, London, 1833.

Webster's New Geographical Dictionary, G.&C. Merriam Co., Springfield, Mass., 1980.

World Almanac, 1983 Edition, Newspaper Enterprise Association, Inc., New York.

World Guide, Rand McNally & Co., Chicago, 1953.

World Travelog, C.S. Hammond & Co., Maplewood, N.J., 1960.

Catalogs

Sources include catalogs published by:

Gibbons — Stanley Gibbons Publications Ltd., London, England.

Michel — Schwaneberger Verlag GmbH, Munich, Federal Republic of Germany.

Minkus — Minkus Publications, Inc., New York, N.Y.

Scott — Scott Publishing Co., New York, N.Y.

Yvert — Yvert & Tellier, Amiens, France.

Zumstein — Zumstein & Cie., Bern, Switzerland.

Philatelic References

Attwood, J.H., Ascension: The Stamps and Postal History, Robson Lowe Ltd., London, England.

Billig's Philatelic Handbooks, HJMR Co., North Miami, Fla.

Bleeker, Tom R., Japanese Occupation of the Dutch East Indies, Philip Cockrill, Newbury, Berks., England.

British Local Stamps, Catalog of, BLSC Publishing Co., London, England.

Dehn, Roy A., Italian Stamps, Heinemann, London, 1973.

Dougan, Charles W., The Shanghai Postal System, American Philatelic Society, State College, Pa.

Hornadge, Bill, Local Stamps of Australia, Review Publications, Dubbo, NSW, Australia.

Linn's World Stamp Almanac, Amos Press Inc., Sidney, Ohio.

Pirie, Dr. J.H. Harvey, Antarctic Posts, Harry Hayes, Batley, Yorkshire, England.

Wood, Kenneth A., This is Philately, Van Dahl Publications, Albany, Ore.